*Hugo von Hofmannsthal's Correspondence
with Countess Ottonie Degenfeld*

Studies in German Literature, Linguistics, and Culture

Edited by James Hardin
(*South Carolina*)

Ottonie Countess Degenfeld around 1906.

HUGO VON HOFMANNSTHAL'S CORRESPONDENCE
WITH COUNTESS OTTONIE DEGENFELD

THE POET AND THE COUNTESS

Edited by
Marie-Therese Miller-Degenfeld

Translated by
W. Eric Barcel

CAMDEN HOUSE

Copyright © 2000 Marie-Therese Miller-Degenfeld

This is an authorized English translation of the German original, *Hugo von Hofmannsthal: Briefwechsel mit Ottonie Gräfin Degenfeld und Julie Freifrau von Wendelstadt*. It has been expanded to include additional letters of Ottonie and omits the letters of Julie von Wendelstadt.

Translated by W. Eric Barcel with Marie-Therese Miller-Degenfeld.
The editor expresses her gratitude to the S. Fischer Verlag
for permission to print this English edition.

All Rights Reserved. Except as permitted under current legislation, no part of this work may be photocopied, stored in a retrieval system, published, performed in public, adapted, broadcast, transmitted, recorded, or reproduced in any form or by any means, without the prior permission of the copyright owner.

First published 2000 by Camden House

Camden House is an imprint of Boydell & Brewer Inc.
PO Box 41026, Rochester, NY 14604–4126 USA
and of Boydell & Brewer Limited
PO Box 9, Woodbridge, Suffolk IP12 3DF, UK

ISBN: 1–57113–030–6

Library of Congress Cataloging-in-Publication Data

Hofmannsthal, Hugo von, 1874-1929.
 [Briefwechsel mit Ottonie Gräfin Degenfeld und Julie Freifrau von Wendelstadt. English]
 The poet and the countess : Hugo von Hofmannsthal's correspondence with Countess Ottonie Degenfeld / edited by Marie-Therese Miller-Degenfeld ; translated by W. Eric Barcel.
 p. cm. – (Studies in German literature, linguistics, and culture)
 "This ... authorized English translation ... has been expanded to include additional letters of Ottonie and omits the letters of Julie von Wendelstadt"—T.p. verso.
 Includes index.
 ISBN 1-57113-030-6 (alk. paper)
 1. Hofmannsthal, Hugo von, 1874-1929—Correspondence. 2. Degenfeld-Schonburg, Ottonie, Gräfin von, 1882-1970—Correspondence. 3. Authors, Austrian—20th century—Correspondence. 4. Nobility—Austria—Correspondence. I. Title: Hugo von Hofmannsthal's correspondence with Countess Ottonie Degenfeld. II. Degenfeld-Schonburg, Ottonie, Gräfin von, 1882-1970. III. Miller-Degenfeld, Marie Thérèse, 1908- IV. Title. V. Studies in German literature, linguistics, and culture (Unnumbered)

PT2617.O47 D44313 2000
831'.912—dc21
[B]   00-037949

A catalogue record for this title is available from the British Library.

This publication is printed on acid-free paper.
Printed in the United States of America.

*This book is dedicated in loving memory to my mother,
Countess Ottonie,
and to all our descendants.*

Contents

List of Illustrations		x
Preface	*Marie-Therese Miller-Degenfeld*	xi
Introduction	*Andrew Zimmer*	xv
Names Frequently Mentioned		xxiv
Illustrations		xxv–xli
Harlekin/Harlequin		xlii–xliii
The Correspondence		1
Index		431

Illustrations

Hinterhör: the main house where Ottonie lived; at right the house in which Hofmannsthal always stayed when visiting.	xxv
Christoph-Martin Count Degenfeld-Schönburg in 1906, the year in which he and Ottonie were married.	xxvi
Ottonie on her honeymoon in Geneva, 1906.	xxii
Julie and her husband, Jan Baron Wendelstadt, in the library in Neubeuern, 1908.	xxviii
Ottonie and Christoph-Martin in their house in Kassel, 1907.	xxix
Julie Wendelstadt's sitting room; here Hofmannsthal gave his first reading of *Der Rosenkavalier*.	xxx
The three sisters-in-law in 1907: Mädy Baroness Bodenhausen, née Degenfeld; Julie Baroness Wendelstadt, née Degenfeld; Ottonie Countess Degenfeld.	xxxi
Ottonie with her child Marie-Therese, one year old at the time, 1909.	xxxii
Ottonie with the seven-year-old Marie-Therese, 1915.	xxxiii
Hofmannsthal with his friend Carl J. Burckhardt and Burckhardt's bride, née de Reynold, at Aussee in 1920.	xxxiv
Hofmannsthal and Mädy von Bodenhausen.	xxxv
Ottonie with Gerty von Hofmannsthal.	xxxvi
Hofmannsthal's best friend, Eberhard Baron Bodenhausen, Ottonie's brother-in-law.	xxxvii
Annette Kolb, writer from Munich, before 1914.	xxviii
Rudolph Alexander Schröder, writer, architect, sculptor, before 1914.	xxxix
Hugo von Hofmannsthal.	xl
Castle Neubeuern, 1999.	xli

Preface

IMMEDIATELY AFTER OTTONIE'S FUNERAL on March 24, 1970, I was asked by a representative of the S. Fischer publishing house what I intended to do with the letters Hugo von Hofmannsthal had written to my mother. I had not realized that those letters were known. They asked my permission to publish them. My mother had told me about the letters, which were sacred to her; now they had become my responsibility. I was sure that neither of them had ever envisioned their letters being published. Also, as I only had Hugo's letters without mother's, my answer to the publisher was that I doubted that letters without answers would be interesting reading.

What was unknown to me at the time was that the Fischer Verlag knew where Ottonie's letters were. Hofmannsthal's son Raimund, always short of cash, had put his father's library and literary remains (*Nachlass*) up for sale. The German Volkswagen-Stiftung, a non-profit organization, had bought the library and had deeded it over to the Goethe Haus in Frankfurt. Ottonie's letters were part of this Nachlass.

This changed my view of the matter and I requested copies of Ottonie's letters and started assembling and editing them. At this time I met Eugene Weber, who, while teaching at Harvard, was preparing Hofmannsthal's poems for the critical edition to be published by S. Fischer. I soon realized that I needed help in my editing, and Professor Weber became my collaborator. I am eternally grateful to him. In 1974 S. Fischer published *Hugo von Hofmannsthal: Briefwechsel mit Ottonie Gräfin Degenfeld*. A second edition followed in 1986 that contained ten further Hofmannsthal letters which turned up before I sold mother's house, Hinterhör.

The correspondence was published keeping the famous poet and playwright and his reading public foremost in mind. I omitted a large number of references to intimate details of the Degenfeld family. In addition, many relatives of both families were still alive, and it seemed possible that some might have been hurt by some of the remarks in the letters. Now that thirty years have passed since Ottonie left this world, I no longer need to worry.

Hugo von Hofmannsthal's Correspondence with Countess Ottonie Degenfeld: The Poet and the Countess is a translation of all the letters between Hofmannsthal and Ottonie. Here my descendants can encounter their ancestor Ottonie and see how she struggled and how, with the help of her friend, she slowly returned to life after her great tragedy. This book contains twenty-three letters by Ottonie that were not published in the original German edition.

Taken as a whole, the correspondence is a period piece of the first quarter of the twentieth century. In these letters one may travel with the German aristocracy as well as with their artist and writer friends from one European capitol to the next. We accompany them from the French Riviera to the various spas, going to theater, opera, ballet, and concerts, while conversing in French, English, German, or Italian – which all understood. The reader encounters a now vanished way of life.

The English-speaking public has little acquaintance with the eminent Austrian poet Hugo von Hofmannsthal with the exception of those who are opera fans. The latter will have seen his name as the author of the libretti for the majority of Richard Strauss's operas. These are: *Elektra, Der Rosenkavalier, Ariadne auf Naxos, Die Frau ohne Schatten, Die Ägyptische Helena*, and *Arabella*. While writing the text for *Ariadne*, the playwright must have been dreaming of his young, widowed friend, Ottonie, so deep in mourning. Greek mythology was the perfect foil to express his feelings toward the young countess. In this opera Ariadne mistakes Bacchus for the god of the Underworld, whom she expects to carry her off. They both acknowledge in their letters that this opera was hers, though it was officially dedicated to the famous impresario Max Reinhardt.

Visiting museums and galleries was also one of the great pastimes of the two, and they were especially fascinated by the work of the French Impressionists. My uncle, Eberhard Baron Bodenhausen, seems to have been one of the early collectors of this art. He was Hofmannsthal's best friend, and it was he who introduced his friend to his sister-in-law Ottonie. I am sure that it was Eberhard's influence that sent Hofmannsthal off to art galleries. He often took Ottonie along, and she enjoyed looking while Eberhard occasionally bought some of these paintings.

To publish the edition in English I was fortunate to meet the Germanist and Hofmannsthal scholar, Gerhard Austin, professor at the University of Connecticut, who was convinced after reading the *Briefwechsel* that it was an important book for the study of Hofmannsthal and a significant text for an understanding of the life of the first quarter of the twentieth century. He and his wife Elizabeth gave me their unstinting help and assistance to bring into existence an interesting book. It seems significant that the grandson of the Poet should write the introduction while the daughter of the Countess is the editor of this book. I owe this grandson of Hugo von Hofmannsthal, Andrew Zimmer, my warmest thanks.

It was a wonderful experience for me to grow up among all these illustrious people, artists, writers, friends of the family. I was always permitted to listen quietly to the grown-ups talk, and to be present when one or the other sat at the piano playing classical music. I am deeply grateful for the enrichment that my mother, Ottonie, gave to my life.

M.-T. Miller-Degenfeld
Barbados, January 2000

Introduction

The Poet

Hugo von Hofmannsthal was born in 1874 in Vienna, the capital of what was then the populous, vast Austro-Hungarian empire ruled by Kaiser Franz Joseph I. The city enjoyed rising prosperity and an unprecedented flowering of the arts and sciences. It was without question at least as significant in an intellectual and cultural sense as Paris or London. An only child, Hofmannsthal was raised by deeply attentive parents, and was taught at home by private tutors until he was old enough to begin secondary school or Gymnasium. While still a Gymnasial student, he began to publish lyric poetry under various pseudonyms to conceal his identity, as students were not allowed to publish. The quality of his verse was recognized by leading poets and writers of the day, and barely upon graduation in 1892 he was sought after by these and other admirers, once his identity was revealed. At the behest of his father, whom he deeply revered, he entered the University, enrolling first as a student of law, continuing a steady flow of lyric poems, but also beginning to write short verse plays, some with mythological and historic characters, similar in form to those made popular in England by poets from Shelley to Browning.

In 1894 he entered the Imperial Dragoon regiment for a year's voluntary service as officer, and was stationed in remote southeastern outposts of the empire. In the next year, he passed his civil service law exam, but prevailed on his father to allow him to abandon law, and to commence a study of romance literature and philology. He concluded his studies in 1898 with a dissertation on the Pleiade poets. During these two university years he published more verse plays, and his first prose works, in short story format; one of these, "Reitergeschichte," drawing on his stint as cavalry officer. Three of the verse plays were done on the Berlin stage in 1899, but were mauled by the journalist critics, and have seldom been performed since. Hofmannsthal was deeply embittered by this response, and wrote little more in that genre. In 1898 he had his first meeting with the famed composer Richard Strauss, in 1899 he met Rilke, and in 1900 he met Rudolph Alexander Schröder, who figures as "Rudi" in this book. In 1901 he submitted a study on Victor Hugo to the University of Vienna, seeking an entry level faculty appointment. Late that year he withdrew his application but only when his father gave his hesitant consent.

Early concerns existed that his prodigious gift for lyric verse might run out, and that the student prodigy's talent would not broaden and deepen into other forms. By 1901 such concerns had been allayed by the output of verse plays, the early prose, and his own realization that his future lay in dramatic playwriting. He bravely realized that the verse plays lacked three-dimensional characters, dramatic counterpoint, and live theater appeal, and would not ignite live audience response. Thus in one year, he made the last of three existential leaps, (marriage and dropping an academic career being the other two) when he set about writing dramas and, somewhat later, comedies for the traditional theater.

In 1900 he wrote a prelude to Sophocles' *Antigone*, and in 1901 began drafts of an adaptation of Sophocles' *Electra*. When it was produced on the Berlin stage by Max Reinhardt, in 1903, it was an instant success. Richard Strauss saw this production, and deeply impressed, set it to music over the next several years. Thus began a famous collaboration between poet-librettist and composer that lasted until the poet's death.

By 1901 Hofmannsthal had begun writing *Der Rosenkavalier,* which in collaboration with Strauss was made into an opera, premiering in Dresden in 1911. Produced by Max Reinhardt, its success was immediate. In gratitude to Reinhardt, poet and composer planned their next collaboration, *Ariadne auf Naxos.*

Also in 1901, at the age of twenty-seven, the poet married Gertrud Schlesinger, a young woman from a prosperous Viennese family. He moved with his bride to the extreme outskirts of Vienna, renting an eighteenth-century house that had been the hunting lodge of a Hapsburg prince. Located in Rodaun, then a small village at the edge of the vast Vienna Woods, it was sufficiently far from the deleterious influence of Vienna's coffeehouse intelligentsia that had preoccupied the younger Hofmannsthal. This Rodaun address, which captions so many of his letters, remained his home for the rest of his life, and gave him a base and refuge that enabled him to work steadily and to raise a family of three children. Here he received visitors in an authentic baroque setting, and could retreat in good weather to the easternmost tip of the property, the highest point of the park-like garden, to a small Palladian pagoda, to write in total solitude.

The Countess

Ottonie, Countess von Degenfeld, was born in 1882, the second-youngest of ten children, and grew up in Sondershausen, a small town in Thuringia, then a multi-principality in central Germany. Noteworthy in this town was a musical academy that drew students from a wide area, wholly supported by the reigning Dukes. Her extended family were members of the landed gentry, and Ottonie often was sent to visit various cousins, aunts, and uncles on their estates. As she grew up, and after her brothers had moved away, she followed the urging of a cousin and was placed in a private boarding school in Charlottenburg, a part of Berlin. She took well to this new setting, away from her family, but able to make day trips into a cosmopolitan city with theater, music, and art, and able to socialize with classmates like herself from the landed gentry. She clearly moved among the aristocracy of the time, with its broad social links to its counterparts in England and France.

The three mainstays of this society were a deep love for inherited land, and managing its farm work; a devotion to the ruling powers, whether duke, king, or emperor, a patriotism manifested in the main alternate livelihood to large farming, that of military service; and a deep religious faith, whether Lutheran in the northern states, or Catholic in the southern states.

After finishing schooling in 1900, the young Ottonie had outgrown the small world of her parents in Sondershausen, and began to travel, making long visits to relatives, old friends, and new acquaintances, chaperoned at every move, as was the convention of the time. At the age of twenty in 1902, while on a one-year stay in England, she learned many of the practical skills called for in keeping a large house. In 1905 she met her future husband, Count Christoph-Martin Degenfeld in one of the many houses she visited. She had been asked to help care for and cheer his elderly father, who had been disabled by an accidental fall. She married the next year, moving with her husband to Kassel, where Degenfeld was the aide-de-camp and longtime friend of Duke Albrecht of Württemberg. She settled into married life, taking part in social events in Kassel, well positioned because of her husband's closeness to the Duke, well liked for her warm, outgoing person, and respected for her interest in her friends and family. In 1908 a daughter, Marie-Therese, was born.

But her husband had been diagnosed with cancer only four months earlier, and died two months later, in his forty-second year. His entire regiment came to his funeral, as did the Duke, who attended his burial in the Degenfeld ancestral estate, next to his father, who had taken such a liking to Ottonie before he himself died just prior to his son's marriage to Ottonie.

Thereafter, Ottonie had what she later described as a complete nervous breakdown. She could walk only with the greatest difficulty; her whole body trembled. She sought treatment and began a year's convalescence in Neubeuern, where her sister-in-law, Julie Wendelstadt, had returned at this same time, having herself suddenly been widowed in 1909. Due to the sequence of losses by early death, Julie and Ottonie began their lives anew, Julie's family having given Ottonie a lifetime residency in a large house called Hinterhör, on the estate of the castle property that Julie Wendelstadt moved into, called Castle Neubeuern. Ottonie and her sister-in-law would live in these two places for the rest of their lives, with but a short walk between the castle and the manor house. They jointly raised Ottonie's daughter, Marie-Therese, and together managed the affairs of the estate, beginning in the summer of 1909. Ottonie was now twenty-seven years old.

As almost always in that time and society, Ottonie and Hugo were brought together by a relative, in this case Ottonie's brother-in-law, Eberhard von Bodenhausen, who, in the eleven years of their acquaintance, had become a close and lifelong friend of Hofmannsthal. Hofmannsthal was now thirty-five years of age. His youngest son Raimund had been born two years before Ottonie's daughter Marie-Therese. During the year of Ottonie's slow recovery, as she was emerging from a largely bedridden state, the visits of Bodenhausen and Hofmannsthal reawakened in her the deep love for the written word, and she began reading voraciously from the poetic works that Hofmannsthal brought into the house. In the early letters, Hofmannsthal, alternately radiant and pedagogic, opened the doors of a literary mansion, one by one, to Ottonie: Goethe, Whitman, Hebbel, among many others. She began to draw increasing pleasure from reading, and spoke her fledgling feelings about these books in many of the early letters. At the same time an emotionally-charged interdependence developed between them, she gaining strength and stability from the range of books — and later the range of music and theater — that were placed within her easy reach by a man wishing to share his own experience of them with her, and he savoring her every response.

Letters

Letters were the dominant form of contact between persons not living in the same community. Telegrams were used for emergencies and bad news. Telephones were only slowly being installed at the turn of the century. Family lore has it that when phone service was put in Rodaun, its metallic ring was so disconcerting to Hofmannsthal that he would run into another room, letting the housekeeper take a message. Writers, in particular, left prodigious correspondences. By way of random example: despite his ceaselessly peripatetic life, D. H. Lawrence, a contemporary of Hofmannsthal, wrote over 5,000 letters, now housed at Cambridge University. After writing fiction each morning, Thomas Mann wrote letters in the afternoon. Letters could be written as the mood of the writer ordained – in deep reflection, out of undercurrents of feeling; lightly, even giddily, breezing along on social patter, with storytelling, in near conversational mode. Letters could be dashed off in a huff, or dragged from the pen over broken periods of time spanning many hours. Since a letter took days to arrive, and the response more days to come back, it was always like striking a sound, whether a single note or an elaborate chord, heard only by the writer, followed by the silent wait for the echo of a reply. Hofmannsthal's sounds in the early letters were yearning and plaintive, didactic and querulous. Ottonie's sounds were purring and thankful, questing and inquisitive. In the war years (1914–1918) the sound and tone of the letters changes, becoming somber and alarmed, their text ever more cognizant of the vast changes taking place in their world, despite official censorship and restricted travel.

The War Years

Like giant tectonic plates, three empires had coexisted, contiguous, in a balance of power, their rulers related by blood and marriage, blessed with extraordinary longevity, without collision or upheaval since 1870, when the last Napoleonic empire was ended by war. The Hapsburg monarchy, the Czar's empire, and the Prussian empire for years avoided collision, but failed to confront internal fission until the assassination of Archduke Ferdinand in Sarajevo. The earthquake that changed the makeup of the European map ultimately struck down all three empires. The social milieu that enjoyed the direct benevolence of their rulers, the broad aristocracy that held so much of the land and most elite military posts, deeply linked to their imperial history for years, was stripped of that benevolence. Their privileges, rank, imperial uniforms were gone, their houses and castles, like Ottonie's in Neubeuern, turned into recovery centers for the wounded soldiers. They were henceforth irrevocably cast upon their own resources. This social milieu with which both poet and countess identified had to adapt to a different world. When war broke out, Hofmannsthal, then forty years old, was called into service to an infantry unit in Istria. Realizing perhaps that this was an inappropriate posting, the authorities furloughed him from the unit and he was transferred to the war ministry in Vienna. He was subsequently assigned to the staff of the emperor's personal and confidential emissary to the Kaiser's government in Berlin. His official duties in maintaining liaison between the two imperial allies absorbed his energies and challenged his organizational skills, later to flower fully in the great task he undertook in founding the Salzburg Festival, with Max Reinhardt, in 1921.

Hofmannsthal's letters of the war years may be the only record he left of this period when he was deeply involved in public service. Interestingly, his service relieved a number of his medical problems, including migraines and depressive states. His letters reveal that his service energized him, and Ottonie's letters to him reveal her resourcefulness in caring for the wounded who were brought to Schloss Neubeuern. Neither questioned loyalty, patriotism, rightness of cause. As part of his official duties Hofmannsthal traveled to the "occupied lands," southern Poland and Belgium. He found solace in Whitman's poems under the pressure of modern warfare. Ottonie learned quickly, reading the war novelist's contemporary accounts. At the time he was reworking *Ariadne auf Naxos*, a play first performed on stage in 1912, and which, again in collaboration with Strauss, was turned into an opera that had its premiere in 1916 in Vienna.

Ariadne auf Naxos

Hofmannsthal wrote the play *Ariadne auf Naxos* between February and April 1911. In its earliest version, it was to be a short play within another play, namely Molière's *Le Bourgeois Gentilhomme*. This piece, popular at the time, has as its setting the great house of a wealthy patron who will invite all his friends to a musical event, a ballet evening, with dancers and singers, as part of a bid for the recognition of the royal court and its nobility. The ballet had been set to music by the composer Lully. The wealthy patron was both the first and the last person on stage in Molière's play, forming its "bookends."

Hofmannsthal unabashedly decided to substitute a playlet of his own for the ballet. He reasoned that the ballet musicale, with fireworks finale, was too thin a plot line, failing to deepen or transform the character of the wealthy patron. So it came that he adapted Molière's play and introduced a commedia dell'arte subplot, with eight traditional characters of this form, and the follow-on subplot of names drawn from Greek mythology: Circe, Theseus, Bacchus, and his own creation, Ariadne. Hofmannsthal retained the figure Zerbinetta from Molière's version, and made her the transition figure that binds together the lengthy rehearsal preparation (Act 1, "Prelude") and the commedia dell'arte characters, their comic antics and stylized foolishness, leading into the emergence of Ariadne, coming out of her cave, and the arrival of Bacchus, stepping off his ship (Act 2, "Opera"). Bacchus comes with pagan god-like attributes, in that he was immune to the blandishments of Circe, the enchantress on another island who had so totally bewitched Odysseus, a mere mortal who could not resist her spell.

The essence of Ariadne is the transformation of two persons. Hofmannsthal uses the word "Verwandlung" (transformation) in a letter to Strauss written in July 1912:

> Transformation is the life force of living; and is the true mystery of Nature's creations; a lack of transformation equals immobility and death. He who wants to live must be able to transform himself, he must forget. And yet we adhere to the past in our lives, because such remembrance is directly tied to those human values to which we remain loyal. This is one of those paradoxes on which our existences are built, like the Delphic Temple, at the edge of an abyss.

The transformation is mutual and immediate, Bacchus shedding memories of his escape from Circe, and Ariadne shutting out any thought of Theseus. There is an instant recognition of past suffering ended, and the metamorphosis of both characters is the high point in the final duet, with bad memories being jettisoned even before the two embark to leave her island behind.

In explaining transformation of the two leading persons as the principal dramatic turning point of this opera, Hofmannsthal could not refrain from contrasting it with *Elektra*:

> My work has been researched, and it has been said that all my life I have grappled with the mystery of this paradox, which never ceases to astonish me. So here once again it is Ariadne standing against Zerbinetta, as earlier Electra stood against Chrysothemis. Chrysothemis wanted to live, nothing more, and she knew that he who wants to live, must be able to forget. Electra will not forget. How could the two sisters have understood each other?

In case the point still eludes Strauss, Hofmannsthal presses on:

> Zerbinetta is in her element when she tumbles from one man to another; Ariadne can espouse only one man, and lives only in the attachment to one man. She tears her costume; this is the gesture of one who wants to flee from the world.

The letter continues on for two more pages: "She nearly died and has been brought back to life, her soul is in truth transformed."

Hofmannsthal never wrote a similar letter to Ottonie. Clearly he knew it was her story, recovery from deep sorrow, slowly being able to walk again, gradually surmounting the multiple deaths in her family of a few years earlier, a transformation to a new person who is able again "to love and live."

In one letter the poet gives *Ariadne* to the countess, as a gift written for her. In letters prior to the war years, she acknowledges how much she loves this play, which was published in 1912 but was not completed as an opera for another four years. A number of the letters attest to Hofmannsthal's care and concern to see that it became a stage and operatic success.

The Postwar Years (1919–1929)

The first years after the armistice brought relief from the stalemate of the war, but they were also marked by extreme hunger, by shortages of food and roving mobs that plundered in the cities. Hofmannsthal became embittered over the turn of events, and blamed the incompetence of the Hapsburg military, and the poor leadership of the emperors and king who lost the war, had to flee, and were replaced by forces and regimes that he did not understand.

The letters then became longer and less agitated in tone. Both poet and countess were now in their middle years. He continued to write in several genres: comedic stage plays, full-length dramas, and three operas, *Die Frau ohne Schatten*, *Ägyptische Helena*, and *Arabella,* in a continued collaboration with Strauss. He began to work again with Max Reinhardt, the impresario who had mounted the operatic premiere of *Der Rosenkavalier*, and the two were instrumental in the founding of the Salzburg Festival, the first truly modern summer festival for all the performing arts. He wrote plays specifically designed for the unusual venues in Salzburg, like the Felsenreitschule, or the Dom Platz, for which *Jedermann* was restaged.

In Hofmannsthal's last five years his health began to decline. Photos of those years show his face swollen, his neck enlarged. He suffered from hypertension and congestive heart problems, in addition to migraine attacks, an asthmatic condition, and an extreme sensitivity to barometric changes. His health was a far cry from his youthful years, when he rode on horseback in exercises with his military unit, and took bicycle tours in the summer of 1897 from Salzburg through the Dolomites to Varese, and again, in 1898, accompanied by Arthur Schnitzler, to pay a visit to D'Annunzio in Florence. Such strenuous activity was now long in the past.

By 1929 Hofmannsthal had been working on the libretto of *Arabella* for more than a year, and decided to revise the first act. He sent it to Strauss, who responded by telegram: "First act is excellent. Hearty thanks, and wishing you luck." Hofmannsthal never saw it. On July 13, 1929, his son Franz committed suicide in his Rodaun house. Hofmannsthal sent a telegram to Ottonie: "Franz has committed suicide, Hugo." On July 15th, while dressing for his son's funeral, Hofmannsthal suffered a stroke, and died a few hours later. Ottonie and a large number of his friends attended his funeral. Ottonie, returning to Neubeuern, said "If only Hugo could have been among us, there for once were nearly all his friends together; how often did he try to arrange such a gathering."

Strauss finished *Arabella* alone, and it had its premiere in Dresden in 1933. Ottonie remained at Neubeuern and was able to hold on to this property by starting a boarding school for girls in the 1920s. She continued to live a very active life past her eightieth birthday.

Hofmannsthal kept no diary. He has not been the subject of a biography. His letters, and the letters from Ottonie, form the most remarkable record of his concerns and work, and uniquely, his emotional moods from letter to letter remind the reader of the dramatic dialogues of his plays, in which moods change swiftly. In that regard, these letters are an extension of his main works, and are more revealing of his emotional breadth and intensity than any of the other collected letters he wrote to friends and persons whom he esteemed. His eagerness to receive Ottonie's thoughtful letters in reply, throughout the many years they continued to write to each other, his highly personal letters responding to her concerns, and expressing his inner feelings, make this correspondence unique, giving the reader a special insight into both Poet and Countess.

Andrew Zimmer

Names Frequently Mentioned

Hofmannsthal Family

Hugo von Hofmannsthal (H. v. H.)	1874–1929
Gertrude von Hofmannsthal, née Schlesinger (Gerty, wife of H. v. H.)	1880–1959
Hugo Peter von Hofmannsthal (banker in Vienna, father of H. v. H.)	1841–1915
Christina von Hofmannsthal (daughter of H. v. H.)	1902–198?
Franz von Hofmannsthal (son of H. v. H.; committed suicide)	1903–1929
Raimund von Hofmannsthal (son of H. v. H.)	1906–1979
Heinrich Zimmer (son-in-law of H. v. H.; Prof. of Sanskrit; husband of Christina)	

Degenfeld Family

Ottonie Countess Degenfeld-Schonburg, née von Schwartz (O. D. S.)	1882–1970
Christoph-Martin Count Degenfeld-Schonburg (Ottonie's husband)	1866–1908
Alfred Count Degenfeld-Schonburg (Ottonie's father-in-law)	1826–1908
Anna Countess Degenfeld-Schonburg, née Baroness von Hügel (Mama; Ottonie's mother-in-law)	1833–1915
Marie-Therese Countess Degenfeld-Schonburg (Baby; Ottonie's daughter)	1908–
Julie Baroness Wendelstadt, née Degenfeld Schonburg (Ottonie's sister-in-law)	1871–1942
Dorothea Baroness Bodenhausen, née Degenfeld-Schonburg (Mädy; Ottonie's sister-in-law)	1877–1970
Jan Baron Wendelstadt (husband of Julie, owner of Schloss Neubeuern)	1847–1909
Eberhard Baron Bodenhausen-Degener (Bockelchen, husband of Mädy)	1868–1918

Bodenhausen-Degener Children

Karin Baroness Bodenhausen-Degener (committed suicide)	1898–1920
Hans-Wilke Baron Bodenhausen-Degener (killed in Kenya)	1901–1937
Julie Baroness Bodenhausen-Degener (Luli)	1903–1951
Christa Baroness Bodenhausen-Degener	1909–1986

von Schwartz Family

Johann Friedrich von Schwartz (Ottonie's father)	1842–1918
Margarethe von Schwartz, née Schröder (Ottonie's mother)	1849–1935
Adolf von Schwartz (Ottonie's brother; killed in WWI)	1880–1914
Albrecht von Schwartz (Ottonie's brother)	1875–1960
Kurt von Schwartz (Ottonie's brother; committed suicide)	18??–????
Margarethe von Schwartz (Eta; Ottonie's sister)	1871–1945
Oda von Schwartz (Ottonie's sister; killed in air raid during WWII)	1883–1945

Friends

Harry Count Kessler	1868–1937
Rudolph Alexander Schröder (poet)	1868–1937
Henry van de Velde (architect, leader in Art Nouveau movement)	1873–1962
Henry van Heiseler (writer)	1863–1957
Annette Kolb, (writer)	1875–1928
Rudolph Borchardt	1870–1967
Carl J. Burckardt	1891–1974
Grete Wiesenthal (dancer, married to Erwin Lang)	1885–1970
Erwin Lang	1886–1962

Hinterhör: the main house where Ottonie lived; at right the house in which Hofmannsthal always stayed when visiting.

Christoph-Martin Count Degenfeld-Schönburg in 1906, the year in which he and Ottonie were married.

Ottonie on her honeymoon in Geneva, 1906.

Julie and her husband, Jan Baron Wendelstadt, in the library in Neubeuern, 1908.

Ottonie and Christoph-Martin in their house in Kassel, 1907.

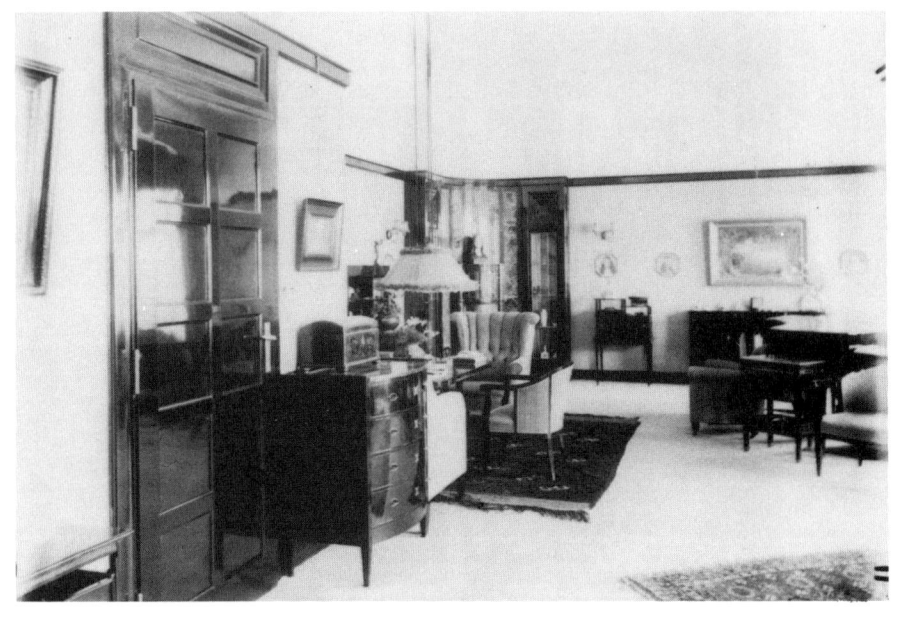

Julie Wendelstadt's sitting room; here Hofmannsthal gave his first reading of Der Rosenkavalier.

The three sisters-in-law in 1907: Mädy Baroness Bodenhausen, née Degenfeld; Julie Baroness Wendelstadt, née Degenfeld; Ottonie Countess Degenfeld.

*Ottonie with her child Marie-Therese,
one year old at the time, 1909.*

Hofmannsthal with his friend Carl J. Burckhardt and Burckhardt's bride, née de Reynold, at Aussee in 1920.

Ottonie with the seven-year-old Marie-Therese, 1915.

Hofmannsthal and Mädy von Bodenhausen.

Ottonie with Gerty von Hofmannsthal.

Hofmannsthal's best friend, Eberhard Baron Bodenhausen, Ottonie's brother-in-law.

Annette Kolb, writer from Munich, before 1914.

Rudolf Alexander Schröder, writer, architect, sculptor, before 1914.

Hugo von Hofmannsthal.

Castle Neubeuern, 1999.

Harlekin

(From *Ariadne auf Naxos*)

Lieben, Hassen, Hoffen, Zagen
Alle Lust und alle Qual,
Alles kann ein Herz ertragen
Einmal um das andere Mal.

Aber weder Lust noch Schmerzen,
Abgestorben auch der Pein,
Das its tödlich deinem Herzen
Und so darfst du mir nicht sein!

Musst dich aus dem Dunkel heben,
Wär es auch um neue Qual,
Leben musst du, liebes Leben,
Leben noch dies eine Mal!

Harlequin

Love and hatred, hope and failure,
Every pleasure, every pain,
All of this the heart can master
Once and many a time again.

But to feel no pain or pleasure,
Numb the ache that was too true,
Kill your heart to ease its anguish:
That I cannot let you do.

You must rouse yourself from darkness,
Even if to newborn pain.
Dearest life, you must be living.
Live you must this once again!

The Correspondence

Aussee, Obertressen, 2 September [1909]

Dear Countess,

For the second time I decided to tear up a rather long letter I had written you. As I do not usually suffer from inhibitions of this kind, I am not quite sure what is at work here. Naturally both letters concerned the matter we had discussed during the sleigh ride we went on back in January. You may have simply forgotten about this, but you do not strike me as the kind of person who forgets, even in regard to an incidental matter. I have thought about this conversation many times during the past month and meant to write you a number of times – prior to the death of poor Wendelstadt,[1] whom I often recall as well. However, after remaining silent for a rather long time, I resolved to write once more in order to explain my initial silence leading up to that point.

It seems as if Eberhard would now like to meet us in October, and apparently Neubeuern is to be the place. I hope this will come to pass so that I will have the chance to see you again.

However, I did not want to see you before first expressing the above, even if I have done so insufficiently.

Faithfully, yours H. v. Hofmannsthal

Rodaun, 23 December [1909]

Dear Countess,

Is it possible that nearly a month has passed since I received the dear words you sent me from Munich? Can it be that I traveled from Semmering, where they reached me, all the way to Berlin and back, to find myself here again – that to this day I have not replied and still won't today, but rather am simply requesting your forgiveness and sending you my warmest regards? The evening your card arrived, I was quietly at work in complete solitude. I was very happy to feel your clear eyes focused on me as I spoke to you. It seemed a very long time, indeed, having put off my reply until the next morning, and then until the following afternoon. But I do believe that I spoke to you at some point during the course of each day. Where might you be now? I wonder if you were able

---

1. Baron Wendelstadt (1843–1909), owner of the castle Neubeuern, and husband of Julie, died suddenly on 29 July 1909 (see letter from H. v. H. to J. v. W from 2 August 1909).

to convince Julie to leave Neubeuern during this time.² I am too tired to write as much as I would like. I hope you enjoy the comedy.³ There is of course infinitely more of the human element to be found there than in the comic opera.⁴ I have also always wanted to hear something – which you alone must tell me – of a personal nature concerning the comic opera. I remember having this question on my mind every time I walked down the long corridor. But then, when we were in your room or the blue room, another conversation always managed to get in the way, and I forgot to ask you. Those were strange days back then. I myself was so lost at times – the physical symptoms, the *sleeplessness*, etc., were mere reflections of this. You also mentioned the lovely books Eberhard sent you. I always wanted to know just what books they were. Please write me again *soon*. I will be here a little while longer before going to Berlin for the rehearsals. The comedy is going to be performed during the last part of January. But there is so much else alive within me.

Yours, Hofmannsthal

P.S. It was a very beautiful and truly memorable day when we went on the big outing. Do you have the French lady⁵ with you now? There is so much I would like to know!

[Hotel Adlon, Berlin–W.] Berlin, Monday, 24 January 1910

Dear Countess,

I thank you from the bottom of my heart for the lovely letter. Not a single day passed on which I did not think of you at least once or even several times, and I felt happy each time I did. Sometime in the course of the next few days, I will send you a copy of my comedy – in shortened or some disorderly yet legible form – in place of a response to your last letter. There is undoubtedly more of me to be found there than I could possibly express in the longest and sincerest of letters. Do take it as something very personal which I send to you, and please don't allow it to pass from your hands. And then, when you have a little time and are inclined to do so, write me about it, about what you find pleasing, or less pleasing, and so on. I have just returned from the first rehearsal. It was really wonderful. You mustn't think it tiring or demanding; it is simply charming, so very charming, indeed – so much so, in fact, that the mere thought of it spurs me on and sustains me in my work when I become weary at times.

---

2. On account of the recent death of her husband.
3. *Cristina's Homecoming:* first performance February 1910 in Berlin.
4. *The Rosenkavalier.*
5. Someone with whom to practice her French.

What a joy it is to have Max Reinhardt, an exceedingly strange, brilliant and, at the same time, fascinating man conducting the rehearsals! (I believe he is one of the strangest and most precious human beings I know next to Kessler.) And then there are all these actors, young men, old men, women, girls, who in the dim light of this ugly, desolate stage are gradually transformed into their characters and who are held together by a bond, much like that between a group of men who are all drunk or facing a common danger. Meanwhile vanities are at a peak and the whole atmosphere at a rather feverish pitch; yet, on the whole, it is a world strangely devoid of the mundane elements of everyday life. The weeks devoted to rehearsing are always wonderful; I truly love the memories I have of them and, even more, the immediate experience.

I am so glad you enjoy reading and that you have acquired the habit of reading several books at the same time. My experience has convinced me that this is the best approach.

I wish – why is it that I prefer to say this rather than write it – that you could familiarize yourself with Balzac, an author to whom, alongside Shakespeare and Goethe, I shall forever remain indebted. If one has only read five of his books, one does not know him at all; only after reading thirty or so can one be said to know him. Whoever makes it this far, however, will undoubtedly read his books again and again. It depends largely on which of his works one gets hold of first. Some of his books can bore the reader or even put him off. He mustn't be read with even the smallest trace of impatience.

First I would recommend you take a look at *La Cousine Bette*, one of his latest and most masterful works – then perhaps *Le Médecin de campagne*, followed by *Illusions perdues*, *Le Père Goriot*, *La Vieille fille*, and so on. There are many inexpensive editions; however, the one that costs only one Franc has miserable print.

Will it be a long time before you write me again?

Yours, Hofmannsthal

P.S. I'll be *here* for about four weeks.

Neubeuern, 23 February 1910

Dear Herr von Hofmannsthal,

I really must explain the telegram I sent you recently, as you were probably very surprised by it, doubly so following your talk with Eberhard about Mädy. The idea of sending Mädy to Weimar came to me because of her much improved physical condition; I thought it would do her a great deal of good emotionally if she had the chance of being together with all of you, even for a few short days. It would give her the opportunity to quietly sit beside all of you and soak in the atmosphere there which is like mountain air for us ordinary people. The thought came to me in connection with the van de Velde invitation, and since Count Kessler, too, was kind enough to ask Mädy to come. However, Mädy felt she might be imposing on you, and that's why I sent the telegram, which I assume was the proper thing to do. She's with Julie now in Nice, which will, I hope, do both of them some good. I am very happy I didn't have to join them. I am enjoying the peace and quiet alone here with my child so much; it's truly heavenly. The spring weather is so gorgeous that I would hate to have to leave.

You probably heard from Count Kessler that we attended his lecture in Munich, although he can't imagine how much this meant to all of us. For me especially it was an experience in the truest sense of the word. I arrived there exhausted and out of breath following a day on the town and having been exasperated by countless trifles. After listening to just a few words of his speech, it was as if an entire load had been lifted from my shoulders. Something so pure and great emanated from him which made all insignificant concerns disappear. It was and will remain for me an unforgettable evening.

And now, thanks again so much for *Cristina's Homecoming*. I rushed straight through it, enjoying it immensely. I am now reading it for the second time at my own leisure. All the characters are so wonderfully portrayed, each in his own way. The captain says such wonderful things and expresses such deep feelings, and Cristina is simply delightful. More about this later.

I briefly saw Eberhard in Munich. He was still very much under the influence of the experiences he had in Berlin, which proved to be so refreshing for him. He immediately told me *how* wonderful the evening of the premiere had been and *how* wonderfully you stood above it all. How splendid it must have been for you feeling so at one with everything, what with having all your friends there and yourself taking on the part of godfather to one of the children of your genius.

I never really thanked you for your letter either. I read some of Balzac's books last year and enjoyed them very much. *Père Goriot*, for example. I have gotten hold of a few more in the meantime. Unfortunately, the French lady won't be able to come, and that after I had made all the necessary arrangements. I do, however, hope to find someone during the month of March because I want so very much to take advantage of the time I am alone. Sometimes an unlucky star reigns over things, and that's exactly what's happening with my French studies. If you happen to find the time, I'd really enjoy receiving a short letter.

With the warmest regards for you and your wife, I am always,

Yours, Ottonie Degenfeld

❦ ❦ ❦

Good Friday, 25 March [1910]

Dear Countess,

This is to bring you Easter greetings there while you enjoy your solitude, which has perhaps by now come to an end. It made me happy to think of you there all by yourself. Everyone needs this from time to time.

I am glad you enjoyed reading the comedy. Whom else would one wish to please besides those one is fond of? For whom else would one write, after all? It's a very curious thing really: although this play was rather a flop, never before did I receive so many kind, pleasant, intelligent, and encouraging remarks. You'll be able to see a shorter, bolder – or perhaps more brazen – version of it in Munich this summer which I completed yesterday (and from which the rather dreary epilogue has been dropped, for one should never state what can already be assumed). You will be astonished how much this play benefits when performed on stage: It has a very lively pace to it, and great cheer and joy emanate from it through the stage settings and other, less conspicuous – yet not insignificant – elements. I also find the characters quite pleasing, especially Cristina. However, I think the essence of the work lies not in the characters themselves (perhaps this may generally be said of my comedies) but in the manner in which the characters relate to each other. The relationships people have are of particular interest to me. Every relationship between two people is unique; it is a highly individual and delicate, yet substantial thing. Understanding this and using it as the raw material of my creations is perhaps my thing. When one's attention is focused in this direction, life immediately becomes much richer and in some respects less of a burden. The individual frequently is weighted down by his own self, but people's relationships, these children of the intellect as it were, float freely above them, some revealing demonic, others angelic faces. They have, just as real children do, something of both parents in them, but they have the capacity to free themselves from their creators and produce that spiritual wealth of the world which hovers above.

You responded to something I said about Balzac. Your comments were very precise, but I had hoped you might address this topic in greater detail by mentioning which books you are currently reading and which of them you are able to relate to more and which less. Then I, in turn, could have taken the matter up further. In cases like this, it is very easy to jump from one thing to another and quite difficult to proceed systematically.

Did you know that I'm seriously considering – this is perhaps extremely presumptuous, indeed absurd – bringing the children to Hinterhör for a visit sometime this summer? They are very typical, well-behaved children and would enjoy rural life, the animals, etc., very much.

And it would suit me very well, as I will be busy in Munich this August in connection with Reinhardt's production of Sophocles' *Oedipus Rex*, which I recently translated. However, this may not be feasible for thousands of reasons, in which case we simply won't do it.

It strikes me as very kind of the Baroness Julie that she invited the musician Varese[6] and his wife – a very young, highly sensitive, intelligent and charming soul – to a sojourn in Neubeuern, even though she has never met them herself. If only the good people would agree to come (they seem to be extremely timid and are perhaps afraid of people), you would have the most delightful conversations in French. Please write me soon, if you don't find it too tedious and are in the mood.

Your friend, Hofmannsthal

❦ ❦ ❦

Nice, Hotel de France, 3 April 1910

My dear Herr von Hofmannsthal,

Today is Mädy's birthday and I'd like to try to write you a few lines. As you can see from the letterhead, my solitude has turned into the complete opposite. I was alone for only eight days, a short time I enjoyed very much. I truly need to have time alone, both for my physical and my spiritual well-being. With every passing day I become more and more convinced that I am truly suited only to country life. During my first few days here the emptiness of everyday life in this area, where not a single sensible word is heard, made me feel completely lost. But I seem to have grown accustomed to this life now, or is it simply going for rides in the automobile every day that has helped me to adjust? We're leaving for Paris this Thursday and will be gone for four or five days. I'm looking forward to this trip because I don't know Paris at all. I wish I had someone who would enjoy showing me all the places one has heard so much about through literature and history. Julie will be too exhausted to do much.

I must tell you now how strange it seems that we have been thinking so alike. My mind was focused on you the whole time, and I was in the middle of rereading your previous letter, when your most recent one arrived. Seldom have I felt that I was experiencing mental telepathy. Thank you very much for your last letter, too. Do you have any idea what you are able to do for me? I don't believe you do. You constantly give me the courage I need to face life. It's so hard trudging along all alone when everyone else is living and enjoying things together in pairs. The fact that you simply assume I take an interest in something gives me the strength and the encouragement I need to keep from wallowing in my sorrow.

---

6. Edgar Varese (1885–1965), French composer.

I am *so* looking forward to seeing *Cristina's Homecoming* in Munich, and I am sure I will enjoy it very much. I thoroughly enjoyed reading *La Femme de trente ans* and have now begun *La Cousine Bette*. I do not believe I have ever read a book in which a man reveals such thoroughgoing knowledge of a woman's soul. I keep asking myself how a man could possibly know so much about a woman's soul! It pleases me that everything about the characters' inner lives is not discussed in detail but instead is simply hinted at. However, there is one thing I do not understand in *La Femme d Tr.*: Why does she take everything – her hatred for a husband she does not love – out on her poor child when she certainly loved the child at first?

What you said about the relationships of the characters in your comedy has given me a lot to think about. You are right, there is something tremendously appealing about these "feelings for one another." One can usually only imagine how much they mean.

Now I would like to respond to the question about your children. I plan to begin living in Hinterhör on 1 August; in other words, I will be living in a partially finished and rather primitive house during the summer. I would be very happy to have your children come for a visit; but if possible, you would just need to tell me exactly when they can come. They could certainly stay with me there for three weeks. However, I only have two guest rooms, so I have to make very exact plans and must know ahead of time, if at all possible. It would be fine if the children came at the very beginning of August. I assume you and your wife will be bringing them? Has your wife had her operation yet, and how did it go? Hopefully fine.

We'll be traveling from Paris to Stuttgart and Boll to see the Reverend Blumhardt,[7] whom you have probably heard of. On the 21st, I will be spending my husband's birthday alone in Eybach[8] and will travel from there to my parents' home in Sondershausen, where I'll be staying until the sixth or the eighth of May. It will be terrible being separated from my child for so long, but I have no choice!

Take care, and do not forget about

Yours truly, Ottonie Degenfeld

P.S. Did you know that Director Schmidt[9] died in Essen? This will have a great effect on Eberhard.

---

7. Christoph Blumhardt (1842–1919), a friend of the Degenfeld family, whose father founded a religious settlement called Bad Boll.
8. Castle of the Degenfelds.
9. A director of Krupp, predecessor of Eberhard von Bodenhausen.

Rodaun, 10 June [1910]

Dear Countess,

I can hardly believe how long – it has been days, perhaps weeks now – I have wanted to write you and failed to do so. You have surely long since returned home.

What I mentioned about bringing the children to stay with you for a few weeks in Hinterhör (rather than Neubeuern) was just a thought. Of course I meant for this to be in connection with our coming there, too, because I knew I would be busy working in Munich for about ten days at some point during the summer. However, I did not know at the time when this would be. I am still not exactly sure when we will be coming. I came to realize one cannot plan something like this on the spur of the moment without first making the necessary arrangements and organizing everything well in advance; moreover, this would certainly be very demanding on you (both physically and emotionally), so I decided to drop the idea immediately. As far as my plans are concerned, I will probably be in Munich for *Oedipus* from about the 20th to the 30th of August – and as a part of the bargain I hope to spend time in Munich as well as Neubeuern. I have an idea for later (this is not the first time I have thought of this): It would be lovely if you could visit us in Aussee alone sometime for five or six days. I really think this would be very nice. Or you might come with the Bodenhausens. We can think about this. Beginning the morning of the day after tomorrow I will be on the Lido near Venice, at the Excelsior Palace. This was not a letter. Perhaps you will nevertheless be so kind and respond with a few lines.

Yours, Hofmannsthal

❦ ❦ ❦

Tarasp Spa Engadine, 24 June 1910

Dear Herr von Hofmannsthal,

You are enjoying Italy and I the Engadine with the same Inn river I know from home, only here it's somewhat closer to the source. We arrived yesterday, we being Julie and I. Although quite long, the carriage ride up here from Landeck was extremely enjoyable. Now we must get used to living by the clock, according to the doctor's orders, which will hopefully bring us lasting benefits. We plan to be back home by 20 July.

The main reason I am writing now is to say once more how much I would like to have your children stay with me in Hinterhör, assuming they would be willing to make do with very primitive accommodations, that is to say, one of the children would have to sleep on a couch. Would this meet with the approval of their loving mother?! I really would be more than happy to have a small crowd of children romping about among the flock of chickens. Marie-Therese would be overjoyed to finally have some playmates. Your wife will certainly accompany you to Munich, which means both of you will have many opportunities to visit Neubeuern. Only it's such a pity this has to be in August, when my father and a friend of mine will be visiting. I would have loved to have had your children stay there with me now. My sincere thanks for the lovely invitation to come to Aussee for a few days. I would absolutely love to at a later date, with or without the Bodenhausens.

We recently brought Mama and the child to Eybach and have installed them there for as long as we are here. We worked very hard to get things ready in Hinterhör so that we can move in shortly after we return. The tiny household will begin running on 1st August.

Unfortunately, I have not had much time for reading recently, so I am looking forward to some quiet hours here. I brought along the new *Süddeutsche Monatsheft* containing Alexander Schröder's translation of the *Fifteenth Song* from Homer's *Odyssey*; I can't wait to start reading it. And Balzac will certainly provide me further enjoyment.

Nature is unbelievably beautiful here. One is filled with admiration when beholding the tall mountains; at the same time, I am overcome by a dreadful longing for the wonderful days I experienced with my husband here in Switzerland. Suddenly, I feel like lashing out in defiance and notice myself becoming quite indignant when the thought crosses my mind that all that twosome happiness others enjoy will remain forever beyond my reach. One feels rather left out when observing all the happy couples together. I apologize for these sighs of sorrow. It was by no means my intention to write this, but it has found its way onto the page – and that is where it is going to stay. I suppose one is not always able to act contrary to one's nature.

Take care. Write me again when you feel in the mood. It is odd how I always know when a letter from you will arrive. I have rarely experienced this before.

Many warm regards,

Yours, Ottonie Degenfeld

[Dolomites Inn, Canazei] 5 August [1910]

Dear Countess,

Twice now I have glimpsed the Inn racing by, and each time I thought of you. We crossed over it, once in Wasserburg and again in Finstermünz, where it rushed along wildly below the road. Sitting quietly beside the driver, one can call forth and, for a moment, retain images of the people one wishes to see. Eventually you lose hold of them and find yourself gazing out into the open space. It is funny how many things hang suspended in the air – in addition to the big, beautiful clouds, which glisten as they cross the sky and cast shadows down below. Once I spied a rake from a harvest vehicle which had managed to get tangled in a telegraph wire. One also glimpses the lovely, old insignia above the entrances to the inns, each of which remains suspended above for a brief moment: gold-plated eagles clutching blue grapes in their bills and white lambs, the emperor's crown, golden crucifixes surrounded by rays of light, black bears, wild men. Soon after entering Italy, the old walnut trees are replaced by the towering peaks of the Spanish chestnut with its thousands of leaves reflecting light; however, all the merry old inn insignias are gone; in place of them, though, each market square contains a beautiful fountain covered by a roof resting delicately atop stone pillars. The women arrive with beautiful, copper kettles for scooping up water. We traveled west to Constance, then south to Brescia; from time to time, in the morning or evening hours, we descended to the low-lying plains or drove along the lake shore; by midday, we were high up in the clouds atop Arlberg or Stilferjoch, where the fields below the road were still covered with snow. What wonderful landscapes the earth has!

The South Bavarian countryside, with the Alpine chain along the border, is very dear to me; I looked out here in the direction of Kufstein and recalled our lovely automobile ride, as well as the walk we took together when you told me so much about the lives of your brothers and relatives.

I remember you once (and on a prior occasion, too) said that life seemed to bring happiness only to two people who are joined together. One should never keep lamentations of this kind to oneself; one must not be afraid to express them, and I understand very well the happiness you mean and how worth the tears it is.

But you are young and good, and you have been endowed with an inner strength, and happiness and suffering have refined this strength, and you can and must see to it that you continue to live your life. I do not say this for the sake of the child – I say it for the sake of your own life, which is worth more than a child's. That which is most sacred and most sublime, most serene and most powerful, is still there for you; it is there for every individual, for the solitary man who is still united with all of humanity – for everyone who lives and loves – and there are many and much that one can love and much and many with which one can join together, and so it must be for you. I would really like to have you here with us for a few days sometime; perhaps this will be possible in September!

Write to me again soon. I believe you have your father and brother there with you and are truly living in Hinterhör and not always in the far too large castle. And let me know how the Bodenhausens are; it has been an eternity since I last heard from Eberhard. I hope he is feeling well after having accomplished so much; I am very fond of him.

Take care. I will be receiving mail here until the 9th and then in Aussee, Steiermark (Obertressen 14).

Yours, Hofmannsthal

Hinterhör, 30 August 1910

Dear Herr von Hofmannsthal,

I would like to take advantage of the peaceful evening I'm spending here alone with my child by writing you a few lines. Hinterhör has become delightful as far as I'm concerned, and I can't think of a time when I was happier since the happy days in Kassel. I wish you could come here sometime and enjoy this wonderful calm with me. I wonder if it's simply having my own furniture in place or the absence of people who don't quite suit one – I think rather the latter – that makes it so indescribably wonderful here?!

I have my father here with me, and it's so exciting the way he enjoys the beauty of our mountains. He takes everything in so completely and is, at the age of 70, much like a young boy.

I also have a friend here who plays the piano, which makes for enjoyable evenings. But everyone is gone today, even the nurse, so I have been taking care of Marie-Therese by myself. She is lying down in her little bed over in the next room. She is like a little angel with her tiny little head of blond curls, and she radiates a wonderful calm. One is never content, and I say, "Oh, if only it could always be like this." And I try as hard as I can to enjoy everything about this idyllic place. Eberhard will be arriving tomorrow and unfortunately will only be staying for a week before going to the Mendel with Mädy. I am very much looking forward to having him here. He is so stimulating, and this is something I also have a great need for. I would really love to come to Aussee for a few days but am afraid this was but once a kind thought of yours that probably no longer exists. I understand very well indeed that your work mustn't be disturbed. However, should you think that I could fit into your circle for a few days in September or October, then let me know.

Thank you for the lovely letter. You evidently understood mine very well. It was an outcry waiting to be – needing to be – released. I have long since regained a degree of calm, almost of happiness. I hardly find time to read, though. I take advantage of every minute of even reasonably fair weather for going out on excursions. I'm doing exceptionally well, and can once again walk just marvelously. Last week the three of us climbed to the top of Hohe Salve; it was incredibly beautiful despite the thunderstorms. On Monday, I was atop the Heuberg for the first time since my long stay there. How I would love it if you broke the silence with your voice this very moment by reading me a few lines of your lovely poetry. Instead, I'll have to read something of yours myself, and then go to bed.

Good night.

Yours, Ottonie Degenfeld

🌰 🌰 🌰

Aussee, Obertressen 14, 6 September [1910]

Dear Countess,

I would have liked to have you here for a visit sometime. There is nothing resembling a circle here at all, if in using this word you meant to refer to people. But the countryside, the daily activity, the little houses inhabited by someone – with whom one might spend an hour chatting – here and there all come together to form little circles, and herein lies a certain magic. I know that you in particular would find your way around here with lightning-like swiftness, and after the first day, you would feel as if you had experienced it all before.

It will be better after all if we postpone the visit until another year, for it's been raining here for nine straight days now without interruption. We haven't seen a single hour of sunshine for the past nine days, and who knows when it will break. In the meantime I have taken on an additional project, and if you were here – and it would be a lovely time – you would certainly want to go for walks and hike up the mountains, but I would not be able to accompany you. We would hardly see each other, and that wouldn't be right. In addition we will almost certainly see each other again soon in Munich and Neubeuern. For, contrary to all expectations, Reinhardt will still be presenting Sophocles' *Oedipus Rex* – which I translated – on the 21st of September. I will be coming for a week to Munich then (and may remain there alone by myself for a while longer). I expect you'll come to town that evening, and then we could go to Neubeuern for a couple of days. Perhaps Eberhard will also be there, in which case everything would, by mere happenstance, fall into place quite unexpectedly. It would make me very happy if you wrote me a line or so to tell me whether or not this would suit you. I hope there is nothing I'm unaware of that might interfere.

Yours, H.

Aussee, 10 September [1910], accompanied by endless rain and fog

Dear Countess,

The Fortuny shawls are no longer to be found anywhere.[10] He isn't making them anymore and is busy with other things. And the remainders have already been sold.

I believe our letters have crossed in the mail. I hope I'll receive a short note telling me something about Eberhard's definitive plans.

Yours, Hofmannsthal

❦ ❦ ❦

Munich, Sunday [2 October 1910]

Dear Countess,

I have made plans to come Tuesday evening. Please make sure you will also be there at the castle. How sad it would be if you weren't present on the very first evening of my stay. Why am I coming after all?

Yours, Hofmannsthal

❦ ❦ ❦

[October 1910]

If one had only sought out
a place in the park
instead of
coming to this
ridiculous,
overcrowded spot.
+ R.I.P.

❦ ❦ ❦

Hinterhör, 25 October 1910

My dear Herr von Hofmannsthal,

You should have seen me when the package you sent arrived. Like a little girl, I ran through the house, one arm raised happily and the other filled with books. The mere sight of them fills me with joy. I thank you so very much. Should I really keep the books of yours that you gave me for my very own? If so, then let me thank you again so very much. I searched to no avail for some more lines of yours, which I unfortunately was un-

---

10. Mariano Fortuny (1871–1949) stage decorator and costume designer living in Paris, made and sold these objects.

able to find. However, I would still first like to tell you how things have been here since you left. Indeed I was immediately very preoccupied with my aunt and spent a delightful week with her; she is a charming, extremely sensitive woman and so indescribably good that I always felt very ashamed next to her.

On Sunday I enjoyed a wonderfully peaceful day here by myself. I went for a short walk alone by myself on the paths quite familiar to you. Afterwards, I sat comfortably in my cozy little blue room and was able to read – first your lovely poems, and then I began *Le Médecin de camp.*, which has something so incredibly peaceful about it that affected my entire being. Julie and Mädy, neither of whom was expecting the other, met and had tea with me here. It was very amusing, and I was happy when they left and the beautiful calm returned. This was the first day in years I had being rid of that harried feeling which I had also spoken to you about. Since then Gaisberg has also come, whom I find boring, but I must not allow this to show, as he is a very dear and loyal friend of mine and also made the last days of Christoph's life so much easier. Last night Mädy, Hildenbrandt, Ry[s], and I went to a concert in Rosenheim; it was very enjoyable and strange. However, the ride there and back was wonderful, and we would have loved to have had you both along. This afternoon I had Mama, the preacher and Hildenbrandt here and now I am enjoying an evening alone here by myself. I cannot tell you how much I hunger for time alone, which is so difficult to come by. Today I feel rather torn by certain feelings I have; how happy I would be to have you here to discuss the new problem that has arisen with me. Julie came up with the idea of going to Paris – with me of course – for ten days starting on the 12th of November. Then I got the notion of simply remaining there until Christmas and completing my French lessons – rather in a Bohemian way. At first, everyone was for it. Then Julie became riddled by a thousand concerns, and now I don't know whether I should follow through with my plans or give in to Julie's influence to the contrary. I immediately fell in love with the idea of staying there alone, and now it's difficult for me to let go of this. On the other hand, it also strikes me as too self-indulgent, and consequently not right for me. Why must a person always have so many scruples instead of just accepting and doing what his instinct tells him to? As you can see, I am not entirely at peace with myself today.

Rysselberghe is departing tomorrow and Mädy on Sunday. Pepino is gone and Hildenbrandt is also leaving this week, so the entire atmosphere here will change, and *we* must also, despite our bleeding hearts, bring our stay here to an end. I sit here a lot now in my blue room and take in its charm; at the same time I feel sorry that you were never up here with me. I really love thinking about your stay here; I regret that you are not here more often. Tell Gerty, however, that this is not the reason I have been feeling sad. I wonder how well you found the children there, and how are you doing? I suppose you have begun working? These are just a number of questions I am asking myself in my mind.

I will say goodnight now. I, too, could chat endlessly with you, but one must also know when to stop. Give my warmest regards to Gerty.

Thinking of you in true friendship,

Yours, Ottonie Degenfeld

🍎 🍎 🍎

[Schloss Grätz at Troppau] 28 [October 1910]
(until the day after tomorrow)

Dear Countess,

It is pure nonsense, but I prefer to write it nonetheless so that it may be said and done with. I have been agonizing over this ever since the night in the train from Munich to Vienna. On the last evening of my stay in Munich, Mädy was somewhat ill-tempered and, as I perceived it, unfair to Karin. I told her this, and then a conversation ensued in which Mädy ran off a list of various things that she "principally" does not tolerate and would never accept. I raised certain objections and, in this context, I think I may have said, "If Ottonie at times talks about her youth," and, "That allows one to see what a wonderful thing it is when one's youth has not been stunted." It could be that I expressed the sentence in this form, but I may have simply said, "When people tell you about their youthful years," while only *thinking* "Ottonie" and imagining afterwards that I had *said* "Ottonie." Shortly thereafter that night in the sleeping car, this turned into a horribly unpleasant and fixed idea which I was unable to rid myself of. I heard Mädy saying at the next opportunity, "Hugo told me you are always telling him about your youth . . . ," and then you would think God only knows what. The whole thing is half mad. For the last ten days, this – perhaps unuttered – sentence has tormented me and forced its way in between me and my thoughts of you. Therefore, it is better that I should write it.

The books which occasionally arrive are not meant to be required readings that intrude upon you. This is not my intention at all; rather they should be your books – is it not the case that the Goethe becomes your Goethe, and the Kleist your Kleist?[11] – for you shouldn't have to borrow these books from the library in Neubeuern, but rather they should remain in Hinterhör as a part of your very existence and, later, Marie-Therese's. I am not thinking of Marie-Therese now, but of you.

---

11. Heinrich von Kleist (1777–1811), German poet and author.

If you can undertake to read everything according to the groups I indicated on the list, a great deal will be achieved. I shall take it upon myself here to recommend and express my sincere hope – in words – that you have a love for order. As you can see, you have removed from me the timidity which held me captive last year; for it was indeed timidity, and not forgetfulness.

Aside from this, it is imperative for the sake of your nerves that you also, in addition to the hours actually spent resting, take one and a half to two hours of your time for reading. And you must be prepared to defend these hours and not to allow yourself to become torn between them and household duties and countless other concerns. (I speak of the months in Neubeuern.)

It would please me very much if you could list what you have read each day in a little notebook. I found myself in a real hurly-burly in Rodaun and Vienna with all the letters, work-related affairs, books, people etc. Here, however, it is very peaceful. I am the only guest in the huge castle and have two quiet rooms to myself. When the twilight approaches, a silent butler brings me a couple of oil lamps and, sometimes, the lord of the house[12] stops in for a quarter of an hour, always very hurriedly. He is a peculiar man and very smart. I have a great appreciation of him and like them both very much.

Unfortunately, I must stop writing due to mealtime. Now you must leave Hinterhör, dear old Hinterhör.
Adieu.

Yours, H.

[Schloss Grätz at Troppau] Sunday, 30 October [1910]

Dear Countess,

Your letter arrived today, and I am enjoying it very, very much. How easy to say: "It is all the same, whether she writes or not." Today after breakfast I was so overjoyed when the servant brought the mail containing your letter. I cannot say anything about Paris at the moment. There is no question you have to go there for a few months sometime – but it had not occurred to me that you might do this so soon. However, as the opportunity presented itself in connection with the trip you are planning, you of course wanted to take advantage of it. (This you did in accordance with the wonderful habit you have of quickly and decisively seizing hold of an opportunity, which I find simply delightful.) If it does not work out, then you will just have to postpone it, that is all.

---

12. Karl Max Duke of Lichnowsky (1860–1928).

A word such as "pleasure-seeking" is too empty to warrant any discussion. You are neither dead nor a nun, but are alive and part of this world and must *sans phrase et sans cérémonie* seek out and find that which suits you in this life, in order that you can develop and put to use your own special strengths, nature's priceless gift to each and all. Whoever considers his life to have come to an end is better off putting a bullet through his head rather than running about as a mere ghost – to do otherwise is but a half-measure or pure hypocrisy, of a more or less blameless sort.

I feel anxious knowing that you have left behind the peaceful house and are now at the mercy of a rather demanding quasi-position with no set working hours. I wish you could find some way to place a limit on these obligations and set aside a portion of the day for reading – but not before falling asleep. I beg you above all else not to choose this time.

Here I have finally managed to write Kessler a letter. I will be mailing it tomorrow.

A very nice letter arrived unexpectedly from Gersdorff. The misunderstandings and gossiping involving Max Reinhardt and him have come to an end, and he will remain at the *Deutsche Theater*. May I ask that you convey the content of my enclosure to Eberhard, so that it may reach him as soon as possible, perhaps even prior to his arrival in Essen.

I am so glad you found a day where you were able to rid yourself of that harried feeling. If it was possible once, then it will *always* be possible. My thoughts of you are never troubled ones. No, they are always very happy. Adieu.

Yours, H.

Hinterhör, 1 November 1910

I must write you at once in order to remove once and for all the foolish concerns regarding your conversation with Mädy. Please rest assured that I would never view anything you relate about conversations as an indiscretion. Rather I am certain that the way in which you expressed yourself struck the proper chord. Nothing – no matter what – you might recount to others could ever shake the tremendous trust I have in you.

I have come to see you as my friend, which is something I do only very, very seldom, so you must trust me, please. The silly matter concerning Mädy, Gerty, and the Russians makes me angry in so far as it does indeed cast a shadow over our wonderful relationship. So in the future please say whatever you happen to be thinking, with or without adding "Ottonie," and there is no need to worry about how I might react. So, enough about that now.

The letter you wrote to Julie was really delightful. It made her very happy. In a way it seemed banal, much like the other letters she so often receives, but you somehow managed to express everything in such a charming manner.

I would venture to say that all of us continue to enjoy the memories of the lovely days we spent with you and Gerty back in October.

You made me feel extremely happy with the wonderful books you gave me. I am surrounded by them as if by dear old friends. They add doubly to the mysterious aura my room has taken on for me.

A terribly unlucky star seems to be reigning over the book list, for the second one has also disappeared without a trace. Marie-Therese is the only possible explanation this time. Mary[13] told me she found her busy completely reorganizing things on top of my desk. Since then, all sorts of things have been missing. I am so embarrassed because I am afraid I may seem very disorganized to you. But then I feel some comfort when I tell myself that you also know me from another side. I just fear that you may no longer remember exactly what books you wrote down and that it is too much to ask for you to write the list a third time? It is really awful of me. I was very excited about the little almanac with Lucidor and discovered many other charming things in it as well.

The recent days were very busy. Hinterhör is gradually being turned over to hibernation; one person after another is leaving. Yesterday Hedwig, then Marie-Therese and Mary, and today Lisa[14] is leaving. It is so indescribably hard for me to leave, and I am going to stay until Friday alone with a helper and will gradually lock one room after the other.

Even in this very short time, Marie-Therese has become deeply attached to Neubeuern. I have never seen the child as excited as she was yesterday when moving back into her old room. I partly feel sorry about this, and yet, perhaps that's the way it should be.

I gave up on Paris due to my philistine nature.

Take care, and give my warm regards to Gerty.

Yours faithfully, Ottonie Degenfeld

Rodaun, 3 November [1910]

Dear Countess,

When I reflect on it now, it is as if my little bout of agonizing over the word "Ottonie" (which I probably didn't even utter at the time) had absolutely no connection to reality whatsoever. The pain and reluctance one

---

13. Marie-Therese's nanny, Mary Angold.
14. Hedwig was the cook; Lisa the maid.

experiences when separated from a person one wishes to be with can assume some very peculiar disguises. It wasn't longing that I felt – or perhaps indeed it was – but rather the feeling that I was suppressing something, and this is where the rather torturous little struggle made itself at home. I couldn't think of you, nor picture your face or even hear your voice. I could recall most vividly images of Winkler,[15] Bernauer,[16] and the beaters of the hunt as well as the faces of the children – but not you. If an image of you, either at rest or moving, flashed before me, then the foolish and empty thought of a possible misunderstanding intruded, like a black hand covering up a lovely picture that one wishes only to behold. After I wrote from Grätz, however, all this unnecessary to-do had passed.

(You have surely received my second letter from Grätz with the enclosure for Eberhard?)

The list of books!

My plan was this: to establish three groups, from each of which one book is read rather without interruption. This is relatively easy to manage and not overly confusing. In fact, each book serves as a sort of respite from the others.

The groups would be as follows: books on history, memoirs, etc.; then those works concerning intellectual inquiries, such as one finds in meditations, letters or other writings of important men; and, thirdly, purely poetic creations. The second and third groups tend to overlap. As regards the first group, we should like to focus on the French Revolution and the phenomenon of Napoleon. In the library you'll find *The History of the Revolution* by Thiers, which serves as an introduction, from a purely historical standpoint, to the *Vieux papiers vieilles maisons*. The memoirs Napoleon dictated to General Gourgaud and Montholon are also located there. A few additional readings concerning this man, without whom the intellectual substance of the nineteenth century would have assumed a very different form, will soon follow. Also included in the first group are the systematic readings of Taine, *Hist. de la littérature anglaise* (library), in light of which you will be better able to view the less significant French literary history epoch by epoch. We will probably see each other before Taine takes you beyond the time of Shakespeare.

I shall include various materials in the second group without suggesting any particular order: the Goethe/Eckermann letters, Goethe's sayings in prose, the letters of Kleist (these make up volume five of your edition and are placed in a very understandable context by the biographical thread which stretches throughout the correspondence).

Balzac's *Médecin de campagne* and *Lys dans la vallée* belong to the third group (a good many seem to escape me now, but I do recall them now

---

15. Butler in Neubeuern.
16. Gamekeeper on the Heuberg.

and again). In addition, there was Gotthelf: We had found *Uli der Knecht* [Uli the Farm Hand] in the library. And Musset. Eichendorff's delightful *Das Leben eines Taugenichts* [The Life of a Good-for-Nothing] was also on this list. You'll gradually come to learn how to read – and skim through – Goethe. This will happen automatically. *Alexis und Dora* is a wonderful poem (one of those molded on classical Greek form). The book about the Willemers will place a rather nice little key to understanding the *Divan* right at your fingertips. I was thinking we could read perhaps *Hermann und Dorothea*, Goethe's most beautiful work, together sometime.

Please write down for me which of the Goethe volumes you still haven't received.

P.S. I would have liked very much for you to go to Paris. And I can understand very well why you wanted to postpone the trip until a later time. But I cannot allow you to call yourself "philistine" on account of this. As bad as it is to thoughtlessly brush others aside with this sort of language, it is all the more irresponsible in the case of oneself. After all is said and done, the word becomes a part of the person, who in turn calmly acquiesces to its power, at which point the description becomes true. You have a free-thinking, agile mind, which is not at all philistine. You never fail to act courageously and decisively, which is not at all philistine. You are eager to engage in lofty pursuits of rather elusive objects and are more than willing to relinquish the position in the corner behind the stove for the sake of a more propitious one, which means you are at the innermost core not philistine. And I do not wish to hear anyone refer to you in this way.

[Reading list Hofmannsthal compiled for Ottonie Degenfeld.]

[List 1]
Memoirs:
Vielles maisons vieux papiers
(along with Thier's *Histoire de la révolution*)
Montholon
Gourgaud
Napoleon
Memorial de. Ste. Hélène

[List 2]
Browning:
(from Smith Elder and Co.)
Men and Women
Dramatic Romances
Whitman

[List 3]
Knut Hamsun: *Mysterien*
Pan
Bibliothek der Romane, Inselverlag
Fontane: *Sämtliche Werke* (Fischer Verlag)
Björnson: *Gesammelte Werke*
Strindberg: *Sämtliche Werke*
Balzac: (attractive edition: Louis Conard, Paris)
Chef d'oeuvre inconnu
Séraphita
Recherche de l'absolu
Louis Lambert
Cousin Pons
Albert Savarus

Poetry:
Balzac: *Médecin de Campagne*
"Curé de village"
"Lys dans la vallée"
Keats
Gotthelf: *Uli der Knecht*
Shakespeare: (try to read when you are in . . .
Hebbel: *Meine Kindheit.*

Literary History:
Demogeot . . . (fr.) (from Rodaun)
Taine: *Histoire de la littérature anglaise*
Dilthey: (will arrive from Rodaun)
Erlebnis und Dichtung
Grimm: *Goethe*
Freytag: *Bilder aus der deutschen Vergangenheit*

Neubeuern, 10 November 1910

My Dear Herr von Hofmannsthal,

Your letter greeted me here this morning after my first night back at the castle. I thank you from the bottom of my heart. Whenever such a lovely letter arrives from you, I always find myself compelled to think of the thoughts (concerning regular and systematic letter writing) Gerty expressed, and each time I think, "Thank God he's no 'Schnitzler.'"

I am starting to get settled in here again, and things are going better than I had expected. I spend a lot of time alone in my room (it's in better shape than it was). Under the pretext of being busy studying my French, nobody disturbs me. So I have a very pleasant and quiet time for reading in the mornings which I thoroughly enjoy. I really want to thank you very much for the new reading program, which does indeed make everything much easier for me. *Le Médecin d. C.* did me a *great deal* of good. It helped me achieve a wonderful state of relaxation. I think it will be one of those books I'll return to from time to time. The characters are portrayed in such splendid fashion all the way through to the very end, and there is something noble about each one of them. Books like this really do help me. They allow me to feel less and less alone and also less unhappy. I am also filled with feelings of gratitude whenever I think of you – the one who makes these quiet and pleasant hours possible – and the genuine interest you take in me. On my own, I certainly would never have taken the initiative required to free myself from all those unnecessary concerns which I deemed so important.

I am reading Taine now. While doing so, I look up new words like a good little schoolgirl in order to make progress in learning the language. The French lady is now scheduled to come sometime after Christmas. You did very well to give me a bit of a scolding. One does grab hold of the craziest ideas, and this can create some real obstacles.

How good that you wrote to Kessler. Your letter I am sure is a good one and will certainly make up for everything that transpired between the two of you.

I wonder if you will be leaving for the rehearsals in Dresden sometime soon? I wrote regarding the seats some time ago but have still not received an answer. Here the season does not seem to want to end yet. At the moment, a couple of honeymooners are here, Bruckmann is on Heuberg and to my extreme dismay, the oft-mentioned Frau Carola is coming on the 15th with her daughter, and it is asking an awful lot of me to enjoy her company without Mädy.

Before moving here, I enjoyed a few days of complete solitude without my child in Hinterhör that were simply *wonderful*. Among other things, I was deeply moved by *Der Tor und der Tod* [Death and the Fool, by H. v. H.], which I experienced with an entirely new understanding this time.

It seems presumptuous of me to tell you about this, but I experienced a feeling of such boundless gratitude towards God for giving the world men who can and may express such things.

I immediately passed your letter on to Eberhard. How wonderful that Gersdorff is staying with Reinhardt. He has already gotten used to working there and needn't again take up something entirely new. Men such as he who have so much to offer really do have a wretched time of it. Sooner or later it seems they are tossed into the abyss which drains them of all their energy.

Finally, allow me once again to thank you profusely for all the lovely books, which have already found a secure place in my heart. My sincerest regards to you and Gerty.

               Yours, Ottonie Degenfeld

❦ ❦ ❦

             Rodaun, 19 November [1910]

Dear Countess,

It seemed so horribly long the last time when you did not write for about eight or nine days. And now again it has been about nine days since I received your letter. The days fly by. I was being torn apart by many letters and other concerns – now I can sense that things are beginning to calm down and fall back into place again. My thoughts are regaining some semblance of order, and images return. A letter arrived from Kessler, to which I had to respond, and then he in turn responded to me. There were certain misunderstandings, misunderstandings of a most extreme sort. I really don't understand it entirely. However, I expect it will eventually become bearable. In time we'll forget about it. It's easier for me to talk than to write about this. I have already gone over everything I would like to tell you in my mind, and perhaps I shall in fact do so at some point.

Strauss was there, too. This was about ten days ago. The premiere will not in fact take place on the 11th. It will be on the 25th instead. This will destroy a great deal – or perhaps almost everything – of the success we had in bringing the production together. (At present, the theater manager still does not seem to be responding to anyone's letters.)

However, I am very happy that, following a round of haggling, he decided not to schedule any rehearsals (at least none requiring my participation) prior to 8th January. All this took place after I had received his letters scheduling me from the 28th of December through the 6th of January and had therefore given up for lost this especially lovely time of year.

             Tuesday, 22 [November 1910]

If only I could truly believe that this will really prove worthwhile, that is my sending you all these books. I have tried to help you acquire a degree of calm. I have also sought to enrich your life and to give you something you could hold onto, so that the richness of your person might truly reemerge from entanglement in suffering and misfortune.

The mere thought of this possibility alone has the power to make me happy. I am not merely sending you randomly selected books. I only hope this will prove successful in preventing you from imposing upon yourself unnecessary confusion and burdens. At times, my soul shudders at the mere thought.

It was wrong – fundamentally wrong – of me to have included the life stories of participants in the French Revolution (*Vieux papiers vieilles maisons*) in this year's selection of readings. This cataclysm, which in fact led to the establishment of the modern-day values we prize, is no doubt the most preeminent of all "historical" objects of study – particularly in light of the figure of Napoleon, the only man close enough to contemporary times to hold a key to unlocking the door to this "great historical event."

The lives of these men are much like fairy tales. They provide us with the most powerful insight into the human condition. Yet in this case, the dark and horrific side is by far predominant. So you must no longer take up these books. I don't know where my head was when I included them in the first list. Both reason and sensibility were lacking, so I ask for your forgiveness.

I was recently reading your Goethe (volume no. 15). It felt rather as if we were reading him together. As you don't dislike my underlining, I took the liberty of doing so to my heart's content. One comes across such glorious passages in Goethe, many of which are quite hidden and virtually unknown to most people. (I am referring here to the last one hundred pages of the fifteenth volume.) Perhaps his lovely little essay, "Lob der Mutter" [Mother's Praise], will convince you to read his life's confessions, *Dichtung und Wahrheit* [Poetry and Truth]. There is at first something rather cool about his depictions, but what wonderful flowers blossom in his garden. And how lovely the figures are: so profoundly resolute and truly present as they are in the soft, gentle light in which they are revealed. One would like to reach out and touch them! And you'll also find great vivacity in the parsonage of Sesenheim and, prior to this point, in the dancing instructor's daughters, and, above all, in the figure of Gretchen. One's heart is truly moved by the entire story, which is carried along by a certain happiness that spreads itself out over all of the wounds life inflicts. One thing in particular Gretchen says has always remained with me. I came across it recently in a book of poetry – and at once, the entire book became very dear to me. "Don't kiss!" she says. "That is too ordinary. Love instead, if possible." Is this not indescribably beautiful?

The more I think about it, the more I am convinced that you should read *Dichtung und Wahrheit*. You should then read another book from the same period (1750–1780) by a wholly miserable man, whose soul radiated remarkable brilliance. These two books compliment one another nicely. Although both works are firmly grounded in the eighteenth century, neither of them is dark or frightening. I'll send you the other book next time; it's ready for its journey to Neubeuern. I would really love to begin another page, but I fear I would then fail to send the letter off, and this would mean I would have to wait all the longer before hearing from you. Please write soon, if possible.

Yours, H.

P.S. Is your Goethe collection now complete from volume I through XV? Please let me know!

Was the second volume of memoirs by a Herr Heinrich von Lang perhaps mistakenly included in the last package of books? If so, I would ask that you return it to me.

The package should contain the following: Goethe, volumes IX and XV, and also a small volume of quotations from Napoleon and selections from Angelus Silesius. I did not accidentally include the little collection of poems by H. Carossa, but rather meant to do so. This man is a young country doctor in the Passau area. I have never met him. We just happened to enter into correspondence with one another. He really does have something of the poet in his blood. And the nice part and what I find so delightful is that he is not a professional writer. Instead, he travels around the entire day curing people of their ailments while occasionally finding time to write a piece of poetry. Despite the great distance between us, he is quite dear to me and perhaps I can be of some use to him here or there.

Neubeuern, 24 November 1910

My Dear Herr von Hofmannsthal,

Even yesterday I could not believe I had not written and thanked you yet. I had continued putting off writing as I was hoping for a letter from you, but even if I had not received one, I still would have written today. The books were partly a response to my last letter. We understood each other very well in this respect. I found the 15th volume in particular incredibly appealing. I began reading – or perhaps I should say leafing through – it as soon as it arrived. Beginning around the middle section, I came across your lovely little underlinings and then felt right at home. I experienced the same thing you did: it was as if we were reading it together.

I also took Angelus Silesius to be a response to a portion of my last letter, or am I mistaken here? I have already read it a number of times but do not wish to write about it yet. New books generally bring me a great deal of happiness, and I do not mean the contents alone. I am childish enough to find great delight in the cute little covers, just as Marie-Therese does in a new doll. I thank you a thousand times over for this. You really do send me too many packages. Even though I feel so ashamed, I am glad to accept everything you give me. I was quite enchanted by the little O. D.[17] that spoke so tenderly, "I belong to you."

You see, unwittingly we understood each other even better, and this on account of my small intellect. I really had enough to keep me busy with Guizot and Taine, as both demanded my diligent attention. It makes a tremendous difference to me if I read a novel consisting mainly of dialogue that is easy to understand or one in which technical terms play the primary role. Anyway, I spent the mornings doing this and read Goethe after teatime. I have been reading *Le lys dans la vallée* the last few days. I find it truly delightful. There is such a wonderful burst of poetry extending throughout the whole thing.

Please don't worry about confusing me by giving me too much to read or mixing me up, for next to your great mind, which soars miles ahead of me, my strong desire – yet modest powers – follows slowly behind and is therefore able to achieve a certain balance.

Speaking for myself, I can say there is no question that your existence gives me endless peace of mind and inner happiness, which is also not without physical effects. I now look forward to each minute of my time alone and no longer race needlessly about the house. Therefore, I am, on the whole, able to relax more than I used to. So please rest assured.

I am so happy that you will – hopefully – be staying at Neubeuern around New Year's. It would really be awfully sad if something were to interfere with these plans.

Saturday: In the meantime I stayed overnight in Munich without having had the slightest intention of doing so. I brought Julie to Rosenheim by sleigh that evening; only there did I realize how eerie the ride would be for her alone and got in with her the way I was, in slippers, etc.; it was very funny. The very next morning I had to come back here, as we were expecting Herr v. Keszycky (the old colonel whom you once met here). After hearing what Kessler had to say, I feared the letter might not be taken the right way. Yet I always hoped that things would quickly smooth over between the two of you. Your next meeting will probably break up any dark clouds that might still be hovering overhead. Any attempt to reach a compromise will have to be the result of your initiative, because Kessler is much too stubborn. Lang's memoirs were not sent here!

I skimmed through some of the country doctor's poems. I found it very interesting what you wrote about him. What a wonderful talent for someone with such a serious occupation!

I read *Dichtung und Wahrheit* with great pleasure last year when I was in the hospital. This helped me to pass the many long hours spent in bed there more quickly and pleasantly.

---

17. H. v. H. wrote Ottonie's name in all the books he sent her. They are still in Marie-Therese's library in Nussdorf, Bavaria.

In Bredeney they are again experiencing hard luck. First Eberhard came down with influenza, and now he is suffering horrible pain from gout; in particular the fact that there were very important meetings he had to miss causes him great despair. We now have six children here. The little one from Frau Carola Schmitz, whom we often discussed, has been deposited here for four weeks and placed under Mary's care. This is splendid for Marie-Therese having to share her Mary and her little things, too, and in the process she is proving to have a really wonderful character, to my great surprise. Frau Schmitz brought the child and thank God she only stayed for a week; she has urged me in the strongest terms to accompany her to Paris, and I declined in equally strong terms. As I unfortunately would have been unable to get rid of the French lady for Christmas, I did not send for her until the end of January.

Take care of yourself now. It's really rather difficult for me to stop writing, but I can't continue chatting like this forever. I, too, very much look forward to your letters.

Yours truly, Ottonie Degenfeld

❦ ❦ ❦

[Südbahn Hotel, Semmering, outside Vienna] 15 [=14] December [1910]

I cannot really write, especially not to you. I have written letters to around 200 people the past few days, and perhaps this is precisely why I am unable to write to you at the moment. Maybe it's also because I'm so looking forward to talking to you and hearing your voice again that the toil and inadequacy of producing written words make me feel so impatient. I wanted to say a word about the books I most recently sent, for they were probably unable to speak clearly for themselves. I should have mentioned this right when I sent them, and now it's too late. Now I have to tell you what I wanted to write.

Der arme Mann im Tockenburg [The Poor Man in Tockenburg] is a wonderful book because it is written from the perspective of the common man. The only thing you see here are *people*. You even have the feeling that nothing besides *people* exists. Yet the nation is still present, hiding beneath and behind everything else. And from within that profoundness that is the nation, the beauty and depth of the soul emerge. This poor man's book serves as a companion to Goethe's reflections on his own life. Thus it connects itself to something that you are already acquainted with and may hence be more accessible to you: For each work must contain some point at which it can be connected to the next one. This is then a powerful force that allows both wealth of soul and peace of mind to emerge.

I can't discuss Novalis now. I sent you a copy containing my underlining while keeping the new one, i.e. yours, for myself. We can of course exchange them later, although the new one really isn't all that attractive. But perhaps I can have it rebound for you.

There are wooded trails here where I imagine you taking a walk, and benches where I see you resting. To hold someone dear is to know who she *is*. I'm not sure yet who you are. Will we really be able to sit together in front of the fireplace twelve more days hence?

Yours, H.

❦ ❦ ❦

Neubeuern, 17 December 1910

My dear Herr von Hofmannsthal,

It was very nice to find your letter yesterday evening when I arrived here alone. I could not stand it in the city any longer and had to come here ahead of both sisters. I was greeted by your dear books upon my arrival. But I have to say, you really mustn't continue giving me such expensive books. I think I will just have to say, "Thank you. But now that's enough!" My warmest thanks for this last package. I am out of breath and tired from the time spent in Stuttgart, which was absolutely full. From the first cockcrow until far into the night people, people and then more people; they all meant well and were nice, but it really was quite a lot. Now all our hands are full here with preparations for Christmas. Mädy said to thank you very much for your letter. She wanted to write herself but is stuck in bed with a cold.

I am very eagerly awaiting the days after the celebration[18] and hope that something will come of it. Your letter was so dear.

With the sincerest remembrances and hopes of seeing you again soon,

Yours, Ottonie D.

❦ ❦ ❦

Rodaun, 22 December [1910]

Dear Countess,

I hope you have forgiven my brusque request. We were not sure what to do when the letters failed to arrive for days on end (we assumed Eberhard wouldn't be able to come or something). I also invited Schröder as our hostess had wished. He would also like to come and sent a telegram asking when *exactly* we would be there. Just five minutes ago, I found out that they're expecting me in Dresden beginning the first week of January! So we do plan to arrive in Neubeuern on the evening of the 28th.

---

18. It had become a habit for a group of friends to meet at the Schloss Neubeuern. This "think tank" is known in German literature as "The Neubeuern Week."

The Orient Express has been delayed, and as a consequence it will be more inconvenient to make the trip than it was last time. We won't be able to leave Salzburg before 7:05 p.m., arriving in Rosenheim at 8:40 p.m. Should we expect a carriage there? Perhaps it would be better not to be picked up should the weather turn out to be terribly cold. In that case, it would be better if we waited the 45 minutes (which would be rather boring) in Rosenheim before continuing to Raubling at 9:32 and arriving at 9:44. So we would be in Neubeuern sometime after 10:00 and could simply have a couple of eggs in our room before going to sleep. If you would be so kind, you still have time to send a telegram giving me your decisive counsel. I do not know exactly how great a toll the Rosenheim trip exacts on man and horse, but you can discuss this with our hostess. Please do forgive this very hastily written letter.

Your remark about my sending you books makes me a bit sad. I am neither able to ignore it nor do I understand it. I thought that we understood each other well enough in this respect and were both aware of the fact that this concerns a well-considered plan, a matter of necessity you might say, which has nothing whatever to do with "presents." In other respects you're not the Sondershausen type! A person gives shawls, luggage, pearl necklaces, pug dogs, and bottles of perfume as "presents," but one gives someone books that he *needs* to have ready at hand. I was immediately saddened when I read that one little sentence. But please *don't reflect* on this now, just *don't think of it*, dearest. We'll discuss it later. First of all I must stick to my plans and send Grimms' fairy tales – which I meant to give you as a Christmas present – to Julie now for Marie-Therese as her own personal storyteller. It is of no consequence *to whom* they belong. I just thought you could read the first few tales aloud to the little girl. Goodbye, until we meet again, if we truly shall. Please don't fall ill – I'm so looking forward to this.

Yours, H.

[Neubeuern, December 1910]

Everything here is so confining the way it's portioned off, and still I can't describe the joy I feel knowing I breathe the same air as you: To not only know, but to see that you are alive! Mysterious indeed, physical presence. It is surely a greater happiness to love than to be loved. Of what concern could it possibly be to you that I might love you?! Dear Ottonie! I am so glad to have this feeling inside of me as I approach *your room*.

Please have me called to the table if I should oversleep.

[Neubeuern, December 1910]

I would be glad to take the carriage if you come along. Please think about whether or not this might be too tiring for you. I think it may be too much.

❦ ❦ ❦

[Neubeuern, 4 January 1911]
Do not read if too tired. Just save for later.

You are so far away,[19] nearly two hours removed from me. Off into the night you are traveling, further into the darkness with each passing moment. And yet you are so close, still so very much here. You appear through a doorway or might at any moment be over in the next room. The air here is filled with your presence. It might be that I find myself sitting down with Julie and the doctor, and there you are by the fireplace, very close to us. When I take Herr Heiseler to my room to entertain him by reading a few lines out loud, there you sit, listening, just like the delightful evening when you sat in the corner with Dabeth crouched down at your feet. And I am unable to comprehend how my eyes manage to proceed from one line to the next while at the same time my eyes remain fixed on you. How is it that my lips are able to utter words, one after the other, while I am talking to you? Somehow everything does seem to work out quite well, and Herr Heiseler also seems immensely pleased.

What is it that I desire? Just what exactly is it that resides here at the innermost core? What is the true nature of this immense attraction of one soul to another? There must be some way to describe this in very simple terms! So that you could feel it enter into you like a ray of light: I really care for you. Yet the "I" in this sentence bothers me. Why should you care that someone feels this way about you? Of course, the man you might love *would be* of concern to you. One should be able to express it thus: "You are loved." And then you would be able to feel it, just as subtly and surely as you feel the other emotions: those nasty feelings of emptiness, loneliness, and melancholy.

But you do know that you are the one and the only one whom someone somewhere in this world cares for very much? You do realize this, don't you? I just remembered how I used to occasionally mention in passing that you are a good person or that you are very kind or that this or that thing about you is very attractive or charming. But none of these specific qualities is of any consequence. It is not because you are a good person that one cares for you, or because there is something attractive about

---

19. O. D. S. had to leave suddenly to attend the funeral of a member of the royal family in Württemberg.

you or because you have a kind and charming personality. All of this applies to you, that I can clearly see. But I am almost entirely indifferent to it all. Rather there is something else underlying all these traits which is truly you. It is your own nature, which is present at every instant, even when you feel depressed or your face appears weary. Once one has perceived you in this way, one cannot help but care for you. Afterwards, one simply longs for – I have to stop now. I have to go downstairs to dinner and do not want to be late. So I say, "Good night," even though I know that you will sleep. And I say, "Please don't wear yourself out tomorrow," although I know that you will. I do not feel any sadness yet today. I am so incredibly grateful that you *exist*.

❦ ❦ ❦

[Neubeuern] 7 [January 1911] noontime

Dear Countess,

Please forgive me if yesterday's letter seems awfully rash and difficult to decipher. I probably repeated words quite a bit and wrote seemingly endless sentences. I was not able to read it over, and Gerty went into the adjoining room to get dressed and talked to me through the door while I was writing you. She is so accustomed to my focusing only half my attention on the "letters" I write that she just assumes one can carry on a conversation with me at the same time. If I had asked not to be disturbed, or if I had closed the door, she would have known right away that I was writing to you. Or I would have had to devise an outright lie, which I am always reluctant to do.

Well, now you find yourself somewhere you don't want to be, and melancholy's grim clutch takes hold of you once again. It is simply glorious here with the Inn and the mountains surrounded by a silver mist. I was out on the terrace again, just like yesterday. Muscadin[20] followed me outside. I found him to be very friendly, and he appears to be willing to spend an eternity waiting for someone, while maintaining a sense of humility even when there is not much hope. Then, all of a sudden, something came over me again, something I hadn't felt since I was a boy. Such a dazed feeling of being lost in the world, of being unable to think clearly – who am I after all? How did I end up here? These walls, the castle the village down below, the heavens and the sun – and this man standing here? *Who* is he? It is indescribably foreign to me, this strange fear. I once had the same feeling as a boy when serving at the school Mass – and I almost cried out loud. But it wasn't that scary today. I saw your face before me, and the longing I felt helped me to regain my awareness. I feel as

---

20. Name of a dog.

if I did not know the meaning of the word "heart" before, whereas now I am suddenly able to understand it. It is as if I were twenty years old again. What strange feelings these are!

I often find myself feeling so incredibly happy. In these moments a burst of joy surges through my entire body – it is because you are so near, so present. Is it just here that I feel this? Will the feeling disappear when I leave? Will I once again feel stifled and exposed to evil as I did last October? I am sometimes struck by a subtle sense of delight, very similar to the pleasure derived from the sweet smell of violets or fresh grass that is borne to one on the spring breeze. I believe it was in fact the few brief words you spoke in passing which were accompanied by kind glances directed my way. We talked about the unanswered letters people keep in their desk drawers. But the fact that you were once again holding my old letter (the short note sent from Munich in which I wrote "Why else would I be coming to Neubeuern?")! It is impossible to consciously recall an image of this kind. You simply enjoy it whenever it decides to return.

I have received quite a number of letters and telegrams recently. It is indeed rather a large pile. But at least there are things I "must" attend to. I will be going to Munich tomorrow evening. There are a number of rehearsals[21] I have to go to after spending a day or two dictating to a secretary, so I'll be there in Hotel Marienbad until Thursday. Julie won't be by herself, though. Fräulein Kolb and another lady will be coming, and Mädy will also have returned by then. I wrote down my address, but you know that I don't *expect* a letter from you, right?! You mustn't ever write me for my sake alone. Neither a glance nor one single word, nor ever a meeting do I wish to enjoy thanks to your having told yourself: "Oh, the poor man, he craves it so much." You won't ever do this, will you, Ottonie? It wouldn't be difficult for me to sense it, and I would truly feel *humiliated*.

I would love to continue writing. It feels as if you were here listening to me, and sometimes it does not, but what of it? You surely can sense that someone somewhere – this word is coming up too often.

I have to go for a sleigh ride with Herr Heiseler and a Frau von Döring. How far from here you must be by now. You are probably already walking around among those dark-clad strangers. So far away from me.

Yours Hofmannsthal

❦ ❦ ❦

---

21. For *Der Rosenkavalier* in Munich.

Stuttgart, 22 Mörikestr., Sunday evening [8 January 1911]

The long day is over now, and it is almost 12 o'clock. I am lying in bed as I begin to write this letter. I do not know whether or not I will finish it today. But I do have to tell you *how* happy I was this morning to be greeted by your letter. It was *very* kind of you to respond so quickly and *so* appropriately. The sentence, "You *are* loved," shows me just what strong feelings you have for me. It is the ultimate expression of one's emotions, I think, when one person reveals his entire soul to another *without wishing for anything* in return. I cannot describe how moved I feel. Yes, I realize now that what you write and tell me is meant *only* for me, and I am glad to listen to everything. Everything you express makes me feel so happy, and I hope that this in turn may be of some benefit to you. What wonderful days we spent together! I wouldn't want to have missed even the first few rather hard days, for otherwise the following ones would never have turned out as they did. Now we must continue to live together in the letters we write – that, too, is lovely. I have already read yours many times over today. But just think how horrible it is that I don't know exactly where you are or what your plans are. I imagine you in Munich, but please do let me know where you will be going after this.

Yesterday was a terribly long day. I was almost dead when I arrived here. But the commotion in Warthausen was not as bad as I had feared it might be. Nobody there was really overcome by grief, which certainly made things easier. I have felt dreadfully tired and have had to say "No, thank you," to everyone. I spent the entire afternoon resting and was unable to read a single line. Nobody here is aware of my presence yet, and I wish I could depart without being noticed.

I just thought of something very strange! I wonder if you will be staying in Munich for a few more days? If so, we could travel as far as Erfurt together on Thursday or Friday. I could also take the daytime train. But you will probably be gone by the time this letter arrives. From here, I only need to travel to Erfurt and not all the way to Halle. Good night for now. It's time for me to at least try to get some sleep.

Yours, Ottonie DS.

P.S. If it is possible to travel together, it would be best to keep Friday in mind. If we intend to travel during the daytime, you would have to arrive here the evening before and spend the night in Hotel Marquardt. We could then board the train together, without of course letting anyone else know that we are acquainted. If it suits you better to travel at night, then we could meet for a few hours in one of the sleeping cars.

[Hotel Marienbad, Munich] Tuesday, 10 [January 1911] 4:00 a.m.

Dear Countess,

I can probably write for only about ten more minutes before being disturbed. Then I have to go listen to one of the singers, visit the Bruckmanns and finally take Gerty to the train station. She has to return home to be with the children.

Your letter arrived this morning after the car was already waiting out front to take me to the rehearsal. I really wasn't "expecting" it and was very happy when I saw it there. In the car I began reading, calm and content; then I came to your suggestion and was suddenly struck by the unbelievable possibility of seeing you! I had always had a vague sense of longing when imagining the day on which we would by chance be traveling in the same direction. I had always envisioned two trains – you in one and I in the other – rolling along beside one another across dark landscapes. And now this *wonderful* possibility shall come to be! I still can't believe it. Something inside continues telling me: "It won't come to pass!" But I am still so happy that you thought of this, and I *do not* believe now that you happened upon this idea *simply* for my sake – at least not for this reason alone, which is what I had always feared.

After I finished reading the entire letter, I felt light-headed due to the sudden rearrangement of the thoughts in my mind. Then the car let me out in front of the theater. I walked through the dark hall and there in a harsh and glaring light sat the man who plays the piano; there the men and women, homely everyday folks, acting and singing my words. It was strange to hear my own words bellowing out of their mouths. Then, again, a phrase borne on the waves of melody made its way to me and enchanted me. And in between, I saw the map from the guidebook: Erfurt, Halle, Reichenbach, my destination. At the same time, in the twilight, these images circled senselessly around me, but your words seemed to sparkle inside of me like tiny little stars. Time is short, so I will try to finish telling you everything I have been thinking about as quickly as possible.

Oh yes, the possibility of traveling together at night. I can see you tiring. Then we say good night to each other, but neither one of us is able to sleep. I can see you leaving the train the following day before disappearing wearily into the cold, gray mist. No, that is not how I wish to see you. So let's not travel at night, but rather during the day. But I wonder if you are really up to this? Think about it some more and don't feel any obligation on account of my enthusiasm. I'll be leaving here for Stuttgart (Marquardt) on Thursday evening. You can cancel these plans by telegram up until noontime Thursday. You could also have a servant telephone in a cancellation from the post office up to an hour before departure time. You would not have to mention my name, but need only to telephone H. Marienbad and tell them that the mail should not be sent to Stuttgart. I explained the meaning of this to the personnel. If you don't cancel the plans, I will board the same car in the train traveling directly through or to Erfurt on Friday morning. Or should I board a different car instead? Perhaps you can let me know in the Marquardt. I won't look for anyone on the platform and will leave if *nobody* is there, unless you instruct me otherwise. It would be very sad to travel alone with no news of you.

I have to finish now. Adieu, and see you soon (even while writing this, I can hardly believe it will happen).

Yours, Hofmannsthal.

Stuttgart, Thursday [12 January 1911]

Here is a small token intended to welcome you upon your arrival in the dreary old Marquardt.

If there is no car traveling directly to Erfurt, then we will just have to board the one heading for Berlin.

In that case I would most likely spend the night in Erfurt. I wouldn't arrive home until midnight, although I would have the entire evening to spend in Erfurt. I will notify them of my arrival on Saturday morning in any case. I graciously accepted the two lovely books, so beautifully adorned, which arrived today.

So goodbye for now,

O. D. S.

P.S. Don't refuse the travel pillow. It was sent to the correct address.

[Amtshauptmannsschaft Auerbach im Vogtland]
Sunday morning [15 January 1911]

Dear Countess,

If you ever find that you have to take a trip and don't tolerate train travel well, there is nothing I can recommend more highly than the company of a certain little Thuringian Fräulein. I do not know how she manages to do it, but she is somehow able to heal migraine headaches, not only while accompanying someone on a trip, but afterwards as well. One is then able to travel along the craziest routes all alone in overheated or underheated compartments. For example, it is no great burden to travel from Erfurt to Reichenbach via Leipzig with nothing to eat but a single apple all day long. And you arrive at your destination without the slightest trace of a headache, and even your eyes feel clear and healthy. This blissful joy simply remains, much as it must be before the gates of heaven or for a happy child at Christmas time when he turns over in bed knowing that the Christmas tree is there. This feeling is so wonderful that one must be careful not to speak of it too often. Sometimes it wells up inside and a faint hint of light transforms itself, suddenly appearing in the form of some particular recollection, a sentence, a fleeting moment, or as an image of the time we shared together out on the frozen balcony in Erfurt. Then the flood recedes, leaving behind a much happier heart.

It is precisely in this manner that one must not speak to one woman about another. But when you get to know this dear creature from Thuringia and perhaps spend some time living with her under the same roof, you will quickly dispense with any possible criticism. In fact, you will come to view me of all people as the person least acquainted with the young Fräulein.

And yet I shall insist that I know her very well. It is a great joy knowing her, and my truest wish is to become even better acquainted with her. Yet I do see her for what she is, and not in some other light. She is by no means an imposing figure: If you were to wrap her in Schröder's blanket, then all of a sudden there would no longer be any Fräulein there – she would vanish from sight quicker than you could cover her up. Her voice is not particularly attractive by any stretch of the imagination – indeed a little rough. Yet after spending but a single day listening to this voice, one has no desire to ever hear another. In fact, one can't bear to hear another. She really does have quite a curious way of speaking: Her voice reveals a North German origin; however it also contains strains of an acquired Swabian or Bavarian accent. Truly neither fish nor fowl. I suppose it depends on the individual, whether or not he finds delight in hearing her speak in such a strange accent. She certainly doesn't have the most beautiful hands either. But to kiss them upon greeting her in the morning and evening is a pure delight. You're probably asking yourself just what *exactly* is so unique about her and whether or not it might be described without babbling. But I would prefer to address this in another letter. For now, let it suffice to say: If you encounter her, please be kind to her. But I do not suppose I really need to tell you this, for it will come naturally. Something about her just compels one to treat her kindly. It's also perfectly fine to tell her now and again, in whatever language you like, "*que l'on l'aime profondément,*" or "*che le si vuol bene,*" or "that one is very fond of her." But this must be expressed naturally without any pretense. One's comments may touch her, but they mustn't burden her. Life has burdened her with unimaginable suffering, and this is perhaps exactly why one must adore her without reservation.

And one other thing, dear Countess. She is as careless as a schoolgirl and pays absolutely no attention to her health. She's also stubborn and won't listen to anyone. She goes to bed without heating her hot water bottle, and even when it's a mere 15 degrees outside, she'll still linger at the skating rink chatting endlessly, so that each person in Sondershausen feels that *he alone* is her best friend. She pays no heed to the fact that cold air is bad for one's nerves and doesn't seem to realize that we deprive our souls if we maltreat our bodies. You go ahead and try your hand with her. She won't listen to me and doesn't believe a thing I say. But I suppose it's really none of my business anyway. I am simply very fond of her.

Adieu, dear Countess.

Yours, Hofmannsthal

❦ ❦ ❦

Sondershausen, 16 January 1911

Can you believe that the Thuringian Fräulein was so eagerly anticipating a letter from a certain gentleman, who just happened to be riding in the same train with her? And that she also skips through the cold house in her robe (after sneaking out of bed) early each morning to see if the mail has arrived and then shuffles, dejected, back to her room? It is all the more silly, for this Thuringian Fräulein must have known that a letter couldn't possibly arrive until afternoon. No sooner has she finished reading it than she starts chattering away in a letter of her own, describing *how* happy she is that the travel companion arrived *without a headache* and was cheerful and quite chipper while starting the sleigh ride. And she hopes that he will feel just as chipper when he meets his Marschallin.[22]

The little Thuringian Fräulein has once again transformed herself into the daughter and the sister, reassuming duties that she had given up long ago, such as giving comfort and consolation to her father.

Unfortunately, it is going to be rough going this time around. I have come to realize that father's melancholic tendencies comprise a much more substantial part of his character – and always have – than I had believed. With him it is a true illness, and all that might prove helpful would be an occasional change in his surroundings and some new company; or perhaps here again an improvement in his poor financial situation. If, instead of just scraping by, he only had a few thousand additional Marks, *perhaps* he would be better able to shoulder his other burdens, but only perhaps. I really would like to help the dear old man so much. I feel so powerless, though I keep telling myself that everything is all right as long as I am here. But when I have to leave the house, he will be right back where he started. Can you see now how I am much better at letting myself be

---

22. The lead role in the opera *Der Rosenkavalier*, which had its premiere in Dresden on 26 January 1911.

helped, or are you so much better at doing this? But why should I expect you to understand this any better than anyone else? Now I think I understand, though. You in fact have a greater capacity for this, a deeper understanding of things, and are probably less selfish and more prepared to give of yourself than others are.

I only do this when I am together with him. But it is probably much more important to write him regularly in order that I might truly become a part of his thinking, for then I could be of some use to him now and again. I found out from Neubeuern how lovely Marie-Therese's birthday was and *how* happy this all made the child. Mama's condition fluctuates; the days are bearable, the nights less so. Mädy writes that Julie's nerves are gradually becoming very drained, and she was hoping to be able to leave soon, which of course will only be possible once I am back.

Take care then, dear travel companion. I have not experienced such a pleasant trip for a very long time. I wonder if we will dare to do it again sometime!

Faithfully, the Thuringian Fräulein

❦ ❦ ❦

[Sendig Hotel: Europäischer Hof Dresden–A.] 17 January 1911, evening

I can already tell this is not going to be a good letter. Of course it will express my thanks and the *terrific* happiness I felt upon finding your letter here a couple of hours ago when I returned from a grueling rehearsal. But it will nevertheless be somewhat deficient, rather stupid and probably quite inadequate due to the exhaustion I feel. Continually having to stand and talk while attempting to extract something worthwhile from those miserable creatures can really make a man feel terribly weary. Then one notices for the first time that one really loves one's creation and is truly joined to it by invisible threads. *How* sad we all were yesterday morning at the first rehearsal, how terribly sad. I feel so sorry for Strauss, such a tremendously strong, somewhat gruff yet extremely sensitive man so near to tears. It really would be a depressing endeavor were Max Reinhardt not involved. It's amazing how much he manages to help us. The man is tireless, always on the go from 10 o'clock in the morning until 11 o'clock at night. He begins on the stage and then continues working back at the hotel. He treads so softly. He is silent, almost imperceptible, yet so very effective; he is a magician in the truest sense. I have a very special fondness for him, quite different from what I feel for my other friends. And yet, isn't one fond of *every* person in some respect? Whenever I like a person and can feel the effects of his charm in addition to finding him rather remarkable, you come immediately to mind, and then I wish to see the two of you together. I often think to myself: If only you were sitting here watching us from the dark parquet. You might find it entertaining. And I would just love to come down from the stage to take a seat beside you; I surely would feel no more tired than I did recently following our trip.

Ottonie, I waited for the arrival of your letter with such longing and was so happy when I found it here – oh how happy I was! I felt a very subtle and foolish, unjustified hope and anticipation – no, not anticipation, just hope. It was a hope accompanied by a guilty conscience due to the presumptuousness of thinking you might have written without first awaiting my last letter. Before the evening rehearsal, I lay down and slept for a while. Then somebody came knocking at my door on three separate occasions. And each time, I awoke with a start and the foolish hope that it would be a letter arriving from you. Each time, it was nothing but a telegram from people wanting tickets for the premiere. There of course are not any left. (I keep "yours" in my pocket and shall hold onto it until an hour before the opening. However, I am not really expecting you.)

I am so happy the distance between us is so small at present. You seem so near, so accessible. You cannot imagine how grateful I am that we are not separated by half of Germany. My life would seem so gloomy if you lived in Kassel, or some other place like Essen or Bremen. I must truly be thankful that everything is the way it is and that I have been granted such a splendid fate: to have found you, to have been able to assist you, to be allowed to see you; and to find happiness in our periodic encounters, in recollection and in longing.

Ottonie, what childish nonsense it is to call me "selfless." Am I to accept this praise for something that could not be further from the truth? I just love you, that is all. Why is that selfless, or devoid of desire? Do I not constantly desire something? To see you, to hear your voice, to have you near me? Or to infuse you with thoughts of me, to make you smile, to sit beside you and wrap up your poor little cold feet, or to take in your face with my eyes, whether you're close by or separated from me by many miles of darkness at night? And right now, at this very moment, Ottonie, am I not writing you for my own benefit? Is it not my intention to feel that you are listening to me, to perhaps bring your thoughts to focus on me or on *that which you are fond of*? And behind all this, does one not find the fiercest longing for some answer, for the eternally unspoken.

[The last page of the original letter is missing.]

[Sendig Hotel: Europäischer Hof, Dresden–A., January 1911]

I beg you: Please write me *soon*, even if it's only a few words – just *soon*! Ottonie, I've been thinking a great deal about what you said about your father in your last letter, and I would like very much to find the most appropriate words for expressing myself, in order that I might truly speak to the crux of the matter. There is nothing in the world that I can relate to more than to the concern one has for the trials of one's father. In the past my worries about my father nearly carried me beyond the brink of madness, and perhaps that is why my father always enjoyed such serenity, while I all the while placed an excessive and indeed unnecessary burden on myself. Ottonie, if only I could express my thoughts in such a way that they might be of some help to you – but I fear that the wretched physical exhaustion I feel shall interfere with this attempt. However, this is what I'd like to say: You should only give as much of your good-natured kindness, enthusiasm and sympathy as you can. But you mustn't exceed these limits by trying to become a participant in the very being of another person. It is impossible to take part in another's sufferings. To try to do so is a wanton act that will just result in the squandering of one's own inner strength while being of no service to the sufferer. One mustn't seek to shoulder the burden of another man's tribulations, for they must remain a mystery to us all. A person must never attempt this, for he will only destroy himself in doing so. And do not be carried away by wishful thinking to believe that you can penetrate the dark shadow cast by another man's suffering. Don't torture yourself with the thought: "He would be happy if only he had some more money! Couldn't I, as his child, see to it that he had some more money!" This is not the case. That would change nothing for him. Just think about it for a moment. You have such a blessedly sound sense of the truth, of limitations, and of what is right. Please remain true to this. You won't misunderstand me, will you, Ottonie? I hope what I say does not grate on your ears and that my words do not seem too cold-hearted. If only I could spend an hour or so talking to you! I am sure you would not misunderstand my spoken words – I am certain of this. Or is it just that you like my letters more than you do me? Should I in fact be bitterly jealous of my own letters, just like poor Lucidor?[23]

Good night.

H. H.

Sondershausen, Wednesday [18 January 1911]

My very dear Herr von Hofmannsthal,

Just have a look at an example of why one really should heed one's intuition! If I had done so, you would have found a letter from me upon your arrival, and all the horrible waiting and unnecessary disappointment

---

23. Character already conceived in his mind for a later libretto of the Strauss opera *Arabella*, premiered 1933 (see letter of 20 January).

would have been avoided. However, it is unfortunate that a woman feels a need to restrain herself; this ruins many good intentions.

I cannot tell you how delighted I would be to sit beside you in the dark theater. And how happy I would be if my presence could remove some of the unpleasantness you're experiencing during the opening rehearsals. But as I am unable to be there, I want at least to write to you.

You wrote a *very* kind letter, even though your mind was exhausted. (I feel this came straight from a very warm and kind heart that was unaware of its body's weariness.) Please be assured that I understood you very well. Nothing you said to me regarding my relationship to my father seemed harsh. On the contrary, it simply revealed how well you understand my feelings. You are right about everything you said, but it is very difficult accepting the fact that there's nothing – absolutely nothing – one can do to change this. I know how impossible it is to carry another person's pain or to share it; indeed, one must endure this alone. But you can get help from someone else which strengthens the ability to shoulder the burden, as I well know, for I have experienced this through you. However, I doubt that I am capable of providing such support to my father. Please do not worry about me, though. I won't get too involved with his problems and will try to accept things the way they are.

I feel very happy knowing that Max Reinhardt is there with you. He, as well as Strauss, will certainly be able to help guide you past the initial pitfalls of the first few days. I imagine the beginnings of such a production must really be awful, what with people who are essentially strangers – and moreover disagreeable, but this is only because you haven't yet discovered their own particular charm – distorting one's *own* creation. It will surely improve, bit by bit. You will gain interest in the participants, and after everything falls into place, everything will round itself out and turn out to be charming. I would adore coming on the 26th, but considering everything we've discussed, it's better that I suppress this desire. Do you know what I have been relishing for the past few days? It's the feeling that, despite having seen all of Ottonie's unappealing traits (and she, too, sees them clearly, in addition to her many other faults), you are still fond of her because you love the little soul residing inside her. And that makes this childish Ottonie indescribably happy. Should I also tell you if I like a certain man's letters better than I do him himself?! This is very difficult to explain. No, of course I like him very much and prefer talking to him in person and I especially like traveling with him. But what I really don't like is missing – his company and being off somewhere where mail cannot reach me. Should I continue explaining why I like him so much? Because he also loves the dust upon the flower petals and would not think of placing the buds in a greenhouse in order to see them bloom before their time. And this is what separates him from other men and serves as a sort of balm for a wounded heart. But if I am to be brutally honest, I would probably have to say that while I am awfully fond of him, I do not love him; I am not only fond of his letters but I do love them directly. And as I say this, I realize that if I love his letters, must I not also love his soul, and him? For surely his soul reveals itself in his letters?! I am not sure. I would have to think about this first. Take care.

Ottonie D.

˜ ˜ ˜

Sondershausen, 18 January 1911

It was about an hour ago, just before your telegram arrived, that I sent a letter to you in Dresden. There is a chance it will reach you in Berlin before you leave. It certainly is a good thing you will not have to be at all the rehearsals leading up to the 26th. Is it as pleasant and migraine-free traveling with Max Reinhardt as it is with a certain Thuringian Fräulein? Or did you have to travel alone?

Do you know how much of my time I spend thinking about you? First I read your letters over and over again until the next one arrives. Then, by the time I finish writing you, the day is over, and once again, I find I have focused my attention almost entirely on you. I find time here and there to read *my* delightful Stifter, which is just what the doctor ordered again and again. He puts me in a terrific mood every time. At the moment, everyone is seated around me reading a book, including my mother!

I wish you were in possession of the last letter I wrote before this one. I would be able to write a much better one now if I were not so worried about the last one possibly having lost its way without any hope of ever finding its owner.

Rarely have I felt that I wrote such a poor letter. I almost feel like tearing it up. But I promised myself recently I would never do so again, so I might as well mail this rubbish as well. The dullness of this letter is most likely due to my present surroundings, so it would not help trying to fight it.

Yours truly, Ottonie D.

˜ ˜ ˜

Sondershausen, 19 January 1911

I have spent a long time tonight talking to you in my thoughts. I just wish I could have done so in reality. I have thought about how you objected to my calling you selfless and now agree that you are probably right. Everything you do for me is ultimately the result of the love you feel for me. However, back in the beginning, when you only wrote on occasion, it had nothing to do with love but was most likely simply a matter of the tremendous sympathy you had for this poor, shattered woman. Indeed, you were quite selfless in the way you treated me. But there's really no point discussing why you are so kind to me. The end result is the same either way. You have been a great help showing me how to live my own life again, just as other people do. There is no question I do not have as strong a desire to live as I might, because I often feel a *terribly* powerful longing for the man who was always there for me. And when this happens, there really isn't much joy to be found in living until I make up my mind to take solace in you, either directly through your letters or through a book. I am so grateful to you in these moments. I am thankful for the help you have given me in overcoming the gloominess, melancholy, hopelessness, and loneliness that I felt. And do you realize that I could never have done this by myself? If I lost you today, I would sink once again to the horrible depths of despair as I had done previously. That is why I ask that you please continue to be there for me just as you have been. I think I was also concerned about this prior to your returning to visit Neubeuern. I became fully aware of this tonight for the first time. So you see, I, too, like you for rather selfish reasons hope this will never change.

Yesterday I think *I* was the one who wrote stupid letters, even though I wanted so much to send you a nice, cheerful letter to Berlin. Right now I am making every effort to be of as much help to my father as I can, for he truly enjoys having me here. I will just have to accept that this is all I can do. It is very strange returning to the old way of life one has come to grow so unaccustomed to. But at the same time, I am content the way my life has turned out, despite the great sorrow I have experienced, for if I had not met Christoph, I would have remained in this small circle, which would have been awful!

Adieu for now. It is really a pity I will not have a chance to speak to you before we are separated by a great distance again. I hope you will have occasion to come to Munich again.

Yours truly, Ottonie D.

❦ ❦ ❦

[Hotel Adlon, Berlin–W.] 20 January 1911, 12:00 noon

Dear Countess,

How delightful everything was one week ago to the day!? In what direction was the dearest Thuringian Fräulein traveling? I think the train was passing by Würzburg when she stood up and said: "That is certainly a lovely town. I have never really seen it before because I've always traveled at night." How near and yet how far removed this lovely day now seems. I believe it is somewhere beyond the realm of time, along with the days we spent together last October. It was no less lovely than they – indeed, perhaps more so, and it also had more to offer (for those who were present). And to remind us that it's been exactly a week, the Marschallin and all her companions will be traveling to Sondershausen today. She will certainly pay warm regards to the Thuringian Fräulein and hopes to be well-received. I hope these dear women will become good friends in recognition of the affinity they share with one another somewhere deep within themselves – despite very different blood lines, personalities and fates. (Their similarity to one another lies in the fact that they are both very natural, sincere and level-headed creatures.)

And the poet who created the character of the Marschallin is very happy that the young Thuringian Fräulein shall – of all people in the world – be the sole possessor of his book[24] (the so-called proof copy) eight days before a single one of the roughly 10,000 curious people has a chance to get his hands on one.

It was very kind of you and I found it touching that you sent me another letter here in Berlin yesterday after you had already sent a letter to Dresden following the arrival of my telegram. I was *so* glad when I found it there this morning. Why do you call it a *poor* letter, when in reality it is such a *wonderful* letter. I enjoyed very much *feeling* as if I were there in the family room where everyone sat reading with the "Fräulein," who also had a book, right in the middle of it all. That is the *old* Ottonie, Miss von Schwartz, the same young girl who traveled to Kassel and Erfurt and God only knows where else. If she was not accompanied from the start, somebody usually joined her aboard the train at some point or met her during a layover. It was never the right one but only the youth of the little Thuringian Fräulein.

I then began to worry about the other letter languishing somewhere in Dresden. I felt the way one might towards a living creature caught in a helpless situation, and I resolved to telephone Dresden if it didn't arrive by 5:00. It was a quarter to five when it finally got here, which meant the evening would have some substance to it. That same evening I also had a nice conversation with Strauss (who still strikes me as a remarkable but completely alien person, as if he came from another planet). We discussed the many lovely projects we might collaborate on for years to come. I kept thinking about how often we will have to meet to discuss things and that Munich would be the only suitable place in the entire world. I felt very happy, and from time to time, a soft voice inside me – or perhaps it came

---

24. This first edition of the *Rosenkavalier* was sent to O. D. S. inscribed: "To the Thuringian Fräulein H:H:" It still is in Marie-Therese's library in Nussdorf, Bavaria.

from somewhere else – would say the same thing over and over again: Ottonie, Ottonie, Ottonie!

Of course I have not forgotten the letter I received from you yesterday, the one from the night when you "talked" to me. (You really shouldn't speak to me in your thoughts when you lie awake at night. If I should happen to enter your thoughts, just think about how fond he is of you and that there is nothing to be concerned about. And try to be happy about the fact that someone *exists* who loves you and who is there for you, just as a soft breeze is there to comfort the nighttime wanderer. But don't contemplate this or speak of it, and don't ever compose letters in your mind. I beg you above all else, Ottonie, if you like me even the slightest bit, please suppress any thoughts of this kind. Banish them from your mind. This is the one thing I can think of that could cause me to stop writing to you.) There are also the last few pages of the previous letter, the one where you tried to answer my question about whether you might in fact like my letters more than you do me. It was a silly, superfluous and intrusive question, and I regret very much having asked it. However, it simply seemed to find its way onto the paper somehow without necessarily expecting to be answered. For I know exactly how things stand with us, Ottonie. I do not expect anything, and there is nothing inside me – neither feelings, nor desire, nor wishes, nor fanciful thought or dreams – that would interfere with my understanding of things in the slightest. And I am happy, very happy indeed, that you are in this world. Perhaps this is why there was no need to mention it, that is, it was not necessary for those two little words, "not-love," to appear in one of your letters. (However, I am to blame for the fact that these words were uttered, one after the other. My question spawned them. Yet my comedy, which I have yet to write, is probably at the root of the entire matter, along with the strange parallels to Lucidor's letters. But there is a fundamental difference, for Ferdinand is *in* love with Arabella and he *loves* the person inside her revealed in her letters, whom he considers to be a manifestation of her true self. It is of course this belief which, at least initially, causes his downward spiral to the very depths of despair following his discovery that someone else wrote the letters.) I also have here your most recent letter, the one you wrote yesterday. Suddenly I began to laugh out loud (not the first time I read it, however). I was laughing at myself, not you. This occurred at the point when you described me as "selfless," which I of course resisted. And today, when you examine the feelings I have and compare my earlier letters and behavior to those of the present (assuming the earlier at least to have been "unselfish"), I must say that I still do not find this description accurate. For at the innermost core of all my feelings for you is the infinite longing to be of some benefit to this poor, "shattered" woman, to use every ounce of inner strength I possess to keep all the horrors at a distance, as well as the penetrating feelings of melancholy, and whatever else might threaten to destroy her soul. I seek not to pull her over to me, but to win her over to life. This is at the core of what I desire – today, as it was back at the beginning when I only wrote on occasion. I felt a gentle, modest sort of love for you then, as I do now. So nothing has changed. Discussions of this sort and any wish to draw a distinction became a topic of discussion in our letters as a result of the terrible scare during the first few days following Christmas – I was afraid of losing or having already lost you. It's difficult to distinguish between "selfish" and "selfless" when feelings of affection and love are involved.

Then there is the *other* matter, which I believe we can also discuss freely and openly, calling a spade a spade. Perhaps you can respond to this in a letter sometime and thereby help liberate me from something that – sometimes – reemerges from my past like a nightmare. It goes back to my youth and the relationships I had with women I never loved. You see, Ottonie, I am probably as enamored of you as I could possibly be of anyone in the world. (My relationship to my own wife, with whom I have lived for the past ten years, to my father, and to the children is no doubt a mystery unto itself.) I came to feel such a powerful affection for you the moment you told me about the monstrous suffering you had endured, which you recounted with a smile on your face. A part of me belonged to you in moments like those, a part of me that had never belonged to anyone else before. It happened just like that, and by the same token, Ottonie, I am as little in love with you and feel as little desire as I possibly could, while feeling tremendous affection for you. It is as if your face, your mouth, your hands and every bone in your body existed only as an extension of your soul, as if your soul enveloped your entire body, just as the opposite occurs in the case of people whose bodies hide their souls, which appear only on rare occasions. But no matter how soft or tender – by its nature soft and tender – it may be, it is still present nonetheless, that delightful, mysterious attraction. It is not of the agonizing, burning or lustful kind, but is simply there and is glad to lead such a peaceful, quiet existence and wishes the last one hundred words had never been written, for they already sound too loud!

One may have no difficulty realizing that a certain hand would not be so lovely if it belonged to somebody else, while there is still a burst of happiness throughout one's body whenever this hand remains in one's for a split second longer (perhaps this additional split second is just my imagination). I found myself in a state of pure ecstasy each time we stood beside one another – like the time out on the balcony in Erfurt – while never seeking to bring about this set of circumstances on a future occasion if it was not meant to be. I remember looking at your hair a number of times and thinking how lovely it would be if you let it down. But it was never my wish to see this nor did I ever call forth the image in my mind or try to seize hold of it if it happened to reappear, nor imagine what possibilities might come of it. And all of this occurred in a much more subdued manner and was scattered throughout the broad expanse of being, much more so than it might appear when expressed in words. But why should you care about this? Just now that deplorable *idée fixe* – this happens every now and then – I had back in my youth entered my mind. It's the one about there being only two things in the world – attraction and repulsion – and that wherever this subtle, extremely subtle, attraction is missing, one will find slumbering (although dulled by a desire to be friendly) a certain repulsion or aversion. And I realize now that you may very well feel the same way about me as I did about those women, and that you, too, may be covering this up and concealing it even from yourself (as I did) *for the sake of the other person* (whose feelings one does not wish to hurt). I fear that you might someday say to me (on the train): "It is a very cozy feeling when my eyes are closed and I know that you are there." I'm sure I said much the same thing to that one woman, even though I knew it was not true, just for the sake of peace of mind – we lie for the sake of our own peace of mind. (Until she let her hair down and I became aware of my true feelings.) Does this make any sense? Dearest, I cannot write anymore now. I have to leave, although I hate to close with these last few sentences.

If possible I will continue writing later today so that you will have the sense that my thoughts proceed naturally from this point and that this is merely the end of a letter and not a "dead end." Rather it is something I have wanted to say, for it needed to be said because – I'm rather tired and feeling a bit dazed right now, but I would *ask* that you share with me your thoughts if I've made any sense and if it's not too much of a chore. There are a thousand things I would still like to say. Just one more thing – the most important – very quickly: There is something for which I am eternally grateful, and that is the mysterious blessing that your existence is for me, which is something that shall never be expressed in words. For it belongs to a different, entirely different, realm. May I prove capable of helping you, in time, to feel just what you mean to me.

Take care and remain my friend.

Yours, Hofmannsthal

P.S. I will be at Europ. Hof in Dresden beginning tomorrow evening.

[Hotel Adlon, Berlin-W.] 20 January [1911] 7:00 in the evening

Well, we went for a walk through Erfurt. (This is a continuation of the long letter; I have the feeling it did not end properly.) I just had tea with Mechtild Lichnowsky in a charming, well-lit salon in the Esplanade. She is attractive and also a very nice woman. Having you as a friend, or perhaps the fact that I am so fond of you, allows me to feel very comfortable and relaxed around other women. All of these things have some relationship to you while remaining infinitely remote at the same time. I could fall in love any time (not with M. L.) with another woman's physical charm very easily, but this would depend on her being present. But why is it that I still find it so terrible to imagine you as another man's wife or lover? Perhaps because I feel that you would – would have to – take with you your special magic and your soul (you may have been different as a girl), indeed your entire person, without being able to leave anything behind for me. When I think about this, it becomes very clear how dark my life would be, as if every last ray of light were extinguished from the world. This is one way I might lose you. The other would be – possibly – if Gerty were to die. I can imagine this might somehow prevent me from ever seeing you again. What is causing me to think such grim thoughts, though?

In half an hour I will be collecting Reinhardt to go to *Oedipus*. What a charmingly peculiar man he is. We left Dresden together the day before yesterday. We spoke quite differently aboard the speeding train that morning than we usually do. When we're together under those kind of circumstances, we are quite regular "people," not the "poet" or the famous "theater man." If it weren't for him, I would find no pleasure in the theater at all and would probably write novels instead. Usually we just discuss the next project we have planned, but this time we were much more relaxed and discussed other things, such as the women or other people one loves or used to love. We spoke in rather general terms, and I really have no idea what exactly he was talking about. He is the shyest, most modest man I know, and this is precisely why I found it incredibly charming to see what was going on inside of him and to discover what happiness meant for him now or in the past. It really is a wonderful thing that takes place between men when they feel close to one another without the slightest trace of affection. And whenever we paused for a moment, my thoughts returned to the train ride from Stuttgart to Erfurt. The little pillow and blanket were aware of this, too, but they did not say anything.

Good night.

H. H.

Sondershausen, Sunday [22 January 1911]

My dear Herr von Hofmannsthal,

The Thuringian Fräulein gave the Marschallin a very friendly reception. She will love having her stay with her for a while. She would like to say "thanks a million" to the one who sent her the *Rosenkavalier*, which provided her with a few very delightful hours yesterday. I am sure it is going to be just delightful in Dresden, and I hope and pray you have a wonderful evening. I had an idea I would like to share with you. As you probably still have the seat reserved for me, and as I am *unfortunately* unable to come, would you mind giving my ticket to Maria van de Velde? I am sure she would be very happy to know that you thought of her. It is important to me to try to help her all I can, for this is a very difficult time in her life. But I am also thinking of myself here. After all, she will have been with you just before she tells me about everything, which would be simply delightful! If for any reason this does not suit you, though, please do not worry about upsetting me. It is just an idea.

Thanks so much for the long, informative and very lovely letter. It is a pity to spend so much of our time discussing the feelings we may or may not have for one another, so we really should try to put an end to it. But first, I want to remove from your mind the *idée fixe* that you have because of the experiences you had had with women you did not love. It is terribly difficult to express in writing what I would like to say, but I will try as best I can. We will also have to discuss this when we are together sometime. Let us assume that people feel one of two things for each other: attraction or repulsion. Then in our case, I feel, as you do, too, the former. I think you know me well enough to realize that I am much too direct and down to earth not to tell you exactly the way I feel. If deep down inside I were repulsed by you, I could not have written you the letter in which I asked you to travel on the same train with me. I suppose I could have, out of pity, put up with you in Neubeuern. I certainly would have been able to be kind and pleasant enough (but not to the degree that I was). However, I never would have asked you to travel with me. I am no longer so young or immature that I would do something like that. Ottonie Schwartz would have been able to, but not Ottonie Degenfeld. Now let me promise you that I will let you know if I *ever* have any misgivings about you. I know this would hurt you, and although it would be a bitter pill for me to swallow, I would *take* it nonetheless, so you never need to have the feeling: "Could it be that she no longer has the same feelings for me and is unwilling to admit it?"

There will probably *never* be another man to come along and take me away from you, so please don't worry about this either. I am neither searching for nor do I long for him. So, please, let us keep things the way they are. It makes me extremely happy to know that I mean something to you. I have certainly done so many times in the past, so there's no need here to explain again what you mean to me. I will second the Marschallin in saying: "sei Er nicht wie alle Männer sind, dann macht Er mich unendlich glücklich" (Don't be like other men, and you'll make me very happy).

I am so glad that you have such a wonderful relationship with Reinhardt. He must truly be a splendid man if *you* like him so much. I would love to meet him. Maybe you can bring him along on a trip to Neubeuern sometime, and then the lovely thought of performing a play in the park might someday become reality.

I wonder if you realize how happy I felt when I read what you had to say about Strauss. It would be delightful if you often were to have occasion to meet him there. Then we could spend a few hours or even a few days together. This is very selfish of me, because I really should not hope that you begin working with Strauss again so soon, which is very different from the work you do when you have time to yourself. And this is time you need for your own creations. You must not constantly be under the pressure of meeting Strauss' deadlines. In any case, please make sure you allow yourself plenty of extra time in addition to whatever work you do with Strauss.

I cannot help thinking of all the ideas you told me about as we hiked up the beloved Heuberg mountain. I *really* do love recalling that time.

Take good care of yourself. I hope the days leading up to the premiere are calm and pleasant.

Always yours truly, Ottonie D.

🍂 🍂 🍂

[Sendig Hotel: Europ. Hof, Dresden–A.] Tuesday, 24 [January 1911]
(Will be here until noontime on the 27th,
and then at the Hotel Adlon in Berlin)

Dear Countess,

The last few days have been simply wonderful, and for each of us they shall remain unforgettable for the rest of our lives. Reinhardt left early this morning for London where he has business to take care of. As we stood on the staircase and shook hands and said goodbye at 2 o'clock in the morning, he told me he was very glad he didn't have to stay and could depart with this wonderful, untarnished impression that could not possibly be surpassed by anything. The first act was performed the day before yesterday and the third act last night. Never again shall we see it performed *like this* with a total harmony of poetry, music and acting. Something about the whole thing was so tender and subtle and so beautiful that we all had tears in our eyes as we sat watching it in the darkness. It is very strange how at times – on rare occasions – one reacts with tears to *pure* beauty, perfection, and absolute harmony. I remember feeling this way when viewing the Elgin marbles[25] and once when beholding the beautiful landscape at the Gulf of Ithea in Greece. Strauss told me he *always* feels this way when he hears Caruso sing. I read somewhere that tears ran down both of old Haydn's cheeks when he was working on his Masses. It was not on account of his music, however; it was because God had made the world so beautiful.

We spent many long, lovely mornings together rehearsing with the orchestra; I can still see the colorful figures up on the stage with only Reinhardt moving silently among them. And everything became more real, more defined, more elegant and subtle, and ultimately so human. It very much had an 18th-century flavor, as I had never before seen on the stage. This achievement we owed to Roller's incredible talent and dedication. Never has anything quite like this appeared on a German stage: every last detail so pleasing to the eye, much like one of Delatour's pastels or an old color print. And one must not forget the lovely evenings we all spent together from 7 to 11 in the rehearsal room with those three tireless women, the Marschallin (played by a rather opulent blonde), Quinquin, and Sophie, a sensitive and indescribably loveable creature. She is a young woman, or perhaps not so young; she is one of those people whose age it is difficult to pinpoint. I think she is an incredibly charming person, like none the theater has ever known before – so moving, quite helpless, and very much a *Poupée de Saxe* [Dresden china doll]. I cannot bring myself to look away when she is on the stage. The essence of her entire character (and perhaps even more than this) may be found in the way she manages to *elude* Ox – and this she does better on the stage than I was able to in composing the part!

I have to admit that I have the *idée fixe* that you *must see the performance here*. What an ugly sight it would be anyplace else. It is here that it receives that touch of elegance which it absolutely requires. But you should not come just for this reason. Instead, take the train that passes through Dresden on your *return*, where you can stop off to see the fourth or fifth performance at the beginning of February. I will send you a telegram in Weimar with the dates of the performances, and then you'll be able to pick one. I have already discussed this with the manager of the theater and have seen to it that I receive two tickets for each performance. Count Seebach will send them to you at the hotel (for you and Maria van de Velde). You can then depart at 7:21 the next evening; you will find a sleeper in Halle and will arrive in Munich at 8:00 in the morning. Would this be acceptable?

Yours, H. H.

---

25. The Earl of Elgin took these Greek sculptures from the Parthenon in Athens and brought them to London in 1814. Now they are in the British Museum, but Greece is negotiating to have them returned.

❦ ❦ ❦

Sondershausen, 25 January 1911

My dear Herr von Hofmannsthal,
You really are much too kind. I will *definitely* come to Dresden, even if Maria does not wish to go along. I am so glad that you have had such wonderful and memorable experiences. It is moments like these that make life worth living. I was *so* excited by what you wrote. I just wish I could have been there to share this experience with you. I will be thinking of you and everyone else in Dresden tomorrow evening, and I *truly* hope it will be a *great* success for you and for Strauss – I cannot express this in words. How wonderful that the three female characters are so well-cast. What a magical aura it will be that surrounds the whole thing!

I will not write any more today, because this letter will arrive right at the start of everything, when you are busy with lots of people, and you will not have time for distant friends.

Gerty has probably arrived today, so please give her my warmest regards. I shake your hand *as* I did *back then.*

Yours, Ottonie Degenfeld S.

❦ ❦ ❦

[Sendig Hotel: Europäischer Hof, Dresden–A.]
Friday [27 January 1911] 5:00

Dear Countess,
Have to write in a hurry now. The hotel is filled with people – they are even out on the staircases – and there is constantly someone knocking on the door; it is terribly exhausting yet still *very* pleasant. It was a wonderful evening. It would have made me so happy if you could have been here. The atmosphere was so festive, especially in a city this small. Hundreds of cars were driving up to the entrance, and the streets were filled with people observing the scene. Then came the opening and the incredible excitement and, after the second act, the feeling that success was now assured. Afterwards I went to Frau Strauss's box to congratulate her. At that very instant, everyone looked up at me from down below, and everyone in the parquet turned around and started to applaud. People from every corner of the theater shouted their approval. It was a wonderful moment, and I felt very happy, much more so than if I had taken the conventional (and very silly) bow out on the stage. At the end, however, as the audience refused to stop applauding, I decided to make an appearance on the stage so as to not offend Strauss. Then supper was served to around four hundred people I would guess. I viewed everything through a

misty veil. A lot of my "girlfriends" were there; Helene Nostitz looked very attractive, and Mechtild L. was also there and really is a very nice woman. Schröder's sisters, the blonde, Clärchen, and Lina, a brunette, were there as well. Everyone treated me *very* nicely, and Max Schillings gave a speech in my honor; many a princess conversed with a critic, and singers and impresarios embraced. Kessler was nice yet rather nervous, Rudi Schröder delighted yet exhausted. Telegrams raced around the globe, and the dwarf from Bremen[26] was constantly drinking toasts to me. I made it back to my room at 1:30 and slept like a log. We are staying here for the second performance and will be in Berlin by midday on Sunday. What a wonderful evening is in store for you here.

Yours, H. H.

❦ ❦ ❦

Sondershausen, 27 January 1911

My dear Herr von Hofmannsthal,

You will be arriving in Berlin about now, and the entire *Rosenkavalier* project in Dresden has come to an end after the many long weeks of anticipation. It is amazing how quickly things like this come and go. I have not heard anything yet about how everything went last night and can hardly wait for the news.

My stay here is almost over. I will be leaving for Stassfurt[27] (19 Bernburgerstr.) tomorrow around noon and will be staying there until Tuesday. That's only two hours from Berlin. How close we will be again yet still so far, separated by two long hours. I persuaded my father to come along. It will be good for him to experience some different sights and sounds, even if only for a few days. I gave him *Eckermann's Gespräche* [Eckermann's Conversations with Goethe]. He was so interested in it that he had to read certain parts aloud. He seemed to be quite happy and was really very content then. It will be very hard for me to leave him behind.

Julie wrote me yesterday and said that she doesn't want to go anywhere now, so I, too, can remain in Neubeuern. I just shall not have quite the solitude I had hoped for. I am already looking forward to some much needed peace and quiet. It really has become a bit too much for me here. Every day in the afternoon somebody came to enjoy my company, and I of course ended up chattering on and on for much too long.

---

26. Leopold Biermann, a generous sponsor of the arts.
27. O. D. S. went to visit her oldest sister, who was married to the director of a salt mine there.

You know, I am *so* looking forward to Dresden. There is no question I will be going there! I was planning to stay with Maria[28] until Saturday or Sunday, so it would suit me perfectly if there were a performance on the 5th, 6th or even the 7th. I have not been to Dresden either and am looking forward to the chance to see some of it. Should I stay in the *Europäische Hof*?

Well, I am sure you will be very busy in Berlin and will be leading a rather mundane life. Will you have time to think of the country people in Upper Bavaria every once in a while, where the Thuringian Fräulein also lives at present? During the few quiet moments I have had here, I have enjoyed tremendously the charming Stifter you gave me; it makes for perfect reading in these surroundings. His beautiful, poetic descriptions so fully capture everything that goes on here in these circles. It is really delightful to see *what* modest lives these people here lead and how they try to make the most of everything. It is also rather amusing the way people shake their heads at anything new that finds its way from the outside world into their little community – things everyone else takes for granted. Especially when it comes to morals, I am often dumbfounded by the shock that even the most trivial flirtation can trigger. If a young lady tries to outdo her neighbor by dressing more elegantly, it is considered wicked and is the beginning of the end in their eyes.

I love those charming "one-of-a-kinds" that you find only in small towns, among which I have many old friends I need to visit. They are always happy to see me again and overjoyed that I still come to visit like I used to, even though I am now a *Countess*, which they consider to be barely beneath their Duchess here in rank.

Well, now all three of my sisters are home to enjoy my final evening with me. Take care. My thoughts are with you,

Faithfully yours, Ottonie Degenfeld S.

Stassfurt 19, Bernburger [28 January 1911]

I was truly *deeply* touched that you still found time to write me *that* day during all the commotion. *How* wonderful the evening must have been; I am so immensely happy for you and Strauss. It was a pity that I did not find out a bit earlier that you were staying last night for the second performance. I could just as well have gone to Dresden first before coming here. I was just about to send you a telegram; however, as I had per-

---

28. At the van de Velde's in Weimar. Maria's husband Henry van de Velde (1863–1959) was one of the leaders of Art Nouveau, or *Jugendstil*. He was director of the architecture and design school *Kunstgewerbliches Institut* in Weimar from 1901 to 1914.

suaded my father to come along, I did not want to disappoint him and therefore decided not to.

I just spoke to Maria v.d. Velde over the telephone and told her about our plans to travel with her to Dresden. She says that Henry will also be returning on Tuesday from Paris and that he would surely love to travel there with us. Do you think you could reserve three seats for us then? And could you let us know on what days the performances are? I suppose it would be possible for you to come there again from Berlin then?

How delightful it must have been to see all the dear, wonderful people again and to have them there for such a special evening. Whenever the next event of this kind is, however, I do not plan to allow myself to be prevented from coming by such pointless concerns. My rather ordinary parents found it very strange that I did not go to Dresden; I then realized for the first time how truly natural this would have been. But now it is of course past, and it does no good to keep thinking about it.

So, now I have to go to town with both of my nephews – nice, cheerful boys – to buy chocolate for them.

Well, my letter arrived in Berlin a day early. I hope it was not forwarded to you in Dresden; otherwise it will have just missed you there.

Yours truly, Ottonie D.

❦ ❦ ❦

[Hotel Adlon, Berlin–W.] Monday [30 January 1911] 7:00

Dear Countess,

Both of your letters reached me all right. The first one arrived before I did yesterday, and the other got here this morning. What a charming description you gave me of the small town and the Countess there, the young girl who has changed so much while still remaining the same.

It has been exactly one month to the day since the evening of my arrival in Neubeuern. It is amazing how much can happen in one month, and so many wonderful things happened during this past month: first there were the last few days in Neubeuern and then the trip, followed by the rehearsals, and finally the rather puzzling hurly-burly around the time of the premiere. When I left my hotel room in Dresden, it seemed so full of memories. I remember waiting for your letter at the very beginning of my stay, the many sleepless nights, an abominable depression – and then a combination of terrible restlessness, exhaustion and joy all in one. The work itself was the greatest joy: the incredible way in which it truly came together as *a whole*, as if it were not the product of two men alone.

I am so glad you are planning to go to see it. I will of course get three tickets for you or however many you would like. But I do need to know ahead of time, so that I can send a telegram to the management, because the performances will continue to be sold out for some time to come. There will be one on the 4th, and the next will probably fall right on the 7th, as you had wished, or the 8th at the latest. Can I go ahead and reserve the seats for this date? You can reserve a room in the *Europ. Hof*, but just make sure it is a quiet one, that is, not one on the side facing the new building under construction (they even hammer away at night). The tickets will arrive at the hotel in your name on the day of the performance. If a mix-up should occur and the tickets do not arrive before noon, please telephone Dr. Adolf Administration of the Court Theaters, and mention my name.

Dresden is a beautiful town that I truly love. I would have *loved* to walk down the old streets here with you. It is somewhat unfortunate that you will be there with van de Velde, who is so unreceptive to and intolerant of the beauty and greatness of past epochs in the history of art. I hope you will not kill yourself trying to look at everything in the museum. There are of course numerous first-rate paintings, which makes it difficult to *limit* oneself. The new Rembrandt room is superb, and they have done a nice job of displaying his paintings. The Venetian room also contains a wonderful display: two Tintorettos that I love so much, a Veronese, and a Giorgione. The splendid Vermeer van Delft!

I am enclosing a very nice telegram Heymel sent.

Yours, Hofmannsthal

P.S. We are having dinner at the Varnbühlers. I think the only reason I accepted their invitation was because I have somehow come to associate them with Stuttgart.

Stassfurt, 31 January 1911

My dear Herr von Hofmannsthal,

Your dear letter just arrived to greet me on this lovely Sunday morning, and outside it looks like spring. However, when you go outside, you discover that it really is cold. They still have snow in Neubeuern, and Marie-Therese can ride her birthday toboggan every day. Well, today I am traveling to Weimar *by myself* and will be thinking a lot about another trip. Especially when I have to change trains in Erfurt, the train station there will also seem strangely empty. I wonder if I will meet Studnitz?! I think it would be best if you now made a reservation for Saturday; this will certainly suit Henry and Maria as well, as he is still free on Sunday. I may also stay there alone on Monday and take a walk in the nice city and think of what a wonderful time you are having there now.

I am so glad that Julie and Mädy came to Munich. It is so good for both of them to get out again and to hear something different, and they will surely be impressed by *Rosenkavalier*. I cannot begin to tell you *how much* I am looking forward to this. Father wants to go out with me. Take care.

Yours, Ottonie D.

P.S. I will definitely send a telegram from Weimar regarding the tickets.

[Hotel Adlon, Berlin–W.] 2 February 1911

Dear Countess,

What a wonderful day it was yesterday on my birthday! (You of course didn't know that it was my birthday. Gerty and even my father forgot, and so did I until letters arrived from the children.) I had been awake for just a few minutes when the telephone on my desk began to ring, quietly at first and then very loud. I ran to pick it up and was told it is from "Weimar," and then I heard your voice. *How* fabulous it was! Usually one feels nothing special, but then, when you said your name, I was overwhelmed. You were so close, so truly present, like something out of a fairy tale. It was as if I were in Neubeuern and you in Hinterhör, and I could come right over so that we could go for a walk together through the early springtime forest, still bare yet full of pussy willows, crocuses, and the sweet scent of the primrose stalks. All day long I heard a quiet yet ever-*present* voice whispering, "Ottonie." Now you are in Weimar, and I can see you there walking around, through the park, where I know every one of the crooked little paths so well from the walks I took with Kessler. Or you might be sitting down with Frau Förster drinking tea, surrounded by the city's rich culture, gossip and other foolishness. Perhaps you will walk down the narrow streets and pass some of the places where Goethe *died* in the truest sense, more so than in any other place on earth. Some afternoon when the weather is fair, take a trip out to Tiefurt with some of your friends. It is so lovely there. And make sure to visit Goethe's house sometime. But when you enter his study and the room where he died, *please* do so alone, all alone, without the company of a single human being. I, too, would never enter either of these rooms with another person.

There are so many people here I have to meet, which can be rather draining at times – it seems a ridiculous, pointless way to live. I suppose I am simply exhausted and reacting to the uncanny excitement of the delightful days in Dresden. Late last night I received a "birthday telegram" signed by the most unlikely of people: Strauss, Schillings, Julie, Mädy,

Heymel, Bosetti, and God only knows whom else. I am *very* glad both ladies[29] had the chance to participate somewhat in all the excitement and commotion, but I am very, very happy that *you* will have a chance to see the opera performed in Dresden, where it is much more delicate and indeed superior. Every one of us left his mark on this production.

You will not have time to write me from Weimar, but please send me a telegram letting me know whether I can go ahead and reserve two seats for the 7th (I have received telegrams informing me that it is sold out every night) or the 9th, when the opera will probably *also* be performed. I'll of course get two tickets for you, but why is it that you want to bring someone else with you if Maria van de Velde cannot come? Would you not like the peace and quiet of an empty seat beside you and the feeling of being *alone*, just as one is when reading a good book?

A couple of evenings ago I went to the theater to see *Die Ratten* [Rats] with Gerty and M. L. That is the new play by Hauptmann[30] in which there is so much that one should be able to relate to. Yesterday we saw *Othello*, played by Basserman,[31] whose wonderful portrayal truly penetrated to the deepest core of Othello's character. The other actors were rather run of the mill, even second-rate. But it was nonetheless *Othello*, which reveals Shakespeare in his entirety: the vastness, the incomparable greatness and novelty of his work, as if it had just been written yesterday, with a shocking quality to it that is second to none. And then all at once, as I sat there in the dark box, I was struck by an ugly, selfish thought fraught with envy and jealousy: There would still have been enough time to go to Weimar if you had visited Berlin for a couple days and accompanied us here these past two evenings, in which case I wouldn't have felt so strained and empty inside. "Why, why, why," I ask myself, "didn't you come?"

I will tell you about the plans I made with Strauss another time, for you don't have time to read all this now. I just want to let you know that it will not place too great a burden on me.

Yours, Hofmannsthal.

❦ ❦ ❦

[Haus "Hohe Pappeln," Ehringsdorf, near Weimar] 3 February 1911

Although it is almost midnight, Henry and I just finished making the seating list for tomorrow[32] evening. Maria was playing the piano in the

---

29. O. D. S.'s sisters-in-law Julie and Mädy.
30. Famous German author and playwright Gerhart Hauptmann.
31. Famous actor Albert Bassermann.
32. For a banquet given for van de Velde by his students.

next room. I was actually supposed to go to a lecture this evening that Wiecke, who is from Dresden, was giving on Goethe. He was apparently going to be reading *everything* that you had just read to us in Neubeuern. Maybe that is the reason I did not want to go, or perhaps I felt an aversion to listening to someone else read Goethe while surrounded by a large crowd of people. So we decided to stay here, and it turned out to be a *very* pleasant evening.

After waiting in vain for a letter from you this morning, I decided to spend a quiet hour writing one to you. When I arrived at the studio to pick up Henry, he gave me a letter from you that had been waiting there for me the entire morning. So I decided to keep the one I wrote.

I felt the same way you did during our telephone conversation. It was *so* nice being able to talk to you (I usually do not particularly care to talk on the telephone). I was so surprised to hear your voice, especially because I expected Gerty to pick up the phone since you share the same aversion to telephones that I do.

I am thoroughly enjoying the harmony of the house here, where the combination of shape and color is truly perfect; it creates for me a holiday mood when I sit quietly in those beautiful downstairs rooms. One quickly notices what a tremendous effect the surroundings have on a person. At moments like these my room in Neubeuern frightens me.

I really enjoy spending time with both these splendid people. The better I get to know Maria, the greater, or stronger, my fondness for her becomes. Emotionally she is surely going through an extremely difficult time right now, but I believe that no matter what may come between the two of them, nothing could ever really tear them apart. Deep inside they've grown too closely attached to one another. I suppose there are emotional difficulties in every marriage – even between the best of people – that can reach a point of crisis, but one should muster the moral fortitude needed to overcome them.

I will be arriving in Dresden around 6:00 on Monday; on Tuesday I am going to have a look at the city as well as some of the paintings and will be going to the opera that same evening. The reason I want to take someone with me (it will probably end up being Pepino) is that the one thing I *hate* is going to a strange theater all by myself. I would be happiest if someone could drop me there and then also pick me up – but this one could only ask of a *very* close acquaintance.

Henry has to go to Hanover this coming Monday and must then return to Paris on the 9th. His life is terribly hectic right now.

Good night then.

Ottonie.

P.S. By the way, I always have enough time to read your letters, even the very long ones. I hope you will write me in Dresden so that I can talk to you again.

Good morning. It is such a bright, sunny morning today, the first nice day (in terms of the weather) since I have been here. I will be walking down the alley in just a moment to visit Henry in the studio. You will accompany me the entire way, which makes me very happy. We have such nice conversations during my walks. You, too, would find it very nice if you could hear us.

I was so glad to receive your letter yesterday. I do not believe you have any idea *how* happy it makes me feel when you send me a letter of this kind. I am always extremely happy when it feels a bit heavier than usual – which I check before opening it – and then I *keep* reading it until the next one arrives.

But now I should briefly tell you a little bit about what we have been doing here. Right now, there is nobody here whom both of you know. I have not even had a chance to visit Frau Förster N.34 yet, but I'm planning to tomorrow. One evening we went to the theater where we saw *Die lustigen Weiber v. W.* [The Merry Wives of Windsor]; the actors performed amazingly well. Otherwise, Henry's been reading aloud to us in the evenings from a new play, *Les Affranchis*. It's very interesting. We expect to finish it tomorrow. Yesterday we went to Goethe's house. It was truly an overwhelming experience to enter his home and see *his* world – and the garden where he planted every one of the trees and all the things he loved to collect that gave him so much pleasure and finally *his* two *private* rooms. It was an unforgettable moment.

Maria is calling me. I have to go now.

Ottonie.

❦ ❦ ❦

[Hotel Adlon, Berlin–W., 7 February 1911]

Dear Countess,

I was so sad when your telegram from Dresden arrived yesterday evening because I thought to myself in no uncertain terms, "Well, it is not going to work out after all; now she'll be thinking, 'It does not matter whether I see the opera in Dresden or in Munich.'" And in reality, it *does* matter. I want you to see it performed in Dresden *so* much; there my contribution is so evident, indeed everything I could have possibly contributed. You will not find *any* of this in Munich.

Then last night turned out to be miserable due to an unfortunate quarter of an hour spent with Kessler, and then this morning there was no telegram to be found. I immediately started worrying that my message may have arrived too late and you would already be on your way to Dresden. Finally I got through to the studio and then to someone at the house, so now everything is all right. You will spend two relaxing days there with Maria v.d.V., who is very much looking forward to everything, and then a couple of days later you will have the chance to meet the Feldmarschallin.

The unfortunate moment with Kessler was a very uncanny manifestation which grew out of an entirely harmless situation. We had dinner at the Esplanade with the Lichnowskys, the Harrachs and Montgelas, and Rudi Schröder was also there. Then we went together to the "Wintergarten" to see a Chinese group perform. However, we arrived late and didn't get to see them; we returned to the Esplanade and sat there chatting. Then Gerty left, and I sat in her seat next to a rather attractive woman whom I had not spoken to the entire evening. She, however, happened to strike up a conversation with the gentleman next to her, while Kessler was seated on my other side. He told me he was planning to see *Oedipus* the following day and that he expected it would leave a miserable impression on him, and he also *brought up the matter of Craig*.[33] He had some very harsh things to say about Reinhardt; he was awfully severe in the way he spoke and showed a complete lack of insight and fair-mindedness. I did not say a thing, but the entire time I imagined one of us striking the other in the face and the two of us engaged in a duel – I imagined all of this taking place alongside an ugly, yellowish gray wall outside a factory. But I remained quite relaxed and friendly the entire time. (I continued to force myself to think of you and of the walk we took together last autumn; I recalled your soft and kind manner of speaking, dearest Ottonie.) M. L.'s eyes had a frightened look in spite of our speaking very quietly to one another. I managed to remain calm and congenial to the very end, until I lay awake in bed that night feeling enraged and extremely agitated, unable to shut my eyes for hours. As morning approached, I tried *to see things from his perspective* and was finally able to fall asleep. And at one o'clock that afternoon we met again for lunch at Frau Richter's. I was frightened, truly frightened, of myself, of him, of both of us. We met in the vestibule. I said, "Do you know what Gerty said? If we end up dueling with one another because of Craig and you happen to kill me, then you have to marry her." We both laughed. His face was so friendly (when he laughed), and we enjoyed a very pleasant and relaxed atmosphere at lunch.

Frau von Spitzemberg is a very nice and intelligent woman and was a – the only – close female friend of Bismarck's. I very much enjoy talking to her, and she is always very kind to me. It is nice having so many

---

33. Kessler's idea was to have Craig do the scenery for *Oedipus*.

people who treat one with such kindness. I wish I could continue chatting, but it's almost 12 o'clock. Gerty is downstairs in the reading room, but I am so dead tired from the awful rage I felt last night that my eyes are about to fall shut. But it is so much fun talking to you. One comes across so many people here. Yesterday I saw the lovely Anga Douglas, a friend of Eberhard's, in a very amusing situation. Will tell you about it later, in Neubeuern. In your room. Your room! I find I feel completely at ease when standing in a room designed by Van de Velde.

At the beginning of the letter I wrote yesterday (partly in pencil and partly in ink; I began it in the evening and continued writing the next morning), I said: "I am making use of a quiet hour here to write to you." The previous letter never did arrive (the one you wrote before receiving mine in the studio). Did it get lost? Or has it just gotten held up before arriving tomorrow morning?? How nice that would be.

Good night, good night.

H.

❦ ❦ ❦

[Haus "Hohe Pappeln," Ehringsdorf, near Weimar, 8 February 1911]

I still have twenty minutes left before saying goodbye to this wonderful house. I would like to spend a few of these by quickly writing you a short note. I will be going straight to Frau Förster N.'s with Veldes to have lunch there with Kessler and afterwards I will board the train for Dresden.

I received your lovely letter this morning. I shall always think of Kessler and you and you and Kessler together. You cannot imagine how grateful I am that he had a friendly smile on his face and that you're on good terms with each other again. I hope the ugliness of the whole affair will not remain with you. I am very, very happy we were able to discuss this then and that it came to mind and remained with you, helping you perhaps to remain calm and collected. I am glad it helped you remain calm and composed. It is so miserable having disagreements with people one is very fond of, as you are of Kessler.

I destroyed the previous letter, but I am not sure why myself. Certain things in it just did not make sense after I received the answers to the questions I had asked. But I do not believe my letters are so special that it would matter if you missed one of them.

Unfortunately, there is no more time to chat. With many fond memories,

Yours, Ottonie D.

🌹 🌹 🌹

[Sendig Hotel: Europäischer Hof, Dresden–A.]
Wednesday [8 February 1911]

Very dear Rosenkavalier,
My dear Herr von Hofmannsthal,

Roses! I was greeted by lovely roses when I entered my room. I wonder if I was wrong when my mind raced immediately to the Adlon in search of their sender? I hope he will accept my warmest thanks from the bottom of my heart. I just loved the way my room looked when I first saw it. It was as if someone had just passed through it spreading love and care.

It is very strange being here in Dresden now. This is the same city that we talked and wrote so much about, and the same hotel where so many *different* sorts of letters were written.

I had a very nice time at lunch today. I, too, find that Kessler has incredible charm. Even though I hardly know him at all, I still like him very much. I always have the feeling that I've known him for a very long time. Henry was also charming and can be so pleasant and simply delightful. I really do like him *a lot*. It is very hard on Maria constantly being alone. Even all those people who could possibly be of some help to her are gone.

I almost think it is better to be *completely* separated from the one you love, as in my case, than having to deal with the constant coming and going. People are often unable to find the right words to express themselves, and before they have had a chance to get properly reacquainted, it is time to part. I wonder what is harder to bear: feeling how all the thoughts of your beloved slowly turn toward another or physically losing him altogether? I have no idea if there is any basis to my suspicions about the Veldes, but I think the last two years have been very hard on both of them. Now that Henry has enjoyed so much freedom during his time in Paris, he may again come to appreciate the harmony of the life he has at home.

You see, no matter where one is, one is never alone. For example, I just happened to bump into my old friend from London here, Countess Wengersky, who will be traveling to Munich with me on Friday and will soon visit us in Neubeuern. She was thrilled by the *Rosenkavalier* and would like to see it with me again tomorrow. I hope there is no confusion regarding the tickets and that they arrive as expected. I wonder if you received the short note I wrote (the one from this morning). I gave it to mail to a young lieutenant who rode with me for a stretch on the train. It was a rather lonely trip this time. There was no blanket of Schröder's and even less someone who could wrap up my cold feet; no pleasant conversation, and no stop in Erfurt either.

It is already midnight, so I had really better go to bed and read a little bit of *Emanuel Quint.*

Oh, I just remembered, I have not told you anything about the lovely banquet in Weimar yet. We, especially Henry, were terribly afraid the young art students might commit some awful *faux pas*, but everything turned out to be just perfect. They presented their theatricals tactfully and in good taste, and the speeches about Henry were really lovely. I felt so happy for him.

A very dear good night.

Ottonie.

❦ ❦ ❦

[Hotel Adlon, Berlin–W.] Thursday morning [9 February 1911]

Dear Countess,

In this city, even if you have the intention of writing a letter all day long, you can still be prevented from doing so from one hour to the next until finally you go to bed at one in the morning without having written it. You sometimes have the feeling everything is conspiring against you. Whenever I had a break, someone came in to talk to me or the doorbell would ring. When I was at Reinhardt's that evening, he went to the next room at one point, and I was about to start writing a letter at his desk when again someone entered the room. It was the painter from the theater, who had been waiting for an hour to discuss the costumes for *Ariadne*[34] with me. (What is *Ariadne*? I will tell you about it later.) So once again I was unable to write, and somebody arrived in Dresden where there was not a letter waiting to greet her there – and, I fear, no flowers, either! Were there really *no* flowers there in your room?? It suddenly dawned on me tonight: The person I had asked to pick out some flowers for me might not be in Dresden. Otherwise, he would have responded with at least a few words to my letter and the three separate telegrams I sent. How careless this was of me. But it is a very pleasant morning today. You will like the city with its old town squares, the Zwinger,[35] the Hofkirche, the lovely river, and the beautiful, distinguished layout of the entire grounds. How I would love to walk around there with you. Seven years ago I went there for the first time, also quite alone, and very much enjoyed it, except for the drab and rather boring dining room at the hotel! Will you be eating alone? Perhaps Pepino will join you? And that evening

---

34. The play H. v. H. wrote with Ottonie in mind, and which he refers to in another letter as "your Ariadne." He officially dedicated it to Max Reinhardt. The poem "Harlekin" at the start of this book is his message to Ottonie.

35. Famous palace and museum in Dresden.

you will see the performance. I hope none of the singers falls ill. I keep thinking if only none of the backups has to fill in for a member of the cast. I just hope nothing goes wrong.

Then you will leave for Munich, as I will, too – soon, very soon. Perhaps even in three or four days. So once again, we will not be very far apart. This time, I am not concerned about anything, though. I do not see any grim or foreboding tides approaching. Ever since the day in Stuttgart, everything seems to be in our favor. It was the departure from Neubeuern back then that made everything appear so bleak.

It upsets me very much whenever I find out you have destroyed one of your letters. It's as if someone has killed a living creature, and I also feel like you have withheld or taken away something that already belonged to me. Perhaps it is just because I almost never do this myself that I find it so disconcerting.

I quite regretted having written about the unfortunate episode with Kessler – but before I knew it, it was already on the page. I kept thinking, "I wonder what she thinks about my apparent need to tell her *everything*." But then I thought, "I wanted to tell her this, so let it be said." My only hope now is that the two solitary days you spend in Dresden are in no way unpleasant!

Why was it that Maria did not come along?

Adieu.

Yours, Hofmannsthal

❦ ❦ ❦

[Sendig Hotel: Europ. Hof, Dresden–A.] Thursday, 9 [February 1911]

I just finished reading, "I just hope the two days you spend in Dresden are in no way unpleasant." No, they were by *no* means. On the contrary, they were both delightful, truly wonderful days. I have just returned from the Marschallin and the charming Sophie and Quinquin, from your enchanted world – oh, how could I not feel well?! You accompany me with every step I take; we stand outside on the terrace together and watch the ice floating down the river while a haze surrounds the rays of the beautiful sun. I do not believe we have ever spent such intense hours together as we did today. I am *so* glad I *decided* to come here. I cannot tell you *how* much I enjoyed myself that evening. I tried to recreate the atmosphere as I imagined it must have been the night of the premiere; I think I actually managed to do so quite well. I almost thought I would see you there. My God, was it lovely! The three women were unbelievably wonderful. You are right, as soon as Sophie appears, you cannot take your eyes off the stage. I was deeply moved by her magnificent performance. It really is a complete *whole*: the words, the music and the acting!

I wish they would perform it again tomorrow evening so that I could see it again.

Just now when I was downstairs having dinner, a dear little waiter came up to me and asked how my health was. He had waited on me every day in Wiesbaden back when I was so sick. He must have thought I seemed lonely, which made him want to entertain me, so he told me all about the premiere. It was very touching.

I want to keep saying the same thing over and over again: There is just no way to describe how wonderful it was. I am *so* grateful to you for bringing me here. *Your* roses said, "Good morning" to me at the start of the day, and now your letter says, "Good night!" Could there be a better way to begin and end the day? Then, while it was still quite early in the morning, a package containing lovely candy arrived. I wonder who might have sent this? Could it perhaps have been Eberhard?!

I had a look at the city this morning and saw many beautiful sights. I also went to Pepino's out in Loschwitz and had lunch at the Wengerskys' afterwards. I took a rest this afternoon so I would have enough energy for this evening. I am going to the museum tomorrow. I will try to behave and save my energy.

It is a good thing you gave me Dr. Adolf's address because the tickets never arrived. After I telephoned him, they were waiting for me safe and sound at the ticket office.

Maria did not want to go anywhere during the few days that she had Henry there at home with her. I can understand this very well, so I did not even try to talk her into coming.

I really think it is quite right and also very kind that you tell me about everything. In fact, I have been waiting for a long time to hear something about your meetings with Kessler. He was quite casual in the way he spoke about you in W. I wanted to ask more about you or send my regards, but it just was not possible. I think I will go to sleep now. I send you my warmest regards and thanks from Dresden before falling asleep.

Yours, Ottonie D.

❦ ❦ ❦

Neubeuern, 13 February 1911

My dear Herr von Hofmannsthal,

Exactly one month ago to the day, we sat across from one another and, every few minutes, one had to shout "Come in!" loud and clear. Oh, it was such a lovely, jolly time, and we had a wonderful day and evening. How often will we recall our lovely trip together.

I arrived back here around noon on Saturday. Mädy picked me up with the sleigh in Rosenheim. The same snow still lay on the ground that you and I rode across on our way to Rosenheim. That was the lovely day of our wonderful return trip, which removed the dark shadows that still lingered from the previous few days. It is very strange to settle down here again. It is a very different Neubeuern now, much different than the Neubeuern that I left behind. You gave me a very nice welcome when I arrived. Do you know how? Through all the notes you put in my Goethe. I said hello to my books and was filled with love by all the good old friends here in my room. I was so touched by once again being able to feel your presence within all these beloved books.

Julie rearranged my room again. The lights are brighter and the large dresser next to the curtain in front of the entrance to the bathroom is gone and has been replaced by a bookcase. The weather here is absolutely wonderful. At night, it dips down into the 30's, and during the day, we are bathed in sunshine. Yesterday it was so warm that we sat out on the terrace without even having to wear our jackets.

It was so cute how happy Marie-Therese was to have me back; maybe this will lessen the pain she feels somewhat because of Mary's departure. Mary is leaving on Wednesday and going straight from here almost all the way to the Russian border by way of Berlin; not an enviable trip to be taking. I found Mama feeling much better. Presently she is enjoying the company of Fräulein von Reck and Frau von Martens. (I do not know if you have ever met the two of them here.) Fräulein von Reck represents the *Almanach de Gotha*[36] and Frau von Martens religious interests. In the meantime we women dined together and sat in Julie's room, and as a matter of fact I held up wonderfully the whole time and will be going back to my place at exactly 10:45.

I still want to tell you about my final day in Dresden. It, too, was very lovely. I spent the entire day in museums and very much enjoyed the beautiful art. My only real problem was not having enough time to allow each one of the beautiful paintings to make an even stronger impression on me. In the evening Countess Wengersky and I took the train to Munich where we parted; I continued on home alone. Mädy will probably remain here until after Julie's birthday (on the 1st of March) before going to Bredeney with Christa. We will probably keep the three older children here with us until shortly before Easter. I am going to try to plan my time with Baby so that I will also have time to read, but I am not sure that I will be able to manage it. Right now I have a ton of letters waiting to be answered, because, for some strange reason, it seems I have sent my mail only to a single address recently! The clock has struck eleven, so good night for now.

Yours, Ottonie D.

---

36. Listing of German nobility.

Neubeuern a/Inn, Friday [17 February 1911]

Even though I planned to wait for your next letter before writing again, I simply cannot wait any longer, even if this letter never reaches you! Your recent silence makes me feel terribly unsettled. I imagine all sorts of possible or impossible things that might have happened. I've asked myself if you misunderstood something I said or if I hurt you somehow or if . . . ! Oh, there are so many "or-ifs" you wonder about when the letter you've been expecting was not in the mail that arrived twice a day this past week. Actually, a week isn't such a long time, but it seems like it once you have become spoiled by so many letters. Are you perhaps ill, stricken with that horrible flu that is infecting everyone? If so, please write just a few words and let me know that you won't be able to write for the next four to six (or eight) weeks. I will gradually get used to it then.

Mary is gone, so now I am playing Mary. It is going to be rather a strain until I get used to it, especially having to wake up so early with my late hours. It is not all that easy, but it will get better in time.

I really have no idea *where* I might be able to find you. Have you perhaps left Berlin and are back in Rodaun, or have you spent the last few days with Eberhard in the Adlon? Eberhard would have been so happy to have you there. Mädy had a very nice time in Munich, where she made friends with Heymel, Blei and others. This was a good thing for her.

I am trying to settle down here again, but it has been very difficult for me this time. I am not sure why, but everyone here in this house seems like a stranger. My lovely books are the only dear old friends I have. I just happened to open up *Dichtung und Wahrheit* again and started reading in the middle of it, and now I cannot put it down. The wonderful atmosphere in *this* book is indescribable; it is so incredibly soothing and relaxing for my shaky nerves. How sad life would be if there were no poets to leave behind great works for us poor, wretched creatures; it is impossible to imagine.

Take care now. I think I will have this letter delivered to its owner's address after all. I guess I just feel the same way other people do at times and have to release my emotions in order to lift some weight from my shoulders.

Addio!

Ottonie D.

[Rodaun] Saturday evening [18 February 1911]

I can believe you thought I must be sick. This is not going to be a letter. I just wanted to let you know that I am not sick. The last few days in Berlin were terribly busy. Now I am back in my little house where the rooms are semi-lit by the lamps. It is quite another world here together with the children and all the peace and quiet. A storm from the south is moving through outside. It seems the spring wants to force itself upon us. It would be better though if the season remained in transition; I still have so much to do before spring arrives.

It feels as if an entire lifetime lay between my departure and return here. First Neubeuern, then Munich, and how distant yet how near that letter seems, the one that cleared the path for my trip to Stuttgart. Oh, the morning of the departure in Stuttgart. I can see you entering – without looking around – the compartment where I sat with a group of strangers. I feel tremendous joy when recalling this moment.

The last few days in Berlin were nice. Quite a few things ended up being resolved rather favorably. I will tell you what happened. It was the harsh and unfair position Kessler had taken toward Reinhardt. It was this, and not something concerning me personally, that bothered me. I really like Reinhardt very much, perhaps even more than I do Kessler. But who knows!

We all had a nice dinner together at the Harrachs'. Afterwards we went to a bar, and I noticed what a nice conversation those two were having together; at 2 o'clock I went to bed and left them there alone. The following day each of them spoke with a great deal of enthusiasm about the other. The German Chancellor[37] also attended the dinner. I liked him very much and had a long conversation with him. I felt unusually comfortable around him even though he was a complete stranger.

I am glad you found my notes in the Goethe and that they helped you to feel that there is somebody there who is very fond of you, but we will not speak of this. The room was so empty when I put them there, and I so sad. Everything is the way it should be now. There was a barrier between us then, but no longer. Good night.

H. H.

❦ ❦ ❦

Neubeuern [22 February 1911]

I am sending you two nice letters from Eberhard which you will certainly enjoy, just as we have. This discussion with Bohlen had long been

---

37. Theobald von Bethmann-Hollweg (1856–1921).

hoped for and was a release for Bockelchen,[38] who had suffered so unspeakably under the pressure back then and in his mind still does. It is truly unbelievable the speed with which E[berhard] continues to move ahead; there is almost something frightening about this tirelessness. I will be very happy for him if he moves to Berlin sometime *soon*; he would once again feel much more a part of life and often see "people" who mean something to him, and this horrible isolation would come to an end. It is not entirely without concern that I view Mädy's moving there. We women are really all more or less vain; men who court us a little bit make an impression and gain influence, and in the case of Mädy, unfortunately, this happens intensely and rapidly; it strikes me as questionable whether she will always be able to assert herself in this area. Indeed, there was a little incident involving her and Biel yesterday which almost made her swear to me that she never, ever wanted to have anything to do with a man again (except for you). Whether she maintains this resolve, and whether it will become reality, I do not know; I hope for the best.

A thousand thanks for your letter. Seldom have I experienced something as strange as I recently did. I was so debilitated because of your silence (probably also because I had no idea *where* you were). Then on Friday, I suppose I wrote you a *very* stupid letter (which I hope did not "burden" you); on Saturday I realized *how* stupid I had been and that you simply had not had time, and I suddenly felt very calm and content. This must have been about the time when you wrote to me. It is really not necessary for you to write me so often again, but just if you are in the mood. I now realize again that, even if I do not hear *anything* from you for weeks, you are thinking fondly of me, and that is enough.

Mädy left for Berlin today and asked me to send you those letters; however, she would like to have them back sometime.

I am rather tired. So Mary has a difficult job. Good night.

Ottonie D.

Rodaun, 23 February [1911]

Dear Countess,

Your letter arrived here by way of Berlin. I cannot begin to tell you how sad I am about the incredible thoughtlessness and insensitivity which allowed me to behave so inexplicably and utterly reprehensibly! I can't understand how I could have allowed you to suffer such duress and needless agony by failing to let you know of my whereabouts. This would have been the most awful thing imaginable for me had I been in your po-

---

38. A nickname for Eberhard.

sition. I have no idea what I was thinking. And all the while I had been, as always, thinking of you a great deal. Yet I was still not able to feel *any* of your uneasiness. I lost all sense of time during my last few days in Berlin. (I'm beginning to realize how this came about and now I feel so ashamed.) Then I returned home to a nerve-wracking foehn, the children and countless letters that were waiting to be answered. I was terribly disoriented and felt a strange sense of uneasiness. On a number of occasions I fell asleep during the daytime while writing. Thus passed two or three days – or perhaps even more?! I'm so terribly sorry – I know you will forgive me or perhaps already have, but that does not change anything. The ugly fact still remains: I was capable of hurting you and causing you such terrible distress. "This you were capable of," a voice inside of me keeps saying. "You ruined an entire week for her, heaping an additional burden upon her with each day that passed. But would you be able to ease her burden and provide her with eight lovely, carefree days? By no means!"

To think of a person – especially here, one does it so often, and each time is very different, and so full of joy. No matter how often one thinks of a particular person, every new encounter is different and the happiness that accompanies it unique. To be happy you are alive, to truly feel such happiness – at night between waking and falling back asleep or while out in the country – or to simply enjoy being together with the children while thinking: "I *really* will take them to Hinterhör!" And then, that evening, to have all this intruded upon by the terribly sad letter I received. One wishes to run off into the darkness, out onto the road and over the hills until *arriving there*, where one would find someone – a room, a light, and in the circle of light a face, hands, and, in the darkness, a pair of poor, cold little feet waiting to be wrapped up in a blanket. Then to utter a few words; to know that everything is all right again, and to be able to wipe away every bad memory. I can't believe I failed to write you a letter in time to arrive the first or second morning! I realize what silly little thought it was that prevented me from doing so. "When she finds my markers inside the Goethe volumes," I reasoned, "she'll have a wordless message much nicer than a letter."

You spoke in both letters of how strange and distant Neubeuern seemed to you. This frightens me. By no means am I entirely unfamiliar with these kinds of feelings, i.e. returning home and being left to one's own devices, to whatever has remained unchanged. I wonder if it might not have something to do with the unfortunate room there; I don't believe this would be the case in Hinterhör. I return again and again to the part in your letter where you talk about Goethe. I am so happy that a book can give you so much. I know, Ottonie, that you *are capable* of sharing in the secrets of this wonderful gift of the mind. Other people have not been *granted* this ability, but you have. And my *chief* concern is to lead you there and to help you find it. This wish was present from the very beginning in all my words, letters and thoughts. If this had not been the case, I would never have had the *courage* to approach you as boldly as I did. And I don't believe I would have *wanted* to.

Every strong inclination is directed towards some specific end. I am keenly aware of mine, but it cannot tolerate words, nor does it need them. Everything real is formed from something small and inconspicuous. Spiritual healing cannot occur where longing or impatience is to be found, and one who knows love is happy and full of confidence. And that's how I feel when I think of you.

May I tell you one other thing, Ottonie? It's a wholly proper and natural thing for you to care for your child, keeping her close by your side. However, you should allow someone else to sleep in the same room with the child for the *sake of* your own sleep in the *early morning* hours. There are so many people in the house the child must like, and change is not half as bad a thing for children; it's not nearly as important as people may think. But this wee bit of additional sleep is tremendously important for you. You still haven't any strength to spare; your inner reserves are still empty. A sublime force dwelling inside you expects this strength to maintain itself; in fact, it demands as much and wishes to build itself a house, as it does not fancy – nor *must* it – living in the ruins of your life. This force spurns merely eking out an existence somewhere between life and death. Should this force, the only thing which makes life worth living, have to suffer because it has no better or stronger an advocate than I?

I have been concerned now for quite a few weeks that you might not be able to pick up the thread following your return. I wondered if you would continue to spend your time alone reading, and if the little stones would continue to build upon one another, brick by brick. But now I am more than merely concerned; now I am very anxious and indeed I fear that the hands of others will rob you and your days will be spun out *of* you much like flax from a spindle. However, composure is *everything*; awareness, integration and seclusion are *everything*. There isn't a week, not even a single day, one may simply waste on joyless pursuits without having to pay. You mustn't allow a single week, indeed not even a single day, to be wasted without experiencing some joy. The eternal state of crisis which characterizes life is both horrific and magical. There are constantly decisions to be made. How happy I would be if I knew things would begin returning to the way they were last November, when I could feel – how delightful it was – the subtle improvement taking place within you and the gradual increase in your strength.

I, too, must collect myself and literally pull myself back together. (Will it be any easier?). I won't be writing as often as I did while we were away from home; eight days or so may pass between letters. I can't help but feel depressed by the thought that all these letters might be unable to spare you hours such as you had to endure this past week. It is sad to think that you aren't absolutely *certain* that I am there for you. Sad, too, it is that the *feeling* – a warm sense of certainty which has little to do with me – of being loved, the one tiny light in the vast expanse of the world, could abandon you. How empty and sad this makes me feel!

Adieu.

H. H.

P.S. A book of Balzac's, which I hope you will like, has been tied up in Paris for an eternity. Have you finished reading Stifter yet?

Which of the stories do you like best? This I would love to know.

❦ ❦ ❦

Rodaun, 4 March [1911]

Dear Countess,

It is rather hard to bear when countless letters arrive day after day in the morning and afternoon and the one you're waiting for is not among them. I do not *mean* to upset myself through excessive contemplation and mulling over the thousands of possible explanations. But I cannot help feeling uneasy when I know that it has been more than eight days now since I received the short letter you wrote, which was not really a letter but simply an accompaniment to Eberhard's. It must have crossed the long letter I wrote sometime around last Thursday (the 23rd of February) in response to the one you wrote on Friday, the 17th, which arrived here on the 21st of February by way of Berlin. Should I assume that you have not received my letter from the 23rd or perhaps that I may have said something which offended you? I wrote about the child and how you should not allow yourself to become exhausted by wasting all your energy. Can this be what disturbed you? We have occasionally had misunderstandings before, but only concerning the highly awkward and delicate matter of our feelings toward each other – and there was no mention of this in my last letter. I hope nothing I wrote has caused your silence, but *if* so, please tell me one way or another, even if it must be expressed in harsh terms. I will experience less torment than I do from your silence. Also, please be so kind as to answer me sometime soon.

In my present disposition I am not susceptible to excessive worrying or wallowing in fear and despair. My constitution is quite the opposite right now. I have experienced an uninterrupted flood of ideas, full of color, and transparent as if they were cut from semiprecious stones. At the same time, they are characterized by a rich profoundness. I must simply see that I shield myself from the outer world, which I am not always able to accomplish. Yet even if I fail to manage this when I am in the company of others or in the theater, the flood remains unchecked, and I find myself the occupant of two separate worlds at the same time. The two worlds do not wage battle against one another, but are instead like two glass balls that have been placed inside one another, each reflecting and acting upon the other. I'm revealing a great deal to you, and while doing so, I see you so clearly, so manifestly. It is a pure and potent joy *having* you in these moments, moments which nothing can take away from me. Then I feel as if some part of the wonderful experience of being together would also have to be accessible to you and that you would feel how your image – no, more than your image – your actual presence is there in a beautiful, brilliant world, to which it so very much belongs. Yesterday I opened a book of Goethe's poems and happened upon a fragment of *Die Geheimnisse* [Secrets]. In part I hoped to find rest from my overactive thoughts. I wasn't so much reading as I was searching for the hidden meaning – which I also found – of the shapes and images stirring around inside me. I peered into the poem as into a magic mirror. I looked into it with perceptive eyes which at the same time were focused inward and unable to see a thing. All of a sudden I came to a very beautiful passage in which an eternal truth was *spoken*. For my understanding at that moment, it was more than spoken. There was something there, a being, of crystalline purity and beauty, composed of both thought and substance. And then all of a sudden, there you stood beneath this beautiful object, your attentive eyes, both cheerful and earnest, which I love so much. Your entire being was revealed through your eyes; first they were fixed upon the object and then on me – but upon me only in the form of the sharp attentiveness we both lent it. We were bound to one another as if we had taken a wonderful, long walk together in order to uncover it. Each of us pointed it out to the other. What a lovely and joyous moment – did I alone experience this?

Oftentimes I see us walking around together in the real world; we are always following the streets of some strange city. I am not truly familiar with those roads, but they probably belong to the city of Paris. Then we sit together in a small restaurant surrounded by strangers. They are not of the crude, bourgeois types, but the pleasant faces of real life. And these, too, are by no means merely dreams; they are half dreams and half desires that will come to be real, just as real as the evening in Erfurt – yet they are so above reality with their charm and joy transcending everything. Why don't you take a trip to Paris around the middle of April, Ottonie, and make sure Julie follows a few weeks later? Everything can be realized – when it comes to mundane matters – if one truly wishes for it to be. Anything that appears to be in the way is just an illusion without substance and offers no real resistance.

The recent developments in the lives of Eberhard[39] and Mädy make me very happy and are no cause for concern as I see it, neither for him nor her. More and more I have come to feel that a gentle hand is lord of all outward appearances.

So many ideas come to me, and so often! I would like to talk to you about your father and a thousand other things as well.

Adieu. Can we be friends again – if we are not already? How happy this would make me if this were already the case!

Yours, H.

☙ ☙ ☙

Neubeuern, Monday, 27 February 1911
[Sent on the 6th of March 1911]

I am so sorry that I upset you with the two negative letters I wrote. One really should not write if one is in a bad mood. One thing just led to another. First, I was exhausted from the trip. Then I found all these people here I was supposed to entertain, which wore me out all over again. As a result, I could not regain the rhythm of my daily life, and it depressed me that I could not put my finger on the cause. However, this only lasted for about a week. Since then everything has been all right, at least in terms of how I feel inside, for I actually experienced a rough period of rather severe headaches, during which I spent the entire time in bed. It made me sad to realize just *how* little I am able to do and how weak my resistance is after only a few days with the child. Afterwards, I do not have any strength left. I am feeling better today and want to try sleeping with Marie-Therese again, even though I realize this is silly and I probably will not be able to manage it. If I tell you, however, what my reasons are for wanting to, I fear you will not understand me. For one thing, I look forward to the moment each morning when she crawls into bed with me and I can feel the sweet little body in my arms wearing only her little nightgown. You might call it a kind of stimulation that I rarely enjoy, which is why I like it so much. The second reason is even more objectionable, but if I do not sleep with the child, Julie will. And even though I am happy about the relationship they have, I wanted to use the four weeks I had here to allow the child to become used to me again (or perhaps for the first time). I always tell myself that I am not jealous, but in reality I believe that I am. The strange thing about all this is that it is just now becoming clear to me as I write it. I had not thought about all of this before and simply listened to my instincts. Now I realize that I *absolutely* have to begin

---

39. Eberhard Bodenhausen was called to be director of a subsidiary of the Krupp steel works.

fighting these feelings at once in order to nip them in the bud. How could we all live here together otherwise?

A person often says to another: "You really do know me," while he does not even know himself. With every passing moment, his various sides reveal themselves, sides he would never have suspected existed. Very seldom are these pleasant discoveries. You would laugh if you could see me now. I stopped writing and sat here staring up at the ceiling. I am thinking about what I just wrote and keep asking myself if I can really be so mean as to deny Julie this pleasure, the one thing that means *everything* to her. Now I have decided. I will let her sleep in the child's room, but I have to admit, this will not be easy for me. I can imagine how it would not have mattered to me at all back when Christoph was alive, but now I am clinging to the child and her clear, wide eyes mean everything to me. I was never fully aware of this, but recently it has become very clear. Good night for today.

P.S. I wrote this letter exactly eight days ago, but since it is still here and was intended for you, you shall have it. Julie has been sleeping in the child's room for quite some time now, and my jealousy has long since passed. Thank God.

Neubeuern, Monday, 6 March 1911

Yes, you can feel very happy, at least as far as the two of us are concerned, for I am, too, down to the very bottom of my heart. It was precisely the web of such lovely thoughts I had inside me that caused my silence. I was acting selfishly, because I was so glad to be in control of myself again and so happy to have you here (in my thoughts). The time passed while taking care of my child and hence I completely forgot to write. I mean, I could feel your wonderful world you found yourself immersed in with the many different characters hovering above. I knew what lovely thoughts you were thinking at the time, and I decided I would join you. We talked to each other for a very long time, and unfortunately, I forgot to write everything down.

On Saturday, then, I really wanted to send a letter to you but did not get around to it. The Gemmingens (the same ones from Stuttgart) are here and are leaving today; I had to attend to them and to the Countess Wengersky, who at first is somewhat awkward. I sensed recently that you had to be waiting to hear something from me and still did not get around to writing. Your last letter was so lovely and so very kind. How could I possibly misunderstand anything that was only said out of concern for me? No, I no longer misunderstand anything you say. This was no longer possible after our last meeting; even if a dark shadow were to rise up between us, I can tell you right now that it would be a result of my nerves or something of the kind. People must understand each other if they wish to treat each other lovingly.

The few moments I had to myself I used for reading. It was not much, but I was able to spend a few pleasant hours reading the wonderful Stifter. It's quite difficult for me to say which of the stories I liked the most. *Die Mappe des Urgrossvaters* [Great Grandfather's Folder] is filled with such wonderful passages that it immediately made itself a permanent home in my heart. I am fascinated each time I read about the evening at Narrenburg [Castle of Fools] where people from all walks of life gradually come together in front of the tavern — the lumberjacks, hunters and others as well. The story is so full of life and is told at such a good pace that I imagine myself on Heuberg, all of the characters stopping by one by one as it often happens there on Saturdays. Then, after a long week deep in the forest, they would return to wife and child down below. And next you see them all sitting together again in Nussdorf where they first enjoy a drink together. Then slowly night approaches, and darkness descends on the lovers' conversation — it is fascinating how the day ends. Yes, there are many such passages. And I love Abdias and his tenacity, and the love he feels and the way everything turns out: the constant denial of his fate which is apparently necessary for everything else to be held in place together. How very much like real life! Then I read *Werther*; what a powerful force there is flowing throughout the whole thing — no, it is more like a flood. And the reader, too, must endure Werther's suffering along with him. I can hardly believe that a book from so long ago can trigger such intense feelings.

I have to hurry and finish because the dinner gong is about to sound, and I do want to send this off with the next batch of mail. I will write again soon regarding my plans, etc. I have to visit my doctor in Munich at some point during the next few days, because I'm not doing all that well and must find out if I can manage to start the chicken farm, or Paris, etc.

A thousand warm greetings.

Ottonie D.

Neubeuern, Monday, 6 March 1911

I just finished giving the child her bath and tucking her into bed. Now I have to sit here for about another quarter of an hour until she falls asleep (then I can get myself ready for bed). I want to use this time now to write you a little more, but who knows, I may not finish! I just read your next to last letter again and realized that I did not actually respond to it at all in my last letter. You are right to lament the fact that your letters no longer seem to provide me the long periods of calm they once did and that I can still slip back into the way I had been before, as proved to be the case following my return here. But this really isn't so, for even before your long, lovely letter arrived, I had already regained my composure, and it was because of you, because of the books you gave me, that I was able to do so. They have become faithful friends to whom I can turn for comfort. I am enjoying myself so much since I learned to use the free moments I have, a half hour here or there, to quickly read a line that can light up the entire day and make it seem like a holiday. And for this I thank you profusely. This is why I did not even miss not receiving a letter from you last week, for you have created an entire world for me in my room. Do not misunderstand me and think that I could ever be overburdened by one of your letters. This will never be the case. Whenever I feel that you are busy creating your works, dreaming and lost in thought, I know that these thoughts in some small way also belong to me. This, too, makes me feel happy and at peace with myself.

(Have to go to lunch now.) 7 March. Once again you have sent me such wonderful books. I was so happy when I spied the dear little package which has become so familiar. Filled with joy and impatience, I can hardly wait to remove all the wrappings and find out what kind of bright, cheerful friends are there waiting to greet me! I thank you a thousand times over! Your *Werther* is wonderful. I'll have to read it again sometime soon. Just last week I was so captivated by it; I participated in his emotional trials. There were many moments when I was deeply shaken and others when I felt very much inspired. Then I start to wish that we could read and discuss it all together and show each other all the new and wonderful passages. But I remind myself that it's not at all necessary for us to be together, for there is nothing I feel that you haven't felt many times before in exactly the same way.

It was a heavenly day today! All the mountains were covered with fresh snow; only the foothills revealed some patches of green. The sun shone brightly above everything and was surrounded by a deep blue sky above. Irmgard Wengersky, Hansi[40] and I rode to Rosenheim and took the same route back as you and I did at Christmastime. All my thoughts were of the conversations we had back then when everything was so pleasant and one could truly relax; I wished you could have been there with me. And then when I arrived back here for tea and was told of your telegram, I fully understood the tremendous uneasiness I must have caused you and felt very disappointed in myself. How is it that one continually manages to cause another person such stress?! It is simply awful! But I am able to find some comfort in the thought that my letter explain-

---

40. Hans Wilke Bodenhausen.

ing all this must have arrived by now. I could keep on talking like this forever and would still have so very, very much to chat about. Nothing of importance; simply little things one would like to tell. However, I have to close again now, for it is once again the same hour it was yesterday! So please, I promise once more that I will remain calm, even if three weeks pass before I hear something from you. Although I would of course prefer not to have to wait that long.

Ottonie DS.

❦ ❦ ❦

9 March [1911]

Dear Countess,

    I'm a very rich man now in possession of your three lovely letters here. The needless agonizing that occurred during the last few days vanished at once and hardly makes any sense now. I think at this point we have exhausted every possibility of enervating ourselves or each other. For you shall always think I am busy at work, and I will assume that you have already written a letter and just not sent it yet and that I will receive it at some later point along with an explanation of why it was not sent right away – just like this last time, which also made me doubly happy, due to your decision to indeed send it, which I found kind and very touching. There was nothing in your letter (I mean the one regarding sleeping in the same room as the child) that puzzled or disturbed me. Concerns of this sort are very understandable, and it would also make complete sense if you hadn't been able to fight and overcome them. However, as they are now overcome, it's certainly for the better. Julie *should* be granted everything: the tender moments, that subtle motherly attachment to the child – even though it may seem imprudent and peculiar – as well as her inability to view the child with open eyes. All that life has so cruelly denied her should be given to her by *the woman* in whose hands the chance has been placed to soften this bitter suffering, or to renew and compound it. You have no reason to compete for the child. Rather than pursuing the child yourself, allow her to come to you in her own time, as she will, feeling drawn to you by the purest and greatest of all forces. And you need not try to cultivate this force within yourself – for this is none other than the force of life itself – because by virtue of the choice you had to make between death and life, you have enjoined upon yourself the obligation to be sincere and true in striving to realize for yourself life's potential. You chose not to become a larva, half-alive and existing in two very different worlds, but are instead a living being without any bounds, and how could the child, as she slowly becomes a grown woman, resist your magical force? No spell is needed to bind one soul to another; I once wrote you (once and for all) that I demanded one thing of myself, namely, that I should come to know you better and better – from which greater and greater love will follow as a natural consequence. You seemed surprised and conflicted, for you tend to view yourself as a limited and self-contained being. But then you were astonished and compelled to stop and reflect for a moment while in the middle of writing and had to gaze up at the ceiling. For you felt something new and wholly unfamiliar and were forced to admit that there was a great deal inside of you that you yourself were unaware of and which only became revealed after you, semiconsciously, entrusted it to one of your letters. I cannot describe how much I love this letter. It contains no discussion of me. Instead, I find you throughout, so touching and charming, a boundless, living soul. In these moments, it is as if one perceives *everything*, including even the divinity manifesting itself from within the limitlessness of the individual human being. One also encounters the same limitlessness in people's relationships. How indifferent and miserable he must be who conceals his own limitless nature behind unyielding desires and rigid expectations, trivialities and jealousies. Such a man destroys his soul's capacity to experience the joy of its own limitlessness – how greatly I experience this between you and me. I had much before; nothing seemed to be missing, really there was nothing I was missing. Then you entered my life, and something utterly indescribable and unfathomable became a part of it. And now, if I go a few days without receiving news from you – this vibrant and constantly rejuvenating feeling of your presence – it is unthinkable *how* deprived I feel!

It is almost impossible to describe how connected I am to you through my work. When experiencing moments of deep fulfillment, one hardly realizes what is happening – one thing, or one image, is constantly replacing another. It is a kind of lasting experience that one is scarcely aware of. Then suddenly, as if reflected by a mirror, I glimpse the image of certain parts of your character racing towards me – I see you smiling at me in the form of a perceived truth or some other image, again you greet me, and before I know it, you are gone, pulled up and away as if you were part and figure in a dance.

I do not like it one bit when you accuse yourself of lacking in strength and begin struggling against your own body. Yet it is my primary concern that you take care of yourself, and I am not so troubled by a few bad days, as long as I know that there are certain rules you will not fail to heed. No one can be certain of just what the soul and the body must contribute and accomplish in the case of each individual, but the health of either unquestionably depends upon that of the other. It is the same as with Münchhausen, who miraculously managed to pull himself out of a deep ditch by his own hair. There are many things I am able to perceive, and I have many hopes and concerns regarding you – when wishing for this or that – but whatever has to be done must come from you yourself. You are very fortunate to have Neubeuern. Hinterhör would be even better, but one without the other would not be a good thing either. Paris would be wonderful; I have examined myself to see if this is truly my wish to see you there. Now I know what a tremendous and indescribable joy this would be; I really do believe it would be the right thing. If it does not work out, there are still a thousand other things. A vacation on the Mediterranean would surely do you and the child a great deal of good – and, I believe, Julie as well. I can allow myself to point out something like this, as I shall certainly not be accompanying you, except in my thoughts. If we do not see each other in Paris, I can stop by in Neubeuern for a couple days along the way, although this would not be the same.

Stendhal is a free spirit; he's agreeable and bright. He would be a perfect addition to your circle of friends. Maybe you can read the novel sometime, just as you would one of Balzac's. One need only leaf through parts of *De l'amour* without reading the entire book. It contains anecdotes, reflections, wisdom and a burning love for love itself. Some of it you may find astonishing, but I do not believe anything will offend you. Somehow the Thuringian Fräulein needs to find a way to make friends with this gentleman. Adieu.

H.

˜ ˜ ˜

[Maximilianstraße 25/I.] Sunday, 12 March [1911]

I cannot describe how truly wonderful it is to receive such lovely letters and to know that one can make another person's day so nice by writing a letter. Your letter arrived yesterday morning just as I was about to leave Neubeuern. I forced myself not to open it until I was aboard the train. Then I felt as if I had company, as if the two of us were there together. You wrote a while back in one of your letters: "Would you be able to ease her burdens and provide her with eight lovely and carefree days? Never!" The "never" should without question be replaced by a "yes." I am a completely different person when I feel the thread taut between us. I feel much more like a human being, and not just a living creature. I really have to say, it is wonderful having you, and even more wonderful that we both feel the same way and both feel our ties are strong! One should simply enjoy it, indeed make a conscious effort to enjoy it, without trying to tinker with anything. I recently read a passage about friendship, in particular the inequality found in friendships, in *Vielleicht, vielleicht auch nicht* [Maybe or Maybe Not] about how one of the friends is usually the giver and the other the taker. I could not help but think of us! Although you did say in your last letter that I also give you something (what a terrific claim!!?), that is, give in terms of being just the way I am (without having any goal in mind). Ever since reading this, I view friendships in a totally different light.

Well, I went to see my doctor again yesterday. He has admonished me to take especially good care of myself, recommending lots of sleep, short walks now and then, and I have to put on some weight. It cannot hurt to give it a try! He advised against my plans to raise the chickens but approved the trip to Paris. Although I doubt very much if anything will come of it because Julie must be my first concern now. She is well overdue for a trip and does not like to travel without me. However, she cannot leave just now because of Mama. Oh well, we will just have to see how it all turns out.

I have already spent quite enough time in the city and am glad that I will be able to return tomorrow to the country. Last night I even went to a little supper at the Schzencks' (he was not there, thank God); this required a tremendous effort of will by me and indeed it was not even worth it. It is awful *how* life in the country makes one awkward, the way one is afraid of ever meeting new people one does not know.

Mädy wrote enthusiastically of her stay. She will be coming here again on the 18th and staying until the 9th of April, as Bockelchen is once again travelling for an extended period, to Berlin, London, Riga.

Well, good night for now. I am tired, but as I very much want to send this letter off (even though it is short) tomorrow, may it bring you many warm, friendly greetings.

Yours, Ottonie D.

P.S. I am looking forward to the two (?) days you will be spending with us, in case we do not make it to Paris.

[Maximilianstrasse 25/I.]
Wednesday [15 March 1911] 10 o'clock in the evening

The Baby is here, a pity the nurse could not be here also. Sorry 'you' has come [*sic*], do you feel a little bit of it? No, nothing, because you must talk *so* much with all the dreadful people. I don't like them cause they keep you so.[41]

I wonder if you were not given my telephone number, or had you not returned home yet?

Tomorrow – in the morning – when these lines say "good morning" to you, then give "2536" a ring and let me know whether or not we might

---

41. This paragraph was written in English and seems to be a kind of inside joke.

meet each other somewhat earlier; if not, then I can also keep busy with other things I have to do.

I *hope* you finally sleep well then, as I also intend to.

I received a short note from a dear nurse this evening as I sat waiting in the carriage to go to the station.

Many warm regards from close by, Ottonie

Rodaun, Saturday evening, 18 March [1911]

Whenever I receive a letter in which a person reveals himself as he truly is (and as he usually does not reveal himself), I have the same experience I do when reading a beautiful passage in a book containing some profound truth – I always wish I could show it to you that very instant and share with you the joy I feel. To this end I shall include the letter Heymel wrote me, which will allow you to become acquainted with him as the kind of human being he really is, and you might therefore approach him with even greater openness and trust, if he should ever happen to cross your path. Deep inside he is a kind, gentle and extremely sensitive man. His letter concerns the death of Rudi Schröder's mother. I would be very happy if you wrote Schröder a few lines. I know what a help it can be when the *right* people write at times like these. And the *right* people are by no means necessarily those whom convention considers to be "close to one." So perhaps you'll write him, or perhaps not if you should have any reservations about doing so. It's only natural for me to hope to establish ties between you and other people who are important to me. His address is: Horn bei Bremen, Schwachhauser-Chaussée 365. *Return* Heymel's letter sometime when you have occasion to, that is, just give it to me when we are together rather than sending it.

You say you like feeling the strength of the thread that binds us together. So, too, do I. When I feel your presence, I am so content and feel truly enriched, and everything I do acquires a certain rather mysterious *character*. I am not always able to understand how a certain thought, premonition or hope may be related to you, nor can I say what meaning such a relation might – or should – have for our life here on earth. But the feeling of this relationship is incredibly salutary – it's the most gentle and subtle feeling of anticipation and sense of having some purpose that one can imagine. The degree to which I feel your presence varies tremendously. Whenever I feel I am close to completely losing my hold on it (like the ten-day stretch last fall when I couldn't picture your face or hear your voice and had to manage without any sense of inner stability on top of everything else), it is a very agonizing feeling of emptiness I have. I am happy to say I have not felt this way since.

The various shades of such an experience are countless, ranging from the subtle, salutary feeling of being accompanied by you to a more sublime and absolute awareness of your presence – sometimes I could perceive from a very great distance the possibility of a presence with the power to make me feel thoroughly happy while separated from one another physically; that's what I mean by knowing a person, and it was in this sense that I once, or on a number of occasions, said that *knowing* and loving are one and the same thing. Everything you gave me (I refer here to the many forms your incredible kindness has assumed) you gave without *realizing you were doing so* – yet I realize this is not entirely true when I stop to think about it. For the fact that you didn't shut yourself off from me, that you were able to begin talking to me *the way* you did last fall, was crucial. I'm speaking of the touching manner in which you so freely and openly spoke about yourself, telling me of your happiness and your sufferings without actually intending to do so – you did so almost involuntarily. It was without a doubt this which bound me to you – the fact that you allowed me to perceive you the way you are. I don't find it surprising or difficult to comprehend that you do not quite realize how much you mean to me. It is no wonder this simply manifests itself here or there in one of my letters like an astonishing bit of news. However, I do believe, assuming I am not entirely devoid of significance for you and my affection is not without some value, this must indeed awaken in you some sense of what you mean to me. This must allow you to regain from within yourself a firm and unwavering sense of confidence that your horrendous sufferings are indeed behind you. I know very well, however, that this must occur gradually and without my attempting to effect such a change in you and without longing or impatience on my part or anything else of the kind which I may feel.

I am also exceedingly fond of everything you have told me about your childhood. The little Thuringian Fräulein is an incredibly adorable thing. Do not think me engaged in an act of worship, for I see things just as they are. I think we can agree that I see you as you are. I have written letters in which I said you *know* that I see you as you are. Ottonie Schwartz is by no means an angel. She is sure of herself and enjoys the courage of the inexperienced. She is kindhearted and utterly sincere, which, however, does not preclude her from telling a little fib now and again. Moreover, one might say that she possesses the truest form of courage, namely, moral courage; she has the wholly unique gift of being immune to self-deception or to the attempts of others to deceive her, along with a very generous portion of curiosity. This curiosity is perhaps her most striking quality. She finds herself a seat in the darkened theater simply out of curiosity and takes the most ridiculous trips and things like that, yet all of this she does without ever compromising her inner self in the slightest. Do you find this an accurate sketch? This person of course no longer exists, yet for me she is very much alive and in some way she belongs to me.

If I continue chatting, this letter will drag on forever and will never end up being sent, and I'm already none too happy about the five, six or seven days that will pass before I hear from you again. Of course, it has been a good four days since I received your last letter. It was rather short and appeared to promise another would follow right behind it.

I have already written three or four responses to various letters in my mind which were even longer than this one here. It is rather a mystery to me, however, the way one day after another passes by. I cannot even account for them all myself. My time has simply been spent lost in thought, which gives rise to images and associations, including chains of pure thoughts and recollections, which other, confusing thoughts occasionally interrupt – this consumes quite a few hours of my time every day now – and among all of this another one of those letters slowly begins to crystallize in my mind only to slip away the moment I am ready to write. I am also really writing something, and now and again I answer a letter requiring an immediate response. At times, somebody comes to pay me a visit, such as Poldy Andrian yesterday evening. He will be the new consul general in Warsaw, and it will probably be years before I'll see him again. Today I was suddenly called to the opera for a rehearsal, and around noon, the children suddenly came upstairs and wanted me to *read to* them, which I could not refuse. It is amazing you have never seen our little house here, Ottonie! I know that if you *do not* come to Paris – I do not even want to let this thought enter my mind, for it is my truest wish that you will. (I will explain why in my next letter, that is, why I promise myself such wonderful things from time spent together under these circumstances. There are good reasons for my expectations; I examined them very closely, and they are indeed legitimate.) But if it should not come to pass, then you will have to visit us here in June and accompany Gerty and me on a little eight-day trip to a certain part of Lower Austria. One finds many very old places in this region, many monasteries and beautiful churches, vineyards and gentle valleys. But now I must return to that which needs to be put into words: Sunday morning.

What I wanted to say primarily concerns your trip to the doctor and the advice that he gives you. I am certainly very happy that you are concerned with your physical health and that you are not allowing yourself to cross the border between sickness and health. However, one additional word: I am not overcome with confidence by the idea of simply looking after yourself, etc. Most doctors and even specialists have much too little appreciation for and no real understanding of human nature, for the uniquely subtle and profoundly mysterious relationship between body and soul. They speak of "eating" and "sleeping" and "nerves" and "thoughts" and "strength" and "functions" and "pain" – as if each existed independently of the other! It is as if one had not even the slightest power to cause or regulate the other; as if one were incapable of interfering with the other or even destroying it. (I believe – i.e. at the moment that I write this – I am just becoming aware of how much time I have spent contemplating your physical condition, i.e. not in the manner of a doctor and not with respect to specific details, but rather in terms of the whole by way of what one calls intuition.) To tell you the following: Seeking to improve your condition by taking better care of yourself, eating more, sleeping more, etc., seems to me no different than the advice of the typical doctor who says to a heart patient whose shaky nerves are causing him to tremble all over: "Avoid becoming so worked up about things!" All you can do is to avoid doing more than is *necessary*. So continue to refrain from such things as sleeping in the same room with Marie-Therese, which ruins your sleep every morning. There are other activities you should refrain from as well, such as one in particular which I am able to see much more clearly from my perspective and the danger of which I can understand much better than the doctor in Munich: You mustn't continue to overextend yourself through excessive devotion to the guests of the castle or by giving in to this awful propensity women have of squandering their energy; they chat with others or toddle about, talking a quarter of an hour too long or writing *one* too many letters at the very moment when your nerves demand rest. I can see now that I will not be able to touch on everything in a single letter; there is simply too much that is worth mentioning, but such a discussion demands considerable attention to detail. The next time we meet we will simply have to take time to clarify this point. I can tell you right now that I will not allow you to refuse to discuss this, for it is this matter which makes all my attempts *to help* you seem futile and thus turns my relationship to you into a farce. The whole thing with all the books was simply an attempt to give you some peace, i.e. a truly salutary, inner peace (similar to that acquired through prayer). In contrast, I do not attach any value to the calm one is supposed to achieve by forcing oneself to lie in bed, as then frightening, dark or fragmented thoughts will race through one's mind.

For now I am concerned again and "above all else" with your relationship to Julie. Here, too, I have certain objections to raise, regardless of how you may receive them or how unpleasant you may find this letter as a result. This concerns you *above all else* (in every possible sense, even in a very deep and serious sense). Julie is incredibly kind and good and also very unselfish, but precisely because she is unselfish and has, so to speak, given herself up (which was perhaps the only way the woman could save her soul), there can exist between the two of you only *one* kind of relationship: one in which you are the leader. This should, however, not only relate to intellectual and moral questions, but must also include the way in which you conduct your lives. Nothing here can be separated from anything else; they all belong together. Julie exhibits a tendency which I have met with before. In an act of somber and modest defiance against a cruel and inconceivable fate, she has consciously made herself into a Danaid who scoops water into a sieve even though she *recognizes* it is a sieve. If you simply gather up what is left of your small reserve of vitality in order to simply give it away to someone else (even should it be dear Julie), thus reducing yourself to 0 (zero) again and having to start all over from the beginning – and so on repeatedly, *ad infinitum* – then Sisyphus truly does stand alongside Danaid, and the mythological underworld is complete. That is why it is impossible for you to accommodate Julie *on the whole*. Her compass will always point in the direction of leaving things the way they are, sputtering on, and *s'abstenir et se maintenir*. A person like you, however, must continue to move forward if you do not wish to be destroyed. If there is something in particular you must do for Julie right now, then by all means do so, but afterwards somebody else must be found to take care of the old lady. Otherwise you will just wear yourself out again, and the whole thing will become an endless circle.

All of this is of course indirectly related to Paris. If we spent just ten or eight or six days together in Paris (with your feeling adequately well), I know that I could be of some benefit to you – and there more than anywhere else in the world. This has absolutely nothing to do with sentimentality; I hope you realize this. If I knew you were able to lift yourself up and that everything was going the way it should and that you could regain your former self, I swear, for two or three years I should not give you a look nor sound a single note of discontent.

If you are not well enough for the trip to Paris, which might very well be, something *substantial* must still step in to take the place of the worthless hours of rest. This could mean Moeller[42] or – what I believe (perhaps incorrectly) would do you as much good – a month-long vacation at the seashore, somewhere in the South where there is a lot of sun.

Adieu. I really think I should stop now.

Yours, Hofmannsthal.

---

42. Swedish doctor who first treated O. D. S. in her illness after Christoph's death.

Neubeuern, 20 March 1911

This is the letter that got misplaced.
I found it resting peacefully in my folder.
Another one is nearly ready to be sent.

Well, here I am again in the nursery waiting for Baby to fall asleep; I enjoy using this time for writing to you. Today is the last time I will be looking after the child; Mary will be back tomorrow. In some respect, it will be very difficult for me having to do without all the lovely moments, for I have enjoyed my weeks here *very, very* much. But on the other hand, it's good that it is coming to an end as I have not been doing that well physically. I intend to start paying awfully close attention to my health now and taking good care of myself physically. This will not exactly be any fun, although I know it is necessary, which I have now come to understand and accept.

Unfortunately, however, I have to give up *all my plans* and stay here. So *please* do stop by to see us; I am so looking forward to seeing you. And it will not be necessary to play the rabbit game this time, since it's already been taken care of – all *too* well in fact. The weather is so spectacular; we have had a lot of sunshine and the flowers, those darling little children of spring, are blooming wherever you look. Today I was alone with Baby and Dicky[43] in Hinterhör; the hour we spent there was so lovely. I sat in front of the house and looked up at the snow-covered mountains, and remembered the autumn of 1910. All the beloved moments together came to mind, what we had discussed here, what there, and it seemed everything was covered by such a delightful scent; it all came back to me. Something so magical surrounds the entire little place there which always forces me to be kind; whether I like it or not, I have to get rid of anything inside of me that is or tries to be nasty. There's also something about the *small* dimensions of everything there that gives me such a sense of calm. It's so peaceful there watching the chickens pecking about and the pastures with sheep and their little lambs and the contented Heiss couple.[44]

I really do not believe I fit in with high society, for all my instincts draw me back to this quiet little place. I also decided today to go there a lot and to enjoy as much as I can. At first the locked-up house gave me a horrible feeling, but little by little I still managed to discover the good points, although often a bit late.

Well, now we have all said our good-nights, and everyone has wandered back to his quarters following Mädy's hilarious stories about her stay in Berlin.

---

43. Marie-Therese's pony.
44. Farmers in Hinterhör.

I haven't been able to read much lately aside from the few minutes I spent alone with Baby. I looked through your Novalis and found so much kindness and tenderness there, so many of the same experiences and sufferings that I, too, know. How difficult it is to find a way out; I think this is becoming clear to me now for the first time, and there are still many hours in which I ask myself: "Is it even possible that I'm still alive and am really living my life?"

I have not had the courage to begin reading Stendhal yet; I want to wait until I have more time. I hope I will be able to plan my days the way *I'd* like to now.

I recently read some of *Vielleicht, vielleicht auch nicht*, and can you imagine how horrible I found it. I had to stop right in the middle and was unable to continue despite the many wonderful passages. I wonder if some part of me is afraid of the passion expressed in it? I am not sure yet.

Good night. I have to go to bed.

Yours, Ottonie D.

❦ ❦ ❦

Neubeuern, 21 March 1911

Today was our godchild's[45] birthday, and we had a wonderful celebration in the child's honor.

While writing to you yesterday, I was so looking forward to this morning because I was certain I would receive a letter from you. How surprised I was when I did not find anything on my desk! I knew the mail had already arrived. Then, just as I was about to write a quick note before going to lunch, I found your lovely, long letter. My warmest thanks for including the nice letter from Heymel. It was captivating and allowed me to gain some understanding of what the Schröder family was going through. The things people have to endure! I wrote Schröder a few lines; it was not much, but it came straight from the heart. At times like these there are very few letters that *really* mean something to a person. One receives so many, and all of them say the same thing. And with every letter, one has the feeling, "He has no idea what has been taken from me, only from me." Everyone seems to think his pain is especially severe and bitter and different from anything anyone else has ever experienced. It is very peculiar really; all of us must go through pretty much the same things, yet each person's experience is somehow different.

It meant so much to me getting to know this very sensitive side of Heymel. How easy it is for me to sympathize with him now. He, too, is one of those people who is always in search of something and will proba-

---

45. Christa von Bodenhausen, Eberhard's youngest daughter.

bly continue wasting a lot of his energy on misguided values. We didn't even notice each other the time he was here. In fact, he, Blei and I sat for the longest time in front of the fireplace in Jan's room but could find absolutely nothing – not a thing – to talk about. I was so tired that it took a great effort to muster a "yes" or "no," which usually did not even come out at the right time. As a man, there is a certain charm to his ugliness, and his lively character and fiery boyishness are quite attractive. He is probably right in thinking that he makes a good impression on the female sex. Since we are on the subject of men, I really must tell you that I find Blei is thoroughly second-class in every respect, and I very much hope I will not have to enjoy his company here again.

Do you know who made a terrific – and lasting – impression on me? Kessler. I cannot help but delight in the memory of the lunch we had together in Weimar. At first, a very embarrassing conversation about religion (which came up in reference to the book by Gide) took place. Frau Förster-Nietzsche of course believed all religion belonged to the past, and Kessler, not knowing my innermost feelings, felt I may have been offended, whereupon he made such charming remarks refuting Frau Förster-Nietzsche and putting everything in its proper perspective. I shall never forget this moment. I desperately hope that all the bad feelings between the two of you will forever become a thing of the past.

Well that's odd, isn't it?! I wanted to write about all sorts of other things and mainly to respond to your letter, and here I am discussing Blei and Kessler. How did I get on the subject of them? Oh yes, Heymel, the fireplace, Blei, and the subject of men in general – an agreeable subject, Kessler. After all this, it is now late, and once again I must go to bed.

Friday: It was so scatterbrained of me to send you the wrong letter. It was just that I absolutely wanted you to hear from me. I was up very late with Baby, and then I ran quickly to my room before lunch to try to make it in time for the mail; I did not look before placing it in the envelope. I certainly can feel your disappointment: you held the letter in your hand with joyful anticipation, feeling it already belonged to you, and then you opened it only to find this! I am terribly sorry. Now this letter, too, has been lying here for two days, and I wanted so much to send it yesterday. However, just as we were about to part that evening, Julie and I got involved in a conversation that lasted until midnight, and I was the subject of it! A certain disagreement came about regarding my health and how best to treat it. Julie felt I was too indifferent on the one hand and that I was also wearing myself out with all my studying and reading. I felt certain she didn't understand me at all and thought to myself: "You'll have to continue fighting every day for your own time, the time alone that you need so much." The feeling of being so completely misunderstood weakened me to the point where I lost my composure and was unable to hold back the tears (which made me feel depressed all over again since she appeared to be right about the poor condition of my nerves if a mere conversation like this could arouse such emotions). To make a long story short, the discussion lasted forever. But perhaps I did convince her to see certain things as crucial to my life, or perhaps I should say, to regaining my life. She always tries to explain to me that our life has come to an end and that we no longer have a right to expect anything. I said this is a lie we tell ourselves. Then that moment came which never fails to infuriate me; it is when somebody believes there is something inside me that is not there at all. For instance, a certain positive quality, a virtue or something of the kind, that I know I do not possess. Julie claimed I run myself ragged from dawn until dusk, and that all the self-confidence that others were able to feed off is gone, and on and on.

So you see, there are moments when only you can give me the courage I need to not simply say, "Yes, and amen," to everything for the sake of peace and harmony while continuing to crawl along the same beaten path with a hundredweight tugging at my heart. Then I think of you, and I tell myself: "If there is someone who tries so hard to help you through your pain and agony, someone who devotes so much of his energy, time and love to you, then you must be of some value, both as a human being and as a soul."

You see, that is just the way I am. I always have to tell you everything right away; I have such complete trust in you. (It would be awful if this were not the case after all the comings and goings between us.) Your last letter in particular was such a great help to me in shedding light on Julie's personality. I had never thought about it this way, but I think you are right. Perhaps the denial of her own self was the only way for her to survive. Please do not assume, however, that there is any real discord here in the house. I am terribly fond of Julie, and she perhaps even more so of me, because she needs me more. Nor can I expect her to understand me entirely. Even if in some small way I am to assume a role of leadership in this relationship, I still cannot do so entirely because of financial considerations. This is terribly hard to explain. Particularly here, where subtle shifts may occur at any time, and one must show great tact.

How awful: it's time for the mail again, and I want to at least send off this portion of the letter. I will try to continue writing later today, but do not be disappointed if I do not manage to. Something often gets in the way.

With many fond thoughts always,

Ottonie D.

Neubeuern, 24 March 1911

After all the conversations I have had with you (I do not mean the letters), I often end up forgetting something very important, like letting you know that your letter arrived. It was because I had just spoken to you – in my thought – about your letter numerous times and assumed you had heard everything I said. I am sure you have by now received the letter (with all my tales of woe) I sent today and realize that yours was not lost.

Well, Julie and I have reached a truce along the following lines: I have agreed to take care of myself exactly as I am supposed to for the next four weeks. If I am doing better then, I probably will go to Paris after all. I will not mention anything about this again. I no longer look as bad as I did; you will find me looking just as always. I had myself weighed today and was 105 pounds, which isn't all that light for my height.

You are absolutely right that feeding me and sending me off to bed will not make me fit again. I need to regain inner peace, and then everything will improve; and recently I have been unable to rid myself of the concern about my father.

You actually gave a pretty accurate sketch of the little Thuringian girl. That's just how she was, a real rascal! And strangely enough, people liked her anyway, which I could never quite understand. Just today, I had to think back to this time. Everyone was so outraged by Luli,[46] who's at that age where she tends to fib. I tried to reassure the others by telling them that I know I told lies as a child, like when I claimed to have practiced or worked, even if this was only partially true. After all, ice-skating, and swimming in the summer, or something else always lured me away. And in the end I turned out to be a reasonably honest person, oftentimes even too honest.

At times I have extreme difficulties due to the severe criticism I subject myself to. Yet in a way I am glad, for someone who imagines herself to possess qualities she does not have is almost too silly to be taken seriously.

You know, I think I am quite familiar with your little house, although I would still like to visit sometime if things work out. Your idea about taking a little trip is lovely, though we would have to find another man to come along, don't you think? I mean a companion for Gerty – Rudi Schröder or somebody like that. Groups of three are never that good.

Julie told me about your letter today. She would love to have the little family with the baby and it would be good for me on account of the French conversation; however, I feel it would be better to have them here at the beginning of June because when I am in Hinterhör, the dear little couple would be of little help to me.

---

46. Julie von Bodenhausen.

I wish I had you here with me now, especially today, so we could chat about everything I cannot talk to anyone else about – not even with Bockelchen, who would not have time anyway. Today was a day without any guests. I had been so looking forward to the quiet afternoon; and then again came another very unfortunate trip to church in Rosenheim which took four hours. I so long for peace and quiet that I will, on the one hand, be very happy once Mädy and the children have left. I do not suppose this letter makes very good sense – but I really have the feeling you must receive it nonetheless.

I am going to go to bed now. You do not have to respond right away if your work, etc. is taking up a lot of your time. I promise not to get upset.

Yours, Ottonie D.

Neubeuern a/ Inn, Oberbayern, 28 March 1911

Since I will be leaving here tomorrow, I will try to say everything in a few brief lines. I will be in Munich tomorrow and will travel to Eybach on Thursday, that is, to Ulm tomorrow and will spend the night there. I will be in Eybach on Thursday but have to return to Munich that same evening because the house in Eybach is still too cold. I would love to spend that night there all by myself, but I must give in as all are opposed.

It is amazing what longing can lie slumbering – no, not slumbering, more like screaming out loud – inside a person. I have often felt this way since he was taken away from me. Often I am so overcome by despair, I wish I could leaf through the pages of my life as one often does through a book in order to find out what happens at the end. I find it very, very difficult living alone. By alone I mean without the man one loves with one's entire heart. To really love someone seems so very hard for me – but once it happens, then completely or not at all.

That is how it was with Christoph, whom I loved deeply from the first day we met. There was something about him that *compelled* me to. I miss him *incredibly*, and *whenever* I try to distance myself from this love, I simply end up with a fresh wound in my bleeding heart. I *have* to stop. I am too sad today and do not want to make you suffer along with me.

I would almost like to burn this letter, but then you would be sad. So I will send it.

Good night. Many warm regards,

Ottonie D.

Rodaun, 2 April [1911]

Dear Countess,

We had a lovely spring day a few days back; the gentle wind was almost mystifying. I took a walk and thought about many things, i.e., my imagination forced a lot of thoughts upon me. They returned to you, over and over again. I talked to you about so many different things and wrote you a rather long letter in my mind. Then I went inside to write you a real letter when the one you wrote before your trip to Eybach arrived. It was filled with incredible pain and beyond all comfort, so naturally mine remained unwritten. Anything I might have said seemed wretchedly inadequate and trivial – even worse than trivial. What could another person possibly say to you when you were repeatedly carried *away* by each new wave of grief and when your soul, which so desperately longed to be held together in one piece by the comforting power of love, instead prefers to suffer rather than to splinter away in life's misery. What could anyone possibly say?!

However, I am writing again now. I have gradually found the thoughts – or they have formed inside me – that have given me the courage I needed. When I contemplate how this recent breakdown gradually came about – the exhaustion from tending to the child, the constant concern about your father, the agony you felt due to the misunderstanding with Julie, the springtime – when I think of the cumulative effects of all this, I understand how you must have come to loathe every aspect of life – although not *permanently*.

I am glad for the sake of your personal freedom that you have decided to go to Paris. I doubt, however, that you will actually follow through with it. Therefore, I would like very much to come to Neubeuern for a few days. I do love you very much, but alas, what is that to you! I understand very well.

Yours, Hofmannsthal

N., 4 April 1911

During the last few days it has become very clear to me just *how* complicated a human being is when taken as a whole; that is, even though it has become clear, I still do not quite understand it. You were *forced* to participate in all my mood swings (I wonder if it is a good thing to burden others with this?) and to realize what despair I felt when I left here. What a great change took place, however. Even my very first night in Ulm all alone brought me closer to myself. Then I took an early train from Ulm the following morning and arrived in Geislingen where the sun was shining brightly, and I took the beloved walk from there to Eybach. Finally, I was all by myself! All the melancholy left me, and a wonderful peace blew towards me from the silent valley. God, how beautiful it was. I experienced everything for a second time, the first walk Christoph and I took there together, the plans we had made – how many of them there were – in full awareness of our happiness – then came the end. All of a sudden, I was no longer sad. For a long while I sat at his grave covered by the many flowers and felt happy. Is that not strange? I was truly happy.

But I could not understand why I felt happy. Was it because I had finally found peace – inner peace – again?! Can you imagine that my thoughts of Christoph and of you melted together into one? You were both tremendously helpful to me. I was deeply ashamed of the despair I had felt. It seemed so pitiful and small of me, so excessively woman-like. Because I was physically exhausted, I wished I had had somebody to care for me, not like Julie, however, but the way Christoph used to, so that I was not even aware of what he was doing. I missed him so terribly at this moment and even thought there might be another. I have gotten a hold of myself again now and keep saying – this is how I really feel, too – that it would not be the same and that I could never endure living with another man on a permanent basis. And you mean a great deal to me. The main reason you mean so much to me is that I have become so accustomed to opening myself up to you so completely and revealing everything. I did not want to write you about all this, but once I start, everything ends up on the page looking quite different from the way it did a moment before when it was still inside of me. Then, for a brief second, I have the feeling: "No, you can't send this letter." But then I am inevitably reminded of a sentence you wrote in one of your letters: "I feel as if something that already came to belong to me is taken away." So I decided on the spot that you shall receive each and every expression of this soul's ups and downs.

I had stopped here. Meanwhile, a letter arrived from you. I just read in it that you plan to visit here for a few days. You cannot imagine how happy this makes me. You are very important to me, because there is no one else I feel understands me as well as you do.

I have to go to Munich again tomorrow for two days with Julie, who will then be traveling on to Stuttgart to celebrate a silver anniversary;[47] she will be staying there until the 10th We have a very, very boring couple with us here who will, I hope, be leaving soon so that you do not have to meet them. At Julie's request I had to consult a doctor again (which is

---

47. Julie, having been lady-in-waiting to the Queen of Württemberg, had to attend the Silver Jubilee of their Majesties in Stuttgart.

completely ridiculous). He wants to place me in a sanatorium because of low blood pressure (I am not going to go, though).

Mail call. Addio.

Ottonie D.

P.S. (I am not going to say anything to Julie about your letters mentioning your plan to visit, so you will have to write to her yourself.)

🐞 🐞 🐞

Neubeuern, 7 April 1911

You provided me with some exceedingly enjoyable days by sending me *Le Rouge et le noir*.[48] It is a fabulous book! The concise dialogue and the instant comparison with each new character are incredible. One has the feeling the book could have been written by one of the moderns. The scenes in the seminary are so wonderful, and so is the merging together of the two women at the end. I cannot express how much I enjoyed the whole thing.

How strange my last two letters must have seemed to you! Or can you delve so deeply into another person's soul that you are able to grasp the depths of one's moods as they swing at times over an abyss? I took the children to the station this evening. Karin's tears refused to stop; that's how difficult it was for her to say goodbye. She has turned out to be so charming during the past quarter year, but unfortunately she and Mädy get along worse, if anything, and she really suffers because of this. How we would have loved to keep the child here longer.

8 April. The peaceful house is so soothing. If only it would once stay this way for a while, but then there is always another dull person arriving here whose company one must tolerate. Hinterhör then becomes even more enticing. There I might even be able to elude my mother when she comes to visit. As an excuse we plan to say that I cannot have any guests there because of my health and that it is to serve as a sort of sanatorium for me this year. I will be very happy if this works.

I will finish now. I just wanted to give you a sign of life.

I hope you do not feel that I am clinging too tightly to you? The thought suddenly occurred to me yesterday.

Strauss is in Vienna. So I suppose you will be going to town quite frequently, with Reinhardt being there as well. I hear the dinner gong.

Many kind thoughts from,

Yours, Ottonie D.

---

48. *The Red and the Black*, a novel by Stendhal.

[Rodaun] Sunday [10 April 1911] evening

 I do not know why, but the *Rosenkavalier* has been a terrible strain on me (the performance was yesterday evening, which was very good and, except for the Marschallin and Sophie, much better than in Dresden). I feel completely dead, the complete opposite of the way I felt in Dresden. Strauss was here today, and I just finished reading to the children from the charming *Melusine*. I was so exhausted that I almost fell asleep. It is 6:30 now, but I think I am going to have to go to bed. Perhaps it is the cruel, lingering winter that wears a person down – the icy, gray sky and this depressing north wind that sweeps over the blossoms lying flat across the frozen ground.
 Emotionally I am doing very well; I am just tired. Even though this is not really a letter, I would be very grateful if you wrote me something.
 Now the thought of seeing you is so fixed in my mind that I cannot escape it. I will be in touch with Julie. I have warm thoughts of you, as always.

                Yours, Hofmannsthal

❦ ❦ ❦

[Rodaun] 14 April [1911]

Dear Countess,
 Even if you cancelled our plans now, I think I would still come. The impatience to see you, to hear your voice now that I have *indeed* made up my mind, is too great to postpone it until another time. I am not even very worried about strangers being there, if, in God's name, strangers must *always* be there. For it is so wonderful when we have a free moment to ourselves and I am able to come to your room or you visit me in the green room where nobody can see or find you. What a delightful day it was we spent alone together! We should not think of how few days there will be, if even *one* day can be so rich and beautiful.
 I will announce my visit to Julie. Please have Winkler check the timetable to see if it corresponds to the following plans, and write me *right away* when you have an answer. I will be traveling Saturday evening and will arrive early Sunday morning around 7:00 or 7:30 in Munich. I shall require an additional 30 to 40 minutes for a possible delay and customs check, and then I of course will return immediately to Rosenheim-Raubling. Would this be possible? I hope so! I'm incredibly busy with all sorts of projects. I have writing that I need to complete, various dictations, and suddenly thousands of people have announced their arrival and want to see me.

I simply cannot *believe* that we will be walking together across a spring meadow in eight more days.

Yours, H. H.

❧ ❧ ❧

Neubeuern, 15 April 1911

I was hoping, just a little bit, that I might receive a letter from you this morning. I am reading *Wilhelm Meister*[49] with tremendous interest and enjoyment. I am at the *Confessions of a Beloved Soul.* How often I find myself in the middle of a particularly lovely passage wishing you were here so that we could both enjoy discussing it. I am always amazed by the expression of one's innermost feelings found in this book. How simply everything is expressed, things one often does not even dare admit to oneself. It is splendid the way Goethe manages to penetrate so deeply to the core of a woman's soul. I find it tremendously enjoyable reading about these experiences and taking part in them. You are often here with me in my room at these times. (Even though it is not too cozy here, we are still content in each other's company.) I also have long discussions with you when I am in the middle of a lovely passage. There is so much that you bring to my attention, and I try as best I can to see it all. The danger that I might have to cancel my plans with you seems to be over. A visit from Frau von Ahlers here in Neubeuern appeared on the horizon; she is the last person I would like to have here when you come. I can bear her alone as a result of the fact that I continually withdraw myself, but I would have endured any such misery for your sake.

Big Fat Egon is here with a friend who left last night to hike Wendelstein at 3:00 in the morning. Dabette will also be coming today with a friend of hers and Miss Smith, so now you'll be able to picture our Easter gathering here. On Monday we are also expecting Frau von Heiseler and her son and Nele and Puppi van de Velde for the Easter egg hunt. Unfortunately Marie-Therese is still sick in bed; it has turned into a rather bad case of bronchitis.

They are constantly having trouble in Bredeney. Eberhard and three of the children are also sick in bed with the flu, and it will not be long before Mädy has worn herself out, as Frau Bauk is on vacation and the English nanny is new. So she decided to send a telegram asking for Mary's help, but I cannot possibly send her there, as I must be careful with myself and conserve the strength I have.

I hope you were able to overcome your exhaustion and now have enough strength to return to work. I am looking forward to hearing what

---

49. Novel by Goethe.

you have been doing. I love to hear you tell me about the beginning of one of your new works and how things come and go in your own world. I could listen to you talk about all this for hours on end.

Do you still remember the walk we took one evening in Hinterhör? The moonlight shone through the trees as we reached the top of the road, and then you spoke to me so beautifully of the moments when greatness comes and causes a whole world to arise within one, and then goes away again, leaving behind a nameless feeling of grandeur. Whenever I come up that way, I hear your voice again. In such moments I am truly happy to be alive and find it is all worthwhile after all.

About when do you plan to go to Paris and for how long?

I did not get any further yesterday, and now I have your letter.

It will be wonderful having you here so soon!

I will write you everything about the train schedule, but I have to hurry now because I want you to receive this letter tomorrow.

We are just about to hide Baby's Easter eggs right now.

I am thrilled that you will be visiting so soon!

It is a beautiful day this Sunday. I spend a lot of my time lying outside in the sun.

Ottonie D.

❦ ❦ ❦

Neubeuern, Friday, 28 April 1911

You won't believe what marvelous luck I have had since you left today. Mary and Baby were drinking tea in my room; I had invited them in so that I would not feel so lonely, it was *lovely*. I asked Mary what she thought of our staying in a tiny, tiny little flat in Paris, which led to some very amusing ideas, and we had a lot of laughs. Baby heard how I said, "One room for me, one for you and one for Baby." She then asked, "And where is Hofmannsthal's room?" Then we quickly returned to our tea (10 minutes), and then I rested in my room until dinner and am already in bed now at 9 o'clock, as I looked a bit like I had a headache (so the others thought); I acknowledged this right away and took advantage of the opportunity to disappear.

I still have a feeling of complete happiness, I could almost say because of your presence, and do not wish to think that tomorrow you will merely be here in my thoughts and not here in the house. We really had some wonderful days; unfortunately they passed much too quickly. I can still not imagine that I am not to see you again now for six to eight weeks, at the very least; neither do I want to think about this, but rather continue to feel happy about the recent pleasant hours.

I have only one request from you; please, please do not allow yourself to become *too* upset when thinking about my situation here now; this will change in time, and until then, I intend to do everything I can to improve things as much as possible. Just having discussed it all with you and having felt the understanding you showed me once again makes everything so much easier for me and more tolerable.

Just imagine that Aida is almost a blessing now, as Julie is wonderfully occupied with her – and that there are no beds to take care of here, so I already feel free for tomorrow. I read some of the delightful new Balzac and found that Veronique's fate is somewhat similar to mine, that is, in being constrained.

Right now you are traveling from Augsburg to Geislingen; I can easily imagine being there with you, as I recently took the same train to Ulm, on my trip to Eybach. Now you are traveling the entire night and, I hope, will be able to sleep a little and not talk too much to me. By no means do I want to be a cause of unrest for you, but rather a pleasant, even if perhaps a sad, thought. I suppose I could continue chatting with you like this forever, but that certain spot in my eyes tells me to say goodnight.

Yours, Ottonie D.

Saturday

Aida is my good fortune, Julie drives and walks with her, and I can enjoy my peace and quiet, so it will be another good day. I lay outside for a long time in my little spot, and all the attraction I have for others completely disappeared. I wonder if it did not come from you? Many fond thoughts constantly travel to a certain hotel in Paris.

Neubeuern, 1 May 1911

You know, our new postal system is horrendous; beginning today until the 15th of July, we are going to receive mail only once a day and this via Brannenburg because the road to Raubling is closed due to construction. So it makes absolutely no difference when you post letters to me; arrangements will, however, probably be made so that Julie does not see the letters beforehand.

It seems that you have been gone from here for an eternity now, and when I count, it has only been three days, hard to believe. It was really wonderful your being here. I enjoyed this so much and still spend time reminiscing. It is really very different once you have seen and spoken to the other person again; you become so much closer to each other right away, so very different than when simply writing letters. I am already looking forward to the fact that May will soon be over; indeed months often pass by very quickly, and then you will be able to come here again in mid-June. Then in July I will *definitely* come to visit you. This way we will still be able to spend a lot of time together this summer; *how* lovely this will be.

Yesterday was quite cloudy, but I still lay outside wrapped in blankets reading the entire day – it was so wonderful being alone that it must be counted as a good day, today, too. I am beginning to realize how marvelous it is having Aida here; she is a great help to Julie and spends the entire day with her, which she loves *so* much, and never before did I have so much control over my own time. I also believe she is going to stay here for at least another two weeks, if not longer.

I am not going to Munich tomorrow; Julie is unable to come along, and I need her at my fittings, so unfortunately I will not be able to go to my concert either. However, I really do not wish to go to town twice in a row, as it is so very peaceful here now.

I wonder how you are. Do you feel at home in the little hotel? God, how I would *love* to be there in Paris with you, which would do me so much good. Do you know what I often had to think about? Whether we both may not have viewed my life here in *too* dark a light and whether most of the blame does not lie with me for the way things have turned out? If I become a bit more inconsiderate, in time the others will simply get used to my doing more of what I want to, and then things will be much better and manageable. At any rate, your presence here made it clear to me that I must do something myself to resist the forces seeking to take control of me in order to save myself – and I am trying very hard now to do so.

However, please do not let yourself feel sad when you think of me, for I am doing very well right now, and you are the main reason.

I want to throw this letter in the post office box myself now – it is 9:00 p.m. – so that the servant does not always see so many letters being sent to you.

With the most faithful thoughts from your,

Ottonie D.

❦ ❦ ❦

Hotel St. Anne, [Paris] 1 May [1911] evening

Dear Countess,

Your letter – which arrived today – was so kind and lovely and did me as much good as anything possibly could have; I thank you very much. I would like to respond to you immediately, but this is going to be a bad letter. I could not write yesterday or the day before; it just was not possible. I could not even send you the little reminder, namely, that the Kreisler concert will be on the 2nd of May. I felt so unutterably sad here in this foreign city with the mass of people, all the arrangements and intricacies meant to make *life more pleasant and more enjoyable*. And now hovering above all the faces there is *one*, and behind all the shop windows, again there is *the* face of the one person I wish to help but am unable to. This can magnify one's sadness infinitely, finally leaving one feeling stiff and numb.

Ottonie, please do not think I am so madly in love with you that I cannot help but see your face everywhere I go. It is not at all like that. It is just that I once again have the tormenting feeling of being absolutely powerless. In the sleeping car I talked half the night – or more than half – not with you, but with Julie. It was a rather grim conversation, characterized by confusion, distortions, and ill-feelings, such as one never experiences during the day. I could feel myself *ruining* everything beyond the point of all repair, but I could not stop.

Your letter is wonderful. The one part where you said you yourself believe that everything will change and *improve* is so comforting. It is almost too absurd that you should comfort me. What a silly thought! My mind is not focused today, forgive me. And above all, please do not read more into my present state of mind than is there. *Please*, let us not carry on endlessly like a couple of mirrors hanging opposite one another.

Here the resources for one who is depressed are inexhaustible. I have spent many long hours walking the streets that are so full of life, from one section of town to the next, crossing bridges to the opposing bank, going up and down the boulevards, and then to a theater each night. I was so tired, I almost fell asleep. Then I would sleep for eight hours straight without turning over, so there is no need to feel sorry for me.

Now I am going to get dressed for the *Variétés*. It does seem possible to stay in this little hotel without being noticed by any of the *gens de lettres* or *gens du monde*, which makes all the difference in the world.

Good night, H.

Neubeuern, 4 May [1911]

It is a beautiful day today, simply heavenly. I am sitting out on the terrace writing letters, and along comes Winkler the postal angel with a letter from Paris. I was afraid – I was sure – that once you found out about my situation here, it would have a profound and lasting effect on you. I knew it would become worse and worse the longer and farther away you were from here and from me. But then there will be moments when you will tell yourself it is exaggerated and not as bad as it seems. And, please, do not budge from here, for you'll have found the right place. Since you left, I have enjoyed one nice day after another. The solitude has been heavenly, whether I am reading a book, looking out over the wall surrounding the terrace or just recalling the last few lovely days that were delightful and so precious. We do not have any guests; how nice to be alone. Schmitz Aida left suddenly on Tuesday evening. A telegram arrived from Schmitz, and an hour later she was in the carriage to Rosenheim. It is so lovely here now, and Julie has been so kind. She leaves me in peace to do what I want, and if we should have more time by ourselves here alone, it will do me a great deal of good, for then I will have all I really need. All of a sudden the idea came to me of why we (Mama and I) should not simply move to Hinterhör when Julie and Baby are in Tarasp. We will do so eventually, though not before the end of June, because I am going to wait until you have been here first, for unfortunately I do not have room for you there. I am getting impatient as I wait for my mother to tell me whether she will be coming now or not. Then I want to decide whether you should write to the Vareses to come in June and July. Julie will probably leave with Baby on the 6th or the 8th of June. I am very much looking forward to the tranquil months that await me.

On Tuesday, I drove alone to Heiseler's for tea, and what a nice trip this was. You sat beside me faithfully the whole time and told such lovely stories (much nicer than your conversations with other people that night in the sleeping car). I wish I could somehow send you some of the wonderful inner peace I am now enjoying. Yet long before this reaches you, you will have grasped it. Please believe me that I have the strongest intention of arranging my life the way I find it necessary for me. The dinner gong!

I realize only now for the first time following our discussion of everything – I have truly come to see it for the first time – what it is that often makes life here so difficult for me. I now realize that one must be inconsiderate to a certain degree in order to achieve a proper balance in one's life. When Julie finally comes to understand that each of us has very different needs, a great deal will be won.

I read *Le Curé de village* with a tremendous amount of interest. I must say, you were lucky once again, or rather, you are very good at picking out what is right for me. Now I have gone back to *Wilhelm Meister*.

Can you recommend a book for me to give to Mary? She only wants to read things that are really good (in German of course), but she is not yet able to read much containing language beyond that of everyday conversation. Our postal system is in horrible shape at present – this letter I am writing now (2:00 p.m.) will not begin its journey until 10:00 tomorrow morning.

I want to lie down now for a while. Later we will drive to Hinterhör with Mama. It will be her first trip since last fall. Enjoy becoming immersed in the splendid beauty of the city, and whenever you think of me, picture me lying in the sunshine on the terrace, outside and partly inside as well.

Yours truly, Ottonie D.

🌺 🌺 🌺

Neubeuern am Inn, 6 May 1911

Why is it that I always have to write you? I simply know that it makes you happy when a letter arrives from me, and I feel the same way when yours arrive, so that's why I continue writing you so often.

Julie and I were just out in the rain in Hinterhör (like the two of us that one evening). On the way back we began talking about you and me.

7 May 11. I told her that I would be going to stay with you for a few days this summer, and then she said this would definitely not be a good thing for me to do because of my health, which I of course disputed. I told her everything about your plans to stay here and that she was behaving ridiculously, like a peeved governess, etc. – all in a very calm and friendly manner. She felt I had spent much too much time with you and that it was natural for this to upset her, considering how it came across to everyone here. In response to this I explained that the time we both spend together is something very different indeed from what goes on between a teenage girl and a lieutenant. I told her that I *also* benefit very much from my relationship with you, more so than from any other, and that I therefore *do not care at all* what silly Belke or Aida thought about our relationship. I continually made a point of telling her that you and I would both be here again and that I would spend *just as much* time with you as always and could not care less what other people think.

Then she tried to tell me that it is only my imagination not being able to benefit emotionally from anyone else. As a counter example I mentioned *her* head-shrink, Frau von Martens. However, we still parted on entirely good terms, and I intend to talk to her about this again sometime so that she will know *exactly* what kind of relationship we have.

I really feel sorry for Julie; it would be so good for her if she had someone who could be for her what you are for me. I almost think she longs for this but will never let it happen on account of her terrible prudishness, which other, hypocritical sorts have so strongly impressed upon her.

I am *so happy* here now. I so enjoy being alone here and view this as heaven's special gift. In this respect, Julie is again very nice; I moaned so much about the constant guests, and she now writes to everyone to tell them they cannot come. However, I, of course, do not begin to serve as a replacement because I am not around her enough.

Tomorrow we are going to Munich and will be staying there until Wednesday. I am going to see if I cannot catch a good concert or a nice play in the theater.

Marie van de Velde wrote that she will be in Paris with Henry next week. Everyone is going to Paris. *How* I, too, would love to go there now, if only I could! I really hope you have a good time there and can be alone as you wish and that the weather is nice for taking walks. You have already been there for a week now; the time will pass very quickly, and then you will be coming back and stopping off here for a visit.

I will be very happy if I can manage to move to Hinterhör by the end of June or early July. As soon as I am there, I feel very different and much more independent. I am also going to try to keep my help with me there into the fall for as long as possible and would probably stay there until the end of November then.

Poor Eberhard is still suffering excruciating pain in his foot; Mädy wrote today that it has still not improved much, which of course directly affects every other part of his life.

Take care now. I *hope* very much to receive a letter from you tomorrow before I go to Munich.

With warm regards, Ottonie D.

❦ ❦ ❦

[Hotel St. Anne, Paris] 8 May [1911]

Dear Countess,

These days I am *unable* to write you a letter, but I prefer to express myself briefly than to create an embarrassing and confusing situation by being silent. Ill feelings of this sort have in part physical causes, or perhaps they are simply emotional and produce physical effects. However, as it is grotesque to take along such *humeur noire* to the theater or the racetrack, I will leave here Wednesday evening and will arrive in Rodaun on Thursday evening. As far as I know, I will still be meeting Reinhardt in Vienna (his company is performing *Oedipus* there.)

If my being there really prompted you to think certain things over and gain some understanding, it was an incalculable gain. Also having the *will* to carry them out, which nobody, not even Eberhard, could do for you. It is a matter of drawing a distinction between your individual self and everything else and protecting your modest rights and freedoms. There was nothing to gain from the way you deliberately put yourself at the mercy of everyone and endured chronic depletion of your limited strength for the sake of life's trifles. Nor was there any more room for hope.

It would be very kind of you, if you have the opportunity, to casually discuss the unexpected tones used by your sister-in-law when she and I were together during my last visit. The memory of this is no less agonizing than were the actual events. You may say she did not *think it through*, but one is obliged after all to *think about* how one treats close acquaintances. The way Julie strove to make clear to me on two or three separate occasions that she finds it regrettable that you gave up your regimen for the sake of our relationship was – for a well-bred woman, which Julie no doubt is – almost a bit too extreme. The fact that you are not a little girl and Julie is not your mother (nor your husband) makes the situation all the more ridiculous, although no less unpleasant. The same may be said of the *manner* in which she approached this subject when we were alone – once with the book that had gotten wet and the other time with the servant. *This isn't the way things are handled.* It would be terribly difficult for me to visit Neubeuern again anytime soon. And doing so in her absence would almost be impossible – after all, she is the lady of the house. It all boils down to certain *nuances*.

I have asked myself what she might be thinking. I do not get the impression that she is oblivious to it. This is unlikely when one so completely neutralizes someone who comes four times a year for a week's visit – indeed, his presence is simply *removed* (in an intellectual sense) or at least everything is undertaken in order to achieve this, so that others find themselves in an awkward situation; this is fit for children of seventeen but certainly does not suit us. I also remember your telling me once in the winter that Julie, following my first visit that fall, delicately raised these issues in a conversation you had, while also revealing what may be called an excessive preoccupation with them.

I am sending my thank-you letter to Julie with the same mail. Well, now I have written it, and perhaps it is a good thing to have expressed it.

Yours H.

[Maximilianstrasse 25/I.] Wednesday [10 May 1911]

I wonder if you are still unable to write me? However, tomorrow morning I suspect I will indeed find a letter from you that was first sent to Neubeuern and by then will have been sent back here. I am already looking so forward to it but do not want to be disappointed if it had not arrived.

I was just in *Mme. Butterfly* with Dabette; neither one of us had seen it before. It was such a good performance; the little Butterfly was very charming but *so* sad.

Unfortunately there are few performances in the theater this week, nor any concerts either; in this respect I have had bad luck. I hope you are enjoying Paris very, very much and are seeing a lot and experiencing many things; later I will be happy when you tell me something about it. Of course I would prefer to experience some of this myself with you, but that is not possible this time.

Actually you must have received quite a few letters from me since you left. Do they really reach you? This must be the fourth or fifth one.

Dabette says Henry seems to be having a lot of difficulty with the theater. This would distress me very much; I just hope that something will come of it and not once again be a failure for him. After all, too much depends on it for him. Now Henry has all three women, who are more or less in love with him, together in Paris – a strange situation; it seems he is unable to escape anything.

Good night. I have been lying in bed for some time and should try to fall asleep; maybe I will be able to now soon. In the meantime, I send you many warm thoughts,

Yours, Ottonie D.

❦ ❦ ❦

[Maximilianstrasse] Friday [12 May 1911]

How sad I am that Paris, with all its beauty, did not have the power to overcome the negative impressions. During all these days I have felt how you were unable to deal with this. Please do not continue to *work* yourself up into a state again. I have spoken to Julie about this. She was completely unaware of what she had said; and in spite of everything, she could not resist this terrible tendency women have of allowing themselves to be guided by feelings they have not thought through. Could it not also be that deep within her heart lies dormant the feeling that she must always do without something (in friendships, as well). *Please* let us not be harsh towards her; everything, especially in her life, was simply a bit out of the ordinary, and this is whence moments do spring as we experienced most recently.

Just think, you were traveling by way of Munich and I was here, so we could have spoken to each other, *too* bad. Only now have I received your letter. I can certainly understand that you do not plan to come again soon, so perhaps I can make arrangements to come to see you for two entire weeks at the beginning of July; *how truly* wonderful that would be. I am almost happy that you are back. Gerty, the children, Reinhardt, Papa, they will all remove a weight from your shoulders without realizing it. But right away I have an ulterior motive: as you have shortened your stay in Paris now, then maybe it will work out for both of us at the same time after all. Oh, if only I could take a walk with you right now down to the Inn river and chat and chat; then you might be able to forget all the nonsense and confusion.

I was all alone in the theater yesterday and saw a very amusing play; it was *so* delightful.

Tomorrow we will travel to Miesbach; where the carriage will meet us and drive us home from there.

One thing can and must make you feel better, that our days were such truly lovely days for me, from which I benefited enormously and continue to benefit.

Very truly yours, Ottonie D.

❦ ❦ ❦

Rodaun, 16 May [1911]

Dear Countess,

This letter from Eberhard just arrived and I find it extraordinary – his lovely whole character stares at you – that I have to send it along even though he did not give me permission, although he did not forbid it either. What could be better, or more agreeable, than becoming aware once again of one's friendships, of the fondness and sympathy one has for another person. As he is not throwing away my letters but rather plans to save them, this is an indication that he finds some kindness in them despite the dreary state in which I wrote them. (Do not let it bother you that he refers to Marie-Therese as "Fratz," a word he apparently picked up from my letter; there is no negative connotation to the word in Austrian German. I often use it when speaking of or to my children.)

You must not think I wish to be overly harsh or unfair towards Julie. Not at all. At this very moment I can picture her charm, her touching feminine and girlish manner, and her kindness just as vividly as the unfortunate way her mind works, for which her fate (as well as her predisposition to some degree) is to blame. It is probably more important that you maintain the upper hand here in order that a firmer foundation for my continued relationship to Julie may gradually be achieved. This would be better than my trying to avoid her as much as possible and for us to only meet somewhere else, which would greatly hamper our ability to see each other. (It is strange. I *know* now all of a sudden that you need me and that it would be a true loss for you no longer to have me. When our visits in Neubeuern were so unexpectedly threatened – at least it seemed to me to happen very unexpectedly — I became keenly aware of this, whereas before it was just a matter of sentimentality.)

I wrote Julie from Paris. It was a very friendly letter, yet a touch different, somehow cooler or sharper than in the past; I also added that my encounter with Frau von A. is not an experience I would have wished to have. Once you know when you would like to have the Vareses visit, then Julie will certainly have occasion to write me.

Have you decided when you would like to have the Vareses visit? I *hope* it has been decided they will visit Neubeuern sometime very soon. It would be absurd to postpone such a positively good thing just because I *might* be coming. Now one other thing: I believe it has been determined that you will be visiting us, if not for a full two weeks, then at least for ten days. But we had always had the second part of July in mind, and now you're talking about the beginning of July. I will not be in Aussee at the beginning of July, but rather in Rodaun, where you would have to travel three times as far. We always discussed Aussee. Please think this over. I can adjust my schedule to yours, but I cannot change it at the last minute. Think about this, as well as the Vareses' visit, and make it clear to Julie that you will stick to your plans without sacrificing your nerves to the "fickle air" there as Eberhard so rightly calls it.

My atrocious state of mind in Paris was probably the result of something more than just the visit to Neubeuern. During the weeks prior to this meeting, I slipped into a kind of despair regarding you. This was not directly related to your letters, however, but to that which I truly felt lay behind them: the most vicious circle of irrationality regarding your physical health and the surrender of your spiritual self. Whereby, when I say "irrationality," I roughly mean what Julie would call rationality.

In Paris I reached the horrible point where the minutes — in the theater or at the racetrack for instance — indeed the seconds of *this* black hell seemed to extend into years. Your letters were unable to provide me even the slightest joy. (Is it not better to avoid — always avoid — writing: "I am writing because I *know* that every letter I send brings you terrific happiness?") They did not interest me in the slightest, and nothing you said had an effect on me, even though you informed me you were doing better emotionally and had acquired the strength and determination to make some changes. Once I got back here, then I took such great pleasure in the first letter I found on my desk. How happy it makes me to feel that something so trivial as two very ordinary plays can mean something to you. It makes me happy and moves me at the same time and then again, it is a very natural thing. And the artificiality of denying the pleasure one derives, the emptiness of such self-imposed restrictions, seems so unnatural. I am looking forward very much to having you here in my world for two weeks. I *know* it will be beneficial to you.

The birds are singing, and the little lilacs I planted myself are starting to bloom. Max Reinhardt was charming and had a lively imagination as always. We'll be playing *Jedermann*[50] in Munich this September. I have a lot of ideas for the *Frau ohne Schatten*.[51] I'm adapting a delightful Molière piece for which Strauss is composing the music. I am also preparing my comedy. We can go for walks in Aussee and sit together in the little peasant rooms when you are here.

Adieu.

Yours, H.

P.S. How absurd and repugnant it is to compare me to an old female "soul mate" of Martin's! How silly everything becomes "when it must be discussed." Yes, I received four or five letters while I was in Paris.

Rodaun, 26 May [1911]

Dear Countess,

Is the little thread hanging listless and sad, all the way down to the ground? I received your letter from the 18th but none since then. The one from the 18th was short. It informed me of your trip to Stuttgart but made no mention of whether you had received a rather long letter I'd sent shortly before this. Yet it must be in your hands by now, or perhaps not at all. And that would be bad, quite bad indeed, for it contained a letter from Eberhard which was so beautiful, yes, a real blessing to me. That is why I included it in my letter, however it was not meant for anyone else to see. If only I knew whether you received it.

Well, now I am sitting here way up at the top of the steeply sloping, somewhat overgrown garden. The birds are singing, the jasmine is about to bloom, and the few rhododendrons I have are beginning to reveal their large, radiant blossoms. The birds are singing, and I feel as if you will momentarily approach, holding a book you found downstairs in my room, where you'd be sleeping if you were here, as Kessler once did. And in the evening we would take a drive into town to go to the Russian choir with the many voices of boys and men. We would drive home at night and enjoy the house, all the rooms filled with a cool, damp scent. The following morning I'd tell you all about the little opera, *Ariadne*, which Strauss is pestering me to begin. Telling you the story of it would bring it to life and allow me to look forward much more to working on it. Then we will take a drive through the country, and I can show you *my* countryside. But wherever are you? I feel that I am calling you and nobody's an-

---

50. *Everyman*, an old English mystery play. H. v. H. rewrote it for German stage.
51. Libretto for the Richard Strauss opera.

swering. Have they all taken you away from me? Has that ugly sadness taken hold of you again, so that it no longer seems worth the effort to free yourself? Are you that weary? Was I so incomprehensible to you during these dismal weeks? Is it not worth it to try to hold the thread taut?

Suddenly Varese wrote. He said he was planning a trip to France with his wife and child from late June to late August. But he remembered the importance I attached to his wife's presence during the visit to Neubeuern, and he asked how everything stood with the plans there and whether it would be possible to combine both trips. I do not completely understand what he means. I think he may mean he would send his wife there before the end of June or perhaps after the 1st of September. There is probably not enough time left to arrange for the first possibility. I have no idea what your plans are. I do not know anything about you right now. I hope you will not be robbed of the little time you have to yourself in Julie's absence. Would it be acceptable then to propose a two-week stay in September to little Frau Varese, just so you have the opportunity to get to know her? And so that, once the ice has been broken, she could be received for a longer stay some other time?

Eberhard's letter meant so much to me, more than words can describe. This deep yearning for peace. It is a curious game he plays with life, or that life plays with him. (I hope the letter was not lost.)

Mahler's funeral[52] was the other day. I stood surrounded by the mass of people at the open grave and threw some earth into the pit. I felt terribly sad for him. I could feel the bitter gravity of this irretrievable loss. Then, while leaving, I suddenly understood that people would also experience a loss if I were to die, and perhaps someone would feel sad about me the same way I do about Mahler, whom I had only spoken to once before in my life. The incomprehensibility of a life such as my own was, at that moment, no burden at all.

Take care, and do remain my friend no matter what!

Yours, H.

[Rodaun] 4 June [1911]

I think one is always able to feel exactly what lurks behind a person's silence. There is no coldness behind mine, no thoughtlessness. It was simply the necessity of holding myself together amidst the growing tension surrounding a *small* piece of work I had promised Strauss [*Ariadne auf Naxos*] and wanted to put behind me. The difficult projects are the small

---

52. The composer Gustav Mahler (1860–1911).

ones: to call forth life within a small, confining space, to arouse the heart's sympathy while at the same time remaining firm and "distanced."

Rousseau's *Confessions* were in the package you found (or perhaps not?) in Neubeuern. It is because of the first third of them, from his youth, that I love them and pass them along to you. You should stop following the episode with Madame de Warens. I was at the Odéon in Paris one afternoon and saw *Andromaque* there. I felt you were there with me sitting right beside me. During the intermission we went outside and took a walk under the arcades, where books are displayed and sold; we bought this book there.

I wrote Madame Varese today and told her that she cannot be received in June or July, but in the last few days of August.

I would be so grateful for a letter like the ones you used to write back in the old days.

Adieu.

H.

❦ ❦ ❦

Rodaun, 23 June [1911]

Dear Countess,

A tooth fistula is a true nuisance. It is painful, and, being so close to the head, it restricts one's imagination and even the ability to think. Thus one has no desire to write. It happened during our trip. We got back on Wednesday, and I no longer have any pain. The sun is very strong and the sky so bright. A playful summer breeze has stripped the roses of their petals. It is lovely sitting up here in the little garden house and completing the text for the little opera. Bacchus has landed on the island and is approaching poor, deserted Ariadne. She takes him for Hermes, the Messenger of Death. He lets her believe this and carries her off.

The "trip" consisted of a little drive to ancient sites along the Danube in Lower Austria, where one finds beautiful old churches and monasteries, farms from the thirteenth century, and in the midst of everything, the big, yellowish green river – this was the trip I had invited you to take with us. A "fourth person" also came along for Gerty, a young poet[53] of true talent whom I like very much. So there were four of us altogether. Whenever we came across a beautiful church tower, a deep-set, ancient courtyard, or the walls of a vineyard providing a nice glimpse of the river, I thought how wonderful it would be if you were here and I could show it to you. But then again, when a warm, listless wind blew relentlessly down the Danube or a powerful storm shook the old inn during the night so that

---

53. Max Mell (1882–1971).

one was unable to fall asleep until morning, I was glad that you had not come along – just like Eulenspiegel.[54]

But now you should be here. The house is nice and cool, and the garden filled with a sweet, warm scent. I have enough unwritten stories in my head to be able to tell you a different one every afternoon – but you are not here and will not be coming either! How restricted you are there, as if you had sold your life to those people – and what have they given you in return? Today I feel as if I could never again bring myself to go there. Then I think of Hinterhör, and it seems possible – we will just have to see.

I will be picking you up in Salzburg on the 20th, perhaps with an automobile or perhaps not. Then the following day we will travel to Aussee one way or another. For exactly eight days! Has this been measured out? Measured according to plan? By the governess, the highest authority herself?? Eight days can be a lot, but in fact it is really very little. It will rain on five of them, you will have a headache on one of the others and the next one will be ruined by a guest who blows in unexpectedly – quite a stingy allotment we have received.

Will it be nice? I do not know – how can one know? But of course it will be nice, really wonderful, for you will be coming *home* from your ridiculous exile, from Nowhere back to Somewhere. You are coming to an absurd little bird house, where everything is rather disorganized, to visit people who belong to no particular kind at all, and you belong here with them. We shall live rather without regard for reason, propriety or rules of any kind. If you would write me sometime soon from the little bench behind the house – that would be nice.

Your friend, H.

[Telegram] [Rodaun, 24 June 1911, 11:40 a.m.]

Many thanks for your kind letter Have not been entirely well Will write very soon.

Hofmannsthal

---

54. Till Eulenspiegel, a rascal in medieval German folklore. Richard Strauss wrote a tone-poem with this title.

[Rodaun] Tuesday [4 July 1911] evening

What a beautiful day, what a beautiful evening! All is clear – happy, harmonious. I wrote the last line of *Ariadne* today. Does Ariadne love Bacchus? Not an easy question to answer. She thinks he is someone else, Hermes, the Messenger of Death, coming to take her away. His mistaken identity remains: the mistake is so wonderful.

If you would like, I can tell you a story every morning and every afternoon – a fairy tale, an actual occurrence, a story of fate, a puppet show, a mystery play.

Does the empress have her shadow yet? I do not know. I have not had time to think about her. Perhaps she has one down in the underworld where she makes her home. Here is another play: tomorrow Jedermann and his girlfriend come to the table. All are eating and laughing. No one hears the eerie sound of eerie bells, but he alone, Jedermann. Then, all at once, the lights go out. Do you know the story of the woman with the little dog? Or of the boy, Euseb? Or the one about the fifty-year-old Prince? Or the one about Dominic Heintl's daughter, who had a twin? Or perhaps the one about Baptist, the servant, who had so much luck and great misfortune? You do not know any of these because you are a castle maid who just sits around in Neubeuern, and you are only remotely related to a very, very nice little Thuringian girl, whom I shall fetch from the train station in Salzburg two weeks from now. Do you know yet when the train will arrive in Salzburg? I will check this right away.

There *may* be a room for you in Aussee, but certainly at the very least a nice reclining chair. You will find things a bit disorganized in terms of the housekeeping. You will also find a poet named Schröder, a dancer, a painter,[55] a lantern for the night-time, lime-blossom tea from time to time, and, always, a friend. We have two governesses here, but they are not for you. Write me sometime!

Yours, H.

❦ ❦ ❦

[Telegram]   [Rodaun, 6 July 1911, 11:50 p.m.]

Any change would ruin the plans I make from day to day. Troubled. Request letter.

Hofmannsthal

❦ ❦ ❦

---

55. Grete Wiesenthal (1885–1970) and her husband Erwin Lang (1886–1962).

R, 14 July 1911

I could not find time to write you due to my work and correspondence. Such a trifle as your going to Munich to see that operetta gave me more pleasure than you can imagine.

Now this: I never had anything else in mind than that we would spend the 20th in Salzburg – a city I just love – which I am looking forward to showing you, and then continue on to Aussee on the 21st.

Sometime in the very near future I will reserve – as Salzburg is overcrowded – two rooms for us in Österreichische Hof. I will tell the owner, who knows me very well, that I will be picking up a friend of my wife's who lives in Bavaria. Your "governess" need not catch wind of this; Gerty would never think of mentioning such a minor detail, which is of no concern to anyone in Neubeuern.

It would be best if you arrived by noon, or in any case, if you went to the Österreichische Hof, had lunch there and then rested in your room. It will be very difficult for me to arrive by noon; I will not be able to make it until afternoon. *In any case*, please send me a telegram at "Aussee; Obertressen 14" on the 18th or the morning of the 19th at the latest, letting me know for certain that you'll be coming on the 20th and which train you will be taking.

We will be taking an automobile to Aussee tomorrow. The children are already there.

Many very kind thoughts, H.

🙶 🙶 🙶

Hinterhör, 14 July 1911

It is often frightening the way the days race by, and one is never able to complete all one would like. For example, I have wanted to write you for a number of days now and yet have not managed to do so.

Mama and I went for a very nice drive Wednesday evening. We left at 6:00. It was so beautiful that we kept on driving and eventually came to Austria and drove past the Schweigen. Do you remember the first sleigh ride we took together? I kept thinking about you the whole time. Some of the things we talked about came to mind, and I would have liked to drive further on into the brightly moonlit night until I found you. Then the poor old woman sitting beside me began telling me about the incredibly sad youth she had. Her mother, whom she loved so much, left one day never to return. From this point on, she was surrounded by a mass of dark clouds. Then she fell silent, and each of us must have leafed backwards through the experiences of our lives. How rich I felt there next to her. I have received so many wonderful things and so much kindness. I felt so much older than this poor creature whose life was filled with gloom at every turn.

At this point my thoughts returned to you, and I felt so happy to have you. I was looking tremendously forward to the 20th, which no longer seems to be in danger. I have made it clear to everyone that I am going to Aussee on the 20th, come what may. So I will be at your place a week from today; should I believe it!

Yesterday you sent me some wonderful books. Thank you so much. I think I am rather childish in some ways. For instance, whenever I receive new books from you, I always have to take one to bed with me and read it the same evening, as I did yesterday. Well, I do not have to go along to Eybach, which is very nice; I have only to take Mama to Munich, and then she will be continuing on alone with her maid. Julie will be joining her the next day with the "Wunderkind"[56] so that Mama will not be alone.

Nele and Puppi van de Velde are here with me now; they are extremely nice children whose company I very much enjoy; they spend the entire day playing with the animals and are always able to entertain themselves.

I have to hurry and write a letter to Maria van de Velde but just wanted to give you a sign of life before I come.

With many, many warm thoughts,

Yours always, O.

Hinterhör, 4 August 1911

Has it really just been a single day since we parted, just one single day! It seems like such a long time since we were in Salzburg. When I was resting in bed today after lunch and was by myself, I had to keep repeating to myself again and again that it really was only yesterday that we parted. God, what a wonderful, splendid time it was! I shall enjoy recalling it very much and very often. Might you perhaps be asking yourself if I have regrets, if I regret a single minute of this entire time? Don't even ask. Or better yet, let me answer you with a resounding "no!" Whatever I gave, I gave with pleasure (although I am also astonished at myself). That it is not all different, you know almost better than I do. But also believe me when I tell you that I like you very, very much, even more than I did two weeks ago. One would surely have to be content if one always had such an adorable nurse.

---

56. Marie-Therese.

Aribert[57] is leaving tomorrow, so it was good that I came back. He was here for almost the entire day and will be having breakfast here again tomorrow before leaving. I have not seen Egon[58] yet; he just got back from Heuberg this evening. He is staying only until Sunday. Julie wants to go to Munich this week with Luli – I mean next week. I have not said anything about our plans to see each other yet; I first want to wait and see which day they choose to go, and then I will say that we had made tentative plans some time ago. I hope that I can come then without them. But, after all, she does not enjoy my company either, for she is not coming along to the theater, and afterwards we will stay out for as long as we like. But, as I said before, I am hoping I will be able to find a way around this.

Were you also able to take the last part of the trip without getting a headache? And what did you end up doing? Maybe you met Reinhardt after all? Nobody asked me much of anything about our trip. Everyone was at the station, two carriages full of people from the castle came to pick me up. The children were overjoyed, and Baby could not be separated from me. Actually it is quite nice when everyone is so happy about one's return. Yet somewhere inside I feel a tiny bit empty, but I will get over this soon. Near my bed I found my beautiful, beloved Hölderlins; I had completely forgotten about them. Did I ever tell you that I am truly fond of them and often leaf through them? It is really wonderful the way I, through you, am able to become somewhat united with all these good and great minds and how they then help me to live my life. One would have to be happy being a poet thinking that there may perhaps live at some later time – when one is no longer around – a little creature who will absorb and cling to everything that has gushed forth from one's mind. I think it still would have to mean something even if it is only a little, inconspicuous creature, simply because it is a human being.

The letter (van Gogh) made such a strong impression on me. I think you should publish the third volume of prose after all if you find time.

I am going to take the second volume to bed with me now. I still want to read whatever I can find in there about Wassermann.

Good night, good night

Ottonie

---

57. Aribert von Gaisberg: friend of O. D. S.'s husband.
58. Count Egon von Beroldingen, a Degenfeld cousin.

[Garmisch Park-Hotel Alpenhof] Saturday [5 August 1911] morning

Dear Countess,

Our performance (*Figaros Hochzeit*)[59] will be on the 10th. I hope you found your little *Wunderkind* very loving, well and happy. Perhaps she really will become a *Wunderkind*, and later a soul who, whether free or fettered, is always kind and always sensitive – whether she devotes herself to somebody else's life or refuses to do so. And perhaps she will never be wishy-washy. Should one wish for her such a fate? This would surely have to be paid for with a great deal of suffering.

There are still a few things you should see in Munich, including the studio of a young sculptor we might visit.

Poor little Heymel no longer has a car. He sold it along with the horses. But he is still in good spirits. I saw Max Reinhardt for an hour. He is charming: his seriousness, the way he listens, it is all quite unique. (At first sight he seems rather ugly.) *Jedermann* will *probably* be performed in Munich, sometime around the end of September.

I have to go see Strauss. If only one could know how somebody looks this morning around the eyes and the forehead with all her rather untidy hair.

Yours, Hofmannsthal.

🙶 🙶 🙶

[Hotel Seehof Tutzing] Tuesday, 8 [August 1911]

Dear Countess,

I was very glad to receive your little letter this morning. I cannot tell you what a of jumble of discussions, reflections, thinking things through, not sleeping, and more discussions I have to endure right now. The dear, wonderful days, everything good and dear so far away; I, too, so removed from myself. Thursday will bring everything back, right? Including myself.

Afterwards I will have to go straight home and finish everything because the first performance of *Jedermann* is in the middle of September! How good that you will not have the Vareses there now and will have time for yourself. The beautiful weather, it is implacable! The beautiful moon! Will we ride around a bit in the moonlight Thursday night?

Would it suit you to pick me up on Thursday at 1:00 at the Marienbad? I will be downstairs by the door. Or write and let me know where I can meet you! I do not quite know the exact address of the little flat.

I have slept in a different bed every night – in Salzburg, Munich, Garmisch, Eibsee, Tutzing – and altogether so poorly!

---

59. The Marriage of Figaro.

Where is the little forest, "Ottonie," the peace, the little house, the candle, the lamp . . . ?

After all, everything is as it is. If Max Reinhardt did not exist, my whole existence would have to be rearranged completely.

The twenty-four hours with the Strausses were a long, continuous, horrible nightmare. These boorish, half-insane, deathly strange people. Characters out of a dream – who are they?! How did I ever become involved with them? How unbelievably strange. What people!

Adieu.

Yours, Hofmannsthal

🍀 🍀 🍀

15 August [1911], 1:00

Dear Countess,

I should do well to take a walk now – the virtuous ballet girls[60] are waiting – but a thunderstorm is approaching. Gerty is chatting with Erwin, so I have time to quickly write a few lines. They will of course be much less good than those I wrote into the air during my morning break from *Jedermann*. Those words I plucked from the air around me – they were born of the air and again buried in it. Everybody seems hard at work here, and once again very intent, very exact. The forest has an entirely different face; so has the sky, which is dull, sultry, cloudy – yes, serious, too. And there are the ballet girls. One must constantly ask oneself: What can you possibly *say* that won't offend them?! They are unable to comprehend the idea that one prefers taking a walk in a group of two or four rather than in an odd number. I tried to explain it today in passing and was met with icy silence. They will be leaving again on the 17th. I believe Gretl is wholly satisfied with everything we have accomplished.

The scene with the devil for Pallenberg[61] is now complete. I think it will be amusing. Everything has contributed to this flavor, which the thought of Pallenberg helped to make possible. Tomorrow – the day after tomorrow – I'm going to work on the "good deeds"[62] scene for Frau Eysoldt. After this, I will be a bit more flexible. I will only have to find the words to round off the pantomime.[63]

I long for freedom. I must often force myself to work on this present project, but the next one will be a delightful change of pace. I will once

---

60. Grete Wiesenthal had young ballerinas there for rehearsals.
61. Max Pallenberg, actor (1877–1934), performed role of the devil in *Jedermann*.
62. A personality in *Jedermann*.
63. H. v. H. wrote *Amor and Psyche* for the dancer Grete Wiesenthal.

again be at one in a magical sort of harmony with myself *and* with everything else dear to me.

These twenty minutes between the Main and East stations are very precious to me because I was able to see somebody smiling, who seemed almost content. Mary has to leave? It frightens me *et pour cause*,[64] in the light of what transpired in March.

Yours, H.

❦ ❦ ❦

Hinterhör [18 August 1911]

I just got back from a lovely evening walk (it is much better alone than in groups of three or five) during which I wrote you a letter in my mind. I want to write it now so that it will reach you in Aussee. Mother, the sisters, Mary and everyone left for Heuberg this afternoon and will be staying until tomorrow afternoon. I sent the van de Velde children away last Sunday and then enjoyed some wonderful, peaceful days until Thursday; every now and then someone came for tea, but I was alone in the morning and evening. It was so wonderful.

It was with particular enjoyment that I read the chapter about Ben Jonson in the book by Taine, and now I am reading Shakespeare. It is amazing the wealth of thought that one is struck by. Shakespeare's greatness is almost incomprehensible. I especially enjoy reading Taine, as I have become much more accustomed to his style. The considerable effort I put into the first volume is already beginning to pay off.

You returned home a week ago today. How nice the two days we spent in Munich were. I like thinking of them. The beautiful pictures will not disappear; at moments some come to mind very vividly. Sometimes when an especially beautiful picture or sculpture has made a very strong impression on one, one has absolutely no need to possess it, for it is already so much a part of you that it remains forever impressed upon your memory. That is how I feel about the two Greco pictures, the one with the snake in the middle of it and that of the kneeling Christ. And also the little one by Degas with the two ballet girls. I do not quite understand how this happens to be in this place, however, the movement and the colors are right in front of me. I am very grateful to you for showing me all this.

Now you are surely working at a feverish pace. I so hope you will soon be done with everything you are committed to doing. I am so happy for you about the next project which will certainly proceed as you expect. Isn't it almost too much, everything you have to do just now?

---

64. And for a reason.

I recently spent a very delightful afternoon with Robinson.[65] We had tea here at my place and went for a walk. He told me what a powerful impression *Jedermann* [Everyman] made on him and on America in general; it only dragged on a bit too long for him. Then he told me that Ruth St. Denis[66] spent a long time studying the Egyptian costumes at the Metropolitan Museum in New York this winter before performing her Egyptian dance, which he said was wonderful. Surely she will perform it here in Europe this winter as well. I would love to see her sometime.

We still have not had a drop of rain here. Everyone yearns for water. Here in Hinterhör one day, we did not have a drop of water. It was a crime to even think about taking a "bath." The weather is still absolutely perfect and truly wonderful in the evenings. This evening, Mädy and "our godchild" were expected at the castle. Yes, Mary will have to leave soon, whenever her mother is allowed to leave the hospital. I am keeping my youngest sister here, who has already become very good friends with Marie-Therese; things will work out very nicely this way, and there will be no collapse as there was in the spring. It seems questionable, however, whether I will be able to come to Munich for several days then, but perhaps for a day now and then.

How do you like Erwin's "Gerty?"[67] Anything to it?

Give my regards to everyone. I think about Aussee a lot. In me it lives on as it was when we were there together, that is, there aren't any clouds hovering overhead and nothing is dismal or overly serious.

I'll write you Eberhard's address tomorrow.

Faithfully yours, Ottonie.

❦ ❦ ❦

Aussee, 23 August [1911]

Dear Countess,

Your letter was so kind and revealed the true abundance that is in you. So much about it is wonderful, and it is just what the doctor ordered for someone who has suffered torment for the past eight to nine days. Your letter failed to arrive during this time, although many others did day after day, demanding an immediate "answer or explanation," instructions, or a decision or intervention of some kind. New ones arrived *every* morning and *every* afternoon. And answering them was such a drain on my time and nerves, as if, driven by malice, one had cast an unwanted search light into an open camera just when the new film has been placed there and

---

65. Edward Robinson, director of the Metropolitan Museum in New York.
66. American dancer.
67. Erwin Lang painted a portrait of Gerty.

asks for nothing more than the peace and quiet it needs to reveal its object's beauty. Oh, pure and undisturbed thought which provides a glimpse of emerging forms and images in which one can feel oneself and the world and satisfy both – how wonderful! It would be frivolous to expect it to be this way all the time, though. This period, however, was by no means devoid of some very lovely hours. One evening I went for a walk by myself. It was a very brisk walk – up and down hills – and I happened upon a little valley I had never seen before. There was a house – in complete seclusion – behind which there was a deserted rift in a salt mine that had been left half-buried. The house was empty – completely empty – and its doors half-open. In one of the windows were red flowers that had a witch-like glow. In front of the house, large, majestic looking chickens with large round eyes walked back and forth pecking food and completely ignoring the stranger among them. On my way home everything was beautiful, and while walking downhill, across slopes and meadows, I saw you. Yes I saw your full radiance from within and without. I felt your presence in the world and inside me, felt very clearly the gentle balance in our relationship to one another which gently hovered overhead in the air.

Words cannot express how wonderful I find it that you have come to feel this way about Taine's writing. Both this fact and the lines you wrote about Greco's paintings live on for me, continually reemerging in my mind. I would like you to keep – gradually – reading Taine until you reach the part about Milton, but don't go too far beyond this point so as to avoid blurring the image of this wondrous time – beginning with Spenser and ending with Milton – not covering too much too quickly. Then, as soon as I am able to send some more books from Vienna, I'd like for certain volumes to truly become a part of you. In addition to Shakespeare, this would include, for instance, the "faithful shepherdess" and the wonderful little poems Milton wrote. I find it touching – in a very mysterious way – that news about the dancer, St. Denis, reached me through you. Perhaps this little letter of mine may reach her by way of you as well.

Gretl played *Amor und Psyche* for me in the woods yesterday. I was deeply affected and enchanted by the richness of her imagination – what a charming and, in the darker moments, almost gruesome invention, filled with a free-flowing abundance, penetrating intelligence and force. It all brings this together into a unified whole, each element in complete harmony with the others. An image so full of life penetrates the deepest depths of one's heart, yet they disappear the very moment one enjoys them – just as life itself does, in which everything is true, and tender and pure. I have truly participated in three different art forms this year – music, drama, and dance – and not at all by design, but rather by mere happenstance.

I would very much like for you to read *Wahlverwandtschaften* [Elective Affinities by Goethe], and then I'll send you the wonderful book *Goethe über seine Werke* [Goethe on his Works]; there you'll be able to read what he himself and his contemporaries had to say about this wonderful book. I do not know what else could provide me a deeper intellectual atmosphere, and atmosphere is important; one must be able to exist in it, in spite of somber moods.

I still remain hopeful that the agonizing need to continually write letters back and forth will lead to the onetime performance planned for Munich, which has been confronted by 1,001 different obstacles. But it is still only hope, and not yet certainty.

Yours, Hofmannsthal.

❧ ❧ ❧

Hinterhör, Wednesday, 23 August 1911

You have so much to do, so I would at least like to write you a few lines. I really think about you quite a lot – and indeed with pleasure. Do you notice this? Mädy was here today and asked me: "So how was it in Aussee?" So I had a lot to tell her. At the end came: "Say, has H. perhaps fallen in love with you a little bit?" Answer: "Oh, no, God, he just sort of likes me." "Yes, and has he never kissed you?" Answer: "No, only my hand of course." She was full of admiration and said how good this was of me, etc. (I really did feel pretty mean, but it's better this way.) I told her a story that everyone knows: *pas mon genre* (is not my style), and she believes it, too.

Mädy said I definitely have to come to Gastein for two days and asked if I would like to come when you are there, which I answered with a firm no, saying that I had just enjoyed you long enough.

I tell you all of this so you are fully aware of the atmosphere when you meet her, the same for Eberhard. He is staying at the Hotel Austria Bad Gastein.

Apparently I have talked so much about the wonderful Grecos that Julie went to town today with the Robinsons to see them.

It turns out Mary really must go to England on the 29th. My sister will be staying here, which will be a great help to me; only we won't, that is you and I, be able to see a lot of each other, which I find rather sad. Do you realize that I find this truly sad?

I read the lovely letters of Charles-Louis Ph.[ilippe] in the Revue; I liked them so much, I could write you volumes about them, and this is the truth. I will show you this when you come. Oh, God, if only you would really, truly come, it would be *so* wonderful. Bockelchen plans to be here beginning the 16th, probably until the end of Sept. So it might work out after all for a few days in Neubeuern – or if you could stay in Hinterhör, that would be too wonderful; better to not even think of this.

I am so happy for Eberhard that you have made it possible to go to Gastein; after all he seems to be very happy about this prospect. Mädy is going there on Monday and will be staying there during the entire time.

My guests here are not pestering me much; they *constantly* go for long walks and are afraid of getting on my nerves, they read and write at a distance, which works out very well.

Good night. Many, many dear regards to Gerty; I like her so much. However, I wonder if she still remembers me.

Many kind regards,
Ottonie.

Hinterhör, Friday [25 August 1911]

It is amazing how much a letter sometimes can mean to a person. It is as if it gives off light and brightens up a long, hard day as well as those that follow. Even if one was completely satisfied, almost happy, beforehand, all at once the "almost" disappears, and one is truly – truly and completely happy. This was the kind of special day your very, very kind letter brought me today. I just adore this letter. I wonder if you wrote it in the woods while taking a break from your work. It seems to have brought the scent of the forest along with it!

I must have somehow sensed that you were about to suggest I begin reading *Wahlverwandtschaften*, for I went downstairs late Wednesday evening to fetch it and took it back to bed with me.

I will continue with Taine (I love him so much) as you suggested, stopping then after Milton, which will unfortunately be tomorrow.

Did you know that I never would have thought it possible that becoming engrossed in all these wonderful things – books, paintings, dramatic art, music (when available) – could give me so much and is nearly able to replace that which fate had seen fit to rob from me?

This world has so many great things to offer, and once one begins to see it and take it all in, one can learn to *live* and not only vegetate.

Do you know what I simply love about our relationship?! It is that you are always there somewhere and that it does not bother me when we are not together. On the contrary, it's so heavenly knowing that we are connected to one another – but in a very subtle way. It is not a painful connection, but a most delightful one. I do not long for you at all, although it would be wonderful to have you here; however it is almost as nice receiving letters. I suppose you cannot feel this as deeply as I can because you get short-changed in our correspondence.

The Robinsons are gone, but I am going to send him the letter for Ruth St. Denis and ask that he forward it to her. How I would love to see her if she were to perform one of her new dance routines in Germany.

It is a pity Mr. Robinson is gone. I like him very much. He is somewhat older, but he would almost be my "type."

I enjoyed our conversations very much.

I will be going to Munich for the *Orestie* on the second and *Orpheus* on the fourth, that is, if Frau Lindemann still can get seats. I have specially arranged the trip so that I can take my mother along, giving her a send-off on her trip home. Will you all be coming to Munich as soon as sometime around the fifth? Because you said something to Mädy about going to Gastein around the end of this or the beginning of next month and something about wanting this to coincide with the trip from Munich to Gastein? It just seems like it's coming up so terribly soon.

I am using a pencil because I am already in bed and not because I'm sick or something.

Well, good night for now. Much belongs to you of a certain

Ottonie.

P.S. I will not be returning here from Munich until the fifth, so perhaps we can meet each other there.

❦ ❦ ❦

Aussee, Thursday [31 August 1911]

Yesterday toward evening I had such a powerful feeling of your presence, more than I have ever felt it; I was consumed by it. Then, as the rain poured down on the roof just above my bed during the thunderstorm that night, the delightful feeling became more and more pronounced. Closeness or presence? I'm not sure what to call it. It's not a physical presence. It has something to do with your approaching with great receptivity. I perceived your very being – that is it really. It is a matter of perceiving your being, which is in no way directly connected to your physical presence. You are often there, very close by, and I would wish to perceive your being but that I am not granted. I lay awake and felt the suspense building as the feeling grew, becoming stronger, more pronounced, more true – while everything remained the same the whole time. Somehow the vision of a distant countryside surrounded by a strange light was associated with it all. It was a distant, yet cheerful *presence*. I had many revealing thoughts, but I retained nothing save an enduring sense of happiness, encouragement. It was surely the life of your most recent letter sustaining itself in this semi-dream. I love everything about this letter; it seems so kind. It provides an assurance of a positive inner state. And the lovely, very simple way you begin to feel, in a way I sometimes do, what I, trembling, restless, sometimes see as the only possibility. And what you said about Taine; everything taken together is right.

I sometimes think about the scruples, personal restrictions and reluctance one has – rather dark moments these are. Everything seems incredibly *good* the way things are now, so touching, so magical – I cannot express it any other way. (At the same time, I don't deny that certain moments full of pain may arise. However, this is all much more mysterious, much more wonderful, than one could ever imagine.)

(I will have to hurry up and finish writing so that this can still be sent off.)

If you have come to love Taine, then everything I wished for has been achieved. Please continue reading him to the end. Then you shall never have any difficulty rereading the parts concerning this great epoch.

(Months ago) once when reading through Charles Louis Philippe's letters I had vivid images of you. Something in them caused me to make a connection to you – and now it's come to be.

I hope the book, *Goethe über seine Werke*, as well as Vollmöller's[68] *Orestie* have reached you by now. I will be in Gastein (Hotel Austria) beginning tomorrow evening until Monday afternoon. There I hope to find a telegram announcing whether *Jedermann* will be performed in Munich. But *at any rate* I will be returning here from Gastein for a week. Should *Jedermann* end up *not* being performed (which I believe to be a very likely scenario despite Reinhardt's good intentions), I have nevertheless made arrangements to travel with Papa and Gerty to Munich around the middle of September so that I may be spared the uncertainty of not knowing whether or not I will see you. Further, I am also seeing to it that I don't have to pose for the sculptor Behn in September. Instead, I will schedule him a time in November or December and will travel to Munich "for this purpose alone." I proposed to Papa a short trip to Berlin and Copenhagen for the end of September. Then I will spend a few days with Gerty in Bremen on the way back. In any case, I will stick to my plans to meet you in about two weeks time so that we, too, don't lose sight of one another – hopefully not for weeks on end again.

It would be lovely to receive a pencil letter in Gastein.

H.

---

68. K. J. Vollmöller, author and translator.

Sunday, Hinterhör, [2] September [1911]

There is no longer time to send a pencil letter to Gastein, but instead, these lines will greet you once you return home to your lovely little house. If only I had you here; I would like *so* much to chat with you about so many things, especially now. You are certainly all enjoying this incredibly beautiful moonlit night together in G.; I am happy for Bockelchen, knowing that he has you there; however, I cannot deny that I would indeed much prefer to have you here. Actually I would have liked to remain outside, but as I wanted to write you a letter, undisturbed, I decided to lie down in bed.

It is almost *too* wonderful picking up on the lovely little signs that someone (whom one likes) is devoting his attention to you. So I could not help feeling very moved when *Orestie* arrived. It was very kind that you thought to send it to me beforehand.

Well, we went to town yesterday. *Orestie*. I am still so *excited*! Reinhardt really did a splendid job with it. Words cannot express how wonderful and gripping it is. My mind is still full of thoughts of *Orestie*: events, images – one is followed by another, and inside me I can still hear Moissi's incredibly moving organ sounding out. The splendidly *charming* organ together with *this* play – no, it was not play; it was life that he showed us. I will never forget the impressions I received there. Oh, the excitement of the thousands who sat listening! There was something magnanimous about it. What a pity it would be if you two do not manage to hear him. Actually I was planning to go into town on Tuesday again to see *Orpheus*, however, as you are not coming to Munich now, I am going to send my sister there with Müller.

I made Müssigbrot[69] happy today by giving him a ticket to the *Oresteia*; he was smiling from ear to ear. We did not get back until this evening, so just received your letter also. I was sure I would find it here and let it welcome me. It is so ridiculous that I always forget right away what I've written you; so of course I cannot remember what I said in my last letter – what may have made you happy, and what did not. But what does this matter. There was something about the last letter you liked, and that is good enough for me.

Just like Bettina Brentano,[70] I sacrificed a beautiful moonlit night to the *Wahlverwandtschaften*. I was so happy I did not read it for a long time and had *never* before really understood it. It was a *vast* treasure and rarely has anything made such a *deep* impression on me. Often it is frightening how profoundly Goethe understands people's souls and how he stirs subtle,

---

69. A coachman at the castle who was an enthusiast for literature.
70. An admirer of Goethe.

hidden feelings within you which you hardly dare to acknowledge to yourself. It is very interesting reading Gräf's book at the same time.

I very much like Abeken's discussion of *Wahlverwandtschaften*. It is a book one can read over and over again, each time discovering something new. It grips and carries one off. It's so stupid writing all this; I would love to discuss it with you and tell you about all the wonderful passages that took complete hold of me. I feel I should read it again right away in order to absorb everything I found there. Surely each person reads the same book in a different way, depending upon his understanding.

I am as happy as a little child that you wrote, "Finish reading Taine"! You know, I was just about to return to him because I could not bring myself to part with him so quickly.

What wonderful plans you have made – two trips to Munich before Christmas! Should I really believe it?! It is almost too good to be true. And then I hope you will be coming at Christmas. I am sure you discussed that in a friendly manner. It is so nice looking forward to seeing and talking to each other again. Getting letters is *delightful* (do you know how much I like getting certain ones?), but I suppose it is even more pleasant being able to talk to each other. It was not half as nice yesterday at the Maximilianstrasse[71] as it had been last time; also being with "nurses" seems better than with "mothers", who give you a powder right away. Should I keep on chatting like this, or quickly, quickly, say good night.

Mr. Robinson wrote that the task of forwarding the letter is rather a hard commission and can't be taken care of all that quickly. That is, he has to search for Ruth St. Denis, who is on tour in the States. But he said with enough patience he will manage. Gretl will also be performing soon. Please tell her how often I have thought of her and wanted to send very best wishes.

Have you perhaps thought of asking Wassermann to sign the *Schwestern* (the sisters?) Please do not forget this, for otherwise he might be offended "if the Countess asks so little about his works."

I wish you a very good night. If you think such kind things about me, then just continue doing so.

All yours, Ottonie

P.S. Julie is being so nice to me now and does not disturb me at all, so I am very happy – if it will only last! Unfortunately a bit of a chill has set in between her and Mädy, and it happened as a result of the "Wunderkind." Mädy touched her at her sorest point with a silly remark she made. Ridiculous!

---

71. Address of a small apartment Julie kept in Munich.

❦ ❦ ❦

[Bad Aussee] Wednesday, [6 September 1911] 10:00 a.m., park bench

Recently I was extremely restless and so close to sending you a telegram with each passing hour until the lovely, kind, little pencil letter *finally* arrived here this morning. Yet this came so late if it was indeed written Sunday evening – and didn't arrive until today on Wednesday. And the whole time I was so sure mine would reach you *before* the trip to Munich. I expected to find yours each day in Gastein – then back here on Monday it did not arrive, nor Tuesday morning, nor Tuesday evening. It's always agonizing feeling so impatient when experiencing a *general* feeling of restlessness. You won't have any difficulty understanding how I feel right now. There's so much I have to try to bring together and so much to think over. I'm certain now I can't make it to Neubeuern, not even for a couple days – but I do know that I will be in Munich for four days. Eberhard will be inviting you to come to Gastein. I am not sure if you'll accept. However, *if* you do, I hope more than anything you'll arrange to visit during the last part of his stay in Gastein – then return with him and Mädy on the 14th, but not straight to Neubeuern. Instead, I hope you can stay with us in Munich for a day or two, which I will urge Eberhard to do as well. We will be in Munich from the evening of the 13th to the evening of the 17th, which can no longer be changed. Reinhardt's last message included the *decision* not to perform *Jedermann* in Munich. We will be following through with the plans we made a long time ago to take a little trip with Papa in order to amuse him. So we'll be in Munich for four days (it won't be possible to fit in a trip to Neubeuern during this time) and then to Berlin, and Copenhagen. I will be in Bremen with Gerty the first week of October to visit Schröder. Then I want Gerty to accompany me on the way home via Munich-Neubeuern. I think it's a good time now to spend a few days with Gerty in Neubeuern again – indeed it would make things easier having her along. On the way back from Copenhagen/Berlin I will be going to see the pantomimes in Berlin and will discuss all the essentials of *Jedermann* with Reinhardt. I hope to be able to find a couple of quiet months for myself to work on the comedy. If you *do not* come to Gastein, you will at any rate still be in Munich from the 14th to the 17th, right? Even if it turns out that Eberhard and Mädy *will not* be staying in Munich (which doesn't seem likely to me)?

Gretl has been gone from here for a long time – she has been in Berlin for days now participating in the most taxing rehearsals. She has taken on a great deal, almost too much. There is nothing more I can help her with – nor Erwin either. The poor boy was ill the last few days here – a high temperature and extreme weakness. Everyone was trembling with fear (this was around twelve days ago). Then his fever left him, but he was paralyzed on one side of his face. The one cheek was completely stiff, mouth contorted. He had to travel to Vienna in this condition, weak and miserable. The doctors reassure us it has nothing to do with his brain and that it is rheumatic; he should be over it in a few weeks. He was very sick this past winter and has never recovered – he was constantly overextending himself and draining every last bit of his nerves. Good thing he's 25, so he should be over it in a few months.

You are always so quick to forget what you wrote in your last letter and ask me what about them I look forward to, what it is that moves me so and makes me happy. Do you really mean to ask me this question? The feeling that a person whom one is fond of is living her own life, that she has come back to life, and hearing that you almost feel happy – perhaps only a few hours at a time, but still these few hours exist. The lines you wrote about the moonlit night – knowing you were there, feeling you under the moonlight in this peace, yourself undisturbed, the peace and quiet flowing about you, through you. The *life* you revealed when absorbing *Orestie* and trembling with joy afterwards – the sign of inner life, *your* life. The loss of that rigidness, the lovely, very moving attachment you felt to a book you came to love and wish to read again. The same thing may be found in your eyes when they observe something – and are *free* – as well as in the movement of your hands. What else is there to say? What could be so astonishing about this? How could I fail to be happy, to not be deeply moved inside and to gaze towards a Hinterhör I dreamed about.

I feel this way whenever I think about it and must look up towards the sky. I feel in my thoughts or when my eyes choose to turn in the right geographic direction of the sky – not praising God – this word just slipped into my pen but it is not the right word. What you said about Julie – that she's figured out what's necessary and is willing to come to terms with it – means an extra bonus and is indeed an unexpected gain. Every single person who has had the chance to listen to or watch your *Ariadne*[72] likes it very much. It makes me so happy when anyone talks about it; to me it seems as if we are looking at each other.

Write soon, please!

H.

Bad Gastein, Friday, [8 September] 1911

It really did not work out well at all with our letters this time, in both directions, because people are being sent here to me on Wednesday. I am very glad that I at least sent you a telegram before I left so that you had

---

72. Here H. v. H. acknowledges that he wrote the libretto with O. D. S. in mind.

some idea of where I would be. I made a very quick decision to take a short trip here, mainly as a matter of principle in order to show Julie that I'm free to move around as I please. Actually I really did not like having to leave Marie-Therese alone with my sister; I am not completely comfortable with the idea of this. If M.-T. happens to come down with the sniffles (which is not taken lightly in our home), this would be held against me *forever* (it would be attributed to the Schwartz craving for pleasure), but right now, this is of much less importance to me than demonstrating my freedom.

How strange it is to travel to Salzburg and *not* have someone there waiting for me. Instead I spent an hour there, then to pass Hellbrunn with its Morgenpark and the entire dear place – alone and yet very happy at the thought of Salzburg. But did you know that no trip without a "nurse" ends migraine-free – not even a short trip to Munich?! It is strange, but that is the way it is.

It is lovely here. I am very much enjoying Bockelchen, who is cheerful and kind. I wanted to write you yesterday, but we went for a long, leisurely walk together all morning, chatting about all sorts of things. Afterwards I had to rest for a while, and then we hiked to the "Green Tree"[73] and did not get home until after nine o'clock. I was dead tired then and slept wonderfully the entire night. The air here is magnificent, kind of like in Aussee. B. was rather upset at first because I said I felt too shut in here and preferred being on the lake, but today we were in Böckstein. I drove there alone in the automobile and then we walked back together, and then I really found it *wonderful* there, simply splendid in every respect. I have the same view from my room here that you two had when you were here; it really is very pretty.

The Bockelchens remain overjoyed by the thought of your being here and are very moved by the friendship you show them by your willingness to travel so far to see them. He seems *much happier* with his position now, which of course is plain to see in everything he's involved with. I hope the time spent in Gastein will allow him to have a better winter health-wise.

Both of them are very *impressed* by *Ariadne*. I felt like I was being given a wonderful gift when Eberhard made *such* charming comments about it. I really feel like I am a part of it – do you think this is presumptuous? Well, it really does not matter!

I am *very* sad to hear that *Jedermann* will not be performed in Munich, but I suppose this would have been *too* much of a good thing for me in a single year. Will it be performed in Berlin this winter? So you won't be coming to Neubeuern. That *really* is a pity. But, of course, there is nothing to be done about it. We were all looking forward to seeing you. Bock-

---

73. Famous hotel and restaurant there.

elchen does not think he will be able to make it to Munich. He has to be careful with his follow-up cure and needs a lot of rest. I am also thinking of going to Munich on the 13th, and then we could meet each other there on the 14th and I would return to Hinterhör on the 15th. But please think about whether or not my presence there might be more of a disturbance to you as you will have so much to discuss with all sorts of different people. And knowing that I am there and that you might not be able to find a free moment would surely be distressing to you, or would it not?

It would be very nice if you came to Neubeuern together sometime. Only Mädy would also have to be there; otherwise it is out of the question in my opinion, even with Gerty. There could well be moments that would only be unpleasant for *all* of us.

Poor Erwin. I feel so terribly sorry for him and Gretel and thought for a second about maybe inviting Erwin to Hinterhör where he might regain his health with the proper care. We could discuss this the next time we are together. How horribly difficult it must be for Gretel having to work in Berlin with all this on her mind.

Your letter was so dear today. Yes, I understand very well this self-debilitation; indeed I experience it myself much too often. I hope for your sake that you first have the days in Munich behind you so that you feel calm when leaving to go on the nice little trip. And then hopefully there will be nice, pleasant moments for the comedy, during which you will feel very happy. This letter is dry and dull, however, I want to say good night and to bring it to a close, so that it can still be sent off with the other mail tonight.

Thinking of you a lot,

Yours, Ottonie.

P.S. Should I receive word that Marie-Th. is not entirely well, I will of course have to go home and leave out Munich.

[Bad Gastein] Sunday [10 September 1911]

Your letter to Eberhard arrived this morning, who right away sent you a telegram. You probably were astonished that the date of my stay in Munich is different from the one in my letter from yesterday. Eberhard found it very silly of me to stay here for such a short time. As the fresh air is doing me so much good and I am sleeping so well, relatively speaking, he urged me to stay longer. I am doing them a favor then in that I will be able to take Karin, who is coming here on Wednesday, with me back to Rosenheim. It may be that you prefer I not come until later; then I suppose everything you need to discuss will be taken care of. I will arrive then at 3:50 p.m. in Munich; maybe you could meet me at the train station; we could go to the flat, where I could spend a moment getting ready, and then I would come along to see Gerty and Papa. However, this is just a vague suggestion, which can be arranged completely differently from the way I have things in mind right now.

I urged the couple[74] to go out by themselves so that I could have a quiet afternoon for myself. I spent the entire morning taking a walk with E., who told me about his affair in Berlin and wanted to know what I thought about it from a woman's point of view. I must admit that I find it entirely all right for him, also that he is fully able to explain it to Mädy, should the unfortunate circumstance come about that she happens to find out. Of course he must never admit to her the entire breadth and depth of his involvement there, but rather must view everything more casually, as one of many such instances. I also find that E. himself is profiting *immensely* here, and I suppose it is this inner harmony that he now exudes, which has attained such a state of peace (in contrast to the never-ending seeking in the past), not only stems from a better position in Essen, but in large part also from the rest that he finds there. I find that Mädy benefits tremendously from the whole thing; E. has developed such a kind disposition in the past two to three years, whose source I suppose is in his complete satisfaction in Berlin, of course next to the improved situation in Essen. I think the feeling of still being able to completely infuse such a young creature with oneself as a mature man who has been married for years must provide one with a tremendous feeling of satisfaction, indeed, make one feel younger and refreshed. Following this conversation I told him some things about our relationship to one another. I found this to be a very good opportunity, and E. can be *so* useful, especially this winter, when I intend to go to Berlin for *Ariadne* (my Ariadne), that I believe you would only approve. He understood everything so very well and was so happy for me to have you as I do, that it was just delightful.

It really is so wonderful to be with people with whom one feels a deep understanding and to discuss and deal with things in *such* a way that one sometimes escapes from the trivialities of everyday life. On the other hand, I don't experience anything of the unpleasantness every day in my little idyll in Hinterhör either, for you have made it so lovely for me there with the wonderful books as well as by always writing me new, *dear* letters. I felt again today by the way I spoke of you to E., *how important* you have become for me – may this *never, ever ever* be ruined. While writing letters I always look out the window; it feels as if I am outside, oh, and I find it so beautiful and wish that you could sit here with me, enjoying everything together and then you could tell me a story. But it is not agonizing for me to be alone, for inside I am not at all.

---

74. The Bodenhausens.

Well now I want to read something from the *Wahlverwandtschaften*, which I love so much. Please write me again soon; I *enjoy* your letters *so* much, but if a lot is piling up for you now, don't write, for above all I do not want to cause you anguish by making you feel you have to write when your time is so precious.

Yours truly, Ottonie D.

🍎 🍎 🍎

[Bad Aussee] Monday, [11 September 1911] 5 o'clock

I have four minutes left before the mail is picked up. Your second letter just arrived. I'm very unhappy that it supplants the first one as regards Munich. So you won't be there on the 14th and not on the 15th – not until the evening of the 16th! And I'll be leaving the evening of the 17th. This makes me very sad. And all the while I have *nothing* to do there. There's *not a single* person I have to meet. I'll be stuck there four days for no reason. I arranged all this so that I'd have a chance to see you; otherwise it would be much easier for us to travel to Berlin by way of Vienna. I thought we could go see *Orpheus* some evening, but it's all just the same. Your seat will simply remain empty. Each day you spend in Gastein is certainly good for your health, but hopefully you'll end up coming on the 15th, okay, and I will pick you up at the station!

I will find a line from you in Marienbad, won't I, when I arrive Wednesday evening.

Yours H.

🍎 🍎 🍎

Hallstadt, Noontime Tuesday, on a bike ride [12 September 1911]

Dear Countess,

Was driving with Wassermann through the mountains – he was looking into the water and probably had no idea I was writing a letter to a countess. We have been having a wonderful time here recently – how I wish you were here.

You cannot begin to picture the landscape here with the many transparent shadows, the reflection of the mountains in the water, and the playful little waves collapsing against the shore! Every tree and every house stand proudly *in their own* quiet splendor – *what* beauty there is in the world!

Also yesterday morning your first letter arrived. It seemed a bit strange, but that doesn't matter, I thought to myself; it is a result of the unfamiliar surroundings in Gastein and the different room where she writes her letters. I took my bike and rode through the woods down along Grundelsee [Lake Grundel]. Someone was playing Beethoven in one of the villas. It was lovely the way it sounded through the still, sunlit air. As I rode along the lake, I talked to you, wrote you, and thought about your letter. You had many lovely things to say – about Salzburg and *Ariadne* and about Eberhard and what you find appealing about him. I sat down on a tree stump and leafed through an issue of the *Revue Française*. I came across the name "Charles Louis Philippe," which brought me back to you again. I sat there reading, just thinking, and I felt happy.

I recently went for a walk alone one evening. The moon had not come out yet. It was dark and rather murky, even nicer than it had been; it was indescribable. The strong presence of the little houses, and here and there a tree greeted the man who approached. The country here is filled with both a past and a presence for me – my youth seems so near, yet without there being a trace of longing or sentimentality. Here I am, here I live, and here I shall die. And just as it does now, the darkness overhead will rest itself against Mount Dachstein, and still, I am attached to everything; I belong here just as it all does. The sound of folk music rang out from somewhere in a ravine down below. Everything was there, for once and forever.

My dear, I was much too rushed when I wrote you the short letter yesterday. This was hasty and selfish of me. I would rather I had not written it. Go ahead and stay up there in the pure mountain air while we are having such wonderful, sunny weather. Do not come until the 16th, or not at all. We will see each other in October. No, not at all, indeed by no means should you wish instead to stay up there a while longer if I happen to discover a very nice, very cheerful letter from Ottonie D. in Marienbad. Ottonie *D.*, not without the "D" of course. In a number of letters of recent weeks you were careless enough to forget the "D." "O. D. S." would also be quite pretty, especially on luggage. Or perhaps simply "D. S." without any trace of a first name! However, the best thing to write would be: "Administration of the Country Residence, Hinterhör; Raubling Post Office, respectfully." Yes, this would be the best way to sign your letters!

Oh, it really doesn't matter, if only you see to it that you *live* a bit. The harlequin sings it better than I express it in words.[75] Just *do not* come then! Eberhard wrote me a very sincere and touching thank-you letter. He makes much too much of me as a person. I'm really not so special at all, oh God I'm not.

Then you just will not come to Munich period. (In which case you will have followed my well-considered advice.)

Adieu, love.

H.

---

[75] Cf. the poem, pages xlii–xliii of this book.

❦ ❦ ❦

[Hotel Adlon, Berlin–W.] Tuesday, [19 September 1911] 7 o'clock

You can't imagine how *wonderful* the pantomimes are. We'll be leaving in an hour to go see them for a second time. Gretl is enchanting, so moving, all in one, revealing a tremendous wealth of expression. I was so afraid I'd think it was awful, and then afterwards of course, I was twice as happy and in high spirits. Really, the *whole* thing is good and right. Erwin's contributions have been terrific, each one perfectly suited to the performance. It is all much better, much more powerful and convincing than in the script. Lili Berger[76] is very attractive. The "rich young man" is a very elegant, handsome man. The people in the audience clap along in accompaniment to him.

And what has been happening here? Absolutely nothing. The premiere was rather flat. After five weeks, nobody will remember this, and it is slowly becoming a great success and will be performed throughout Europe, England, America. The agents have a sense for this ahead of time and are making large offers (up to 20,000 Marks for one month). Everyone is pleased. The telegram was completely unnecessary, all the headaches and also the 25 minute train delay!

We had a lovely lunch today. Gretl, Erwin, Lili Berger, and Gerhart Hauptmann, who just happens to be staying here in the hotel, were there, as well as the painter, König. Tomorrow we're going to a premiere in the *Lessingtheater*. We'll be leaving Thursday evening and arriving Friday morning in Copenhagen – Hotel d'Angleterre. The pantomimes contain such beautiful, yes nearly perfect, moments, especially when Amor brings Psyche back to life. And then in the bedroom, where the woman who had been tied down glides across the room, so dreamlike and fully within herself. I wished so much you were there, and Gerty said, "If only Ottonie could see this." We were able to create something truly wonderful and good and true in which possibilities were realized, and this makes me very happy.

In these moments – it's strange – that sinister torment, the terrible shame that had plagued me ever since that moment in Munich disappeared, and since then, it hasn't returned. One should never think, "One thing has nothing to do with the other." There are indeed very mysterious, very profound relationships between things.

Erwin will be very happy and touched if someone would be kind enough to send him an invitation to Hinterhör. The poor, handsome boy, all disfigured. Gretl, too, will be very happy. Possibly this could be ar-

---

76. Dancer who danced the part of Amor in *Amor and Psyche*.

ranged for the beginning of October (around the 5th). Gerty also liked him, and all is well. His address is: Pension Bruhn, Nürnbergerstrasse 65. Adieu, adieu, adieu.

H.

[Hotel d'Angleterre, Copenhagen] Sunday [24 September 1911] evening

Day after day a lovely little pencil letter has still not arrived, neither here nor in Berlin. However, Gerty received a charming little card containing much information and many kind words about how well one is feeling, etc., so I am calm and content.

I can't write now either. I'm acting as a travel agent so that Papa's little rest and relaxation trip will be properly arranged for him. As a result of this and the change in location, I feel very worn out, and my head is nothing more than an empty casing. Our stay in Copenhagen has come to an end. We'll be in Berlin tomorrow evening and will stay there until the 29th. We'll be seeing Reinhardt's production of *Penthesilea* with Moissi and Eysoldt (in the meantime someone in Hinterhör will remain in close contact as she reads *Penthesilea* and skims through Kleist's letters, right?), and afterwards we will leave for Bremen. This is all just a roundabout way to reach Hinterhör. Good night there.

H.

P.S. Address from the 26th–29th: Berlin, Hotel Adlon.

[Telegram]   [Berlin, 27 September 1911, 11:30 morning.]

Confused by continued silence I don't dare announce a visit there Would be very grateful for a short telegram Hotel Adlon

[Hotel Adlon, Berlin-W.] Friday [29 September 1911]

I still have not received the short letter you sent to Copenhagen. I am going to try claiming it again. Well, we're leaving for Bremen (Hillmanns Hotel) this evening and I think we'll be staying there for four or five days. Rudi sent a telegram saying he plans to have a group of skilled musicians play his new quartet for us on Sunday in a house he has grown to know quite well. Is he not a multifaceted being? I am so glad that all the people who are meaningful to me are gradually coming to mean something to you, too, and that they also exist for you and you have such kind and spirited recollections of them. And how I love that you are learning French! (I don't mean for there to be a trace of blind adoration here.)

Hauptmann's very handsome twelve-year-old boy just knocked on the door with his *Stammbuch*.[77] I wrote my favorite saying in it for him: "The whole man must move at once." And while I write here in the reading room, Erwin is sitting outside in the Adlon lobby, pale and strained, negotiating with English agents about whether Gretl is to receive 28,000 Marks for a month's work in London or only 24,000. Yesterday we planned to go to the airfield with Vollmöller to watch his nice, little nineteen-year-old brother fly a plane, but the weather turned bad and it was cancelled. Instead we went to Wagner's lovely Japanese shop, and we came across a very handsome Chinese coat there. It was given to Gretl as a gift, and she was as happy as a child. Gretl is also performing another magnificently charming dance *in addition* to the mimes. It's a Hungarian dance, with a folk-like character to it – she wears pigtails and the atmosphere is very jovial, sensuous and cheerful. It's very charming and very graceful. The audience applauds like mad, and I thought to myself about twenty different times, with each new movement: "You should be here, Ottonie, watching this!"

Yesterday evening we enjoyed a pleasant, quiet hour with Max Reinhardt. We were alone with him in the little theater restaurant and made plans, plans and more plans. The summer after next we're going to present Euripides' *Bacchae* in the twilight of the ancient Vindonissa Theater outside Zürich. Gretl will lead the choir of hundreds of torch-bearing, young girls. And who will be watching? Of course! Even if Julie believes that's *not* a good enough reason to take a trip to Zürich.

I will leave the very best for the next time we are in the woods. It concerns yesterday's performance of *Penthesilea* – and not Frau Eysoldt. The role was played by a young, upcoming actress named Mary Dietrich – how well I've already become acquainted with this name! This is not just a matter of wishful thinking; it's rather as if she has already become the great actress she will be in the future. She's the best thing to come along since Moissi and would make a wonderful partner for him. She'd be terrific as the princess in my comedy, as the "Good Deeds" in *Jedermann* (alternating with Frau Eysoldt) – and who knows what else?! Frau Eysoldt fell ill. They gave the young creature forty-eight hours to master her role. She cries, doesn't want to continue, changes her mind, goes out onto the stage, so young and slender and beautiful – of the innermost spiritual beauty. She plays her role and is able to carry away the audience along with her. There are moments when she manages to bring chills up and down one's spine. She was called out onto the stage four times by the wild

---

77. Autograph book.

applause. It was wonderful to be there. I then went to the stage door and told her how well I thought she performed. She came out, this earnest young girl. Her father was there as well, and her mother, in from Mecklenburg – from their estate – arrived too late. They were excited yet seemingly calm. What a strange, triumphant beginning.

Erwin and Gretl are delighted to have received such a kind and charming letter from Hinterhör, however, he is really not able to visit right now. One has to realize that he is simply unable to.

It would also be very nice to receive a letter like this in Bremen.

With love (of the non-smothering variety),

H.

[Neubeuern, 12 October 1911]

Dear Countess,

Perhaps you will find the time to skim through your Stifter some time and dig up a story for me that is significantly shorter than *The Mappe* [The Folder] and that you like. And then also try to find "Die Ruine" [The Ruins] and "Die Fischlein in der Pfanne" [The Little Fish in the Pan] in *Hochwald* [The Timber Forest], please, and write it down for me in the handwriting that I, despite everything, find very legible and dearly love.

I close with my best wishes, in which you are very close by, so close as if we were separated only by a small area of space and the ticking of a clock in a cozy room off somewhere with an autumn landscape outside that we both delight in.

Yours, H.

[Rodaun] Friday evening [20 October 1911]

I have the feeling you're in Munich and this letter will have to wait for you. Or perhaps this is not the case. The period of transition was incredibly easy for me this time. We were traveling, and the following morning here we had the same bright, somewhat misty weather and just the same cool warmth. The autumn is beginning to consume the spring intruder, and winter will soon arrive with a single blast, here and there. The distance between here and Hinterhör is not all that real or concrete; it seems insignificant to me now. If nothing – no unexpected obstacle – came along to block the path so to speak, one could make it to Hinterhör in one and a half hours by bike from here; if the road's covered with ice, then two and a half hours by horse. It wouldn't be possible to make the trip every day, but easily a couple times a week.

Everything went smoothly today. I had no trouble writing Max Reinhardt and was able to express myself the way I wanted to. We saw Behn[78] in Munich. I could see a lot of what was going on inside him through the tone of his voice and his facial expressions (without actually talking to him), all the fragility, peril, pending doom. I can also understand very well how Gerty manages to soothe him. And I suddenly understood why I could never be jealous – even if she were to give herself fully to someone in this way. It's because everything in her – of which she herself is not aware – is directed towards doing good.

Afterwards – Behn had to meet someone, apparently a woman – the three of us kidded around quite a lot. At Bernheimer's[79] I took along a beautiful, blue Chinese silk blanket. Mädy wanted to know what I needed it for, whether as a tablecloth or on a bed. (I really don't need it at all. I just thought it was very attractive and decided to take it.) So I said to Mädy: "I need it for travelling. When one spends the night with a girlfriend in an ugly hotel room in Nordhausen or Bebra or Sangershausen or Probstzella, one needs to have a blanket like that along." Mädy said I would first have to pick out from among all my girlfriends one with the proper hair color to match the bright, light blue color of the blanket. Then Gerty said that wouldn't be difficult because, according to her, I have girlfriends with every sort of hair color in many different cities throughout Germany. To this Mädy quickly added that she could easily believe that and that she thought I was in love with them all and that that was the strange thing about me. Then I said, "Yes, of course. With all of them at the same time, just like I'm in love with both of you at the same time. So you can see the 'at the same time' here is no problem at all." Then they both laughed and were very charming.

I find it all very puzzling, though. I can't even come close to putting my finger on any of it. Could there in fact be some truth to it or none at all? Who am I really? And how is it I have come to wonder about all this? And am I making too much of it or not? What characters! In any case, I certainly do have a charming wife and a delightful girlfriend. Now I'm able to see her, very distinctly; I haven't lost sight of her – I see her running and standing, getting tired, resting against something, then jumping up and walking around all about. I just love her, when she is afraid and when she is happy, when laughing or when she has a serious look, with-

---

78. Fritz Behn, sculptor.
79. Famous antique and decorating shop, in both Munich and Venice.

out desire and yet with a little bit of desire – but always *gently*; she is hurt by anything that is not gentle. I just really do love her, you know the one.
Good night.

H.

P.S. And as far as the others are concerned, besides these two, that's just a game. By the way, I find relationships with men are just as puzzling.

❦ ❦ ❦

[Rodaun] Wednesday, 25 October [1911], 7:00 in the evening

Well, these awful "gripes" have found their way into another letter and into my memory again, too; especially in trying moments, they're numbingly painful to endure. Perhaps it would be completely unbearable – thoughts of mine like this can become *excruciatingly* agonizing – were there not also something trivial and truly laughable about it. Right after the first negative thing you wrote, a very distinct thought formed in my mind: "Strange that she isn't concerned with how I take this. I would find this odious, but that is what she said, and it didn't seem to bother her." This is how the letter continued, with my rather fierce attempt to make clear to myself this symbolic opposition between Beethoven and a conversation about income tax fraud. I was quite alarmed and amazed – once you finally cut me off, but I was also satisfied to a certain degree. Now this won't ever happen again, of course. Regarding the matter about the letters (the ones that had fallen out of the file in N., a state of disorder that you'd never find here), I gave an extremely detailed verbal answer between two and three o'clock in the morning last night (I imagined writing a letter), and I don't wish to repeat it – it's too great a strain. I'm trying to get the most I can out of each day now. I enjoy quiet hours here, especially in the evening. I alternate between reading various rather difficult books, among them both translations of Homer (to which I am devoting a great deal of my attention), etc.

Gretl is also leading a serious and austere life now. Erwin said she is dancing every day in front of a horde of philistines, which is very tough indeed. Sometimes she feels like she's tunneling through a sinister mountain – Miss St. Denis felt this way, too. Gretl lies in bed for long periods of time and afterwards is rather morose; she goes to the theater and cries while putting on her makeup; and then she dances very well, however, and goes to bed, etc. London will be more tolerable for her than Dresden, and she'll be taking a break in February.

As a second work of Shakespeare's you should read *As You Like It* in place of *A Winter's Tale*. It's impossible to describe the tenderness found there, and it's so cheerful and down to earth.

Hebbel's diaries are on the way to you along with Shakespeare. Just give it a try. If it weighs on you and seems too great a bulk (similar to Cesar Birotteau), then stop right there and write me a letter letting me know. However, I anticipate quite the contrary, like with the letters of Lenau. It's not necessary to be acquainted with Hebbel beforehand. The reading of this incomparable diary would amaze one still more had this strange, dark man burned all his other works – in which are hidden the secrets of his life – and only this diary along with a few fragments of his letters had remained extant. It will be worth a great deal if you are able to endure reading it. It is a mirror, from which a single face observes you – and at the same time, the entire world. If you are unable to bear the sight of this face, then just put down the mirror. If one were to read Hebbel's diaries and the story of Lucien Rubempré's youth (*Illusions perdues*) at the same time, some strange parallels would become perceptible and with it the aroma which pervaded the most important decades of the nineteenth century: the 1830s and 1840s.

I have a number of things to write today, so I have to stop now. Just because no mention is made of fondness does not mean the letter was written without emotion. Being really fond of someone means being able to understand him, becoming truly aware of the other person's individual existence; I have felt this again very intensely in recent days.

Good night.

H.

P.S. Has the Gräf book turned up??

[Rodaun] Wednesday, 1st [November 1911], evening

The evenings here are long, peaceful and pleasant. When the children have gone downstairs, it is possible to read a difficult book and to try to approach higher, purer intellectual insights. It is a forward movement, slow and uncertain, and from time to time an uplifting experience. And then one finds oneself slipping back again, back down like pebbles down a cliff. It is astonishing how feeble my mind is when it comes to absorbing certain things. However, I know the proper thing to do and will not relent. Here, too, one can find the answer after a number of years. Plato and Kant, these two names encompass everything I strive to really understand. It is amazing how such objects of one's aspiration can fit into the most intimate and barely comprehensible of one's own insights – the former addressing the latter as if some prior kinship were involved. I am neither capable of formulating this in words nor even thoughts.

I wanted so much to write to you a couple of evenings ago. I almost felt as if you were staying here in the blue room; I could hear you climbing the stairs. Yet sometimes one must do what is harder and less pleasant, and so I wrote to Julie. I hope it was the right letter. A letter is a small thing, yet no word expressed is entirely without effect, and they all become, one way or another, a link in a chain. I wrote while thinking of you – and also of her – but I did not feel constrained. A rather difficult matter will have to be dealt with in the relatively near future. It's true, isn't it? We both know in advance that it will have to be overcome, right? Each time you walk from Hinterhör back to the castle, you can remind yourself that my unhappy existence and the powerful affection I have for you are the cause of everything which I will now express and which might test your patience. You must always remain the more generous one because you're the stronger one, and I'd almost venture to say, the happier one, or at any rate the less wanting. I am unhappy that I am unable to express this more aptly, with greater warmth, and more in such a way *that* it could be of some help. My head was in better shape the day before yesterday! On Sunday, it was dull. I wanted to clear my head and went to town alone to the opera. I had a corner seat in the back of the parquet (they performed the *Fliegenden Holländer* [The Flying Dutchman]) and I paid little attention to anyone or anything, and suddenly I was able to spin a terrific plot to *Frau ohne Schatten* before my own eyes – and I gained some of the intimacy with the characters that had been lacking for me up to this point.

That little Mädy! The little thing constantly shakes and is so easily thrown off course. I wonder if I should send a letter to her in Bredeney once in a while or better not to? The nurse is asking the baby for advice. The baby can answer in German or English. Of course it's permissible to write in English. Strangely enough, this will not warp the face in front of you. Carolin does not mind this either; she has so little time now anyway that she is not able to skim through letters very carefully.

Good night.

H.

P.S. It may be that something else from Vienna was addressed without your first name. Perhaps you have thought to notify the post office in Neubeuern that such mailings from Austria are intended for you and not for the castle.

P.S. A short letter just arrived from Munich. What does "Yours truly" mean? It comes across as rather foreign, precisely because it says so much, more than one may have intended or should have – perhaps it is simply because it came from Munich and not Hinterhör.

I wonder if Reiher's performance went well? And what a kind letter Eberhard sent! How lovely! I hope you have a good morning today. H.

Rodaun, Saturday, 4 November [1911]

Well, once again a very kind, truly lovely letter had to be summarily torn into a thousand little pieces and discarded and now can never be read again. And all this because, once again, it ended with the three very unfortunate, wholly incomprehensible words, "Very respectfully yours." How is it that these words find their way into this pen and onto the page at this point in the letter? (Because they never occur in the pencil letters.) "Very respectfully yours." This is well-suited to the letters I write to Gersdorff. In this case, I even try to become accustomed to writing this, for it's perfectly suited to our friendly relationship based upon mutual respect. It would also be just right for a letter written by the wife of the head of an administrative district to an older lord of the manor who is deserving of great respect and with whom one is not well-acquainted. However, at the end of one of your letters to me, I am truly unable to see or understand it. Nobody could understand it! This is the point at which everything comes to an end! The nurse no longer understands the baby, nor the traveler the Thuringian Fräulein, nor the poet the lady of Hinterhör, and neither does the friend understand his girlfriend or anyone else for that matter! Ask Mary sometime at breakfast – no, perhaps it would be better during the afternoon tea – whether she would give somebody a kiss to whom she writes "Very respectfully yours" in her letters. Or, looking at it from the reverse, whether she would even... give someone a kiss, whom she . . . . Ask her about this in general, at the afternoon tea. "No," she'll say, that wonderful Mary, who is virtually faultless and is able to utter such delightfully silly things about the chicken coops[80] and their creators. "No!" Mechtild would say; "No!" little Helen would say; "No!" Annette would say; "No!" Mädy would say; "No!" little Clara would say: "No!" Lina and Magda would say. All my charming girlfriends – be they blond or brunette – all of whom fit into a Chinese silk robe, they would all say: "No." And there the lady from Hinterhör would be left standing, all alone feeling rather abashed. She would have to let down her thick, deep-brown hair in order to hide behind it. She'd have to wrap herself in her newest, deep-blue blanket decorated with white birds of paradise and hide away in the chicken coop. Now that's the question, whether the chicken Goethe and the chicken Stifter and all these many-feathered chickens would admit such an intruder, and whether they wouldn't become angry and impatient, cackling: "Very respectfully yours, dear lady! Very respectfully yours! Very respectfully yours!" For *this kind* of style will not convince these beautiful chickens to allow themselves to be plucked. So, adieu then. What sort of a letter can one write anyway when one is in such a hurry

---

80. O. D. S. had a three-tiered bookcase, a gift from H. v. H, that one could turn around to get at the books easily. M.-T.'s nanny Mary called it the "chicken coop."

and still has to write Gersdorff and Strauss, has to go to the station, and must dine at Yella's[81] with the Bruckmanns.

Very respectfully yours,

H.

🌿 🌿 🌿

[Rodaun] 9 November [1911], evening

My Love, the entire content of one's thoughts seems so close. It all seems so easy to say without any need to reflect, so easy to make all the necessary connections and then respond. Yet a great distance separates these thoughts from their expression in written form. And whatever does find its way onto the paper is never the original thought but rather a version of it. I won't say anything – I have *already* said it all.

We went to the theater together last night – Gerty came along, too. It was a pleasant experience; the play was well-performed by attractive, very capable people. It gave you pleasure, and your pleasure became my pleasure. Before we said good night after arriving home, I told you: "This is the second time now you've said you want me to tear up your letters and not save them. So this really does seem to be your wish. If this is what you want and if it will make you feel better, then how could I possibly refuse." I immediately threw out the last one you sent me in addition to a few others I had at hand. I will continue to do so from now on, and at some point in the near future, I shall gather up the rest and burn them. This has nothing to do with what you wrote; I simply want to do everything in my power to see to it that none of your wishes remains unfulfilled.

Again you were here during the day. A short but nice letter came from Schröder. It was a very touching letter written at three in the morning in which he told me that I need not wait to hear from Gersdorff. After breakfast, you took both letters and placed them inside your book to read through later. Dear little Herr Mell had come for lunch. You liked him. He's overworked right now and looks rather pale and worn out. He hasn't gotten over the death of his poor little brother yet. You went for a walk with him afterwards, which made him very happy. Meanwhile I wrote a letter to Georg Franckenstein; it's really beginning to take its toll on him being all alone and so far away from home. Gerty had received a letter from Erwin. Then Mell went back into town. We remained seated in my room, and soon it was evening – oh, what nonsense! You are in Hinterhör and I am here, but I am very fond of you.

---

81. Gabriele Baroness Oppenheimer, old friend of H. v. H.

The first rehearsal of *Jedermann* is scheduled for this Friday – you are very dear to me, Ottonie; of course you are unable to realize this – Gersdorff wrote this to me in a great hurry. However, that does not necessarily mean that it will be performed *before* Christmas because Reinhardt is busy working on three separate projects right now. (Very dear, but why should you care, after all? It's your nature to prefer loving someone rather than being loved like most other women want to be.) It may drag on into January, in which case it could spoil this lovely time of year for me. I will perhaps have to leave Neubeuern rather early – yes, you are very dear to me. Why did it suddenly dawn on you when the chicken coops stood there? I'd be delighted to send you a few more chicken coops, but I fear this would cost me Mary's favor. A very nice letter also arrived from Annette this morning. She wrote three very lovely, very dear words: – . I would never have dreamed of hearing this from her. Without even thinking about it, I imagined myself writing some trite phrase such as, "Good night, dear friend."

I can't bear it when people give her the *Insel Almanach* when it's already waiting with the O. D. inscribed for you!

R., 16 November [1911]

Dear Countess,

Sometime in the next few days you'll be receiving a parcel from a Viennese art dealer containing a few color lithographs that I think will go well in Baby's room. I placed the order four of five days ago, that is, before I could interpret your failure to write as I now must.

It is of course very embarrassing that an otherwise unremarkable mailing will now create the impression that I am trying to force you to not forget me. In any case, I would ask that you attach no special significance to this parcel.

Yours, Hofmannsthal

Rodaun, Tuesday [21 November 1911]

We won't discuss it anymore. It had nothing to do with a misunderstanding but rather the feeling that it was at least *possible* that we were once again becoming distanced from one another as was the case back in September. And the thought that I might be unable to bear a recurrent feeling of this sort caused me tremendous despair. It is the feeling that a certain hostility over which you had no control was beginning to enter our relationship and would ultimately dissolve it. You obviously couldn't have had any knowledge of the unfortunate extenuating circumstances that were involved, namely, the fact that I had promised to deliver a project by a certain date. Therefore, I had to work on it and was unable to write a single line (or even to read) while agonizing over when I might finally hear from you again. Meanwhile, contrary to all expectations, the rehearsals for *Jedermann* began, and I had to miss the first four or five of them, which are very important. But say it is so, Ottonie, tell me that you will resolve to never again wait until the 17th to mail a letter you wrote on the 11th!

Most unfortunate of all was that you wrote a short postcard to Gerty, which destroyed any *hope* I had that you were perhaps ill and thus made it impossible for me to inquire personally.

Listen, Ottonie, it would be *so* wonderful if you could somehow make it to Berlin for the last few rehearsals and the premiere. I have invited Julie; I'm sure she would have no trouble understanding if you came as well! We can just say you were invited by Eberhard! It would make me so very happy if you were here; and I would do everything necessary to make sure it's not too stressful for you. But please let me know *soon*. Gerty won't be coming until the dress rehearsal, around the 29th. There is one scenario under which I would prefer you not come: if this would make it impossible to come in February and take the trip to Stassfurt!!

Adieu.

H.

❦ ❦ ❦

Hinterhör, 21 November 1911

That would be fine if I could just quickly come to Berlin! Why are these things so out of the question?! but alas, one does not live alone on this planet and so one has sometimes to bow to its rules. I can't tell you how I would *love* to come, but I must not think of it and send you a few words instead, to welcome you in Berlin.

So did *Jedermann* finally arrive all of a sudden then, or had you already expected it when a letter arrived from Gersdorff some time ago? Too bad that Julie is not Mädy; then of course I would be able to arrange to come without my family in Sondershausen needing to know anything about it, for it is possible for me to go to Berlin (without my family in Sondershausen) *only* if they don't know anything about it. However, all this is impossible with Julie. Moreover, I promised her I would go to Stuttgart with her. She has not accepted this offer yet, but she hasn't turned it down either. Well, in any case, it is not conceivable.

You must have received my letter in the meantime, otherwise you would not have sent your telegram; and with it, the gloominess between us has blown away. However, it is strange indeed, how we immediately and so acutely feel – or rather sense – when the thread connecting us is a bit limp. As I had occasion to write to Eberhard, my thoughts were more directed toward him, and I was therefore somewhat removed from you. Otherwise I *could* not have left the letter lying around.

Julie was just here for tea with Pipo and Keszycky, who is going to Berlin this evening (I wish I could have traded places with him). Of course your telegram arrived right then; however, my instinct told me not to open it in front of them, and instead I discretely put it away. Julie of course knows that it is from you, or no, she might also believe that it is from Eberhard. She really is a strange person. Recently I told her that Eberhard proposed that I make an investment, which I *of course* agreed to do. Several days later, she says she does not understand how I could have done this when it might be lost; hence it was extremely foolish of me, according to her, to take such a risk when I have *so* little money. I responded that Eberhard would indeed probably suffer the consequences, as he had advised me to do it *without* my asking. She found it completely *ridiculous*, my taking advice from Eberhard. I explained to her that I did not agree with this at all and that there are very few people from whom I would take advice, and he is certainly one of them. A total blank! But why am I bombarding you with such uninteresting details anyway, especially now when you must be thinking of a thousand other things besides the affairs of the lady in Hinterhör.

When is *Jedermann* going to be performed? Will I find out soon?! However, I hope so much *Ariadne* is not also going to be performed now? Then I think I would have to come after all, then Bockel would have to *pro forma* say he invited me. Actually I am expecting a letter from you tomorrow, and with *such* certainty that I think I will be very disappointed if there isn't one. The one I sent you last Sunday will have arrived today.

I am reading *Une Caprice* now with Mrs. Banck; it is also very wonderful. I now know that I would very much like you to read works of Alfred de Musset to us if you come at Christmas. Could things in Berlin ruin Christmas? They mustn't under *any circumstances*!

I did not find much time to read today or yesterday. I have such an incompetent seamstress here, and she always comes and disturbs me; now she wants to know this, and then that. Now Mary has gotten the situation under control, once she found "that it was really too trying for the Countess," to always be separated from such wonderful books simply in order to get all her old rags fixed.

Can you imagine I am really making some progress with my French. Mrs. Banck helps me quite a bit, for, after all, one cannot learn any language without knowing a few rules. Like a schoolgirl, it is also a lot of fun for me when I really understand something – when to use the imperfect and when to use the passé définis.

Well now you are going to throw yourself into the whirl of events and have long talks with Eberhard and, I hope, good rehearsals. However, the first few days will be awful; I will be thinking of you very, very much and would love to lighten your load.

So, good-bye now, much love, Yours, Ottonie

🐛 🐛 🐛

[Hinterhör] 23 November 1911

I am rather tired, and I am almost afraid it might be better if I did not write and yet I very much want to.

I feel like everything drags along sometimes and at times am even at my wits' end. Do you know I only came to realize yesterday for the first time what your trip to Berlin means? A premiere, a true premiere, and once again I should not be present, that seems impossible!

So now you have to deal with all the horribly difficult early rehearsals with all those strange sounds emanating from the stage. However, things will improve and get better with each day. I would so much love to be there.

I am *terribly* sorry to have caused such dreadful feelings for all these past weeks. This must not ever happen again. I had no idea not hearing from me could have this kind of effect on you, and I am much too fond of you to hurt you in any way. I really like you so much and wish you were either here (right at this moment) or I could be there with you; then I bet I wouldn't feel tired anymore.

The lovely pictures for Marie-Therese arrived today. Thank you very much. The child is overjoyed about her new belongings. And her mother is moved by the wonderful memory of a lovely moment we spent together one beautiful morning in Hinterhör.

I am trying to picture you in the Adlon now constantly. Do you . . . have to meet with people now, or do the few moments you have to yourself really belong to you?

Good night. In me is such a yearning for you. Ottonie

🐛 🐛 🐛

[Hinterhör] 24 November 1911

I am so happy! *We are* really coming! So a couple of ladies from Neubeuern will be dropping in on the morning of the 30th. Julie decided without any prompting – I did not say a word – to make the trip to Berlin and to invite me. Is that not wonderful! I feel so happy. She only wanted to spend a single day there, but I requested that we at least try to be there by the 30th. So would you please reserve two rooms for us in the Adlon?

Very simple rooms with a bathroom, we do not need a salon. Then we would also like to have simple good seats, if possible not too far in front, but not next to people like Mechthilde L., etc., if possible. Please reserve the rooms at the hotel in my name, as Julie wants to be there incognito.

I am in a big hurry now so I can mail this letter in time.

With many very kind thoughts,

Yours, Ottonie

❦ ❦ ❦

[Hotel Adlon, Berlin-W.] Saturday [25 November], 7:00 p.m.

Your letters arrive now from so far away, so very far away. They all seem so removed, every one them. This makes me very sad.

Our rehearsals last the entire day. I am not sure how it is going to turn out; perhaps it will be no good. The stage may be too large. There is no turning back now. We will be rehearsing tomorrow as well. Tuesday and Wednesday nights will be used for putting the stage in place, preparing the lights, and tending to other technical matters. Theater!

I cannot help thinking of little Fräulein Schwartz, who scurried past the old porter at the Sondershausen theater as she blew him a kiss. I find her very likeable. But where is she now? Where are you, Ottonie?

Imagine, Kessler is also here. Reinhardt spoke with him yesterday evening. I have not written him – I have not been able to – in months. So he will find out that I am here now. He may be leaving the day before my premiere, which also saddens me.

And now you will be dragged here for only 24 hours, and that when it is hard to predict one's mood. Will it be worthwhile? When I think of the three nights you will hardly sleep a wink, of your weary face – and the fact that I will be to blame for this – I feel terrible. We will not have a chance to see each other under these circumstances. However, from what you wrote in your letter, you seemed to be looking forward to everything. It seems like it has been months since I read this letter. I have reserved the two rooms. I will also reserve your seats. You can cancel both by sending a telegram at the very last minute if need be.

I wonder if you are able to sympathize with me when I feel extremely sad. Perhaps not. Your own sufferings may have been too profound and too real for you to do so.

I wanted to send the baby different pictures. Please *do not* have those framed. You might as well burn this; I will send it rather than be silent.

H.

❦ ❦ ❦

My Dear, I think I wrote you a very rude letter about an hour ago. Throw it away immediately – possibly before reading it, should this one arrive first. I just found the letter I received from you today and read it through again. You wrote some very dear and kind words in English at the end. Suddenly I could *feel* your presence so intensely.

I'm going to write a few lines to Kessler now to clear up that ridiculous misunderstanding we had the last time we saw each other. I have recently received quite a few very touching letters from Eberhard. Adieu! See you soon – really?

H.

❦ ❦ ❦

[Hotel Adlon, Berlin-W.]

Good night, Ottonie. Your letter was very touching. How kind of you. This time I'm the one who's moved.

Gerty said I showed very little tact this morning when complaining about people who attach themselves to me in order to obtain tickets, and thought you might have thought this applied to you. Do you really imagine it bothered me ordering a ticket for you, the one whose presence gives me the greatest happiness?

Good night. How I wish I could knock on your door and give you your ticket. I'm afraid to because of Julie. Your room here is just as poorly situated as the one in Neubeuern!

Good night now, for the third time.

H.

❦ ❦ ❦

[Rodaun] Friday, [15 December 1911]

Possibly you may still be able to recognize my handwriting. I just missed a train for Vienna, so I have a half hour's time to kill. I was able to sleep a while today unlike the past three nights. This was probably due to all the work I did in Berlin, and also now I have a huge amount of correspondence, roughly fifteen to twenty letters each day; in addition there are difficulties with Reinhardt's attempt to launch *Ariadne,* excited cables back and forth between Berlin and London, everything too hurried, needlessly under pressure, and I sit right at the center of it all, hoping to balance everything out. However, I want so much to have a little peace and quiet for myself, to sit here quietly – just six to eight weeks of peace and quiet, to collect my thoughts; this chance will come again. Yesterday I was exhausted; thoughts raced through my mind while at the same time appearing so formless, and unreal, that I laid down in bed in the middle of the afternoon; there I remained until evening and even read your letter in bed. Of course I also have a silly cold. On top of this, the weather is horribly dark and overcast. But enough complaining for now.

Gretl is truly a charming person; it's nice to have her here again. Her zest for life is wonderful. If I feel any better tomorrow, we're going to go to the theater with her and Erwin. Then, as always, we will say, "If only *Ottonie* were here!" Kassner[82] is also very pleasant to be around. You'll have to meet him sometime soon.

It was wonderful, the second performance of *Jedermann*, exactly one week ago today. That people such as Strauss would have tear-stained faces, I never would have imagined. Van de Velde was also captivated and seemed to wholly enjoy it. I was very happy. He's such an agreeable man! But please do give me the Christmas present of no longer referring to him as "Henry" when speaking to others about him (when talking to him yourself you can of course call him this). There's no room here to list the 37 different reasons why, but, *please*, do me this favor! I know that you will, aside from forgetting to now and then. It's such a charming name, "van de Velde!" And the sound of "*Henry*" spoken in a Sondershausenian French is so hideous when it suddenly appears in the middle of a German sentence − or at any time! It has the same effect as a school uniform, like pure antics! I also wouldn't be able to tolerate your *calling me Hugo*! It's just too demonstrative!

Yours, H.

[Rodaun] Monday, [18 December 1911]

I am terribly afraid that I may have, as a result of mental exhaustion, expressed my wish for a silly little Christmas present regarding the name "Henry" rather clumsily and thus may have upset you. However, I'm too tired now to apologize properly. So please forgive me and think of it as *nonavenu* until the next time we have a chance to talk about it. I ask for permission to brush aside a couple of things today because I have the most agonizing nightmares regarding all that I fail to accomplish during the day. Behn has revealed himself to be rather a shy and sensitive man and would, in spite of his great desire to do so, not come to Neubeuern after Christmas unless he receives another special invitation (which I find entirely appropriate). Would you be kind enough to pass this on to Julie

---

82. Rudolf Kassner (1873–1959), philosopher and writer.

W. or would you prefer I write her myself? (His address is Mandelstrasse 8.) Also, the tickets I ordered for Keszycki were most certainly misplaced by the hotel. I first noticed this as I was about to leave. It's *terribly* embarrassing! Now the old gentleman is sure to think the worst of me! Would you take it upon yourself to write him (at Kurfürstendamm 47) that you took the tickets from me and forgot to send them! I would be very grateful to you.

I won't add anything personal here because I do not have enough strength to focus my concentration on you for more than a second right now. I'm so looking forward to Neubeuern and a little *peace and quiet.*

Yours, Hofmannsthal.

🌣 🌣 🌣

[Neubeuern, 31 December 1911]

When you're not here, the house is so empty. Oh, *how* empty it was a year ago. You were traveling through the dark night on your way to Warthausen, completely surrounded by darkness — and I was here. It's a *warm* emptiness I feel here today. I found the Musset in the billiard room and took it upstairs to your room. I felt so happy as I stood there in the empty room. I could have kissed the table or the door posts — I am so very fond of you. I'm completely overcome by the feeling of your presence, for which I am so grateful; in the absence of this feeling, your presence is so faint, and the feeling I have in the absence of your physical presence so filled with longing. Now I am here and can see you so often; I am enraptured, to the depths of my heart, when I hear your footsteps approaching. One wonders, "Who's that there?" But I know ahead of time. The fact that I hold you dear is not all that special — I! Who am I anyway? Behn is working on a bust and face — it is apparently to be of me. Ottonie encountered a furious and nasty man running through a corridor in Berlin — that, too, was supposedly me. I do not really know who this "me" is, but *it* certainly is enamored of you. That is what I always used to write when I wrote to you from this desk, and this is what I wish you for the New Year.

Your friend, or perhaps a stranger.

🌣 🌣 🌣

[Neubeuern, 31 December 1911]

I cannot begin to tell you how glad and happy I am. No words can describe how grateful I am to you. It's as if the sun rose after many long hours of darkness. There is so much I would like to say, but the words still frighten me. However, that is just because I can't see you.

Vienna, Saturday, [13 January 1912] morning
(before returning to Rodaun)

How easy it is to be separated when the feeling of togetherness is still so strong – one feels so enriched and happy thinking of the many hours spent together. The thought of the many lovely hours we spent together still makes me very happy.

The trip here was pleasant and passed quickly in no time at all; I chatted with Gerty. She, too, is a delightful friend to have. I find it lovely the way she talks about you, leaving no question that she likes you, and her understanding knows no limits, for she never asks "Why . . . ?" – and has no reservations, not even at the deepest depths of her soul, just like pure spring water – and none of this requires any effort on her part; as everything is in her case, it's a matter of instinct, and there's never the slightest trace of "doing someone a service." The very notion of "doing someone a service" has a bitter taste to it. In short, I suppose we're all rather strange people. We were so bright and lively when we got off the train, much livelier than on the way from Rosenheim to Munich. (Sometime "someone" will take this train to Vienna, feeling *equally* chipper and cheerful.) Because Erwin and Gretl live so close by, we also went to visit them at their place for an hour or so. Gretl was swimming in all the success she's had in Vienna, where everyone falls at her feet. In her dressing room, you can hardly get past all the excited archduchesses; she is filled with excitement, as cheerful and high-spirited *as could be*. We got a *firm* commitment from both of them for the end of May – for Rome and for Aussee and then afterwards Salzburg, that is, you'll also be coming to Salzburg on the 25th or 26th of July. We're going to rent the house now – how happy I am about *everything*! Now is finally the time of my "youth," which had to come sooner or later, don't you think? Indeed I am *yours truly*,

H.

In town, Wednesday [17 January 1912]

Oh, to receive such a beautiful letter! Christiane brought it to town along with a bunch of others. I must thank you at once, though I can only find this silly little card.

There is so much I would like to tell you! It makes me very happy when Kassner speaks so fondly of Neubeuern and the ladies there. I have scheduled my meeting in Dresden for the 18th. Then I can either "wait" or go to the Nostitzs' for a couple days – it is wonderful to think that we will see each other in February, in April, in July, in August, in October, etc., and so on forever! At night I have been thinking about the reading list I made for you. I cannot tell you how glad I am that *Illusions Perdues* is not turning out to be a failure.

Much love, H.

❦ ❦ ❦

Monday [22 January 1912] evening

Is it possible for four or five days to pass while all the while one comes so close to writing a letter on about ten different occasions? All the sentences stored up inside – one wants simply to write them all down, but then along comes something which must be written immediately. And then again there's something else! There is no time to even leave the house to go for a walk or even to visit an ailing priest. One believes to have gained an extra hour, and then it is already gone. Finally, you feel so weary, weary from all the letter writing – I no longer want to make these black marks on the white paper. You think the other person knows that you've spent so much time thinking about her; you check the table every morning for an envelope with black edges . . . .[83] You waste a lot of time; finally you must simply admit to yourself that it's for the money. And in the end money means being able to sustain one's life, secure one's freedom, not being dependent on *anyone*, and being able to raise one's children. Money also makes possible your children's freedom, even when they're past the age of twenty. Money is the little house in Aussee, the train ticket to Dresden. So I really cannot complain. Sometimes it can confuse you and test your patience, this constant feeling of having empty obligations; it resembles the work of a chambermaid. Yet then along come months where one is free to do what one pleases. And there is also work such as Eberhard's, consisting of an abundance of scrap and so little ore.

This was an unfortunate beginning which simply found its way onto the paper by accident. To you I write as if I were thinking out loud.

I visited the parish priest today, a poor man, fifty years old; he sits there at home by himself, ill, and nobody looks after him. Whether sick at home or on the way to Davos,[84] he's always alone. How rich one feels by comparison, almost sinfully, frighteningly rich. You come home to a charming house, your wife inside, surrounded by harmony, and there is always a certain modest, unspoken gaiety in the air. The dear children –

---

83. Stationery used by a person in mourning.
84. Tuberculosis sanatorium in the Swiss Alps.

you can hear them downstairs, and you're upstairs beside the lamp contemplating something, thinking about the "strange child" sitting there (in *Frau ohne Schatten*) crying. If you ask why it is crying, it will sing:

> However should I not cry?
> The woman has no shadow
> The emperor will turn to stone!

And, suddenly, everything disappears.

One has all of this! And very close by are the letters – so dear that you are reluctant to burn them from one day to the next. A clear word and a wonderfully clear sentence do so much to create a balance between things. A flame burns inside me, but whenever this almost otherworldly calm is missing, it begins to flicker – yours burns quietly, radiating perpetual light. To avoid shutting oneself off – to stand before the world with no inhibitions, to live, to *once again* live amongst the living; to reach for a hand when that hideous darkness (which has no substance to it; it is a mere breakdown in one's strength, a sensation of death) spreads itself out across everything. All of a sudden I understand why it is I who can help you – why *it* has sought me out and sent me to you. I can understand it better – better than I can explain it – as it manifests itself inwardly in the form of a feeling which penetrates me. Perhaps it's because I understand the relationships between things; everything is intertwined, not as a confusing knot, but as an intricately woven web. And I know, more than many another, the pattern the threads have assumed. I can be patient, where another would be impatient, and I don't lose heart when strange gaps appear in things, when one thing is inextricably linked to another. Perhaps my hands are able to remain steady when others begin to hurt.

Will I really have you all to myself for three days? From dawn 'til dusk, in a strange city? We can look at paintings and listen to music, and when you're tired, I'll read something to you, will feel you resting – if only it will come to pass! Have you spoken to Mädy yet? I have the feeling you already have. Then I can expect you on the 19th, right? And you'll stay with me on the 20th and 21st, right?

The meeting in Dresden will *probably* be on the 18th, although it's not yet certain. Strauss, Seebach, Levin and I have been sending each other countless telegrams back and forth regarding this. Even if it turns out not to be the 18th, it is all the same. I will come on the 18th – from Prague where I will be giving a lecture – and wait there for you! How happy I would be to wait for you, Ottonie!

It is unlikely we will be able to see Gretl perform; she will be in the Austrian province then. That is, unless you come to Berlin for a day on the 28th, the 1st or the 21st of March, in which case I would wait for you. We can discuss this later. So I will either travel to Auerbach on the 22nd, or with you to Berlin, in which case I'll visit the Nostitzs' some other time. Don't write now telling me it will not work out!

Please go ahead and send all your unbound books (you do not need to include a note) to Dr. A. Kippenberg, Kurzestrasse 7, Leipzig. When you do so, however, send *me* a list of them. You should, of course, keep *Illusions Perdues* if you are still in the middle of reading it. (Do not forget about Mary's Christmas book.)

Good night.

Yours, H.

(P.S. A "long" or "detailed letter.")

Neubeuern, 23 January 1911

My dear Herr von Hofmannsthal,

It is so much fun to once again write this wonderful and long-forgotten salutation. One has to think back quite far to the last time I began a letter with this address. It is much nicer the way it is now, don't you agree? You know, it seems like such a long time since I received a letter from Rodaun. Although it has only been a week since the last one, it does seem so long after one has gotten used to chatting with certain people on a daily basis! But in place of this, a lot of lovely Balzacs arrived yesterday accompanied by the dear blue-red Schillers, all bringing along such warm greetings. All was received with many thanks and gave me enormous pleasure. My ugly bookcase keeps getting heavier, yet it alone provides the room's only sign of life.

Last night we read aloud some of the nice Mozart letters to each other again, and everyone enjoyed them very much.

Did you know that the painter couple are thinking of moving to Braunenburg permanently? They would rent the house there where the Lampes used to live and sell their own house. Julie was planning to leave for France with M.-T. on Friday, and today the child suddenly came down with a fever; it had already reached 38.6 degrees[85] by noontime. I hope it will come down soon and turn out to be nothing more than a mild cold. It is always frustrating when this happens, especially so right before a trip.

Good night. It is nearly midnight already. Ottonie

---

85. Centigrade; 101.4 F.

24 January 1912

This morning I found tremendous pleasure in a *very* long and dear letter. I certainly enjoy those really long letters from certain gentlemen in Vienna. Too bad I know so few of them! It's highly questionable, however, whether anyone else could write letters *such as* these. My intuition told me that you've been busy working and that the time drifted along without your having the chance to tend to correspondence. Still I've been thinking about you the whole time. I feel that I, too, come along when you go to visit the ailing priest, and I also want to help him pass the many long days. The days are racing by much too quickly for me now; that is because I have had too little time for myself recently, as I have had to devote lots of my time to Julie before she leaves to go on her trip and we had a lot of things to discuss. Baby's doing better. She no longer has a fever and just a bit of a sore throat; in spite of this, Dr. Glaser does not think she should have any trouble traveling. Mädy is going to Munich with Julie tomorrow and returning the same evening. Then she is leaving on Monday to visit friends in Meran for a week. I'm always very glad when she has the chance to spend time in different surroundings and experiences new things. Although I am always able to maintain her high spirits, it takes up a lot of the time I'd much rather spend reading. Just as I say this I see the notes attached to the reading list you were so kind to put together for me, and I must say, "God bless you." You of course know *how* much I enjoy these books. I am looking forward to the peaceful week ahead.

Yes, it is still going to be the 19th at this point. Should your meeting not take place on the 18th and you decide to come to Dresden on the 17th, then I could perhaps come on the 18th. It would also be possible for me to arrive in Berlin at around 6 o'clock on the 2nd, but then I would have to leave the evening of the 3rd the very next day, as the 3rd is the latest date I can return because Mädy wants to leave on the 5th. Perhaps you will have work to do in Munich and then we could return together. As you can see, I still try to arrange to spend as much time with you as possible before we have to part. Will this be a cause of concern to you? In that case, it would be best if you stopped by the Nostitzs' on your way to Dresden, and I would make sure not to come before the 19th. Would it *perhaps* be possible to ask Reinhardt if he could present *Penthesilea* either on the 23rd or the 3rd? If it's possible to see Gretl on the 2nd, I could still make it to the play on the 3rd and go straight to the station afterwards. I suppose you'd have to call this adventurous, right?

I'll be sending my books to Kippenberg tomorrow as well as a list to you. I can't wait to get them back! Mary's very happy that her book is going to be bound, too. Well, good night; it has really gotten to be late.

Yours, Ottonie

❦ ❦ ❦

[Neubeuern] Friday, 26 January 1912

Winkler just finished packing the books for Leipzig, and here is the list of them you wanted to have. I think I am becoming very spoiled. First you give me all these books and now you're even having them bound for me! That's terribly kind. I wonder if other people have such good friends?

Well, my little baby left for St. Moritz today. She still has a bit of a cold, which hopefully she will get over soon. Mary looked lovely, and everyone here misses her already.

We're enjoying a spell of real spring-like weather. All the snow has left us.

I'm in somewhat of a hurry since I still have to write a few letters and want to take everything to the station with me.

Much love.

Yours, Ottonie

❦ ❦ ❦

Rodaun, 27 January [1912], evening

People who live and wish to live, dear Countess; people who enjoy their Balzac and love their Walt Whitman, who revere their Goethe and find pleasure in reading their Musset; people who place their toboggan on a horse-drawn carriage, who fall off and leap back on to their feet; people who keep others in high-spirits and at the same time secretly look forward to a week of peace and quiet; people who know how to use a timetable and are able to make the best of their knowledge of geography and stick to their plans, who would like to go to the Wintergarten on the 2nd of March and the theater on the 3rd under the pretext that it's Papa's birthday – such people are of course, seen from a distance, completely *terre-à-terre* and *extraordinarily* dull. Strangely enough, however, when seen in greater detail, they are incredibly dear and lovable (more precisely: they "must be loved" for some mysterious reason) and *touching*. (The latter is wholly incomprehensible, but it is a fact.)

And I must also tell you how very nice I found it that you thought of suggesting that I arrive there earlier, on the morning of the 18th; it was very nice that you did so without being asked, and I will gladly (if possible) take you up on it. Because, aside from matters related to my chief concern (which will hopefully resolve itself!!), nothing else seems to be falling into place. Reinhardt is apparently still in London, and Strauss, who really can be an unbearable creature, has been wrangling with Seebach. So there may be no gathering in Dresden on the 18th at all (other than a very unofficial one). The poor Russians[86] will probably finally make a guest appearance in *Vienna* from the 23rd to the 29th of February, which means that I may have to shorten my stay in Berlin to two days and return on the evening of the 24th. However, I did receive a telegram today informing me that they will be coming on the 12th, in which case everything would be all right after all. At any rate, I'll be in Prague on the evening of the 16th, where I will be giving a lecture (as part of a program that Gretl and I are conducting to aid feeble-minded children). On the 17th, I'll be in Dresden, and I am already looking forward – more than I can say – to seeing someone arriving there, someone shy and remote who will "possibly" be *somewhat* friendlier later.

Yours, H.

P.S. The lovely poem about the bird[87] who laments the loss of his wife will be difficult to find on one's own, but it shouldn't be any problem in Dresden.

[Rodaun] Tuesday [30 January 1912]

How lovely! I felt so happy when I found the little pencil note on the table this morning! I wouldn't have dared look for one of your lovely letters so soon.

It was the 16th of January – these days belonged to us, yesterday and the day before, and the two days in Auerbach, days that were filled with nothing but thoughts of you. Whenever I see that house again this year, how I shall find all of this – and only this – at every turn.

Then there was Dresden – and Berlin, where we wrote so much to each other. There was one time in Berlin when I spent the entire day in the hotel and did nothing but write: "Dear Countess, dear Countess." There was also one day when I received three letters. It's all so improbable – you and I. Here is today's letter. Did you send it to me? I find myself picking it up as if it weren't meant for me. Yet it still makes me very happy. The day before yesterday and yesterday I had to spend the entire day working on the play I promised to write, *Jedermann*, always Everyman, and never Fräulein Everyman. I thought about you a lot but

---

86. The Diaghilev Ballet.
87. By Walt Whitman.

couldn't allow myself to set aside my work and replace it with stationery. I took a walk through the house in Hinterhör, moved the furniture and hung a painting on the wall that belongs to you (it has ever since a certain day); I was afraid of disturbing its modest harmony. The white picture frame seemed obtrusive, and I found myself obtrusive. I was afraid of moving something out of place that might have been identified with Christoph in some way. You were nowhere to be found there – I was alone. Then I went over to the castle to look for you. I found you, dear, dear, dear Countess.

I have to stop now. We're going into town to Yella O.'s, where I will tell stories about the trip to Rome, have tea at the Taxis',[88] and tell stories about the trip to Rome. We are going to see G. and E.[89] this evening, and then I'll really tell stories about the trip to Rome and will mention in passing that the fifth member of the party is *a friend of ours*, a young woman from Bavaria – which is not true; she's a Fräulein from Thuringia. At night I will think to myself, "Mama D. and her cough!" and will be anxious about Dresden.

Adieu.

H.

❦ ❦ ❦

Rodaun, 3 February [1912], evening

My Love, the last sentence you wrote in your letter made me rather sad. I so longed for one of your letters, and then you wrote of the loose thread holding us together – if you feel this, then it is certainly the case. I think you were worn out, perhaps a bit exhausted at the moment. Also, do you know *how* long it has been since you sent me a letter? Of course, it is because so many different things have taken place this week that it seems like such an eternity to me. Is it just a week or has it not been much, much longer since you wrote me? Raimund has not been well since the week before last; when we went out there on Monday we found him in an unbelievably miserable state. His skin had a wax-like yellowish hue to it, and he was completely apathetic and didn't even recognize us. Although he didn't have a fever, he suffered from an abnormally low body temperature which continued to persist. The very first thing I thought of was a dreadful illness that, once one has it, is not *dangerous* – how harmless "*dangerous*" sounds – but absolutely deadly. Then the doctor told me he had been thinking of the same brain disease – it didn't dawn on Gerty, thank God. None of the other symptoms was present, however. He was

---

88. Prince Alexander of Thurn und Taxis.
89. Grete Wiesenthal and her husband Erwin Lang.

already able to get out of bed today. Oh, the hours one spends under such circumstances walking around and thinking through every last possibility – I also thought about you, in a different manner than usual perhaps, yet still very intently. I read the letter you wrote after the child had died – and I read my response; I asked you not to come until a later date perhaps. Well, he's alive and doing very well. It turned out *not* to be any of those *symptoms*. In the meantime so many letters and messages have arrived. Reinhardt agreed to produce *Ariadne* – in the meantime that absurd Strauss upset everything and began to set things up in Stuttgart. Levin, the good fellow, realizing that letters and messages wouldn't help, went straight to St. Moritz – when was this, Wednesday? Everything is in a state of confusion right now, and I still haven't received any news. Every fifteen minutes a telegram arrives – nothing but telegrams expressing approval, from strangers, politicians, and others, regarding a political essay I wrote (very much an exception) in response to an outrageous poem by d'Annunzio which was directed against Austria. In the meantime, in order to force myself to relax, I read a great deal of Homer and a lot about Homer, and also wrote about him myself. These were peaceful hours. I often thought to myself how wonderful it would be if a letter arrived now. There was also a very happy moment – when was it? I can no longer remember, but it was a letter I received from Eberhard letting me know that he was able to find a car we could use. I got out my map of Italy, and we took a lovely drive around the entire area. Meanwhile, I was worried about my father. (Our pediatrician in the city – those are about the only friends he has. He nearly died; as of yesterday, it began to look as if he would make it.) I now have a great need for *fresh air;* there's no snow on the ground here; it always melts right away. We're leaving Monday for a four-day stay on the Semmering. If I were to get a little pencil-written letter there, a lovely little letter. . . . How odd, Ottonie, that you always seem to drop me when I'm not feeling well or not quite up to par and that you are quite unaware of this. The force that guides you is certainly correct – you need happiness, and nothing else. And, Ottonie, it makes no difference to me if I have to spend a day waiting for you in Dresden, but does this mean you will spend one day less with me? If this must be, then let's not talk about it.

If Levin takes care of everything, then I will be in Dresden with Reinhardt beginning the evening of the 17th. If I do not have anything to do there on the 18th, I could find something to keep me busy in Leipzig on the 18th and 19th, but hopefully this will not be necessary. In Dresden we will of course be staying in the lovely Hotel Bellevue. Bring a warm coat with you for car or sleigh rides – this is lovely there. From the evening of the 15th to around noon on the 17th I will be in Prague at Hôtel Blauer Stern. From the 5th to the 8th, Semmering, N. Öst., Südbahnhôtel.

If I could only see your eyes or touch your hands for a brief moment. Your letter arrives from such a far away place!

I am so fond of you. H.

[P.S. on the back of the envelope:] Photos were sent by G. W.[90] IV. Alleegasse 2.

❦ ❦ ❦

Rodaun, 3 February 1912, evening

I am terribly afraid I wrote you a bad letter this morning – I was in such a hurry. Now I can see every sentence before my eyes and am frightened by what I see. It would not be necessary to retract anything if I simply had the chance to *say* it all to you, but I went ahead and wrote it, and everything comes across different when it's read rather than when it is heard. Can't I make you feel for a week or perhaps longer the way I am sometimes able to make you feel for a couple of days? (I do not mean what you feel for me, but for life, and through your life, for me.)

This thread which "is not taut at both ends" – have you really let go of your end? Finally, I received a letter from you after so much time had passed – you've become very weary of writing me. Write me soon if possible. Write when it's convenient for you.

Good night.

H.

P.S. There was no *bitterness* in what I said, namely that you *must* find joy and must not be exposed to anything else. I am quite convinced of this! I sometimes feel, however, that I am still able to give you much happiness. In Dresden, as I gathered a few books together in the corner to read to you, I felt so happy.

Did you know by the way that Gretl already left our car for Italy? She *has* to go to America in May, but Erwin will surely stay here, and Gerty says she is sure she will make arrangements for him to accompany us. That would be very nice, for a group of four is much, much better than five. If Erwin can't make it, then Schröder will – building castles in the sky! I can't believe that right on my birthday you wrote me such a cold and unfriendly letter. I'm going to burn it right away.

Ottonie!

Good night

❦ ❦ ❦

---

90. Grete Wiesenthal.

Neubeuern, 4 February 1912

If I could *only* have you here to let you see how very, very ashamed I feel. I see myself being so *abominably* mean to you, so cruel. Every time when you are sad about something, I can feel it, but — always the wrong way.

I really believe that I am by no means a sensitive person; otherwise it would not *always* turn out like this over and over again. You know, I really am rather frustrated with myself today, not because I wrote that nasty sentence, but rather that I was able to feel *this* way. If only *you could* be here right now, now, when we could enjoy so much peace and quiet, and the beautiful snow, this would do you so much good; we could talk to each other, and then I would no longer find myself so loathsome.

How horrible this flood of reflections must have been when looking at the poor little sick darling; how wonderful that he is more or less well again. Then the concern about your Papa, everything squeezed together all in the same week, and on top of this, the complete absence of your "girlfriend" — you know, I would cut her off a bit, this person.

Did I really not write for that long a time? I thought it had been five days at the most between my last two letters. Maybe the feeling of not having anything of substance to write kept me from writing; in short I find this not very nice and cannot understand myself. We really are strange, we human beings, able to move so quickly from one world to the next, so indecisive and so unsteady.

Tomorrow you are driving to Semmering; I love the thought of this so much, to know where you are always makes me so happy. A bit of relaxation will surely be good for Gerty, too, after all the excitement.

I can then, as we have discussed up to now, depart from here on Sunday evening (18th) and arrive in Dresden on the morning of the 19th. On the 21st, I must go to Berlin; there I thought for sure you might travel with me, for then we would be together until the 24th after all. However, if you have a talk with Reinhardt in Dresden, you may no longer have any reason to go to Berlin and may want to go home; maybe you could even write me about this beforehand, because if we are both in Berlin together, we should stay in the same hotel, right? But when I am alone, I stay with some of my Stift friends. However, as I must tell Julie when I am leaving, I would really like to know beforehand.

Thinking of you faithfully and lovingly,

Yours, Ottonie

P.S. I wonder if you can feel that I am very fond of you!

Neubeuern, 5 February 1912

The dear sweet lines I got today make me even more ashamed. I cannot tell you *how* miserable I am in all my feelings. It is the first time that I recognize myself as an abominable egotist, never never never giving – but *always* taking from you, taking in a matter of fact way as if it ought to be so and yet I don't see how to change it, because my feelings will always be wrong in the same moment as I only realize it when too late. It is really distressing, because there is no way of curing it. I am so sad in regards to you that I absolutely lack the courage to pull the cords. Your letter from yesterday could not hurt me at all, I felt the truth of every word so strongly. But it touched me to the bone. It seems that I need now and then a little "shaking up" to show myself the feelings I have for you – then, I see that there are many. Only two weeks and we see each other, talk to each other, what a blessing it would be. So dreadful the idea that months would have to pass by without a hearty touch of hands.

Only Gretl has bailed out, *what* a pity; but of course it really is better with four than five. I very much wish Erwin could be the fourth. Eberhard was very quick with arranging the car; he really is very good with things like that.

If I did not have the feeling you should have yesterday's letter by this evening, I would almost like to send a telegram, but that always attracts attention here. Just imagine, I have been thinking of your birthday the entire time; it must be his birthday sometime around now, but I could not remember when it was; I hit it on the telephone last year and now I feel twice as sad.

Many, many thoughts wander towards you without interruption from

Yours, Ottonie.

Tuesday, 6 February 1912

Again I want to write you so that you know my thoughts are always with you, and I wish you would think of me lovingly and forget this cold, unkind person – who is called Ottonie. Can you do this? Yes, I know *you* can, and you can do so quickly, much quicker than I ever could. I do like you very much because you are always so touchingly kind to me – at times I do not like myself at all.

I went for a wonderful walk today from Nussdorf along the entire Inn dike. My little cousin came with me and talked about the birdies and everything else she knows about the woods. I half listened to her and half thought about someone else and heard him say many, many things, about *Frau ohne Schatten*, and then about *Jedermann,* or perhaps the lovely words he spoke on our final morning together, when there was still some snow left on the ground. We had found each other again and felt very close. Or someone pricked her ears up upon hearing the same voice say "Italy" – the same one that had spoken to her along the same lovely Inn dike. And a Thuringian Fräulein heard everything that was said and strangely enough it remained with her, and suddenly reappeared and always accompanied her. How nice it is to have such delightful companionship! Then one asks oneself why everything cannot go on like this forever. Why, why must the silly Thuringian Fräulein be so alone at times? She does not know the answer to this question and tells herself "thank God" it's not like this today.

Illusions perdues was really wonderful. It was unbelievable how many beautiful passages I came across in it. I will have to tell you more about this sometime. Right now I'm reading the last part of *Gaudissart*. Did you know that in two more weeks to this day we'll be able to chat with each other and won't need to write?!

Good night, good night.

Yours, Ottonie.

Rodaun, Thursday, [8 February 1912] evening

Three letters just arrived very quickly, one after the other. The first one came in the morning the day before yesterday. I received it while taking a walk. I stayed back so I could be alone while I read it. The southern wind nearly tore the pages right out of my hands; rain drops fell from the trees, and now the letter looks as if tears had fallen on it, which makes it seem even more touching than it would be otherwise. There are no traces of tears to be found on the second one, but there are some short sentences written in English that make me feel so sad and sympathetic. Today on the way to town I wanted to sit by myself in a coupé in order to read through both letters again. Instead, the porter gave me a third letter as I was about to board the car. The thoughts that went through my mind during the two hour train ride were one continuous response and took the place of the long letter that I could not write. Between Wiener-Neustadt and Baden I came across a passage you wrote which revealed great timidity; it was long and full of doubt – about me and my ability to *truly be of some benefit to you*. I wanted to ask, "Yes, *who* is coming to meet *whom* in Dresden?" Should one follow through with these plans if there is so little which could possibly provide you some warmth and support and make you happy? Yet this question was never asked (I'm talking about a letter that was never written), and now I'm sitting here at my desk and the ticking of the clock is the only sound to be heard here in the quiet of Rodaun (that is, after the three children have fallen asleep). I have here in front of me the three letters you wrote; they appear to be at home. All the self-reproach found there, the accusations, have become subdued, like children who cry themselves to sleep, and suddenly my mental probes and the fear I have appear before me: Can I hope to give something where something may not be taken? Everything just disappeared. All I can see is your face, your being alone in the world. I can't help but be especially fond of you *because* this is the way *you appear* to me. Everything else is hairsplitting. And if, when in the presence of the man you're meeting in Dresden, your loneliness is mollified even a little bit, a great deal will have been achieved. So just come and meet me there! (There was one part of the letter where someone might have thought it necessary to ask you *not* to come. *How* empty everything would seem if this were the case, and how pointless the whole trip up north — what a cheerless, difficult trip it would be.)

I do not have anyone I have to meet in Dresden; there's no chance *Ariadne* — with Reinhardt, Stern, Hempel and Destinn, and Strauss as the director — will premiere in Dresden. It will be in some other German city that you'd never think of. I agreed to go to Prague, where I will be lecturing on the 16th (I will be staying in Hotel Blauer Stern). I will be traveling to Dresden (Hotel Bellevue) on the evening of the 17th because it is lovely spending *one* day waiting for someone. However, if you are unable to arrive in Dresden on the morning of the 19th and not until the 20th, then I have no idea how I would spend two long days there all alone. Perhaps I would go to Leipzig and we could travel to Berlin together on the 21st. I write this even though I am not sure I believe it.

I would stay in the Adlon by myself or, just the same, in a smaller, less well-known hotel or guest-house; perhaps you could suggest a place.

Good night.

Yours, H.

❦ ❦ ❦

Neubeuern, 9 February 1912

Is there anything in my letters that could possibly have hurt you! I await with tremendous longing a word from Semmering every time the mail arrives, but none comes. Now you are back home. I wonder if you might be able to write me from there? I really hope so. But if this is not possible, then it's better if you don't force yourself; otherwise it's painful.

It's spring here. Today we went for a long walk; it was so incredibly wonderful and incredibly beautiful, *how* I would have loved to have you here!

Eberhard just wrote that Hotel Bellevue is the honeymoon hotel for all of Germany and that I would be sure to meet some people I know. Would it not be better then if we stayed in another one in Dresden? However, if it means a great deal to you, then we'll just go ahead; I don't mind. Then Eberhard also wrote that if we want to stay together in Berlin, it might be better to stay in a guest house instead of the Adlon. However, it isn't quite clear to me why, for in a big hotel, one is only "Mr." after all; who can know who all is staying there, right? One must only be a bit cautious by not arriving in the same carriage and not standing around together downstairs in the lobby; rather each of us should exit the hotel alone if possible. It's just that it seems impossible to me to stay together in a guest house or in a small hotel; then someone will find us there together (one takes the chance). It would be much more conspicuous than in the Adlon, where *you* always stay, and so do I, when I go the Stift reunion.

10 February 1912

I came this far last night. Today I received your – unfortunately – rather sad letter. What can I say? I simply *cannot* give you up; yet it seems, you cannot take me *completely*. Where does it come from, where is it, where does it lead, oh, if only I knew! If I were more completely, or more partially, what should I wish? – Hugo, I would just like to talk to you again sometime, to be with you, to let someone explain it who knows me better than I do. Yes, then should I really not come to Dresden? Should I understand this and have enough strength to deal with it like that? No, I truly do not have it, and hence I am going to come, and you must once again take me *as* I am. One thing, however, I do not understand – that you *can* bear to. This is precisely why I am so terribly fond of you. You know, for a moment I was afraid of coming to Dresden (not because of the two of us), afraid of meeting someone who would probably not want me to be there then, and that Julie would then find out, and as a result, our entire relationship, which we worked so hard to patch up, would once again collapse. However, now I tell myself, why not, if one is never willing to take a risk, one will never arrive anywhere; and now it's over, and I am simply looking forward.

You also wrote about the hotel in Berlin; of course I already told you what I think yesterday. Naturally we must not reserve adjacent rooms, but that doesn't matter anyway in the Adlon. In Dresden it might be better to stay in the Englische Hof or whatever it's called. As you will already be there the day before, you will be able to see whether a lot of people are staying in the Bellevue and can still send me a telegram. (I just remembered this is not necessary; I will have my mail forwarded to the Bellevue, and if we stay somewhere else, I can have it picked up. The way it looks now, I will be in Dresden Monday morning; I will let you know what train before leaving.

So then goodbye, you occupy my inner self entirely, can you feel it?

Yours, Ottonie

❦ ❦ ❦

Rodaun, 12 February [1912]

Yes, yes indeed you should come, Ottonie, and how! How certain I am of this – and how fond I am of you for deciding to do so, to be here, to really be here! I feel desperately afraid, as if surrounded by darkness, whenever you begin to seem unreal to me, when you fade away like a shadow and when everything becomes a puzzle, an intractable contradiction – when it seems so idle and presumptuous to want to help you without a grasp on you, and without the one thing necessary for giving – and receiving – help: mutual affection. I search and search for what you might be able to feel for me, and it seems I find nothing but contradictions at every turn. Many things appear to reveal a great deal, and others nothing at all; on the contrary, they destroy or displace the former. The words speak a different language than does the subtle, unconscious behavior; the hands react differently than the lips. And uniformity of the person, internal coherence, and constancy are so wonderful. When there is love, there is also endless patience, and now I feel that I could have waited for years for your charming smile, for the gentle pressure of your hand – and now everything is so different. Sometimes I long for days *past* when I was no more than a stranger to you (am I less so now?). But you loved my letters – and now they, too, no longer have an effect on you; everything has changed. This frightens and saddens me terribly; I think about it day and night. Not all night long, but half the night; not all day long, but half the day. I can't describe the agony I am forced to endure when you continually – in November, December, and now – forget about me. But why should I not endure this agony if only that *something* I once spoke of is still there – for you?!

Sometimes I feel as if there were absolutely nothing there at all (I speak of the feelings you have for me). If you were only half there! Or entirely there! But you aren't. I must take you for what you are. I can't stop loving you – neither will I. But now I must see you and talk to you soon, while accepting you as you are. I will come to do so again, and I always will. But please understand that I sometimes find it extremely eerie and frightfully absurd that you can – if at all – only like me because . . . .

Ottonie, my dear, I am looking so forward to you and to every moment we spend together – when you look at a painting, when we take a walk through the old city streets in the evening or at night, staying in the same hotel together. There are so many little things I am looking so forward to. Ottonie, I would like very much to stay at the Bellevue Hotel, and of course, it is all a matter of chance. (Say, is our nemesis still in Dresden?!) And the Bellevue is so nice and cheerful and the new little rooms there are lovely – you enjoy things like this and will like it very much there, whereas rooms in other hotels are horrible, dark hovels. And then each of us can write a separate letter to the Adlon. And in any case, our rooms will be miles apart, and we will not be as noticeable in such a large hotel. By the way, we do not have to eat in the Bellevue when we are in Dresden; there are some lovely restaurants there, but if you prefer to eat somewhere else, I think the Savoy is supposed to be quite nice. Send me a letter in Prague, yes? You will, won't you? At any rate, please let me find a few lines from you in Prague (Blauer Stern) this *Friday*, alright? I'm so restless and so impatient. I think if you ended up not coming – I don't know what I would do! I would go straight to Neubeuern.

Yours, H.

[Rodaun] 14 February [1912]

I am very much afraid I may have frightened you with something I said in the letter I wrote you the day before yesterday, something very harsh that revealed profound struggles or the pains of agony – it's all gone now. I am filled with joy and anticipation and a touch of apprehension about whether or not we will really have two days to ourselves without that hideous corridor from which the sounds of approaching steps can always be heard. We'll have the chance to take walks together in a strange city and to sit beside each other in the theater or concert hall – I am so very happy! Will I discover a little letter when I arrive in Prague? (The name of the hotel where I will be staying is Palace Hotel and not Blauer Stern, as a certain "Gerty" indicated in a telegram she sent.) By the way, Gerty knows that we are meeting each other in Dresden. She is much too nice and open for it to make any sense to hide something from her; she understands everything very well, and it all makes completely good sense to her. So tomorrow, that is Thursday evening, I will be in Prague; Friday evening I will be giving a lecture, and on Saturday I will stand around and will not yet feel like I am waiting for someone. I will go to Dresden that evening and will take a walk in the city on Sunday, at which point I will no longer be able to tell myself that I'm *not* waiting – in addition, it will be Sunday and the shops won't even be open. Oh, God, if only I could believe that you will really be coming Monday morning!

Adieu.

H.

[Hotel Adlon, Berlin-W., 22 February 1912]

I think I am all better now, and I continue to stay in bed as I am supposed to. Good night. One cannot help being very, very fond of you.

H.

❦ ❦ ❦

[Hotel Adlon, Berlin-W.] Monday [26 February 1912]

Dear Countess,

It is so lovely today, so bright and cheerful, and I hope it is just the same in Sondershausen and that you are also enjoying it.

It was so absurd of me to lie in bed in Berlin instead of taking you to *Viel Lärm um nichts*[91] — which is supposed to be very charming — and giving you the feel of having a nice little trip. We simply met under very unfortunate circumstances. When one is feeling well and the sun is shining and one reflects on people, then one knows exactly what those people do and do not need. Ottonie, I think you need to spend a lot of time in Hinterhör, and in addition to having a reading schedule, you need some peace and quiet. Perhaps a little automobile trip and a small dose of Gastein or Aussee would do you good. I hope that the books, or more precisely, that which these books contain, will in time truly become a part of you — not as a sort of fairyland beyond this world, to which it would be unhealthy to flee, but rather as something which provides enrichment to your life and which exists in harmony with it as a guiding force filled with overtones and positive connections. This world should truly be a part of your life, illuminating everything in it and thus expanding and intensifying your experiences. It seems probable that the world of the intellect (which something inside you has always sought) may indeed enter your life at this moment to help you to begin living a life that is not mere vegetation.

Here I was disturbed. I had to dine with Strauss and am very tired and can hardly collect my thoughts, and yet I don't want to tear up this letter or leave it lying here unfinished so that tomorrow morning you won't be without a sign in Sondershausen that there is someone who thinks of you (as lovingly as ever).

Last evening I sat in my room and could not think of anything except spending the evening here — then I heard a knock at the door. Who's there? It was Reinhardt. He stayed for two hours and seemed just as near as well as remote as he always seems to me. Once again we offended one another. In spite of everything — we came to an understanding — this man has a very strange appeal to me. Relationships between men are just as mysterious, puzzling and intriguing as those between men and women. I

---

91. *Much Ado about Nothing.*

feel that I must have caused you a great deal of confusion entirely forgetting how little you know me. Don't respond to this, but write, and remain as kind as you always are.

Yours, H.

❦ ❦ ❦

[Hotel Adlon, Berlin–W.] 28 February [1912]

Yes, you were entirely correct: it really is very much like in Paris. The only difference is that I have work to do here and spend the evenings in Reinhardt's theater. Today I'll be having lunch with him, so much better indeed. Kessler sent a telegram saying that he won't be coming; I am glad, for the only possibility right now is for me not to see *anyone*.

Now I'm beginning to wonder whether or not you will still be coming here on the 2nd. It seemed before you half-promised to, but *you didn't promise to* and neither should you if it will cause you any difficulty or require too great an effort. If you do decide to come, that would of course be wonderful; we'd have the evening together and could see Gretl or *Viel Lärm um Nichts*, which really is an enchanting performance. Perhaps we could both go see Reinhardt rehearse on the 3rd and depart together that same evening. If you will be coming, please send me a line letting me know right away, or even better, send a telegram if feasible. And also send a telegram right away to the hotel – which is always overfull – to reserve a room.

Today is the day of the birthday,[92] which has been on my mind a great deal. I am going to a lovely concert this evening that Strauss is conducting.

Yours, H.

P.S. Both of the Schröder sisters told me about the very similar experiences they had the evening they spent with Collier, which differed greatly from his account. The way he behaves around women seems rather ordinary and American to me now, and I would *very much* prefer you no longer wrote to him if it is all the same to you.

❦ ❦ ❦

[Sondershausen] 14 March 1912

I was so *very, very happy* to receive your telegram today. It removed the oppressive fear that was causing such a tight feeling in my chest. *How* I would have loved to be together with you and Eberhard in Berlin! However, I am very happy for both of you that you had a chance to spend this

---

92. Seventieth birthday of O. D. S.'s father, Hans von Schwartz.

time together. I wouldn't have done well in that environment; it's precisely being surrounded by large groups of people that I can't tolerate now. The birthday party was delightful. Father was incredibly moved by the overwhelming love and kindness everyone showed him. I am so happy to find him *so* much more chipper than he was last year, and he has also regained his old sense of humor.

I am staying here now until Wed. and then will probably spend one day in Weimar. Friday in Bamberg and Saturday Neubeuern. Maybe, if you have time and feel like it, I will find a word in Weimar on Thursday at the Veldes; otherwise not until back in Neubeuern is rather a long time, but I would not like you to take great pains to write me a letter. I would *rather* wait for one. Mädy will be staying now for the entire month of March here in Neub. Therefore I no longer need to hurry now. I am *so* happy about the telegr.; I must say once more, I was afraid of my own letters that I had written to you and can now sense something between us which has become freer. Am I right, or am I just imagining this?

How lovely that you will have been able to see the Russians perform. I wish I could be there with you tomorrow evening. Now you are traveling; I really think about you a lot.

Good night, it is late now, and I have already been lying in bed for a long time. Giving you a kiss on your kind eyes,

Yours, Ottonie

❦ ❦ ❦

[Rodaun] Tuesday [5 March 1912] evening

Just a short note which Max Mell will take to town shortly. This is the only way it will arrive in Weimar by Thursday. Yes, you understood my telegram very well; that's exactly what I hoped to convey, that is, the gratitude and happiness I feel. This short trip was completely different from the one to Paris; it was a lovely symphony, at worst with a somewhat bizarre and intricate second movement! The last few days here have been so delightful with all the people seeming to come into bloom. Again and again I found myself alone with someone. Last night it was Strauss from eleven to midnight, and for the first time, I think I was able to *understand* him. The following day I had lunch with him and Reinhardt at the Levins'. He played and sang for us from *Ariadne*, the Bacchus scene. One must say he truly is a genius, and Reinhardt is so enchanting. Then, all at once, Gretl appeared and spent the entire evening with us. She was very different than in Prague, so witty and wonderfully natural; it was a lovely way to bid one another farewell. While they were still there, the telephone rang. It was Eberhard. On our last day there, we had lunch with Eberhard and Schwerin; that same morning I received a lovely letter from Julie, which was really very touching. After lunch, while walking and chatting with Eberhard at the Tiergarten, both of us suddenly said, "*How* blessed we are!" He radiated a certain pure, natural self-confidence and a sense of triumph. Then we went to the station. In Vienna, Gerty was so charmingly feminine as I had hardly ever known her before; she was drunk with delight over the Russians and in love with Nijinsky. I spent the following two days in Vienna, where I went to the theater in the evening and to the hotel where the Russians were staying during the day. I am going to work on one to ten or perhaps 100 ballets for them! They say I'm the only person who understands them. They're engaging Gretl for next spring as well as Frau Rubinstein. I wonder what all is awaiting us! And you will watch and enjoy it! Ottonie!

Good night, good night.

H.

P.S. It is impossible to write about Nijinsky. Gerty, I and Erwin will have the *entire* automobile trip to tell you about him.

[Rodaun] 12 March [1912]

Through the Russians I felt I was in a sort of fantasy world; everything I saw had a golden shimmer. Now I must return to the real world, and to help me do so, I have resumed my study of Homer and shall now finish the essays I began writing about *Homer*. Reinhardt will still be coming to Vienna on the 28th to present *Jedermann* and then it will already be Easter and April, and on the 28th of April, three people – soon to be joined by a fourth – will depart from Munich for Trient, Verona, Bologna, Pisa, Arezzo, Peruggia, and Assisi. I have had the map on top of my desk for some time now.

I have decided to no longer expect to receive letters from you and to not become the slightest bit unsettled when I do not hear from you. I read in Mädy's letter that you returned looking well and rejuvenated.

I hope you found a letter in Weimar on Thursday (the 7th), one that I wrote on Tuesday evening. Hope the two small bookcases[93] from London made it safely to Neubeuern. (Liberty has informed me that they were indeed sent to the correct address.)

I also hope you received your bound books in good condition. Stendhal and Mary's Oxford book were mistakenly sent to me.

---

93. Ordered at Liberty's in London, and located in Marie-Therese's house in Bavaria to this day.

I hope you have not completely given up reading and are taking some time out for yourself; I would be terribly sad if this were not the case. This is of course the most important thing for you.

I have once again completely regained my health; I have been sleeping superbly. I wrote two ballets for the Russians, one of which I've already sent to Strauss. A very talented young Frenchman[94] will be composing the score for the other one.

Good night. I am tired, but very content.

H.

[Hotel de Castiglione, Paris 12, Rue de Castiglione]
Friday evening [March 1912]

Your letter arrived today. Thanks so much. You know, I very innocently spoke to Julie about the automobile trip we are planning, and she *didn't say a thing* about it. It seems she finds it entirely acceptable that we travel together. Have we decided on the 28th now? Will an automobile be available beginning on that date? Or would it also be possible to leave on the 1st of May? God, I truly can't believe it will happen, but I am still looking forward to it with tremendous joy!

At first I was *so* disappointed in my stay here in Paris, but today was a wonderful day. I enjoyed a *splendid* moment in the Louvre when I saw the *Victory of Samothrake*. What stunning beauty! We also saw some magnificent paintings – God, it is so beautiful! Later we went to *Museé Cluny*. I was very taken by the thermals, and this right in the middle of Paris! And also the marvelous goblins. Oh, there are so many *lovely* things to see!

Yesterday we went on a lovely auto ride to Malmaison and drove back through the Bois. I sat alone beside the chauffeur so that I wouldn't have to talk, which was also nice. I find Paris so captivating. I would really like to take a walk with you sometime through the narrow streets here and then have a look at the paintings and go for an occasional drive in the country.

A very nice letter arrived yesterday from Schröder. He is *seriously* considering taking a trip to Italy, if not with us, then by train. At this point, however, he still seems to be planning on traveling in the car with us. He will *of course* be coming along in Julie's mind. Should we not at least take him part way?!

Henry will be here tomorrow; I am very much looking forward to seeing him. However, I am afraid for him of everything that might appear.

---

94. Darius Milhaud (1892–1974).

Unfortunately, Rysselberghe's away now. It is very late, so a very good night.

Yours, Ottonie

P.S. We will be staying here until Tuesday evening.

❦ ❦ ❦

[Neubeuern] 22 March 1912

Well, we found our way back here from Paris. Unfortunately, both Julie and I have some strain of influenza; I have been told to stay in bed by Dr. Glaser. Julie has been in bed since yesterday. I just wanted to let you know that Mädy left for Graz today with her little Hügel cousin[95] whose father died of a heart attack yesterday. Mädy will probably return on the 27th or 28th and perhaps telegraph you when she arrives in Vienna. It would certainly make her happy if you or Gerty could meet her at the station. She will have many very unpleasant things to attend to there.

I feel like it has been a long time since I last heard from you. Are you perhaps also ill? If so, then maybe Gerty could write me a card – not a telegram. Mädy's address is:

Schloß Reinthal; Post St. Peter bei Graz.

Have to close now. I'm unable to collect my thoughts.

Warm greetings,

Ottonie

❦ ❦ ❦

[Rodaun] 1 April [1912], evening

Before I am able to feel close to you again, I must first regain some sense of myself. So much has transpired during the past few days, and as is always the case with me, everything is interwoven. It's difficult for me to separate a part – or myself – from the whole.

I'm very sorry to hear that you have been so ill! I just found out from the letter Mary wrote me. At first, I thought you had just gone to bed with a bit of a fever and headache and felt no need to worry. Now I'm beginning to feel concerned about the automobile trip we planned. Are you sure you will be completely better in four weeks? It has the possibility of being a wonderful trip, but I don't want to think about it yet. I have even forbidden myself to glance at the map or to picture the names of the cities, the distances between them, or the routes we'd take.

---

95. Huberta Countess von Hügel (1898–1915), niece of Anna von Degenfeld.

I wrote a letter to Schröder about four or five days ago asking him to send a telegram right away confirming that he will depart from Munich with us on the 28th. Now he is not answering me. However, I believe you said he wrote you that he would like to accompany us and is already looking forward to it. Erwin will not be able to come, at least not at the beginning; he has army service. Perhaps he can join us a couple weeks into the trip. He will probably be returning from Berlin soon; Gretl will soon be boarding a ship now. I have not heard from her in a long time.

How long can it have been since I wrote you? It must be perhaps ten or twelve days or even longer.

2nd evening

Well, I wanted to tell you a little about the days and evenings spent here with Strauss, with Reinhardt and, earlier on, with Mädy, who was so cute and touching in her manner. Then there's Moissi,[96] whom everyone here spoils; all the royal ladies enjoy following him around. After the performance of *Jedermann*, people ran into the manege and pick up the flowers that fell off the table during the party to keep as mementos — there's so much I wanted to tell you! But not now, I'm not able to.

What a poor man, our pediatrician and my father's good friend. They are about the only people who are Papa's friends. The poor man returned from Meran recently, sick again, and had to undergo another operation; he spent six days teetering between life and death, and today it looks as if death is gaining hold of him. A man so full of life, such a kind and intelligent doctor always so encouraging of others. It's hard to imagine what this will mean for Papa. It will be difficult for me to leave him here all by himself in May!

My head is so full, I am not able to write anything more at the moment, as much as I would like to. However, I can think pleasant and warm thoughts of you and of Eberhard, Mädy, and Julie. People mean so much! What is life?!

Good night.

H.

P.S. I am sending you a couple issues of a magazine containing a short novel by the young poet Max Mell,[97] whom I like very much. I would also like for Eberhard to read them. I think it is very good; it reveals the touch of a gentle and, at the same time, firm hand.

---

96. Alexander Moissi (1879–1935), famous actor in Reinhardt's troupe. First to play the title role in *Everyman*.
97. Max Mell (1882–1971), poet and playwright, great friend of H. v. H.

Neubeuern, 4 April 1912

God, I'm so happy to finally have a few lines from you. It had been three weeks since I last received a letter from you, and your letters mean *so much* to me – you have no idea *how* much. Especially during the time when I was really sick, I found myself waiting to hear from you; I really felt miserable and continued to wait for a letter from you each time the mail came – but always to no avail. First I told myself this was because of the essay you were working on and then *Jedermann* – of course I quietly said to myself inside that he always used to find a minute to write a few words; so it must be that he simply *can't* right now. That's also why I did not dare write to you. I thought this would just make things worse and remembered everything we had discussed regarding these kind of situations.

Hugo, again I have realized *what* you mean to me. It is very strange and very hard to explain. I thought our inner bond had been broken and that I had lost you, and I was so sad you *just cannot imagine*. I am able to admit this to myself now as the burden has now fallen from me like a bad dream. My life has become *so* rich because of you, and so – in some sense – happy.

I must tell you, on the very evening you wrote me, I also wrote you – the letter is still in my folder, but I didn't have the courage to give it its marching orders. I think this was for the best, for it was much too sad.

I've been thinking a great deal about your Papa, and the death of the good doctor! Might it not be best if Papa came along with us on our car trip instead of Schröder? I would be *very* happy to chat with him, and Gerty would have you there to talk to. The four of us together would be so nice. Or would this weigh too heavily on you?

I have been feeling better since yesterday. While I was ill, I of course lost the two pounds I had struggled so hard to gain by eating more, but I hope to gain it back soon. I am also very much looking forward to our trip – if it will only come to pass!

It's *delightful* having Eberhard here. We went for a walk this morning in the *beautiful* sunshine with a snow-covered landscape and green pine trees all around us. We talked a lot and very fondly about you. He's traveling to Berlin on Sunday with Mädy, where he has a full day ahead of himself at the dentist's there. Then they will all be returning to Bredeney; it will be very strange for us without Mädy here. The dinner gong is about to sound, so addio. With many loving thoughts,

Yours, Ottonie

P.S. Schröder wrote me the following on March 11th: "What's going to become of our heavenly plans to take a few automobiles to Italy? I suppose it will remain a mere castle in the sky, etc., etc. In any case, I intend to make my way to Italy, even if I have to ride in a shabby train."

❦ ❦ ❦

Easter Monday [8 April 1912]

I am so terribly sorry, Ottonie. It was nothing but – is nothing but – a lack of strength on my part. My strength does not extend beyond my immediate surroundings at times like these. This expresses itself as a fear of writing; the sentences were scarcely willing to leave my pen. It soon will pass: it's spring and great demands are placed on one's strength, that's all. It was so foolish of me not to write. As Mädy constantly spoke of you, I felt as if you were close by, indeed present, and I assumed that you would have the same feeling once Mädy arrived back there where you are.

I can't write much more at present. Please take care of yourself and get well in time for the trip to Italy and for sunning. Try *to avoid* any problems with Julie. It's almost unbelievable how *hurtful* and unfriendly Schröder has been. I wrote him on the 25th of March, expecting to receive confirmation that he'd be coming – how could I have expected otherwise? – and asked him to confirm our plans by telegram if possible. I didn't hear a thing from him for *13 days*. Finally I sent a telegram *à bout de mes nerfs* to his father inquiring as to Rudi's whereabouts. Then he (Rudi) sent me a telegram saying he couldn't go on the trip because of his sister's wedding, piles of work, and other things he had to do. I find this incredible. I am not going to include a note when I send him my *Homer* essay.

Who shall the third person be now? I guess Max Mell is the only possibility. You will like him very much. Erwin's army service will be over on the 10th of May, and he may join us after that. Would you find it unacceptable if it were just the three of us for the first ten days? Gerty does not seem to find this idea at all disagreeable. I have to go to town now.

Please send me a few lines.

H.

P.S. I never would have let three weeks pass like this if I had been able to send a telegram. A telegram of a mere twenty words truly provides a feeling of being in contact!

❦ ❦ ❦

Neubeuern, 9 April 1912

A few of your kind words manage to lift an entire iceberg from my shoulders. I am only sorry that you are about out of strength; it seems you took on too much recently and haven't had a moment of rest for months now. I hope the automobile trip will not be too taxing but instead will give you a chance to relax. Actually, I find the idea of the three of us being alone together very charming. Gerty and I will be happy to share you between us, don't you think?! However, I of course do not wish to stand in the way if you wish to bring young Mell along; *whatever* you two think is best will be fine with me. What you told me about Schröder is unfortunate. However, I wouldn't continue being mad at him. Everyone knows that Schröder is rather slow and bumbling with his responses, and then his sister's wedding interfered – very much against his wishes – with his plans. One simply has to show a great deal of patience towards friends. While Eberhard was here, he also had to wait for days for a very important reply from Henry van de Velde which he still hasn't received. Instead, van de Velde wrote me a letter during this same time in which he made no mention of Eberhard. We said to each other, "That is just the way these artists are, and you just have to accept them the way they are." You will just have to see good old Schröder the same way, too.

I am feeling *much* better again. I drink a lot of milk and eat eggs in order to gain back the kilo I lost. Julie is also well again; it took much longer in her case. Right now my brother is here, who will also be staying until I leave for my trip with you, which is very nice; and tomorrow Mr. Morton, a friend of Julie's, is coming. Throughout May van de Velde will be here in order to keep Julie company and to work here. This is of course *very* agreeable to me. From the 16th to the 20th. I will be with the child in Stuttgart; I will be staying at the Hotel Marquardt on the 20th, in Bad Boll near Göppingen until the 23rd, and then back here.

It was delightful having Eberhard here; he, too, enjoyed the chance to get away from everything for a few days. He was amazingly cheerful in spite of the problem he had just had with his tooth. It is delightful to feel how the whole house breathes easier as soon as he is here. I like him very much. Well, today poor Mädy is beginning her life in Essen again; it is *terribly* difficult for her being away from us. The children will only gradually join her. I find the short story by Mell is *very* well-written. So does Eberhard. Would you like to have it back?

Yours, Ottonie.

P.S. Well, good night – do rest well. Julie and Ottonie are getting on well!

Tuesday [1912]

Today, following a virtually sleepless night, your pencil letter arrived and made me very happy. All at once, I was able to conjure up a vivid image of you. It is awful that we are both so down right now. However, I am counting on being completely well and *alive* for the 28th. Do all that you can to get better yourself. Spend a day in bed; it does wonders for one's nerves. What is dragging me down so low is the work involved with *Ariadne*; having to stand between Strauss and Reinhardt, the whole notion of "differences," and this in the case of such a delicate thing which is the product of love – and to explain the dynamics, to ponder the letters that must be written, all with a mind that is already exhausted.

Of course, this should not be as great a burden as it has been, and neither would it be were I not still feeling the effects of the wondrous exhilaration I experienced in Berlin in addition to suffering from a cold, which is now on the wane. I love you very much (really). What delight and beauty have entered my life because of you. Adieu.

H.

❦ ❦ ❦

11 April [1912]

Your letter is so nice and kind; it completely rejuvenated me! There are things that truly weigh me down at times and cause me to stiffen and falter and even to feel impoverished, so much so that not even the most steadfast resolve allows me to display some strength or warmth towards anyone beyond the limits of my immediate surroundings; this is a very dark experience. There have been times like this throughout my life, so far back as the age of fifteen. They have somehow become less harmful over the years. Perhaps they are extremely profound and very mysterious forces which are so oppressive – it might be something appearing to be quite ordinary on the surface, which, mysteriously, has a tremendous impact on my constitution: the weather, this sluggish spring, held back in spite of the juices rising in the stems about to blossom; one stormy day after another, unremitting cold and storm, dark winter clouds – snowflakes when everything was so alive and ready to blossom. We had one day of Spring, on Easter Monday; it was extraordinary the way the chestnuts' branches with their limp leaves about to burst into bloom stretched out into the open space; everything had opened up, the entire world lay before me. You, too, belonged to this world. I do not want to and neither can I have you for myself – I wish for you to exist as a part of the world and to live your life there. You are still not leading the life you might, although you are closer to doing so than in the past – do you really think I could wish to let you go? That is also why I am clinging so tightly to the automobile trip we have planned and hope we will be four – the right four, whom we will manage to find. It has been determined that Erwin will come to join us from Meran (he has weapons training there). So we will be traveling alone for approximately the first ten days, possibly in the company of Mell, whom you will like very much. There is just one thing: I cannot say yet whether we will be leaving from Munich on the morning of the 28th, which I would very much prefer for various reasons, or on the 1st. However, please make sure you'd be able to arrive in Munich on the evening of the 27th in any case.

Aside from showing a lack of manners, for which friends forgive each other even if they cannot understand, I found it so absurd of Schröder – because of some kind of hypochondria and self-inflicted torture – to deny himself something he would so thoroughly enjoy and which may not come along again for many years. I asked Gerty to write him a letter along these lines, to which he responded yesterday with a telegram requesting patience for one more day and saying he would do everything possible. I almost think he may come after all.

Papa's situation is still unresolved and indeed rather agonizing. His doctor and friend is by no means dead, as you presumed, but rather is still caught between life and death. His strong constitution and healthy heart have withstood everything astonishingly well. Every single day he runs the risk of hemorrhaging when his dressing is changed, in which case he would die instantly. If this can be avoided, then he will have been healed, and not just temporarily, but permanently. In a few months, he would be fully recovered and capable of the same level of activity as any other normal person. This is indeed a rather trying situation. Hopefully it will finally come to an end; word has it there are still about ten critical days remaining.

I find the tolerance you and Eberhard have for such incomprehensible behavior – the kind you attribute to van de Velde – admirable but baffling nonetheless. At any rate, I would implore you not to view it as belonging to the character of an artist, whereby in truth there is no connection between the two (such conduct is more likely to be associated with dilettantism or simply stupidity and unmanliness). If anything, artists should be more humane or at the very least not less so! For it is less than humane to trample on and test the nerves of one's fellow man, and, in any case, it is below a man's dignity to tolerate such treatment for the sake of other, redeeming qualities a person may have. That everything goes wrong in the life of someone who habitually behaves like this is to be expected. It is simply repulsive how unaccomplished he is in the art of life.

On days such as these, books about Napoleon are tremendously valuable to me and are practically the only thing that has some meaning. I just read the history of the year of 1814 and the *campagne de France* (which took place between Leipzig and the abdication), perhaps the greatest chapter in the history of his life. Everything began to give way at this point: France's resolve, his generals' nerves, their horses, the canon, the rifles, and everything else, except for him. The necessity which carried these events forward is truly indescribable. There is a profound and grand symbolism to it all that not even the feeblest of minds could fail to recognize. I have ordered the *Rémusat memoirs* (1802–1808), which I will send to you one volume at time.

It really is rather depressing that you follow through with the reading plan (on which so very much depends) so fastidiously every fall, only to let everything fall by the wayside once spring arrives, allowing week after week to pass without making any mention of what you're reading. There's a newspaper in the package of books I sent you the day before yesterday which contains the essay I wrote about Schröder's *Homer*. Please send it to Eberhard on my behalf as soon as you finish reading it. You may keep Mell's novella – the many superior qualities of which may become even more clear to you upon a second reading (it's about the only good peasant story that I know of) – there to perhaps use for reading aloud from on occasion.

I hope both bookcases have been removed – I urged Mädy to see to this – from the room in which they don't belong at all and that they have been wrapped and stored until your arrival in Hinterhör. It is of course very childish of me, but I was bothered that you unpacked them there and even more by the fact that you did not think to put them away afterwards; for what makes them so lovely is that they are perfect for the type of wood and dimensions found in your room in Hinterhör. The older I become, the more – almost disproportionately – something *hors de sa place, hors de propos*, bothers me – there is nothing I can do about this, however, hence the force of my objection to your use of "Henry" back then. That's also why a letter from you as well as your manner – when your countenance reflects the way you are inside – can make me feel so happy; and herein lies much that is real, proper and vital, so perfectly suited to life. Perhaps my essay about *Homer* will help you to understand this better.

I hope you remain well and will write soon.

Yours, H.

R., 17 April [1912]

I am very happy you wrote me a few lines; I was beginning to think you had fallen ill again. There is only one thing I need to mention today: I think we'll be leaving at about 8:45 a.m. on the 30th from Hotel Marienbad. I'll be busy to the very end and will hardly be able to make it to Munich before the 29th. Now, about your luggage. In the car you can bring along a carry-on suitcase (not the size you'd take aboard a ship) in addition to the *necessaire*.[98] You will have to check the larger suitcase – the

---

98. A small suitcase.

one you're sending by train – to Brixen (in Tyrol) no later than the 26th (use express or rush mail). But how will you cross the Austrian border with it? Please talk to Schenker or some other agent about this; you can either attach the key or perhaps it would be best if you have a servant take your luggage from Neubeuern to Kufstein, where he can check it through customs and straight on to Brixen. Please talk to Mary about this right away so that she'll be able to remind you of it when the time comes. (We *won't* be traveling to Innsbruck by way of Kufstein in the car.)

Also, please bring a large and heavy carriage blanket to Munich if possible, as we do not own one ourselves. (Also bring some automobile goggles for yourself.)

I will let you in on a few things regarding this summer. The Salzburg Mozart concerts have been canceled this year. Gretl and Erwin plan to arrive in Aussee circa the 25th, so I hope you can make it around the 2nd, 3rd, or 4th of August, if this suits you. The automobile trip will end in Munich on the 25th or 26th of May. This should help you in making plans. Mell is as happy as a little child. I am almost beginning to believe myself that we will actually be taking this trip.

H.

Rodaun, 10 June [1912]

We just arrived here the day before yesterday (the evening of the 7th). We had to postpone departure for Paris, in part because of Diaghilev's[99] request and also because Gerty needed to rest for a few days following a very severe throat infection and high fever. She spent more than half our stay in Paris in bed in the little room we had looking out over the Rue Castiglione. She is quite healthy now, however. In order to cheer her up, Mariano Fortuny presented her with a lovely evening coat made of light, black velvet covered with golden flowers and other decorations. One night in my hotel while Gerty was suffering from a high fever, I had several nice conversations with Reinhardt, one of which was particularly nice. I am awfully fond of him. Everything is fine with Kessler. Suddenly I've come to see him in such a way that I feel terribly sorry for him. The tension he had felt has disappeared. The entire man is filled with talent, and yet there is something crucial missing – how horribly sad. First I am going to work with him on the ballet for the Russians. It's a biblical subject (*The Joseph Legend*)[100] with costumes à la Paul Veronese. For various reasons

---

99. Serge Diaghilev, owner and director of the Ballet Russe.
100. Pantomime written by H. v. H., music by Richard Strauss. Premiere with the Ballet Russe in Paris, 14 May 1914.

Orest and *La Mort du jeune homme voluptueux,* my two completed subjects, are going to be set aside until 1914. I went ahead and promised Reinhardt I would write an entire pantomime for him; working with him is simply too wonderful to resist. The only way men are truly able to communicate with one another is through their work.

Among the 2,000 letters I received here were a few very kind and touching lines from Mädy. Gretl is in South Tirol, with Erwin and the child; apparently she is well.

I feel well rested, more so than I have in years; my nerves are perfectly fine.

An anonymous political article came from Borchardt that I find truly exceptional.

That you should have happy and rich memories of our Italian trip was the reason we went there in the first place. I am planning to pick you up in Salzburg around the 25th of July. The second Rémusat will soon be arriving. Today I am sending you Browning (*Ring and Book*), which you will perhaps find is very accessible now with its extraordinarily Italian setting.

H.

❦ ❦ ❦

[Hotel de Castiglione, Paris 12, Rue de Castiglione] Sondershausen, 17 June 1912

I am not in Paris as the heading might lead you to believe but rather once again a Thuringian Fräulein, here in the peaceful and humble surroundings of the old house. At present we must let everyone enjoy our company; relatives and old friends constantly come to admire the "Wunderkind." Then they discover that the fairy tale about the Wunderkind is no fairy tale but reality – I wonder if it will go on like this forever!?

What do you think about the constant craving I have for pleasure?! I was with the Veldes and other Weimaranians in Lauchstädt on Friday to see *Gabriel Schilling's Flight*. The whole experience in the sleepy little town was delightful, this mass of elegant, and some not so elegant, people; the little park there with a pond on which a few self-reliant swans confidently glided past us – it truly belonged to a different world. Then, filled with anticipation, we arrived at the theater. The audience was awfully quiet during the first three acts, and then all at once, after the fourth act, they broke into an uproarious applause which lasted until the end.

I didn't care for the play myself. I found the characters of Luci and Maurer *very good* and superbly portrayed, but the part of Schilling was too morbid and there didn't seem to be any conflict, as he does not really love either of the women. At the end the doctor ruins everything by declaring that he had always had these feelings inside him and now they finally revealed themselves. I can imagine the whole thing would be much better as a novel and better able to shed light on the characters' feelings. As a play, however, it is really a series of conversations, in part very good ones.

Afterwards we all returned to Weimar; we had a very amusing time together staying up to the wee hours in the Russian Hof. I returned here on Saturday.

I met Rathenau in Lauchstädt, and Studnitz and Nostitz sent a telegram in the end saying they could not make it as she or his father was ill (I cannot remember which one). I felt very sorry about this because I would have liked to meet her so much.

Thank you very much for the Brownings. I read the first volume yesterday and found it very interesting. I recently read some of Goethe's *Italienische Reise* and especially enjoyed the part about the arena in Verona. It is delightful the plain and simple way he describes it all.

It's impossible to continue writing with everything going on around me here. One sister is making lace, and the little wooden pegs constantly rattle against one another, and next to her the other sister is reading to Baby. Baby is really enjoying the Grimm fairy tales now, which I read to her almost every day.

Addio. Many warm regards,

Yours, Ottonie.

❦ ❦ ❦

Rodaun, 26 June [1912]

I often think about writing you and want to very much but do not manage to. There's simply not enough time. I *must* concentrate and need to spend a good deal of time alone; the hours race by and nothing comes of them. But this nothing is in fact worth much more than anything else. At times it seems paradoxical being a poet and a human being at the same time, a contemporary of others, a husband, father and man of the house at Badegasse 5. Thoroughly incomprehensible.

I made every attempt to be as outgoing as possible on the automobile trip, which did me an immense amount of good (I can still feel it's benefits). Everything around me was stripped of whatever significance it might have had. I thought you would understand this (during the trip), but you made an unfortunate remark – attempting to sum things up – on our last day in Kufstein. I wished I could forget it the very moment you uttered it; in fact, I did manage to forget it. Nothing in the world could bring me to recall the precise content of the remark now, but it showed me that you didn't really comprehend what actually lay behind my behavior. One must never take me *à la lettre,* but this has nothing to do with trust or a lack thereof.

For a period of a few days, I was absolutely baffled by what you said about Browning. You said you read through the first volume and found it "interesting" – this deadly word people of this world use to mask their inability to grasp something; I thought it possible you would find Browning difficult to understand and might gain nothing from reading him. However, if you did understand it – as appears to be the case – then a new and truly extraordinary mind has entered your horizon, a mind which exposes life in a new and remarkably magical and disquieting manner and is a world unto itself. When you used the most obtuse of all imaginable words to describe the turn-around that triggers the experience of the same phenomenon in every person who is not obtuse – were you perhaps tired and distracted by the various trivialities which intrude upon you there? Indeed I must admit that I found your description rather depressing; I felt like one does when one realizes one has lost one's way. It's strange that I somehow feel that you are in some way receptive to matters of the intellect during the autumn – also in Italy I felt this way at every important juncture. However, the various forms of intellectual *abaissement* have simply woven a very treacherous web for themselves in your life; at times the machinery of Neubeuern takes over, at others *corvées*, like the stay in Paris with Julie, and again soon those family get-togethers – and yet *everything* depends, Ottonie, upon your not *vegetating* in some other, less lugubrious form of existence, but rather you must live, continue to develop, and move *forward*.

Yours, H.

P.S. I still have quite a few blocks of the nice stationery left but have almost run out of envelopes. Perhaps you could send me another 50 or 100 of them!

❦ ❦ ❦

[Hinterhör] 6 June [=July] 1912

I'm all settled in back here in the golden sunshine of Hinterhör! It's simply *too* lovely here! We still feel excited about everything in and around the house, and we are all as happy as could be. The castle is empty, which makes it even more delightful being here. Now I wish you were here, but that's *too* wonderful to imagine!

I can easily believe I wrote a rather dull-witted letter in Sondershausen. First of all, I generally don't write very good letters, and there they end up being twice as bad. My mind was filled with nothing but thoughts of all sorts of people that I had to attend to in one way or another.

The Browning in particular so enchanted me that I read all day long; I kept reading further and further without *being able* to stop – which doesn't happen to me very often – and then I go and say it was "terrifically interesting" – what a stupid thing to say. But that's me! Here today, however, I'm feeling so good that nothing could make me sad. On the contrary, I'm very cozy here at my desk and have two lovely little new cabinets in which I have placed many lovely things from a dear friend, and they greet me in shared memory of the wonderful hours spent together this past year. Perhaps I have misunderstood them all, but I am certain they do not hold it against me and instead say to themselves, "She simply enjoys us in her own way," and are happy they mean so much to her and are able to benefit her – indeed to have returned to her her entire life.

You also wrote something about some comment I made about you in Kufstein. I don't remember what it was I said; nothing comes to mind. And the only memories I have are of the delightful times and wonderful moments I experienced throughout the entire trip. The only thing I can still remember about you personally is that you were so kind to take care of everything the way you did, and otherwise, only that the way we toured Rome didn't appeal to you. That's everything! Please don't continue to think about this anymore.

Oh, I must tell you, *today* life doesn't seem so burdensome. I wonder if this will last? It's so lovely in the afternoon (right this second) when the sunlight streams through my yellow curtains; everything shines brightly as if bathed in gold. It really is lovely here. My *Ferienkinder* have already arrived and the van de Veldes are excited about being in Nussdorf.

So, addio, then.

Yours, Ottonie

[Hinterbrühl, Hauptstrasse 19] Tuesday [9 July 1912]

I certainly am glad the postmaster thought to have your lovely letter forwarded to me here rather than sending it to Aussee. It has once again given me some idea of how you are and what your days are like now. I was already very grateful for the telegram you sent. Before, I had been telling myself, "She is such a kind woman. How is it that whenever life is not treating me well, she, through deliberate silence, does everything possible to make it more difficult or impossible for me to achieve inner peace? This is by no means trivial. It is easy to say, "Get back to work now!", but one must in fact leave behind this world and enter a completely different one, while removing the thousands of threads by which it hangs: father and children and the home and business as well as correspondence and all the rest which cannot be broken. It requires careful handling with gentle, steady hands to undo all this – temporarily. One can only hope to accomplish this. In recent years, there have been very few days, a few isolated instances, that I can say were truly productive. I was no richer in the past than I am now, indeed perhaps poorer, and no doubt lonelier. But I more often benefited from a certain indescribable inner harmony between the external and the internal, between my inner self and the world, and without this, I do not wish to live. What is everything else by comparison? The lonely man who leads a one-sided life more readily achieves this kind of harmony. However, I do not regret being like other men and having children for whom I provide a home, even though this part of my life is alien to me at times.

Everything you tell me about being alone in the house and about the books provides me more happiness than I deserve – *assuming* I deserve anything from you. I understand now what you said in the letters you wrote from Sondershausen. You made some beautiful and very loving comments about Browning. He has certainly been done justice if viewed as a man whose mission it was to elevate you above the tedium of everyday life.

I have already forgotten what it was we were talking about in Kufstein, and even more so if it was not meant to be taken as an intelligent, serious, or significant observation.

I enjoyed very much being back in Rodaun. The countryside there is also more beautiful than words can express. When I am old, I will continue to explore the Rodaun area and still shall never discover everything it has to offer – but you must become acquainted with this region before more years pass. I look forward to wandering through the valleys here with you. Is this now a promise? The children and the servants have arrived in Aussee. We are going to wait a few more days until the bustle of unpacking boxes and trunks in the little house is over; then we, too, will go there. My mother-in-law will be arriving there on the 14th and staying for about two weeks. So I will plan to pick up a girlfriend of mine in Salzburg sometime during the last few days of July. Will that be all right?

Adieu, Ottonie. I am very fond of you. Do you really have kind feelings towards me? Or what?

Your friend, H

❦ ❦ ❦

[Hinterhör] Sunday [14 July 1912]

I reserved Placci's rooms at Hotel Marquard beginning on the 15th. I ordered them immediately after returning from Italy, including a room for you, which can be canceled at any time should you wish to stay somewhere else.

We got back from the Heuberg yesterday evening. We spent three delightful days there with all the children and also had beautiful weather. It was so wonderful lying there on the meadow and watching Baby prance about among the flowers. Any depressing thought I might have had soon disappeared, vanquished by the beauty of nature up there. Just as we were about to leave, your letter arrived. It was especially kind. It seems that Hinterhör is somehow able to make everything sound more innocent, everything that departs from there and whatever returns; it is such a blessing.

It is mean of me to remain silent so often, but in Sondershausen I had the *distinct* feeling that I could not write the way I wanted to, and this made it impossible for me to write anything at all. I should have simply sent you a telegram.

I also think you must know by now that the reason I am silent is not to show you how I feel inside, but rather simply because I cannot write at that particular moment. It no longer bothers me as much as it used to when you let a couple of weeks go by without my hearing from you. I know then that something is keeping you very busy.

Today is another glorious day. Everything in and around me is so peaceful, and the children are delightful. *This* is how I wish to live all the time, a little outside of the world and without any worldly ambitions, and without snobs. I am of course very content now, as it is still peaceful at the castle, which does mean I have more work to do, but there are fewer people and less supervision. On Saturday Julie will be back; I wonder, will you be coming to help her with the matter concerning the fountain,[101] or is your life filled with too many distractions right now, which I suspect? Otherwise you could of course stay for several days, and we would then travel to Aussee together around the 25th. I can stay until the 4th; on the 5th, I would like to be back here for Puppy's birthday. If it suits you better because of your mother-in-law for me to come later, then I will simply forget the birthday and will come from the first to the 13th. I definitely have to be back on the 15th, as I am expecting my father then.

At the moment, I have an awful lot of letters to write, however, this does not bother me at all. There is an unfortunate person, for whom I am searching for a position, and I have a lot to write for this, which I hope will ultimately yield a positive result.

Did I ever tell you that I spent a *delightful* day in Degenershausen with Mädy and Eberhard? It was so very, very nice, the three of us there in the wonderful seclusion of the woods.

---

101. In memory of her husband, Jan, Julie presented the village of Neubeuern with water coming from a spring on her land and a fountain in the village square.

Well then, addio for today. Do not torture yourself by worrying about me, and do not feel you have to write – do so only if you feel the need. I no longer wish to be a burden on you; rather I would prefer to be like a little butterfly that flutters quietly above your shoulder now and then when you are sitting down on your little bench out in the woods.

Yours, Ottonie

🍎 🍎 🍎

[Hinterhör] 27 July 1912

I am so terribly sorry I had to write you about decreasing the length of my stay in Aussee, but there was nothing I *could* do about it this time. I know *how* horribly unpleasant it is for you when plans one made a long time ago have to be changed. That is why I waited so long to see if it might not be possible for me to avoid going to Eybach, but it just was not possible this time. Please do not take this to reflect a lack of desire on my part or an inability to stand up to others. It simply was not possible.

I will try to leave Eybach on the afternoon of the 7th, perhaps traveling as far as Salzburg. Then I could leave for Gmunden the morning of the 8th if you're able to meet me there. I do not have a train schedule here with me to check the times. I just worry that I may have a rather long layover in Attnang. As far as I can recall, one always has to wait there a rather long time for the connection. Would it be possible for us to meet there? Or is that too far to ride your bike? Of course you should do whatever is most convenient for you.

Yesterday I was on the Wendelstein with my children, descending on foot and lunching at the Heиselers', where we also met the Veldes and Lampes. It was a delightful day. I am expecting Velde for supper this evening. Unfortunately, he has to leave Monday and will be gone for eight days. He is really a very agreeable person and very nice to have around. One always has a good time in his company.

My life is completely devoted to the children for now. I enjoy their energy and how they show their love in such charming little ways. This together with the calm of Hinterhör makes me very happy. Often one feels quite rich; one might even be able to share some of this with others. I am surrounded by such harmony right now: my cozy little room where I write letters, all *my* books, and even Sisi, who always tries to lift the burdens from my shoulders. I often think, even if *much* has been taken away from me, I still have a lot left, which I am just now learning to appreciate.

Take care of yourself now. I will be going to Eybach on the 3rd.

A thousand warm thoughts,

Yours, Ottonie

❦ ❦ ❦

[Postcard]   [Bad Aussee, 1 August 1912]

I never thought for a second that it was your fault or due to carelessness on your part, but rather simply the result of unfortunate circumstances. Of course, I could not really understand what you wrote in your last letter about why you simply have to spend three days in Eybach and why you cannot do so from 27th–31st July. However, you can explain this to me later. I only could not accept your choice of the 4th as your departure date not knowing that Gretl will most likely be arriving then. I will have a look at the train schedule and send a letter to you in Eybach. I do not believe you will have a *substantial* layover in Attnang.

If you would like to spend the night in Salzburg (Hotel Österrr. Hof), then you will have to send a telegram two or three days in advance to reserve a room. I would appreciate it very much if, in addition to the *Rémusat*, you could also bring along Shakespeare (the volume containing the sonnets) with you as well as *Der Arme Mann im Tockenburg* and Novalis' *Hymnen*.

I hope you continue to feel at peace. I have a very clear head right now.

Yours, H.

❦ ❦ ❦

[Postcard]   Aussee, Sunday, 4 August [1912]

Gretl is still not here; we expect her any day. There really is no train in the morning that runs from Salzburg with a connection to Gmunden. So take the little local train (*Salzkammergutlokalbahn*) which leaves from Salzburg at 8:05 (if that is not too early for you?). You would travel to Strobl, where you would arrive around 10:29 (Strobl is a very nice spa). I will make sure to be at the station before you arrive. We could have lunch in Ischl – maybe I can manage to find an automobile in Ischl. Would this suit you? Check your luggage in Salzburg (the larger suitcase) straight through all the way to Ischl, or Aussee if possible.

Please send me a telegram.

Yours, H.

Aussee, Wednesday, 21 [August 1912]

It has already been a week now since you left! Yet here surrounded by this countryside I still feel such a close connection to you. We are only separated by a few mountains and valleys after all, and it is no problem traversing them in one's imagination! I sometimes feel that you are over in the very next room.

We just had three beautiful, sunny days — true summer weather. The four of us lay on blankets on the ground in the woods, and I read Homer to them.

These days Gretl was so unbelievably tired and exhausted. She was unable even to walk the shortest distance, no further than out to the carriage. Mentally, she was sharp as a tack. She could visualize her entire life. It felt very strange, which I can believe. Yesterday she began to regain some of her strength. She suffered from nervous exhaustion, which one so often feels when one starts to relax.

Erwin returned on Monday. I see Ilse now and then — it is amazing, however, how little strength an attraction of this kind has when it is based solely on a pair of eyes, a mouth, and the outline of a person. I cannot begin to tell you how peculiar I find this.

Eberhard, the good man, seems overjoyed and very touched by the fact that we are planning to visit him. I decided on the 31st and 1st. We will travel to Salzburg with Erwin and Gretl, and then they will continue on to Tyrol.

You are reading Keats, *The Pot of Basil*, now, right? After this, read the sonnet he wrote in the *later* part of his life (he died at the age of 25).

Adieu.

Hugo

P.S. It was wonderful having you here, and everything went fine, the way it should.

[Hinterhör] 22 August 1912

How time flies! I have meant to write for a very long time now but just could not seem to find the right moment. We had to take advantage of the few good days to be outdoors and go on excursions.

Yes, it was indeed lovely in Aussee, even if it was a little short. I have such fond memories, especially of a couple of walks we took together. They must have really been wonderful; we surely felt very close to each other. One never forgets moments like these and continues to benefit from them in countless ways. I think you are entirely right: Beautiful eyes, pretty hair and an attractive figure are wonderful to look at, but the moment they are gone, one is left with an empty feeling when there is no soul behind it.

How lovely that Gretl had such a fabulous time. She has incredible charm when she expresses herself through her eyes and gestures. At such moments she reveals something from deep within her. She gave me a great gift by telling me about her whole life; they have helped me to view child-rearing in a completely different way.

Yesterday Mary took Karin to Salzburg in order to send her off to Gastein, where she will actually be spending several days alone with her father; however, I think Mädy will follow as soon as tomorrow.

My "dearest" Steinitzer[102] is here as well as Mädy's friend, Heinrich. We play tennis whenever we get the chance; it is very nice having both of them around for this. It is a pity Gerty is not able to be here as well.

Addio. My warmest regards for all of you.

Yours, Ottonie.

❦ ❦ ❦

[Bad Aussee] Friday [30 August 1912]

Gerty read your letter while lying in bed. She had another bout with angina and still has mouth and gum infections and a bit of a fever. Unfortunately she has not seen Erwin and Gretl the entire week, except for 15 minutes this morning before they both left. It all began last Sunday, a beautiful night with the moon veiled in mist. All of a sudden, Gerty no longer felt like sitting outside, and by the following morning she had a high fever. It placed rather a damper on the cheerful time we were all enjoying together. We had planned to accompany both of them to Salzburg before continuing on to Gastein. Now, of course, I will be traveling alone by myself to Gastein. I plan to leave this Sunday, assuming Gerty's condition improves enough that I feel comfortable leaving her alone.

We still enjoyed many happy hours together. It is very true indeed – even if I have often expressed this in jest – that it is Gretl's intellect, and this alone, which captivates me about her. It is her understanding of things and the stories she tells – she told quite a few during this past visit – about her childhood and the experiences she has had. Bit by bit I read aloud to them well over half of the *Odyssey*. Beginning with the part about the Phoenicians, I did not skip over anything, and on many an occasion I read two or more songs in one sitting – this on dark, rainy days. With all the concern over Gerty's poor health – she, so fainthearted, often softly crying alone – this then was the best hour of the day.

---

102. Friend of O. D. S.'s husband, apparently in love with her.

I will be happy if I can make it to Gastein as planned; I am looking forward to it, and I know Eberhard is as well. I want him to believe that where there's a will there's a way.

I feel your stay here was much too short – I often think I still have your visit to look forward to. Then I realize that it has already passed, and it is as though a passing cloud had veiled the sun. In July I felt rich, full of plans and expectations – August produced nothing; now much depends on September.

Once again they make your mother-in-law stay with you; I find this rather unnecessary. I would very much appreciate a letter telling me what you are reading now (which would allow me to send a few additional books related to the ones you are currently reading).

H.

❦ ❦ ❦

Aussee, 5 [September 1912]

It worries me that you have once again been saddled with the old lady[103] in the little house there during this eternally dreary weather, with the sun nowhere in sight. Now and then I think about how Mädy tried to explain to me that there is nothing to be done about it, that everyone simply must do his part, and that you are now healthy enough and have the strength, etc. However, I do not believe you are healthy enough. I am hoping this is just the modest beginning of something much greater – that is why I am worried. Your daily routine seems so very arduous to me. There's always something you have to do every moment of the day. You can never enjoy a meal alone and have no time for yourself to go on a pleasant walk with a book. Perhaps it is not as hopeless as it seems. The rooms there are quite cheerful and cozy. Perhaps you do have a few hours to yourself when you can read, etc. Please write me concerning this if possible – but, *please*, do not write me when you are having difficulty concentrating, as you did on many an occasion this past spring. I was able to perceive the weightlessness of your pen as it glided, almost unthinkingly, across the paper. More than anything else, I would like to know if you are finding time to read and if so, what exactly, and also whether or not you are engrossed in it and able to really enjoy it. I do not know if you have acquired enough of a feel for Goethe and Shakespeare to be able to make a smooth transition from one to the other. Make sure you read *Measure for Measure*, which I find to be one of his strangest works. It has some truly divine passages. Then read *Othello* at some point, too, but only when you can really concentrate. It would be a crime otherwise. In addition, you

---

103. O. D. S. had to take care of her mother-in-law.

should also read the *Rémusat*. Please write me the name of the publisher of your Browning edition as well as the name of the edition itself, if it has a special one.

Eberhard was delightful. The most enjoyable time we had was a conversation while taking a walk; I forced myself, despite the bleak skies and rain, to tell him *tant bien que* about *Die Frau ohne Schatten*, which I managed to describe very well. For the first time, I saw the whole thing before me, including the audience, and was truly moved by the beauty of this creation and its human content. My own insight into the whole as well as Eberhard's comments provided me with a wealth of details and directions which I have since made a point of jotting down. Now I can honestly say that the entire poem exists in me and has, in a certain sense, been saved.

Gerty is beginning to recover finally. If the sun would ever decide to shine for a couple of days, she would be completely well. My father is here now, but I doubt he'll be able to stand it very long. It's been raining almost continuously for the past four days (and nights).

I am now going to finish writing the introduction to *Die Deutschen Erzähler*, which they are waiting for me to complete. Once Gerty is able to travel (in five or six days I expect), I will escape to the region around Bolzano, or Venice, or wherever the sun might happen to be shining. What is so painful is when one's productivity is artificially suppressed by nature; in this weather all is dark and cold and there is a great deal of unrest in the house.

Adieu.

H.

P.S. I was struck by what you said about not perceiving or feeling the other half of the world. It was less tangible to me, something much more vague, much more insubstantial. I feel it can only be healed from the very center of one's being, from the soul.

[Hinterhör] 15 September 1912

Finally, I am going to write you a letter. However, I am not sure whether I will be able to finish it today. Please do not worry about me. I am *so* full of energy right now and am able to accomplish a great deal of what I simply could not do last year.

I of course have not had much time alone recently; our little house here is completely full, what with Mama, my father, two nieces and on top of this, Mary's brother (however, he is staying in a place called "Villa Rosa" in the nearby village) and also two new maids. Nevertheless, I have had a very easy time taking care of everything.

I went to Munich with Father and the two girls on Thursday afternoon. I just happened to read that *Jedermann* was being performed in the Hoftheater, so I took my whole crowd along. It was wonderful! I got a lot more out of it than I did at the premiere, where all the excitement made it difficult to enjoy the real context of the play. Of course, you could not compare it to the performance in Berlin in any way, and yet one was captivated by it from beginning to end. There was not a moment when we felt that it was dragging. I think you could perform *Jedermann* in a tiny little flea-pit, and it would still have just as powerful an effect on the audience. My father was so *deeply* moved by it that he refused to go see another play with us the following evening. Instead, he returned to Hinterhör alone. He asked me to offer you his most sincere thanks for this great work and I was to say this in my own best words. I am so glad I brought him along. As he is a very religious man, I was concerned that something said on stage, such as hearing the "Lord's Prayer," might offend him. I was *so* incredibly happy when I saw how thoroughly gripped he was by it.

The next morning, I took him with me to the *Alte Pinakothek* where we looked at the beautiful paintings. And again, in addition to my own enjoyment, the excitement he felt for the first time in a long while made me incredibly happy. He is a very appreciative audience. It was a particularly lovely collection they were showing just then – wonderful paintings by Rembrandt, Franz Hals and others. I thoroughly enjoyed myself and shall always remember this day.

You asked what I am reading now. Actually, one can hardly call it reading. I occasionally have a look at Hebbel's diaries or the Rémusat, which always helps me to relax. Things will probably remain a bit hectic until Mama moves into the castle, but I am having no difficulty managing everything.

Eberhard will be coming tomorrow. I am looking forward very much to seeing him, but as always, it will only be a short visit.

I can *well* understand your flight to a sunny place. It is so dreary and rains *every* single day. Since I returned from Aussee, we have had only two nice days. I would also love to leave everything behind and head to Italy.

Smith, Elder & Co. (15 Waterloo Place) has published *The Ring and the Book*. How wonderful that *Die Frau ohne Schatten* is being brought back to life! I often remember what you told me about it, and I always had a special love for it. I am looking forward to the time when you seriously begin to work on it.

For now good-bye, and do enjoy the sunshine.

Yours, Ottonie

[Hinterhör] 22 September 1912

Yesterday I enjoyed a delightful hour, thanks to you. Eberhard brought me the foreword to the *Erzählungen*. Once everyone had returned to the castle – Mama is a little unwell, so she went to bed early – I sat all alone in my lovely little blue room and felt so very close to you. It is a wonderful introduction to these stories. Everyone is going to love these books.

A few days ago, a splendid case of fruit arrived from Bozen. I must assume you are the kind gift-giver, for I cannot think of anyone else there I am close to. So please be kind enough to accept Madam Hinterhör's sincere thanks.

Now I have a question for you which we discussed here yesterday and would like to hear your answer: If you and Strauss are content with this proposal, and if you would like to have a place where all friends could meet after the *Ariadne* performance, it could be arranged at Fritz Gemmingen's house (if he agrees), or also at another place. We would just have to be absolutely certain that you and Strauss would both be there. About how many guests might we expect you to bring? Perhaps ten to twenty or twenty to thirty people? It does not matter how many as long as we have a general idea. First you'll have to ask Strauss if he finds this acceptable, and then you can let me know. We would also make firm arrangements to have Putlitz and the Schillings come. Please do not take us along. Of course, it is up to you how many guests you would like to invite. We would just need to have some idea how large a number it is going to be.

Do you have enough sun there for you to be able to work? It is cold here, and we hardly have any sun. Eberhard is full of energy and very dear. We took a lovely walk together and talked about many things.

Well, addio for now. I have to go back to the castle, where the Wolffs will be today as well.

Sending a thousand loving thoughts,

Yours, Ottonie

Schloss Gandegg im Eppan [26 September 1912]

The two lovely letters you sent make me feel as though you were *here*. Even without them, I can feel your person and almost feel your presence, which is always so natural and so very kind. The scent of your soap on Erwin's and Gretl's hands adds to the feeling in a peculiar sort of way. What a strange way to touch others by sprinkling one's own scent about. All of a sudden, I feel like traveling again to Erfurt or sitting on the bench near the meadow where the sheep are grazing.

My prose work is coming along, or at least it seems to be. However, here, too, it is cold and dark. We will leave on Sunday, Gerty for Rodaun and I for Munich. I will be there in the "Marienbad" from Sunday evening until the 15th, or at least I plan to stay until then. You will come to visit me there for a day sometime, right?

I must also tell you how incredibly happy it constantly makes me that you are going to be in Stuttgart. Please do not ever let my foolish playing around *prevent* you from coming on such a day. You cannot imagine how much you are a part of my life.

It will be impossible to have a semi-private party on the first night (evening of the 25th). There will not be ten or twenty, but more like 150 to 200 people, whose hands I will have to try to shake and who cannot be left out (there were 400 in Dresden). I cannot allow them to feel that they are being neglected. There is only one possibility: to dine in the largest room at the Marquardt and for you, Kessler, the Taxis (Marie and Titi), Margit Zichy, Schröder, Gretl, etc., to sit at my table.

Maybe I will find a little note in the Marienbad.

Yours, H.

❦ ❦ ❦

[Hinterhör] 8 November 1912

How quickly things take a different turn from what one expects. When I arrived back here from Munich Sunday evening, I found Baby rather tired and pale. She had come down with a high fever and diphtheria on Sunday. Praise God we passed the most critical stage last night. The thoughts that go through one's mind day and night at times like these. It is a terribly strange feeling when one vividly imagines the worst of all possibilities. I felt as though I were falling into a deep abyss, and it became clear to me how everything I do is ultimately done with the child in mind. She is so touching in her illness.

I am *very* happy we are still here and not in the castle; there everything would be discussed before a decision can be made, which is a tremendous drain on one's nerves. We are obviously completely isolated from everything here; there is no Sisi, or anybody, coming to visit us. This allows for a degree of peace which we never had here before. Nobody here knows that it is really diphtheria. Instead, we have let them believe it is the mumps, for otherwise we would immediately have had a huge ordeal on our hands with the local authorities and the precautionary measures that have to be taken. We can do without that additional burden.

I began reading *The Brothers Karamazov* yesterday and of course am unable to stop. It is incredibly wonderful and good.

We have real winter weather now – 22 degrees and a beautiful snow landscape with lovely sunshine.

I often think of *Ariadne*, and whenever I do, all the problems that weighed so heavily on her are lifted, and the only thing that remains is the wonderful memory of this evening. Have I ever really told you *how* much I love *Ariadne*? I am sure you knew this anyway.

Take care.

Yours, Ottonie

❦ ❦ ❦

[Rodaun] Sunday [10 November 1912]

I found your letter here yesterday evening when I returned from town. The painting by Hodler was propped up against the side of my desk; it arrived at the same time. Strangely enough, instead of causing me worry and excitement, your letter allowed me to feel your presence. I felt the purest joy knowing that you exist. It was so wonderful, and I have felt so grateful all day. Nothing is more foreign to you than attempting to provide a sketch of yourself in a letter, which still portrays you incredibly well: the concern and, at the same time, the composure you show; your enjoyment of the peace and quiet and time by yourself; your mention of the lovely, cold, snowy weather; the nice transition you made to reading the sublime and indeed almost sacred Russian novel; and your comments about *Ariadne*, which I find almost embarrassing. All this together forms the totality that is you, and I cannot express how much it means to me having found you. In a sense, my second life began after I met you. One thing I am sure of: I may continue to be your friend, indeed I must, yet at the same time, I realize that I am hardly (and then, only on occasion) deserving of you and the friendship you have shown me (while enduring my idiosyncrasies and many faults).

I was in unusually low spirits here, but this has passed now. Gretl and I recently spent a couple of simply delightful hours together. I also received an extraordinarily charming letter from Borchardt and another very charming one from Helene Nostitz revealing great warmth. I am truly enjoying both of my paintings (the one by Hodler and the other by Picasso)[104] as well as two that Erwin painted this past summer.

---

104. A landscape by the Swiss painter, Ferdinand Hodler (1863–1918), and a self-portrait by Pablo Picasso, painted 1902.

Just now in this rather eerie moment I feel – no, I know – as if we had lived a long time ago; and reliving this in my mind, I also feel that much beauty surrounded us in this life.

I am trying to avoid sending telegrams. I feel very calm now, yet would like you to send a short note as quickly as possible.

Yours, Hofmannsthal

❦ ❦ ❦

Rodaun, Wednesday, 20 [November 1912]

I make a point of not being frightened by physical illnesses, especially those of children. What could one possibly hope to accomplish otherwise? However, last Sunday evening, after 36 hours had passed without a response from Julie to a telegram I had sent, I became very unsettled. Actually, perhaps I was more – or less – than unsettled by this. I began pondering things, and it quickly became clear that a single thought formed the basis: As insignificant as the child is in the picture I have of you and your nature, it would nevertheless be quite difficult to imagine your life without her.

As far as my investment of *feelings* in you is concerned, I am never quite sure what you are trying to say. This concerns the relationship of one person to another and the attempt to bring out something of immeasurable value. One man may take his lessons from Christ, and for another, it could be Goethe or, just as well, Walt Whitman or Rembrandt. And I cannot imagine what purpose art could possibly serve other than to continually preach this message *with* a thousand different voices. To grow wiser also means to gain a stronger and more secure grasp of *this*.

I can almost sense how wonderful your hours spent alone will become once the anxiety is completely gone.

With Dostoevsky, the *Erzähler*, and your approach to Goethe and Hölderlin, you must have the entire world around you, as Noah did in his ark – I hope so anyway. I saw Gretl for a moment; she seemed rather tired, but in every respect more mature and improving, almost visibly so. I very much enjoyed the meeting I had with Hauptmann; everything about this man is so pleasing and good, including the happiness he feels due to the worldwide attention he is receiving now. I think we may visit him together in Italy sometime. In fact, I virtually promised him we would.

Yours, H.

Rodaun, 25 November [1912]

I am going to send you this[105] for now instead of a long letter which I will not have time to write today. These days I wrote down the memories I have of Raoul Richter[106] (he is the man who died while we were in Italy), that is, the recollection I have of the single meeting we had in Aussee back in 1896, which had significant meaning for me. I hope it will bring some joy to his mother and brother.

As of yet, it is not possible to say when *Jedermann* will be performed in Dresden due to the illness of two of the performers. I am hoping, however, to be able to stick to some time between the 5th and 10th of December, which means I will probably be traveling to Dresden on the 1st. I will be staying at the Nostitzs' in Auerbach on the 2nd and 3rd and in Berlin and Dresden from the 4th to the 11th. I will be in Darmstadt the 12th and 13th, the 14th in Frankfurt, and back home after that. I will give you the exact dates later.

I almost believe that your life is rather pleasant now and that your nights are peaceful and undisturbed. I hope this is indeed the case.

I will see Gretl this evening, probably for the last time. She is going to Budapest.

The political situation is still just as grave, perhaps more so than ever. My military service is no longer planned for Pola,[107] but for somewhere else. Most likely I will only have to serve in the case of a war with Italy, which I hope we will be spared. Fighting a war on two fronts is serious enough as it is; we do not need a third.

I hope all of us will truly be together at the end of December. How do things look for Eberhard, should it come to a war?
Adieu.

Your friend, H.

[Auerbach im Vogtland, 2 December 1912]

It seems as if it were only yesterday that I left behind the little rooms here where I make myself at home – the bedroom and the tiny little study with its white furniture and a few small stacks of books and magazines here and there. And yet it has been nearly two years. At that time, I had arrived here from Erfurt by way of Leipzig and thought I might find a letter from you waiting here for me, but there was none to be found. I felt so

---

105. An article called "Der Wanderer," which deals with part of his trip to Greece.
106. Raoul Richter (1871–1914), the philosopher.
107. The port for the Austrian navy in the Adriatic sea. After WWI, it became a part of Yugoslavia.

close to you back then. My thoughts anxiously searched for you in the world out there – and it is very strange, Ottonie, how when I find myself searching for you today, I feel as if I must look for you inside myself. First I would have to clear a path – downward, further and further – leading to my true self, and there I would find you, too. What I felt back then was love, and nothing else. I am not quite sure what to call it now. It is something mysterious that refuses to speak – a certain mysterious unity of souls perhaps? Yes – and longing, too. There are very strange, inner connections between things sometimes. Experiencing wanderlust, homesickness, happiness, apprehension, tenderness, while still wanting something more, or perhaps not even this, but rather? The desire to *see* even more, to feel even more alive, to look out beyond one's own horizon, to feel one's self – whose? Whose? Everyone's! Who is everyone?! It is all very obscure. Silly little letter – yet powerful feelings and thoughts, without any longing to speak of. Just intense feelings and thoughts.

Dark times these are. We simply must persevere. First we, and then perhaps our children. I cannot wash my hands without seeing the countless bloodied, maimed and crushed hands before me.

The Nostitz's are very good, upright people. She is a kind and courageous woman.

I wish I knew what books you are reading. I will be in Dresden (Bellevue) until the morning of the sixth, and then in Berlin (Adlon).

Good night, good morning, or whatever the case may be. Adieu.

Your friend, H.

❦ ❦ ❦

[Hotel Adlon, Berlin-W.] Thursday [12 December 1912]

The six days and evenings I have spent here with the Russians and with Reinhardt in his theater and alone with him in his home have been wonderful. Kessler has been kind and seemed relaxed. What an evening we had yesterday with the incomparable Nijinsky and everyone so happy and excited – Strauss, Liebermann, Reinhardt, all united in joy. I do not have a very clear head at the moment, for Strauss just finished giving us a little recital. And the figure of Josef has been just as misrepresented as Zerbinetta[108] – however it can still be salvaged, as it is still only a sketch at this point.

I am going to Levin's as soon as I finish writing to you to talk everything over with him. From there I will go directly to the sleeping car, and tomorrow I will be in Darmstadt, where *Jedermann* is premiering with Moissi; I will be staying in the "Traube" Hotel and will return home

---

108. Joseph, in the *Legend of Joseph,* and Zerbinetta, a figure in the opera *Ariadne.*

straight from Frankfurt on Sunday night. I wonder if the quarantine you have been under will reach a timely end? I thought we could travel together to Vienna, i.e. Rodaun, for five or six days at the beginning of January. During this time, you will have the opportunity to feel relaxed while seeing the Russians perform a few times. Yes, we will certainly do this, that is, if a war does not break out.

Have not heard a word from Gretl. She is in Budapest. Concern about Erwin is surely weighing upon her as well.

Adieu.

H.

Rodaun, 13 January [1913]

Burghausen is a place I know very well, and I have always wanted to show it to you. I was there during the summer twice before when the weather was scorching hot. We went swimming in the pond below the castle and spent the night in the old inn there.

I felt unsettled during the first few days back here, which is typical for me. Two entire days I spent writing to Eberhard, which resulted in my feeling rather depressed and coming down with a migraine. It is quite hard to depict such a condition in a business-like sort of manner by tearing a loveable human being apart to visualize on one side the true person and on the other side the sickly distortion in the hopes of painting a semi-clear and well-ordered picture; the subject seems so sad and trivial. This caricature of an artistic activity has really unnerved me.

15 Jan. You will have received the Dostoevsky by now and begun reading Raskolnikov. In between, I would like you to take time out each day to read something which will help you quietly muse about things for a few moments; Dostoevsky has surely led you far away from yourself. Take a look at Goethe's proverbs written in verse, and alternate between reading them and his *Sprüche in Prosa* (= Maxims and Reflections). Also try reading Novalis' *Fragmente*, and see how far you can get and how much of this becomes a part of you without struggling too hard. As you are a true woman and can only manage to see the world through the eyes of men, the world of the intellect must compensate for what would otherwise be made exceedingly difficult or even unattainable as a result of certain circumstances. In this house full of women you are in constant danger, and this must constantly be counteracted.

Please do reacquaint yourself with your Whitman. Schröder's *Deutsche Oden* [German Odes] would be easier to understand if you were to read them aloud, each two or three times – no more. This will help you to see and to recognize the superiority of his poetry, the purity of his thought, and the sensitivity of this man, as well as the *correctness* of every last detail he gives – and then you will really enjoy it.

I hope more than anything else that you set aside certain times of the day for all of this and that you stick to them. One and a half to two hours a day spent filling the Danaids' leaky water jars is more than enough.

Your friend, H.

❦ ❦ ❦

14 January 1913

I feel a need to write to you. I do not know what or why, but I seem to long for you a bit inside – long to have you here, to go for a walk with you, to walk for hours in the wonderful winter weather, to chat with you, to sit quietly beside you. As none of this is possible, I am writing you this stupid note. I think about you a lot and *have been* reading Raskolnikov.

Annette[109] is here with us now. She has many pleasant things to say and kindly plays the piano for us in the evening. Then she comes to my room, and we chat. During the day we do not see her, as she works then.

Physically, Mädy is feeling better and is thinking of perhaps going to St. Moritz on Saturday; I hope we manage to convince her to go. At the moment I am very much in her favor, and she would like most for me to spend all my time with her, which, however, I do not do. Yesterday I was in Munich to see my doctor (Professor); I have had a lot of pain recently and was afraid another operation might be necessary. However, he found everything to be all right and claimed it was exhaustion, that my body was very weak and I would need uninterrupted peace and quiet and a lot of rest in bed. I think he is only partly right. It is simply hard for me to settle down in the house here, and this time, it was too pronounced right at the very beginning.

Have you perhaps found the peace and quiet in Rodaun that you so longed for, or have the Russians already taken hold of you?! You do not need to write me. I understand perfectly what letters mean to you. I have warm thoughts for you and would like to believe you think the same of me.

A thousand warm greetings,

Ottonie.

❦ ❦ ❦

---

109. Annette Kolb (1870–1967), half French, half German, a writer.

Sunday evening [Beginning of February 1913]

My thoughts have often turned to you during the past few days. Suddenly I began to worry about you a bit. Are you back home now? Where are you anyway?

Somehow it seems to me you do not realize that you have locked me out of your life, yes, completely locked me out for a fortnight, as you did not give me your address. You did not even include one in the letter you sent from St. Moritz, and ten more days have since passed.

I received a very nice letter from Annette (which consisted of two separate letters) about *Ariadne* that made me very happy. It is very strange how the enthusiastic and spontaneous acknowledgement of a single person can compensate for the obtuseness of thousands. She said the performance in Munich was lovely, especially by Frau Bosetti. She will not be returning until the 2nd of March, however, so it is better for you to see it then.

I am leading a rather quiet life, and in spite of it, nothing much seems to come of it. Of course, one can never be so sure. Often the most toilsome of times are not the most fruitless. I can often envision distinctly what I am capable of achieving, within my limitations – however, I am not completely confident of my ability to fully realize this potential.

If I were certain you were at home and had the peace and quiet needed to concentrate, I would ask you to take Chamberlain's book about Goethe to your room with you – Julie would not even be able to read three pages of it – and to begin reading it.

Good night.

Your former friend, H. H.

The same one you met in the train two years ago, about this time, when you were traveling from Stuttgart to Sondershausen.

[Privat Hotel Caspar Badrutt's Erben, St. Moritz-Dorf]
Sunday [Middle of February 1913]

I am still here! Your lovely letter made its way here yesterday after following me around for a week. Yes, it has been *such* a long time since you last heard from me. Imagine, I have been ill. I had a strange throat infection – no fever, but a very weak heart. I came down with it the day of my departure, that is, the day I had planned to depart. But as miserable as one may be, here one recovers just as quickly. I feel completely well and fresh and will be able to travel tomorrow. I am going to Konstanz, will be seeing Binswanger[110] there, which Mädy does not know, and will be at home

---

110. Dr. Binswanger, owner of a psychiatric clinic.

on Wednesday. Then I hope to have as quiet a time as possible before really going to Paris at the end of March.

But to think that I could exclude *you* from my life! I thought about you *so* much this entire time and would have given so much for a short note. I was strangely disconnected from everything and wanted more than anything else to die — I had but one wish: if only I could pass on quickly.

Now I am alive again, and am very happy. This *wonderful* sun is simply splendid and so many bright colors sparkle in the snow, and above it all the brilliant, blue sky; it really is too lovely.

Mädy is doing much better physically; however, emotionally, she is, of course, not much better. We registered the boy for the 1st of May in Zuoz,[111] which will certainly do him a lot of good, as well as Mädy.

I am so glad that things have quieted down for you now. Every fruit ripens in time. You just do not always notice it happening right away.

God, how fond I am of you! I really could not go on living without knowing of some kind of connection to you.

Good night.

         Your as always unchanging, Ottonie

🍎   🍎   🍎

         Rodaun, Friday [21 February 1913]

"Afraid" is not the right word; it is more concern. I have been very concerned about you for a long time and now once again. Are you back now? And if so, are you staying in that huge castle, not really at home? And with the old lady there and the many servants and all the long, empty corridors? Yes, I am worried. I would like to be there with you to make sure you are not racing up and down the stairs. Is your heart really, truly sound? What was wrong with it anyway? What could it have been? No fever and a *very weak heart*, when you had always had such a healthy heart and a pulse as regular as clockwork! Do you think it was because of the high altitude? But that never bothered you before. Or perhaps your heart was not functioning properly, the heart muscle itself, I mean. Could it have been that the heart muscle was infected? Was that it? If so, you have to be extremely careful for at least six months afterwards. You must not climb stairs, not even a few steps, and you need to spend a lot of time lying down. I really do not think that *could* have been the problem. Otherwise, the doctor would never have allowed you to travel. You also mentioned Paris — but what *could* have caused it?! And are you sure you're over it, completely over it? There is no longer a hint of it? And what is it

---

111. A famous boarding school for boys in the Swiss Alps.

like? Does it happen when you overextend yourself? Or in the morning after you get up??

I wish I could be there with you. I would like to pamper you and take care of you in every possible way. I'd quietly enter your room and leave just as quietly. I would return with a book and read some of it aloud to you. Then I would put a cover over you, take off your shoes, undress you and put you to bed, like a child. I would sit beside your bed. How I would love to! There are ways to show one's fondness for another – all of a sudden I understand it. I can feel it, and see once again that I am not useless to you, not only not from your perspective, but from all around. Ottonie, should I come? Is your life the same as it always has been? And I, the one who looked forward so much to your having a quiet time for yourself! What will you be reading now? Perhaps that "Goethe" (by Chamberlain) is too difficult. But Whitman, Whitman is never too difficult; he is always there. No matter where you happen to open the book, you will find him there; he provides the reader company. He is so present, a living breathing creature, an open eye, a human companion. He is incredible, and we both do not know him yet, although we both love him. We have scarcely entered the edge of his sphere, although he is as vast as the sea. There is a poem of his, with his name written above it – on page 31 – that is like a primeval forest. Shall we enter it together?

I have read quite a few books the past several weeks about plants, animals, and about people with illnesses. However, in the morning or evening or during the twilight hours in between, I always pick up Whitman. A truly incredible book! "Drum Taps" and all the other poems he wrote during that bloody war, which he himself experienced as an orderly, as a friend of the sick, and one who cheerfully offered love and comfort to the dying. What glorious poems! Read them one after the other. Read "Seashore Memories," "Song at Sunset" (page 338), "Poem of Joys." Pick out any one of them to read, and proceed from there to the end or the beginning of the book. Plunge yourself into this wonderful, rich world – I am glad you are in possession of this book. It is somehow like a guardian of life and joy. And will you please write me soon – about your illness – everything. Tell me the whole truth, please, Ottonie?!

Good night.

🌱 🌱 🌱

[Munich] Saturday [February/March 1913]

You have no idea what a wonderful gift you just gave me, another new gift. It was superb! I went all alone to see *Ariadne* and enjoyed it *so* enormously. I really find it wonderful to have such a dear friend who is able to create something so marvelous. I simply love *my Ariadne*.[112]

Just imagine what a nice thing happened to me. I had written Franckenstein a few lines and asked him to please reserve a ticket for me to be picked up at the box office. When I went to get it, it was presented to me as a gift. I was so surprised and right away felt it as a kind of greeting from you. Oh, if only you could be here next week. I have to stay here with Hansi from Tuesday to Saturday; he has to go to the hospital to have a tonsil removed. Imagine *how* nice it would be to go to the theater together each evening, etc. What a bore that Vienna is so far away.

Tell Gretl that everyone misses her in *Ariadne*. I also think Jeritza was much better than Fay. Bosetti was enchanting, so graceful, and her voice and her acting are just right. But the whole thing is *simply* superb!

And now, good night, dear friend.

Yours, Ottonie (who is very fond of you, as always!)

❦ ❦ ❦

Rodaun, 15 March [1913]

So far away from each other? With no way to be united? Dearest Ottonie! I wonder where you go walking about now. Along the Inn? Are you tired? A little bit of that March weariness is in the air, in the wind, and in the sun – here and everywhere else, too. You will not place too many demands on yourself just now, will you? Take it very easy and don't try to do too much, and tell yourself: "Later." Even those among us who were not so ill in the Engadine are feeling weary now.

How can I give you an idea of what my life has been, for many months now? It has a different rhythm than what you are accustomed to; it is much quieter and more reflective. Working – can one really call it work? Thinking, feeling – introspective feeling and seeing, vague, dull, everything disconnected – a book, looking through the book and into the world. And then the window pane clouds up again. My days are very calm, with an occasional visitor now and then – Mell, Kassner, but not very often. Mell is intelligent and very nice. He takes great pains over his work; however, if nothing comes of it, he sets it aside. He is an upright, gentle, and hard-working man. Now and then we go to the city and listen to a singer or watch a play. We recently spent an evening at the Taxis', just the two of us alone, and Ferdinand Lobkowitz, the heir to the title, a

---

112. Here O. D. S. acknowledges that H. v. H. wrote it for her.

musician — ten times more a musician than a prince — played Beethoven's *opus 31* for us. (Where was the good Annette — far, so far below!) Then he played selections from the *Hammerclavier* sonata, the adagio, heavenly — words cannot express it. To imagine living and never hearing this! It was just an accident. We asked to be invited again sometime with him alone — Monday — I will ask him to play exactly what he did the last time.

So you are going to Paris. I hope so. To hope. Hope. My hopes. Perhaps hope is better than love, which I felt for you from the very beginning. Hoping you will become free, free inside, relaxed in every joint, everything flowing freely — no longer stiff, no more fear, your body no longer paralyzed with horror. And, moreover, you as you are: the very same one who writes meaningless letters, etc. What a wonderful thought, at least it is for me.

Does the thought ever enter your mind of how grand it would be rapidly, as if in flight, to visit old sites again? Gubbio, Orvieto — to stand next to the door of the church in Lucca or to touch the tomb of Ilaria? I had that same thought. By chance, it will become reality. Strauss asked me to join him and step into his car in Verona on the 29th and drive with him to Rome by way of Bologna, and then along the coast to Rimini and Pesaro. From there, we would return by driving over the Appenines, descending at Gubbio and traveling on to Rome through Perugia and Terni. Then I am going to travel alone for a couple of days to Tivoli, where I shall spend the night. Then I will spend a week at Borchardt's with Schröder. Strauss is going to pick me up there, and I will be back in Rodaun before the 20th. I feel this trip will be a kind of solitude; Strauss, of course, will be without his wife. He is mostly lost in thought and does not talk much. I think it is the right thing for me to take this trip. Gretl will be in Monte-Carlo during this time; she may expect me to visit her there, but I will not be able to, nor do I wish to. I have not had the energy to write her during this entire time. She has been gone since the end of January. First she was in Hamburg and now in Berlin. Because of the customs, Gerty decided not to send her the little girl's dress; it arrived after Erwin, too, had departed. In Berlin, a new play by Sternheim, Reinhardt — to me they all seem so strangely far removed.

Adieu, Ottonie. In spite of it all, please try to write me sometime.

Yours, H.

P.S. I wonder if there is some way to help Gersdorff; he is going to be unemployed and penniless beginning in June. (By no fault of his own. Edmund R.[113] is letting him go because he does not have anything planned *outside* of Austria for the immediate future.) I thought of the Queen of Naples or perhaps Steinitzer. God only knows. He can speak and write

---

113. Edmund Reinhardt, brother of Max, and his business manager.

English, French, and Italian and is a tremendous worker. He is also tactful, has organizational talents, and is exact and discreet.

P.P.S. There is an incredibly beautiful poem (it is impossible to fully grasp it on the first reading) called "Sleepers," which you will find on page 210.

❦ ❦ ❦

Neubeuern, 22 March [1913]

So now I *finally* will write you again. Otherwise, you will no longer be able to recognize my handwriting.

I was so sorry to hear that you were not at all well and had difficulty working. I hope this has long since passed. However, the transition from one season to the next is always very difficult for you. I think I also suffered some from the disagreeable weather, which always causes me to get these annoying migraines. I am feeling better now.

I find the possibility of meeting you in Paris simply *delightful*. *This* would make me so happy. God, then we could wander around together, look at the paintings without any disturbance, and take walks through the park at Versailles. *How* wonderful this would be! Now I am very nervous about whether or not Mädy will truly be operated on during the last part of April and not the beginning of May so that I at least have the month of May to travel, either to Rodaun or to Paris. I occasionally ask her when she will be coming, but unfortunately, she *never* gives me an answer. Otherwise, she says she is doing well. Eberhard is leaving for London today. Agnes came down with appendicitis of all things at Mädy's.

My father has been with us for a week now. He is happy and very pleasant to have around. Maria van de Velde will also be staying until the 6th of April. Henry experienced a turbulent time as the object of all sorts of intrigues by Mackensen, the painter, the Minister, etc. It seems Schröder was also involved; everything has calmed down now, although it is not yet completely over. This is just meant for you.

I am going to Munich on Thursday and will try to make plans to see something with Stauffenberg. On Friday, I will be traveling to Boll to pick up Karin there. I have to go to a confirmation ceremony in Stuttgart on Sunday (I will be staying at the Gemmingens', Mörikestrasse). Monday I will be in Lorch, Tuesday in Eybach and not in Munich until Wednesday; I will be back here on the 2nd. On the 21st I will be going to a concert with the Wolffs in which her brother is singing and which is being conducted by a friend of Eberhard's. I have spent my time reading some of the older books like *Ivanhoe* and *The Vicar of Wakefield*, as my mind was too weary for anything else. In the evening, we read from *Bismarck* by Emil Ludwig, which was really quite good, also in that one could summarize all the interests.

Thank you very much for the books. I hope yours which I returned have arrived safely.

Warm thoughts, Ottonie.

🍂 🍂 🍂

[Grand Hotel Baglioni Bologna] Sunday [30 March 1913] evening

There is something curiously eerie about traveling along the same path as a year ago. The weather is just as it was then. As before, we left Verona today, had a view of the river from downstream, turned right at Villa-Franca and passed by the Towers of Mantua and then Carpi, the little town with the large castle made of brick. Then Modena, then there is the view of the mountains before reaching Bologna. Strauss and I walked along the same hilltop outside the city; we looked below; he talked about everything imaginable. There is something endlessly pleasant about his voice and manner of speaking, and of his gestures. I thought of you as I answered him. It made me laugh to think that there are at least three people who will always find pleasure in *Ariadne*: you, Strauss, and I.

All of a sudden it dawned on me that you must be ill, that this is the only possibility. Otherwise you would not have left Neubeuern without a word to me and neither would you have once again (!) left me without an address where I could reach you in Paris. So I am certain you are – or at least were – ill. I was only partially aware of this in Rodaun. Each day that passed, I thought a letter would arrive from you. I was also sick in bed with a fever at Easter; the following few days I was incredibly dull-witted and weak. I can become very depressed and debilitated so suddenly; I do not know if it was the touch of fever or the March weather, or perhaps it was something inside of me, which I never can understand. Tell me, could it be that you never received the letter I wrote you about a week before Easter? It was a very nice letter. Ottonie, where on earth are you? Write me a letter. The day after tomorrow I will be in Perugia and I will be gone before it would reach me there, so go ahead and send a letter to me in Rome (Hotel de Russie). I will be there from the 3rd to the 7th. Yes? Could you possibly be so very ill, Ottonie?

Good night. H.

🍂 🍂 🍂

Neubeuern, 7 April 1913

I have been rushing around all over the place before sitting down to write you. The short trip I took was full of variety, but it was a cramped schedule. Unfortunately, I could not meet with Stauffenberg, as he was very busy and also had to cover for another doctor. I was very sad, because I would have very much liked to see something with him. Then once I was here, a telegram suddenly arrived from Julie saying that she would be returning with Baby. There was of course a great deal that had to be done and straightened out, for nothing of what I had planned to do in her absence was finished.

Baby returned so happy, never have I seen her so full of joy to see me again and to be back home. She is at a very charming stage right now and seems quite fascinated by me.

I am very sad indeed to hear that you had such a bad time. Do you think things will improve soon? Would Schröder not be better able to help you through these difficult times than anyone else? I truly hope that you are experiencing a good period again.

Yours, Ottonie.

❦ ❦ ❦

Lucca-Monsagrati, 14 April [1913]

Dearest, I am so sorry you are there all alone or have only the company of other Germans – Steinitzer of all people, whose mind is constantly on "home" and other boring topics. I am also puzzled that you have not mentioned the Rysellberghes[114] and Van de Velde in any of your letters; through them it would be very easy and would require little effort to establish some ties to the French. I do not know anyone there, at least not anyone who would show a young woman around. Kessler with his 10,000 friends and acquaintances would of course be the man to ask, but I am really not able to write to him now. Aside from a meaningless postcard, I have not had a sign of life from him in months. God only knows what may have offended or upset him again. I hardly think of him anymore; I believe I have finally lost him as a friend. But why don't you write to him yourself at "15 quai de la Tournelle." He likes you very much; he will be delighted to hear from you.

It is beautiful here, unbelievably beautiful – enough to make one feel happy. It will be very hard for me to leave here and I shall do so longing to return. The little house, so secluded and homey; it seems completely removed from time. The lovely, quiet valley surrounded by steeply sloping hills covered with olive trees from top to bottom. The heather, which grows as high as a man, has already begun to bloom and the figs and lemons are ripening. The two people here, man and wife, so pure and filled with the passion of pure intellect, so far removed from the bleak, wretched, confused world in which – or too close to the edge of which –

---

114. Theo van Rysselberghe (1862–1926), Belgian painter.

we live our lives. Something about this place is so beneficial to me. A subtle sense of happiness moves me when I rise each morning – Rudi feels the same thing. A very strange and very meaningful letter arrived from Eberhard, steeped in a struggle for survival; it was as if a faintly glowing meteor soared across the peaceful valley. We human beings! I always love you, Ottonie.

H.

P.S. Please send a letter to me in Rodaun, even if it is dry and dull. Just let me know what you are doing and what you have seen.

P.P.S. Were you able to ask Steinitzer about Gersdorff?!

❦ ❦ ❦

Paris, Continental, Saturday [May 1913]

Once again, so many days have passed since I last wrote to you.

I settled into a very nice routine following my first week here. I found a young man who takes me around every day in order to practice my French. He has shown me a great deal of Paris. Steinitzer was soon shoved off; he is only allowed to join me for a walk on Sunday mornings and otherwise is permitted to decorate my room with fresh flowers when I am not around. I have met Kessler several times. He was ill all winter long since arriving in London, and I think it was quite serious. (He was afraid it might be throat cancer, which his father apparently died of.) He is feeling better now but still takes great care. I bumped into Heymel on the street one day and have seen him every now and then. He gave a delightful party in a charming little restaurant.

I stroll around in the city by myself a lot or go to the Louvre or inside churches. I am enjoying my freedom immensely. It is *not* so easy to make friends with a French family; one receives a formal invitation, and that is it. Unfortunately, the Rysselberghes are not here. He is off painting in Granada. I had a wonderful day yesterday at Chartres; I took my young man along to speak French all day. Now the weather is great for trips in a car through the surrounding country, which I enjoy very much. Mädy is coming here next week to shop for clothes and will be staying for a week. Right now, she is in Zürich with Hansi.

A morning all alone in my hotel, where no one comes to bother me, or an evening, is delightful. I feel as free as a bird – more so than I ever did in my life. I went to Théatre des Champs-Elysées a few times. It has become very respectable and the performances are well-attended. Unfortunately, it is never very full, and people have said Astruc[115] is going to be nudged aside, which is probably nothing but a rumor. However, he does

---

115. Gabriel Astruc, French theater producer.

make very silly mistakes like scheduling performances which then do not take place. Or the starting time in the paper may be eight o'clock, but when one arrives, the doors are locked and the play does not begin until 9:00 – and things like that. I am so incredibly looking forward to the Russians, who Kessler says will be performing all these new pieces. I assume it is certain you will not be coming? I am once again the true Ottonie Schwartz here. If somebody asks me, "Have you seen this yet?" I answer, "No." Would you like to come along?" "Yes!" That is how I end up going everywhere, which is simply wonderful!

Many kind regards, Ottonie

❦ ❦ ❦

Continental, Sunday [May 1913]

We will be returning to Neubeuern a week from this Monday. Julie arrived a few days ago. My lovely stay here in Paris is coming to an end. I have benefited a great deal and have particularly enjoyed my time away from the family.

As van de Velde was only here for a short time and also was not feeling well, I did not ask him to go with me to have a look at the Picasso. Instead I went first with Rysselberghe to Vollard; we went twice in vain, as he was deeply involved with a sale, and hence we were never able to talk to him. However, he did give us a *rendezvous* for Thursday, but claims he has very little left. Kahnweiler[116] did not have anything left except a small head, which was nothing special. He said he had already sold all of that period. By chance I know an acquaintance of Picasso's, who is going to let me know if he has anything left in his studio. Then I will go straight there and have a look. I just hope I will be able to find something that you would really like. I have gone to quite a few dealers and seen lovely works by van Gogh, Gauguin, Bonnard, etc., but they are already selling at terribly high prices.

Boris Godunov,[117] which I saw a few days ago with Schaljapin, made a tremendous impression on me as a picture of Russia.

Take care.

Yours, Ottonie

❦ ❦ ❦

---

116. Vollard and Kahnweiler are art dealers where O. D. S. tried to find a good Picasso at a reasonable price for H. v. H.

117. Opera by Modest Petrovich Moussorgsky (1835–1881).

[Rodaun] 28 May 1913

That was very dear of you to respond with such kindness and great self-control to a truly awful letter – yes, I realized what an awful letter I wrote and suffered a great deal because of it; and yet, it was not as horrible if read the way it was meant to be read. However, I somehow felt – knew – you would not be capable of understanding it in this way. Therefore, you were left to shoulder the full burden of this awful letter by yourself. I feared you would not answer me at all or would send an accusatory answer. Instead, you sent me this, which did me a tremendous amount of good. I see your radiant face before me, while all the terrible, faceless images which do not belong to the natural order recede into the background. I can see you so vividly, can take you by the hand – not physically, but in a different sort of way – and pull you towards me, close to me. We again occupy the same world – together.

There is a reason for your silence about Kessler: you have nothing good to tell, so you do not say anything. When I am able to hear it from your mouth, it will be much easier for me to bear. I can see that I must force myself not to think about this unfortunate man. I believed he was my friend, a friend of mine and of that which exists inside me and manifests itself through my work. He, too, believed he was – and wanted to be – but was unable to, not permanently. Something simply got in the way.

I have to see you, Ottonie. Make me believe that I will see you. (It has not been good for us, the way these past four months have passed.) Let me know when you can come to Aussee. I will arrange to make it possible whenever it suits you. You will be near me and very loving and not the slightest bit a burden, no more than a feather or a flower would be. I will work and will completely be a part of my work, yet I still will find time to return to you every day. Do not be too rigid now; just let me know when you can come, will you?

It just dawned on me that if possible, I will come to Neubeuern for a couple of days at the beginning of July – but this has nothing to do with the other plans.

Your looking for a Picasso for me was very kind and loving, and there is nothing wrong or boring about going to art dealers. Possibly you might still find a picture – if not, nothing will be lost.

Adieu.

Your unworthy friend, H

[Hotel Continental 3, Rue de Castiglione, Paris] Friday [June 1913]

I had a truly splendid evening with the Russians. Seldom has anything made such a powerful impression on me. It was the new ballet[118] with music by Stravinsky and choreographed by Nijinsky;[119] he really came up with something entirely new. It was very powerful for me, like something of Hodler or Gaugin, or van Gogh. At the same time, it is in no way a copy of all these, but completely original. There was a mixed reaction to it — both hissing and applause. However, it will win out in the end, just like *L' après-midi d'un faune* did last year. I am very happy I was able to experience it.

We managed after all to find four Picassos at Vollard's. Two of them are paintings of children; in one of them, he is holding a dove in his hand, with a ball lying beside him, and in the other, the child is seated in a chair — not as good; there is also a woman wearing a yellow blouse; not so important. So in my opinion (as well as in Rysselberghe's), the best painting left is one of a nude woman lying on her back. I am enclosing details Rysselberghe wrote down which will perhaps give you a general idea. I would take the first child painting or the nude. Perhaps Vollard will be able to send them to you. All further efforts turned out to be unsuccessful, as at present all the older Picassos have been bought and are not for sale. We had another amusing encounter with Vollard, which I will tell you about later.

We will be leaving Monday evening, and I will be in Neubeuern until the 16th. Afterwards the child and I will be going to Sondershausen for a two-week stay and will not be arriving in Hinterhör until the 10th of August this year, because I have to spend all of July in Eybach and must be there to celebrate Mama's 80th birthday on the 6th of August. So it won't be possible to have you visit Neubeuern for even a couple of days in July. There is also no way for me to come to Aussee before the beginning of September, but then you'll no longer be there. However, I might meet you somewhere else, that is, if you will be spending the fall in Tyrol or someplace else again.

There is nothing good nor bad to report about Kessler. It is simply a matter of indifference, which is better to talk about in person.

Good night. It is very late now.

Yours, Ottonie

---

118. *Le Sacre du printemps.*
119. Vaclav Nijinsky (1890–1950), dancer in the Rusian Ballet.

[Südbahn-Hotel, Semmering] 16 June [1913]
Will be back in Rodaun tomorrow

I do not think I will be able to write you again until I receive a letter in which you tell me – oh, I beg you to! – that you burned the letters I sent you in Paris, assuming you kept them. Especially the one very unfortunate letter, which was not even real – that ghost of a letter! Once it has been burned, it will truly have been destroyed – forever. For it never really existed.

I spend my time here alone and am able to accomplish a lot of work in these peaceful surroundings. As the evening approaches, I take a walk and afterwards I read – I am enjoying *Faust*, the second part, so very much. What a divine piece of work, this feast of feasts; semi-weary, I pause to think – I look into the valleys and up steep mountains; the ridge above comes into sight, and I see forests and many tiny worlds. How I wish I could picture you and *see* Salzburg (our first time), the walks we took in Neubeuern, also the short evenings we spent together in Munich last October. What lovely times, although they were too few and too far apart. Then an emotional vexation became unbearable, too severe – am I supposed to go without seeing you nine months out of the year?!

I wanted so much to pass through Munich on my way to Italy back in March. How I would have loved to! But I came down with a fever and was too weary, and then there was no time left. And you were away, so far away. On the way back, we passed by the *deserted* valley.[120] So it will not work out in July either; can you come visit us at the beginning of September, Ottonie? It will be beautiful in Aussee at this time of year, I am certain! Do you think I am mean – more mean than I am kind – because I can write such letters as I did? But I am *kind to you*, am I not?

I have been working a lot recently; perhaps it is something which you will take pleasure in. I simply delight in your happiness and the way you express this happiness, like in the letter you wrote me about the new ballet you had just seen. There you are so entirely yourself to me – so lovable. I no longer have your last letter and cannot remember your plans; I hope I am correct in sending this to Sondershausen. Gretl has been in Südtirol for some time now. It feels as if I have not seen her since January and have only said "adieu" to her a few times. I thought about the possibility of luring Gretl and Erwin to Hinterhör – and we could stay in the castle – for a few days sometime in August (she has to be in Berlin again at the beginning of September). However, I suppose your mother and who knows who else will be there then?!

H.

---

120. Refers to the Inn Valley and Neubeuern without O. D. S. there.

[Hotel Österreichischer Hof, Salzburg] Friday, 4 [July 1913]

You write a kind and loving letter, while with the sweetest smile breaking the back of these final three months of summer. Is it not ghastly to be spending three months in Aussee (July, August, September) — and you are unable to arrange to come for even a week?! It simply was not possible; I am not angry when I say this, just a little sad. I do not want to — I *cannot*, not now — think about October yet, at which point another summer will have passed; this time in life that has always been so precious to me ever since childhood will be gone. Month after month goes by — finally a year or two or three or four — and we have yet to see one another.

And here I am with Gerty in the certain hotel; I walk along the same ridge overlooking the city and down those certain steps — not at night, naturally — and everything seems so distant and at the same time near and beyond my grasp.

The last letter you wrote to me about the Russians and how much you enjoyed their performance suddenly enhanced your entire stay in Paris for me. I knew at once why you had to be there. This was not as obvious from letters you had written previously.

The weather here is weighing me down. It is overcast and damp, indeed oppressive, and my head is like a clouded mirror. Only occasionally, when things become clearer, are the fragile images inside me illuminated by a more brilliant light.

I do not expect things will improve any time soon, so we simply sit here. I would have liked very much to take a few excursions. I long so much for the sight of a crystal clear lake filled with glowing reflections and surrounded by towering trees which stretch upwards into the deep blue sky. Will I ever see this again? In any case, we will be going to Aussee in four or five — or six — days from now.

Adieu, Ottonie. I have been so happy reading *Faust* during the past few weeks. I thought I might read the entire book aloud to you in Aussee sometime. One thinks one knows it but really has no idea.

I am filled with very remote, very cumbersome thoughts and feelings. Of course, this will pass in time.

Adieu.

H.

Eybach near Geisslingen a/St., 6 July 1913

You make me terribly sad with what you said in your letter! How can you speak of the possibility of not seeing each other for *years*? How awful that would be! Something like this could never and will never happen. The following few months are unfortunately, however, completely full, but maybe I can find a week at some point when I could come for a short stay. I felt obliged to spend a week in Gastein with Eberhard. He sounded so depressed in the letter he wrote about being there all alone. It does not suit me at all at present, but it was the first time he really asked me to do something for him, so I did not want to turn him down. However, I do not want you to feel sad when you think of me. Imagine that I felt some happiness because I felt sure that some part of *him* belongs to me, and I must truly mean something to him if the idea of not seeing me for ages depresses him so. And right then I felt so drawn to you and was very happy. I wanted to take you in my arms and tell you, "Relax, everything is all right."

If only you did not always have to know so far in advance exactly *when* I am able to visit. But otherwise I suppose you would not be able to make any plans, right? There is also much I do not know as of yet about how things will take shape. Since I have been in Sondersh[ausen], Mary has been in England and will be staying there until the end of October. My sister will be here then, but I cannot leave her alone the entire time with the child and the people I occasionally have here either. In any case, you know that, if there is *any way* I can, I will come to see you at once. You seem to think it would be very easy for me to live without you, but here you are terribly mistaken. It is only when I sometimes have to wait a long time for a letter that I tell myself, "Just get used to it. That is the way life is. One cannot continually take while giving nothing in return. Otherwise, the well goes dry." Or I say, "Do not make a burden of yourself." Men want and must move freely without constraints; one must not cling to them, especially not to those with delicate souls and great tasks to accomplish.

How lovely that you enjoyed *Faust* so much, and *how* happy it would make me to sit near you and listen to you read it. Stupidly, I did not really bring anything decent along to read – only Whitman, who is *wonderful*, and Annette's book, which I have already finished. I liked it a lot. Just now I am reminded of a lovely evening in Paris when I went with Henry van de Velde to meet Rilke in a small, old-fashioned restaurant. The three of us spent such wonderful hours together. Everyone left feeling happy about the time spent together. Rilke had such kind things to say about the *Exemplar*; I felt so happy for Annette. Indeed I experienced many lovely moments in Paris; I have benefited greatly from this wonderful time and have only one wish: to go there again next May for four or five weeks. I have gotten off onto a completely different subject, however, from what I actually wanted to talk about. I thought I, too, should begin reading *Faust* again in order to catch up to you and enjoy what you have been enjoying recently.

I am all alone here with the child; she is sleeping in Christoph's room with the open door, and I look in on her as she lies there so peacefully. Yet at times I hear an anguished cry inside me lamenting all that has been lost. However, the bitterness is gone, and I feel more able and willing to accept. Being alone now without the old lady is good – the sorrow she feels is so much more powerful here where she feels her loss so much deeper. Without wanting to, one can easily become bitter and at odds with things. Is it not strange how years of one's life can suddenly seem to vanish when one returns to a certain place; sometimes here I feel as if everything has just happened.

Mama and Julie will most likely be coming on Thursday. Mama was not feeling very well, and I hope it is nothing serious. Now good night. You seem so much closer to me when you are in Salzburg. But how you must suffer with the awful weather we are having. Another wet summer like last year's would be horrible.

Addio, for now. I am *so* looking forward to your next letter. It was *so* dear of you to write me a letter for my arrival here.

Yours, Ottonie

❦ ❦ ❦

St. Gilgen, 11 [July 1913]

I imagine you know where I am sitting. (I do not mean my sister-in-law's little house where we are staying for a few days – rainy days, of course – until Franzi is over the mumps and the little house in Aussee is once again cozier.) I mean the country here, which you know well – we came here once before. And the lovely St. Wolfgang by the lake, where we relaxed together in that strange, noisy room there. Bright, sunny days like these are *reality* for me here, while the dark, gloomy days seem so unreal; then I, too, am gloomy and very foreign to myself. But that's just the way it is. However, it is childish to spend a lot of one's time thinking about such things, and I am careful not to. When one pauses to reflect on the value of the world and on human life and also considers in which manner tens of thousands of men are dying, what is this world? And that there exists something like Siberia which has suddenly descended upon my soul through the fantastic book my sister-in-law has here: the memoirs Dostoevsky wrote while spending ten years in a Siberian prison (forced labor camp). (The book shop in Munich will be sending you a copy in a few days; I ordered it for you after reading the first fifty pages.)

It is very peculiar this weakness I have. Although I am always able to regain a firm hold on the raw materials out of which I construct what for me is important and permanent, they always seem to somehow slip out of my hands. And there I sit, helpless, dumbfounded, like a lost child, until the moment arrives when the world, and much more than the world, is reconstructed before my eyes.

You should be able to find a copy of *Faust* there in the castle or the little volume published by the Universalbibliothek should be available in Geisslingen. You will be receiving something from the Insel Publishing House which will be a much greater help to you in reading *Faust* than anything I could ever say. It is a small volume of letters containing the remarks of Goethe on his own work throughout his life; in particular, I find what he wrote during the last years of his life very moving and incredibly captivating – the way he decides to leave this entire work locked away in his desk, unpublished, waiting to greet some later generation. Incomprehensible, the greatness and originality of this work, which will never be replicated; and it is, after all, the incomprehensible which nourishes the soul.

You spoke of Annette's book, which I have meant to speak to you about for some time, only to forget over and over again; this was after I had finally read it in May and felt so deeply touched by it, as I still am today. It is highly original – there is so much in it which no one else could have possibly written. The tenderness you will discover there is unbelievable and at the same time the figure of the "Exemplar" is portrayed with tremendous clarity, although constructed of incomprehensible elements. At the same time, this work can by no means be characterized as a powerful or forceful piece of literature; it is indeed so "true to life," and yet strangely touching. After having had the book for months and then finally reading it, I wrote her a very animated letter. I find it odd she did not answer me. Could you perhaps ask her sometime (or even in a letter) if she received it? (I mailed it to Sophienstrasse 7. That is the correct address, isn't it?)

How lovely it was for me to be informed of all the little things you experienced while in Paris – such as the dinner with Van de Velde and Rilke which you wrote of. What a joy it would have been for me and how insignificant the distance between us would have seemed had you kept a little diary and then sent it to me (a few short words about what you experienced and whom you met now and again) every two weeks instead of the letters, all of which were much too vague and cheerless for one who is always so afraid of truly *losing* the other person and feels utterly incapable of reinforcing the ties weakened by destiny and physical distance.

It is as plain as could be that you had no choice but to grant Eberhard's request. Everything else will take care of itself, and I did not really mean what I said about not seeing each other for two or three or four years. I do not know if Eberhard would want me there at the same time (a letter may have arrived from him in Aussee). In any case, it would be better if Gerty also came, because four is better than three. However, I cannot – nor do I wish – to concern myself with future plans right now; I only hope that the weather improves and the children recover and that one could work and enjoy spending some time outdoors. Mell is coming in August. His intellect and strength of character have become more and more a means of reconstituting myself.

Adieu. Write me again soon.

Yours, H.

❦ ❦ ❦

Eybach near Geisslingen, Wednesday [Summer 1913]

I wanted you to receive these lines days ago, but Mama arrived here with Julie, and my sickly brother-in-law along with his orderly, and last but not least, Miss Martin, which means there is a huge crowd here together. Once again, I hardly find any quiet time for myself, especially as I now spend half the afternoon sleeping. I am getting to be nice and plump ever since I learned how to sleep straight through an *entire* hour. You certainly ordered some lovely little books for me, which I was so happy to receive! I had a delightful time reading Boccaccio's tales as soon as they arrived, and it is wonderful reading the little Goethe book before beginning *Faust*. I am already looking forward to reading it again. The weather here is also so-so. One must pay for every nice day with several days of bad weather. I hope, for your sake, it will improve, as I know how much of an effect the weather has on you, and here it gets plenty of rain during normal years as it is.

So you were in Salzburg (St. Gilgen). I can still picture everything from back then when we crossed over the little lake on the way to St. Wolfgang. That was a delightful time, probably among the loveliest times we ever had together, and we had beautiful sunshine as well.

I am planning to write to Annette about what you mentioned in your letter. Please give me the address of the castle outside Bozen where you stayed. Friends of ours would like to go there for their honeymoon.

A thousand warm regards.

Yours, Ottonie.

❦ ❦ ❦

Aussee, 16 July [1913]

I am nervous about having sent you Dostoevsky's book, *Memoirs from the House of Death*, before first reading all of it myself; I have since come to realize that it contains a great deal of suffering which you may find very depressing. Of course, that is not what the book is really about. It contains something infinitely greater which stands out above everything else; yet, you may still find it too hard to read, in which case you should simply set it aside. If, however, you are able to read it and take in the nearly inconceivable greatness there, then please do not read pages 315–417, *whatever you do*.

I spend the long, peaceful morning hours in your room over in the other house as the rain, once again, falls incessantly. I find the atmosphere there very friendly, where fairy tales, both old and new, and imagined fates come to life. After nine long months, I dared for the first time to return to the tale I began writing last fall, which I found had a rather happy and lively beginning to it – and which yearned to be resumed! Perhaps I will be able to pick up the thread where I left off, however, first I want to finish the other project or at least the first draft.

Wassermann is here and, as always, he works diligently and never takes a break and is cozy, yet never smiles. The Franckensteins recently said they would like to have me over for tea, so I am going to walk there across the damp, gray, windswept countryside.

Have you received the books yet? Perhaps you will be able to read the second part of *Faust*, keeping in mind that each act is a complete work unto itself: the events at the emperor's court, the Greek Walpurgis Night, Helena – and the less substantial fourth act and the majestic final act. Each one is a fairy tale, an adventure, a delightfully refreshing fable.

Adieu. H.

[Postcard]   Aussee, 23 [July 1913]

Now I am closer, but you have moved so much further to the west, which I am not at all pleased about. I wish you were still in Hinterhör, alone with the many wonderful books there. This would make me happier. The sun never shines and the children have the mumps, so one must find some way to amuse oneself. I have continued writing the short story I began last fall, the one from the little room in the Hotel Marienbad. It might turn out to be rather nice, if one only had some talent. I have been writing a lot; my brain is overactive. I have to be careful about my nights; that is why I am writing you on such a small piece of paper – it is almost 10:00 o'clock! I think I may use the same little room to write in this October; would this give me the chance to see certain people, or will you be ordered into service again, God only knows where — will you race off to Meran or take language lessons, etc., etc.?

Do you have any idea *when* Eberhard would like to have me visit him in Gastein? I would like to know ahead of time; then I will plan to take the time, even if it proves to be difficult. I long to see him again. I care for him very much.

Yours, Hugo

P.S. The name of the castle is: Schloss Gandegg, which is right beside St. Michael-Eppan; it is an hour from Bozen with the Überetsch train.

Eybach, Sunday [29 July] 1913

I took a short trip to Bebenhausen with the child to visit friends of Christoph's. I found the few lines you wrote here when I returned. It is great to hear that you are working on the old story again, and how lovely the thought of your going to the Marienbad. If only it will truly happen! I sincerely hope I can go to Munich then. Are you not planning to come to Neubeuern with Gerty?

Just imagine, since yesterday I have been living in complete isolation in two rooms with Fery. All of a sudden he began to vomit and had the shivers and a temperature of 103.3 (39.6 C). As scarlet fever is going around the village, one is of course anxious and very careful; however, today he really does not have much of a temperature but only a bad cough. I hope it will turn out to be just a bad cold, otherwise I will have to ride with him in an ambulance to Stuttgart, where the Geisslingen Hospital also sends its people. The boy is a touching patient, so dear and sweet. Julie had just left for Hinterhör and will return at the end of the week. She is not doing all that well either; she is supposed to take a mud-bath cure, so I might have to forget about going to Gastein. Mama is eagerly anticipating her 80th birthday, and as Eberhard will be there, too, it will be even more meaningful for her.

Thank you very, very much for all the books. The little Insel books are perfect for here; so convenient to take along. I have read all of them except for *The Death of* [Ivan] *Ilych*, and I enjoyed them all *very much*. I have a lot of jobs here besides looking after the house, and that with both children here without Mary. However, I feel very healthy now and am able to manage everything *without much* effort. So your children still have the mumps, the poor dears; it is very painful. We have had nice weather for the past few days, though it is doubtful that it will continue. I have not heard anything from Eberhard for ages now, but I am going to ask him about Gastein.

Good night. I am tired. I spent all day reading den *Kleinen Lord* [The Little Lord] to the children and did not sleep much last night.

Yours, Ottonie.

P.S. It is so good to know where you are working and that my thoughts can find you in the little room. Would love to stay there again sometime. It occurs to me that we should take another little trip together with Gerty or whomever, and then we could really be together again – but when?!

❦ ❦ ❦

Aussee, 3 August [1913]

Because you like books with underlined passages, I have just sent you the volume of Goethe's letters which I had just finished reading that day. I did not have anything else handy that was underlined. This was the most difficult period of Goethe's life, the one following his return from Italy (from the age of 40 to 48). He came back home and found an aging Frau von Stein (who must not have been a very kind woman); the Duke and Duchess estranged from one another, each unhappy in his own way; an embittered Herder, also towards Goethe (one of the darkest chapters of all); the petty, absurd little town, and a very *bleak* outlook all around with the Fatherland threatened by hostile foes and sentiments. In the face of this he had to live his life. *How* he was able to do so is both awe-inspiring and comforting, like everything about this man. There is no need to read all of the letters; leaf through them until you come to the ones I have underlined, and read towards the end or the beginning from there. His understanding of young people, whom he treats like his own sons, is really wonderful – Fritz von Stein and Max Jacobi, for instance; I intended this book to serve as a counterbalance to Dostoevsky's. I am enclosing a lovely story by Lagerlöf[121] which I found very stirring and which you can perhaps read to the boys. I bought it for myself a few weeks ago to read on the train on an extremely dark and rainy day, which made for a very nice afternoon at the time. Oh, the countless dark, rainy days we've had since! You can scarcely tell what time of year it is. And much like a child, I depend upon the joys of summertime! The summers left such strong impressions on me as a child, and now it's the only time of year that really matters to me. There is nothing I can do to change this at this point. From my childhood, I can hardly remember anything – except for Christmas – about a single winter; however, I can recall just about every day of summer. The past few days here have been particularly wretched; it's muggy

---

121. The Swedish writer Selma Lagerlöf was commissioned by the King of Sweden to compose for his children a tale describing the geography of this country; the result was *Nils Holgerson and the Trip of Wild Geese.*

and dark, even during the day. I even had to put my story aside; everything is standing still. Reading alone helps me to get from one day to the next: the expedition Stanley[122] undertook to liberate Emin Pascha. His march for nine months (this caravan of half-starved men), back and forth through the dense jungle inhabited by evil Pygmies, and while marching, their only background music were the final gasps of the dying. It is amazing what a great man – for he must be counted among these – is able to endure.

You at least brought the Whitman with you, did you not? He, too, is a vast primeval forest which cannot be exhausted. However, it is not inhabited by evil Pygmies poised with poisonous arrows.

Yesterday Müller-Hofmann, the young painter, arrived with his wife; we are letting both of them stay in Erwin and Gretl's room this year. (I am using your room as a study; Mell will be staying in the other room upstairs.) I knew him in Vienna, was much taken by him and also am aware that he needs help, so I decided to offer them a place to stay. I had never seen his wife before. She's a *Northern German*, as you would say. (What I would give to hear you say this or some other silly little thing in that funny accent of yours!) She arrived here in a black silk dress and a flowing black crêpe veil; he wore tennis clothes even though it was pouring rain. I greeted them and found his wife truly awful from the very first moment. Everything about her was extremely harsh: her voice, her nose, just everything. We had invited them to dinner for their first evening here, but immediately after they appeared, dear old Gerty had to run and show them the way out. After a long, dreary day on which I was unable to write a single line, I simply could not bear the thought of being enclosed in our little dining room with that woman. So they were uninvited, ushered off, and the roasted chicken, still warm, was sent over to them along with the following excuse: "The host has a migraine." (I have not seen the woman since then, and it was understood from the beginning that they are to run their own household.)

I wrote you about this so you could enjoy a little chuckle. I am enclosing a short letter in which a certain sentence has been underlined. You will understand right away what I mean, Ottonie, won't you? Please, do not ever again express something like this to me so *directly*. You use virtually the same words every time, and it sends an awful shiver down my spine and makes me feel very distant from you. It was sentences like these in the Parisian letters that caused a huge gulf to open up between us.

Everything you write about yourself, even the most trivial of details, is of tremendous interest to me. I find what you have to say very moving,

---

122. Who met with Livingston in darkest Africa.

and this allows me to feel closer to you. You will understand, if you wish to!

                       Yours, H.

🌣 🌣 🌣

                [Bad Aussee] 19 August [1913]

 An unexpected sign can produce great happiness, as did the letter I received from Annette Kolb today in which she mentioned having bumped into you on the street "yesterday" in Munich. Now, once again, my thoughts know where to find you. They have been wandering aimlessly during those recent dark and gloomy days. Now I feel that we are again surrounded by the *same* vast firmament. Today it is shining brightly, and it belongs to both of us: from atop this towering mountain, one can see as far as Chiemsee, and with a decent telescope, one can even make out the Heuberg. Only a vague and uncertain feeling guides me towards you in Ulm or Eybach.

 Eberhard has written me some very lovely letters. I also feel his presence much more distinctly when there are a mere 100 rather than 1,000 kilometers separating us! We have decided to drop my idea of going to Gastein; instead, I, along with Gerty, will go to visit him in Madonna[123] on the 10th of September. I suppose there is little hope of finding you there? No, you will have your instructor with you then; Gerty thinks that he is a real boyfriend and that you flirted with him in the letters you wrote from Paris. I do not think so at all. If this were the case, I would almost like the idea of it! (You must not misunderstand me, however; it is *true*, but by no means *à la portée de tout le monde*.)

 Now about October. You asked whether or not Gerty and I were planning a stay at the castle. I can tell you right now that the only reason we would not come would be if I were in deep despair over my work, which will not be the case at all. On the contrary, I'm very captivated by the story I'm writing. Anyone who truly understands it will see it as a net capable of enveloping heaven, earth and hell – I have no thought but to pursue it, in Venice in September, and in the little room in Munich in October. Does this meet with your approval? If I knew it gave you even a tiny bit of pleasure, I would look forward to it with great anticipation. And you would come once or twice a week, and I could relate to you what had been born in the meantime; and we could go to the theater together. It would be just the way it was when we first met, and that is the

---

123. Madonna di Campiglio, a resort in the Austrian Tyrol (after World War I in Italy).

way it should be, for one must never forget how to begin anew. Mother Nature, too, is constantly reborn.

I think you also owe me a small sign of your friendship after these nine long months, and you surely could manage to present this before X and Y.

Yours, H.

[Bad Aussee] 1 September [1913]

It was a week ago that we stood atop the mountain in Gosau, an area which I wanted to show you so much. (You have actually seen very little of the natural beauty where I live here. What a powerful effect it had on Eberhard; he could not help but utter the lines Schröder wrote in his elegy to me.) The children were with us on the mountain as well as the young painter, about whom I will have a great deal to tell you. Everything seemed surrounded by an incredibly poignant glow. I saw the Venediger mountain yonder, as it gazed into the Inn valley below – and you were still not there.

Are you there now? Through a conversation with Eberhard, I learned that Julie is there. But your entire day does not go to waste, does it? I hope you find time to go for a walk in the country and to read a book while relaxing under one of the trees. The paths you take, beneath which tree you rest, the time of day, which book – oh, how I would love to hear all about this! However, I realize that I will not.

But it is good, yes, very good, that you like the idea of my arriving in October with my work – and you seem to understand that this is a way, perhaps the only way, for me to visit *you* (otherwise, I would remain in Italy). And you also know (and if you don't, I will tell you) that while you like my company, I enjoy seeing you more than any other person in the world. After I am through working, we will go to town – all of a sudden, it seems as if it exists only for your sake – the little restaurant, the opera, which will be very good this year under the direction of Walter[124] – and the streets and automobiles. And you will come and check on me regularly and go and come again, won't you? In the name of God, I will also take a 24-hour trip to N. sometime. Will I receive another letter before we leave here on the 8th of September?

Yours, H.

---

124. Bruno Walter, conductor of the Munich Opera.

[Grand Hotel Britannia Venice] Sunday [21 September 1913]

I am so happy about Munich. I enjoy thinking about being there more so than here or some other town or place, for Munich affords me the only opportunity to see you regularly, again and again, and to combine this with true productivity and to couple that with some time to myself. In other places I would not be able to see you this way; that is why I would be so happy if you, too, would say that you like the idea of Munich; pray, say it again, and *soon*, because I would like to depart here already on the 28th and maybe arrive in Munich on the 29th. I know for sure that I can work there in that little room; it has the atmosphere I need, and in every other place, I would first have to recreate this atmosphere for my work. And the evenings there are so pleasant; I have so many fond memories of them.

I just hope the fact that the Lindemann flat no longer exists is not too much of an inconvenience for you, and I also hope that Julie will accompany you only sometimes, but not always. Couldn't you introduce the subject by simply mentioning that I will be staying there and that you are planning to take several trips to Munich during this time? I assume we have moved beyond the children's diseases, as far as Julie is concerned? Eberhard, the dear man, wrote me that he has not seen you looking this well in years – words such as these make me happy for weeks at a time.

Yours, H.

❦ ❦ ❦

Hinterhör, Tuesday [23 September 1913]

Should I say again *how much* I am looking forward to your coming? Oh, I will just go ahead and say it once more, because I find this simply delightful! I completely agree with everything you said about Munich; one can really spend lovely evenings there. I simply explained very matter-of-factly that you will be coming and that I will also be going there a number of times, which everyone seems to have accepted.

I was with Julie at Frau Lindemann's for the last time from Thursday through Sunday. I was actually planning to go there again on the 28th, but perhaps I can postpone it until the 30th so that you have time to get settled in. I have to leave from Munich to pick up Mama in Eybach and then take her back with me. I will then quickly expedite her to N. How long are you planning on staying in Munich? Mädy and I recently had a very nice time together with Rilke at the Hotel Marienbad.

The weather, however, has been dreadful for the past two days – rainy and overcast. It will seem twice as bad to you when you return from all the warm sunshine. Unfortunately, I saw Eberhard only for a brief moment – I am really terribly fond of him. Mädy will be in Munich until tomorrow. Here it is still crawling with people until the 1st of October. Hopefully things will calm down after that, although I am feeling *so* well that it does not bother me at all.

So, auf Wiedersehen for now. Someone is looking tremendously forward to seeing you in Munich.

Yours, Ottonie

🍂 🍂 🍂

[Hotel Marienbad, Munich] Sunday [28 September 1913] evening

The wind shifted to the north this morning, and I was filled with hope for both us. The wind has shifted yet again and is now blowing in from the south, although I remain full of hope.

I wish for nothing more than to love you – but *you*, the same one I knew before – you have taken her away from me, drawn a veil over this person, and I cannot find her.

My work is going so-so. There were moments when I was able to visualize things, and could almost feel them. It was that way yesterday in the Rembrandt room at the Pinakothek, and there were also moments when I was able to hear – truly hear for the first time in a long while – yesterday in the opera for instance.

Well, now I am going to go to *Salome*[125] tomorrow without you; I have tried to invite Wilhelm Stauffenberg to use the extra ticket if he is free. He is working here in Munich again, in the hospital on the left bank of the Isar.

So, will it be Tuesday? Or not until Wednesday? Or Thursday? I hope not that long.

Good night.

H.

🍂 🍂 🍂

Eybach, Monday [29 September 1913]

Well, we will certainly be leaving on Wednesday, that is, if nothing comes up at the last minute, which I do not anticipate. We will be arriving in Munich at 3:30 and will drive straight from there by car to Neubeuern. I will not be able to stay in town because there are a number of things I have to arrange for Mama in Neubeuern. At any rate, I will return as

---

125. Opera by Richard Strauss with libretto by Oscar Wilde.

soon as possible. As I write this letter to you, you are at the opera enjoying *Salome* (I wish I were there, too).

I took a lovely walk in the woods today where the leaves had already turned into many beautiful colors; the weather was nice and I thought a great deal about the two of us. I wonder if one should try to mend a relationship – of any kind – once it has been damaged?! I will be the great loser – but that always seems to be my fate.

Good night. Yours, Ottonie

🍂 🍂 🍂

[Hotel Marienbad, Munich] Wednesday [8 October 1913] 11:00 p.m.

It was the south wind that blew, Ottonie, when you wrote this letter; and a very strong south wind, while you sat in the woods thinking about the two of us. I am no friend of this type of *reflection* on your part. The situation regarding our relationship is very different than a sad, terribly general sentence you wrote in your letter might lead one to believe. I am sitting here, and it is raining outside, and I ask myself if you are in Hinterhör. An hour ago, I was still at the opera; Annette sat next to me, and I asked myself if you were feeling well.

During the past days, I have been slightly ill, but only physically. Neither my state of mind nor the powers of imagination were affected; I was able to work reasonably well, and I believe I have some good days ahead of me.

I was able to locate Wilhelm Stauffenberg. He looks like a "ghost;" one wonders if he will live a few more years. He spends the entire day working at the hospital; he is free Saturday evening after eight and comes to see me. I do not think I can bring myself to mention your name to anyone else right now.

Come, please come, but let me know beforehand.

Good night.

H.

🍂 🍂 🍂

[Hotel Marienbad, Munich] Sunday morning [12 October 1913]

It is gradually becoming rather difficult for me to keep on waiting every time the mail arrives – without seeing you – there was no answer to the letters I wrote you (I mailed letters to Eybach and Hinterhör). I was in a miserable state physically; I lost four kilos of weight and nearly all my working days, which is worse. I found out last evening from Frau Wolff that you arrived in N. "all in one piece." What are you doing to me and to yourself, Ottonie? Please come here tomorrow, or Tuesday at the latest. Make sure you are here Tuesday evening.

Yours, H

❦ ❦ ❦

[Hinterhör] Monday [End of October 1913]

I so long for a few kind words from you, but none arrive. I finally thought you might be sick, but I no longer believe this, for the Wolffs were here yesterday, and Hanna told me she received a letter from you, which I was glad to hear. You must have just been busy with things, and now I would also like to thank you for the *Casanova*, which I take as a greeting letting me know that you are still thinking of me.

Our days in Munich were good indeed. I am so glad that you are there for me again and not in some far away place. You know, I can understand very well now why you look forward so much to getting a few lines from me, even if you know beforehand that it will be dull and will upset you. It is just good to know that the other person is still alive and doing well. I have recently had the mail brought here from Neubeuern every afternoon which I had not done for a long time; I do so in the hope that there will turn out to be a little letter from you.

Hanna again looked charming and was sweet and kind; he, too, is so nice and pleasant. We were at the castle from Saturday morning on. My cousin Konrad Degenfeld arrived here suddenly early in the morning and brought us over there. We had a very amusing evening; Pepino used a projector to show us pictures accompanying his songs (which he illustrated himself, priceless); he sang along with each one. Before this came Steinitzer's trip through East Asia. He took terrific pictures, especially wonderful were those of the primeval forest. Old Keszycki was there as well as a very nice and handsome Baron Dörnberg, a former son-in-law of the Baron Schenk, whom I believe you have already met here.

After a few days of horrible south winds, the weather here now is beautiful. We spent the entire day outside. Unfortunately, we were not able to get good seats for *Falstaff*, and as it did not fit our plans yesterday, we are planning to go there for the next performance.

I have enjoyed reading Casanova very much. His charming love stories never cease to entertain me. The one about the French lady wearing a soldier's uniform is delightful. Otherwise, I dip here and there into my Goethe, the *Römische Elegien*, and things like that. Just now I would like so much to have you here; we could go on lovely walks together and spend time relaxing here in the house. I think you would enjoy it, too.

We expect Mary on Thursday. Baby cannot wait to see her; she really is an adorable child. I had a migraine today, and it was so cute the way she looked after me. She has a very kind heart but absolutely no imagination; one has to accept that.

My Ludwig von Hofmann is *so* beautiful; it hangs right above my desk, and I must constantly stare at it and feel very happy about it. Do you still remember our beautiful Leibl at Caspary's? It is truly wonderful that such a painting exists, and I often picture it in my mind.

I believe that good paintings have more of an enduring effect on me than beautiful music does.

Well, good night, for now.

Ottonie.

❦ ❦ ❦

[Rodaun] 2 November [1913], morning

You truly are a courageous woman to have written me again. I should have responded to you a long time ago, and in a much nicer and longer letter than this will be, but I will finish this quickly before beginning to work. If only it were possible to put right down on paper – or better yet, to send it over the hills and mountains straight to a certain little house – the thoughts one has expressed silently to oneself or in a quiet whisper. We have days of the most miserable foehn imaginable recently, without a single break. It has been unseasonably hot, and the summer-like air continues to blow across the sky above the bare trees and dead leaves below. Constantly one had a headache and awful nightmares and kept sticking letters into the wrong envelopes! It required a great effort to maintain a semi-tolerable mode of existence.

Othello was once again performed very well two evenings ago. Again one was filled with sympathy for the poor, wretched creature (I am referring to Othello, not Desdemona). Like always, Iago's voice was as horrific as it was magnificent, and his death, again, crept up on the audience in the course of the prologue to the fourth act. However, something emerged from the festive and moving passages of the music, much like a bird soaring up and away: it was your presence, your face, as you never see yourself in a mirror – and as I am unable to find it when I *search for* it inside myself. But unintended, how beautiful and dear and true it appears – when it does!

I am pleased that you were able to make Casanova's acquaintance all alone – without a mediator. His autobiography, which I find a marvelous book – *everything* about it – has given me a hundred good hours. Yet I hesitated giving it to you, as easy as it was for me to give to Gretl, who took it along on trips for an entire year. Now start with chapter two in the volume I sent you; it discusses his affair with the captivating Henriette. Continue reading from there, about Paris, Vienna, etc.

Adieu.

H.

🌰 🌰 🌰

[Hinterhör] Saturday [29 November 1913]

It was so dear that both of your letters arrived just now. Especially your lovely comment about the *Divan*. I really am happy to have a friend who is continually able to give something new and wonderful. I am once again a poor little soul, lying in bed tired and miserable. For the sake of thrift, I wanted to have a tooth removed in Rosenheim instead of going to Stuttgart, but when it did not wish to be removed after the fourth attempt, my courage was gone and I left. The injection made my face swell up, which hurt terribly, and to top things off, I poisoned myself with too much Veronal. It doesn't really matter of course, but it is very draining, and I have practically no resistance.

Tuesday. Well, I didn't get any further the other day. I am out of bed today for the first time and am feeling better now; my face is still a bit swollen. Today I feel like reading again.

How wonderful that you are able to work. Meanwhile Gerty and the little boy are having their portrait painted, too. This sounds so homey, as if you have settled down for the winter.

My oldest sister is staying with me; she is very quiet and dear.

I really hope your friend does get better. I find one often hears that old people have a hard time dealing with death, whereas it is easy for young people to leave this world.

Addio. Deep within my soul I think of you. Can you sense this?

Ottonie

A meeting with Fink[126] seems impossible. My friends asked him to come to their flat, but he has not shown up; so I suppose one will have to do without him after all. I hear that Yella O. was at the Bruckmanns, so I suppose they will provide her with a chauffeur?

Charles de Coster has shown up; a thousand thanks. I will make his acquaintance in the coming days; only my head has to be somewhat free of the morphine again.

I enjoyed *Casanova* very much; I would love to read another volume sometime.

What you wrote was really *so* dear (I just now read your letter again). For years now, these November days really have belonged to you alone

---

126. Banker in Munich.

(as far as I am concerned). Here I am living together with all my books; and this reminds me of what you said about this or the other thing, and I wait in these tranquil surroundings for letters from you, again and again.

Ottonie

❧ ❧ ❧

Rodaun, Wednesday evening [late November 1913] (do not return!)

This is for you so that you will feel motivated to keep the *West-Eastern Divan* on your desk and to read each of the books separately (one at a time) and enjoy them, for this most sublime and unusual intellectual/sensual/spiritual creation is worth even more than the Leibl picture – which now also hangs on the wall in front of my desk in all its splendor.

I am working diligently now (the awful south wind has ceased, but instead we have thick fog). I am trying to write the fairy tale[127] – while I am completely removed from the opera. I work during the morning and evening, and the hours in between pass very quickly – Faistauer paints Gerty and Raimund in the mornings; she wears a dark purple house coat and the little boy a garish red one. The colors will certainly turn out to be very beautiful. F. is the man who is so good at painting flowers. Gretl is lovely and very cheerful; she has a nice, spacious apartment and is very happy.

My dear friend, Christiane Thun (the sister of the Countess of Neipperg, but this does not tell you much about her), lost her husband following many sad, long years of illness. My old, 93-year-old friend, Herr von G., is also ill. He seems somewhat better now, but will he pull through? I would be terribly sad if I lost him. And can you imagine that he is afraid of dying? – how strange!

Casanova. What a unique character! I am glad you have had such a merry time making the acquaintance of this impossible gentleman. Do you think at some point you would enjoy another volume of his adventures?

Again you have written to me – you are truly a courageous woman – and everything in that letter gave me pleasure. I am going to read it through once more and then shall burn it.

Good night.

H.

❧ ❧ ❧

---

127. After having finished the opera drama *Frau ohne Schatten*, H. v. H. wrote the text as a fairy tale.

[Rodaun] Monday [December 1913]

It is hard to comprehend, Ottonie, how so many days could have passed so quickly – there was not a single day, however, on which I did not answer your letter in my thoughts. The thought is never missing, nor the desire, nor my sincerest wish to send something – something better than a mere letter – to the place where forests and foothills surround a little house. Somebody lives there – but who? Why, you, of course – you, a living – no, there is something too remote about this word; perhaps my – no, what do I mean by "my?" Yet, you are in a sense mine – or shall we say it is simply you! What is missing, however, is the strength, that little bit of additional reserve, needed to accomplish anything beyond a few hours of work; this eludes me now. I do not even have the energy to sit and listen to a concert all the way to the end. I just do not have my full capacity now, that is all. I suffered a recurrence of the same malady which was treated much too lightly and amateur-like in Munich. Now I have a strict doctor, starve myself rather comfortably and consistently, and in a little while it will all be over. Strangely, everything appears to me as through a thin veil, except my work. Sitting peacefully in an old armchair, I seem to be hearing gloomy music while other people stage unpleasant, absurd little dental adventures, poisoning themselves with Veronal or partaking of morphine.

Ottonie, let me put it this way: Sometimes your manner seems so uncanny, indeed horrifying – I am speaking of the way you underestimate your own worth. Can it be prudent to treat oneself like this? And as strange as it may seem, it is precisely this which is so essential to your kindness and the charm you possess!

We buried my old friend[128] last Sunday. His life ended peacefully and without pain. He made many wise, intelligent, and subtly ironic observations even during the last few nights; then he lay there, peaceful, unmoving, and every room of the house filled with flowers. During the funeral, a strange, restless south wind blew across the brilliant sky. The graveyard is situated at the foot of the most beautiful, rolling hills; All Saints' Day decorations still rested on all the graves, and the many flowers sparkled in the sunlight as never before. The ancient Jewish chants[129] had a celebratory quality, yet were severe in a way and very foreign to me; the coffin was carried to the place where his beautiful sister rests. She would now be nearly 100 years old; I was her friend when I was 20 years old and she 74, during the last few months before her death.

Ottonie, my dear, write down for me on a little piece of paper which of Balzac's works you own as well as the publisher. (I recently spent a few

---

128. Max von Gomperz.
129. Though H. v. H. was partly of Jewish descent, he was a Roman Catholic.

evenings reading *Eugénie Grandet* before falling asleep.) There are certain of his books that I would like you to have, but by no means a single one too many. Have you been reading in the *Divan*? Has it been a long time since you had a look at Goethe's *Sprüche in Prosa*? Or Novalis? Or Hölderlin? All three of whom must continue to remain your living friends!

Good night, Ottonie. I speak these words softly into the night but send them to you in your house.

Please throw away my awful letters – please do! And make me believe you have done it.

Good night, Ottonie.

Your friend, HH.

P.S. Could it be that Price Collier[130] has died? One almost envies him.

❦ ❦ ❦

R., 4 December [1913]

Where are you, Ottonie? Day after day goes by, and I continue to wait eagerly for a short note or some sign – but I do not hear a thing. I so long for the sight of your face as it is when you give me a friendly smile. Have you left me for some faraway place? Don't you care that I am still here? Did I overlook or fail to notice something again?! I feel like crying out into the night: "Ottonie!"

The address on the photograph was written in ink in your handwriting – so you cannot be ill. Is the child ill? How sad that you could not send me a short note, a note containing the titles of the Balzac books. Why is it that I always see you far off in the distance with your head turned away from me (your hair is so pretty – what an unusual style) as you walk down a long, white corridor with no end in sight and with numerous doors, all of which you pass on your way.

Where are you anyway? Can't you hear me? How can two people treat each other this way?!

Since returning from Munich, I have been, not exactly ill, but close to it. I have very little strength. All this time I have not found the strength to write Reinhardt the friendly letter I had planned to; I have so little energy left. Sometimes there is something pleasant about this; everything seems so fragile , so weightless, as if visible only through a veil. Last week I was also in bed with a fever for a few days. I will get better soon enough. Now – behind a thin veil – the rehearsals of *Jedermann* are taking place.

---

130. American writer and collector.

There is still so much I would like to tell – but to whom? Who could possibly be listening?!

Ottonie!

H.

❦ ❦ ❦

[Hotel "Baseler Hof," Munich] 7 December [191]3

I am tempted to say, "Dear One," but I am not going to do so because it might hurt your feelings. I feel so bad that you did not get my letter. I put it in the mail along with a letter to Velde. So, just like you, I, too, have been waiting all this time to hear a few words from you. But what could have happened to my letter? I hope I at least tore it up when looking through some old letters. But you, poor dear, suffered again as a result. I am sitting here in the theater expecting to hear *Tristan*,[131] but it will not start. We have already been waiting twenty minutes. I am like a child; I have never before heard *Tristan* and am so excited! If only you were here next to me, we could at least chat.

Nothing came of my *Tristan*! Can you imagine, after waiting in vain all this time, it was cancelled, as both Barry and Fassbinder[132] were suddenly indisposed. So one had to go home – everyone was sad. I also felt sorry for poor Cle[133] as the theater was overfull; there was not a single seat to be had. Julie is also here in town with me. We have some shopping to do. I am leaving tomorrow for Stuttgart to have my teeth taken care of before Christmas, so I will not have to worry about being in pain during the holidays. If everything goes smoothly I hope to return Thursday.

Yesterday Heiseler's play was performed, which we could not decline to see. Afterwards there was a reception at her parents' home. It was very pleasant sitting together with van de Velde, who seemed to be doing very well; he was cheerful and seemed to be quite happy. Taube[134] was also there, the criminal who wrote the *Verborgenen Herbst*.[135] We had lunch with both of them and Nele[136] at the Wolffs' today. As always, we had a very pleasant time there.

You know, it is really very disquieting that you have been feeling ill for such a long time. Have you still not completely recovered? What are you going to do?! I am really *very* frightened. Is there not anything concrete that can be done? However, I know you will have found a good doc-

---

131. *Tristan und Isolde*, by Richard Wagner (1813–1883).
132. Opera singers.
133. The conductor Clemens von Franckenstein, old friend of H.
134. Otto von Taube, German writer.
135. Lost Autumn.
136. Oldest daughter of Van de Velde.

tor and will do exactly what he tells you, and Gerty will take very good care of you. Perhaps you could manage to write me a few words soon letting me know if you are over your fever.

I will be returning on Thursday and will be staying here for a few days. On the 18th, young Herr Josten (the brother of Frau Wolff) will be giving a recital here. He has selected a very good program and I hope his singing will do it justice.

It is always so much fun for you to hear that somebody likes me, and I was just told that I had a secret admirer in the person of an officer who was once at Neubeuern. So that is how one comes to have devoted hearts scattered throughout the world without even knowing it. I just thought it was very amusing and said that I found an entire day was plenty of time for me to make a conquest and that I usually only needed an hour to capture a man's heart. (That sounds a little conceited, doesn't it?)

I finished reading *Till Eulenspiegel* a few days ago. I think it is *wonderful*; it is *so beautifully* written. For me, a truly great book.

Oh, I wish I could quickly be there with you right now so that we could chat together. Perhaps we will be able to trade places sometime; I could sit at your bedside, or are you up and out of bed and simply trying to get enough rest to recover from being so exhausted? It would be horrible if you could not come here for Christmas! Could this possibly happen?

Good night. I have to hurry downstairs with the letter now so that you will be sure to receive it before too long.

With the warmest regards,

Ottonie.

P.S. No, my head is not turned away from you, and my eyes are looking directly into yours. Several days ago, when I woke up, I could feel how our hands let go at the end of a handshake, and it seemed so sad that I could only imagine this and was unable to touch your hand in reality.

[Postcard] [Munich, 8 December 1913]

I own the following Balzacs:

La Cousine Bette
La Maison Nucingen
Le Père Goriot
La Vieille fille
César Birotteau
Les Employés
Le Colonel Chabert

Le Curé de village
Histoire des treize

Société d'Éditions Littéraires et Artistiques
Paul Ollendorf
50, Chaussée d'Antin

R., 12 December [1913]

Just a few brief words to let you know that I am completely well. I spend most of my time in town because of the *Jedermann* rehearsals. I am only here for the morning and still have nine other letters to write and a lot of telephone calls to make.

The one letter you wrote a while back (the next to the last one) really must have gotten lost! I just hope we can be sure to travel after Christmas. We are planning to leave here on the 28th and can stay until the 3rd or 4th.

Should I, that is, may I invite Müller-Hofmann, on behalf of the lady of the house, to come and stay for two or three days? (From the 30th to the 1st?) Would this be all right, or are you planning to invite him yourself? Please let me know as soon as you can.

And what about Schröder? I do not have time to write him. Would you perhaps do this?

Gretl often talks about how "delightful" it would be if Ottonie could come to Vienna in February.

Erwin, along with a few young painters, organized a very pretty black and white exhibit where I will be giving a lecture at 4:30 this afternoon. Why don't you come, too! Gretl, Kassner, Wassermann, Yella, etc., will also be there.

I have to close now. Do not forget about M. H. and Schröder.[137]

This is no letter at all. Please throw it away immediately.

Yours, H.

[Postcard]   Sunday [14 December 1913] evening

I suspect you have long since returned – the letter I wrote you, a very short one, was sent to Hinterhör. In it I asked a question to which I would appreciate an answer sometime soon (regarding Müller Hofmann). I do not like writing you so many of these dull notes; you might think that the

---

137. Arrangements for the annual meetings in Neubeuern.

dullness has some meaning, but it means nothing at all. It is simply because I have just been writing New Year's wishes here and do not have much time before going back into town.

I will be leaving for Munich from Neubeuern on the 4th and will be there through the 6th – and you with us; I hope that has been arranged (I asked for tickets to *Ariadne*). Afterwards I may be spending a week in the mountains of Tyrol with Reinhardt and Spiegl (and Gerty). I would so love to have you come along, even if you can only stay for a few days! Let's plan on this, shall we? And we will pretend it is a spur of the moment decision! I had lovely memories of the house at Mörikestrasse 24 as soon as I began reading your letter.

Good night.

H.

❦ ❦ ❦

[Postcard]   Rodaun, 21 December [1913]

Now it must be true and it is probable as well as improbable – yet to me it is quite otherworldly, yes ghostlike – that in eight days we will be sitting face to face.

I tell you, Ottonie, this time, I not only am looking forward to being with you, but also being in Neubeuern. So many truly wonderful things have happened there – spending a day in the amiable company of all those dear people is worth a lot. The morning hour, at dusk and then the evening hours – this means so much! I invited M-H to come on the 30th; he is a man who is very dear to me.

We plan to travel at night this time, arriving in Munich before 8:00 in the morning (on the 29th). Then we will take the next train leaving for Raubling; if nothing changes, then I will not send another telegram before we leave!

H.

❦ ❦ ❦

[Hotel Adlon, Berlin–W., 10 January 1914]

This is Berlin and the Hôtel Adlon, and still I am sitting quietly here alone in my room and have the time to write a letter at my leisure. It is 7:30 now, and Gerty just left with Spiegl to go to the theater. I have to get dressed later to go to see Reinhardt, who is expecting me in his lovely, quiet little house. We lunched with Eberhard, who was overjoyed about his meeting with Borchardt. Then we went to Strauss' for tea, and he listened attentively and graciously to the first act[138] – there really is something invigorating and truly vibrant about Berlin.

And now about our snow. There is no question that Reinhardt can leave here before the 25th or perhaps even the last of the month – at which point, however, he really does want to leave. He plans to go wherever I suggest, perhaps Salzburg or Lofer, or a bit higher, such as Arlberg; at any rate, it will not be too far from Neubeuern. The question I have to ask myself is whether I want to return to Vienna on the 16th and then leave two weeks later for the mountains, traveling through Salzburg – I would do this only if I knew that you would also be able to come then, as well as now. What do you think? Please write me about this right away! Then things would fall into place with Reinhardt so that we could be with him and Spiegl without the presence of Reinhardt's wife,[139] whose company Spiegl cannot tolerate because "she doesn't deserve to be there." (She will also be too busy at the theater to get away anyway.)

Reinhardt really does exhibit a certain flair[140] Although I have never mentioned you to him, the first question he asked me was about how you were doing and when it might be possible to see you again!

You really are my one constant girlfriend – that is, as far as Reinhardt is concerned. Oh God, and you are for me, too, as far as my heart is concerned, or however one should put it. Here I am again sitting in the old Adlon; once I spent a whole day writing to and receiving letters from you. In thirty-two pages, you informed me three times that you do not love me and that is the way it remains; in short, everything is fine. In the meantime you tried to run away from me but did not succeed – you will never get rid of me.

The days in Munich were lovely. Your proximity makes my days so rich somehow – it is like the background of a superb, tremendously colorful painting; and although one is not certain where she is, one is sure to feel her.

For me, the few days I spent in Munich were a very festive time. Eberhard told me today that he finds my fairy tale extraordinarily beautiful. Again, I asked him why exactly, but he was unable to say.

Ottonie, if only I knew *how*, in what way you have friendly thoughts of me; if I had an idea of this, I might suddenly fall madly in love with you, or perhaps not – perhaps not at all.

Do not forget about Stauffenberg. You promised me you would take him for a walk, so please make sure that you do that.

---

138. *Die Frau ohne Schatten.*
139. The actress Else Heims, whom Reinhardt later divorced.
140. "[F]lair" appears in English in the original.

Adieu. Soon I will turn forty, which is twice as old as twenty, but only one half of eighty. Yes, I certainly have a mind to come up with this! Adieu, adieu.

Your "faithful" friend, H.

❦ ❦ ❦

Rodaun, 21 January 1914

I am so certain that we are going to be able to see each other again soon that I have become lax when it comes to writing, much more so than I typically allow myself.

24 hours later, Thursday evening

Well, once again, this lay unfinished for an entire day! I plunged right back into my work after returning – I did not want there to be an unproductive transition period. I always return from Berlin feeling much encouraged. Reinhardt's aura does me a great deal of good, where so many wonderful things are within one's reach – *Hamlet*, *Lear* (Moissi as the jester was unforgettable; that is, I only saw one of the rehearsals, but it made such a strong impression on me that I do not want to see it again!), *Tasso*, in the first row of the *Kammerspiel*, only a few feet away from the actors who experience and speak this; Eberhard beamed as he said, "It is like being in heaven!" He was absolutely right.

Again you had more kind words to say about my fairy tale (just begun). In front of a wonderful little antique statue in a museum, Eberhard said to me, "You see, this is what your fairy tale is like." That is really much too generous a compliment – although it is encouraging and good.

I did have a wonderful time there, although life eventually turned upside down; one always ended up going to bed between 3 and 4 o'clock in the morning. I came down with a little malady and had a fever for a day; it was nothing serious. In fact, I have been over it for a long time now.

Well, it has been arranged with Reinhardt and decided that he and Spiegl will arrive in Munich on the 31st. Our *rendezvous* will be held some place close to Salzburg or Innsbruck; I am assuming that you will be able to catch up with us no later than the 2nd or 3rd because the entire trip is not going to last a long time! Please write me a few words about the weather there and let me know which volume of Hebbel you are missing. God, I wish I could have written more!

Yours, H.

❦ ❦ ❦

Neubeuern, Saturday [24 January 1914]

As I had not heard anything for so long, I began to think that nothing would come of our trip this winter and started to plan a trip to Rodaun in the spring. Just yesterday I had reserved rooms for Baby, Mary and me for the third in Munich. Following a web of intrigue, I had to change all my plans today after all and will instead allow Baby to go to Davos on the 3rd, where I do not need to accompany her since the Gemmingens are there. I will meet all of you then wherever it may be on the 3rd. The weather here is wonderful; since you left, we were able to go sleigh riding, etc., everyday. In the morning it's always in the upper teens, and today we had the most splendid sunshine. Mama just said the weather is supposed to change sometime soon according to the weather reports, but of course they usually predict the opposite of what actually happens.

Müller-Hofmann was here for several days, was nice; he became popular with everyone. Now he plans to leave for Bremen soon. Mädy is in bed after having pulled a tendon skiing. I gave her *Der Idiot* [The Idiot] and with it she is so well-occupied that not even the bed makes her feel miserable, as it always does otherwise. Baby also received skis and is skiing very nicely; she skis down entire slopes by herself. You should also have your children start sometime soon, if there is enough snow. They learn so incredibly fast and have no difficulty at all unlike adults.

So we will see each other soon; I hope you are not afraid of our meeting. I am looking forward to this, very, very much.

Many fond regards,

Yours, Ottonie

I am missing the second volume of Hebbel.

Rodaun, 2 February [1914]

Papa had a better night last night. He is still seriously ill, however, and we have all been very apprehensive. Spiegl just sent me a telegram saying that Reinhardt will not be able to leave before Wednesday or Thursday. Now I am hoping that we will manage to leave on Friday, although we just put Raimund, who has a pretty high fever, to bed.

I hope you will not be impatient. I would like very much for us all to meet in Ischl, or if not, then Berchtesgaden. Let's hope it works out!

Adieu.

Yours, H.

Neubeuern, 3 February 1914

I received the little card today. I am *terribly* sorry that your Papa has such a serious illness and that you have been so concerned. I hope he is much better by now and will soon have completely recovered. I can imagine what a stressful time this must be for you. And Raimund sick, too? I hope it is nothing serious. Please do not worry about me being able to come. Any time is fine; it does not matter when, at least not up until the 16th. By then I will have to be back here.

We accompanied Baby and Mary to Kufstein today; from there, they will be traveling by themselves to Davos. Afterwards we walked to Oberaudorf. It was beautiful. We are continuing to have simply splendid weather. Gerty's letter arrived just as I returned from Berchtesgaden. The three of us went there to visit the Wengerskys for a few days. Berchtesgaden is lovely; that would be very nice if we could all meet there.

I ended up not writing a letter to Eberhard because he sent Mädy all the details of her trip on the same day and also invited her to come to Berlin for the last four or five days of his stay there. So I am just going to leave it up to them.

We are all doing very well here. Only the separation from the child was hard for each of us, and she felt it, too. It just takes a while to get used to.

Please do not feel any obligation to write me immediately – I realize that you have to go to town a lot and also want to finish your work.

I hope we will end up getting together sometime before the winter is over.

Yours, Ottonie.

P.S. I think I will try to arrive a couple days after Reinhardt so that you can have him to yourself at the start. Is this all right?

[Postcard] Rodaun, Wednesday [4 February 1914]

Annette, who is sitting beside me playing the piano, once again had such wonderful things to say about the Grand Hotel in Berchtesgaden. So I decided to send Reinhardt another telegram about this. Reinhardt and Spiegl will be leaving tonight or tomorrow night. We hope to depart by Saturday at the latest. Please make plans to catch up with us on Monday, as we can't be away for too long because of Papa. Annette wants to go to Neubeuern this Saturday but only if she can be certain that *you* will be there, too – which I do not understand at all! Will we really be together in the snow?

H.

❦ ❦ ❦

[Das Grand Hotel Kurhaus Berchtesgaden] Sunday [8 February 1914]

Please see to it that you never again leave us in limbo like this for no good reason, but simply because of some ridiculous and completely senseless fuss there at the *** castle! I have been waiting (for you to arrive) before reciting to everyone something wonderful and new – but we are only going to be here for four or five days on account of Papa. Have you forgotten that you promised us you would arrive during this time and that this was the only reason I asked Reinhardt to come to B.? And do you not realize that this must also be viewed as a social commitment in the eyes of the *** castle that one must adhere to just like any other if nothing urgent arises?
Mad!

HH.

❦ ❦ ❦

Neubeuern, 20 February 1914

I wonder when you arrived back in Rodaun? It was *so* very nice in Berchtesgaden and my only regret is that we had such a short time there together. It has been a very busy week here with all sorts of people coming and going. We are expecting the Ludwig v. Hofmanns, Lampe, and the Heiselers to arrive tomorrow, all of whom wish to stay here in the castle; Steinitzer, Stetten and perhaps Müller-Hofmann as well. They all decided to come at the same time, which is in a way much better than having them all here one at a time. Julie is finally going to be leaving on Wednesday; it took her forever to get ready. I am continuing to incubate the chickens which I actually enjoy. The weather is very mild, almost too mild, but Maria and I still go for long walks every day. I like her a lot and wish she took things a little more lightly, for she would have a much easier life if she did.

How is your Papa doing now? I hope he is feeling much better and that you are no longer worried about him.

I finished reading my volume of Esmond which I enjoyed very much. I hope to soon find the second volume. Right now I am reading *Jeanne d' Arc*. It is well-written, but I have not gotten very far with it yet.

Please give me Gretl's address so I can write her and ask what music she wished to have sent.

Thinking of you and the charming time we spent in Berchtesgaden with great fondness,

Yours, Ottonie

❦ ❦ ❦

Monday evening [End of February 1914]

I am all by myself here at home, working; Gerty is in the city, and the children are sleeping. Everything comes to life when I am alone; more ideas and associations form themselves than my brain can follow. I did, however, manage to also write a few more pages of the fairy tale (*Frau ohne Sch.*).

You wrote that you found the trip to be very nice; I did, too, although not entirely *as regards us*. There is never enough time – it takes three days or more to get close to each other again. Did we ever really reach this point during the last trip? I do not believe we did. It was as if everything had come to an end during Christmas in Neubeuern, and we did not have much time there either. Then along came Munich. For me, the days we spent in Munich were the last time we were truly together.

I am very glad you got to see Reinhardt in this type of environment, it really makes me happy. It is simply an additional thread that is woven into our fabric – which fabric is that? Well, I suppose you could call it the fabric *of life*.

I am worried about Eberhard and Mädy; I do not know how else to put it. Have you by chance received any news? I wrote to him but (naturally) did not receive an answer. I am reminded of this at least ten times during the course of a day.

I already put the Esmond volume in the mail for you. It is a book which brings to mind again the English character, something one loves heartily in spite of all its drawbacks. The description of Marlborough is truly brilliant – as much of it is. (For instance, the duel in which Castlewood falls and the events that precede it. It is almost impossible to narrate a better story.) May I ask you to return Vandal's *Avènement de Napoléon*? I only know part of it. I also see here *Rémusat Memoires* (just the 2nd volume). It seems you have volumes one and three. I would ask that you to please let me know so that I can keep things in order. (A lack of order among books is a very bad thing.)

Unfortunately, certain volumes of Hebbel's diaries are unavailable (according to the publisher).

Also, would you be so kind as to inquire (through Jan's Dutch relatives)[141] whether or not it would be possible to obtain one of the Javanese string instruments (most likely a guitar of some type) at a low price ? The Javanese use them in their village theaters.

Good night. I am very tired. A dog is barking, stars shining above tiny white clouds, and the smell of spring is in the air.

---

141. Jan Baron Wendelstadt's mother was Dutch.

There was no calm and relaxed moment during our last meeting; not a moment when one could feel relief, now was there? I said too much about Julie that did not need to be said, a sickness that always strikes me at the *beginning* – I probably should not have tried to combine everything, *tant pis;* so I will just *have* to see you again soon.

Good night.

H.

P.S. Sometimes I think that our relationship would lose something if it were not for the misunderstandings and the pain they cause. Maybe this is just the product of a somewhat weary mind. Do not say (or think) that you are *terre à terre*. There is something in each person which is the complete opposite of *terre à terre*; it is a matter of not letting go.

The fairy tale allows me to think – and see – many more things than I could before.

Good night for the third time now. Why did you write so completely *pleased* with our last meeting in your letter? How could this be? Why? Please answer this question.

❦ ❦ ❦

Neubeuern, Friday [March 1914]

It was really rather silly of me to try to hide from myself that I was not entirely satisfied with our visit by expressing myself in neutral terms in the letter I wrote to you. I thought only I felt this way and that you returned home from Berchtesgaden completely satisfied as a result of your work. I felt like a typical woman incapable of ever being content. I felt ashamed and at the very least did not want you to notice it, and as a result I ended up doing exactly the wrong thing. I thought that if I admitted this to you that you would be apprehensive about our next meeting from the very start and unable to concentrate on your work with me around. But now I can express very candidly that I thought the trip itself was lovely, but as far as the two of us are concerned, I went home feeling as though something were missing. However, you should know that because I now realize that you had the same feelings, I feel better and much happier about things. The entire time I felt a certain emptiness; there was something missing. It was simply the fact that we were never really on the same wavelength. We are alone here now, Mama, Maria v.d.V. and I. The atmosphere here is very cozy. Everyone has something to do and is living her own life. Maria is busy taking a cure. Julie had to cancel her entire trip at the last minute to leave for *Celerina*, as Mädy sent a telegram saying Hansi was ill and that she planned to go see him if Julie did not. So Baby will also be leaving to go there today. After receiving Julie's telegram ("Hansi is up out of bed"), it seems to me that Mädy was once again exaggerating things. We have not heard much from Bredeney recently. It seems Eberhard does not take the operation too seriously and so far is doing quite well. Even Mädy seems to be quite courageous in coming to terms with the waiting period that lies ahead.

You know, I do not think I am going to be able to come to Rodaun now. I cannot leave here and later it seems Hansi will be coming here to recuperate, and then I have to go to Bredeney to pick up Karin in place of Mädy, and I also have to be present at the confirmation of a godchild of Christoph's on the 22nd of March in Stuttgart. So unfortunately March is going to be pretty full for me. Therefore my only hope is that Mädy's operation will at least take place right after Easter so that I at least have the month of May free, either for Rodaun or Paris.

When will Schröder be coming? Müller-Hofmann was here on Sunday and had a great deal to tell us about Bremen, about all the work he did there and what a delightful time he had. The Hofmanns were also here; they are both *very* charming and dear people. They kept asking if you were going to be in Florence again sometime; they would like you to visit them there.

I will send you the books presently.

Thanks for the *Esmond*.

Yours, Ottonie.

❦ ❦ ❦

Rodaun, Monday [Mid-March 1914]

It has not been a good time for me recently; this is the only reason I have not written. My creative power seems to have retreated deep inside of me – and this makes me unable to face life from one moment to the next. That tender awareness which allowed me to perceive things and to show understanding has disappeared – a feeling that has always accompanied me in the past. It is never entirely clear what causes this deterioration – most likely it is the transition from winter to spring with all these damp, dreary, listless days. It will certainly pass at some point; one must continue to wait quietly and be patient.

I busy myself as much as possible with my work; at times thoughts and images still flash through my mind like lightning. The other day I was able to relate very clearly to G. W. the tales I had formed in my mind in Berchtesgaden. She received and understood them so completely which showed me that, on the whole, they are good and not run of the mill. Something very beautiful lies hidden in this silent form of poetry. I constantly find myself groping for it, as if searching for a trap-door that I must open. Whether or not I shall find the right one and will have the strength to lift it remains questionable.

If I were able to accomplish more during these quiet periods, I would then enjoy leaving home, traveling to new places, etc., more than I do. Right now I am thinking of going to Paris from the 12th to the 22nd of May; maybe we will see each other there. I was very glad you noticed something was missing during our stay in Berchtesgaden – and that you felt empty afterwards. It is these kinds of trepidations, disappointments, and the keen perceptiveness and anticipation that foster the *life* which exists between the two of us – otherwise it would be dead.

Have you heard anything from Eberhard? And what about Mädy?

Your reading – I don't know exactly what? Have you read the strange books by Knut Hamsun (*Mysterien*, *Pan*)? I believe the books that I am reading now, all of which concern the East (the Buddha, the Upanishads), would be a little too hard. In any case, you would have to read a series of books like these, for nothing can be gained from reading any single one of them. Have I given you any of Lafcadio Hearn's books about Japan? If so, which ones?

Yours, H.

[On outside of envelope:] No word yet from Schröder

[Südbahn-Hotel Semmering] 27 March [1914]

I have transferred myself here for the time being in order to put an end to a slow, arduous spell that continued to drag on. Schröder, whom I had been expecting from week to week ever since the 20th of February, asks me today if he can come now! At this point, I had to request that he postpone it until some later time.

You must be on your short trip now – perhaps I will receive a few words letting me know if you have had a chance to see Stauffenberg. I would of course be very glad to hear this.

There is one more thing I should mention: It looks as if I will be in Paris without Gerty this coming May (12th to 22nd). She no longer wishes to go on trips like these and is happier staying in Rodaun and playing tennis, etc. If you were there, too, it might be as it often was in the past, and perhaps I would once again grow fond of Paris.

I have been brief because I want – and need – to hold myself together, maintain my concentration and focus on my writing altogether.

Adieu.

Yours, H.

[Postcard] [Vienna] 18 April [1914]

I am no longer feeling poorly as I was back in March. However, my story is still not at the point where I would like to have it; I hope I will not have to set it aside. Nature right now is truly enchanting, and in addition, life is full of many pleasant diversions, due to the presence of Reinhardt. We see him quite often and are planning to take a trip to Dürnstein (the little old town on the Danube) for 24 hours tomorrow with Gretl, Erwin and him. Schröder will be arriving on Monday and Moissi will be coming here for lunch on Tuesday – such is our life now; we spend every day this way. I am going to reserve my room at the Crillon in Paris beginning the 8th of May and plan to stay there for twelve days, I hope with you? No, seriously, when will you be arriving? Will you be there when I arrive? That is all I wish to know.

Yours, H.

Rodaun, 25 April [1914]

The presence of Reinhardt was a great pleasure – I also benefit from Rudi's, though in a completely different way. After having read it aloud to him, it appears that those parts of the fairy tale with which I struggled so hard did not turn out so badly after all and that I must simply continue this way.

Gretl was already not feeling quite well on our little excursion; toward evening she always ran a little temperature. Now she has been in bed for the past four days with a temperature of 39 degrees[142] from morning to night, and the doctors have no idea what it could be.

I reserved my room in the Crillon beginning the morning of the 9th. I am very glad you will be arriving before I do. I hope you are able to do all sorts of things that amuse you and will on occasion allow me to join in this life of yours. My life there will not exactly be uncomplicated; that is why Gerty will not be coming along. She thinks it will be easier for me not having her there, which is probably true.

I do not wish to say anything about Kessler. If one wished to express it in harsh terms, one would have to say he is a fool, a poor fool, and from time to time, an intolerable fool. He has, as the result of the most ridiculous pomposity, dragged himself down so low that now it seems he finds himself in a deplorable situation. I am holding my line with regard to him and hope to be able to keep it this way. It was very stupid of me to do what I did (drawing him into everything, due to my own naive good-

---

142. Approximately 101 degrees Fahrenheit.

naturedness), but now I am on a *tour de force*, which I intend to see through with decency and generosity.

What I have written seems somewhat diffuse due to Rudi's playing the piano a few feet away. If possible, do have friends get you a ticket for the premiere[143] on the 14th. Should I be given two, which is really my just due (however, I do not wish to demand it); then we will give yours away. Does the little hotel near the Madeleine have a name? I hope nothing else will interfere with my plans.

Yours, H.

❦ ❦ ❦

[Hinterhör] Friday [May 1914]

The little hotel is *so* tiny that it does not even have a name, but it does have an address: "14 rue de l'Arcade." If I do not like it there, I will move to one of the many other hotels and leave my address for you at the Crillon. I will be going to Eybach for a few hours on Tuesday and will leave for Paris from there that evening.

Poor Gretl, I wonder what could possibly be causing it. I hope she is over her fever by now.

Mädy will be arriving with Hansi tomorrow for a few days. Judging by a letter from Eberhard, he seems to be rather run down. Everything he says sounds so sad, although nothing in particular has happened that would explain this. Maybe you could find time to write him a few short words – he is always very happy when he receives your letters.

Good night. I will see you soon. Yours, Ottonie

❦ ❦ ❦

[Postcard]   R., 6 May [1914]

I will be arriving at the Crillon Saturday morning if nothing interferes at the last minute. Then, if you do not mind, I would like to meet you somewhere for a brief moment on Saturday between 5:30 and 6:00 to discuss something. Is there anything special at the theater on Sunday or Monday that you would like to go see with me? If so, please get the tickets, or for any other evening between the 10th and the 19th.

I hope to find a message at the Crillon.

H.

---

143. Of *Josephslegende*.

R., 16 [June 1914]

My love, there is no need to worry about my recent period of silence and even less to think that you are not dear to me – I was simply unable to write. All sorts of reasons kept coming up, too many for me to relate them all. I was very despondent (least so in Nauheim, but then all the more). Gradually one returns to oneself and finds one has managed to pull oneself together. The picture of you I have inside me is always untainted in its beauty. I benefited tremendously from your company in Paris – strange, how much a part of my life you have become. If one were to die suddenly, it would be strange and very painful to think of why more of you had not been given to me. By "not more," however, I mean something different than it might appear on the surface. If I could see you returned to your self, fully able to experience life again; to simply know this, without seeing it, no matter whose hand it was that led you, even if you were met with new sorrow, confusion, and failure, then I would accept being removed from your life, stricken from your memory, and would consider myself fortunate. For my feelings for you are entirely pure now, yet also strong, and hence in one respect, they do not allow me to fold my hands in my lap and renounce them.

Every now and then Gerty hears something from you, so I believe you are in N. now without Julie. I am probably going to go to Aussee ten days from now, the rest of the family a few days earlier. If I can think that you will be coming any time later, my life will become richer.

Yours, H.

❦ ❦ ❦

Neubeuern, Monday [ca. 1 July 1914]

There has not been a day in weeks now on which I did not think of you, especially while lying in bed in the evening. When everything around me has quieted down, my thoughts always return to you. Then I always intended to write you the next day and even made plans to do so, and again I felt so horrible not to have done it and decided again not to write. I do not even know myself why I decided not to. Something inside me was intent on holding me back. Finally today, thanks to the splendid, hot, sunny weather, the peace and quiet on the lovely terrace here at Neubeuern allows me to get around to doing this.

We have not heard anything from each other for a long time now. However, the last letter you wrote was so lovely; I am now quite content to do without all those that are written simply for the sake of writing.

I am certain I will be able to come to Aussee but am not yet exactly sure when it would be most convenient. It is always having to go to Eybach that seems to break up the summer and interfere with other plans; and my mother will also be here from the end of August until the 20th of September. At any rate, I truly want to come, so I suppose it will work out somehow. We have been having beautiful summer weather here for some time now and are all enjoying it very much. It is the peak of summer, and we have had a flood of guests; every room in the house is taken. I have been feeling so well that I was able to take many long day trips, like when we went up and over Heuberg on our way to the top of the Hochries and then down to Aschau, as well as other similar trips. We are planning to climb Heuberg in the moonlight tonight and watch the sunrise tomorrow morning. It has been five days now since Julie left with friends of hers to go on an automobile trip to the Mendel and Madonna and then back across the Dolomites. We are expecting her back on the 14th. Then on the 15th, she and Mama will be going to Eybach and I will be moving to Hinterhör with Baby, Mädy and Beaulieau.

The death of the couple who were heirs to the throne was a horrible thing to happen. Now poor Austria has such a heavy burden to bear. Will the young one[144] be able to handle this position of such great responsibility?!

Take care. We really belong together.

Ottonie.

[Postcard]   While passing through Vienna, 28 July 1914

Believe me and please tell all our friends that all of us here, down to the very last woodsman, have undertaken this project and *everything that may come of it* with a true resolve, indeed with joy, unlike any I have ever experienced before – or any I would have ever thought possible. I shall enter the Home Guard tonight. Perhaps you can send me a few lines in Pisino (Küstenland), P.O. Box.

Yours, H.

---

144. Archduke Karl, cousin of the Kaiser and his successor.

[Hinterhör] Sunday [Mid-August 1914]

My dearest Gerty,

I do not know if this letter will reach you, but I have to try and write you. We all share your worries about Hugo. Do you know where he is stationed? Let me know how I might send him a short note. Did you decide to stay with the children in Aussee, and is Papa Hofmannsthal there with you and how is he doing? I am *terribly* concerned about everything you all are going through; perhaps you could write me sometime.

Oh, this war! It is horrible to think of all the human life that goes to waste, but *the* solidarity that has come about as a result is a truly sublime and grand thing. All of Germany is bound together like *a single* family, which Austria is very much a part of. I have two brothers and forty-two cousins who are taking part in the fight, many of them young volunteers. One trembles out of concern for them, but one *must* have courage. We women certainly don't want to take a second place to the men when it comes to courage and the willingness to make sacrifices; we wish to do all that we can to help defeat the enemy.

We have partially turned Neubeuern into a hospital. I will take care of the enlisted men. We have arranged the old part of the castle so that there is room for twenty-two to twenty-five soldiers. Then there have been two to three beds placed in all the guest rooms for the officers' use; we will be very busy now. At the moment we are sewing shirts and knitting socks for the wounded. We are still in Hinterhör, but as soon as the wounded begin to arrive, we will move into the castle.

Mama will be remaining in Eybach for now with my brother-in-law Fredy and his servants. Eberhard was a member of the cavalry's levying commission and wrote that everything went extremely well.

Our people here reveal great courage and enthusiasm as they leave for the war; one cannot help but be proud.

Take care of yourself my dearest Gerty. Let me know something about Hugo as soon as you can. You know *how much* he means to me.

Faithfully and with love,

Yours, Ottonie

[Postcard]   Vienna I, Elisabethstrasse 6, 22 August [1914]

Letters sent to Pisino Küstenland where I was stationed at first, will no longer reach me. I would be very grateful if you sent me a short letter here. I was transferred from my regiment to the Ministry of War (Army Welfare Office) at the beginning of August. I would appreciate any news you have of Eberhard's whereabouts. Schröder was sent to Wangeroog

(Navy Division). Erwin Lang was sent to Galicia, Müller-Hofmann is most likely in Lorraine, and I assume you are at your parents' home.

Gerty is with the children in Aussee.

May God watch over us all.

HH.

Please send an *open* postcard.

[Hinterhör] Sunday, 30 August 1914

A letter I had sent to you on the 27th of July was just returned. I sent it to the Aussee address and Gerty forwarded it to Pisino. I am afraid you may also not have received the letters I sent after this and may be thinking you have a very callous friend. However, you must realize that especially at a difficult time like this, all my thoughts are with you every hour of every day. I thank God for the letter Gerty sent me last week. It put my mind at ease, and now I know that you are not involved in the fighting, which probably pains you very much, but those of us who love you can rest easier now and simply feel it is a godsend. What a marvelous time this is now! Victory after victory hurries toward us in our peace and quiet. And yet this peace is hard to bear, for one would rather be there in the middle of it all where one could be of more use and benefit to the cause. It is the possibility alone of helping the cause, here too, that keeps us going.

I received word from my oldest brother[145] a few days ago. He is fighting in Belgium, and my younger brother[146] must also be there. Unfortunately, however, we have not received word from him personally for some time.

My dear Dr. v. Boot from Kassel is one of the first people I know to die in battle. It is terrible, the distress and countless tears this war brings for all.

Thank God everyone who goes out into the war does so with such enthusiasm. Everyone here who must stay behind is deeply saddened and can hardly wait for his turn to come.

Our hospital is ready now. It turned out very well and will, I hope, soon be occupied.

Take care and do not forget that in a peaceful little corner of Upper Bavaria a gentle woman's heart is constantly trembling for you and *your* hardships as well as for the Fatherland.

Ottonie.

---

145. Albrecht von Schwartz.
146. Adolf von Schwartz, killed on the French front in 1914.

❦ ❦ ❦

Vienna I, Elisabethstrasse 6 [beginning of September 1914]

Dearest, I am not able to write you a real letter right now. The anxiety about our army, which for three weeks has been confronted by a host of more than 600,000 men, is too enormous. All those very brave people there! Oh, what an awful feeling, martyrdom – now more than ever not to be among them. One surely is of some use no matter where one is sent; possibly one could manage – on the other hand – oh, perhaps nothing will come of it, and one must endure this feeling of being physically inferior – it all persists, day and night. One views everything hidden behind a dark veil which minimizes all – even one's own wife, children, everything. Then, on top of this, expressions of sympathy for the individual! Poor Gretl has not received word – not a single word – from Erwin since he left. She has no idea whether he is dead, seriously wounded, in a Russian prison camp or . . . .

I have a question I would like to ask you now. Please respond as soon as possible after you discuss it with Julie. Please send me an *open* letter and write "open" on it.

It could be that I will have no choice but to arrange for Gerty, the children and my father to leave Vienna for the West in four to six weeks from now. I suppose there would not be any room in Neubeuern? Or possibly even just for the children?

One of the larger servant's rooms would do for all three of them. After all, who would think of comfort under these circumstances? Papa's housekeeper, a very good cook, would accompany him. I thought about renting a little house for him and the rest of us in Brannenburg – one with four or five rooms that are easy to heat. Please think this over. It may turn out to be unnecessary. But it is better to think things through calmly beforehand than to find oneself in a state of panic once it is too late. Is Dr. Glaser there? For Papa, I mean. Or maybe it would be possible to stay in Markt Neubeuern? This would not be as good as staying in Brannenburg I suppose?

I hope you can give me an answer soon.

Yours, H.

P.S. Strangely prophetic, my extreme despondency in Paris. Having to cry each morning upon awakening.

❦ ❦ ❦

Eybach Geisslingen, Monday [September 1914]

You will have received our telegram by now. That was indeed a sad letter you wrote. I hope none of your fears proved to be founded. In any case, you must know that there is always room here for your entire family. All of Hinterhör is at your disposal, and if Gerty finds it too large a place to run, we can always find something in the village. There are a number of flats available that are nicely furnished. Dr. Glaser lives in Brannenburg, and has a car and is able to come here on the shortest notice. There is little room here in the house, as we have offered to convert it into a hospital and have received official approval, which means it will probably remain full during the winter months. However, as Gerty is very skilled at running a household, it would probably be better for your Papa to live somewhere where he wouldn't be a guest and could order what he pleases. As *much* as we would love to have you all here, I must say that I hope this will not happen. The fighting in Galicia must really be terrible. We have also suffered horrible losses. Every day I hear of additional friends and acquaintances who have fallen in battle. It is of course no different here. Weeks pass during which one does not hear a thing from relatives. I am glad my brother is in the safety of a hospital at least for a time, but this is *very* difficult for him.

It does not look good with Mama; an agonizing condition and so variable. I am going to Munich today to pick up Marie-Therese and will then stay here for an undetermined length of time. Mädy is in Degenershausen with Christa and Luli. The wife of Heinrich Mutzenbecher is with her, a war bride. Hansi is in the sanatorium in Königstein, Eberhard is terribly busy in Essen.

Everyone wishes he could multiply and somehow make use of every last bit of his strength. We must indeed hold our chins up in order to provide ourselves and those around us with moral support. Julie, too, is devoted to all of you and ready to help if need be.

Yours always, Ottonie.

Vienna, 27 September [1914]

Dearest, I have received several, maybe all, of your wonderful, kind letters. I replied a number of times, most recently in an open letter addressed to you (which Julie may also have read). I received a telegram signed by both of you in response, and then the card arrived in which you told me that your youngest brother died fighting for the Fatherland and that the oldest one is seriously wounded. My premonition was directed towards you during this time. I saw you strolling through your parents' home, comforting your father. Now, because of your other duties, you cannot be with him; God will send comfort – will have already provided him the comfort he needs. How much I wanted to try to write him, but letters from strangers are not worth much.

When I was free for an hour recently, I wrote Julie a letter. (I sent it as an open letter to the Eybach address. Perhaps you went through the mail and had a chance to read it; I would be very happy if you did.) I thanked her for her willingness to take my family in should such a need arise and tried to (so that she will not think I am out of my mind) elucidate for her the monstrous tenseness we feel under the present circumstances, which even in Germany cannot be fully comprehended. We have not seen anything of this kind since the Turkish Wars – the Napoleonic Wars in 1805 and 1809 were child's play by comparison. Deep in my heart I am confident we will pull through. I have less confidence in the men who will have to undertake the immensely difficult task of representing our interests at the peace table. It is precisely the lack of intelligent men of character outside the army (an age-old Austrian defect) which makes the situation here so exceptionally difficult to bear.

Gretl is good and very brave, though she is without news from Erwin since the 4th. Her brother-in-law, the husband of Lilith, Herr von Forster, is being held in a Serbian prison camp.

My thoughts are with you.

Yours, H.

❦ ❦ ❦

Eybach b/ Geisslingen a/ St., 24 October 1914

With all there is to do here it is hard to find time to even write a few brief words.

Thank you very much for the kind words you sent me. How strange that you were able to sense it. His death was horrible for my parents! Horrible for all of us. It is so sad when the circle of such a vibrant family keeps getting smaller and smaller. But you cannot imagine how glorious and sacred the death of a son fallen in battle is even for my mother, so much so that not even she dares to lament his loss. My father is wonderful. His old heart remains strong, and his childish faith, coupled with his fervent patriotism, allows him to quietly accept this newest tragedy. He has so much to do as State Delegate of the Red Cross – so do my mother and sisters, a true blessing at a time like this.

It is so very sad for us siblings that there are now fewer of us to share our childhood memories.

Here, too, it is difficult. Mama has been doing better for the past week now, so we hope we can move back to Neubeuern during the first part of

November taking Mama along. It will be a difficult trip. I wish we already had it behind us. It is questionable whether we will be able to separate Mama from everything here again, but we hope we can.

The war is terrible, yet also grand. The terrific successes here in Germany now, as well as yours in Austria. There have been so many great feats. What a magnificent man the commander of the Emden must be. It is glorious to be a part of this and every day one hears so much. Your and Schröder's poem is *so very* beautiful. Eberhard is going to have it printed, and we will include it in the packages we send the soldiers; thus many hundreds of dragoons will receive a copy from me next week and will have the chance to read your beautiful greetings. What would one not be prepared to do to help the soldiers in whatever way possible? We work from dawn 'til dusk, yet still, one feels as if one should be able to accomplish so much more.

Thank God Albrecht is doing better. He is allowed to get out of bed again but is of course still very weak. He received the Iron Cross, about which we were all overjoyed.

On Wednesday I am going to Stuttgart with Baby for several days to see the dentist, etc. We will be returning on Saturday and then hope to go to Neubeuern the following week.

Last week we were in Geisslingen to bring something to drink to a hospital train. I helped take care of the wounded and saw *how* well-organized everything was there. Only we remained in the train by mistake and had to ride along to the next stop.

Take care. I *hope* you are well.

Many warm regards from,

Yours, Ottonie, who doesn't wish to be forgotten entirely.

Vienna, 28 October [1914]

You probably have no idea how often I think of you, Ottonie, or how often I see your figure pass before my eyes or see you seated in the little room in Paris or walking along the road between the castle and Hinterhör. I cannot tell you how vivid the images are of all those who hold a special place in my heart. Nor how often I talk to you, Eberhard, and Rudi Schröder – over and over again while caught in the middle of this vicious circle of worry and activity. I am on duty all day long; such endless masses of material pass through. Now and then, the impatience and shame I have felt as a result of not being stationed at the front have eaten me alive. There have been week-long stretches that nearly drove me crazy. Now, however, I try to tell myself that I could not hold up physically if I were there; here I am able to do much more, and, as a single individual, relatively speaking, I can accomplish more.

Everything seems so dreamlike and yet more real than any imaginable reality. It has been another month now since we have heard from Erwin. They are dragging our officers off into the deepest depths of Siberia, all the way to the Mongolian border. The hand of God reigns over everything, and Gretl is holding up splendidly. Willy Müller-Hofmann has received the gifts you sent and was also awarded the Iron Cross, as was Heymel.

The mere thought of Eybach makes me sad. I wish you were back in Neubeuern. I often think, "If only God had already seen fit to take the old woman."[147]

I would very much like to continue writing, but I have to report for duty.

Hugo.

🌣 🌣 🌣

Neubeuern, 18 November 1914

We have been here for almost two weeks now. I am so grateful that we managed this difficult journey and that I have Mama here with me and that she is feeling well. The departure from Eybach was horrible. The old woman cried miserably; I had to remove her by force against her will. It was terrible.

During our last few days there, another Degenfeld cousin put an end to her life by jumping off a cliff. On the outside, she seemed a wholly rational person, whom one would never have thought capable of anything out of the ordinary. She had had religious delusions and finally became convinced that she had to sacrifice herself for the world's sins. She believed people had very little regard for the sacrifice Christ made and it was up to a woman to die for the sake of all.

These were terribly stressful times, the war outside and no rest in one's personal, everyday life. I am constantly reminded of your prophetic tears in Paris. May we indeed achieve a true victory and not ultimately be forced to make peace because of exhaustion. Hindenburg's[148] most recent victory was marvelous. It is amazing how much a *single* victory means for the morale of entire nations.

All of our friends who are stationed on the front continue to show tremendous confidence in the letters they write. We, too, want to arm

---

147. Ottonie's mother-in-law.
148. General-Fieldmarshal of the German army on the eastern front, later second president of the Weimar Republic.

ourselves with patience, although it is tough when one thinks of all the sacrifices the poor boys over there are forced to make.

I can imagine how horrible it must have been for you not to have joined the others at the front. However, you are surely able to contribute *a great deal more* in your present capacity!

I am sure you have heard about poor Heymel; apparently he's in *very bad* shape. Eberhard found he had gotten much worse during the two weeks he hadn't seen him. Have you written to him again yet? This would certainly make him extremely happy.

Our hospital is not very full – the few men we do have are receiving *very* good care.

Monday. This letter has been lying here unfinished for a long time now. In the meantime, I visited Campenhausen in his internment camp[149] in Traunstein. Such an institution is not a very pretty sight. Thank God he just telephoned to say that he has been set free, i.e. he is allowed to stay in Traunstein.

Müller-Hofmann always seems to be very confident in the letters he writes. We send him a package now and then. If Gerty would like me to send a Christmas package to him for her, tell her to send me a card right away.

Take care. I think of you a lot and very often.

Yours, Ottonie.

❦ ❦ ❦

Rodaun, 14 December 1914

It was the 3rd of December when I met you for the first time in Hinterhör – Kessler was there, before the birth of Marie-Therese, on a misty, damp winter day. The two Baltic barons recounted stories of the Estonian Revolution. How long ago this now seems, almost as if it belonged to the biography of totally different people.

I was rather worried not to have heard anything from you for such a long time. I was keenly aware of the hard times and worry you endured; then the telegram arrived from Klärchen containing the news of poor Alfred's death.[150] (He received my letter before he died. I'm so grateful to Mädy for telling me, "It's high time you write." The remorse, the self-reproach and the pain one feels about everything that couldn't be put right remains, but at least he received my letter and enjoyed it.) Then I received

---

149. Campenhausen was an ethnic German from the Baltic carrying a Russian passport. Despite his being a guest at the castle, a zealous Austrian border guard arrested him. Suddenly some of Neubeuern's international guests had become enemy aliens.

150. Alfred Heymel.

your letter on the 28th. It was dated the 18th. Strange, letters from Bavaria take the longest, whereas those from Essen take only half the time.

Just this sign of life today. It is very late and I am tired, so I will have to close. You must not, however, imagine me feeling miserable or gloomy. On the contrary, I have a clear head now and am in a positive state of mind. Since the war began, I have not had a single day like those back in Paris – I am sorry we are not together now, also because I would certainly not be a burden or cause you any suffering, but would in fact be able to cheer you up. I recently read aloud to some of the ordinary folks, office employees and the like. I read some of the Grimm fairy tales, *Machandelboom* [Juniper Tree], and the *Geselligen Lieder* [Songs of Friendship] by Goethe. It was very nice; I look forward to continuing to do this now and again. I am rambling on about myself in the hopes of distracting you a little bit. After all, a person would go crazy if all he talked about were the war. I will send you several things in print next time. Have you been reading Goethe?

Good night. I am often with you in my thoughts.

Your friend, H.

Neubeuern a/Inn Oberbayern, 5 December 1914

How excited we all were that Belgrade fell! Especially since everything takes such a long time on the Western front, each new success has a special meaning.

Van de Velde was here yesterday. He talked a lot about Heymel, whom he nursed in his last two weeks. Poor Heymel must have suffered terribly. He had open sores from his stomach all the way up to his mouth. The only way he could take anything was after being numbed all the way down his gullet with cocaine or something like that.

They still could read your letter to him. He was probably no longer able to understand it entirely, however he did say "dear letter."

Henry believed that Heymel was unaware he was dying right to the very end. His humor continued to shine through and light up the room, and for hours he told stories of the war and other times in his life. Perhaps these very last hours were the best ones of his life. Frau Heye was apparently very *touching*, and Heymel was extremely happy to have her there.

Van de Velde has been having a lot of trouble in Weimar and will probably be going to Berlin. Maria and Thylla are in Degenershausen for the time being and are also going to remain there for now. The life of Henry and Maria has, indeed, as far as I hear from Mädy, changed a great deal, and Frau Lampe has entered into this marriage as the third party, which Maria is aware of. How this came about right now, I do not know, but in any case, H. said he could not continue to lead this kind of life with Maria. The war has of course outwardly provided a mantle for their current separation.

Last night you were so close to me, holding my hand as only you can, and we spoke at great length. You have no idea how often my thoughts wander to you and how much you are able to help me, especially in this often very difficult time. There I am surrounded by all the books and as I pick up one of them, I am filled with great joy. As I read on and on, I am so grateful and happy that I can read.

Mama has been feeling somewhat better the past few days – not much better of course, but just a slight bit. Still, it makes us very happy. Seen from the outside, I am naturally the same as I always was; for when I allow my wings to droop, the mood of the entire house sinks to a very low point. My brother is here now. One of his wounds is still open, but he is able to walk again quite well. He has already been out hunting and hopes to perform garrison duty by early January. To bear the thought that he will soon have to return to the front requires all the courage one can muster, and above all, that he *wants* to go. It would be too much for all of us if we lost him, too. Here I am again thinking these dark thoughts while at the same time trying to banish them.

We continue to receive good news from all our friends and acquaintances out in the field. Müller-Hoffmann's last card arrived yesterday, and it seems that he received the parcel I sent him in Gerty's name.

Take care now. I am happy when I think of you.

Yours, Ottonie

❦ ❦ ❦

Rodaun, 2 January 1915

When Gretl returned from Munich, where she saw and spoke to you, she still carried with her a warmth which had not yet cooled off completely, and I was convinced that you are still alive – convinced in a way which is simply not possible from reading a letter. However, it is starting to become somewhat shadow-like again.

Eberhard seemed to imply in his letters that it would depend on me this time (as I am unable to visit him) whether or not he comes here for a couple of days. Just when I had taken him up on this, a telegram arrived saying "unfortunately unable to come." At that moment, I became truly aware for the first time just how much I had been looking forward to seeing him and how frequently I am in need of his personal involvement and counsel. I was very disappointed and still am. I've come up with an idea, though. Listen to this. It seems to me it would really be the most natural thing in the world if you came to visit here for four or five days in place of him. How I fit this in with my present duties, etc., is my own business. You could either stay here in the house as Schröder does from time to time or next door at Stelzer's.

I believe you will decide to come, that is, I believe it would be hard for you not to without arousing in me the belief that the relationships I have with all my German friends remain intact only in so far as I am able to follow them wherever they may be, which is not the best way to maintain a long-term friendship. I will be expecting a reply.

I think we must prepare ourselves for a long war. However, at this moment, the only thing I perceive (one cannot constantly remain focused on all the horror) are the immeasurable gains we've achieved both intellectually and spiritually.

I am happy when I find some time to read in the *Hyperion*. Take the volumes of Freytag's *Pictures of the German Past* which deals with the Thirty Years War, Frederick II and 1813 – that is a good book to read in these times.

I would love to see you walk through the front gate right now.

Your friend, H.

❦ ❦ ❦

Neubeuern, 8 January 1915

The few sparse letters we write each other now still seem to cross each other in the mail. But your letter served as a very kind greeting on my return from Munich. The thought of my father depresses me, too. It appears that being the head of the Red Cross there is becoming too much for him, coupled with the pain of losing his son. He also longs very much for me. However, I feel I cannot leave Mama now, who clings to me very tightly and is in need of my moral support. Everything lay like a heavy stone upon my heart when along came your letter, which was more cheerful than usual and which acted like balsam. I have asked my father to come here now; I hope he can take the time and do so.

As far as my coming there is concerned, I would simply *love* to, more than you can imagine, but I am not sure it will be possible. I think it can be managed, that is, if Mädy were to come here and take my place at Mama's side, then it would work out very well. However, as Mädy has now once again reached the point of collapse, she will probably do it. *When* I will be able to come, I cannot say right now, but I will come if there is *any* possible way.

Take care. You are very close to me today.

Yours, Ottonie.

❦ ❦ ❦

Rodaun, Sunday [10 January 1915]

The sad letter you wrote on the 5th arrived yesterday evening. I hope you are feeling a little more cheerful now. I was very worried not to have heard anything from you for so long, and I went ahead and wrote you a while back. It is strange you did not mention this letter, but perhaps it arrived in N. while you were in Munich. In it I urged you to come and stay with us here for a few days in February and spend some time with us, and I can only reiterate this now. I cannot imagine that *they* would not be able to do without you for a few days once the hospital is in running order – what would happen if you fell ill?

As the entire situation here is so unpredictable, I have no idea when I will be able to leave again. Eberhard wrote me a rather sad letter. He said the longer this job continues, the less capable he feels and must cry a lot, etc. I want to write him a letter today and try to cheer him up. Particularly at a time when fate is dealing so harshly with the lives of hundreds of thousands, as if they were a mere bundle of straw, each individual must recognize the value of the individual even more clearly than he might otherwise.

Not long ago, I experienced the purest joy while reading several of Keller's novellas set in Zurich. You should read them, too. And have another look at *Hyperion* sometime. I hope more than anything else that you have not lost sight of the importance of *committing* yourself to occasionally spend a few hours by yourself.

There is one odd thing about a very kind letter from Julie: it seems now she is outwardly just as friendly and well-disposed around the invalids. (The letter ends here.)

❦ ❦ ❦

Neubeuern, 26 January 1915

Can you imagine that a letter I had written to you during the first days of the war was just returned to me. It was strange during all the cold and snow we have here now reading what I had written with great excitement during the first days of the war in the warm, sunny weather we were having at that time.

Well, I will be leaving for Berlin on Friday in order to spend a few days with Eberhard. Will be staying in Berlin until the 3rd of February at Frau von Keszycky's (Kurfürstendamm 47). I will be at my sister's on the 4th/5th in Stassfurt (Bernburgerstr.19) and in Sondershausen from the 15th to the 19th. I would then – if it is all right with you – arrive in Vienna on the 20th and could stay until the 24th. This is my plan. Whether or not it will work out depends on Mama's health, etc. I will have to go there, to Vienna that is, on a Sunday sometime anyway in order to check on our boy,[151] who is not free on any other day. I hope it all works out this way from our side and that it suits you as well.

Mädy has been here for a while now. She said she was feeling somewhat down at home; she is feeling better here.

I am looking forward very much to being able to talk to Eberhard again.

Is Gretl still in Berlin, and where is she staying (so that I might meet her sometime)?

Mama is doing quite well at the moment. If only things stay this way.

Many warm regards.

Yours, Ottonie

Rodaun, 6 February [1915]

You told me you might come to visit me and repeated this to Gretl. Nevertheless, I shall not think of it too often so that the disappointment will not hit me too hard.

On the other hand this may be the moment in my life when I could truly benefit from your visit, more so than at any other time.

You are probably aware of the intensified passport regulations. In order to enter Austria (and also to return to Germany), you must have a passport containing a photograph, and the photograph must be (with respect to the owner's identity) authorized and stamped by the authorities, etc. Your father will not find it difficult to arrange for you to receive such a document from the authorities in Sondershausen in case you do not already have one, but it's *imperative* that you have one when you come. I assume you will be arriving in Vienna (on the Northwest Train) sometime in the morning. You can then take a taxi to South Station where quite a few trains leave for Rodaun (every 20 to 30 minutes) via Liesing or at least as far as Liesing, from where you can make it to Rodaun in 10 minutes (by taking another train). We live at Badgasse 5, next door to Stelzer. You can check your suitcase to Rodaun at the South Station in either case, even if you yourself only travel as far as Liesing. (For not every train arriving in Liesing has a connection to Rodaun (located along a secondary route), however, the suitcase will arrive with the next train.)

Will you really be sitting down here in these very rooms and walking across the snow-covered yard and examining the books I have stacked on the shelves here . . . ? Who could possibly know?

---

151. The young cousin Fery Count Huegel was in a boarding school in Vienna.

Good night. Send me a telegram around the 15th or 16th, please. Letters sometimes take an awfully long time.

Yours, H.

Sondershausen, Wednesday, 10 February 1915

I would like to ask you a direct question about something. I now realize that it would be terribly complicated traveling from here to Vienna. I would have to leave here by 11:00 a.m. and change trains four different times before arriving in Dresden, where I could board a sleeping car in the evening. So I thought it would be better if I gave up the idea for now and came instead sometime in March or April from Neubeuern, as it is much easier traveling from there. However, if you have *really* been looking forward to my visit so much and would be disappointed if I did not come, I would be *glad* to make the difficult journey knowing it will make you happy. Please send me a telegram then "only" after you receive these lines – now or at some later point. I also think I might be able to stay a bit longer if I came in the spring. Perhaps for a week. I will leave it completely up to you and let you decide what you would prefer.

The two days I spent with Eberhard were simply wonderful, unfortunately much too short a time, though. Eberhard has been feeling terrible, indeed sad, which is partly a result of Mädy's terrible nervousness. I am tremendously fond of him and want him with all my heart to have more peace and happiness there at home.

Gretl's dance as a peasant girl was *very* enchanting; she did it beautifully. The bride's dance was not as good, not quite convincing enough. Unfortunately, I did not have the chance to speak to her.

I have been traveling around quite a lot recently and am happy to now have a moment of peace here. My father is so happy to have me here and feels better as a result, too, although he really has aged a lot during the past year. I want more than anything to still give him all the love I can, the good old man.

I will look forward to hearing from you then and ask that you please not consider me *at all* but only yourself.

With love, Ottonie.

R., 7 March [1915], evening

From day to day I am waiting for an hour of inner peace – but in vain – life remains heavy-laden and unpredictable or even becomes all the more so. At the moment, the great pressure and uneasiness we feel (concerning the question of Italy) is so great that the only reason I have decided to write is because I find it too agonizing to let you go too long without news from me. And also because it is the same for me when I have to wait such a long time to hear something from you. However, this is only a means of keeping in touch and not a true letter.

Now and then I say to myself: "When this time finally comes to an end someday and we see each other again, it will seem as if we all have just emerged from the grave."

How many weeks has it been now that I have wanted to write to Eberhard without being able to bring myself to do so? It has been months since I heard anything from Schröder. Kessler came here with a delegation from the Carpathians[152] on his way to Berlin. He looked amazingly well and never before did he appear as handsome and masculine as he does now. He has grown into his uniform and the entire present situation and has many nice tales to tell. Of course, his group fared no better than the others in its attempt to cross the northern edge of the Carpathians (except for the one in Bukovina), and the wonderfully bold offensive planned from the southeast is essentially a disaster – despite tremendous achievements and sacrifices.

It turned out to be a good thing that you did not come now. I had a very bad cold and was in bed then (around the 20th); during that time my father, following some bad weeks, had an attack similar to the kind your mother-in-law had a number of times. His feet would no longer carry him, and one hand went lame. It seems to have remedied itself in the meantime, and the doctor hopes and promises a total recovery to his previous state, which was only rather mediocre. One must simply learn to accept this like everything else. How should old people be able to make it through times like these unscathed?

It is always a pure joy for me when you write.

Best wishes from Gerty.

Sincerely yours, H.

P.S. You have mentioned the wounded you have there in your letters. Who are they anyway? Is there no one of distinction among them?

---

152. Mountain range in the former eastern provinces of Austria where the war raged.

[Hinterhör] 3 May 1915

It has been ages since we heard from each other. It almost seems impossible. I hope to see Gretl when I go into town this Friday and to find out how you are, what you are doing, etc. Thank God the military situation here has improved a great deal during the past few days to the point where one feels like there is more breathing space, which must make you feel better in Austria, too. I received a letter from Eberhard yesterday containing some very comforting words, also with regard to Italy.

We are having unbelievably beautiful spring weather; it is like something out of a fairy tale. For days now the sun has been shining from dawn 'til dusk, and the vegetation is so lush. It is hard to imagine in these peaceful surroundings here that death and destruction are the rule in other places.

My brother has been back on the battlefield since Easter and we are of course all trembling with fear for his life. Father is here with us now to try to recover somewhat from the grief he has endured during the past year. I met him in Nürnberg and we had a look at the beautiful old town together. However, he still felt rather miserable and was unable to really enjoy it. He is doing much better now, and he has regained his ability to experience a feeling of enthusiasm.

I often wonder how your Papa is doing.

What would you say if I came for a short visit after Whitsun? Would the last few days of May suit you? I would *really* like to come if I knew that it would give you even a tiny bit of pleasure. Perhaps you can respond sometime soon.

Take care, and many warm regards.

Yours, O.

❦ ❦ ❦

Aussee, Obertressen 14, 21 August [1915]

One must become reaccustomed to writing letters. However, I was not so far away from you during this time as you may have imagined. I once read in Goethe that he divided his girlfriends into those who remain alive for him *per distance* and those who do not. You belong for me to this first category. It is simply a case of having been constantly – and still being – focused on external events as a result of the worry, grief, hope, and a sense of community one feels, as long as the end does not appear near – of being unable to dedicate oneself to one's own sense of awareness and to that which constitutes one's own true being. At the very least I feel as if I am barred from my own inner self and barred from the countryside surrounding me. I am here and yet not here. There is much I have to do, but there is a deeper layer consisting of everything related to my own work, which I hardly dare contemplate – even though the possibility exists. To offer a brief account of these external considerations, I can tell you that I returned from the occupied territories at the end of June to find my father feeling weak and miserable and breathing with difficulty; he even slept poorly in his wheelchair. For a time it was questionable whether it would be possible for him to travel to Ischl. It was his most ardent wish to leave the sanatorium; finally, a date for the trip was set which worked. He has been in Ischl now for about three weeks and is living reasonably well. I have been relieved of my duties for an undetermined length of time as a result of the intervention of one of the highest of all government offices. In keeping with the spirit of this order, I might be assigned to the Imperial and Royal Commissioner of the Imperial Government in Brussels for a time beginning around the end of September – until then, I can pretty much rest assured that I will be allowed to stay here. In connection with this, I wrote Eberhard a letter about two to three weeks ago asking where I might see him now or at some later time, however I have not received any answer. Is he ill?

A written copy of a speech by Borchardt, "Der Krieg und die deutsche Selbsteinkehr" [The War and Germany's Self-Examination], reached me here. It has made the strongest impression on me of anything written in the German language since the beginning of the war. I felt truly happy to be able to count this man as well as Schröder among my closest friends and also to be one their closest friends.

Have you had a chance to look at this brochure (the speech)? Did Eberhard by chance send you a copy? Or haven't you seen it yet? Please write me about this immediately.

During the first few months, the book by W. Whitman meant more to me than one could possibly imagine a book could mean to a person.

Gretl announced completely unexpectedly that she will be arriving tomorrow. She plans to stay for five days. It has been a year now since she said goodbye to Erwin – by the way, the news we hear from him is always reasonably positive. For no particular reason I have been hopeful for the past few days now that peace lies ahead somewhere in the foreseeable future.

Perhaps this is foolish of me.

Yours, H.

P.S. I have wanted to ask you something from the very beginning of this letter: Would it not be possible for you to come for a week around the beginning of September?

❦ ❦ ❦

Degenershausen, 9 August [1915]

I am alone here with several of the children and will be returning this evening to Neubeuern with Baby and Fery. I want to use this brief little moment of peace to write you a few lines; I have meant to the entire time now, but people were constantly converging upon me from all directions in order to "enjoy" me. Now your letter just arrived, and I want to answer right away.

I, too, am very depressed about your father's condition, for I know *how* you must be suffering, as I of course have known for so long and so well all about your relationship to him. I hope the fresh air in Ischl will be of great benefit to him.

Now about things here. Degenershausen is lovely, a truly charming paradise with all the woods surrounding it. This is the one place that provides a rare sense of calm — wherever you look, all you can see are the green meadows and woods, green and more green. Courten's[153] art of uniting the courtyard and farm buildings with the house has helped the appearance of the house immensely, and Eberhard has done a great deal here in a short period of time. You will have to come here sometime. Maybe at the end of August, when Eberhard will be here for two weeks from the 28th to around the 10th of September.

Eberhard showed me your letter, which he has probably already answered. Again he had a lot to do here and there and told me that he would unfortunately not have time to meet you anywhere where he had to travel, as he *must* now stay here for a while.

I would just love to come see you and had been meaning to ask you about this for a long time. However, whether it might be possible during the first week of September is something I cannot answer today, not from here, because Julie *has to* at least go for two weeks somewhere away from home. I suggested that she come here on the 23rd of August; then she would hardly be back in Neubeuern before the 10th, and with our hospital, we cannot both be away at the same time. Would my coming be all right with you from the 15th to the 22nd of Sept., or do you plan to be gone by then?

Eberhard had a copy of Borchardt's speech sent to me in Neubeuern. I will read it when I return and am looking forward to it very much. It had the same effect on him as on you. It made a very strong impression on him, and he told me it was the best and most wonderful thing he has read about the war. In connection with this, we have been discussing Borchardt a great deal recently and have all come to the conclusion that we are fortunate to know a man like him or to know that he exists.

---

153. Count Carlo Courten was the architect Eberhard employed when renovating Degenershausen.

You wrote me something so precious about your relationship to me which made me feel so good. One feels so deserted now, everything around seems to be dying; and never has one had such feelings of being totally alone as in these days of this raging war. I can well understand why you are scared and do not dare to delve into your innermost feelings, which do make up the core of your being. It is probably best for now to deal only with every day work, for everything else has become so confused.

I have to close now. How lovely it is that Gretl will be spending a few days with you.

Well, I would really *love* to come and hope that we can find a time that will be mutually agreeable to both of us.

Yours always, Ottonie.

🙶 🙶 🙶

[Bredeney bei Essen-Ruhr] 14 October 1915

Dearest, so now the war has brought me here to this place where peace and friendship had beckoned me so many times before. I sit here quietly in this cheerful guest room on the second floor that you yourself once occupied and feel calm and collected, as I have not done for a very long time. I have a feeling of happiness as I breathe the air of the great German country struggling for world domination and can truly say to myself that I feel a part of this air and this country. I feel close to everything that is dear to my heart – which includes you, from whom I of course never felt removed, indeed to whom I often felt very close in times of great stress. Were you able to feel this?

Once peace is achieved, we will experience an indescribable feeling of deliverance, and this ironclad weight will finally fall from our hearts. No people has ever had to endure *what* we have to, not even during the time of the Napoleonic Wars. I already feel a quiet sense of deliverance today, a small taste of the peace to come, by being able to send you this letter without 422 Austrian and Bavarian officials reading it first. Do you still know him, Ottonie, the one who is writing you this letter? I became a new man around fifteen months ago, much like a glove that has been turned inside out; I am now up to my ears in political matters. Would you still recognize your friend? Oh, sure you would, right on the spot! From Hinterhör, we would take a few steps in the direction of Bibiana. We would carry a book of Hölderlin's poems along with us. We would enjoy lovely conversations and quickly would feel very close to one another. Our first few steps would take us past the bench where we sat together that time when you said to me, "I would not have believed that I would ever allow another man to say that to me again." I had told you that I was happy that you were a part of this world – whatever happened to all of this? And yet, *it exists*, Ottonie, and we shall not lose it as long as we are still alive (after that, who knows?).

Another example of this was when I was in Salzburg in September. I was there for three days. It was because of the mail that I could not ask you to come there. (Communications were completely cut off for three weeks, so that I was unable to send Strauss, whom I wanted to meet there, either a letter or telegram.) But on the other hand, I did not really want you to come there then. I had brought together a group of people to discuss certain political issues, so we would not have had an opportunity to spend time together. One evening Gerty and Christiane and I walked toward the Mönchsberg; we had started at the fortress and lost our way. Suddenly we found ourselves near the big restaurant to which the lift leads. We turned trying to find the road back to town when I noticed the bench where we sat together at night that time, the first evening I picked you up on the way to Aussee. How this bench looked! How something spoke – of you, of me, of both of us at the same time. How lovely and nostalgic it felt, and yet really it was simply lovely, transcending any sense of wistfulness.

My love, I would so like to see you again soon, but I realize that the only way I could return here or come there is via Berlin. If I can sort things out with my very "semi"-official duties, in which I would like to include you (and which, to summarize it briefly, Eberhard approves of), I will have to be in Berlin for at least two more weeks beginning in mid-November and will have to return there every now and then. At the present time I have nothing to look forward to except that you will, when you have an hour to relax, write me one of your dear letters sometime soon at the following address: Office of the Austrian-Hungarian Commissioner; Baron Franckenstein; Brussels 51; rue de Spa. However, you will have to make it an open letter again.

Would it not be possible to toy with the idea of coming here to Rodaun once in your life for a little while sometime in January or February? However, this assumes that I will not be sent somewhere unexpectedly by the military in the meantime, which I hope will not happen.

For the first time I have a chance to see Eberhard as the Eberhard *in Essen*. He is kind, as always, and to me, the truest of friends. However, he is very weary and has absolutely no desire to talk. He is so in need of rest that I believe we should wish for him nothing but an abundance of peace and quiet in the future.

Your friend, Hofmannsthal.

[Fritz Töpfers Hotel Prinz Friedrich Carl, Berlin N.W.] 2 January 1916

Dearest, the letter you wrote on the 29th, which arrived here today, the 2nd of January, made me very happy. It was as if I heard your voice again for the first time in a long, long time. The previous letter you had sent simply made me aware of how far away we are from each other, while this last one gives me the feeling that we are still alive and still there for one another – which is truly wonderful. There is presently so much that stifles people; one is no longer one's own master. It is a hard school we are going through. Yet we surely do not want to keep ourselves apart as a result of our own doing: If we want to come together, then surely we will. But letters, which mean so much, are no help right now. But dearest, I do not like it when you tell me that you cannot come to see me because you have to "take care of" Marie-Therese. For how could a seven-year-old child who is as well-behaved and reasonable as Marie-Therese, possibly still need taking care of?! Especially in a house full of people! All you have to do is to leave a few volumes of Goethe for her and make sure that nothing of Casanova's is lying around, and then depart. Right?

Dearest, seriously speaking, I have an official position here which allows me considerable freedom but also requires a great deal of responsibility. I cannot tell for sure how long they will keep me here. I will probably be going home in two to three weeks and returning here at a later date; this seems to be most likely. Later they may give me another assignment. I can probably expect to be home for Easter, that is, around the end of April – but this is not certain.

8 January [1916]

This letter has been lying here unfinished for six days now, and during this time I have discussed so many difficult matters with some horrible yet shrewd politicians – in between I also heard and saw some wonderful things, such as kind faces of men (women no longer exist). Last night I heard a wonderful performance of the *Eroica* – deepest secrets in the greatest clarity. Strauss told me afterwards that he had conducted it only for me and that he had never before experienced it as he did then. *The Rosenkavalier* had been performed a few days earlier. I happened to be free and decided to go. I enjoyed it very much. It was such a lively performance and the elegant aspects were clearly evident. You once mentioned this, and I remembered the words. You are right: and it made me happy. I felt like you were sitting beside me, just as your shadow sat beside me back then in Dresden during the rehearsals. Do you still remember when this took place? You were in Sondershausen; it was then that someone had just discovered you were such a Thuringian Fräulein.

I am going on and on as if there were no war and as if we both were still alive. I thought about the *possibility* of returning home via Munich. I thought you could come there for a couple of days. But why bother, since everything always turns out differently than one expects? You would have Julie with you in Munich or would be someplace with Julie. In short, it is always "Julie, Julie, Julie," the same old melody I simply cannot tolerate in connection to you.

So why don't you help us – by first sending a nice letter! It may be *very* nice in Rodaun around the end of April – but you will be coming with Julie, right? Then she will leave, and you will stay here? Or what would your plans be?

Do you read in *Eckermann* every once in a while? Or Goethe's *Sprüche in Prosa*? Or Whitman? Or – or – or? I am imagining you now in the two little yellow rooms. I like that thought. I wish I had not waited six days to finish this letter!

Your friend, H.

P.S. In your previous letter (the one before last) you wrote, "'Dearest' friend." What an awful sight to behold, this adjective reducing its lovely noun, destroy it. You must not write that ever again. Am I not in *reality* your true friend?

Indeed!

[Fritz Töpfers Hotel Prinz Friedrich Carl, Berlin N.W.] 19 January 1916

Months have passed, dearest, since I last heard from you. This could not be helped, so there was no choice but to accept it. Now, however, I wrote you on the 5th, and we can be close again because there is no one in between us who can open our letters. I find it very surprising – and upsetting – that you are not writing again.

Dearest Ottonie! What is wrong with you? Write me a letter.

Your friend, H.

[Fritz Töpfers Hotel Prinz Friedrich Carl Berlin N.W.] 7 February 1916

Dearest, this cannot be a letter, but I still want to inform you of a certain matter so that you are not left hanging in the air.

I am not away, as you had suspected (and thus will not be returning) but rather I am still here and thought (assuming I am not given orders to the contrary) I still might have work to do here until the 20th. I hope, if you come here to visit Eberhard, that I might extend this for another week, so that you will find me here when you arrive at the *end* of the month – and then I can perhaps also arrange for us occasionally to have a look at a painting together, to go to one of Reinhardt's rehearsals for an hour or so, for which I have no free time right now under my present schedule. (I only mention this because your letter paints a picture which reminds one of peace and being in control of one's own destiny.)

I just hope that Mädy is not here then, for E. finds her terribly exhausting to be around, so much so that I prefer not to see him under these circumstances. I am of no use to him then, and I must try to save whatever energy I have in order to continue to be of some use.

I can tell that this will seem like a cold letter to you. I cannot help it. It would not do any good to wait any longer before writing it because nothing is going to change in the next few days. It is always difficult for me to make the transition back to the real world – and added to this strange relationship we have. We must both bear this ourselves, don't you think?

Yours, H

[Fritz Töpfers Hotel Prinz Friedrich Carl Berlin N.W.] 10 February [1916]

I believe you have received a disagreeable letter from Berlin. How can such people exist?! And that people correspond with them?! What for? One must have a great deal of patience with these people as well as a sense of humor. Please, have both and simply come here for a visit; then the rest will take care of itself. No – what kind of a letter is this?!

How can I possibly send it?!

Your friend.

[Fritz Töpfers Hotel Prinz Friedrich Carl Berlin N.W.] 16 February [1916]

Dearest, I certainly hope to be here on the 4th and for some time thereafter and to be able to show you something beautiful around this time (the final rehearsals of *Macbeth* and *Malade imaginaire*) – but if you postpone things again for another two weeks, everything will be spoiled.

Yours, H.

[Fritz Töpfers Hotel Prinz Friedrich Carl Berlin N.W.]
Sunday [27 February 1916] 6:00 p.m.

Dearest, can you believe that I have thought about writing you the following two lines for the past three days from dawn to dusk and can't seem to find even a minute to do so! Well then: I will be going to Leipzig Tuesday afternoon and will be staying at the Nostitzs' (Wiesenstrasse 5) and returning on the 2nd of March, in the afternoon, the same day as you (so that I will be back here that evening).

I asked myself whether you might be traveling the Dresden-Leipzig-Berlin route on the same day, and hence would be on my train in L. But I suppose this would be an unnecessary and doubly long trip for you. And then there is also reason to fear the trains will be overcrowded, in which case we would not even see each other. Otherwise there is really nothing to worry about; as far as I am concerned, nothing particularly bad will happen, as I have not had any headaches since the war began and never feel tired, although I do not fall asleep before 2:30 in the morning. I am also very friendly with everyone, including women, as *parti pris*, because there is already plenty of evil in the world. There was a very charming little party by candlelight at Reinhardt's this evening; with Mozart quartets and an enchanting little dancer as well. It was very nice when Reinhardt suddenly said to me, "What a pity the Countess Degenfeld is not here." Do finally come here!

Yours, H.

P.S. It is a very good thing that you are Eberhard's guest or else nobody's guest at all; so I can no longer *un*invite you!

❦ ❦ ❦

[Fritz Töpfers Hotel Prinz Friedrich Carl Berlin N.W.]
2 March [1916] 11:00 p.m.

Dearest, through a gardener I sent you a few flowers and a letter, to be delivered Thursday afternoon. Apparently you did not receive them. I telephoned at 8:30 to be told that a Countess D. had neither arrived nor was she expected. I got there at 9:45 and was told by the lift boy that you were staying there. I wanted to knock on your door, but instead of Julie, Eberhard, with whom you are living *en famille*, prevented me; so I will hardly be able to approach you on the spur of the moment without a very *in-depth* analysis of the "when" and "where," which is Eberhard's way. However, I decided not to subject myself to this kind of treatment the very next day. I have tickets to a performance of *Macbeth* for the two of us tonight. Please call me (I already asked you to in the other letter) between 10:30 and 11:00. The way you seem to discuss things that only concern you and me with Eberhard – such as traveling via Leipzig for instance – is quite incomprehensible.

I hope you have not changed so much that we will not be able to find each other.

Yours, H.

❦ ❦ ❦

[Neubeuern] 1 April 1916

The most splendid gifts have arrived here in my enchanted land of sunshine – it is like something out of *A Thousand and One Nights*! First a fantastic carpet[154] appears, so *unbelievably* beautiful that I find myself standing here admiring it again and again; it makes the whole atmosphere seem so festive. Then along comes Ali Baba[155] to enchant me on my lonely evenings, while my thoughts wander towards the one who bore all these gifts, and I feel happy knowing he is still alive somewhere in the world.

Again the weather is incredibly beautiful today, so beautiful you truly cannot describe it in words. The mountain tops emerge gradually from the sea of fog, and everything is radiant in the sunlight. I just returned from a little morning walk through the park, which is yellow from all the cowslips.

Unfortunately this precious time alone will soon be coming to an end, as I will probably have to go to Dresden on Thursday to pick up the child. It is truly painful having to leave here now.

Mädy is in Berlin now. I hope no major storms will erupt there.

Greetings.

Yours, Ottonie D.

❦ ❦ ❦

R., 30 May [1916]

What in God's name has happened with us anyway? Has there been a misunderstanding? This time I really cannot figure it out. You told me in Berlin that you would be coming to Austria with Julie sometime later in the spring to stay with us for a week. I waited the entire month of April for some sign, then in May from one week to the next. I have done everything I can to arrange to stay here longer – I was so sure in my mind that you would be coming – and have been so happy that we have had such lovely spring weather: I already pictured you in the rooms here and imagined you walking through the garden. During this time you have exchanged letters with Gerty about governesses, and each time a letter arrives I ask if there is any news about when you plan to visit, but there never is. Neither have you said that you wouldn't be coming, so I continue to assume that you will be. You said that you have your father there.

---

154. A loan until H. v. H. could move it home to Austria.

155. H. v. H. had sent her a 1907 edition of the *Arabian Nights*, for which he had written an introduction.

I am happy for you in this respect, but I still cannot figure out what has become of your trip.

Well, May is now coming to an end, and you simply fail to appear without saying a word. I thought about this for a long time today while sitting outside in the garden; I cannot understand it. Please say something. One other thing: I might be able to arrange to be in Munich for three days around the 10th of July on my way back from Warsaw via Berlin. Would this mean I would be able to see you there?

Your friend, H

P.S. Has the Van Gogh[156] by chance arrived yet as it certainly should have? Does it make you happy?

❧ ❧ ❧

[Neubeuern] 14 June 1916

When I returned, and "my carpet," now used to its place, greeted me so lovingly, I remembered instantly that I was to send you the measurements. But on Friday and Saturday I was still in too much pain from a migraine headache, and then Gerty's telegram arrived last night. It is 3 1/2 meters in length and 73 cm in width. If you enjoy and delight in its precious blue and yellow and salmon tones half as much as I do, you will be very happy to be the owner of it. I never enter my bedroom now without giving it a very loving smile and even am childish enough to enjoy walking on it in my stocking feet and feel pure bliss from its soft, silky touch. It was a pity that my head completely ruined my last day in Vienna and that, because of this, my return visit to Rodaun had to be canceled. However I really have *very*, very fond memories and am so happy to know now how and where you live. I constantly see the charming house with the beautiful light, the lovely staircase and the green roof of leaves, through which patches of sun entered; and again I can feel who you are and have somewhat removed the burden, which I suppose I myself had erected between us – partly out of stupidity, partly because of other, not very nice feelings which should have no right to exist!

I hope you have received *Die Lästigen* [Annoying People][157] by now (I gave it to the hotel porter to mail to you). I had a delightful time reading it, and I was only sad not to be able to take it along in order to enjoy reading it again every now and then. It is simply delightful, very graceful and very charming. Oh, how I would have loved to have spent eight days with you out there at your place, I can really feel how wonderful it would have

---

156. H. v. H. had bought this picture in Germany. As he could not take it to Austria because of the war, he had it sent to O. D. S. to keep for the duration.

157. Play by H. v. H.

been. However in any case, I intend to fight, if necessary, for my autumn visit. Thursday we rode in a Balkan train, the most unpleasant way of traveling you can imagine, which I would urge you to avoid. One is continually harassed, be it by the military, or customs agents who search everything. There are no papers in the world, not even from the highest legations, that can spare you this plague, which is not offset by the shorter hours one travels.

Everyone here, except for Christa, who has a mild case of the measles, is well. Egon Beroldingen is here from Verdun for a two-week visit.

Auf Wiedersehen. Best regards,

Yours, O.

ỡ   ỡ   ỡ

[Bad Aussee] 1 August [1916]

I have gotten hold of a book that, when I have time to read, is incredibly captivating and very enjoyable: it is the letters of van Gogh to his brother in two large volumes, which I am reading letter by letter. One lives with this man – one lives both in this world and in his intellectual sphere, forgetting the many horrors, without escaping them – by climbing to new heights. While reading this book, I always had you there seated next to me, reading along. I wrote a letter to the bookseller in Berlin three days ago asking that he send it to you. I hope it will arrive around the same time this letter does.

I traveled from Warsaw through Berlin on the way to Garmisch around the 15th and then through Munich on my way back. The evening of the 19th in Munich I find a letter telling me that I could have seen you! However, it was so firmly impressed upon my mind that you had told me in Rodaun that the month of July was simply booked full and that nothing could be done to change this. So there was no doubt in my mind you were stuck in Eybach.

In Warsaw I once sat beside a Swabian, Count Brandenstein, son-in-law of Zeppelin, at the governor-general's table. He had heard of Eybach and had met Christoph Martin a few times – I was glad to speak these names out loud, and I thought of you there walking around.

That you have been in Rodaun and Vienna! Now this seems so lovely to me – and so far away. Right afterwards another dark and dismal period followed – for weeks then I was not able to write a letter. Then came the colorful, shimmering impressions of Warsaw – the strongest ones I have had during the war. It was a bizarre situation being "the famous man in the foreign land" in an atmosphere like summertime in Paris, with everything at a feverish pitch – yet still full of hope, with a somewhat better view of the future. Not everything was entirely grim there.

And now these summer days, this radiance, the bright, sunny sky, the little houses here. It is as if one had eaten lotus blossoms and were lifted off into a dream world – and what is happening in the real world? It really is not possible to describe.

This you know: *Ariadne* will be on the 4th of Oct. Before that, I hope to be here; I think by the 28th of September (even if my stay is not uninterrupted). You know what I wish for and how very much. I suppose the reason you will give to the authorities for taking the trip is family matters – which should suffice?

Yours truly, H.

❦ ❦ ❦

[Postcard]   [Rodaun] 8 September [1916]

As your letters gave no clue as to what your present address might be, I sent a telegram to Degenershausen (you seemed to be on your way there) requesting you be notified that we are expecting you to arrive on the 2nd of October. Please make sure that you do come, and do not come later (the première is on the 4th of October) nor for too short a stay. It is no longer possible to keep up with each other's life by writing letters until the times improve, so we must endeavor to see each other and must have the will to allow whatever would interfere with our plans to recede into the background. However, certain inner constraints, which I discovered to my great surprise from a certain letter, are so absurd that I do not even wish to contemplate the possibility that there might be any substance to them.

Yours, H.H.

❦ ❦ ❦

[Hotel Adlon, Berlin]

[Note written to O. D. S.:] Julie's wedding,[158] 9 December 1916

1. See to it, please, that you leave on Tuesday and not Monday evening, for if I am to be the friend of a maid in the castle, then it must be one who occasionally has a day off.

2. Tomorrow evening you will please go with me to see Reinhardt's production of *Kabale and Liebe* [Cabal and Love]; I reserved seats for us.

3. I would like to pay a little visit to your father tomorrow if it would suit him.

4. I am ready to lunch with Bockelchen tomorrow (or maybe not?).

---

158. On this day Julie married Hans-Wolfgang von Herwarth-Bittenfeld.

5. Monday morning we will go to look at something in Potsdam.

6. I am at home; please come to see me for a little while around 9:30 or 10:00. I am waiting (again see No.1.).

Yours, H.

❦ ❦ ❦

[Postcard]   Rodaun, 12 February [1917]

Please do not worry about the fact that once again something (or it is not so much something but rather "that a certain something") has gotten in the way. (I never expected things to be any different and knew "it" would end up this way at exactly this moment.) But it makes absolutely no sense to be concerned about particular things at a time as difficult as this. I presently have influenza and had to postpone my trip and would not be able to see you in Berlin anyway. My plans to stop off in Munich have also been postponed for awhile. I will stick to the 13th to 17th of March and have no doubt that you will be needed in Eybach during this time. May God soon give us all a different kind of world in which we can live for the rest of our lives.

Yours, Hugo.

❦ ❦ ❦

Rodaun, 24 May 1917

You cannot help but come to the conclusion that I have not thought about anyone or anything and that my silence is an expression of this. In fact it is quite the contrary. Ever since I began to assume that you had returned, I have actually meant to write every day, but the internal and external complications are such that thoughts like these continually appear and disappear, like a piece of driftwood out on the high seas. The monstrous situation the world finds itself in seems to drag on with no end in sight, and on top of it, there are continual distractions here that interfere with my ability to concentrate and finally – precisely because it continues to be held in check – there is an urge to be productive which stubbornly demands expression. My desk is filled with unanswered letters, political articles I had begun, outlines for new works, notes for comedies – Strauss, who wants to have his *Bürger als Edelmann* [The Citizen as Nobleman] *à tout prix* and Fischer, who also *à tout prix* wants to publish my political essays and at the same time, if possible, the third volume of my prose. Also, a small suitcase is packed for a trip to Prague. This is how you must imagine my time passing from day to day, but never without positive results. Because of the trip to Prague, I also cannot ask you if you could come to

Rodaun in June, as I very much wanted to. I do not know how long I will have to stay in Prague; this depends on factors which are still to be determined. I am going to take along the "fairy tale" (the tale of the woman without a shadow) and the new, i.e. as yet unwritten, social comedy,[159] and I hope, in addition, to take part in political discussions, and to have time to work on these in the mornings and evenings.

I have thought about so many things, such as how we might be able to see each other. It will not be possible to invite anyone to Aussee. The official regulations are too strict. I thought about the possibility of Rodaun at the beginning of October. I have gradually come to hate encounters that depend on the irregularities of the railways. After you had left Munich, and I no longer had anything to do with the police, I enjoyed some wonderfully peaceful days. I was rather irritated by the contrast.

Yours, Hofmannsthal

[Neubeuern] 8 June 1917

How nice to once again hear something from the place whereto one's thoughts continually return . Now I know again what you are doing and hope that, in spite of the political matters you had to attend to, you found some time in Prague to work on the fairy tale and also on the comedy.

Here we have fairytale-like weather, superb sunshine, everything is blooming in rich splendor, and finally even the long awaited rain has arrived. Reluctantly I am going to Munich for a few days to let Karin and Christa be painted by Zumbusch. Eberhard was recently in Munich for a day, and we discussed everything. My father was here for a few weeks; he is going to meet me later in the city, and then we will be going on to the Eibsee together for two days before he returns home. The 3rd of July is Hansi's confirmation, in Degenershausen, which I must attend; I will probably stay there the first week of July. It would really be nice if we could meet again in October – could it possibly be during the second half of the month? Or is this already filled with other plans?

We are expecting the baby[160] here around the middle of September. I wonder what Gerty says about this? How I would love to chat with her sometime about everything.

I received a subscription offer from a magazine, *Marsyas*, a few days ago in which I recognized many of the names. It is a pity it is so terribly expensive.

---

159. *Der Schwierige*, a play about a returned war veteran.
160. Julie was pregnant.

Can you imagine my father is quite enamored of your van Gogh. Every day he comes to have another look at it. Life is good here among all the flowers and the Japanese golden sky and the *Wahlverwandtschaften*;[161] this is my life right now.

Addio now.

Yours, Ottonie

❦ ❦ ❦

Aussee (Steiermark) Obertressen 14, 11 August [1917]

Without your being aware of it, it almost always happens that you write me at the moment you are about to leave, so that I have no possibility of giving a prompt answer, which I would always like to do. This also leaves me with the strong impression that you live your life in a perpetual and futile rush (a fact which obscured all our most recent encounters), and I must then make an effort to tell myself that there are times when you lead a calm and collected life. And yet to be completely collected, to have an inner tranquility, to be at one with yourself, is the root from which everything – religion, culture, love and happiness – sprouts.

Becoming more and more one with myself, the interlinking of old and new spheres of my life, increasing clarity, attentiveness, strain; it is also this which provides purification in my present life. This one and the same Aussee view, me as a man of such variable earnestness with so many different occupations, who nevertheless always remains the same. Whoever is something and remains true to himself and continues to develop. This is what I feel in every letter I receive from Mell, who in his very pure manner accepts his fate to be a soldier and even revels in it.

I was granted a strange experience: I was sent a letter of a 36-year-old man, up to now unknown to me; he will mean a lot to me, this I can tell in advance. It is almost getting to be too much. There must be a balance between that which one receives and what one gives, but sometimes the balance of the scales shifts considerably.

I wrote Eberhard a very long letter. It was not a typical letter but more a monologue, and I made a point of sending it during the time I knew you were there and sought to address several points in connection with your presence there. I was fairly certain you would respond to this, for I thought you would recognize my intentions. At times like these, when all of one's experiences are overturned, one cannot help but deviate from the norm in order to send some sign or greeting, and one hopes to be understood.

Yours, Hofmannsthal

---

161. *The Elective Affinities*, by J. W. von Goethe.

❦ ❦ ❦

[Neubeuern] 13 August 1917

I did experience or understand the letter you sent to Degenershausen the way you meant it and certainly took it to be common property. But my response continued to be long in coming, as I saw an opportunity for sending a sealed letter, and even though it probably did not turn out to be any different, there was still something very tempting about the idea of writing to a single person and not a whole world of strangers, so that is why I decided to wait. I felt so happy knowing that you were feeling so rich within yourself and able to spend an extended period working – these peaceful waves managed to reach me. You cannot have any idea how I can sense what you are feeling; oftentimes it is so pronounced that I feel deep inside of myself whether you are living in harmony or are caught in the back and forth of difficult struggles – this means everything to me.

I have not had a hectic time but rather following my short trip, which consisted of a delightful time in Degenershausen together with Eberhard, I allowed myself to spend two wonderful days on the Starnbergersee and have felt a rare inner calm here. I lived in paintings. In the library I found Meier-Graefe's book on the history of the development of modern art, and through it my mind disappeared into this wonderful world which built a bridge for me from Delacroix and Manet to Leibl and Liebermann. I now realize for the first time how much I can benefit from spending more time on this subject rather than always simply snatching a free hour in Munich to look at a painting. I also was in Munich and went to Caspary's and searched for something for you. He had a little Géricault *a currassier*, but it was not so good that one felt one had to have it. However, he told me that he could arrange to have a large *currassier* delivered to me that he has in Holland at the moment; it costs 40,000 Marks. I said it would be better not to go to all the unnecessary trouble of having it shipped if we really were not sure whether or not my "friends" would want to have it. It is apparently quite a large painting that would fit with your others. He also has a little still-life of an apple by Renoir, which is charming but very expensive – 20,000 Marks. There is a lovely Picasso but it is not one for you. I saw a Slevogt there for the first time that you might like to have. It is a painting of a countryside dipped in sunlight; Caspary said its value would certainly climb to 25,000 again. It would, of course, only be as a second choice if you wanted to invest additional money and after all you have a certain interest in Slevogt.

Then I also went to the unbearable Thannhauser, who unfortunately ruins all his pictures by being so disagreeable. However, I am going to go there again sometime soon because he has a lot of good paintings, and if I am at leisure, assuming I am fortunate enough not to run into him, I am sure I will find something there. He had a lot of Renoirs which were also cheaper than Caspary's as far as I could tell. The latter also said he might want to trade a Hodler. I very much enjoy browsing around, but just now I seldom find time to make it to the city, as one can no longer feel comfortable leaving Julie alone, for it is now the final stage. She will be going to the city at the beginning of September. I will be grateful beyond all bounds when all of this is behind us, for it is impossible not to feel frightened when thinking about it.

It was also very sweet how you asked about "my" van Gogh, and if you might be able to have it. Of course I will have to give it up, for I must not deprive you of its wonderful aura any longer; it gave me a great deal. Never before had I been fortunate enough to be in the presence of a (I was almost about to say "person") painting like that in such an intimate way for an extended period. I am so grateful to you for this. With this painting you gave me much inner peace and lifted my spirits during this long winter, which was a truly difficult time for me. I only hope that you, too, will continue to love it as I have. And the screen I so love, should it also embark on this journey? It was a blissful world you provided for me, both on the outside and inside. Wherever I may look, I am always greeted by you; when I go upstairs and have but a few minutes, I find there right in front of me a Delacroix album, and I start to leaf through it or the *Talenten* and find delight in the charming drawings by Meid or something like this. In the evening I sit in bed reading Hebbel's poems, which I have just recently come to discover although it was a long time ago that you first gave them to me. Sometimes one may be reading something but only much later come to appreciate it. Besides this I have been reading a lot of Goethe this year and it enriched me so much. I have seldom experienced a time that has truly given me so much work to do and at the same time so much peace. For the most part, this is probably because Julie is no longer an emotional burden on me; I have freed myself of her and no longer have the feeling of constantly having to be responsible for her, and now I can see for the first time how much this held me back and burdened me in the past. Outwardly, however, I continue to live as I always have – but I am free. Everything is a gift from me to her, and not the fulfillment of a duty; I am no longer bound in chains. In a certain respect, I can see her suffering out of concern for me – but this no longer holds me captive as it once did, for I simply tell myself, "This is what you yourself wanted." It is good indeed that things have turned out this way because I can once again flap my crippled little wings.

You know, Hugo, I am really very happy living in my little world knowing that there are a few people somewhere to whom I have emotional ties. And the paintings that exist, paintings that make one's life so rich, even if one does not own them – yet the fact that they are there, in addition to certain other things, make life worthwhile.

Sometimes the war is so powerful that one cannot achieve – or figure out how to achieve – any distance to one's own life at all; yet there are still wonderful periods of happiness in all of this. I am sorry that I do not have much luck in the letters I write you; it seems I always pick the wrong moment and thus give you the feeling of my being scatterbrained and not at ease. Unfortunately, I am just not at all the type for letters, which is particularly painful for me, too, at such a time, as the thread leading to the other person often seems to be torn as a result – which certainly is not the case at all. I envy those who are able to say everything and fully express themselves in just a few lines. It is a gift which unfortunately has been completely denied me. Baby just walked in and asks to whom I am writing, and I tell her to Hugo and that I said I would send the painting and the screen; then she wrote the note to you which you will find enclosed. She made me promise to send it along with my letter; just take it as childish prattle which is of course wholly inconsequential.

I discussed the matter of Borchardt with Eberhard and convinced him to try to look at it from a somewhat different perspective. We then wrote him a card together, which should serve as a bridge to him; I hope he also understood it as it was meant.

It is wonderful that you found someone who means so much to you; how enriched your life will be through this experience. And Mell is still alive, still a soldier. How long ago, the time we spent together with him. I can still picture him in Florence when we were all so tired and he returned from town in the blazing heat with some postcards he still had to send to his parents. He was really very nice.

Now I should say goodbye, I suppose. What do you think we should do about the picture? Is there any chance you might be coming to Germany and if so when? Should I have the Géricault brought in from Holland? This also reminds me that Caspary has a snowy landscape by Courbet. It just does not seem cheerful enough. You are certainly familiar with the motif: a grotto with little in the foreground, and a lot of brown and white to it.

Good night.

Ottonie.

❦ ❦ ❦

[Bad Aussee] 21 August 1917

A letter from you of course, due to your nature, never means as much as a word, a gesture, or even your listening to something, however I found the last one you sent me was lovely and I thank you for it very much. Now and then it seems completely absurd to me that you constantly appear to be free, and in reality you are not. You are not here where I am and could not spend time with me during my stay here while leaving the child in some little house; you are not here in the afternoon at teatime or in the evening when I am reading something. Well, things are as they are. Whenever I can feel that you have recaptured those things which make life worth living, then, for a time, I am completely content. I feel as if I were constantly trying to blow on a fire, while from the opposite side an unwelcome and powerful wind blows, and once it subsides, another person, J. W. (J. H. now),[162] has only one thing in mind, namely, to throw sand on top of the fire with both hands in order to smother it. I fear once I have taken a liking or a disliking to something or someone it is for good; I most thoroughly hate this J. W. For me she embodies that which is truly immoral – not something simply highly indecent or scandalous, which everyone can recognize from afar, but rather something much more subtle, much more wicked, which is the continual betrayal of higher values for the sake of base concerns; it is the continual hypocrisy she displays before the world and herself. I would like to – and then the ugly box would burn to the ground. But first fetch from the library a few bound volumes of *Kunst u. Künstler* [Art and Artists].

It makes me extremely happy that you have come to understand that in order to reach that which is *truly real*, one need not always wait for the reality that comes with standing before the actual paintings – there are also other ways of cultivating such an interest. This is the second time now that I have spent the summer living in the constant presence of Poussin, i.e. with a written volume about him and a book of small, dark photographs which nevertheless are a piece of heaven.

I wrote to the *Insel Verlag* and asked them to send you the Meier-Graefe volume about Corot and Courbet right away. The marvelous Courbet! To own something of his – just something! But no snow. That is the last thing I would want. Please go to Heinemann's sometime. Do you remember? We were there years ago. It must be something that you fall in love with at first sight – just do not be rational about it, be irrational! By no means a Slevogt. He is past history for me; even when sketching I find him vulgar. Just continue to search for something for me. Here I do not see a single painting year in and year out. I believe C. to be the worst of thieves, but never mind. We are *counting* on seeing you around the middle of October!

Yours, Hofmannsthal

---

162. The former Julie Wendelstadt's new initials, for Julie Herwarth.

Aussee, 21 August 1917

Dear Marie-Therese,

Thank you very much for the lines you wrote. Please make sure you always write me what you really think, and I will do my best to do the same, and someday we will become good friends. I would *so* much like to have the painting in my house for a while. Do you know that I left a little room completely bare without any pictures in order to hang this one there? And I am sure your mother will be glad to lend it to me, but we will leave the screen there with her for a while longer and perhaps she or I will find a painting that she is very fond of. Then we will send her that one instead of this one and later we can trade sometime. Is that all right with you?

Many regards to you from Gerty and also the children.

Your friend, Hofmannsthal

❦ ❦ ❦

Aussee, 15 September [1917]

From a letter Mädy sent, I have been informed of the events[163] that have transpired there. I think of you constantly but am unable to write about all this now. The work is exceedingly straining and the results as yet entirely uncertain, however I hope that something real will ultimately come of it.

Now is the last moment that the Van Gogh can be sent to me by normal means. So I would request that it be sent to Berlin within the next two weeks. Means of shipment: freight or express freight with insurance of 25,000 Marks. Please telephone Caspary or a carrier in Rosenheim if you need assistance.

The address to send it to is: Geheimer Kanzleidiener Grünägl; Berlin Wilhelmstrasse 75.

The following must be written on the crate and especially on the dispatch note: For Count Bernsdorff; Emp. German Embassy, *Vienna*. Please write *Vienna* very clearly and underline it because his uncle is in Constantinople and if the shipment goes there by mistake, the painting might be lost.

Yours, Hofmannsthal

P.S. Please send me a postcard notifying me as soon as the shipment is gone.

P.P.S. I am definitely expecting you to come around the middle of October!

---

163. Julie nearly died giving birth.

❦ ❦ ❦

[Neubeuern] 14 November 1917

It has been almost eight days now since I left Rodaun, but my mind is still there. I have been wondering whether Cari has said goodbye to Helene[164] yet in his own strange way, and much more. Did you have a look at some nice paintings when you were with Geiger? A pity I didn't come along because I very easily could have. After all, my train didn't leave Vienna until after three o'clock.

Well, now Andrian was there with you and must have told you a lot about Berlin – but I hope he didn't talk too much in that Warsaw accent! Mädy and I were discussing Andrian when Karin said, "The one who wrote *Der Garten der Erkenntnis* [The Garden of Knowledge]." I was astounded that someone had heard of it. She liked it so much and was thinking the whole time that you surely must know him very well.

I was just reading some of Borchardt's poems; they really are fabulous and can make you forget completely the gray, overcast day. I like "Sestine der Sehnsucht" [Sestine of Longing] and "Der traurige Besuch" [The Melancholy Visit] very much and many others, too.

Do you realize how enjoyable it was for me to stay in Rodaun and what happy memories I have? All the feelings that I left with continue to brighten up my days here: Claudel and his magical Orient, and George's wonderful poems, all made a very strong impression on me. I still think about Pannwitz[165] and what he must have told you in his recent and very detailed letter. I can hardly imagine what inexhaustible depths he penetrated this time with his great mind.

I am already looking forward to spending a few days in Ischl in January and hope it will indeed work out.

By this time, you must seriously be considering leaving, and are sure afraid of being in Berlin; just make sure you bring along everything you can think of. Eberhard will be there for a while, but not the entire time. He will be in Essen the first of January and has a "vacation" (as we call it) until the 1st of April.

Mädy is here. She was planning to stay for two days but caught a cold and is stuck here now.

Take care. Please write me and let me know how Reinhardt enjoys the company of Stani, Cari, Helene and Antoinette. All right?

Many warm regards,

Ottonie.

---

164. The two main characters from Hofmannsthal's play *Der Schwierige*.
165. Rudolf Pannwitz (1881–1964), writer and philosopher.

[Rodaun] Monday 19 [November 1917]

From the charming Pannwitz letter I've enclosed here, you'll see how happy he is to accept your invitation to come to Neubeuern and how much it means to him to know that he will be able to spend these winter weeks in pleasant and stimulating surroundings, which for him means a place other than the miserable little room in the Fürberg inn. Please write him yourself as soon as you can and let him know when he may come. It will be important for him to know in arranging his work schedule. I was very surprised when I found your letter here this morning and realized that you still had not departed and that we can still discuss everything.

The past week has been busy and belonged more to the external world than I would have liked. However, at least I had completed the second act[166] prior to this – during the time following your departure.

Andrian wasn't here at the time, but I have since seen him and also Ferdinand Colloredo, whom I am very fond of, and Mensdorff, Redlich and a few other essentially political friends. One is rather *d'accord* with Berlin, especially with Kühlmann.[167] I will also have considerable personal contact to him because he recently hired himself a private secretary, a rather strange outsider, whom I have known for a long time and get along with very well.

I will be arriving at the Adlon Monday morning and will be spending my first day there with Eberhard. Please do let me know right away there by mail if the shipment, or rather express shipment, has been sent and if not, let me know whether or not you could have the Van Gogh shipped to me in Berlin by an officer traveling there or by some other means; then I would finally have it. I will send you a telegram containing the address. If for some reason you should be forced to improvise when sending it, then address it to: für Hofmannsthal an Kunsthandlung Glenk, Unter den Linden 30.

Yours, Hugo H.

P.S. The poor Nostitzes have suffered a great misfortune. On the day they were to depart they lost a child, the third one of the boys, who was the very picture of health. He was dead within two hours after having been given the wrong medicine.

---

166. Of *Der Schwierige*.

167. Richard von Kühlmann (1873–1948), Secretary of State in the Berlin Foreign Office.

[Degenershausen] 27 December 1917

I am finally able to write again. I have had a busy schedule since leaving Rodaun. I was in northern Germany at my parents' for a time and returned to Neubeuern only to have to leave again quite unexpectedly as soon as I got back. Karin had searched for a place where she could work as a nurse; unpleasant experiences were connected with this and made it most disagreeable for us, but I cannot write about any of this in these open letters. I was forced to take a sudden trip to Berlin that caused us all a great deal of anxiety. As a "certain" gentleman[168] arrived again suddenly after his vacation had come to an end, I decided – very quickly – to leave the morning of the 25th to fetch Christa and bring her here. I'm thinking of staying here until the 2nd, at which point the air back home will be pure once again.

Here we are having a cozy time; we take walks through the snowy forest, watching the large beech trees being cut down, which let out woeful gasps of pain as they fall to the ground with incredible force. First, however, I must thank you for the *Writings in Prose*. I enjoyed the *Begegnungen* [meetings] immensely; it's charming and so, too, none the less, is *Die Furcht* [Fear]. How beautiful and so completely you are the Greek pieces, especially the first two. I thank you a thousand times over for this *very lovely* Christmas greeting.

Now about Pannwitz. I was not able to write to him yet, as our plans for the winter were still uncertain. That is, Julie's plans for the winter were still uncertain, and I first had to wait until I consulted with Müller,[169] which resulted in the determination that Julie will have to stay in M. throughout January, so I think it will be all right for P. to come and I will write him about this from here. I really would not like having him and Julie there together. Eberhard is very upset about this.

Eberhard is deeply moved, especially by his first book,[170] and we of course talk about him and you a lot. During my short "stay" in Berlin, I had a wonderful evening at the *Don Carlos* and paid the new goddess[171] a visit when I went to the museum; and I again very much enjoyed the splendid exhibit they had of the gorgeous antiquities in the downstairs wing. The image I have in my mind of the relief of the dancers is intoxicating. Seldom have I felt so excited and happy as I did on this day in the midst of these wonderful remnants from this great period of art.

Eberhard has now left Essen. His mind was of course full of memories of the many experiences he had had there, and now he has his freedom. It

---

168. Julie's husband, Herwarth.
169. Prof. Dr. Müller, gynecologist in Munich.
170. Pannwitz's.
171. Nephrotete, the Egyptian head, recently appeared in the museum.

was indeed a moment to let out a sigh of relief. Now they are hard at work on the apartment in Berlin with a nice and splendid architect who seems to have a good feel for interior design.

I wonder if you have received my beloved painting yet, or is it still on the way? I am sure it will make you happy to have it there in the lovely little town flat, or will it end up in Rodaun after all?

Please tell Gerty that I will write her sometime soon and also Christiane. Here I must finally write some of the countless people to whom I owe letters.

How do things stand with Ischl? Are you still planning to go there and, if so, when? How is your work progressing? Have you begun writing the third act of the comedy? Give my regards to my friend, Cari, and the lovely Helene.

Take care now. May 1918 bring us many lovely and fulfilling days together – this I wish for myself, and for you a blessed period of work.

Yours truly, Ottonie.

❦ ❦ ❦

[Rodaun] 10 a.m., 9 January [1918]

Just a few lines this morning before I begin working because afterwards it will be one thing after another as always, and then the few lines will remain but as a thought that never receives written form from one day to the next.

Back in December I often thought about writing you and telling you about the time I spent together with Eberhard and with Borchardt and Reinhardt – but something kept holding me back. It's almost impossible to explain, and yet it was after all entirely clear what it was: the simple fact that you were always someplace else, and I could sense without really knowing it.

Pannwitz visited here before Christmas – only for three days, but as always it was an epoch unto itself. It's incredible how he sets my productive energies in motion and how I regain a sense of my own self and am able to resume work on things I began long ago. Fragmentary pieces suddenly appear as a potentially unified whole, and then I become what I always should be.

Indeed, I am without a doubt experiencing the most productive period I have in fifteen or twenty years. To begin with, I must leave off working on the third act of *Der Schwierige* and start organizing the ideas I have for a rather strange drama (a heroic-mythical tragedy);[172] it has brought along with it into the light of day another old complex of mine, so that I am only

---

172. *Der Turm* (The Tower).

able to preserve the time I need for the "fairy tale" with considerable effort. However, I indeed manage to salvage this time and am making progress.

(If only it were more than 11 to 12 degrees in my room during the morning — oh, how many plaid blankets and boas you would need!)

I just rose and walked around to warm myself up, which led to the following chain of thoughts: Yes, the Van Gogh is here. Thank you very much for being so kind and going to all the trouble. It is a beautiful painting. For the past two weeks I have also been the owner of an incredibly beautiful painting of a blackamoor in a red shirt with a turban in fabulous colors and an aigrette feather that can hardly have been painted by anyone other than Rembrandt. On the whole, however, the painting may have been done by one of those close to him, Aert de Gelder or whoever.

But now let me return to Pannwitz: He is going to be drafted in January; however, Nostitz, who was extremely impressed by the man, is taking great care to address this matter. Later, at the beginning of February, it would be his greatest wish to come to N. for a few weeks. He has a good feeling about you and the place there, which certainly will not prove to be unfounded.

I cannot even think about Ischl. To do so would cause me to become divided within myself again. It would be much better for me to go somewhere *alone*. But that is not possible right now. I will be in Berlin from the 17th to the 21st of February and then in the various cities along the Rhine for a week, and back in Berlin for the entire month of March. I hope you will be able to come there then!

Yours, H. H.

❦ ❦ ❦

[Neubeuern] 24 January 1918

Our letters have crossed in the mail; yours has given me the feeling that you are very near, and I can sense that you are accomplishing a lot of work. At the same time, however, I've had the feeling ever since that awfully warm, unreasonable spring-like weather we had that it must surely have slowed you down. Pannwitz also seemed to be very happy from the letter he wrote me about the time he spent at your place, which meant a great deal to him. I'm looking forward to seeing him and hope that he finds here the right mood that he needs in order to work. He writes such wonderful letters and expresses his thanks for things that he hasn't even been able to enjoy yet, as only he can.

He just brought back into the light of day new worlds existing within you which I had known before in an older form. I'm glad the fairy tale at least hasn't been completely lost; I love it so much and am sure that it will become something truly wonderful. And you own a blackamoor with a heron's feather, you lucky thing! Congratulations! I'm also very happy for you and am looking forward to making his acquaintance some time next year.

Right now we're enduring *a great deal* along with Karin.[173] I have to go to Berlin for a week this Sunday, or it might even be somewhat longer. That is why I asked Pannwitz not to come before the 10th, which he probably won't mind one way or the other. There I will be staying in the Adlon.

Good night. I just read your *Maria Theresia* again and enjoyed it very much.

Ottonie.

P.S. Many warm regards to Gerty and the children.

[Neubeuern a/Inn] 16 January 1918

On my last day in Degenershausen your well-traveled letter finally reached me; it was *so* lovely, a *true* letter, such as only you can write. Eberhard was tremendously happy and spoke so charmingly and with great modesty of the friendship the two of you share. At this time, he was reading Pannwitz and was of course deeply moved and enthralled. All in all we had a wonderfully peaceful and harmonious time. Eberhard was very relaxed and natural in his manner, knowing that he wouldn't have to return to Essen, and as a result he enjoyed everything twice as much here as he would have otherwise.

Unfortunately they once again have new problems. Karin seems to be very ill after coming down with the measles toward the end of December in the hospital where she was working as a nurse. At first everything was normal, but a short time ago she had a relapse and now is apparently in awfully wretched shape, with a constant fever of 102.2 to 103.6. E. visits her out there every day I think; if only it does not move to her lungs again! Please tell me, if you would — E. told me that Pannw. has tuberculosis. Is this true? Does he bring up a lot of phlegm, or any at all? I ask only because of the two children I have here whether he is already in an advanced stage, which, however, I cannot imagine; otherwise I, too, would have certainly heard something about it.

Rudi has apparently come down with pneumonia in Bremen. I hope he will be better soon, and I hope everything else will turn out to be exaggerated.

---

173. The oldest Bodenhausen daughter suffered with deep depression, and committed suicide the following year.

At the moment we are a very small group here. It's very relaxing for everyone and I'm enjoying myself very much.

I must tell you again how much we liked your volume of prose. Eberhard read aloud from it almost every evening. They're unbelievably beautiful, indeed, truly timeless pieces it seems to me.

Good night now. As always I send you my warmest thoughts.

Yours, Ottonie.

❦ ❦ ❦

[Neubeuern] 15 February 1918

We had such a *wonderful* evening with Pannwitz that I feel I *must* tell you about it right away. He is simply splendid, so rich, so pure, so benevolent towards himself and others, and it is wonderful breathing in the life-giving air that surrounds him. Yesterday evening when he arrived it was perhaps at first the way he moved and spoke that caused his outer persona to fall away, and one felt terribly insignificant next to this powerful intellect – and I was afraid as I thought to myself, "How is this going to work out, and how will the poor man stand staying here with us?" Today, however, I no longer feel worried. I think he will enjoy his time here, and our lives will be tremendously enriched.

So you are in Berlin now. How lovely it would be if you could also be here. Yet I'm awfully glad for Eberhard that he will have you there. He really needs to talk to you again sometime about the things he has on his mind.

What do you think of the idea of Schröder first coming here for a rest before going to Degenershausen. I can imagine this would be good for him, especially right now when he could spend time with someone like Pannwitz. Why don't you talk to Eberhard about this when you have the chance and also to Clärchen Heye if she is still there.

Pannwitz did not want to be alone during his stay here nearly as much as I had thought he would. He takes all his meals with us and did not seem to like my offer to have his breakfast brought to his room very much at all, so I decided not to bring it up again. Between meals he of course spends his time by himself. He was very enthusiastic when he spoke of Redlich,[174] with whom he got along very well and whose company he finds very pleasant.

I must say once again that I believe we will both continue to enjoy each other's company.

Warm greetings,

Yours, Ottonie.

---

174. Josef Redlich, lawyer and politician.

❦ ❦ ❦

15 February 1918

How strange: right after a conversation with Pannwitz about Grillparzer, your parcel arrived. A thousand thanks. It really is so lovely talking to P. His presence makes me feel incredibly happy, and he had such wonderful things to say about *Ariadne, Rosenkavalier*, etc., today.

❦ ❦ ❦

[Neubeuern] 18 February 1918

Well I went ahead and sent a letter to you straight to Berlin as I felt I really had to tell you right away how Pannwitz arrived and how well we were getting along, but you would have realized this without my telling it — he is wonderful to be around. We never stop talking, and if I did not have my duties here at the hospital which call me from the breakfast table, I think we would still be together once lunch arrived and on and on into the night. It really is so wonderful with him that one never needs to explain oneself; he understands absolutely everything about one, virtually down to the last detail, or *usually* at least better than one does oneself. You have tremendously enriched me through his entering into my life — but he, too, feels happy here, which is so wonderful.

Gradually he is relaxing, and I am convinced he is happy here. We get along splendidly. Aside from you and also Eberhard in a sense, I have never met anyone else with whom one is able to resonate as well as with him (this occurred with Christoph in a different sort of way). Since Pannwitz has been here, it feels as if we are surrounded by a new world, as if we were lifted above the earth by the width of a hand.

Yesterday evening he read us *Die Befreiung des Oedipus* [The Liberation of Oedipus] and, oh, *how* he read it! It is a wonderful and so typically Greek world, and the way it closes to form a ring is marvelous. This was followed today by *Der Tod des Empedokles* [The Death of Empedocles] — which is equally wonderful. We have so many things planned we'd like to do that I told him even years would still not be enough time.

He does not wish to work here on a fixed schedule but rather to have a break from everything and to take whatever comes as it comes.

Now I heard from Eberhard today that you were ill, will not be going to the Rhine and will not be coming to Berlin until later. I hope you are feeling well again and are able to work. I heard about the new plans; it sounds good.

So good night then.

Yours, O.

❦ ❦ ❦

Rodaun, 27 February [1918]

I knew you would get along well, but after having read the letters now, the two you wrote and one from Pannwitz, I can see that everything went very well indeed, and this makes me very happy. Among his (many) great gifts is one which seems to me to belong to the most rare and precious to be found among men, and it also allows him to gain an increased sense of himself, greater awareness and greater hope, just like the wonderful atmosphere in Asia Minor, where nothing appears closer or further away than it is, but rather all things are revealed as they are – within reach and connected each and all to the other in all their glory. Nothing makes me happier than to think of Schröder arriving at this time and being able to share in it all. If you just set your mind to something, it usually works out; typically it is simply a matter of one not having the will. Write to Schröder yourself. I am just not sure what his address is, however it will reach him right away if you send it in care of Clara Heye; Bentheimstrasse 7; Bremen.

The longer you can keep Pannwitz there, the better. I am certain I will be able to get in touch with Gandegg for him, however I do not know if he will be able to move there right now or perhaps not until Autumn. There is one other thing, too. I kept thinking you might come to Berlin the last week of March and be able to see the dress rehearsal of *Bürger als Edelmann*,[175] and other things. Perhaps this will all fall into place if we are blessed with good fortune. You could either keep him there until the 20th of March or have him return in April to meet with Schröder. (It is of course my feeling that he must not ever get together with Herwarth.) Please send me a letter about this to the Adlon, at the end of next week.

Yours, Hofmannsthal

P.S. I asked Frau P.[176] for a list of the most embarrassing garments, etc., they are missing. The situation is miserable, more so than you can possibly imagine! "As Rudolf is down to only one nightshirt now, I gave him 'mine' (singular) to take with him to N." Perhaps you still have some of Christoph's things! I will do all that I can from Vienna for the three women, three children and Herr Mauracher. I wonder if he might not, under your supervision, be able to take some things out of storage in Munich. It can only be the result of carelessness that everything is located there and cannot be retrieved. Sorry!!

---

175. H. v. H. translated Molière's play and arranged it for Reinhardt.
176. Frau Pannwitz.

P.S. Christiane lies in bed with a bit of fever, a bowl of cherry compote, *Hamlet* and, beside her, a photograph of Gretl. She asks, "Is Ottonie going to marry P.? And does she know that he already has three wives? Or doesn't she care?" Raimund says, "Why should that bother her? They're all someplace else!"

🌣 🌣 🌣

[Neubeuern] 1 March 1918

Well, Eberhard spent two days here getting to know Pannwitz; they found a path to one another and had the most delightful conversations with very positive results for many different political writings. Pannwitz is going to completely revise some of the things he wrote, which Eberhard will then bring to the appropriate places, especially to those for which he himself had once been selected. Pannwitz also very much enjoyed Eberhard and through him came to see certain things differently than was previously the case.

Eberhard is so looking forward to seeing you and especially as Mädy will be here for one or two days, to whom a good conversation with you will mean so much after all the terrible problems she has had to face during the past few months. You can always find just the right words which keep helping to ease one's pain long after.

I do not think I am going to be able to come to Berlin. I need some more peace and then there are also things that make life very unpleasant for me through the presence of certain of my relatives there. Do you think you might be able to come for a few days when Schröder and I are in Degenershausen for Easter – I am dying to see you again and it is difficult to do so in Berlin with the continual hunger one experiences there.

We are learning an awfully lot about the Hyperboreans, the Blue Flower-Zarathustra and this entire philosophy – and are trying to understand something of the age of Dionysus and many other things; at times it can be somewhat demanding. However the spheres in which this man is at home are so pure and beautiful – although they often feel like cold glacial air. And then I feel a longing for *your* humanness, which is so warm and cheerful and makes me feel so happy. In any case, our lives have been deeply enriched by the presence of Pannwitz.

He wrote a very charming essay about Goethe the politician which Eberhard took along to have printed right after he left.

Addio for now. Have a nice trip and if you have time, send me a few words.

Yours, O.

P.S. Pannwitz wants to have Eberhard read through his political work first before it is printed, which is probably a good idea.

❦ ❦ ❦

[Hotel Adlon, Berlin-W.] 17 March [1918]

Dearest, I have wanted to write to you for days now but could not seem to get around to it, as I always seemed to be in such a rush with so much to do. (Inside I have longing, such great longing, to be alone, to go for a walk out in the countryside, to dream the dreams of the "fairy tale" – and then again there is an inhibition. I will just give you the bare essentials very briefly.)

My first few days here were really dreadful, and Eberhard was the cause. He completely darkened my life; his own unbelievable ballast was oppressive. To have seen him together with Mädy, followed by his depression, was terrible for me – and at the same time very profound – a friendship has its dark moments just like marriage. It is over now, but I certainly do not wish to come to D.; I dread the very thought of it, and there is also no possible way I could come. And now the last few days of rehearsals take place and the premiere is on the 3rd. And this is precisely what constitutes that strange, magical world of mine; I simply can't give this up for the sake of that never-ending and horrible world of reality. I had of course expected you would be coming to one of the performances, perhaps on the 6th, but then I was forced to feel the hundredweight that, as always, is attached to little things like this and to listen to how it's "hardly possible" because of the grimace that horrible person Julie would make. So I think I must now accept that I have lost you to these people; everything ends up being poured into a dark vat with no bottom, and it is time this came to an end.

The hints you dropped about something having happened with P. when he was there are also horrible! What was it?! I do all I can so that people can have a nice and enjoyable experience, and they make their lives miserable. It's awful. It seems so pointless: one creates something from light and joke and music and dance, and you cannot see it so that Julie will not make a face, the old witch!

All right then, all right – it does not matter, just let it be. Once P. has left, please send him this letter *open*. Do you really think P. is the same type of person I am down to every last little detail? As you said in the first letter you wrote? That was the most perplexing thing anyone had ever written to me. So adieu. Adieu. Adieu.

Yours, H.

❦ ❦ ❦

[Hotel Adlon, Berlin-W.] Good Friday [29 March 1918]

You really are a very, very nice, sweet and kind little woman; very little is wanting, oh so very little indeed, and you would make the most charming girlfriend one could possibly wish for. And then I went ahead and wrote you such an awful letter, and you were able to sense that deep, deep down inside, it really wasn't that awful and wrote me the nicest reply one can imagine.

And now here we are — spending Easter together just as we should. Oh, *how* glad I am that I am not in D.! How fond I am of my little room here, No. 375, and the opportunity to be alone, and the little slice of bread with bacon I have for supper, and the soup I had at Borchardt's[177] and the confusion of the rehearsals that never seem to be quite right — and everything else! And *how* relieved I have felt since Eberhard left. I must say, dearest, it was very difficult for me to stand being around him this time. It was just like a marriage. (What a good thing for you, in all seriousness, that Christoph died early on; being married is much too difficult.) No, but it really is so: *Sometimes* a dragonfly can carry a melancholy fawn on its back, but not all the time!

I feel a terrible load upon my shoulders when a thing presents its cheerless and weighty side to me: it was just such a stroke of misfortune that news about an episode involving P. had to come to me by way of Mädy's miserably contorted face — and on top of this the burden of Eberhard. How grateful I am to you that you have the strength and the will to dissolve such things, how truly grateful, Ottonie. You will tell me about everything — for you're coming to visit, aren't you?

I once wrote you a letter from another such little room in the Adlon, on and on three times a day it seems. And now here we are, both of us still in this world, and we perhaps don't know each other as well as we did back then.

You wrote that you often talk to Pannwitz about me. How could this possibly be? What is there to talk about? There's certainly nothing special! I'm rather ordinary. Do you even know if I'm good or bad? And in what respect am I good and in what respect bad?

At times I loved you very much, that is, I *saw* you, had some sense of who you were, and loved, through you, the mystery of the world. But I don't believe there is any way I can bear indefinitely sensing how your life continually becomes mixed up with those of others; it seems so horrible. Confusion of any kind is very much at odds with my nature — I cannot describe how much I love that which is pure, the individual character of things and the delicate harmony which exists between all creatures. How-

---

177. Borchardt's, the famous Berlin restaurant, not Rudolf Borchardt's.

ever, these constant entanglements horrify me. How wonderful the dead are, so pure, so alone for themselves.

There was a moment when all of a sudden, as if struck by lightning, I understood why Eberhard wants to have you there in the future, or *has* to have you there – not now and then but rather on a regular basis:[178] He can't bear living with Mädy, and it's only tolerable for him when you are also there. [. . .] This good and strong man lacks something essential, but I don't know what to call it.

Dearest, the premiere is on the 9th. You will not be able to stay this long, I do not believe (if you are coming as early as the 5th) – also, it is nearly impossible to sustain life; just make sure you bring provisions along, eggs and so on, so that it will not be necessary to go through the awful ordeal of eating in these dreadful restaurants here nor to worry about how to sate one's hunger. (Now, since I have been alone, I have gotten over it completely; I'm able to manage without thinking about it.) However, the premiere is also the least nice of everything. The final rehearsals – which I can of course take you to – with no set length of time are much nicer.

Please, relieve me of one concern! Getting hold of tickets to the premiere for *someone*, including E. – least of all for E., who is so painfully sensitive in regard to all matters of secondary importance.

Adieu. Are we really going to see each other?

H.

🌣 🌣 🌣

[Hotel Adlon, Berlin–W.] Friday [5 April 1918] 5:30

Unfortunately I have to leave here by 6 o'clock today; it is too late to change my plans now. I'll be back sometime between 7:00 and 7:45, and Borchardt (Eberhard, too, of course) is expecting us at 9:15: there is something he would like to read to us. Please come to the rehearsal with me tomorrow at 11 o'clock. It will last until half past two. In the evening (8 o'clock), unfortunately, I have to go to a social gathering. We are going to see a very nice private collection together Sunday morning and to the theater Sunday evening. The dress rehearsal is on Monday. I would not recommend you stay for the premiere; I do not think it would reinforce your impressions of the rehearsals but rather would dissolve them.

Yours, HH

---

178. Eberhard had recently bought a house in Berlin, where his new job took him. While arranging the house, the top floor was being fixed up for Ottonie and Marie-Therese to live there.

❦ ❦ ❦

[Hotel Adlon, Berlin–W., 6 April 1918]

We will see each other tomorrow then around 10:45. I accepted an invitation for lunch at Levin's; I assume you will be lunching with Eberhard, but please, not before 1:30. At 4:30 I will pick you up at the hotel to go to tea at the Borchardts'; from there we can go directly to the theater and then from there to Reinhardt's. I managed to make it through everything without getting a migraine, even though the rehearsal lasted until half past six.

Good night. H.

❦ ❦ ❦

[Hotel Adlon, Berlin–W., 10 April 1918]

It is strange how well I am feeling, and I will certainly sleep tonight. Please take these two etchings of the *Lästigen* with you to Neubeuern. Good night.

HH

❦ ❦ ❦

Sondershausen, 1 May 1918

I was thinking of you a great deal just recently, and only the next step to reality in the form of a letter was not easy while together with my parents. Just now I received a letter from Eberhard which included the passage you wrote to me. Please rest assured regarding this matter; I had already written P. very plainly from Berlin back then, and as he did not respond, I have *completely* stopped corresponding with him. Then last week he sent me – *without a word* – two articles that he had promised in Neubeuern to send. So he realized that I would no longer write to him, which is of course good.

Should I ever see him again, an entirely different language will have developed between us. At any rate, I am completely through with him and would only worry about this if I thought it placed too great a burden on you. The only other thing I wrote to P. back then was that I told you *very little* about what he said to me because I did not want for him to feel embarrassed around you. I would very much prefer if you did *not* speak to him about this; I find this *too* grotesque. He of course also sees everything differently than other people, so I think he's got hold of the idea that it was always I who started everything. I have *often* told him all that you tell me through E.; he did not hear me, so now his vanity must realize that I am simply disregarding him – which to him will seem impossible. If you accuse him of anything now, then I will truly appear to be a liar in his eyes, which I in fact am, since I have told you everything. Mention me to him as little as possible; this is best. I only wrote him that I told you about his family circumstances, just as he wanted me to.

As *Der Bürger* [The Bourgeois] is still on the repertoire, I am happy that it is doing well for Reinhardt. I intended to return to Neub. on the 6th but hear now that Julie will be there with her husband until the 13th, so that is why I am staying here this long. I will be back in N. on the 14th.

Many regards, Yours, O.

❧ ❧ ❧

Rodaun, 16 May 1918

I have been thinking about you continually and am unable to write you from one day to the next, and am still unable to now.

We both have suffered an incalculable loss; what is there one could possibly say? It does not even help to think about it. In this case tears are worth more than thoughts.

We both really are his bereaved survivors.[179] The two of us and a third person were, during the last few years, the ones who brought him the most happiness. He died while leading a rich life and while the capacity to experience happiness was still able to offset the other, dark side. This is good. The last letter he wrote me two days before he died was full of joy.

I can hardly think of you without feeling terribly afraid for you. I hope the thought of the child gives you something you can hold onto for support. The child is good and dear. I have an indescribably good feeling about the child, not just at this moment, but always. I believe I will gradually come to play a significant role in the child's life: not as Eberhard would have, but in a different way that can also be of some benefit to her. I feel that we are attached to one another beyond all description in words, Ottonie, very firmly attached, in a special way, but I don't know how much this is able to help you.

I wrote two letters in March, which I have already asked you to destroy. I would ask you once again to do so, if you have not already. Now I am also able to understand myself through a part of me which allows me to feel presentiments. Back then I had the feeling that Eberhard's death was very near; it happened very suddenly one morning when he was sitting in my room and enveloped me for days in a dark shadow of rather odious fear.

---

179. Eberhard von Bodenhausen had suddenly died of a stroke.

The authority of the newly relieved officials, which made it impossible to renew expired papers for travel abroad, ended on the 15th, so I could go there and probably should. But I can't. It was laborious and very slow in coming, but gradually I was able to work again; that something was *there* again, and again I, too, was there for it. I can't and mustn't continue to destroy it again and again, or else I will destroy myself. How awful the years 1914 to 1916 were – no, I cannot and I must not. Eberhard would not have wanted it this way. I must preserve this one thing inside of me, through which I am able to live in a more sublime sense – and it is *constantly* threatened, so unspeakably threatened by the requirements of life, which can be so heavy-laden and bitter, with no end in sight.

If possible, send me a few lines or a telegram sometime.

Hugo.

🙠 🙠 🙠

[Degenershausen] Whit Monday [20 May 1918]

Hugo, we are all sitting here together. Rudi is right beside me playing the piano *so* wonderfully, so very beautifully. Outside everything is bright and in full bloom, and he who would have loved this all so very much is no longer with us! Oh, how he would have enjoyed having us here with him at this time of year when his Degenershausen is the most beautiful, and now this is to be forever more without him, forever more – it's so awful. However, he is well; he looked forward to leaving this world, but it is so terribly, terribly difficult for us. Poor Mädy is extremely courageous and tries to keep going, and, surrounded by all of our love helping to bear the load, she will manage to. My heart cries out horribly for him, and this eternal, never-ending dying that surrounds me – I often think I will not be able to stand it any longer. Now one must once again begin to come to terms with things – to endure the pain. Eberhard meant so incredibly much to me; I always knew this, but now I truly see for the first time, *what* he meant to me: a place of rest. I believed I was essential to *his* life, and now I see how essential he is to mine.

This winter following the Pannwitz affair, he wrote me such a *wonderful* letter in which for the first time he truly told me everything about what he feels for me – I can't tell you how happy I am to have this now, and I am *glad* to view the entire matter as a thing of the past, for the sake of Eberhard's letter.

I cannot tell you what it means to have Rudi here, what he meant and means to all of us; we cannot express it in words. With a love that never fails, he made wonderful preparations for *everything* and made a true festival out of Eberhard's burial. We hope to keep him here for another ten to fourteen days or so, and then we will experience a great emptiness for the second time. He is so tender and understanding and then the next moment very funny, making us all laugh with his silly nonsense for minutes on end. Borchardt was also wonderful, and he spoke some very great and beautiful words at the grave. I do believe there's a feeling carrying us all right now; it is the love we all share for Eberhard and the feeling that no one, whether he knew him well or had only briefly crossed his path, will forget him. Indeed, you have also suffered just as great a loss as we have; he always referred to you as his "best" friend. Oh, Hugo, he loved you so much, and you always meant so much to him. Borchardt put it so beautifully: "Now we must endeavor to become ever more mature and more calm, so that we can in part serve as a replacement for Hugo of what Eberhard was to him." And it seems Rudi says at least once a day: "Ottonie, we must see to it that all of us only grow closer to one another as a result of this – in order that we may replace for one another this loss." It is in this that one may take comfort: in the knowledge that those with whom he surrounded himself have also become part of our family and that they don't wish to leave us, now that he is no longer here.

I was in Berlin for two days in order to open up his desks; I sat in the room there in the Adlon once again which was so very much *his* room. Absolutely everything there was exactly the way he had left it, and I often thought he *must* be returning soon now to pace back and forth while telling me about his day and that all this sorrow was surely a dream – yet the dream remains reality. He was rather finished with everything here and had gotten everything all ready for Mädy and the children. His executor, who will also continue work on everything, was his former secretary. He told me that he would also continue to carry on Eberhard's accounts, i.e. also yours, until such time that you prefer otherwise. Herbst (that's his name) is a gem and a splendid legacy with whom all is in good hands.

It is my job then to first of all stay with Mädy this summer and to see how everything develops.

Take care. We mourn together this friend to both of us. If only I can hold onto you now.

O.

P.S. There's another concern I have that is extremely depressing to me. My father was operated on for cancer three days ago. If only he can pull through this or at least not have to die an agonizing death.

Rodaun, 27 May [1918]

We really must be connected to one another in some strange way if I had such a strong foreboding that your father's death was near, which I also expressed to Gerty.

And so, too, it has come to pass, Ottonie, and you must stay after all. It always seems to return: that little old song of the Harlekin.[180] You are a living being, and life is good for you; it is bright and warm and the world does not wish to miss this, and neither do I. How wonderfully you are revealed in Rudi's letter, and how wonderfully Rudi is in yours. I often struggle for hours on end musing about myself, wondering just who I am and what I am. I contemplate having become alienated from people, completely alienated – then I recall Eberhard and you, and Borchardt and Rudi. Who brought you together after all, and who would have held you together, if not I?

You must take me the way I am, Ottonie. "Do you wish to live with me here in my heaven? As often as you may come, it shall always be open to you!"[181] This is all that I have to give.

Come to me then as often as you would like, often, again and again; this is all I can say.

Mädy, the children there – there is absolutely nothing more I can do to help them. How little I am able to help my own children, how little!

Life's confusion continues to intrude again and again – while I wish only to give life to the wonderful impressions I have inside of me! During these awful weeks I wrote what is probably the most charming chapter of the fairy tale: about how the emperor comes to the unborn children. I did not take a single day off. A few months ago, Eberhard told me these imaginary realms of pure harmony had very little, almost nothing, to do with life, and that it made him happier than anything else to know that they were there and that new ones would continue to come into being. I think of him a hundred times when I'm at work on something.

Mädy wrote me a very lovely letter; yes, it was very lovely – and yet it seemed sentimental and forced. Your words are never sentimental or forced at the most fundamental level.

The art of life – the older I get, the less capable I become, the more embittered and awkward. Money. Your letter brings me to this. It foists itself onto everything and pursues a man, even in his dreams: in my opinion it is almost a monstrosity for an artist to be concerned with such things: matters of house, children, paying taxes, the cost of a kilo of butter, etc.

I can hardly describe how kind and good and practical-minded Gerty is. The whole thing (I refer to the pressure of the present age) could hardly have come at a more critical time for me than now. *Everything* is at stake for me in this year, i.e. my livelihood as an artist. Borchardt finds himself in the same situation.

---

180. See poem at the beginning of the book.
181. From Schiller's poem, die "Teilung der Erde" (The Division of the World).

Financial matters! First the matter involving me. I would be glad to have Herr Herbst continue to tend to my account there. There's not much to tend to by the way. First one must determine where the missing one third share is, i.e. one must find the records concerning this. I'm including an enclosure, which I would ask that you pass on.

The second matter must be handled with the utmost sensitivity and only under certain circumstances. I leave it entirely up to your discretion. It concerns the 20,000 Mark gift to Pannwitz which you already know about. It has not been *carried through* yet. This was pushed back at my request, and Dörner made a note that 10,000 Marks were to be transferred to me on two separate occasions, once at the end of 1918 and again at the end of 1919. I subsidized the people in 1918 and paid their overdue debt. If Eberhard's gift is to be omitted, then I of course must assume the responsibility for the years 1919–1921. You are familiar with the situation there unlike me; it will of course make a big difference whether Eberhard's enormous income is there or only his property, which is certainly not enormous. If perhaps half of the gift were to remain intact, then it would free me from any responsibility for the next year and a half, and that would be a great help.

The whole thing weighs all the more heavily upon me ever since this miserable man, through his absurd behavior, cut right into the true source of the joy and sympathy I had felt, in particular the length of time he continued to adhere to such an absurd, grotesque position. I do not want to have to see him again for a long time, however I can't let him starve to death. Think about it for a while, and deal with it *properly* and as you see fit, without taking into consideration any sentimental feelings you have involving me – if only you hadn't had these last March either!

HH.

🌿 🌿 🌿

[Degenershausen] 1 June 1918

Thank you very much for both of your letters; it means so much to me having you there. I will always come to you. You are certainly aware of this, for I don't believe I could live without you. (Please don't take this to be sentimental on my part, but rather just as I mean it.) I neither want to nor may I burden you, and please don't let me be a burden when you think about me. I am doing quite well physically; I am just somewhat tired and as a result of this tiredness, which was particularly bad during the first days following my return here, I wrote Gerty a rather gloomy letter. Things have improved somewhat now – I spent several days in bed and thus had more time alone. The *Divan* and the accompanying notes have helped me a great deal. I hope and would like to reach the point again where I can *enjoy* living — anything else is really not right.

He should not have been taken away from me right now, my father. I was so looking forward to seeing him if he would have come here.

You know, Hugo, I feel so horrible about the financial concerns you have. I would like so much to talk to you about all this sometime. Try to free yourself, or is this quite impossible? It's so difficult in writing. I can't say anything yet regarding the Pannwitz money, as they're not yet sure here about financial matters because the will hasn't been opened yet. Eberhard's salary of course only extends until the 1st of July (close of the fiscal year), however I think Mädy will be able to bear at least half the burden. I will write as soon as I know anything about this. I have not heard anything else from Pannwitz since Berlin, i.e. I no longer open his letters, so I'm also not aware of what is going on there; of course one can't allow him to starve.

Borchardt wrote today that he will be here during the last half of June, which will be wonderful for us, as everyone is already worried about Rudi being gone. He wrote a wonderful poem. What a dear man he is! Oh, Hugo, if only we weren't so far apart and could quickly get together sometime and talk. I realize that everything is at stake for you now and that you must be completely free of any burden in the coming years.

Yours, Ottonie.

❦ ❦ ❦

Degenershausen, 9 June 1918

It is Sunday morning here, and the sun is shining brightly; everyone is working feverishly out in the field in order to gather up the hay, but it neither seems like one is working nor does it seem like a Sunday here. One feels so empty and gloomy despite the sunshine; I suppose it is particularly bad today, as Rudi has left us and we have to rely completely on ourselves now. I cannot begin to tell you, Hugo, *how much* he meant to us, especially to Mädy, whom he always knew how to handle just the right way, whether by showing great understanding for her feelings of grief or by making one of his funny little remarks. Now everything falls on my shoulders alone — will I continue to be up to the task, as it is very hard on me, too? Eberhard would have turned fifty on Wednesday; he still looked so young to me in Berlin. When you're able to, write Mädy a few kind words again sometime. You help her so much by doing so and therefore me as well. Oh, Hugo, how wonderful it must be to have work like yours, which offsets the trials and tribulations of life. So you've been working on the fairy tale — *how* lovely. In my mind it is one of the most beautiful things you've written.

Rudi wrote a wonderful poem for Frau v. Kühlmann and another one for the visitors' book here which was *so* lovely; I'll copy it down for you.

Take care. Do not torment yourself by writing a letter to me. I know that we both share the same feelings right now.

Yours always, O.

P.S. My only wish is to finally have a sense of inner peace, and now my brother is returning to the war, and I have the feeling that he, too, will likely fall because I love him so much.

> So muss ich denn den Berg für lange meiden,
> Den Hügel meiden, den wir fromm geschichtet,
> Da wir umglöckelt vom Geläut der Weiden
> So gern den Blick ins offene Feld gerichtet.
> Ins offene Feld! Und Er, der nun bescheiden
> In schmaler Kammer schläft, der nun beschwichtet
> Mit Geistern wandelt, – ach nach Geistersitte
> Bleibt er für immer, Geist, in unsrer Mitte!
>
> Nehmt meine Hand. Und sei's zum Bundeszeichen
> In seinem Namen, der uns eh verbindet,
> Soll unser Keiner aus dem Dienste weichen,
> Des Feuers wartend, das er angezündet.
> Ob wir verstreut nach aller Erde Reichen,
> Hier bleibt der Grund, da unsre Wurzel gründet.
> Nur wer da dient, erwirbt sein richtig Leben,
> Nur der ist *reich*, der es vermag zu *geben*.

7 June 1918　　　　　　　　　　　　Rudolph Alexander Schröder[182]

Degenershausen, 13 June 1918

Gerty's letter arrived today; I am sorry to find out that you did not receive my letter in which I told you that Herbst would provide precise answers regarding the financial matters. We sent this letter to Herwarth, who was supposed to expedite it unopened, as certain information about your account was included. It also contained a letter from Rudi. After this,

---

[182] Translation: It's time for me to bid the mountain farewell / To shun this hill which we piously erected / While in the ringing of these meadows' bells / We gladly held our gaze directed. / Into the open field! And He, in modesty / Asleep in his small chamber, now at rest, / Walking with spirits, and as a spirit guest, / He remains in our midst, eternally. // Now take my hand. And let it be a token / In his name, who once bound us together / Not one of us shall avoid this service: / To tend the fire which he set aflame – / Though life divides us, even scatters / Us all, here is the earth where our roots did grow / Only he who serves attains the life that matters. / And only he is rich who is able to give.

as far as I can remember, I wrote you twice. There are problems with the money for P. as Eberhard only has his personal wealth left, which was not that much; his salary had suddenly ended; it was not that high this year, as he hadn't received anything from the new project. I spoke to Herbst about this (on my own); he did not think the executors of the will would be able to approve this amount and that it would be quite impossible from the present account. I feel terribly sad that I could not do anything more here. M. has no knowledge of my receiving a letter from you; the one to Herbst he just handed over. I would have to withhold all of your letters to me because of the one sentence. Couldn't we receive something from Redlich or someone as a subsidy for P. (of course I suppose it won't be easy to come by an amount like that from E.)?

Yesterday Eberhard would have turned 50; he was still so young really and often so boyish. We have lost a great deal.

We are expecting Borchardt on the 17th. I hope he really comes; he would be such help to me in supporting poor Mädy. She tries so hard at present to put on a good act, but inside she is filled with despair – oh, Hugo, and there is so much from the last few years of his life she does not know.

In a strange way I fear for the time you spend working. I wonder if you have found the inner calm you need in order to complete the fairy tale? It sounds so easy, a "fairy tale," and no one has any idea what it means to master it.

Take care.

Yours, O.

❦ ❦ ❦

Degenershausen Ermsleben Harz, 26 June 1918

I simply must write you again even though it is so soon, or would it be better if I did not? If it will make you anxious receiving my letters, then do not answer me, and then I will know that you need to be left in peace now, especially by me. However, there is one thing I do want to tell you, and that is that I am glad you found Pannwitz again, especially now, after you, too, had lost a great deal. I was very afraid the entire time in Berlin that the ridiculous episode involving me might have spoiled how you felt about him, a man who can still be worth so much to you in particular and vice versa. It is a crying shame that I was not able to smooth things over.

Having Borchardt here is wonderful. I never would have thought that he could feel so at home here and be so incredibly humane. Yes, he's of course very different from Rudi, who was soft-hearted and helpful in carrying the burden of everything and funny at the same time. Borchardt is rougher, more masculine, yet he shows terrific understanding. I had a conversation with him one evening and was shaken by how he carries his life and his love and takes every hardship upon himself with a delicacy that leaves one *deeply, deeply* moved. Perhaps I was particularly affected by this now because I can still feel the other, violent feelings in every bone of my body.

Fortunately he will be staying for three weeks; he reads such wonderful things to us – like his *Armer Heinrich* [Poor Henry], which is incredibly beautiful and tremendously pure. Then on another evening he gave us his last, great lecture in Mannheim, *Der Dichter und die Geschichte* [The Poet and History]. Oh, Hugo, what wonderful men you have brought us; this is truly your achievement. Indeed, we think and speak of you almost every day, and the love Borchardt has for you is immensely beautiful, with great and supreme feeling and deep understanding. Eberhard is always among us whatever we may be doing; one often feels he is laughing along with us or at one of us.

Mädy is courageous, however I would not dare leave her alone right now; after all she needs somebody she can lean on for support. I think we will go to Neubeuern again at the end of October, as Mädy and the boy must spend the winter in a place of high elevation. Thank God for the wonderful position Rudi has working,[183] and he received a *very* nice reception from everyone in B. I am so happy for him!

Warm regards, O.

Rodaun, 30 June 1918

At first the only thing I was able to see in the letter you wrote was one single word: "October." So I will have to manage without you for at least this long then! Dearest, that is what is so difficult for me to bear, this burden which continues to mount and mount: eternally having to do without those people who belong together with me and never having these people here to whom I am able to give something – from the same reserves of creative imagination that not only nourish hundreds of figures, but also that which belongs in a different sphere – which always only appear as these black marks written on white paper, which tie men to me and me to men – and constantly being up to my neck, to my lips, in a real and near perpetual concern, darkness, confusion, chaos, horror: the senseless jumble. I am not fainthearted; I always manage to move beyond this, but you cannot begin to imagine what consequences it had for me mentally and emotionally and spiritually having to live through these past four years here in Austria – and what this meant for me as an Austrian. Borchardt

---

183. R. A. Schröder was sent as a delegate to the German Embassy in the Hague.

understands this, as he does everything; he will help you to understand as well.

So you will come to see me in October if the world still exists then and if it is still possible to travel – it's impossible to know how it will be then, but the purest of things, the only thing, which resides within us, must also help us to get past this intact. Just don't leave me here alone for too long – not forever!

When I think that Borchardt will be there with you for a number of weeks, your future again seems to be bright, and this in turn allows me to share in this brightness. Do let me have a copy of *Armer Heinrich*, Ottonie. Is there not a girl there, a child, who would copy it down for me by hand – and the Mannheim lecture, too? I will also receive something else later, something I was promised – the eulogy Borchardt gave at the grave – right? The books I was supposed to receive have not arrived yet. You must not constantly make me do without the one thing from which the very core of my being is able to nourish itself, that which, as I am already forced to manage without the conversations, would be my only form of conversation. And the years pass on, these prime years of middle-age, the most important.

I am very moved that you thank me for Borchardt's being there with you. For all that is good about this you have only yourself to thank; he writes wonderful things about you (see below), the loveliest words, and the truest that one could attribute to you. I wanted to write them down for you, but then something held me back, a sense of shame; I cannot do it – perhaps I'll show it to you sometime, although perhaps you would be embarrassed to read it, and yet his words contain the purest and most delicate of truths.

Words cannot describe how happy it makes me when I can bring people together who are worth more to me than anything else in the world – the impatience that can thus be conquered and, time and again, obscurity, cruelty and sharp, sudden judgments; while it may have at one time nearly made my heart stop to read a letter of Eberhard's in which he bitterly misjudged Borchardt, this only lasted for a moment, thank God.

Just as Borchardt is there with you now, so I had imagined it would be when P. was there; that's exactly what I had intended. I was thinking more of you and of your happiness than of his when I sent him there. And then everything turned out differently. Inside I was filled with the terrible aftershocks of these days in Berlin; it was indescribably difficult for me to have to see him. I wrote him and said that I knew about everything. I expressed myself in harsh, scathing terms; I could not have done otherwise. He wrote me a very nice reply, and I felt then that I could see him once again. It was as if an iron clamp had been removed from my chest. He came to visit and stayed a day and a half. The time passed without our saying a thing about these events; not a word was uttered, and there were no questioning glances. He read some of his more recent essays to me and free renderings of the most ancient oriental myths. I was once again exceedingly impressed by this person: his strength, uniqueness, and the tragic, paradoxical character of his life. In the meantime a letter had already arrived from him; I didn't read it at the time. I was happy to be able to tolerate his presence and indeed that he seemed more calm, more mild in some way, as if covered by a veil. Then another letter of tremendous scope arrived; both of them together provided a kind of rendering of everything, of his life among men in general, of his connections to people there in Fürberg; the clarity of the entire picture was wonderful, and yet a certain distance was preserved; it in no way forced itself upon the reader. You were referred to in a very subtle manner without being mentioned by name; it is almost impossible to say how often you are the topic of discussion as opposed to something else more general. The enormous shock he feels as a result of his encounter with you is becoming evident, also the lamentable position of having brought about these circumstances through no fault of one's own as an object of one's own fate; there were faintly perceptible lamentations about the incomprehensible and contradictory – so it always is that the object of one's love who does not return this love shall remain incomprehensible. I have not forgotten the other, terrible, and violent side of this; it weighs terribly heavily upon my soul – but there is a certain blindness inside him which conceals from him this side of his actions; he just feels it is his fate to act in this manner, to covet so much, to intrude completely upon the lives of others. To completely change the other person, to breed new souls, is his greatest dream; the horrific element of this remains hidden from him, and that is his blessing. It seems very strange to me. I see him in double vision: with your eyes, just as Borchardt, too, describes him in his letter with merciless severity, which is wholly just; and then I also see him as he sees himself and loves himself and as he asserts himself as a creator in the most dreadful conditions of poverty with this trusting love he has for himself and as he binds people to himself, so that their bodies nearly become joined to his as one, and yet he still feels lonely and complains about being alone. At the same time something of his being surrounds me. I can't describe it: it's not the love I have for Borchardt, not the quiet, indescribable trust that Eberhard instilled in me, not the cheerful awareness that the thought of Schröder gives me; it's completely different from all of this, and yet it gives me courage and strength to know that he exists. This occurred in one of the letters he wrote me: he complains, without seeming bitter, that I judged him so harshly in connection with what transpired in Neubeuern; he finds that I would only possibly be justified in doing so if I knew everything that had happened down to the last detail and that I in fact hardly know anything at all, for you yourself supposedly wrote him, following your encounter with me in Berlin, that you told me almost nothing about these days in Neubeuern.

How peculiar it is now this little knot you have tied: You are a person who is incapable of willfully telling the slightest untruth; then in this case for some reason you said something that was technically a small falsehood, and immediately confusion ensues – or confusion would ensue, however, when it comes to you, there is nothing that could confuse me. I am going to let this and every other matter pass and will never talk to him about these things again or only from a great distance providing for a cathartic effect. But I would like this to be brought to some kind of a conclusion by your initiative. I would like you to return the letters to him unopened in a box through Bernsdorff – to the Fürberg address, and include a note in which you tell him that there was never any division within yourself, never a contradictory message in your behavior towards him, never anything mysterious (which he wrongly believed to be present) and thus no negative change of heart towards him after he had left; rather the feelings you had inside were the same all along: you sought to understand and hoped to understand and to help, allowing that you might soon become friends; however, you rejected his attempt to force upon you something more and clearly turned away from any such overtures. Seek counsel from Borchardt. Get it clear in your own mind how you will put the gentle and stern facts into this epitaph without overdoing the simple way you have of expressing yourself; and put an end to it, in your own mind, too, by using delicate words and not through that dark silence, which will always seem ambiguous to the passionate man, because he wants there to be ambiguity.

Take care, and think of me. It is wonderful knowing that you are close to one another. Eberhard is here with me as he is there with you; he is with us and indeed is feeling carefree, while we here are weighted down. This he has earned.

Just imagine what you will do for me if you send me one of Borchardt's things, whatever it may be!

The address is: Aussee Steiermark Obertressen 14 beginning on the 10th.

Hugo

P.S. Herbst wrote me a letter along the same lines as yours; his discussion of matters related to P. was extremely tactful and sympathetic.

There is of course only one solution: the entire burden must fall upon me. I will beg from various people until I can gather enough resources to cover the amount needed for the years 1919–1920. This will be difficult in two respects. First, that which has been so difficult to obtain will only enable the eight people to remain in constant hunger without exactly starving to death under present conditions (which have worsened tremendously since the end of 1917), and while one claims to be able to provide for their needs, they themselves must work tirelessly begging for assistance wherever possible. Secondly in approaching all these people, half-strangers, as I am now forced to do (a moderately well-to-do man such as Redlich is able to give me one twentieth of what I need, no more; I must not trouble Frau Yella O. with anything right now; among other things she carries the burden of a children's home); the many letters I must direct *égards* towards those people who are presently very much rubbing me the wrong way at a time when it's really a matter of survival; and in that I have isolated myself from the world and avoided becoming mixed up in its affairs during a time when there is so much pressure from the outside and such a great productive capacity on the inside.

Constantly having to describe my situation in the letters I have written in the past three weeks is extraordinarily debilitating. I would ask you, after discussing it with Borchardt, to write to Rudi about this new state of affairs. Describe my situation to Rudi – but not so that he himself will offer to help. I know he is not in a position to do so, neither do I wish him to. Perhaps he can win over a few people or even only one – first of all to understand P. – and then it might be possible to approach this one during the course of the year 1919 for a request of modest assistance.

P.S. This is not the only such burden I must carry, and that is why I can feel the pressure tenfold which Eberhard, without being asked, wished to remove from me by means of a single line, the good man!

[Excerpt from Borchardt's letter:]

Her magic resides in her tireless and temperate benevolence towards others and her unflagging concern for their well-being. She provides comfort and healing the moment she uncovers a want within her circle. How wonderful that there are women who, while no longer young girls, fulfill their mission in the world because there is no man, either husband or lover, who restricts them or makes them dependent. One cannot imagine them without their freedom, for a confining relationship can only result in their destruction.

[Degenershausen] 11 July 1918

Borchardt just finished reading "Durant"[184] to us – it was wonderful hearing it for the second time! Everything is so concise, so compelling and yet tender – truly sublime.

Hugo, your letter was *immensely* valuable to us; you were so very present in every one of the lovely pages. Borchardt was in Berlin for two

---

184. A poem by R. Borchardt.

days at the time the letter arrived, and I could hardly wait for him to return and to share this joy with me. We had five wonderful days alone without Mädy. I felt so light and free, as I had not for quite some time; it's so easy to discuss everything with him. No, Hugo, we will not abandon you, and you will not abandon us, for indeed we have become permanently attached to one another. The eulogy at Eberhard's grave is in the process of being printed. Borchardt of course couldn't bring himself to write it down, but we did finally receive it. I will send it to you as soon as it's ready. It will appear in *Wieland* as a counterpart to one by Meier-Graefe, which is not really good.

Borchardt cannot give us his lecture, "Dichter und die Geschichte," either, as it is not complete, and he only has one copy of *Armer Heinrich*; in short, you are certainly familiar with how inhibited he is when it comes to things of this kind. At first he promised to give me all sorts of things for you, but as soon as one would like to have them, he has nothing to give. I cannot say why this is so; even he cannot seem to do anything about it as much as he would like to.

He told me so much about his lovely girlfriend, which seemed to come very easily to him; it is marvelous how he is handling everything. He very much hopes to make it to Vienna sometime in the course of the summer. You will surely see each other then.

He was very helpful to me regarding the Pannwitz matter. I am much more relieved about my role in all of this, except for one small part, for which I blame myself, for this man really is extremely complicated.

I am going to write Rudi regarding several people who might be able to assist you.

Next week Kessler will be coming for one or two days and will certainly be feeling rushed, as always.

Hugo, Eberhard's grave is so beautiful; it is so plain at the moment, and often I sit out there trying to get clear in my mind that there lie the remains of what we once knew as his body, and it seems so impossible that he is not seated beside me, for indeed I am talking to him quietly in my thoughts. However, there is no response! Mädy was with the boy in Berlin at the doctor's, who thank God discovered that his lungs were once again clear; only his heart is not yet quite as it should be, and his general condition is still delicate. Therefore he will have to remain here for now, and we will then look for a place in the mountains for the winter, where there is a combination of as much sun, fresh air and good food as possible. Mädy continues to be brave; she does not look good and is still fighting a physical collapse. I hope she is still able to for a while longer.

Oh, Hugo, if we had had our wish, Borchardt and I would have left immediately to come to see you, but instead we must continue to be content making plans. However, I will certainly be coming this autumn and am looking *so* forward to it and to everything we will have to tell each other. It is embarrassing that Borchardt wrote such touching things about me; he views me through rose-colored glasses.

Take care. In my thoughts I picture you in beautiful Aussee. How I would love to move into the Rosa villa,[185] if but for a few days, and in the evening (as it is just now) in my mind I can see the beautiful pine tree in the meadow as I look out the window, and behind it the mountains (which I really do miss here).

Truly yours, O.

❦ ❦ ❦

Bredeney Essen, 14 August 1918

Here we are faced with a sad task, having to dissolve everything where Eberhard spent the most difficult years of his life. How many battles he had to wage here on countless fronts. What a truly lovely place to rest he had prepared for himself; all the rooms are filled with his aura, too – everywhere there is a sense of harmony. It pains one so to destroy all of this, to pack away perhaps for years to come all the colorful paintings[186] he loved so much; how terribly sad, and yet nothing can be done about it. Degenershausen is full, and so too Meineweh, so we're storing everything in his third estate, Tierbach,[187] until Mädy has decided where she will spend her winters. We can't decide this yet.

Mädy's energy never ceases to amaze me. Even here, where it constantly seems her heart is about to give out and where she has become so keenly aware of what it means to be without Eberhard, she always seems to pull herself together at the last second. It really would be cruel to leave this truly extremely dependent creature standing alone on her own two feet. Whether she will ever learn to accept his death seems highly questionable indeed!

I received a nice, long letter from Borchardt a few days ago; the poor fellow got food poisoning from a bad meal and had several bad weeks; apparently he is doing better now. He writes beautifully about the feelings he has for his beloved. Actually I wanted to send it to you, but quite a few of the things he says about me are expressed in overly glowing terms, which I find embarrassing. I had also hoped for the services of Petra, his scribe, but he says, his typist has left him in a lurch. Otherwise I would have simply passed his writings on to you; however, I fear it's a hopeless situation; unless one tears them out of his hand, he will not give them up.

---

185. House in Altaussee where H. v. H. spent his summers.
186. E. von Bodenhausen was a collector of French Impressionists.
187. Degenershausen, Meineweh, and Tierbach were the Bodenhausens' estates.

I am so glad that Andrian has come to the *Burgtheater*,[188] which after all must surely be pleasant for you, too, in many respects. I'm just so amazed that he completely gave up his career in politics.

We waited several days for Kessler in vain. As always, he did not come. He was unable to move from Berlin for weeks; people always remain the same.

We found a deeply moving diary of Eberhard's here in which he revealed the same character traits he did elsewhere: diligence, kindness, humility, idealism!

This Saturday we will be returning to Degenershausen. Is the summer going well for you? Are you able to work? It would make me happy to receive a few short words about this. I hope you received my last letter. I forgot to send it express mail.

Forever yours, O.

Degenershausen Ermsleben Harz, 26 October 1918

I have the feeling nothing is going to come of my planned trip to Rodaun this year. Such dark clouds[189] are beginning to overshadow all sides that one does not wish to leave the country, and I think I should rather stay here for now. It will be *terribly* difficult for me to renounce our being together, especially this year after all that has happened. What a strong need I feel to be able to talk to you there sometime; being together with Gerty and Christiane would have also done me a great deal of good. I can't help thinking that it may be fortunate that Eberhard does not have to experience all that we are undergoing right now and that he was permitted to depart at the right moment.

Neither is Mädy's situation a pleasant one, for she is to cross the border into Switzerland on the 13th. Oh, how much she does leave behind!

Right now my brother is here, but unfortunately he has to return to the battlefield soon. Again we of course do not have any news from Borchardt and Rudi; they always seem to disappear, and we lose sight of their whereabouts.

If things should clear up here, then I will come right away.

Many warm regards, Ottonie.

---

188. H. v. H.'s friend, Leopold von Andrian, left his political life as a diplomat to take over the management of the Imperial Theater in Vienna.

189. The Russian Revolution, which began in 1917, started to spill over into Germany, and actually broke out on 7 November in Kiel.

[Postcard]   Rodaun, 6 November 1918

I would be overjoyed to know where you are. The letter you wrote on the 26th of October arrived here on the 4th of November, right at a rather turbulent moment. Things have calmed down here now, but the situation is very difficult in terms of money and food.

I sent a letter to you in Degenershausen a few days ago; it contains something I would ask you to pass on to Herbst, of whose whereabouts I'm also not aware.

Really I constantly feel uneasy about Borchardt; I saw B. B.[190] She is very pretty and very nice; however, she told me very little about Borchardt, and what she did say I found disturbing. He obviously finds himself in a dangerous situation. Perhaps you have heard something about him! I would also like to know where Müller-Hofmann is hiding so that I could give him a little help financially.

                                                                             Yours, Hofmannsthal

❦ ❦ ❦

[Two postcards]   [Degenershausen] 25 November 1918

I received your card – I am going to speak with Herbst later. The letter I had been expecting just arrived as well; oh, how happy I am that you are all doing well, as we are, too. We are sitting on an island here where new waves of upheaval arrive *only* by way of the newspapers. On the 7th of November, that is, right at a very critical time, Borchardt was here, which was a *great* help to us. He stayed for a week; we were *all* in bed with the flu. He read some wonderful passages to me from "Durant" which I was not familiar with, and we had pleasant conversations. He burns with longing for Billy. He talked to me a great deal about everything. In Berlin he spends a lot of time with Schröder's niece and also with a small group of friends from Bremen. However, in a certain respect, your fears are probably legitimate. We, too, were struck by something about him which seemed to indicate a tremendous uneasiness. He is most eagerly awaiting the peace so that he can leave at once as the first man to go to Italy. I write cards and hope that they reach you.

We are still being detained here. Baby was already in Neubeuern; she had to return, as everything appeared uncertain there due to the possibility of occupation by the Italian troops; food was also too hard to come by. Well, now I hope to finally land in my own little port this spring – will it be possible?! Mädy could not make it into Switzerland; she is still here and experiencing a particularly difficult time. When will we ever see each

---

190. Sibille Blei, actress ("Billy").

other again?! I am so happy about everything you write about yourself. Give my regards to everyone, especially Christiane.

Ottonie.

❦ ❦ ❦

By courier   Vienna, 26 November 1918

Dearest, it is rather agonizing to have no idea where you are at times such as these – to not be able to picture your surroundings. How I would love to think you were in Hinterhör. But for years now you have informed me in every single letter that you (at about the time one could send a reply) are off to somewhere else, i.e. "probably" somewhere else, so that one's thoughts constantly go astray.

Well, the entire world is collapsing. Perhaps the private lives of individuals will also become simpler now; perhaps present circumstances will completely eliminate this pathological excess of possibility – then people may come to their senses and rediscover themselves to some degree, and I can finally imagine you sitting on the little farm and not always as a hurried slave to a world moved solely by material, and never intellectual, concerns.

You wrote to me on the 26th of October, a month ago today. At the time the letter arrived, 2,800 people were dying of the flu each week in Vienna; four of the seven of us here were bed-ridden. In addition there were constant alerts against looters and shooting in civilian areas, once in Brunn and another time in Liesing, and everywhere thousands of loitering, starving prisoners of war, and escaped criminals, hundreds of them, roamed the little villages (where one used to eat so well, as I always mention) – all of them hungry, freezing, threatening, and at the same time revealing *au fond* an astonishing good-naturedness; otherwise it would have been even worse. The rest, the more general matters, you know from the newspapers. The future is extremely uncertain; should one survive, find something to eat again and not have to wander around in dark, ice-cold houses, then one will, despite everything, feel as if one is living in paradise and will in some way also have become wiser. Throughout this entire time Goethe has been incredibly valuable to me, and I constantly talk to Eberhard about everything. He is happy that I never lost my head, not even during the most absurd days, and that I never lost sight of my convictions (including the political ones). I reproach him for the stubbornness of all North Germans to whom you just cannot say anything regarding these matters (in Austria everything has turned out as I had been telling everyone it would since 1917, which no one wanted to hear at the time). If only he were really here – but he would have to be healthy. Being ill the way he was, I think, as you do, that it was good for him to have been spared this. In all of this there is something I indeed find liberating; I have truly learned to hate and to despise everything which is being turned upside down now. However, Liebknecht[191] is merely a continuation of Ludendorff;[192] thus weight must be transferred from the Northeast to the old Southwest, and Germany must once again become Germany after the terrible case of Prussian stubbornness, which continual injections simply aggravated further and further – leading all the way to the dreadful conclusion.

It is the farthest thing from my mind to excessively ponder financial concerns; I take it as a matter of course that there will be very strong, legal incursions into the small savings I have accumulated. I trust by the way that Herr Herbst, to whom I would request you convey the content of what I write here, will take all the precautions he deems necessary within the confines of what is legally permissible. If, for example, he finds it appropriate to transfer my cash credit of about 60,000 to his own account or to place it somewhere else for safekeeping, then I would ask him to be assured of the complete trust I have in him. I would ask that he perhaps cancel the loan from Söhnlein and Cie. if he sees fit. Losses of interest earned or something of the like doesn't concern me in the slightest; what I want is for the nullification of my savings to be averted if possible.

Please write me an open card telling me how things stand with you and the little girl, and try to keep your spirits up. I am looking forward to our next meeting.

Yours, Hugo

P.S. One more thing for Herr Herbst: it would be perfectly fine to transfer my cash credit to my longtime friend and publisher S. Fischer in Berlin (Bülowstrasse 91) and to credit it interest-free to my account with his publishing house. Someone there would simply have to notify Herr Fischer that I request of him this friendly favor.

Degenershausen Ermsleben, 16 January 1919

From your letter to Herbst and Gerty's to Mädy, I can see that two of my letters to you did not arrive; in addition I also wrote two simple postcards. I think I made the mistake of not sending them express. I received your letter from the 26th of November a few days before Christmas; it seems you are emotionally unattached to all the great upheaval which, by

---

191. Karl Liebknecht (1871–1919), leader of the Socialist Party.

192. Erich Friedrich Wilhelm Ludendorff (1865–1937), German general, involved in right-wing politics at that time. During the Revolution he was hiding in Schloss Neubeuern.

contrast, has left us so shaken. I had not expected you to feel otherwise; from our walks together in Rodaun during the last days of Autumn, I was, after all, aware of your views about the old regime, which you felt had to be overcome. I can still recall the exact moment when I anxiously asked, "Is Germany then to cease being a monarchy, something that is unthinkable for this people?" And now it has come to this in one fell swoop. One asks oneself, probably to no avail, where this all will lead to and how we are to emerge and find solid ground. If we can all rise up and, as decent human beings, perhaps tell our children the truth instead of lies, then a great deal will have been gained. At any rate, I do not want to join in the complaining; I find it so undignified. This incredible fate that has closed in on Europe is probably not entirely undeserved; we cannot overlook this. Indeed, we still find ourselves very much at the beginning, I believe.

Personally, of course, we were at first touched by this new wave only through the newspapers. The solitude of the forest surrounds us as a warm, green, protective cloak. Mädy has probably explained how and why we have all remained here. We'll be staying here at least until April and then *hope* to *finally* land in Hinterhör – will this be possible?! I so long for the secluded little house, and once we do make a start of it there, then I hope it will be forever.

Borchardt recommended a wonderful book to me, *Die polnischen Bauern* [The Polish Peasants], by Reymont, which I enjoyed reading very, very much. One can truly smell the soil in it; it is really marvelous! Recently I have found Stendhal – *Vie de Napoléon* [Life of Napoleon] – especially interesting to read and also *Die Revolution* [The Revolution) by Carlyle. I'm trying to get a picture of what the Revolution was like back then, and quite a few things which I had not been aware of have now become clear. I bought Treitschke's *Geschichte des 19. Jahrhunderts* [History of the Nineteenth Century] as a Christmas present for myself and just began reading it with great interest.

I heard that Borchardt gave his lecture about Petra. The critics, as one might expect, apparently had a negative response to it; however, I hear that many people were very much impressed, and are asking him to come to speak everywhere. He remains silent, which is the only thing he can do. So much is being said about it right now, such negative things at that, and to what end?!

Take care. Think of me every now and again.

Yours, Ottonie.

P.S. I have not heard anything about Müller-Hofmann; and I really don't know whom to ask to find something out.

Rodaun, 6 February 1919

The letter you wrote on the 16th of January arrived nine or ten days later. So it's still possible to correspond with one another, to be there for one another. Around the 15th of January, I wrote a rather long letter to Hans Wilke. It would mean a lot to me if I knew that this one, too, was not lost, for a letter of this kind reflecting moments in time as we experience them cannot be replicated.

I am striving to hold my friends together, to arouse in each of them the feeling of a mutual attachment. The news I received about Rudi (from a letter Borchardt wrote) is not good. They saw each other, and he was shaken, both mentally and physically, shaken to the very core. And this was still before the more recent incidents that occurred in Bremen (which may by the way, as many things of this kind, affect one in close proximity less than one reading about them in a newspaper report). However, Borchardt himself, I must say, has me more concerned. There is a restless quality to his letters, a sense of despair and reservation, which I know all too well as a sign that he is experiencing great difficulties. I fear that base and disgusting material problems are combining with the terrible whirlwinds of his inscrutable inner life. You have come to grow fond of him now and can share my concern. Now he is always staying in different places, first with Wolde[193] and now in Potsdam at Pension Starke-Rettberg. I am worried about him, and not without reason. Could you write to him? And perhaps ask him to come to D. for a time? I have the feeling that someone must intervene from the outside. Everything about him is taking on that certain strange physiognomy. So, too, his relationship to S. B.[194] They wrote me about his love for the girl. He writes her, as she tells me, and would like to take her for his wife. Not for the first time. To which she responds, trying to let him down gently. Believing that it will make him happy, I mention to him that I saw the girl a couple of times. He writes to me in response that that is no longer of interest to him and that the girl has vanished from his memory; he says he will manage to absorb the blow, etc. It is all so spasmodic, so dark; indeed, it is terribly hard on me. I would be happy if I knew that you saw him again.

One more thing: I have finally gotten hold of Müller-Hofmann. He is in Munich, where he finds himself in the most deplorable situation imaginable. Poor fellow. He is painting plates, which a friend of his fires and they then try to sell. I sent him some money, as much as I could, on the spur of the moment — I try to do what I can; I'm surrounded by *nothing but* people in this type of situation. Now I have finally gotten rid of Pannwitz;

---

193. Co-founder of the *Bremer Presse,* in which H. v. H. took great interest.
194. Sybille Blei.

rather it is Hebra[195] who has relieved me and taken him on himself. Perhaps you know someone you could write to who would be willing to send a few hundred Marks more to M. H. if you ask. This would make me happy. His address is: Willy Müller-Hofmann; c/o Gräfin Holnstein; Isabellastrasse 25 IV, Munich.

I have wanted to read *Die Bauern* by Reymont for a long time. I am glad you get so much out of it. Wasserman's new book is much stronger than one would have ever suspected he was capable of writing. Strauss spent last week here. We vigorously expanded the project for the Salzburg *Festspielhaus*, just as Reinhardt would have it. I hope we will have a very nice performance of *Faust*, Parts One and Two,[196] there in 1921.

Do you have the third volume of Nadler yet? You will find it very enjoyable!

Yours, Hugo

Degenershausen, 27 March 1919

Surrounded by suitcases and boxes – a situation of total unrest – I quickly send you this note to let you know that we are going "home." If the new strike does not prevent us from leaving here again, we'll depart on Saturday. Mädy has been in Weimar for several days now, where Luli is to be confirmed on the 6th; it's going to be hard for Mädy spending this day without Eberhard and without one of us, but one is only allowed to enter Weimar for a compelling reason.

It is good that we will be leaving when she is gone; otherwise it would be too hard, and the best thing of all is that Rudi really did send two letters several days ago promising he would be coming in about four weeks; however, it probably will not be this soon. Then he plans to spend a few weeks here and to visit me afterwards. It surely would be wonderful if you could also come then or if Rudi and I came to Aussee. He writes that he has gone through a terribly difficult period emotionally and that he needed peace and quiet and time away from Germany in order to pull himself back together. Now he is able to get a lot of work done. We are all looking forward very much to seeing him. No answer from Borchardt yet despite the many letters and invitations *urging* him to come. (No one can approach him. It is such a pity; he surely could very easily stay there.) Müller-Hofmann was not able to come, as he is absorbed in work on a big painting. I hope to get some money for him, although it's difficult now, as *everyone* who has some is overextended.

---

195. Wilhelm von Hebra, writer living in Neubeuern.
196. This did not come about.

Take care. Whenever you wish to think about me, you can find me in the dear old little house.

My sincerest regards to everyone,

Yours, Ottonie

🍎 🍎 🍎

Rodaun, 14 April 1919

I thank you so very much for the letter you wrote on the 27th of March. It was such a joy for me – to at least hear a little something about the few people who really are a part of me. Oh, to remain constantly separated!

I would have responded sooner, for it has been ten days now since your letter arrived, but I have been ill the entire time, with the flu, etc., and a constant, low-grade fever in addition to feeling rather weary. If only the sun would decide once to shine for a few days straight!

In the meantime another letter arrived from Borchardt; it was very animated, almost too feverish in fact – this time even his lovely handwriting appeared quite frantic. He has all sorts of plans and again a new publisher; he wants to publish thirteen volumes – if only there will end up being one! Tell me, Ottonie, did he really continue reading more of "Durant" to you in Degenershausen than he did to us in Berlin?

Well it was exactly one year ago that we said adieu to one another. I cannot remember when it was that Eberhard and I said our last goodbye. Did he leave before me, or I before him? Thereafter I received two more beautiful letters.

Yes, life and death! Do you remember the charming Finnish Swede whose acquaintance I had made and of whom I had grown so fond? She was marvelously well-educated; I saw her in Kristiania for the first time, and again in Stockholm. (Surely I told you about her back then: her name was Frau Odhner, and she was a Griepenberg by birth.) She would sometimes write me a letter, and then Christiane entered into correspondence with her and thus had a "friend" in her, and she was looking forward to paying her a visit next year – suddenly, two days before Christmas, a telegram arrives from her husband: "My dear wife died yesterday of the flu."

Christiane is so excited that you want to have her come to Hinterhör. And I will also be very happy if you do it. I am certain she will not be a burden to you; she is a sensible, uncomplicated creature, and that is the best thing about her. And she would benefit immensely, in a thousand different ways. You could teach her quite a few things, for she does have quite a few little bad habits and tends to be careless, and now is still the right moment to correct this; but Gerty really is not a very good teacher, and it truly is more difficult for mothers than for someone else. When do you think you would like to have her? In July? And do the regulations allow for you to have someone there as a guest? The poverty here is truly awful; and each region cordons itself off from the others. I rather doubt that we ourselves will be allowed to travel to Aussee, and by no means with guests – oh, certainly not with guests. After all, we have nothing to eat; now even the horse meat, from which we have subsisted for the past year and a half, is no longer affordable and no longer available. But this misery will pass in time – and again one will find some way to exist – whatever it may be, as long as one is not constantly pressed by material needs.

You wrote to Gerty that I should not allow myself to be weighed down by property taxes and other such things. I really believe you hardly know me at all and have very often misunderstood what I said. I truly loathe money, Ottonie; everything having to do with money I loathe: earning money, having it, and managing it I loathe just the same as paying taxes on it and parting with it – I dread every single contact with it. Until I was married, I had no idea that money even existed; how I would love now to be able to forget this, to live in a world without money, while providing only the most basic essentials for the children. What do I care about the dreadful stuff?! How horrible the "good years" were as well; and this whole world, and the castles that looked like beer halls and the beer halls that looked like castles. And everything: whether or not one has this or that house, or furniture – or paintings – when it comes down to it, I am so indifferent to it all. My entire life depends upon very, very different things – the climate above all, and having time to myself. Spending the entire winter huddled together with Gerty and the children in two rooms because we had no source of heat and no lights – this takes a great deal out of one's nerves. Oh, God, to sit down in an old tower or in the middle of some partially collapsed ruins in South Tirol or in Italy; how wonderful it would be – and the food that I really like to eat costs one and a half Liras a day; and to always wear the same suit, and the same old shoes, until they fall off, is what I love most of all. So that is not what is weighing me down, for God's sake.

Please do write me again *soon* – about whether you are really there and what is going on with Rudi.

Yours, Hofmannsthal

P.S. It doesn't make me at all happy that you have started reading Treitschke. It is this man's damn narrow-minded and prideful disposition which has brought on all this well-deserved misfortune.

Have you had a chance yet to look at the third volume of Nadler, which contains the beginning of the 19th century? He is wonderful. Has Rudi read Nadler? Make sure he becomes familiar with him!

I have been wondering whether Hebbel's diaries and letters are among the books you have? Please let me know. If not, I will have them sent to you from Berlin.

Several weeks ago, before I was slowed down by my silly illnesses, I took Whitman with me while strolling through the meadows here; I benefited considerably from this.

I saw Mell now and again. He is working on a charming book comprised solely of short stories, a kind of story of his youth. It is as lovely and clear as the pebbles and the trout at the bottom of a crystal clear brook.

Have you by chance seen Wassermann's new book? People have all sorts of opinions about it; I myself have none. The older I get, the more difficult it seems for me to have an opinion about anything, with the exception of that which is very *good*.

[Neubeuern] 27 April 1919

Can you imagine, I really truly am here, indeed; I am finally here in my beloved little house, and it's delightful, or rather, it is going to be. On the 6th of April we, that is Baby, Christa, Puppy[197] and I, arrived in Neubeuern; I began right away to arrange things, for after having been closed for five years, you can imagine how horrid it looked here. Suddenly one night we had to move here. Everyone slept on mattresses on the floor. We lived for several days in this muddle; then everyone except for Puppy and me moved back to the castle, and now we are hard at work arranging everything. It is a good thing we have so much to do right at this moment. We are completely cut off from North Germany and have not received *any* news from there for almost three weeks now, not a single line. Would you be kind enough to inform Mädy that we're doing well and that there is no need to be concerned about us. All sorts of things are happening, but nothing dangerous. Tell Mädy to also write to Sondershausen and Oldenburg about what she hears from you.

Your letter arrived in the middle of our complete isolation from the mail; I was so happy to hear from you and to find out that at least you are doing well. That must really be dreadful spending the winter without wood or light and all so close together when you want to get some work done. We had it good there in the Harz; we still had everything we needed and lived in seclusion! But I cannot tell you anything at all today of how things will turn out, whether Rudi can still come visit me here now, or Christiane. Everything is so vague right now. Who could possi-

---

197. Helen van de Velde.

bly know if we will have anything left or not? I will of course manage my life, and if I must earn some money, then I will take in young girls who wish to learn something about running a house and so on.

No, Hugo, I know very well that you can manage without money, that you can live, perhaps, or rather would much prefer to live, without money in a dump somewhere under the southern sun; however, the thing that I would always like to relieve you of is the agony that money causes you – having to concern yourself with it.

Yes, Borchardt did continue reading more of "Durant" to us than he had back then in Berlin, a splendid continuation which I hope he will finish. As far as all his plans are concerned involving new publishers, I am afraid not much more will come of them than has up to now.

I must tell you, I did not get very far beyond the beginning of my Treitschke – not because I did not enjoy reading him, but because I really had too much work to do in Degenershausen, and now it seems it's a good thing I stopped.

Yes, I have Hebbel's diaries; only unfortunately I lost the second volume on one of my trips here from Vienna. Julie just received the third volume of Nadler. I am going to borrow it from her and will read it once I have finished decorating the house.

I read Wassermann's most recent book. There is indeed something quite strange about it; when reading it, one often has the feeling that he knows you. It certainly seems to be the most interesting book he has written. I myself do not have a strong desire to read it again, as I very much do in the case of the *Polnischen Bauern*; I simply find it a *marvelous* book. You really should read it. So often I find myself thinking of it. If the scent of the soil in spring should fill the air again, I can at once picture entire scenes from it, or on a rainy day – oh, and so on and so on.

Do you know what makes me extremely happy now? The Japanese screen! I am afraid, Hugo, I will not be able to return it to you very soon. It is like a painting to me; and every aspect of it is so beautiful. I wish so much that you could appear here – oh, just once, if only for a brief moment. You, too, would find it cozy here with me now, and warm. I cajoled some cherry branches into bloom near the stove, and now the entire house is filled with cherry blossoms and, oh, how happy they make me, and how much I am enjoying being at one *with myself* again.

Good night then. I hope you receive these lines. Could you simply send a card to let me know?

Warm regards,

Yours, Ottonie.

P.S. Despite everything I have a tremendous trust in the future – if only I may hold onto my little house and the harmony I feel within myself.

❦ ❦ ❦

[Neubeuern]
Whit Monday [9 June 1919]

Do you find that the longer you have not seen people, the more you long to be with them? Often now I have such a burning longing for Eberhard, and instead of becoming more used to not having him, I feel just the opposite. So often I feel like a garden in the countryside without a fence, with nothing to hold onto. That has been missing to this point: one's own, self-contained world, and the dividing line, which helps one to become aligned with the outer world. Eberhard was such a fence; he provided a feeling of protection and through him I was always able to face things anew! Here I often feel very intensely what it means to go through life without a man, feeling so alone inside whenever I am surrounded by the dear young people, which is delightful; and it makes me happy, indeed, to be able to give a great deal to them. However, I really do miss the exchange and taking part in the work of a true man (here in the castle, too, I get to view only a grotesque caricature).

It is just awful that you are also unable to come here and I can't go to Aussee; I could make your stay here so warm and cozy now and had so hoped to have Rudi here sometime soon and thought you would also come then. Now we have these horrible regulations that forbid us from having any guests here.

Did you know that Borchardt is in love with Rudi's little singing niece and they want to get married? If he didn't write you anything about this, it is better if you don't mention it; I don't know if Rudi knows anything about this yet either. Rudi is not in Degenershausen yet, and they were already expecting him there by the beginning of May; I suppose he will again have a hard time leaving the Hague.

My life has finally reached port now, which is more wonderful than I could hope for. My little house is warm and cozy the way I was able to arrange it with very modest resources; the people are very nice and touching the way they look after me, and I am completely free of the castle, which is best of all. Just imagine no longer having to fear the court, being able to travel without essentially having to request permission and needing only to pay a short visit there on occasion. And then later being able to have guests that suit *me*; oh, if things stay this way, that is, if they are not disturbed by external factors, then I will be very happy.

Today I read such lovely sonnets by Keats, truly wonderful, and last night the one about the sea, the waves of love, with its charming introduction. Hugo, it is wonderful how you are able to bring a person into such close contact with beautiful things. Just now I am so interested in

Grillparzer's[198] life. How wonderful it is to be with all my lovely books again, in this world that you surrounded me with. Reading here is really wonderful; it is tremendously joyful here. And as I no longer read newspapers following this humiliating offer of peace (because I get so indescribably worked up), the Spartakists leave us in peace here at the moment – who knows for how long. In this way I am living in my own world, consisting only of flowers and my wish to have you, Rudi, Borchardt, all of you, here.

I have talked about myself so much, but how are you doing now and what are you working on? Please, if you have time, do write a few lines to

Yours, O. D.

❦ ❦ ❦

Rodaun, 11 June [1919]

Your letter from the 27th of April arrived on the 10th of May. Once again it has taken close to a month. The passage of time, even of particular events, has become especially baffling ever since 1914.

Christiane has written you in the meantime. I very much hope that she will soon receive word that you can have her come and stay for a while. The most likely possibility would be sometime in July, because in the middle of August, it would be more difficult for me to do without the little one who serves as my typist. However, it is incredibly important to me that she spend some time completely surrounded by the atmosphere of Hinterhör, and I cannot begin to tell you how much she is looking forward to this. The child has a sense of the people with whom I am truly connected, and consequently she feels attached to you and, in her imagination, to Borchardt as well, whom she has never met; undoubtedly his poems will, once she learns how to read them, provide her with a tremendous presence. A letter Mädy wrote made me happy, as it made frequent mention of Borchardt; she indicates that he is experiencing an especially sublime feeling of joy which allows him to resist the general state of misfortune – and a further indication of a person who seems to mean a great deal to him and of whom I should have already heard but have not – if this does not refer to you; on the other hand it seems to me that it's someone else. The name "Marel"[199] appears, which I have never heard; and finally there is even an indication that he would like to come visit me soon. However, this is all indirect; and I'm about to leave (that is, sometime between the 6th and 10th of July), assuming Aussee will be willing to have us. I went ahead and wrote to the government agency in Tirol to request a

---

198. Franz Grillparzer (1791–1872), Austrian poet.
199. Schröder's niece, Marie-Luise Voigt, soon to marry R. Borchardt.

residence permit for myself. I am a bit tired and weak from being ill and could use a few weeks of solitude in the crisp mountain air. However, it is highly unlikely this request will be granted.

Even if they do let us travel to Aussee, it is out of the question that we shall be allowed to bring a guest with us, including Yella.[200] The regulations have become exceedingly strict in our land of hunger. (Will you be allowed to invite Christiane? Does she need to have any other papers besides a passport? What foodstuffs should she take with her?) I thought of the following plan then: The premiere of *Frau ohne Schatten* in Vienna is scheduled for the first of October. Please allow me to count on your being here (i.e. not for the first performance, which will be accompanied by hundreds of unpleasantries, but rather for the second one) and staying with us here in Rodaun and going to Dürnstein or to Aussee, in short, spending at least two weeks with us (1 to 15 of October). I cannot stand always being separated from the people who belong to me.

Write me soon, first and foremost about yourself, and then also what you know about B. or Schröder; it keeps me alive to hear a little bit of news.

Yours, Hugo

P.S. I am working on the next to last chapter of the fairy tale; it is shaping up nicely but demands a great deal of effort. For my strength is reduced.

P.P.S. Do you own the Meier *Classiker-Edition* of *Kleists Works*, one volume of which contains the *Briefe* [letters]. I read them while I was ill, and once again they left a strong impression on me. I would like to have the ones you do not have sent to you right away.

Perhaps the library at N. has Michelet's *Histoire de France*. The Germans unfortunately have nothing resembling this type of book, one which truly reflects the nation's history. Read a few volumes sometime – the 12th or 13th or 14th century. History reads completely differently now since we have experienced the full brunt of its dreadful power. The nation, of course, will easily survive this and may even emerge having attained a higher degree of development. For us as individuals, it is difficult to avoid becoming a lost generation. Borchardt, Schröder – this is my fatherland, and this is my age. Everything depends upon what we make of ourselves!

---

200. Yella Oppenheimer, old friend of H. v. H.

Fusch near Salzburg, 19 July 1919

Dearest, do you realize that I am not far, not far at all, from you and that this fact remains a constant part of my awareness and makes me very happy? That is just how dependent man truly is upon reality, which he constantly believes he can transcend; and I am so tired of continually contemplating the incomprehensible distance which surrounds us – and of addressing this distance. When I climb up a steep path in the woods here behind our house, I look out across the valley which lies in front of me to the north; and I see from the northern valley in front of me towards the north and west, out into the open, and then on towards two rocky mountain chains not far off in the distance; the further, more pronounced one is the Kaiser range, and behind it – how close it is – the Inn flows from Kufstein to where you live, and I feel as if I could grab hold of the little house and hear your voice.

Dearest, it is a strange relationship the two of us have – and it is a special twist of fate that we were brought together and continue to be kept apart without our ties to one another being entirely severed. When I think of those many encounters and separations, the interference by other people, particular circumstances – how eerie, like the days of spring in 1911; then others that were so charming and wonderful. It has been a true odyssey, but the image I hold of you inside me remains untarnished and, how shall I put it, as fresh as spring water which has not yet been tasted. This analogy crept into my pen because everywhere here streams of cool, brightly shimmering water emerges from between the roots of trees and the rocks, and one wishes to bend down again and again to touch with one's lips this unfathomable, crystal clear life. So, too, is the feeling I have of your presence, pure and strong, and as simple as water. However, I must do without you too much. Constantly I wish to expand the sphere of my life, so that it will surround you completely; for you are a woman, and you want to be enclosed by the magic of the intellect – and the ground beneath us continues to move, tearing through the faint outline of the circle and even forcing me from the confines of my true existence – sealing me off from those people who are the closest to me. Years pass in this manner. What a strange life this is. I no longer know if I am young or old, rich or poor when it comes to the most meaningful things. Has everything become skewed, or is it slowly, secretly preparing itself for a good end? Is there something there or nothing at all? There I sit in seclusion, in a narrow, green valley enclosed by a ring of glaciers, hearing nothing but cowbells and falling water, surrounded by thousands of fluid memories of my early youth – is this close by? Is it far away? I know absolutely nothing.

I sometimes have such vivid images of the people I must do without that it is as if I could touch them. I wrote to Schröder a few weeks ago; he scarcely seems to respond. If only I could imagine him staying with you, so close by; I could think of crossing through Kufstein to come there for a few days – in five, six hours I would be there – but all the bolts, all the chains! One must simply bear it. If you know anything about him or if you have heard anything about Borchardt, then please write me. This is the never-ending refrain.

Christiane obtained all the papers she needs, so she will be able to come for two weeks or so when you call her. She needs only to send her passport to the embassy, and then they will take care of the visa for her. The child's wish to be with you and to share your life there is so alive; she is lured by the place there, which is different yet also familiar. It would be so wonderful if her wish could be fulfilled, for after all, one is only seventeen years old once; however, do not force anything if it is not meant to be; nothing good comes of trying to force things.

You have Albrecht Schaeffer[201] there; I am very eager to hear what you are able to make of him. I understand the way you have of seeing a person, and then I am able to see him, too. There were various things of his I found beautiful, some very beautiful, and then there were other things I found dark or of no consequence. He does have a gift for poetry without a doubt, but what is this? It only makes for a difficult life. Is there something more sublime to be found behind this, the delicate jewel, upon which everything depends? You will have a better idea, once you see how the man lives and you experience his own aura. Depending on what you discover, I will either count him among those I respect, or perhaps not. I am not going to allow anyone to impose on me, neither by virtue of momentary fame nor by busy people. However, there where I can hope to find the exceptional, and above all the pure, there I myself will make a gesture, without waiting to be called.

You probably will not be able to guess who it is that I often think about: it is your daughter. I believe I will become a good friend to her later. I recently came across a book here that, strangely enough, I had not read: *Oliver Twist* by Dickens, the famous story of the boy who falls in with the thieves and murderers. I immediately began to ask myself whether it might not be a book for Marie-Therese. The dear people in it are so charming and lovable; of course the bad ones are depicted with tremendous power and extremely graphically – if you give it to her, make sure you read through it first to see if the heinousness may not indeed be too severe and graphic. I recently carried *Hebbel's Gedichte* [Hebbel's Poems] around with me again for a few days from morning 'til night. It is a wonderful book containing a complete depiction of a profoundly dark life; have a look at it again sometime and read to the child one or the other passage – of course not from the darkest ones, but there are many pic-

---

201. Albrecht Schaeffer, writer (1880–1950).

tures of such wonderful purity which a very young soul should be able to absorb; and one must not try to keep from her the *premonition* of darkness, as long as, at the same time, one provides her with the feeling of powers and sanctuaries that are able to overcome the darkness.

I already gave you the screen[202] a very long time ago. Did I really keep forgetting to mention this? I love the little house, and I love the contrast that such a strange and exquisite object can make when placed within four plain walls. Maybe the world will become more congenial, and one will be able to find the *one* lovely painting!

Adieu. Write to me soon – and then I will be twice as happy, but please, please do not tell me that you are sitting in the train or are about to start. You will leave the first half of October open, right? The date cannot be fixed, so try to be a little bit flexible around this time!

Adieu.

Hugo

❦ ❦ ❦

[Hinterhör] 25 July 1919

Yesterday I experienced something so wonderful; it was such a wonderful feeling I had deep inside me, unlike any I have felt for a long time – the Isenheim Altar.[203] Hugo, how magnificent it is; something about it is so incredibly remote and yet so very close by – you think it is a part of the present and yet feel that it belongs to eternity. In my mind I still can see before me the figure of Mary lying stiff in a large white sheet in the arms of St. John; only a genius could have performed such magic.

Then I took a quick look at the Rubens' Cartons and saw two beautiful Rembrandts – the old Turk and the angel who emerges from the darkness; then I left trembling inside with joy. Now it always accompanies me, this brightness, even though it is a dark and rainy landscape I see outside – but what does that matter when, indeed, the world has such glorious things?

I also went to the opera, but it was really pretty bad. It was a new comic opera called *Dandolo*; I felt as if I were sitting in a small town theater somewhere in the suburbs. The actors were poor and so was the libretto, but for me it was all offset by the splendor of Isenheim. Then I arrived home and found your lovely letter, which was such a kind welcome for me here in my little house. You are so near, so terribly near, and yet we will not be able to talk to each other, for Rudi will continue to dawdle be-

---

202. A six-panel Japanese screen, gold background with white flowers, which is still in Marie-Therese's possession.
203. A triptych, painted by Matthias Grünewald (early sixteenth century).

fore coming; in fact, he has not even arrived at Mädy's yet and had planned to go there before coming to see me. However, I certainly will come in October – I will make sure I am free the *entire* time. In fact, I am generally very free and unburdened now; I can arrange things the way I like and enjoy doing so very much. Mädy spent two weeks here; she talked about Borchardt, whom she had met in Berlin and found inspiringly youthful, made happy by the presence of the nightingale,[204] to whom he is presumably already married. They plan to have a proper, bourgeois wedding in Bremen in a church and with a wedding veil and the obligatory, tactless speeches (as B. says). They just wanted to wait out the divorce, which was supposed to be finalized by the beginning of June. Then they planned to go to Lake Constance for a while; this is all I know but hope to find out more details from Mädy soon.

Müller-Hofmann announced his plans to come to Degenershausen; I am sure he will let you know too, soon after he arrives there.

We also went to Kassner's recently, Mädy and I; we had dinner there in his charming, northern house. His wife was not there; he was so fresh and cheerful, so truly wonderful in a world filled with swindle. He gave me *Le Feu* by Barbusse to take along, which I had difficulty reading (difficulty because it is so gruesome); but now I have seen the war, which is terrible indeed. Then we discussed Wassermann's *Christian Wahnschaffe*; he also found it an unpleasant book containing a few very brilliant passages, but nothing more.

I very often read *Hebbel's Poems*; I am especially fond of them, and strange though it may seem, I have already read some of them to the child. She loves poetry, although I do not believe she understands any of it; however, the rhythm is pleasing to her. She is a little creature with a distinct sense of rhythm. We read some of *Oliver Twist* to the children around Christmastime, and Baby was so moved by it that she could not sleep for several nights. She is really a very simple person with all kinds of interests in the practical side of life; she adores spending time with her animals, the little chickens, cats, etc. They are her life's enjoyment. However, she is very sensitive, guarding herself against every form of sadness. I find it so sweet that you think about the child. This autumn when I come to visit you, she will be going to stay with the van de Veldes in Uttwyl on Lake Constance; it will be the first trip she takes without one of us. She is looking forward to it very much.

You know, Hugo, our life here is charming. Everyone has his work, and the children enjoy a lovely, carefree childhood. My brother[205] has brought a great deal of music into the house. In the evening, he always

---

204. Marie-Luise Voigt, because of her lovely voice, studied singing.
205. O. D. S.'s brother, Albrecht von Schwartz, being jobless after the war, moved to Hinterhör, where he tended the garden.

plays the cello, with the governess accompanying him on the piano; now we are also searching for a violin so they will be able to perform chamber music. Of course my brother is by no means someone to whom I can relate on an emotional level; he does not share my interests, however, he is such a helpful and good man, who is always working on something outside that it is nice to have him here. Van de Velde was here as well as Puppy's fiancé,[206] and they got to know each other here, father and son-in-law, and both took to each other very well. It would be *extremely nice* for me if Christiane were to come. I always wonder whether she might not spend all of September here and then go back together with me to Vienna? By then I am hoping our district, too, will be open. We here are the only ones who still do not permit guests to enter, because recently we had such a terrible hale storm which caused tremendous damage, so much so that absolutely everything was destroyed. The vegetables in the garden were doing splendidly; we lived off them, and now there is nothing left and again I have to have canned food brought in from Munich. All the windows at the castle are shattered; the greenhouse is now a heap of rubble, it really is miserable. But what keeps me going despite all the misfortune, which of course thoroughly assails every one of us now from all directions, is the incredible feeling of being here alone by myself – to finally belong to myself and to sit here in this little yellow house. I am almost like a child in it the way I feel such warm affection for every little chair, because it is my chair and because I can place it where I want; I provide every little flowering plant with constant care because it is here with me in Hinterhör.

Well, shall I really be allowed to keep this wonderful screen for ever and ever? Then I can feel even happier looking at it, as I will no longer need to worry about returning it. Hugo, it is a world unto itself; for me, it is *the* picture. I often sit there and turn it so that another panel faces the light; I look at it and become a part of it. Do you find it strange one's being so attached to things this way? Of course, I am also able to give it all back – I am sure I could. But then I would have to have something else in place of it – maybe a great love. But do not think that I am undergoing some curious change and am entering an age when a woman gets foolish ideas – although I of course feel that I have been living a strange life for a long time now and doing without a great deal; however, I understand this and therefore will not do anything silly, such as losing myself; or if so, then only in a beautiful painting or something.

Yes, Hugo, what you wrote about the two of us really is true, the way we always manage to find a way to each other and then to let go of each other completely; this is probably necessary. Without you or your being a

---

206. Jochen von Schinckel, an industrialist from Hamburg.

part of my life, I would not have begun to make of my life what I have, and the rarity of seeing one another, of being unable to share in the experience of your work as was the case during the war, was a great sacrifice for me. Instead there was Eberhard, who often needed me (or rather needed my cheerful nature), also a few nice weeks with Rudi and Borchardt – and even with Pannwitz at the start. But none of them are for me what you are. I cannot imagine being any more deeply connected to someone emotionally; something inside of you keeps me going without any conscious effort on your part. You occupy my thoughts infinitely more than any of the others do. And now I can see you there in the valley walking alone, stopping to look into the water and musing about yourself, about other people and your relationship to them, and asking yourself, "Is this me, or not?!" Hugo, I believe you are still young, very young, yet mature in so many ways; and then one does not know if one is old now, or quite the opposite. And indeed you are rich in the most important, which one's self is not permitted to know with certainty – but others sense it.

You asked about Schaeffer. Yes, well there is really not too much to say. I still did not see much of him (which, however, is my fault). But no, the man really is nothing truly special. In my mind, he does not possess the true mystery of art, he gave me a book of his, *Gudula*. It was of little interest to me and contains only a few true sentences, in my opinion. He does show a love for all that is beautiful and true. Of course, I enjoy every now and then having a person with whom one can discuss a book. On the whole, I suppose he is more a man's man than one for women. I found his wife has a pleasant personality. You may perhaps be able to enjoy a nice walk together sometime, however, he will probably never occupy a larger place in your life.

Well, once again now, I have gone on and on chatting to you, as I have not for a long time, and now I want to stop. For the first time I read something by Kassner, which I was always afraid to do. It was *Der Tod und die Maske* [Death and the Mask], and I found some very wonderful passages. I very much enjoyed reading Rilke's[207] *Rodin*[208] last night.

Say, do you know of a nice book about Beethoven? Kassner strongly recommends a new book by Keyserling; unfortunately I have forgotten the title (it is not *Die Indienreise* [Journey to India]).

Take care, Hugo. When you think of me, know that I am living in harmony and am not in a rush.

Yours, Ottonie.

---

207. Rainer Maria Rilke (1875–1926), poet.
208. Auguste Rodin, French sculptor.

Aussee, 11 September 1919

For a long time I saw before me your letter from the 25th of July, as if I had received it only yesterday. All the sentences fresh in my mind for so long, like good, healthy flowers cut early to make a bouquet and remaining fresh for a long time.

That one may see with one's eyes a thing like the Isenheim Altar is so wonderful, but equally wonderful and rare is the gift you have to fully take this in, the capacity to allow yourself to be filled with it. In general, you are, as is your nature, thoroughly unique and must accept yourself as such. No, the thought never crossed my mind that you were entering any particular age and might take to foolish ideas or to some other fixed pattern or commonplace notions. You and your particular fate are simply one, and I thank God that I have you and wish to have you even more.

You may be right about my still being rather young in a certain respect. I also feel this way whenever I find myself flooded with ideas and images, which to seize hold of not even decades would suffice; or when I am all alone pushing my bicycle through a mountain valley, as I did the day before yesterday crossing over the mountains to Salzburg to meet Reinhardt, one last time to think many things through together; in the magnificent town which is so dear to my own heart, with you close enough to reach out and touch, the moonlit night so beautiful that I did not wish to fall asleep, and I pulled the settee, upon which I had lain, out onto the open balcony, falling asleep, my eyes still open, before waking up again to discover the towers and the beautiful river illuminated by a different light; and soon the ghostly midnight hour, and soon the ghostly morning arrived – who experiences this? A young man!

I am very glad that you are able and want to have Christiane stay with you. This means more to me than I can tell you, and she is also looking extremely forward to coming. She senses exactly who can be of help to her when she needs it; in general, it is one of her finest traits to freely and openly accept and adopt what others have to offer. There is not a bad bone in her body, and she has many good, natural qualities: a natural balance, tact, *bon sens*, also discretion and modesty – but still too little upbringing. She does not know – *au pied de la lettre* – how to walk and stand and sit properly; she often speaks too freely, too much, and is indeed too carefree, regarding her appearance as well, nor does she look at herself in the mirror in order not to see her bad complexion. And as to her disorderly habits, please don't permit them. and do inspect her room every now and then; it should not look like a Polish student slept there. With one word you can accomplish more than we can with a thousand. Gerty is really not an educator, nor can I be when it concerns a girl. However, she will be very pleasant company for you.

One has to patiently accept her bad complexion; it's something between a disease and health. Gerty tried a hundred different remedies and went to doctors and quacks – it only got worse. The most intelligent doctor I believe in said to leave it in peace, else this physical problem will get worse and worse.

She will be leaving here at four o'clock in the morning on the 17th and arriving in Rosenheim at 8:30 in the evening. I suppose it will be difficult for you to have someone pick her up then? Please send me a telegram right away with the name of the inn with which you are somewhat familiar and where she could spend the night by herself; and reserve the room for her there so that the hosts realize she belongs to someone.

Please send a petition with an explanation concerning family matters right away to the police headquarters in Vienna (1 Schottenring) for permission to travel to Vienna and the surrounding area sometime between the 2nd and 7th of October for a two-week stay, and include along with the petition the *10 Crown bill* enclosed in this letter.

Now please send a telegram right away with the name of the inn in R.

Yours, Hofmannsthal.

[Hinterhör Station] 9 November 1919

I wonder, are you still there in Aussee and are you able to work? I suppose so, and I hope the third act[209] is nearing its end. Is it? I wanted so much to be able to tell you something positive about the magazine by now, but unfortunately, there has been a ban on train travel here for some time; therefore Frau Heiseler was unable to come. After the 21st, one should be allowed free travel. That is also why Bärby[210] and Christa got stuck halfway here in Meineweh, so that I also can still not respond to all the questions about Switzerland. It seems there is only one thing that I have managed so far, and that is to find a man for Yella's cows; please tell her, won't you? I will write to her as soon as I have arranged everything with him; as everything must still be put into writing with the man, it will be a long time now before all is settled. I will send a telegram at once regarding Mickelsch's money once I receive word that it has been deposited, so I hope that it has long since reached him.

It was so lovely there with you, Hugo, and it was really difficult for me to return to life here in my brother's world. But the little house is just as charming as it was before and is filled with a delightfully clear sense of

---

209. *Der Schwierige*.
210. Barbara von Sprecher, a Swiss friend of O. D. S., who replaced Marie-Therese's governess for a few months.

harmony. I am really looking forward incredibly to January and to you and Rudi, if only he will be coming. Afterwards I am going to write to Clärchen and ask her to find out whether he is coming. Julie ran across Borchardt in Munich completely by accident; he was there together with Lina for two weeks and is hoping the divorce will finally go through now. All of a sudden without my making an effort another boarder arrived here: Karin, however, probably only for this month. One didn't know what to do with her; Christiane will be very envious of this.

A shipment of books arrived with the new Kassner and Tessenow, which I find is *excellent.* He would surely be someone for the magazine. I have also been reading *Krisis* recently and must say the whole thing is tremendous, despite what Borchardt thinks.

Because of you, I really have made a lot of progress; I am able to see so many of my books in a different light again. Schaeffer immediately wrested the fairy tale from me, so I haven't been able to read it to Baby yet.

How I wish I were still in Aussee; I would be able to take walks with you and listen to the wonderful things you read in the evening. However, it was a good thing that I returned, for the house was already lacking a great many things. Take care. I am grateful to you for so very much.

Yours, Ottonie.

❦ ❦ ❦

Aussee, 13 November 1919

Dearest, I sit here in the dim light, too dark to read and too bright to light the lamp, thinking of you and that I wish to write you now and say adieu to you for Aussee (because perhaps I will be traveling home the day after tomorrow; Schereschewski[211] telephoned; he happens to be in St. Gilgen and has his car with him and would like to take me along) – then I heard a knock at the door and was handed your letter.

Yes, the third act is nearly finished, including the all-important scene with Cari and Helene. I will finish writing it either today or tomorrow, and I have also made the most crucial changes in the second act. Andrian's harsh but fair criticisms were very helpful here: I made some changes in the scenes of the "girlfriends" and left out quite a lot. It was too much of a struggle for poor Toinette; it was almost lugubrious. Then I made the scene with Helene and Neuhoff longer and more powerful; one sees more of Neuhoff and, as a result, more of Helene as well. But now the final scene is much lighter, more suited to comedy, and at the very end, everything is left more undecided and doubtful.

---

211. H. v. H.'s brother-in-law.

You have taken so much upon yourself, Ottonie – Yella will tend to the correspondence on account of the cows and the man; and don't bother about my stay in Switzerland. Please take this very light-heartedly, as a truly minor matter, for I have now come to understand here that I – not without torturing myself – cannot tolerate long country sojourns in the winter. However let's make *sure* we stick to our plans for me to visit Hinterhör and do not create an *embarras de richesse*. Instead, perhaps at first I could be there alone for a little while, and then Rudi and the others could come! It goes against my nature; my entire being depends upon the rich foliage; the dark countryside, stripped of all its leaves, is ghastly, and neither am I particularly fond of the snow. After your departure and then Irene's, I endured five or six wholly miserable days here. I completely collapsed; under the dreary, eternally lead-gray sky, I could hardly make it from one moment to the next. A single morning during such a time seems like a month – one of my funny little crises, and I also had a bit of a fever. What rejuvenated me and truly brought me back to life were the wonderful letters Pannwitz wrote about the fairy tale, one after another. Every day one arrived, so full of warmth and tenderness and boundless encouragement. Then all at once I felt better again, and I was able to work, not only on *this* particular comedy, but also on another one, *my bourgeois gentilhomme*, which has a Viennese quality that you will find very amusing. An enormous number of crucial ideas for this one has come to me in recent days, which at times even make me laugh.

the 14th.

I found so touching your little note that you wrote me the night before you left. I really wanted to get up and say adieu. I woke up at a quarter to three and thought I would easily be able to remain half awake in bed thinking of something for half an hour; then, however, I fell into a deep sleep, and when I awoke again, you had long since gone. That which you wrote about "giving presents," that of course works both ways and is not at all one-sided. I couldn't even begin to define for myself what I receive through your presence. Why should one try to define it anyway? Your presence is a very powerful thing; it is true presence, and therefore neither does its *fluidum* allow itself to be known, aroused or remembered – it is simply there, when you are there, and unfortunately away, when you are away. It is like a very pure and clear water that does quench one's thirst but from which one wishes to drink more and more. It is similar with Gerty – although she is of course on the other hand a very, very different person. Those are the kind of charming, real women, who will, thank God, leave no trace behind at all in the history of literature, not a single letter which would "yield something," no indistinct, shapeless biography; there will be absolutely no chance for them to be compared with Frau von

Stein or George Sand! Several of the most charming of Goethe's girlfriends were like this, among others Minna Herzlieb with the "round little face," of whom people know very little and who was, indeed, the model for Ottilie and thus certainly a wonderful yet completely "uninteresting" creature.

No, Ottonie, you really are a very charming woman; and there is something about you which is so wonderful, as revealed by the fact that, after everything that you experienced, you are able to have an open mind and think well of P. and perceive the greatness in him. I find something like this incredibly moving; in fact, these are the only things that truly move me. One conjures up in one's mind false ideas about the difficult and trying aspects of something like this; it would simply be charming, wonderful and curious, and possible, if indeed it shall be possible!

However, you are at least entirely right about people constantly needing to reacquaint themselves with one another and that one was again just beginning to get acquainted.

I am sending this, by the way, as an open letter. Surely no one will read it, although yours was opened by the censors before it arrived.

You will enjoy Keyserling's book very much. It is a strange book. Only a member of society, coupled with tremendous intellectual training – thus perhaps only a Baltic nobleman – could have written it. *Die Deutsche Lehre* [The German Lesson], on the other hand, which I delve into more deeply each day, is a stupendous wonder of a book; one can say nothing more about it. We want to do everything we can to see that this book makes its way among the poor, confused Germans who have lost their self-esteem, and should lead them to themselves with its wonderful sense of fairness and infinite balance.

And Herr Schaeffer, an average poet, should buy my fairy tale for himself; and let Baby, a terrifically receptive child, have *the* fairy tale right away, so that she might gain some sympathy for a nonexistent friend of her delightfully existent mother.

Yours, H

Rodaun [presumably 19 or 20 November 1919]

Dearest, I am just writing a few lines to say that I know through Christiane that you were once again forced to go on one of those harried trips, which I dislike so much.

It is a constant cause of torment for me now that I burdened you with so many concerns in Aussee. On the other hand, I am now left, for lack of any notification – which I should probably interpret as negative notification – completely hanging regarding the magazine matter; I must therefore treat a number of things as undecided and would probably do better not to prevent Mell from making other plans in the meantime.

The most important thing to keep in mind, however, would be this: I would have to know by the 15th of December at the latest if it would be possible to come to Hinterhör around the 10th of January — it would be impossible if Herwarth, whom I never again wish to see, remained at the castle. Also, would you be so kind as to obtain a room for me through the head mistress of the college in Berlin sometime sooner or later.

I would then first of all like very much to come with Gerty in January and then to stay on — perhaps I would leave from there for Berlin. I would like to go to Switzerland (if the Hodler is finally sold — Burckhardt is, like all very elegant men, terribly ineffective) around the beginning of April and then go on to Italy for a little while.

I hope more than anything that no one will ruin January for us. Have not received a single word of thanks from Rudi either, for the fairy tale, as one might have expected. Neither has an acknowledgement arrived from Degenershausen for the fairy tale and two letters, sent to mother and son. One begins to wonder if these copies ever arrive.

I hope I will have a little news from you. A very profound essay by Pannwitz will be appearing in the December issue of the *Neue Mercur*.

Yours, Hugo

[Hinterhör] 7 December 1919

When I arrived home a few days ago from Constance, Eybach and Munich, I found a huge pile of letters on top of my desk; there somewhere in the middle, almost hidden, lay the dear letter you sent me from Aussee. Right away it made my little house, which was already so lovely, feel so cozy and warm. Thank you very much. Well, now it has also been nearly three weeks that you have been back in Vienna; I hope you quickly overcame the feeling of collapsing, through the help of Gerty's courageous and caring hands. I hope there is not once again too much coming and going and feeling cold and hungry? Bärby and I were about to look for a nice place for you in Switzerland but decided not to after your letter came. I suppose it would be best then if you left for Berlin from here. If so, then send me word here so that I can set out to find a nice, pleasant place there for you to stay.

Yesterday I finally had the meeting with Frau Heiseler. She is going to speak with the publisher on Wednesday, and should he be able to provide the money, I shall go to town on Thursday to speak with him myself, so that at least the preliminary matters can be taken care of before you and Rudi arrive. I really do hope this will be possible, for I am becoming more and more convinced of the need for a literary niche of tranquility to sprout among the other magazines during these hectic times. Keyserling arrived here yesterday. Many thanks. But so many new books! I am completely overjoyed and very proud. However, I probably will not manage to get to them during the next few days, as I am right in the middle of Christmas preparations.

How lovely that the work you continued to do on the comedy went so well and that you found so much enjoyment in your own, special Viennese atmosphere. And then you received such good letters from Pannwitz; how nice of him. There, however, his good qualities revealed themselves, and if one always knows, as you do, just when to remove oneself, then indeed, he will only give of the treasures which he has to offer; and his profound understanding – and his love for your art truly is great and has, indeed, for me, in addition to his brilliance, always remained the link to him, with no sentimentality whatever. I really would like to read them sometime, these letters. Couldn't he possibly discuss the fairy tale somewhere?

What is going to come of the nativity play in Salzburg? It will surely be too difficult for you to go there, and how do things look with Aussee? Will you be there for Christmas? But the plans for Hinterhör remain firm, right? Sometime during the first part of January. Rudi will be coming then, too. I am looking incredibly forward to it and only hope that you will truly be able to feel at home here. Please come at the beginning of January if at all possible because Mädy is coming around the middle; she will be staying in the castle but will of course often be here with us, although I do not think she would be a burden on you here in these healthy surroundings with all of us. I will also try to postpone her visit as much as possible.

Well, addio. Warm regards,

Ottonie.

P.S. I had a nice, capable man for Yella; however, unfortunately she got one herself. Oh well, it may even be for the better. I read lovely letters of Kleist in the evening.

❦ ❦ ❦

Hinterhör, December 1919

As a result of the unhappy forwarding having taken such a long time, this letter from Rudi did not reach my hands until now. As I know *what* a profound effect the contents of it will also have on you, I do not have the courage to try to keep anything from you, for I find withholding such things only makes them worse, as one's imagination then runs wild and is free to roam far off course.

Poor Rudi, poor Borchardt. It is impossible to say whose misery moves one more deeply. I replied to Rudi right away and assured him that, as far as I knew from your plans, you surely would not drop Borchardt, especially not now that he is in such great need of support. I also told him how you had seriously discussed this thing with Eberhard back then. Borchardt must simply be measured by different standards, and if one were to drop him now, then all of his enormous potential will likely be lost forever. The letter Rudi wrote Borchardt is wonderful beyond all measure; what incredible warmth *must* have radiated in his direction from within every word. Hugo, what an unspeakably difficult journey it is, this little bit of time on earth, especially for all those who venture slightly beyond the confines of an average existence!

One thing comforts me in all of this, and that is that you will soon be here, four weeks from today or tomorrow, and that Rudi will be coming then and we will be able to discuss everything and you will hear more about it and will feel less burdened as a result. Today it is of course impossible to say whether Herwarth will be gone again; as he has been back in Berlin for several weeks and will not be arriving here until the 19th, I cannot say anything about this. However, I will let you know right away, but after all, you don't have to see him either, for he really never comes here and of course will not come when you are here. I think it is *delightful* that Gerty is coming, too; I no longer allowed myself to hope for this.

I immediately sent a telegram about Mell, because it is still too uncertain regarding the magazine, especially if Borchardt has become *so* uncertain. I will, however, still go to town during the next few days in order to have the preliminary discussion I already mentioned.

I will write to Puppy again about your Hodler right away (even though you really were not too keen on having van de Velde involved in the sale); she is really quite practical. She'll be going to Zurich after Christmas and can get some information on the current prices when she's there. How much are you expecting at the very least? You could also sell old pieces of jewelry there which do after all bring a lot at the present rate of exchange.

I send this letter with a heavy heart and would ask you, if you are unable to reply, to at least send me a few lines through Christiane.

Faithfully, Ottonie.

[Hinterhör] 11 December 1919

I forgot to include this lovely poem of Rudi's.

I wonder if you might already have received my letter. What I wouldn't give if you could be here right now and experience this magical, sunny winter day with the countryside covered with freshly fallen snow. We could walk outside and talk about everything. It was strange how you sent me Pannwitz's letter about Borchardt right at the same moment my letter about Borchardt was about to begin its journey to you. Pannwitz really is *so* right about many of the things he says there. In general, I find he had (incredibly) good sense of truly everything. He almost always views things so accurately from within his loneliness, so naturally, although probably in too sharp a light. You know, Hugo, a very subtle fear has come over me in recent days; it is that to lose Borchardt would instinctively push you closer to Pannwitz, which, on the one hand, would be completely understandable and to be expected and would give you all the stimulation you need and search for – if only the excessiveness in this unhappy man would not eat up all your time and therefore endanger your work. But is it not true, that this fear is probably unnecessary?

I am still waiting for word from Munich about whether I should go there today or tomorrow.

Thank you very much for the *Inselschiff*.[212] What wonderful things you said in there!

I am sure Mädy has received the fairy tale; however, she is extremely busy furnishing the place in Meineweh, as Anga Douglas has rented the house beginning the 15th of Dec., so she will not have any time to write before Christmas. The boy wrote to me that he had received a letter from you; he is always somewhat bashful about answering.

Many warm regards to everyone, Ottonie.

Hinterhör, 29 December 1919

I come to you today with the best of wishes for the year 1920; may the general state of misery which surrounds us not also embrace your inner, personal world, and may you find the peace and composure needed to continue writing.

Your telegram said that you plan to arrive here between the 10th and 15th; I would like to ask that you wait until the 15th, as this family has the custom of celebrating birthdays, which you find so unpleasant; Baby's is on the 14th, to which the neighbors, who never visit us otherwise, might come; it would be better to avoid this. Gerty is coming, too, right? I asked Rudi to come sometime around the 22nd, so he may arrive on the 30th. He was planning to spend Christmas in Degenershausen but is not there yet; he will continue to have the same inhibitions to the very end. It is still uncertain when Mädy will be coming, probably not before the 25th either

---

212. A magazine published by the Insel Verlag.

since Luli has vacation until the 20th, so the first week here would, indeed, be completely free. I hope it snows by then; right now it is warm and is even raining. We had a lovely Christmas here together in the cozy surroundings. The room turned out wonderfully well; I am sitting in front of my silver tree right now and enjoying it.

So it will only be a few more days now before you are here; I am *so* looking forward to it.

All the best for everyone in 1920,

Yours, Ottonie

❦ ❦ ❦

Vienna, 3 January 1920

Dear Ottonie,

I must quickly express something unpleasant, very unpleasant for me most of all: I am a bit sick, without it having any larger significance, either for the present or for the future; however, my doctor absolutely refuses to let me travel before around the 5th of February. Thus the main concern is: will one be able to travel then? I hope so. Perhaps the very bad situation at present may have calmed down. Second: Could you still use me then for around ten days or two weeks? I hope so. The third matter: Will it still be possible to pin Schröder down (who might be glad to postpone coming until then?!)? It would mean so *incredibly* much to me to see him again during this time in our lives; it is fundamentally important for every aspect of our continued friendship that we should have an extended visit very soon. Please pass this on to him. I do not know where he is; he did not even thank me for the fairy tale – but indeed that does not matter. He should simply stick with me now and also show that he does by coming! Further: Will the people involved with the magazine continue to show so much patience? Perhaps they will, in deference to the technical difficulties. If not, then we will have to drop it.

Borchardt sent a wonderfully cheerful letter filled with pride regarding everything that is in print; he also mentioned in passing that he earned 30,000 Marks last year; he didn't mention anything further about all his trials (I would prefer he did not come to terms with them too soon). Marie Louise sent a very charming and exceedingly sympathetic letter expressing that she continues to hold onto him extremely tightly. She must be a splendid person.

Please do not lose your patience over this unfortunate, coincidental matter and write me soon and help to keep a few people together!

Hugo

❦ ❦ ❦

Vienna, 27 January 1920

My Dear,

The following in the form of a telegram, as I hear someone reliable is traveling to Germany now and the mail is as good as useless (this is the most trying of all that has happened to me during the past five years, more trying than the rise in prices). A few days after I had to cancel my plans with you, Gerty fell ill with extremely severe pains from a gallbladder infection. It started with a period of truly wretched pains lasting nine hours, with me here all alone with her in the attic apartment. Then she was given morphine; the actual attack was soon over, however she still suffers from the after effects, and also has a bit of a fever, etc.

My own health has improved in the meantime. Now I have no possibility to come to terms with Rudi. If one writes or sends a telegram into empty space, it makes waiting for an answer a tremendous strain on the nerves. I think the best way to combine things by far would be if he and I could come to your place for ten days around the 15th of February or so. Reinhardt had a telegram sent to me saying he plans on seeing me in Salzburg at the beginning of March – so I'd be able to save myself the trip to Berlin.

Maybe you can get hold of Rudi by telegram, perhaps through Beuthenerstrasse 7; it is truly vitally necessary that I see him soon.

From Borchardt a beaming letter, almost uncanny, his radiant spirits. He only touches upon what happened with a kind of cavalier attitude. I find the letter more uncanny than encouraging. From Pannwitz awful letters (sparing my person), a crisis of complete madness. He is living with a fourth woman, a girlfriend from his youth. If he does not go mad now, things should gradually improve.

I have not built a simple world for myself. However, one must hold one's head high. Here Müller-Hofmann and Carl Burckhardt are a tremendous resource.

Christiane sends her regards. With the help of a very sensible doctor, her complexion has almost returned to normal. Please send word soon.

Yours, Hugo

❦ ❦ ❦

Vienna, Stallburggasse 2, 6 February 1920

Dear Ottonie, my good Rudi,

The evening before yesterday, I received the lines Ottonie wrote on the 30th of January along with Rudi's letter from the 22nd, which I found so lovely in what it said about the fairy tale, and so profoundly grave and sad in regard to our friend. I was utterly overcome by sadness the following night as well as yesterday; how difficult it is to bear. This is how things stand now: Eberhard is dead, Borchardt's image has become terribly warped, so dark – oh, perhaps forever – although during the two following nights, the beautiful, the great, indeed the *good in the deepest sense*, which I experienced in him the past several years, have once again begun to well up inside me with tremendous force! And Rudi and I are being kept apart on such unhappy terms as a result of the unfortunate web of physical, mechanistic circumstances. Oh, why did Rudi have to be so punctual this one time! If he had come two weeks too late, then everything might still be all right! But now I feel so helpless and disheartened and sad as I hardly ever have before, and further I am not in control of my own life. You'll understand why: For three weeks now Gerty has been sick in bed here in the attic apartment, the pigeon loft, with no kitchen, no telephone (her gallbladder infection was just the beginning; then came additional pain, bleeding, fever) – and I, her only nurse, am sick myself, plagued by an old malady. I should have been resting in bed precisely during these past three weeks, lying down, warm. Instead I have been up at three o'clock in the morning many a night; I walked about feeling frightened. And now the thing is if I should catch a cold during the final stage of the malady, I could very easily get arthritis. And now the express trains have stopped, only unheated trains are headed for Salzburg; departing from Vienna is much, much worse than we came to know in November. I *cannot* travel like this; truly I am so drained that I would scarcely have the nerves needed for packing. In a week to ten days, if I could have stayed in bed in Rodaun for a few days, everything would have been better, and anything possible; and now I realize from a letter and telegram that Rudi *cannot* possibly stay. How is it all going to turn out?! Oh, God! I now hold the strings in my hand which are needed to start up a charming little bimonthly magazine geared solely towards the few of us; it will only be possible if I can discuss it with Rudi – and I really cannot bear to continue to exist so completely alone – however, if I could manage to maintain the productivity of those few people, at least intellectually, then I, too, would be able to further withstand the pressure exerted by this mechanism and could also help the others to bear it – but how can I even begin, if I am unable to see Rudi?!

Not knowing what to do yesterday, I asked him to come here as my guest – but he will not be able to; so again we are torn apart. God knows for how long! Ottonie, could he – simply as my guest on the trip and the rest of the time beginning with his departure from Bremen – visit you again in a few weeks, or in two weeks? (In Germany, I do not believe traveling is quite so hellish.) Then I could rebuild everything with him and could also give him comfort and joy! I am sure of this. How could we *possibly* arrange to meet?! As of yesterday, Gerty's fever has been much lower and the constant pain is less severe; I think in ten days I would be able to travel, but that of course does not help anything!

Perhaps I could meet him in Leipzig sometime later? But what a poor setting this would be by comparison!

Do give me any kind of answer. Find me a solution!

Yours, Hugo

❧ ❧ ❧

Hinterhör, 9 February 1920

It really drives one to despair knowing that you two apparently will not be able to get together, especially at a time when you both need to so very much. As you were not planning to come until the 10th, Schröder had made arrangements to do everything else he had to do in the meantime in Munich, in order to be able to go directly to North Germany when you departed from here. Stupidly Rudi did not bring any kind of identification along with him from Bremen and does not even have the permit required to stay in Bavaria, which now means he cannot apply for a passport for Austria here, and as things presently stand with the postal system, it would take too long for one to arrive from there. I talked with him over the telephone, indeed hoping he would still find some way to go to Vienna, but he said it was quite impossible. I cannot begin to tell you *how* wretched this is for all of us. Rudi and I had really been looking so terribly forward to seeing you; it would have been simply delightful. The warm little house is presently well-supplied with food, and in the evening Bärby and Albrecht play music; Rudi composed several nice pieces for cello and piano – we were so sure that you would recover here in a few days, and on top of this, the weather was perfect. Oh, Hugo, sometimes things start off so well, and then everything collapses right in the middle. Rudi arrived feeling quite exhausted; the whole affair with Borchardt, which of course was quite grotesque in terms of their particulars, had worn him out completely. He hoped to get a clear picture for himself here with you; now I instead discussed everything with him. Whether I was able to help, I do not know, although after several days, he did indeed begin to feel more relaxed and then wrote some wonderful poetry.

Well, now Rudi was wondering on the telephone whether you might not be able to come to Degenershausen during Easter, as he must make Eberhard's gravestone there at that time; if you can, then I might come, too. Rudi has so many commissions he *must* complete, as he now owns his house and must earn enough for himself and Dora.[213] In case you still decide to go to Salzburg after all to meet Reinhardt, you might perhaps join me here afterwards (aside from Degenershausen), along with Gerty, in order to recuperate here a bit? Poor Gerty, what she must have suffered, and surely she is still not completely recovered yet? I suppose you have suffered from malnutrition, or did things improve there?

We are expecting Rudi to arrive again this evening for one day; then I will be able to discuss everything with him again and will soon write. In the meantime, I greet all of you while feeling rather sad and I wish you a speedy recovery. Unfortunately I do not have the Stahlburggasse address and therefore not the one on Elisabethstr.

I am so sorry that P. is so mad again; how will this crazy mess end? Madness!

Yours, Ottonie.

Hinterhör, 11 February 1920

Dear Hugo, your letter that arrived today caused Rudi and me to feel concerned all over again; it is really terrible that poor Gerty had to go through such a difficult time. If only the pain is finally over now and you both have the chance to rest for a while. The circumstances there must really be as miserable as could be, living right in the city without a kitchen and without any kind of special help at all. Unbelievable that everything turned out so wretchedly because Rudi arrived on time for perhaps the first time in his life, despite being ill himself; what an unexpected thing for him to do. Yes, Hugo, at the moment, a reunion unfortunately really is not possible, but there are only about six more weeks until Easter; by then you will certainly be completely healthy. Of course I would be happier if you all came here again, but that will not be possible because of Rudi. Maybe you will also find someone by then who can take you along to the border by car, for traveling is not quite so bad here as it is there where you are. Geiger might possibly have work in Berlin then or might be able to make arrangements for some. If Gerty came along, that would be very nice.

The long letter Rudi wrote you today pretty much tells you everything, so I will only say once more that I hope you are both facing better times ahead and that you no longer despair, because our plans to meet will certainly come to pass in the near future.

Yours, Ottonie.

---

213. Dora Schröder, Rudi's unmarried sister.

❦ ❦ ❦

Hinterhör, 17 February 1920

Rudi's letter could not be sent until today, as I had to copy it again for Rudi himself. I am sorry that you have had to wait rather a long time, but I was not completely myself during the last days; I was in bed with a cold, or otherwise I would have written it sooner.

Then Rudi and I also discussed that it might be better not to schedule our meeting right during Easter but rather roughly two weeks after the holiday celebrations, say around the 21st or 23rd of April, and to stay there for the anniversary of Eberhard's death. That would give Rudi some more time now to work at home, and then it would of course be somewhat warmer there, which obviously would also be better. Mädy knows nothing about you and me coming; instead she should only find out once it is certain. Then I suppose you would send a few lines announcing it to her.

I hope so *much* that it somehow works out, for Rudi needs you, too. Borchardt has hurt him too much in every respect, especially in the area of production, that it is absolutely crucial that someone lift him up again. I have done what I could, although I of course realize that that does not help or mean a thing. Please write him something *soon* about the ode (which Borchardt, mind you, is supposed to have found good). Rudi also has a tremendous need for some sign of love, otherwise he will withdraw completely into himself.

He is such a wonderful person, so loyal, so wonderful the way he expresses everything, that it was a pleasure being together with him. Of course, we also laughed heartily at his crazy jokes, to which Bärby also added a great deal with her equally splendid sense of humor; often they both could not wait for him to finish the last story before beginning another, even better one. They both left us the same day, and Hinterhör has been very quiet ever since. Bärby is a great loss for all of us; I miss this friend, my brother, the ever-ready piano accompaniment, and for the children a very amusing and entertaining teacher. Rudi said she was the nicest Swiss lady he knows, too bad really that she could not stay.

I wonder how poor Gerty is doing now – is she able to be up and about again? Do you have anything to eat there? If not, she should come here to me.

Should Müller-Hofmann travel to Munich, he must not forget to stop by in Hinterhör; please make sure to tell him this.

Then please write me just a line sometime soon about how you feel about the whole question of our meeting, as afterwards I want to arrange a trip to Switzerland for Baby.

I am also very sorry that Pannwitz is acting so crazy again. God, how lucky I am to have escaped him and don't once again have to make a place for the "fifth one."

Take care, Hugo. I wish for better times for you and Gerty.

Forever yours, Ottonie.

🍀 🍀 🍀

Rodaun, 24 February 1920

Dear Ottonie,

I am dictating this to Christiane, as I must once again remain in bed. Altogether now I've already been sick in bed here for the past sixteen days, as has Gerty in the city apartment for almost six weeks now. You wrote that you would like to have her come to stay with you; however, she is not even supposed to get out of bed yet and walk around in her room, thus she cannot begin to think about taking a trip and especially not under the present circumstances.

I received your letter from 17th Feb., and previously the one from 11th Feb., and another one before that, as well as Rudi's long letter from 6 to 13 February. Do, however, always make sure to write open letters please; the authorities there open and therefore hold up every one of the letters you send. I am about to write a long letter to R., in which I will also comment on the *Ausseer Ode*. This fell into my hands, in an envelope, which also contained the deeply disturbing news of the incidents with B. What was I supposed to say about the poem? What is more, such poems of Rudi's, those which are the immediate result of life's agitations, are for me more startling and alien than appealing. Only a handful of men have been granted the ability to create out of agitation something truly poetic. Borchardt manages it sometimes. It is strange that Rudi does not recognize this afterwards.

Now about your suggestions. It is also my sincerest wish to go to Degenershausen sometime, and I would prefer it if we could postpone this until after March. For February and March have been bad months for me during the years following 1917. Therefore, after settling a few urgent matters in Berlin and Leipzig, I would like to plan on arriving in Degenershausen around the 20th or 21st of April. That is assuming the following: that from the start there is no chance that my stay will extend beyond the last few days of April and that my departure will not cause any awkwardness. For I have an opportunity, if circumstances do not take a turn for the worse, to go to Milan for a few days at the beginning of May and possibly to return via Switzerland under the most agreeable conditions for our continued existence. Following these six years of imprisonment in the dungeons,[214] this opportunity means so much to me, and I could take Gerty along, and she could spend two weeks recovering in a little Swiss hotel. This means so much to me that, as uncertain as everything is, I want more than anything in the world to avoid ruining my chances from the outset. The mechanistic recurrence of anniversaries of people's deaths as well as birthdays do not mean anything to me anyway. However, I would very much like to see Eberhard's grave in the spring, when the weather is nice, and if I can also meet Rudi there, then indeed there would also be a prospect of some happiness after so much sadness. Perhaps by June travel and living conditions will be bearable enough for you to come visit us and for us to go see Dürnstein and the Wachau together, as we had planned.

Yours, Hugo

P.S. I was certain that I would fall ill, and had Gerty felt better and had I forced the trip, then I would presumably be lying in bed now with arthritis in Salzburg. Instead, I have only a relatively harmless yet pronounced case of rheumatism along with a little fever.

Friedrichsfelde Castle near Berlin, 17 April 1920

Oh, Hugo, how very difficult life is at times. For weeks now we have really felt nothing but concern for Karin, who no longer wanted to stay at Binswanger's. We had finally found someone who wanted to take K. in when, on Easter Sunday, a telegram arrived from Binswanger saying that K. had run off; nobody knew where. We waited in agony for days until we finally heard that she was at a friend's in Berlin in the Sanatorium Westend. At first, we felt some comfort, but then two days later another message arrived saying that she had also left there, again without leaving any information behind. After several days of waiting, we received the following message: "Karin had accident, request further instruction." After this, we of course had to assume that she was dead. Mädy, the dutiful Herbst (who had arrived in Neubeuern several hours prior to this) and I left immediately for Berlin. A terrible trip, during which one thought of the most unimaginable things, which, however, did not turn out to be the case. A friend received us here at the train station and said that K. was very upset and told her friend that she wanted to commit suicide; however, as she often said things like this, they did not take her too seriously while still informing the doctor at once. However, by the time they came to her room, she had already gone. Nobody had any idea where, until they found out from the police two days later that her fur, her watch, wallet and passport were found at Lake Müggel. Now we are sitting here,

---

214. Referring to World War I.

Hugo, and waiting from morning 'til night and throughout the night to hear whether they finally found her body. It was so horrible in the Hotel Adlon under these circumstances, so Treskow invited us to come here so that we could at least sit in the peaceful surroundings of the enchanting park. Hans Wilke also followed us here. We still have to wait here until nine days have passed; if she has not washed ashore by then, we cannot wait any longer, as one can no longer say where she may have been carried off to. Indeed the latter would be even worse, for it would provide a certain sense of peace having her buried beside Eberhard in the quiet park there. The reason Karin left Binswanger was the beginning of her being legally certified; she thought we wanted to have this done in Switzerland and that it would be easier there than in Germany, which of course was all wrong. The one great comfort for Mädy is that she cannot reproach herself, for I found it touching how kind she always was to her throughout all of the last years and that she always let one of us negotiate with her. However, she is of course suffering unspeakably because of this whole thing; yet I still see it as a deliverance for everyone, for the poor child suffered unspeakable agony and Mädy was always faced with the horrible prospect of having to have her completely confined in the future.

We are going to Degenershausen on Tuesday and will probably stay there for a week. I would like to take Mädy along with me again, so that she does not have to stay there all by herself. Write a few kind words to her.

Are you coming to Germany now; when and where?

Warm regards, also to Gerty and Christiane,

Ottonie.

Salzburg, 8 June 1920

I am so very much looking forward to a peaceful, extended stay there – then you, too, would once again have a little pleasure from my company, of that I am certain.

Now then, the following practical concerns: The German passport office here would be happy to do anything for me, however they *can't* grant me permission to enter Bavaria (everywhere else, just not Bavaria), and neither can the embassy in Vienna do anything without an entry permit from the local district office (Rosenheim, I suppose). Is this manageable? Hopefully for three weeks! Then I would arrive during the last days of July and would stay until 18th Aug.; on the 22nd of August, Reinhardt is presenting *Jedermann* here in the open Winter riding school and requests my presence beginning Aug. 19th. If you can only obtain permission for a two-week stay, which I think would be rather short, then I wouldn't come until around 5th Aug.

Please send me a telegram to Rodaun as soon as possible; first about whether you can obtain it (perhaps through Herr Kanzler) or whether I should try to have the German embassy in Vienna intervene in Rosenheim on my behalf – and if so, then send the permission form to me in Rodaun.

To Mädy I shall write immediately in connection with the very disagreeable impression the muddled commemorative paper for Frau von Kühlmann made on me.

Warm regards, Hugo

🌺 🌺 🌺

[Hinterhör] 15 June 1920

This was one time when something really went quickly and easily. I just went to Rosenheim myself and received the entry permit immediately. The end of July is of course a very flexible notion; I did not wish to tie you down to a certain date, and in the event that Reinhardt should postpone *Jedermann*, you can certainly stay here until the 22nd, and if the weather stays nice.

It was so wonderful having you here; now indeed you have a better idea of how I live and can send your thoughts here at times. Here a very sudden and dramatic change has occurred as a result of Albrecht's sudden departure. He received a telegram asking that he come right away; now the garden is deserted, how sad.

I am looking incredibly forward to your coming here, Hugo, and hope so much that you can work here. Yesterday the American package arrived, two large boxes, which thrilled the entire house. There are really wonderful things; so you won't have to go hungry then either.

Mädy is in Munich, and I am enjoying peaceful days by myself, which is good.

With the sincerest recollections of all of you,

Ottonie.

🌺 🌺 🌺

Rodaun, 3 July 1920

Dearest, I feel truly happy a few times every day when I think about the certificate lying in the drawer which assures me of being able to come to visit you and to spend a few weeks there. Then you, I hope, will also once again benefit from me: only when I am surrounded by peace and quiet, and something or someone isn't tearing me in all different directions, trying to pull me here or there away from myself, only then am I myself, and if it is at all possible for some sense of pleasure to emanate from me, then this is the time.

Meanwhile I have been living like a dog here for the past three weeks, under the perpetual weight of an absolutely terrible weather system, with a barometer which refuses to budge from the lowest reading, and a musty, humid heat causing me to feel virtually the entire day as if I am in hell. I cannot produce a single thought, scarcely an idea, scarcely a letter; the mechanics of my daily life have reached disgusting proportions, like a dog that eerily approaches one in the November fog and looks as big as a horse. At the same time I realize that if only once a breeze were to blow in from the east, and bring a clear summer day with a hot, dry sky, then I could cast aside all this misery in a second.

I am facing a new, rather difficult project; this is indeed always a stressful moment, which other people are unable to imagine (what do we know of another person), however, that is not what is dragging me down so far and making me feel a stranger to myself – rather it is simply this demonic dependence upon the physical world, the atmosphere. The same damp, musty air, which makes it nearly impossible for the pen to traverse the damp paper, turns my thoughts to worms, and causes anxious nights, disheartening mornings, and miserable days. What a peculiar make-up we have.

You posed quite a few questions – about the nation, one's own, over which one cannot stop brooding – that now at times repeat themselves in my mind. However, I believe one should not ask a lot of questions – as with people whose personality one is on guard not to call into question; rather one simply lives with them, the best one can. Reading Nadler will do you good as it will lead you deeper into the life of the nation instead of viewing it from the outside; that is why it has a soothing effect and allows one to forget about asking questions.

You are very right to love big, long novels that are good. One shares in the life of the characters and moves within the scenes; in part one is in touch with the true meaning of it all, and in part, one is lured away from reality. You should always read one right after the other; novels and poems are different sorts of company, but both are good friends. Take from the castle some of Thackeray and Dickens; from the former I read *Pendennis* during the trip with such great pleasure, from the latter, while I was ill, *Great Expectations*. The one shows a marvelous understanding of the world, the other a great imagination; both are indispensable. If *Simplicius Simplicissimus* might be there, then take it along as well.

Order from your book dealer in Munich for me (and yourself), 1) the collection of pieces, and, 2.) *G. Buddhas letzte Tage* [Buddha's Last Days], from K. E. Neumann's *Buddha-Übertragungen* [Translations of Buddha's

Sayings] published by R. Piper Verlag, and pay for it with the small cash reserve I have there. To order books from Berlin is too much trouble, and R. Piper is located in Munich. If I can only accomplish something here, so that for once there is something on paper, then I will be so looking forward to August. I am planning to arrive on the 28th or 29th of July.

Hugo

❦ ❦ ❦

Postcard   Rodaun, 18 July 1920

I hope you received my letter. Since then, the quality of the weather has changed; and my work has advanced.

I expect to be in Salzburg on the 27th and at your place around the 30th, or at the latest the 31st.

The closer it gets, the stronger the anticipation and the excitement, and at the same time, the apprehension that something could interfere again. Send me a short telegram informing me that this is not so and you are expecting me.

Yours, HH

❦ ❦ ❦

[Hinterhör] 30 September 1920

Now we are finally back home, much later than we originally expected. In Switzerland we ended up staying for four weeks and thus did not adhere to our plans. We returned on Saturday and met Mr. and Mrs. Herbst in Munich, who came out with us and stayed for several days. Now it seems quite strange that you no longer emerge from the other house, as the geraniums are still blooming just as nicely and the weather is delightful and the leaves have only partially changed color. Last night your telegram with the inquiry arrived. Well, now I must first stay here for a few weeks; must get my provisions for the winter and must oversee the construction of a cellar. I hope to come to Rodaun at the beginning of November, assuming it is really convenient for you and a burden will not be placed on Gerty as a result? No news from Rudi. Mädy wrote that he left word that he would not be able to go to Austria again this year and asked whether you might not be able to meet him in October in Degenershausen. I wrote back saying I did not think so.

Our time in Switzerland was really wonderful; I very much enjoyed it. The van de Veldes are all gradually moving to Holland, then they plan to sell the lovely house they have on Lake Constance, a pity. In case your friend B. has Swiss friends who might buy it, V. does not wish to make any profit on it but to pass it on, as he took it over, adding only the small construction expenses he incurred.

For Herbst a change will probably also take place now in that he will be entering into a larger business venture in Munich. All of Mädy's things can be more easily managed and improved financially, as he will then no longer be sitting at the other end of the world. He will probably also go to Vienna now and again, which means that you will also have more contact with him in the spring. However, everything will be decided in time, so it's better that you know nothing about this as far as Mädy is concerned.

I wonder, did Deventer, who was in Aussee with Frau Kröller,[215] visit you? Henry had written to him that you were there, but we were afraid the letter might have arrived too late.

Many warm thanks for Christiane's letter; I will do everything the way she ordered it. Next week the blind colonel will be coming here for several days; I hope the weather will remain the way it is so that he, too, can enjoy it. I now also found a notice from the bank here, which informed me of your transfer, but *how* unnecessary, Hugo. I really enjoyed having her so much as my guest and not as a paying guest.

Then if all goes well, I will be there in about four weeks. I would still like very much to come to Aussee, but that's impossible.

Warm regards to everyone.

Yours, Ottonie

[Hinterhör] 15 October 1920

I hope you received my telegram. I spoke to Strauss' second secretary the day before, who said no. It turned out to be more difficult, as a larger sum was involved and more things stood in the way of matters of this kind; however, he said they had begun the process and that there is *no* reason to be concerned, as it is underway. T.[216] was unbelievably busy, as he was offered a rather high-level management position in Munich, which he has taken on. It meant an enormous amount of work for him, constantly traveling back and forth and training his successor; so I hear that it is a mixed blessing. This is the only way I can explain his not answering, although, like you, I by no means find this an excuse.

I wrote him again and am certain that you will have received an answer from him in the meantime.

---

215. Wife of Otto Kröller-Mueller, founder and owner of the van Gogh Museum in Otterlo, Holland, built by H. van de Velde.

216. Tyralla, banker in Munich.

My passport is at the consulate now; however, as the entry permit hasn't arrived from Vienna yet, I am not sure if I will receive the visa now – well, by the end of the month anyway.

Surely you are having weather just as gorgeous as ours, which means it will be very hard to say goodbye to Aussee. Are you better able to concentrate on your work now? If for any reason you prefer I not come to Vienna, please feel free to say so, for I would be very sorry if my arrival should, indeed, disturb your work.

I still have Eckstein here, whom I read aloud to a lot, with great pleasure, for he enjoys it so much. Yesterday we spent an enchanting day on the Heuberg with several other people, it was so wonderful.

Well, I hope that you or I receive a message from Tyr. very soon, so that you are not constantly kept from your work by these agonizing concerns.

With kind regards for everyone,

Yours, Ottonie

❦ ❦ ❦

Aussee, 19 October [1920]

A thousand thanks in a hurry – I have been working feverishly almost the entire day; I am alone with Gerty here. The silly, unnecessary matter involving Tyralla! I do not attach any importance at all to the 6,000 being sent here to Austria, only because you make it seem so simple! So arrange by cable for the 6,000 to be returned to you (rather to me or to you, than to Delbrück); the rest I will take care of.

Rudi canceled out on us, unfortunately. I'm looking *so* forward to your visit! Don't cancel! Send a wire to Rodaun in time in case your permit for Vienna is delayed, however they will certainly still give you a visa without one. Ask Wolde in Munich how he did it, for he was just in Vienna! Also ask him about *Dame Kobold*. Borchardt is with Marel in Horn near Radolfzell in Baden. They are not married as yet (a document is missing) but are very happy. "Durant" and "Verkündigung" [annuncation], one as wonderful as the other – you, too, have them both, don't you? He was planning to come here three days ago to ask my opinion about something; from Bregenz he sent me a telegram canceling, postponing it. What if you wrote him – suggesting he travel with you? In fact, some friendly words to both of them would be nice. One must hold these few people together. So, auf Wiedersehen in two weeks!

Warmly with best wishes,

Yours truly, Hugo

❦ ❦ ❦

[Postcard]   Rodaun, 27 October [1920]

I was working in Aussee up to the very last hour and hope to continue doing so here. I only realized later how tremendously valuable the few peaceful weeks in Hinterhör were for my work. I hope you arrive here around the 12th (14th) or so. During this time I will desist from working on this difficult, main project and begin preparing for the Beethoven speech I will be giving on 10 December in Zurich. I wrote a very friendly letter to Maria van de Velde; she did not respond with a single line. Why is it that, the more difficult the times, the even more unreliable and unfriendly individual people are, instead of the other way around?

Yours, Hugo

❦ ❦ ❦

Basel Rittergasse 20, 15 December 1920

Dearest – I just wonder if you are well again! Your lines seemed covered by a kind of veil, which depressed me the entire time. Perhaps – I hope – I am only imagining it resulting from my being in somewhat of a rush the entire time, sleeping too little, and the dark sky is threatening snow. By the way, there is much that is friendly and pleasant for me in Switzerland, and today I received a telegram from Kippenberg saying that his wife has a severe case of the flu, so he is not expecting me for New Year's. So I sent a telegram to the "Marienbad": "Reserve room evening of the 18th, cancel train ticket to Leipzig."

For I plan to stay one day longer, not leaving until the 18th, and then to stay in Munich for two days (19th and 20th). I hope I can count on Borchardt having given Wiegand the contents of the *Gespräche in Rodaun* [Conversations in Rodaun], as he is – if I can trust your telegram – now in Munich. (Why did *you*, however, give misinformation in the telegram to Gerty, and why, for goodness sake, did you leave poor Marel in suspense by not notifying her right after you arrived in order to ease her mind?)

And now this non-descript from Tyralla. The letter sent to Gagliardi[217] has not arrived. The harm done is beginning to become very serious as a result of the absurd behavior of this man. Everything depends now on Herbst, or whomever you wish to engage, to take the manuscript away from him in Germany as soon as possible and return it to me and then on our forgetting about Herr T. as quickly as possible. (This I would have desired as early as October.) Did he happen to hand over the package in

---

217. Somehow connected to Tyralla.

Munich? And what has he written anyway; what does he have to say, the beast?

That we must correspond about something like this!! Now I would ask you above all else – as I do not know how one can travel from Munich to Degenershausen in a single day – to thus send a telegram regarding this to me in Munich instructing the porter at the Marienbad to get me the *proper* ticket, for the 21st, instead of the one to Leipzig (which I canceled by telegraph, as you know). If only Rudi doesn't leave me hanging!

Please forgive all this. I wish for nothing more than to soon no longer have to correspond with you in this manner.

Yours, H.

❦ ❦ ❦

Degenershausen, 26 December 1920

Dearest, I had not expected to see you in Munich, and so I was not disappointed not to find you there – and indeed there was something wonderfully salutary about the realization that you were geographically close by. Dearest, what horrible, absurd moments I can have, as during my first few days in Rodaun! Can you not only forgive me for making such grimaces, but also quickly forget them?

I am really happy here; I am glad to have Rudi's company and again to be able to lift his spirits a bit (although today, for instance, I am nearly dead on account of the foehn); and the boy[218] – he pleases me so much. I find him more loving and intelligent than I had expected, as well as good-looking; he reminds me of Eberhard in so many ways! The way he laughs and greets you! I am so happy about this. I get along well with poor, good old Mädy; I am so glad I came.

From here I plan to go to Berlin for a few days (30th to the 2nd), then to Meier-Graefe's (Kaiserstrasse 4; Dresden) from the 3rd to the 5th, and to Kippenberg's (Kurzestrasse 7; Leipzig) the 6th to the 7th; I'd like to arrive back in Munich the evening of the 8th.

If it is no trouble for you, please let me find a permit in the Marienbad allowing me to spend ten days in Hinterhör; this I would need for the authorities in Munich. I will be busy in Munich for three days; perhaps you might by chance come to the city during this time. Then I could also come to see you for two more days.

One other thing. If you do not have a postcard there from Fräulein Auguste Adler[219] from Leopoldskron with information about Reinhardt,

---

218. Hans Wilke von Bodenhausen.
219. Reinhardt's secretary.

then write, or rather, please send a telegram to: Fräulein Adler or Fräulein Bernhardt; Schloss Leopoldskron Salzburg (Hofmannsthal, would like to know if Professor R. will arrive at the beginning of January); and wire me the answer to Meier-Graefe's.

Yours, Hugo

P.S. I saw T. in Munich; I did not enjoy being with him; again everything is still up in the air; I am going to discuss it with Herbst.

(On the outside of the envelope) Please forget about sending a telegram to Adler about Max Reinhardt; I have already received an answer.

❦ ❦ ❦

Hinterhör, 31 December 1920

I would just like to say very quickly that I will send the residency permit to you at the Marienbad. I am so happy that the get-together in Degenershausen seems to have gone better than expected after all; and it makes me especially happy to hear that you liked the boy. He really is a dear fellow.

Yes, Hugo, and the grimaces you made; because you have now reminded me of this, perhaps I should quickly say everything for once and then it can be forgotten. You know, I truly suspected it even before I came and that is the reason I asked again; why didn't you simply tell me not to come? I really would have much preferred this; as it was, I had constantly to fight the feeling of having arrived at the wrong moment, and this is naturally very unsettling.

I of course much prefer seeing you less frequently when I have the feeling that you in some way derive pleasure from me rather than experiencing me as a burden. That is why now I prefer to recall the time when you were here with me; it seemed to me then that we both enjoyed each other a little. Well then, now I've expressed it very openly, and now it is over with; and please promise me, if you should once again not wish to see me and don't have room for me, then please always express this openly.

But in closing I must once again thank you many times over for the wonderful Lucidor and the splendid volume *Prosaschriften*, which came just in time for the holidays and lay resplendent on my table. I would really almost prefer that you came here because getting together with Mädy in Munich involves so much palaver. However, I understand *completely* if you do not want to make such a short stop again and would rather travel straight through.

So many warm regards then and have a nice time everywhere you go.

Yours, O.

❦ ❦ ❦

[Dresden, Kaitzerstr. 4] 3 January 1921

Dearest, I will be in Munich the entire day on the 10th, and if I somehow can, the 11th as well, and I hope from the bottom of my heart that I will see your face; however I will not be able to come out to your place after all. This trip really completely took it out of me in every sense, wholly apart from the extreme torment caused by this summer weather in the middle of winter, and I can't now, without wearing myself out to the point of sin, once again (for the eleventh time!) arrive somewhere, unpack, pack, make connections, etc.; I *cannot* do it. The most taxing part of it all was purely moral: the encounter I had with Rudi in D.; both these men, Borchardt and Schröder, each of them puts all of his energies, which truly are not modest, into ruining the picture I have of the other; and so great are their energies, so demonic the ability of both to put forth the most deeply felt arguments, that – I must say it – both have succeeded to a certain degree. One must also be able to bear this thoroughly dreadful side of life, just as one must know how to handle the glorious and enchanting aspects of life.

In Berlin I found what used to be Reinhardt's theater in a state of disorder; it was almost eerie. They are performing – without even having thought to let me know – *Abenteuer* the day after tomorrow and *Die Florindoscenen* (from my first few sketches of *Cristina*), and Moissi will be charming in both parts; therefore I can swallow the whole thing feeling amused and emotionally virtually indifferent. Reinhardt again managed to arrange things so that I will miss him; I am going to miss him in Salzburg, will probably also miss him in Vienna, and he will arrive in Berlin 24 hours after I will have left Berlin. I can't help him or myself; I have to preserve my energies and my production – the rest will take care of itself then.

So I *hope* to see you.

Yours, Hugo.

❦ ❦ ❦

Tuesday [1921]

Dearest, I can understand very well, and yet nevertheless, I find it sad, very sad, that I am passing through here for the second time and cannot see your face – or find a single line (your card did not arrive until today); it is as if you, too, had already died.

The trip was hard on me and the preceding weeks as well, when I had to tear myself from my work, to which I was connected with every fiber. That is also why the weeks of November seem so unearthly to me; I feel as if you had not even been with us – were you here? For how long?

What did we do anyway? However, the summer stands clear and firm before me; perhaps I will be able to return.

Yesterday – last night – I spoke to Reinhardt here. He had come from Vienna; again everything is uncertain there, and it is all up in the air. Perhaps all the beauty will still materialize, or perhaps it has been wasted again.

The magazine affair between me and Wiegand, an earnest, honest and very agreeable man, was straightened out quickly and easily – only the material safeguard has yet to be determined. Mell will remain in Vienna as my secretary.

Yours, H. H.

ॐ   ॐ   ॐ

Rodaun, 22 February [1921]

Dearest, I wrote "forgive my grimaces," and you could have forgiven my grimaces, and then it would have been all right. Now, however, you've taken it up again, and I found your letter here; it traveled from Leipzig to Rodaun, from here to Berlin, and then came back here again. And it was a bit unfortunate, *the way* you took it up again – this turned it into such a problematic situation. I thought for a few weeks how I might answer it without the answer breaking us up completely; in the meantime I had books sent to you from Leipzig; I partly meant for them to take the *place* of an answer. Have you not received them yet, though, for I hear you wrote to Christiane and didn't mention anything about books. Have you really not received them then?

Dearest, in your letter you set an impossible condition. If you do so in earnest, then we can't see each other again for the rest of our lives, neither here nor there. Last summer at your place it was so wonderful; I thought this would have given you an idea of my nature and under what difficult and strange conditions I, too, am living, although I am not a man torn into two halves like Borchardt nor through some dark fate a semi-petrified man like George or Schröder. However, now you place on me the condition that I should in the future, for every meeting we have, be able to provide assurance beforehand that I will be able to focus on you and be *there* for you. Dearest, that is so womanly in the customary sense, so unlike your nature! What made you write this unfortunate letter? How am I supposed to meet such a requirement? No, then I should wish *never* to see you again. This past fall, on the 22nd of October, I tore myself out of a trance , for the sake of that unfortunate speech I was to give in Zurich; I walked about like a bloody infant just separated from its mother's womb – *everything* was a burden for me, I myself most of all. But how do you expect me to again drag myself over into that other world, to figure out whether this miserable condition will last two or four weeks or half a year – and after that, to make or alter "plans" – no! No! No! No!

I thought always you would come here in the fall because you enjoy the city, because that is your little sojourn in the city; and I was happy that you saw people here, Burckhardt, the theater – and as much of me as I can give. However, if you remove from this the harmless elements for all time, the reign of a lucky or an unlucky star, which reigns over every form of productivity – and every inclination means productivity – then you place an awfully strange and heavy burden right on the outermost end of the longer of the lever arms; then it no longer works. And I had believed you were my friend! Tell me, are you really hardly at all? Are you so womanly, so selfishly sensitive? Was there perhaps not a very bad southern wind when you wrote this letter?

Good night.

Hugo

Hinterhör, 2 March 1921

Yesterday I returned from Munich and found your letter here. My, for God's sake, what in the world was it that I wrote to erect such a wall between us? I wanted to bring about exactly the opposite, and *not* to burden you of all people; I do not want to be one of the many people who adds to your stress. It was precisely this feeling – that you, in order to make me happy, to make my stay in town possible, you had to tolerate having me in the house during such a difficult period of work – it was exactly something like this that I wanted to prevent in the future. Because I know *very* well indeed *what* your work means, precisely for this reason, I want to spare you, and indeed above all, not to cause you additional anguish. I really seem to have written at a very bad moment, if it sounded like a demand. I truly believe I *am* your friend; really I would simply like to do everything to help save you as much as possible for your work and for that which you have to give and must give and to clear out of the way any difficulties, which it is in my power to do. However, I have no talent for writing letters and always express myself so horribly stupidly in them, and as a result, everything turns out to be a ridiculous mess. So please do not misunderstand me; in a few brief words, what I wanted to say is to please forget about me whenever your work does not allow time for me, and do not let the thought, "Ottonie needs a little taste of the city," prevent you from doing so; this is what I wanted to say. Naturally I enjoy the city, the nice people, the paintings, but indeed I enjoy it a *thousand* times more when you write that you are in a productive period of work, and that which emerges from this is what I enjoy most of all. That is what I meant and nothing else!

Yes, and the books have arrived, however, not until after I had already written to Christiane. I enjoyed them so *very* much, everything about them; I constantly wanted – everyday I suppose – to write and thank you, but it was like an unfortunate fate, because the whole world seemed to need me. Not a single day was I alone – for the past six weeks my mother here, and in addition there were always other people; and in every batch of mail were letters in which someone wanted something from me, as if all my friends had chosen this time for divorce, and it was always I who was to provide counsel and assistance. Yes, my God, I am simply not able to help everywhere. In addition Christa has been sick since the 14th of January as well as Miss D. and also Julie. There are constant trips to Munich, the last of which unfortunately had the unhappy result that Prof. Müller noticed the same type of bronchitis in Christa that Luli once had, which seriously complicates our little operation here, as she must not have the slightest inkling of this – by no means is there an extra strain to be placed on her studies, which of course means that she can't keep pace with Baby. In short, I am a bit run down and really only wanted to write you a letter when I was feeling calm after having first dealt with all my own emotions; as a result, I am not really writing this. Mädy is not to find out about the entire scope of Christa's situation, although she of course will have to be told about the results. A ray of hope in all of this was the news that Hans Wilke passed his *Abitur* with dispensation. How happy this would have made Eberhard!

An additional little pleasure is that I got 2,000 Marks for Pannwitz from my nice friend in America (who, however, is apparently poor himself). I had asked him in light of the letter from November. It would be best if I transferred this money to your account with Herbst, and you will pay him off in Crowns. Is this acceptable?

Tomorrow I will be going to Munich with my mother and will be taking her to the theater, etc.; on Friday she will be leaving and I will return in order to enjoy some peace until after Easter, I hope. Then I have to go into town with the children for two to three weeks to visit the dentist; however, I am thinking of trading flats with friends so that it might then be quite comfortable and pleasant.

Now please, do not take this letter as a burden upon yourself again, but simply as an explanation of everything.

Yesterday the *Reden und Gleichnisse* [Talks and Parables] of Tschuang Tse arrived. Thank you very much. They have arrived at the very best moment for me; there you are met with so much peace.

Good night, Hugo. Do not think with anger, but with understanding, of this friend, who never wants to create but only to solve problems,

Ottonie.

🌱 🌱 🌱

Rodaun, 15 March [1921]

Dearest, here are a few lines for Hans Wilke, who is with you or will soon be arriving. Let us not speak another word about the other matter. I simply read your letter back then or a few sentences in it with completely foolish eyes.

I cannot write much. There are all sorts of things occupying me which are becoming muddled. There must of course also be times like these, although they are agonizing. The Reinhardt matter – his coming to Vienna for the performance of *Der Schwierige* – all of this has fallen through after countless reversals of circumstances. I must strive here to make the nearly impossible possible; with regard to material concerns, I must almost transcend the boundaries of possibility in order to keep my house here in Rodaun. Losing it – not today, but tomorrow – is a distinct possibility.

The magazine has become questionable again and again. A difficult period is simply taking hold of every individual in so many ways, such is fate.

Dearest, I found the copy of *Die Frau ohne Schatten* in the Hotel Marienbad; all the others please send to the Herbst bookstore if they have not already been sent.

Please keep what you have for Pannwitz there until someone finds a way to reach him quietly without a lot of trouble or paperwork on my part.

With the warmest regards,

Hugo

[Ink blot] Forgive me; I did not notice this until I turned the page over! How naughty – my dear!

H.

P.S. An hour ago someone telephoned me again to tell me that Reinhardt is indeed coming, however, without the actors. *Qui vivra, verra.*

🌱 🌱 🌱

Hinterhör, 27 March 1921

Hans Wilke and I were both so happy to receive your letters and together we send you our warmest regards for Easter. All of us are enjoying these magical, sunny days to the fullest on the meadow here in Hinterhör. Hans Wilke has really turned into a nice fellow and gives me a great deal of pleasure; he is so thrilled to be finished with school now forever that he would like nothing better than to kick out in every direction, like a young colt. At the same time, he is open to all that is good; he takes pleasure in nature and in every good word spoken. We go on wonderful excursions, which is also nice for the girls; my brother and Franzl are also here, and Mädy is swept up by it all. On the 5th I will be going to town with the children for three weeks to finally have their teeth straightened; I seem to have once again been met by good fortune – by finding a wonderful apartment from a Frau König, whom I have never met before. She is renting me the entire flat furnished, is also leaving me her housekeeper there, and on top of this, she is also providing me with food from her farm near Munich. But the most wonderful thing of all is that she owns three *beautiful* Picassos, which I will be able to enjoy during this time. Oh, Hugo, they really are so beautiful. If you happen to have anything to do in Munich, you really must come during this time; we could have a lovely time together.

Wolde telephoned me recently and said that there is still not enough money for the magazine. He will be coming here tomorrow, and then we will discuss whom we can still approach; I think we will manage it. Tomorrow there will be a singer coming as well as a very musical young man from the Baltic provinces; so we will surely have a lovely day with music ringing throughout the house.

It is truly awful that the house in Rodaun is causing you so many problems; if only it will be possible to keep it. And all the trouble with Reinhardt and *Der Schwierige*; it is always you who must endure this ballast; and just now when you need free time and peace for all the ideas that are forming within you. I truly wish that there were someone who would relieve you of all these everyday things, so that you would not be disturbed in your work. Do you already have an idea whether you might be able to stay in Hinterhör for several weeks again this year? And when do you think?

I read a lot of Keyserling to the boys, and we have good conversations about it on our walks.

Herbst was also here, and he has the copies of *Die Frau ohne Schatten* all organized. When is Christiane going to the big city on the Seine?

Take care, Hugo. Warmest regards from everyone here in bright sunny Hinterhör.

❧ ❧ ❧

Rodaun [1st half of April 1921]

That is good and right that someone lent you a nice apartment with three Picassos. You should at least be lucky in *these* respects, indeed, you deserve this.

I see the magazine in this way: either it will come to be, or it was not meant to be. I would like to spare Wiegand inquiries and the like as much as possible, for he is a man who spares himself very little. I hope you get to know him. He is a splendid man. However, I would like you to know (and indeed to tell him this on occasion) that I cannot wait forever for my things to be put to use – I must seek to make money from everything (reprints, individual publications, etc.), so that I remain free in the one most crucial respect (the *what* and *how* of my production). Thus if the magazine is published, i.e. if the first issue of the quarterly comes out no later than October, I can then have large portions of my new drama (the one I began at your place this past August)[220] appear in it in addition to writings in prose, aphorisms, etc. If it does not appear by then, I will have to publish everything somewhere else (because I expect the play to be performed sometime around November), perhaps by the *Insel Verlag* as a private printing, *Book of Friends*. I am going to Lucca and Pisa now (the end of this week) and perhaps on to Rome for ten days. The reason is to be isolated, and to truly find myself, without dealing with letters, lawyers, taxes, misunderstandings and other annoyances. I hope to be able to finish the drama for the most part. (Only the last two of seven parts are missing.) I will be back here again around the middle of May; until then, however, I must feel that the ground beneath my feet is firm regarding this matter (the publication).

At the end of June, I plan to spend three weeks in the higher mountains, perhaps in South Tyrol. I would like to arrive at your place on the 25th of July – if you are willing to have me again – and to stay for at least four weeks, if this is not too long.

Yours, Hugo

Pisa, 22 April [1921]

Seldom have I been able to recall and feel your presence so completely as I did yesterday morning in front of the grave of Ilaria del Caretto in the Cathedral of Lucca. Perhaps you, too, may never be so completely yourself as when you enjoy something beautiful: that is, of course, the most secret power of a thing of beauty: that it is able to unify for a moment our diffuse and scattered self.

I, too, have left my home in order to be alone and to reconstitute myself completely. May I succeed! There have been many trying and bewildering circumstances during these months, and also many a dark moment; and among these, Ottonie, I must count my encounter with Schröder, and yet I

---

220. *Der Turm* (The Tower).

can hardly say how or why. It is not as if his attitude towards me had seemed to change in the slightest; even regarding our tone towards one another, things were the same as always, both in serious and in lighthearted moments. And yet something else happened inside me, which is almost horrifying, and I cannot get rid of it. When I try to analyze it, it seems to involve his relationship to his own country. There is something there which frightens me and almost causes me to grow numb. The chauvinism of the man on the street or of immature people does not amaze me or at most irritate me. Such chauvinistic contortions, however, on the part of a soul of his standing – and to maintain these contortions, willfully, to the point of convulsion, to a point of absurdity – this is so hideous, Ottonie; and in it there is something wicked: it is terrible – and as if using a flashlight – B. pointed this wickedness out to me. I turned him away, I did not want to see it, did not want to hear about it nor to see it – yet I must see it. It is a half-conscious, willful act: a desperate attempt of withdrawal from a terrible case of self-doubt; transferring this, which one does not accord to one's own self, to the nation. How sad! How unhappy! What poor, lonely creatures we are. That I had to recognize this fact – and must pronounce it! But only to you, Ottonie. For, after all, we are connected to one another; somehow we simply do belong together.

Would you like to have me sometime around the 25th of July? First I should, indeed, perhaps I really should, spend two weeks in the mountain air. To go again to Italy in South Tyrol would be too complicated and so far. Now I thought about the Salzberg over Berchtesgaden. There I think it is more than 1,000 meters above sea level. However, I wonder if it would be possible to find a place to stay there. And whether one would receive permission to stay for so many weeks, in Bavaria six to seven altogether, this year?

I will be passing close by you on my way back – but the tiresome old border separates us! Do let me find a line at Greif's in Bolzano, sometime around the 8th of May.

Adieu, Hugo

❦ ❦ ❦

[Postcard]   Rodaun, 18 May [1921]

On the train I happened to hear from Kassner the welcome news that you are well and are still in Munich. You *never* did give me the Munich address – on purpose? The requested reply to my letter from Lucca did not arrive. I also wrote of practical matters. (I asked if I could arrive around the 10th of July, and if I would be able to receive a residency permit for five weeks.) Not a word from Wiegand-Wolde. Should I therefore assume that I am to give up the idea of the magazine? Vague news about

Borchardt through Kassner. How is his wife doing? The child? Is the "Durant" finished?

Many warm regards,

HH.

❦ ❦ ❦

Hinterhör, 23 May 1921

I am really very sad that you did not receive my letter in Bozen, for I sent it so well in advance that I was certain it would be waiting for you there. *Of course* you are always welcome, anytime; I scheduled the children's holiday for the end of August so that I will be able to devote myself entirely to you until then. In the next few days I will be going to Rosenheim and will get a residency permit for you to stay in Bavaria for six weeks; with it I hope you can also spend the two weeks in Berchtesgaden. I am *so* looking forward to your coming, I hope you will be able to work again as you did last year. I wonder, did you find the peace and quiet you were looking for in Italy? Yes, Borchardt and Marel are, from what I hear, supposed to be leaving for Lucca with their son – I have no idea whether or not they will. Seeing Kassner was very pleasant. He is always so invigorating and charming; I really like him a lot.

And regarding the magazine there were undreamed of difficulties in procuring the money, as indeed presently, the financial world has no idea what is going to happen, what one should do, what not; I do not suppose it was ever *this* difficult. Before leaving I asked Wolde to give you an answer *right away*, whether yes or no. He wanted to wait for one more meeting that they were supposed to have during the past week; however, I cannot help but think that it will turn out to be negative.

Christiane must certainly have spent some wonderful weeks in Paris with still more to come. I wonder if she will stop by here? Tell Burckhardt, too, he must not forget his spring visit here; I would very much enjoy seeing him. Julie, Mädy and Luli are on an automobile trip with Kramer-Klett[221] through Switzerland and plan to travel on by train from Milan to Rome and to stay there for two weeks. Won't it be terribly hot?

I had a lot of bad luck with my stay in Munich, as I spent eight days in the apartment and two weeks in the hospital with bronchitis. It was too cold for me with the central heating that did not work; we have become too spoiled for this out in the country.

You wrote in your letter that you would like to stay here beginning the 25th of July and before this to spend two weeks on the Salzberg. Are these

---

221. Baron Kramer-Klett, friend and neighbor of Julie.

still your plans, or would you like to arrive earlier? Please write me about this, as I have travel plans for later, but in any case, it does not matter to me *at all* when; I can arrange everything. Here the weather is gorgeous, and unheard of masses of wild ground orchids grace the fields – some remind one of the tropics in their size and splendor; all the vases are filled with them. I wish you could enjoy it with us. Steinitzer is here and keeps bringing fresh wild flowers and recounts a lot about his travels; how much he has seen!

Take care. My warmest regards for Gerty and the boys.

I hope your work goes well.

Yours, O. D.

❦ ❦ ❦

[Postcard] Rodaun, 29 May [1921]

Please forgive me for writing this way; everything is in absolute bedlam as far as business matters are concerned; it is so chaotic, complicated and tense that I will be *relieved* if the magazine does not materialize right now. (The manner in which one fails to inform me, however, is nonetheless quite thoughtless.) Please give me the liberty to arrive as soon as the 10th of July; I may have to go to Salzburg as early as the 15th of Aug. and will probably not go anywhere before Hinterhör; it is all too complicated.

Oh, you were ill again! And so seriously! Are you completely over it now? No more coughing? Please send me a short message *right away*. Christiane will *not* be stopping by.

Yours, Hugo

P.S. "Halbgerettete Seele" [Half-saved Soul][222] is wonderful, mysterious; I wonder how I could have failed to recognize this when I heard it in Rodaun.

❦ ❦ ❦

Hinterhör, 1 June 1921

I just received your postcard, which I want to answer right away. Of course you are also welcome to come as early as the 10th of July; it is good that I already know, so as to arrange our vague holiday plans accordingly. Otherwise, if you have to be in Salzburg beginning the 15th of Aug., you would again have too short a stay here, for last year we definitely had the feeling that three weeks was much too short; nor should one squeeze one's working periods too tightly together.

---

222. Poem by R. Borchardt.

On the 25th we once again celebrated another birthday here: this time it was mine. I was overjoyed to see *Der Schwierige* in print. I read it aloud to Franzl and a young doctor, who were absolutely thrilled and delighted; it was charming. I am very eager to hear everything you will have to tell – of all the performances, when and where and whether there were any at all. I imagine you miss Christiane a great deal and hence some of the muddle with all your paperwork, and so much remains undone. I hope you will soon find your way through it all again, so that the benefits of your trip to Italy do not disappear right away.

I am quite well again; I still have to rest a bit, which I now can do very easily here. Until recently, we had delightful weather, however, it has been raining heavily for the past two days, so I hope that the rainy period of the summer will soon be over, so that it will then be nice when you arrive.

I am really looking forward so much to your coming and hope desperately that it may be as relaxing as it was last year.

I also find it baffling that Wiegand still has not said anything definitive about the magazine – everything always seems to depend on another person!

Take care. Do not spread yourself too thin in too many directions.

Yours, O. D.

🙶 🙶 🙶

Rodaun, 14 June 1921

Dear one, you can hardly imagine how much I am looking forward to coming and how I now, as the time approaches, feel what it means to me knowing this refuge is open, where *everything* is dear to me. If the climate were also different, then it would indeed be paradise, which of course one should not enter here on earth. However, be that as it may – if it is only close to being the way it was last year, then the gain will be enormous. Even regarding so-called bad weather, I want to say, "Cool, rainy weather does not bother me at all!" If only you are well! Please try to be by the time I get there – I certainly do not want to wear you out.

Allow me, please, to arrive on the 10th. It may be that I will have to go to Salzburg as early as the 12th of Aug. because of the *Bürger als Edelmann* rehearsals.

Please make sure the entry permit is in my hands rather soon; this will put my mind at ease in a world where everything is precarious and uncertain! (I do not mind if H. W. is at the castle; I have seen that it is possible to arrange everything so that such encounters can be avoided.)

Things here are still up in the air, but not without hope. *Der Schwierige* will premiere in Berlin, Munich, and Dresden at the same time in the middle of November. Where is Borchardt? Is the child alive? Is it possible to share in his happiness, to tell him how happy one is? Yes?

Yours, Hugo

P.S. "Die halbgerettete Seele" [The Half-saved Soul] is one of the most glorious poems of this great poet. How could I be so foolish as to not recognize this when I heard it read aloud? I read it again and again with great delight.

Hugo

❦ ❦ ❦

[Postcard]   Rodaun, 24 June 1921

It is with the greatest joy that I hold the entry permit tightly in my hand. You did not enclose any lines! I hope you are not ill; however, as the address was written in ink, it eases my mind. I am looking forward to taking refuge there, more than I can say. I will be arriving on the 10th, or at the latest the afternoon of the 11th; prior to this I will be in Salzburg at the Österr. Hof for two to three days. Will be here until the 5th in any case. Everything is always up in the air; once again a very nerve-racking period for over five weeks now. Auf Wiedersehen!

HH.

❦ ❦ ❦

Eybach, Saturday [25 June 1921]

On my way through Rosenheim I only had time quickly to take care of your entry permit and therefore could not write anything. I wanted to get a few things for the children in Munich; upon arriving here, I found Julie there in bed with a severe gallbladder attack, which had overcome her on her way here. We had to take her to the hospital immediately, where she remains with a high fever and extreme pain. I hope things improve in the coming days, for otherwise she will certainly have to have an operation. I came here quickly in place of her, as my brother-in-law was expecting her, and because of his poor mental condition one must not risk disappointing him, which can cause him true fits.

I hope all the excitement with Julie will be over by the time you arrive. I will be going to Munich on Monday. Unfortunately, you will have to accept a young boy here on holiday, whom I have to keep until the end of July; for this reason your arriving on the 20th would have suited me better, but he will probably not bother us much.

Yesterday I had lunch in Munich with Borchardt and Marel, the two glowing parents. The boy was born two months premature, but they say he is in spectacular condition. He is to be named Kaspar, and from what I have heard, they plan to ask you to be his godfather. He will soon be baptized, and it seems that then nothing more will stand in the way of their trip to Italy. Take care. Tell Gerty and the children I say hello.

I am very glad that you are coming.

Yours, Ottonie

❦ ❦ ❦

Rodaun, 4 July 1921

Dear one, I immediately felt rather unsettled when the permit arrived without a note and thought something bad might have happened. I hope things have already begun to change around for poor Julie and that she may be spared a serious operation!

If only I find you once again in a state of peace there, emotionally as well. The holiday boy will not bother me much; everything is easy in Hinterhör.

I have tremendous longing for the tranquility there; you can scarcely imagine how I get more and more entangled in mundane concerns here.

If I had peace and quiet, in my present frame of mind, I should not want to write one but two new plays each year.

I will be leaving here on the 6th with Gerty, will be in Salzburg at the Österr. Hof from the 8th to 10th and hope above all to be at your place the afternoon of the 11th.

Please let me come, even if you yourself, which is hardly what I hope for, cannot be there on that day. I hope to find a line in Salzburg.

Yours, Hugo

❦ ❦ ❦

Bad Aussee, 7 September 1921

That is wonderful, Ottonie, that it is so lovely and good for you there; it all unfolds in your letter like beautiful pictures. And in October you will perhaps be coming here for a few days, right?

However, it is a terrible pity indeed that you were unable to come to Salzburg; every evening, except for the last one (the one evening sleepy Wolde came), there were outdoor performances on the cathedral square, and again everyone was extremely impressed, and you, who are so receptive, would have been even more impressed, and anyway who knows if you will have another chance — whether it will again be possible to perform *Jedermann* alongside *Das Welttheater* [The Theatre of the World]. You also would have attended a really pleasant soirée in Leopoldskron; you were already on the list. A quartet performed in the wonderful grand hall, and out on the pond atop a float alight with torches, was a singer, and the buffet stood illuminated on the beautiful garden terrace; however, I could not have accompanied you, for I lay in bed with Gerty looking after me. Yes, Ottonie, indeed I must say, Hinterhör in July is not the place for me; I completely collapsed afterwards and became very pale one evening just as on the way back from the Vosslers' that time; then came an attack of dizziness, and I barely made it up the steps and into bed – and I am still not *completely* over it; I am hard of hearing in one ear now and still feel a bit dizzy. Next July I must go somewhere in the mountains with good, fresh air, perhaps Gastein; however, I still want to come to Hinterhör every year, perhaps in May then; we will manage to arrange something, and you must make sure to take a week out for Salzburg. A nice room was also waiting for you this time; many children, including Isepp[223], met each train, *however*, to no avail.

I am content with everything you did for me having to do with the publisher. I just hope Herbst handed over the manuscripts he was holding in safekeeping to T. or Z.[224] right away; otherwise a most favorable opportunity to publish the first issue promptly would have been lost. You must tell me one other thing: whether they agreed to having my writings published anonymously at first or not, and whether experimentally a period of approximately three months could be scheduled for the entire project, as we had envisioned it. Then I should be able to view this with confidence, which indeed comes at a rather favorable time for publications of that kind.

I only intend to work in the morning, first on the fourth act, then on *Das Welttheater*; wherever one goes here in the afternoon, one finds pleasant conversation that keeps one's mind delightfully alert. We have Isepp here in the house; he carves little wooden figures of saints and is as content as a woman working her needlepoint; also, the weather is glorious, with the most gentle sunlight of early autumn, and again the moon is waxing – an enchanting summer.

Do let me know again soon where you are.

Yours, Hugo

---

223. Sebastian Isepp, painter and restorer.
224. "T" = Tyralla; "Z" = Zimmermann, a banker in Munich.

Aussee, 2 November 1921

Dearest,

Until eight days ago, I continued to waver back and forth as to whether I should insist in rather strong terms that you come here, or perhaps not; it was so wonderful and peaceful; then suddenly the weather changed and we plunged from summer into winter; now it has turned into a dreary, wet and misty autumn. Then Isepp canceled, and Burckhardt and his sister canceled; so I let it go, and it was probably for the best; I work nearly the entire day now and it is impossible for me to remove myself from this web. I intend to force myself to finish *Das Welttheater* here between today and the 15th of Nov. (I stopped work on this long play between the fourth and fifth acts, which is not good; one must dam the stream again and again when dealing with such a powerful mill.). In the meantime the premiere will take place in Berlin and Munich; then around the 15th of November I will be going to Berlin – in the meantime, Reinhardt has returned from Stockholm – and I will most likely be in Munich for four or five days from around the 25th of Nov. in order to reach a final decision regarding the magazine matter and, at the same time, Mell's future. As it concerns a circle of people and things here which also mean a great deal to you, and as every little shimmer of kindness and understanding is crucial in a world of confusion, where everything is becoming disjointed, it would make me very happy to have you close by at such a time if possible.

Please write me a word about how Julie is doing if you can and – in the most general terms – how things stand at the castle.

One more thing: Christiane will be going to Munich on the 7th; she will be arriving the evening of the 7th and staying for three to six days. She wants to see *Der Schwierige,* and also to take care of a few things for me. She would be happy to find a message from you with the head porter of the "Marienbad" – although she will be staying somewhere else. I often think of your room! Has the stove been set? Is the hanging lamp there? Are you changing the furniture? Everything should *become* a reality, not mere words. I have the fondest memory of all the hours we spent together in the house; the rest was simply physical.

Yours, Hugo

☙ ☙ ☙

Hinterhör, 22 April 1922

I have a very guilty conscience for having left you without any news for such an eternity! I was terribly busy with Christmas, was constantly in Munich and bought a house in Pasing in order to create a boarding school where seventeen girls can live. I had to see that it was properly financed, which was not easy; also to arrange everything involving the renovation of the house so the children can move in there on the 11th of May. But, Hugo, everything worked out for me so fantastically, with so much wonderful help coming from all sides that I am almost afraid, something like, "I shudder at the thought of the envy of the gods!" Then on the 11th of May I will be taking the children there, and with that the first chapter of my life here will come to an end.

I actually intended to rent Hinterhör to an American, had already begun negotiations, and here again an unbelievable thing happened to me: a man from America,[225] whom Christoph helped to begin his career in business, wrote me that he was now successful and that a small amount of money that Christoph had once invested with him has increased to the point that he is going to send me the interest, and, therefore, I do not need to rent the place. Isn't that wonderful! I had already begun negotiations with an American and, already with a heavy heart, I had come to grips with the idea that I would have to move around like a vagabond, beginning the 15th of May. Now everything is going so well. As all good things come in threes, I also found a valuable brooch which I had lost during Christmas. Are things also going this well for you? How do things stand with your work? Yes, and when and where are we going to see each other this summer? For the children's holiday I am reserved from mid-July to the end of August; however, any other time I can come to meet you somewhere, if this would give you pleasure.

On the street in Munich recently, I bumped into Isepp, who was looking for a restaurant. He had returned from Paris feeling so invigorated and gave such a delightful account of everything that it felt like a breath of fresh air from former times. This winter we had an endless stream of comings and goings here; people who needed some help and there was constant activity revolving around a new connection. Wolja Schmitz got engaged to a Frau von Waldhausen, whom we are expecting today; she is to meet his daughter[226] here. The "agreeable" job of having to break such news to those concerned always falls on me.

Meanwhile I am reading Stifter's *Studien* to the girls in the evening, which they already understand very well and enjoy very much. Could you perhaps advise me of a few suitable books that I could give Hans Wilke for his 21st birthday; I would be very grateful.

How do things stand with Christiane's plans for Germany? Or can you not manage without her? Please do write me a few lines sometime, so that I once again can be somewhat in the picture. Mädy has found a job for Luli's fiancé[227] at Otto Wolff's in Cologne; I am sure you remember

---

225. Otto Haas, co-founder of the company Röhm and Haas in Philadelphia.
226. Tanya Schmitz, daughter of O. D. S's erstwhile friend Carola von Ahlers.
227. Gottfried Baron Hohenberg.

having heard that name from Eberhard. Now Mädy has rid herself of a very great burden, especially as they will also be receiving living quarters – so terribly difficult to find now – along with the job.

Take care, dear Hugo. I would love to know how you are doing and *what* you are working on.

Your ever faithful Ottonie.

🥀 🥀 🥀

Rodaun, 27 May 1922

Dear one, it was entertaining for me to hear that you have even created a boarding school for seventeen girls; it is wonderful to imagine how you did this, for only when you are involved with a lot of people and everyone has some purpose to serve, are you truly yourself. How I would love to be there in July and to listen to you tell me everything in the evening – that the most insubstantial, most incomprehensible of things must keep us apart – the atmosphere. However, it is not possible; I suffered too much this winter from the extreme changes in the weather – an earthquake on the 30th of January, which occurred 8,000 kilometers away, caused me to get an utterly miserable migraine lasting for days. Now once again I am no longer at all myself as a result of these days of south winds; so I must seek out something which is unequivocally good for me now, a place high in the mountains. I will be going to Southern Tyrol with Gerty in mid-June, first to Cortina, then perhaps to Karersee; how much I would still prefer to sit with you in the beloved, strange little house and to write the first and second acts of the comedy [*Der Unbestechliche* = The Incorruptible]. (The one in which the super clever, strong and strange butler evicts both of his lord's mistresses from the house, without the lord of the manor noticing it – it seems to me I must have told you about this once in the morning after our tea when we were walking around the little hill covered with pines.)

That my body's bizarre hypersensitivity costs me so many days! How I would love to be sociable and, alternately, alone, both together, deriving joy from both. But when the wind shifts to the south and the stifling air pushes its way in, I am neither lonely nor sociable and become lost to myself.

Now and then I like people quite a lot, as well as the figures I create, and there is hardly enough room for both.

I have fond memories of Hans Wilke. In him I have a piece of Eberhard; I realize this and am happy in this realization. We invited him here, but he was unable to come.

A good book to give him for his birthday would be the wonderful Kleist edition published by Insel Verlag, including the section containing lovely letters illuminating Kleist's soul.

The children, all three – i.e. if the bank gives Franz a vacation, otherwise only the other two – want to take a trip to Nürnberg via Regensburg on the 8th of July, then to Würzburg and the small Franconian towns, on to Rothenburg; they would pass through Munich around the 20th and would like to look at Neubeuern and to return to Aussee by way of Burghausen-Salzburg.

Who knows, though, if you will be home then!

Well, *Das Welttheater* will be performed in Salzburg in the Collegienkirche (that is, if something church-related or something political or some technicality or some financial concern does not interfere at the last minute), and it will be from the 13th to the 25th of August. For you I always have one or two extra tickets (preferably not the first or second night; then it is difficult!); for others I should probably reserve the seats soon – with the branch office of the Austrian Department of Transportation. Accommodations are taken care of by the Accommodations Committee of the *Festspielgemeinde* [Festival Organization] in Salzburg.

This is a true smorgasbord of a letter – I wish I already knew when I will again sit with you in the little house. The year 1920 was a very good one, the previous ones I remember rather as a disease, through which, however, much kindness glows.

Yours, Hugo

P.S. I have lost Burckhardt[228] for the moment, but one always finds people again; he is traveling around in Italy, and I fear a crowd of people has attached itself to him, some frivolous, some unhappy, as was the case with Wilhelm Meister.

Cortina d'Ampezzo Italy, 5 July [1922]

My Dear, it is correct and good for you to once be away from the atmosphere of your own home for a time – something about one's native land is so eternally stressful and burdensome, and even if we must continue to carry this burden on our shoulders, it is indeed refreshing to cast it off for a while. So, too, am I and can breathe more easily here and have nearly finished the first act of a new comedy (the one about the lord and the butler who drives the lord's girlfriends out of the house)[229] in these ten

---

228. Carl Jacob Burckhardt, Swiss diplomat and great friend of H. v. H. as well as O. D. S.

229. *Der Unbestechliche* (The Incorruptible).

or fourteen days I have been away from home; if I am lucky, I will also wrap up the second and third acts before I go to Salzburg. Then I could write the final two acts in Aussee this August (everything is organized very precisely into scenes), and after that in autumn, the best time for me, I could perhaps undertake to complete the tragedy.

Now about you and Salzburg. I am enclosing a pamphlet containing the opera performances – for which I have no possibility of securing tickets. You will see from the pamphlet that there is a ticket office in Munich, and also one in Amsterdam; perhaps then your host friends there could get tickets for you; it would probably cost 40–50,000 Austrian Crowns, thus very little in Dutch guilders. For *Das Welttheater* I will first have Christiane keep you and Baby in mind for my two tickets for the 18th – I want (aside from the possibility that we will see each other there) above all for you to *see* it, and also for the child to see it, as unfortunately you have already missed *Jedermann*. I believe, if this comes to pass at all, it will leave an impression that cannot be topped. Here place and poetry seem – if my imagination does not deceive me – to combine to perfection. I would really much prefer to have you both come to one of the two dress rehearsals (on the 11th and 12th), for which I have tickets, because it is highly questionable whether I will still be there with all of mine on the 18th: first because I must soon return to my work in Aussee, and also because I can hardly afford to pay for an extended stay in Salzburg beyond the rehearsals and the premiere. If you insist on the 18th, it will be *possible* for Christiane to secure the private accommodations for you that we have for the days of the premiere. It would be best to correspond about this right after you return, during the last days of July. We will be in Aussee then.

Greetings to Henry v.d.V. from me. It is a great loss for me no longer to see him. Just a thought, is there a chance of inviting you to Aussee for the end October?

Warm regards,

Yours, Hugo.

Rodaun, 10 January [1923]

No, not a deep depression, dear Ottonie – this word is too cumbersome – productivity does emerge – sometimes for hours, sometimes for days – only enormous, unpredictable problems concerning our sheer existence, and as a result, problems, confusion, the constant overextending of one's strength, eternal waiting for news from abroad, disappointment, etc. But all of this is very boring; I do not wish to talk about it, however, I have a suggestion. (As a precaution, I will not send this to Salzberg,[230] but rather to Neubeuern.) Burckhardt had invited me for a stay in Switzerland; however, this does not really work out. I am not too well and shy away from such a long trip – and then I will probably have to read my new comedy to Pallenberg[231] in Garmisch some time in February (one must not let actors read a play by themselves; they never understand it). In short, if, as you say, you will be back in N. around the 20th – and "always want to be free for me" – may I then perhaps come for ten to fourteen days soon after the 20th, and may I perhaps bring Burckhardt with me for part of the time? Would that be possible? Could you manage it materially and also logistically? Perhaps one might also invite Schröder (not right during the time when B. is there, but towards the end). Let us strive to manage this! I would so much love to be there with you again! One realizes the older one gets how much one's friends mean. If only Eberhard were here sometimes for a couple of hours! The longer he is lost to me, the more he becomes for me, the good, beloved man!

Yours, Hugo

❦ ❦ ❦

Salzberg Marineheim, Berchtesgaden, 19 January 1923

Your idea is really delightful, and I will be extremely happy if it should become a reality; we would only have to postpone your arrival, for a week, if this is possible. I just received a message from Sondershausen that I am needed at my mother's until the 24th; so if you arrived in Hinterhör on the 26th, it would suit me *perfectly* and then you are welcome to stay as long as you like. Of course Burckhardt can come, too, and Rudi, too, for I am all alone there and therefore have enough room. My little home is running at this point, thanks to the help I received from America and also from the purchase of guilder,[232] as you know; a Swiss may just have to lower his expectations considerably; maybe you should write to him about this right away. What really makes me wrack my brains are your accommodations, as my brother has now fetched his furniture, and the rooms are only very sparsely furnished at the moment; however, I still feel you would prefer this to living in a room that you are not attached to in some way.

---

230. O. D. S. was skiing with M.-T. on the Salzberg.
231. Max Pallenberg, actor at Reinhardt's theater.
232. Inflation in Germany was running rampant, hence all sorts of foreign currency were advantageous.

We will be going to Hinterhör on the 25th, to the Marienbad in Munich on the 29th, and on the 3rd of Febr. to Sondershausen, so now you can always let me know what your plans are.

Here we are surrounded by deep snow and can ski to our heart's content; but unfortunately there is no sun. Tomorrow there is to be a big ski jumping competition to which the most famous jumpers are expected to come.

Take care, Hugo, and please, let's work to arrange this little stay together.

Warm regards to Gerty, too,

Yours, Ottonie.

❦ ❦ ❦

Rodaun, 22 January [1923]

Dearest Ottonie, after having waited forever, I received your truly incomprehensible letter enclosed here, which completely quells any hope I had of spending time with you there, as I so very much wanted to. My love, you are such a dear and kind friend, however, is it perhaps possible that Eberhard was right when he complained about your being so confused? On the first page of this letter you allow me to visit you beginning the 26th, that is, next Thursday; on the second page you write that you will be leaving on the 29th! What, am I to sit there in Hinterhör by myself?! I wrote very clearly and unambiguously that it would be possible for me to stay there sometime between the last days of January and the 20th of February and therefore asked that you postpone your visit to Sondershausen (which you said in an *earlier* letter could be moved to another date) until around the end of February. And you had written clearly and unambiguously in the earlier letter, "After I return from Berchtesgaden, I can have you come stay with me anytime." What cannot be moved to another date is this: around the 5th I must go to Garmisch for a few days – I was hoping to first stay there with you for a few days, and then to return there for another ten days; and I wanted to suggest, as Burckhardt is no longer free, that you invite Schröder to come along for this second stay (10 to 20 February). What is going to happen now? I am at a complete loss. Tomorrow I will be receiving the entry permit for Bavaria due to Wiegand's kindness – I wanted to depart the 27th at the latest; what should I do now??

Please send me a telegram in case something can still be salvaged. It is impossible for me to come at the end of February; in Vienna the rehearsals for the new comedy will begin then. Maybe you will at least be able to postpone your departure long enough for me to be able to spend a few days with you there before the 5th or 6th of February.

Yours, Hugo

❦ ❦ ❦

Munich Hotel Marienbad, Thursday [8 February 1923]

That is, I am staying in the Reichsadler but hope to move to the Marienbad tomorrow and I will find my mail there.

Dear Ottonie, I am so looking forward to being together with you there again soon, to seeing your kind face, to hearing your voice, to feeling your good sense, which is so very agreeable and so very becoming to you.

Schröder wrote a letter – before having received mine – in which he said he would like to meet me around the end of February/beginning of March at your place. I sent him a long telegram today informing him that you have to leave at the end of February and that he must absolutely see that he can visit you, visit us, around the 18th. I am also looking forward to seeing the boy and hope to see him out there once – I am referring to Hans Wilke. Sometimes I feel as if, in many respects, my guardian angel had left me with Eberhard. Hypochondria? Yes, however, my life has become more complicated than I would have ever expected. That I will see you so soon. I will hardly see you, and you will only partially hear what I say – but it will be so cozy there! I am going to finish my business here and in Garmisch and will leave as soon as possible, in four or five days.

Yours, H.

❦ ❦ ❦

Rodaun, 19 April [1923]

Dearest, can it be that in these many weeks following the wonderful time we spent together I have not written to you – is it possible? The strange thing is that I do not even know myself. I am in such a constant rush; during every intermission, I quickly write a few letters; for weeks now I have constantly had a migraine or a toothache or neuralgia. In addition, many different things are surging forward – foreign projects that come up, occupy one, and then disappear. If I once take a walk by myself for an hour in the countryside, I do everything to forget this world and become lost in my dreams; so today I really do not know whether a single one of the letters I often wrote to you in my thoughts in a matter of seconds – whether a single one of them ended up on paper.

Have the little colored pictures[233] of Gavarni (for your staircase) arrived there? Wiegand was supposed to have them framed and sent there. I could have also gotten prints by Daumier, but they were not of his best

---

233. Still in Marie-Therese's possession.

ones, and the subjects, not as harmless as these. I hope that they will look cheerful on the white wall, and French, without being pretentious.

Regarding the curtain, Christiane was unable to work anything out – perhaps we will buy it together sometime in Munich.

I have often thought if I might come there in April; but it just was not possible – and I must do something for my health. So I have asked Burckhardt if he would go on a ten-day automobile trip with me to improve my health or on two five-day trips, to which he agreed. Thus I will be going to see him in Basel at the beginning of May. (I have not forgotten about Marie-Therese.)[234] Please write us a few lines at the beginning of May in Basel at Rittergasse 20. Before this (the last days of April), if I can muster the strength, I will go to Berlin – and travel to Basel by way of Frankfurt or whichever way.

The final weeks of May I will almost surely be in Salzburg (in the meantime Reinhardt will probably have returned from America) in order to work on the pantomime with him which must be incorporated into *Das Welttheater*. During this same time, Schröder plans to be in Fischhorn, and then in Vienna for a week. Might the "little bunny"[235] perhaps be so kind as to allow you to come to Vienna during this time? That would be nice; the house is quite warm, and Christiane's room is available, as is the room at my mother-in-law's! So let us build a little castle in the air!

Yours, H.

❦ ❦ ❦

[Hinterhör] Monday [May 1923]

How wonderful to finally hear a word from you again and to know that you are not ill, even though very worn out by the thousand different things each day brings along with the countless requests. I had indeed still hoped that you would announce your arrival for this time now and had made sure I had no visitors, however, it is certainly *much* better for you to take the automobile trip with Burckhardt; I am *so* happy for you. Just make sure you do really get some rest. I very much hope for your sake that you will travel by way of Berlin; after all, you will again receive quite a few new impressions that will stay with you, and time spent together with a few men like Meier-Graefe does indeed provide such wonderful memories.

I do think that the little bunny would allow me to travel to Vienna. I would really love to come, if it still fits your schedule; I suppose that would be the first week of June, according to your letter. If Rudi were also

234. To ask about a nice place in Switzerland where she could study French.

235. A pun on the friend in America whose name is Haas (meaning "hare" in German) and who is always refered to as Häsle (which means "little bunny").

back from Spain then, it could turn out to be a truly lovely time. At any rate I will at least plan on this time; what a wonderful castle in the air.

At the moment I have pretty much come to terms with a lady from Geneva who wants to place her eighteen year-old daughter with me (for 200 Francs a month). If the Burckhardts should happen to know of another girl, that would be wonderful – but only if you happen to think of it; I do not want to burden you with this. (Two are much easier, as they are not so dependent on me then.)

Yesterday I read Maupassant, the *Yvette* volume; I really found it very good, and some of the little stories, such as "Retour," are excellent. I am leading a charmed life at the moment: garden work, young animals all around, and reading. I am really enjoying it very much. The pictures have not arrived yet. However, I plan to invite Wiegand for next Saturday/Sunday, and perhaps he will bring them with him; thank you very much in advance.

There's really *no* need to bother about the curtain. I just bought myself the white stove. (You will have to tolerate my having named you as the donor to Julie and Baby – along with the remark that you did not wish to be mentioned as such – because otherwise I would have felt obliged to perform various other tasks for which I was not particularly suited.) I hope it will soon be in place. Just imagine that Rudi gave me a lovely porcelain piece from the Wiener Werkstätten [Viennese workshop] for the chest of drawers; it looks really nice now.

Tell me, is Gerty going to Switzerland with you? If not, for as long as you are away, might she not like to come to visit me and to perhaps, if Christiane would happen to be free, meet up with her here?

Tora Eulenburg is at the castle now and is indeed a truly enchanting creature, like a fairy-tale figure from another world, and she is *very* musical; it is a pleasure to be with her.

Heiseler recently came here for tea and told me many very interesting things about Russia.

Well, addio now. Many warm regards, and above all I hope you have a good time.

Yours, Ottonie.

Schönenberg Pratteln, Basel-Land, 14 May [1923]

Dearest Ottonie,

Sometimes a letter can also make you feel very close to a person – in these moments it turns into a figure, and the warmth one feels inside lasts for a very long time. This is how your letter, which I received while still in Rodaun, made me feel recently. I was suddenly able to feel completely what I have in you, and for a long time in Berlin, the feeling of happiness and gratitude remained. And here I have this younger friend, whose presence I enjoy tremendously; how can one so often – when life presents one with such gifts – fall into darkness and despondency? One really has to ask oneself. But that is the way it is.

I never again want to allow a long time to pass without seeing you! Perhaps you can arrange with Gerty that you will definitely come to Aussee in the fall – and in the winter I will visit you again. For now that it is June, I am afraid that I can no longer invite you to come see us; if we were further from Vienna, it would be possible, but Rodaun being the way it is, a guest would require alternating spending time there in the outskirts and in the city; then I would not be able to concentrate or to find myself; then I might once again be overcome by every imaginable confusion and fear – this I cannot allow. If only I could tolerate changing climates better (or if money did not interfere constantly) so that we could meet in June somewhere in the mountains; I would work, and in the evening we could see each other, which would work out so well. But I know of no place.

Yours, Hugo

P.S. I spoke to Mama Burckhardt about the request you made regarding a Swiss girl. Maybe you could tell me the name of the little lady from Geneva; that would be helpful.

❦ ❦ ❦

Rodaun, 23 June 1923

Oh, Ottonie, day and night, it seems to me truly the epitome of absurdity that I will not be able to pack my suitcase in eight or ten days and come to see you – when there I would hold every hour of every day dear to my heart, and in each there would be something meaningful and pleasant. But one is denied this. Ottonie, I felt so happy later that I had suddenly and unexpectedly – without having sent for you – caught sight of you with my own eyes. It is wonderful that you are here, and it was already wonderful that I was not forced to lose you during these eleven years.

I will still think of something: I have to go to some little place about 1,200 meters high in the mountains. I am going to choose one that is not very far from Salzburg, somewhere close to Gastein. You could come there very quickly by way of Kufstein and Wörgl. Maybe – if I feel well – when I have completed the fourth act, you could come and visit me for a week at the end of July? Would this be possible?

Borchardt and Schröder were in Munich. Did you see both or one of them? That your ties to these people have assumed almost a supernatural quality in your life here on earth seems also a gift like something out of a fairy tale.

Please write me a few lines. Scan this letter to Mädy and then forward it to her in a sealed envelope. Gerty likes Marie-Therese very much. I also had a very good impression from our meeting. Suddenly her father's side is coming to the fore in such a delightful manner.

Adieu. Yours, Hugo.

P.S. You never write me – absolutely never – a single word about what you are reading! If you know someone from whom you could borrow one of Proust's novels, perhaps *A l'hombre des jeunes filles* [In the Shade of the Young Girls] or *Du Côté de chez Swann* [Next to Swann], then please do so. At first it is almost too laborious to read, but very strange indeed. No one has ever – or at least not since the seventeenth century – seen the phenomenon "society" in this way or made something like this out of it.

Hinterhör, Thursday [July 1923]

Yes, Hugo, I saw both of them, Rudi and Borchardt. We all went to town to hear Borchardt's lecture on "Der Dichter and das Dichterische" [The Poet and the Poetical]. It would have been worth going there ten times over, even accepting the current hassle of this trip and the adventure of staying in the strange hotel as part of the bargain in order to experience this evening. Borchardt really is an incredible genius. Hugo, just imagine, two days before – if I am not mistaken – the idea came to Wiegand of arranging an evening lecture. Borchardt thought about this a bit in a rather intent manner and then gave enormously of himself. Not only the content, but also the form and not least of all the kind of lecture; I can only compare it to a magnificent musical composition. With tremendous zest, he carried us all into it and then included a moderate yet incredibly lively second movement – before arriving at a fantastic finale. It was a strange audience, full of university professors and students. They were all captivated from beginning to end; I do not suppose anyone missed a single sentence. I was *so* thrilled that I implored him to give us a second evening, and Wiegand chimed in right away, so now everything is arranged for tonight. It is going to be in the large lecture hall at the university; however, I cannot be there. I went from Munich to Eybach to see how Fredy[236] was; I returned, as planned, to Munich last night and found out that Baby had come down with the measles and was brought home [from school] yesterday. Julie is in Stuttgart with Hans Wilke, so I had to come out here right away this morning. The child is lying in bed very swollen and disfigured;

---

236. O. D. S.'s retarded brother-in-law.

she had a fever of 39.5 [102. 5 F] which means we will exceed 40 [103 C] tonight, however, it is certainly not a dangerous illness, but we will have to live through it.

Borchardt will be coming here tomorrow to work in the other house as you do. Marel is going to Italy and will begin moving into the little house near Altieris and hopes to be back here in around ten days. As B. will probably be going to America in November, Marel wants to see whether she might not wait until he gets back before returning to Italy with the children , as it is after all decidedly cheaper here; however, it will be *very* hard in Bavaria to find a little house somewhere in the country where they could stay and where there is peace enough for him to work.

Here now I have your dear letter; I suppose we were all very close to each other in our thoughts. You appeared everywhere in the words Borchardt spoke (of course without being named), both in his lecture and in the conversations. He is as cheerful as always, Marel was charming, and Rudi, sick as always.

Yes, Hugo, it really is rotten luck that you cannot be here with me now, go for walks with Borchardt, discuss things, read, etc. Now all my plans have indeed been short-circuited for the next three weeks; the risk of infection is expected to last at least three weeks, and then I will have to see how the child is recovering; in any case, her vacation lasts until the 3rd of Sept.; if she feels better by then, we must spend some time with my mother and also go to Mecklenburg. In addition we really are expecting Mary to arrive at the end of July now, so I am afraid that my visiting you somewhere in the mountains is not going to work out. However, maybe you can come here in the autumn, depending on how your work schedule is; otherwise, certainly in the winter.

The stove is in place – it was put there last week. Unfortunately it has turned out to be a bit too large, although it is attractive, and the color is nice.

Pictures[237] have also arrived from Mädy, which I am going to hang up tomorrow; too bad you are not here to help pick everything out.

Gerty's letter was forwarded to me; I immediately wrote to the authorities concerning the entry permit for the boys. Most likely, if everything proceeds as normal with Baby, we plan to be gone from the 26th of July to the 17th of August. At any other time, the boys are welcome here; Gerty will just have to decide whether Raimund may come on account of the infection.

Thank you very much for the nice little pictures and to Gerty for the recipe. I am so happy that you took some pleasure in the child.

Many warm regards from

Yours, Ottonie.

---

237. As Mädy's apartment was too small to house all of Eberhard's collection, some of the French Impressionists were loaned to Ottonie.

❦ ❦ ❦

Rodaun, 7 July [1923]

Dearest, I am certainly not frightened by the measles, and I would hope that after the first few days of fever – which I remember exactly from when I was sixteen years old – the difficult period will probably be over for the child. However, please write a brief note on an open postcard, so that I will indeed know how things stand.

One's thoughts travel there so often – and can you believe that? It is childish enough to think that the tile stove is a bit too large, that it is taking up too much space and causing trouble! If only you had brought me along to help pick it out; my eyes are very sure regarding things such as measurements and colors. And *what* wonderful pictures Mädy has finally handed over to Hinterhör; that is also something one would have liked to know!

That one must be kept apart by distance! And I enter the little house so easily in my mind – so often; and without it being any strain whatsoever on my imagination!

I do not know yet exactly what is going to happen to me. In the meantime another one of those matters has arisen involving money, taking time, and very possibly making a fool of one now this: to make a film of *Der Rosenkavalier*.[238] To this end one would almost have to write a novel (with the familiar characters), for the opera itself provides almost nothing useable. At any rate, I am not going to spend more than two weeks on this; then I am going to go somewhere and work on things that are serious.
Adieu!

Yours, Hugo

❦ ❦ ❦

Ramsauerhof Ramsau near Schladming in Ennstal, 2 August [1923]

I have repeated this bad joke so many times that now your letters do not give me as much pleasure as your conversation – and now I must say over and over how happy it makes me to read a letter like this last one. You wrote so beautifully of the death and the life of your sister,[239] and the transition from this touching and serious subject to the modest and yet truly profound joy that your house gives you – the flowers and the pictures you live with – is so easy for you to make; yes, it is in fact easy to make the transition from one to the other, and it is all a product of the

---

238. The film was shown in Dresden in 1926 and was not a success.
239. O. D. S.'s sister Annemarie von Schwartz.

same raw material, the mystery of life. For me, however, this letter is wonderful and truly meaningful, and it gives me great pleasure to know that, if indeed we are not meant to be together at this time, you are still here, so near, with only a few valleys and a few mountain chains separating us; indeed the weather is the same for both of us. And I hold so very deep inside of me a picture of your summer days there that I feel as if I were on my way there now with a book in hand: in the afternoon, we sit for an hour in the hall, where it is as cool as a cellar; once in the morning (what wonderful mornings we are having this summer!) we might go for a walk on the forest path and around the hill a couple of times. That you are still there – that you even decided to stay there! What luck I have, Ottonie, that you have not remarried! Is it cruel of me to say that – selfish? However, there really are so few people after all, who are truly close to me – whom I do not wish to miss – and one of them, my most loyal, most mature, best friend of all,[240] I have of course already lost.

Now I have you – and Yella O. Perhaps you find it strange the affection I have for this old lady; however, if you knew her – which does, however, require time, and I have known her for 25 years! – you would understand this. Then fate had it that I should, in the same year that I lost Eberhard, be given a new friend in Carl Burckhardt, and with each passing year, I can better understand what a tremendous gift this was. And there is still Rudi, and when he is there, as strange as he no doubt is and often very troubled, then one has a great deal. I should also wish to include Mell's name here; I derive the purest joy from his person, and from everything that he produces; I need him much more than he does me. Should I mention Borchardt's name now as well? I cannot, and you of course understand why it is that I cannot! I find him wonderful and enchanting; I have respect for him, and sometimes the most deeply-felt mixture of feelings in the world for him; but I cannot use the word "friend" to describe him. What word can one use to describe him anyway?

Dearest, Gerty says that when the three of you are together – she, Christiane and you – and speak of me, you talk just as one would of a man who is crazy and always recount further examples of my craziness and cannot begin to stop laughing. She told me this once in her charming and natural way, half-humorously and yet partly half-serious and with a shade of wistful sympathy. Is this really true, Ottonie? And must I not be very careful that I do not become a caricature for you and lose you as a result? That would really be horrible. Am I really so crazy – or is it possible to recognize that these are only grimaces and that beneath these lies the other part? And that the other is the real part, as is the case when viewed from the inside? I am starting to feel afraid. If only you could once

---

240. Eberhard Bodenhausen.

see me when I am truly myself – as I am here! Or am I after all only myself when I – as is here the case – am alone fifteen hours out of the day and more than 1,000 meters high up in the mountains? As Hamlet was, conversely, only crazy when a south-southwesterly blew in! Oh, I can hear you saying, now he is acting crazy again; now he keeps talking about things "here," and I have no idea where he is, and he must realize after all that I have no idea!

Here: that is here. "Here" is my attic room where I am sitting. It contains a bed, a little desk and a wooden chair; a few nails on which you can hang your things, a window facing the west – it leads almost directly to where you are – and one facing east; they are called windows, only really they are just attic holes. On the desk there is some clean paper and some containing words. That with the writing on it contains the fifth act of *Der Turm* [The Tower]; but for God's sake, not the actual text, but another one of those "layers" (see the description of Delacroix's way of painting in Meier-Graefe) – I hope by now pretty much the next to last, which one could almost already call the "text." (The whole thing really is, it seems to me, rather strange.) "Blasted!" you will surely exclaim, though. "Now he is praising his own play again instead of finally telling me where then, geographically speaking, this little place is!!" However, that is really extremely simple. Look towards Salzburg with one eye and towards Kufstein with the other, but not so much directly, but rather only in passing in the direction of Kufstein, and then look in the diagonal of both directions, over this way here; not as far as Aussee, but somewhat closer to where you are, towards mount Dachstein, but towards that side, facing Tyrol; take a quick but good look over this way, and here I am!

Dearest, now something serious, though. Is there anything standing in the way of your coming, say around the second half of September, to Aussee? And that one might also try to get Rudi to come for a while then? Should we hope for this? Can we believe it will happen? This is not meant to be *in place* of Vienna, however, Aussee is so near and so convenient! And in the winter, if I may, I will indeed be visiting you first.

Yours, Hugo

Bad Aussee, 11 October [1923]

Dearest,

When on the most miserable of many miserable days of south wind such a dear letter arrives from you with an Austrian stamp; when you are there, whence my thoughts so often traveled to where you were; when you *yourself* "discover" the Porcia Palace (about the most famous Renaissance structure north of the Alps); when in Lienz you soar, philosophically, to the heights of politics and, upon seeing the lovely oxen and calves, suddenly understand that an Austrian is happiest among Austrians — in short, when you once again have the "small fortune" of finding the right people at the right moment and of being with them in the right place, then one feels so alive that one also has the "small fortune" of belonging to you in some small way; and one sits down and immediately writes a reply, hoping the letter will still find you there. (For the one you sent, on Monday (?), did not arrive here until today, Saturday.)

If you did not automatically understand everything, then you would certainly have good reason to be puzzled that you have not received a letter from me since the beginning of August, for exactly two months now. However, there is something inexorable involved here. Back then in Ramsau, where I was completely isolated and completely devoted to that one thing, I hoped I would master the fifth act. But that was not the case. There was, however, something there which was essentially complete, but it did not arouse the belief in my heart. It had looked like the final draft but was once again certainly only the next to last. Therefore it was necessary that this work be postponed until a much more favorable time. The month of August had, as is almost always the case, a negative effect on me physically. There were also a lot of interruptions. I had to spend several days in Salzburg and to attend to a few semi-journalistic affairs. I had very high expectations for the fall. However, with the beginning of September, a true hell began in terms of the weather, which has still not relaxed its grip on me (for other people are not so affected by it). The south winds are unrelenting: for weeks now we have had terribly damp, foggy weather and dark, oppressive days and nights — followed by warm, rainy tropical weather, and now a glassy, thundery heat. Thus have passed forty-five days without my experiencing *a single decent hour*. So as not to allow myself to begin despairing, I set aside for now this difficult work, and as I had promised to give *Die Ägyptische Helena* [Helena of Egypt] to Strauss by the fall, I worked on the first act of it. This has turned out quite well, and with it he has something he can use to compose his music for the time being. It is a long act; the opera will have only two of them and is going to be a rather strange thing.

Now, however, I must (for at some point of course, there will again be a high barometric reading after all) manage the final act. These are not insurmountable difficulties even if they are substantial: generally they are really more of the intellectual than artistic in kind. If I have all my wits together, for just two weeks, then I will master them. (And how could I be expected to bear leaving this work unfinished?) Burckhardt, whose participation in this project is particularly invaluable to me, is coming here on the 20th for a week. (I still thought I might ask you to come at the same time; but now of course it is no longer possible.) I hope we will then have weather which no longer impedes the free flow of my thoughts (to form subtle associations without effort is everything; and such unfavorable weather makes a fool of me). I hope then with him to be able once again to bring back to life the mental picture I had of this act. (Such a mental picture is the most delicate, poetic unity, like a poem in which indeed both the first and the last lines [in so far as it is truly a poem] *must be present at the same time*.) Once I have this ethereal body of the act in front of me and can *believe* in it – then I do not wish to return to Rodaun before I have written the very last line. However, to keep Gerty here that long and to leave the boys alone or in homes of strangers; all of this is more difficult than you can imagine. Here my hopes attach themselves to you: could I come and see you during the very first days of November? All that is necessary is for you to be there – and a room, even if it contains no furniture at all except a desk and a chair. Alone the fact that I have worked there on *this* piece is a good omen and boosts my confidence in my ability to also complete it there. Please give me a very brief answer right away as soon as this reaches your hands. Please give my warmest regards to Herr and Frau Heiseler.

In friendship, Yours, Hugo

Bad Aussee, 23 October [1923] evening during stormy southern winds

Dearest, your telegram made me tremendously happy. How wonderful to know that there is a little house in this world where one feels so at home, as in one's own house. My idea now is this: to finish the second (and final act) of *Helena* here. And at the same time to take advantage of Burckhardt's refreshing and extremely stimulating presence, despite a continuous, terribly oppressive atmosphere, in order to approach *Der Turm* with a new heart – and to create the fifth act. Then to hope for the completion in several peaceful weeks of work at your place. Please write me a word, and tell me honestly if you might perhaps have to leave Hinterhör during the course of November because of plans you have already made. In this case I would not come. I do not wish to have to adhere to a schedule *here* either – but the circumstances are such that I cannot maintain the household or keep Gerty here past the 7th or 8th of November. If nothing interferes then with my being there in November (as I very much hope), then I will of course have to burden you once more with the request that you send me an entry and residence permit from there as soon as possible, because I must obtain a new visa in Salzburg, which requires that I have these papers from Bavaria.

Schröder, who will soon be in Fischhorn but cannot come here (by the way, he – the good man – was apparently very ill during the summer!), asks me whether or not I will be in Hinterhör again sometime. As soon as I have your answer (I am tormented by the fear that you may have to go to your mother's), I will write to him.

I received something from Borchardt's publisher, *Die geliebte Kleinigkeit* [The Beloved Trifle] that I almost found revolting – just as the lecture. However, a book written by a very young man about Hölderlin gave me tremendous pleasure, which Burckhardt now shares. His reading aloud every evening about another day in his fantastic journey through Asia Minor is something so wonderful that it is my dearest wish to have you here each day for this hour. How fortunate that heaven gave me another *human being* right after the death of Eberhard. Mell has his head filled with enchanting ideas for new works; if only Schröder were also closer by.

Yours, Hugo

❦ ❦ ❦

Bad Aussee, 2 November [1923]

Dearest, it is so touching and kind the way you take care of me. The entry permit has arrived. Thank you very much. The air has indeed improved now; I work every day in the morning and in the evening and hope to bring the finished opera[241] with me. It will amuse you. It is a pretty sister of *Ariadne* but has experienced more than she has. Burckhardt's presence is really a great joy. Every day he writes down part of his recollections of the trip and reads them to us in the evening. His eyes are extremely clear, and he sees *everything*; this is what appears so rare and wonderful. How much is revealed then: cities and deserts, coffee houses and ancient ruins, dervishes, gypsy girls, monks, murderers, prisoners, snobs, Kurds, Jews, Armenians – children and animals, bears and gazelles – and everything is seen equally well and with the same seriousness and the same love. This is a man whom Eberhard would have enjoyed!

About my life there: As lovely and cozy as the salon is, I could not complete a task as difficult as the fifth act in a room without a door. For this the other house will indeed be better. Can't my usual room be heated? Also with regard to my sleep during a period of hard work, the house over there is probably better than yours, where I can hear the maid's footsteps after they wake up in the morning. To talk about food when in Berlin the most respectable of people are literally starving is truly indecent. The little piece of meat the head requires twice each day in order to function properly can surely be found in the village. Everything else and plenty of it is of course always available there in the house. Perhaps I should bring along sugar, which I use a lot, on account of the phosphorus.

---

241. *The Egyptian Helena,* opera by Richard Strauss and H. v. H.

I am planning on coming around the 10th and am looking forward to it.

Yours, Hugo

❧ ❧ ❧

Rodaun, Thursday, 8 December 1923

Dearest, once again many days have passed; I have not written you and did not even let you know that I arrived. So much is thrust upon one in the very first moment; I also immediately got sick, as is always the case when I return to the big city from the country. And just imagine, Ottonie, the past Sunday afternoon we buried Reserl[242] at the little graveyard here in Rodaun. This strong, extremely fit, young creature so full of life! Twenty-three years old! There is a very dark relationship involved, both in the tragedies of an individual life and of great peoples and nations. With horror I recognize from the memoirs of Paléologue,[243] alongside those of Tirpitz,[244] and now Conrad's,[245] that all the blame for the actual outbreak of war rests *with us*, Berlin and Vienna – all the terrible foolishness, stupidity, and the failure to think things through; one acted as if in a state of semi-consciousness. One must seek salvation in the thought that the greater the catastrophe, the less destiny has to do with the motivations behind it. (In this way, too, Shakespeare revealed his greatest tragedies: the monstrous must manifest itself, no matter how.) The lesson contained in Paléologue's records, who, for a West European, reveals a great understanding of the mystery of Russia (Mensdorff tells me that despite the imperial, Byzantine name, he is the son of a Galician Jew), brought me directly back to Dostoevsky. I reached without thinking for the *Demons* and can say that I never before understood so well the enormous content of this book (politically, too) – which also proves that I am not yet becoming more stupid but rather smarter. If you already know this book, then read it again immediately. You only think you know it, but do not know it at all; if perhaps you do not own it, then W. will have to get it for you right away.

I hope you are sticking to the schedule of the historical readings; read one after the other without falling into the *torpeur* [anguish] that can overcome one when one does not distance oneself at all from the events of daily life. In any case, I hope you will come here in January after all. There will be rooms available. Only one thing concerns me, and that is

---

242. Maid in the Hofmannsthal household.
243. Maurice Paléologue, French diplomat, Ambassador to Russia during the years 1914–1917.
244. Admiral of the German fleet.
245. Franz Count von Hötzendorf, chief of the Austrian High Command.

that you must have a true *home*, as is not possible in Elisabethstrasse. Burckhardt is living very happily and peacefully – in a nice, clean, quiet room in the Hotel Imperial – and he is even able to work a lot (on what he will not tell me). But it is exorbitant staying there (and is even *very* expensive for him). The package to Heiselers left several weeks ago. Please ask about it again. I will not be able to send the one to Groth-Oettingen[246] until after the holidays. Hundreds of thousands of packages are mailed from here; the only railway line (in peace time there were three of them) is overloaded; everything takes weeks.

Christiane is coming here for Christmas.

I read the second act of *Helena* to Strauss; he thinks it is wonderful; on the whole, I suppose it is good. However, I am still not quite satisfied with certain, distinct parts. I am going to read it to Arthur Schnitzler[247] sometime and ask him for a detailed critique. It must turn out absolutely perfect.

Yours, Hugo

🌰 🌰 🌰

Hotel Post Seefeld/Tyrol, 12 January 1924

Once again you will receive these lines of mine from Tyrol. And again it is enchanting here, the landscape indescribably beautiful. Baby looked too pale to go back to school like that, so I quickly decided to come here with her. Seefeld is almost 1,200 meters above sea level, and it is the mountain air she needs. The sun was shining as we rode through the Inn Valley on our way to Innsbruck; we had a look at the city, which is beautifully situated, the royal residence and the court church, with its silver chapel we saw from the inside. In one of the rooms in the residence there is a picture of Maria-Theresia with her sixteen children; I remembered then the beautiful piece you wrote about her in your volume of prose, which brought me forever so close to this wonderful woman with such great qualities. Baby took great pleasure in everything, which made it nice for me showing her around. The ride up here was also wonderful! Bright, sunny winter weather here, so we can spend almost the entire day skiing. Gerty should be here, too. And it is still very cheap for us here.

Since you left, there has been a lot of Christmas commotion with all sorts of people around; Christian Leden,[248] who traveled to the North Lands and spent three years living among the Eskimos, tells stories of great interest. He cheerfully recounted tales about the strangest of things.

---

246. Friends of O. D. S.
247. Arthur Schnitzler (1862–1931), Austrian author.
248. Swedish anthropologist.

One time, for instance, he spent three weeks with one of the tribes; the oldest of the elders, who had two wives, told Leden he really must not stay there without a woman and said he wanted to give him one of his wives while he was there. Leden did not wish to have her for whatever reasons and explained this very carefully, which the Eskimo did not understand at all; on the contrary, he was insulted, saying, "I suppose she is not good enough for you and she was after all for the white bishop, who came here last year." Is that not quaint! Leden gave two lectures accompanied by slides in Rosenheim and Neubeuern and collected a tremendous amount of money for the emergency food bank; it was his idea not to accept any hospitality without also doing something to lessen the suffering.

Thank you very much for your letter. Yes, poor Resi; I was really terribly shaken by her fate. For you it is almost as if one of your children had died.

Before Christmas I was in Munich for several days and enjoyed a very pleasant evening in the Presse with Borchardt and Wiegand, where the "stove figure"[249] was also in attendance and actually much nicer than I had expected; maybe she had had a particularly good day. Borchardt was bubbling over; he read aloud many of his old poems that he had written during the war.

You asked whether I plan to come to Vienna in January after all. No, Hugo, I feel that this would *only* burden you and therefore I think we should only meet in Hinterhör. One does not always need to have everything. That is good that Burckhardt is really working there in the city, which means you have a *human being* there now. Have you read *Helena* to anyone else yet, and has Strauss already started working on the music? Are you able to work on anything at all now, or are you in part leading a city life?

The packages for the Heiselers have arrived; they were really *very* happy. Many thanks to Gerty as well for also sending something to both of the other addresses. I will let her know when it arrives.

Hans Wilke was here for Christmas and poured his heart out to me regarding the entire matter; I will have quite a few things to tell you about this. His "girlfriend" must be a very smart person and is not without merit. H. W. wanted to take you to see her then, too, but it seems you had a headache, too bad.

Take care, Hugo. Many regards to you and Gerty. Thank you for the letter and the postcard. Baby also asked me to say hello.

Yours, Ottonie D.

---

249. A Fräulein Tiersch, whom they had nicknamed for her size.

[Rodaun] 20 January [1924]

I am so happy that you are somewhere again, suddenly, and that something new is opening up around you. I had just begun to fear for you in some way – and here your dear letter arrives. Never before did I feel afraid when thinking of you; however, it took hold of me this time. Christiane told us during her Christmas visit how all the prices there had suddenly risen – then I became very concerned about your material circumstances. Who knows if you decided to write a letter to Haas; who knows how to keep the castle running – my inability to help you, all this would not leave me in peace.

Monday morning: A completely bizarre story, which threatens the survival of one of my oldest friends,[250] forced me to go to Vienna now and, with the help of the chief of police, I might be able to cripple this, which is like something out of a movie.

See you soon.

Hugo

P.S. Monday, one o'clock: I cannot find the people I am supposed to meet now; meanwhile the good old Gicky[251] died of pneumonia last night.

I would so like to disregard the idea that we should only see each other in the country and no longer in Vienna. Quite the contrary, there were so many good theater performances in Vienna – Moissi, Pallenberg, Massary once again totally bewitching – and as always, I had very vivid thoughts of you. Only it is so hard to find good and appropriate accommodations, to which I count neither Elisabethstrasse nor a guestroom with the Hellman family, who are really complete strangers to you. Please write me again right away, if it does not bore you, also in some detail about Baby.

Yours, Hugo

[Hinterhör] 28 January 1924

Even though it is definitely not customary for the two of us to wish each other a happy birthday, I must nevertheless write you a letter this time for the 1st of February as for some special day and tell you that I am indeed thinking of you more than usual and am so grateful that you exist. There is only one wish that I have, and that is that you may continue to

---

250. Leopold von Andrian.
251. Nanny in the H. v. H. house.

live for a very, very long time and that you still have more good years ahead of you now.

We have descended from our sunny paradise and again find the little house to be very cozy and warm, however the sun has left us, and once again the snow falls quietly, endlessly. Baby will be going to her school tomorrow feeling much refreshed. I have my sister, Oda, here now until the 7th and one of the Gaisbergs for a few days. The little bridal couple Franzl and the attractive, smart, and young Countess Verry have just left; they were like a ray of sunshine. Franzl really is lucky that such a sweet little creature was brought into his life; people call her *Amsel* (her name is Amélie); she truly is like a little bird.

Unfortunately the calculation of my finances revealed that I cannot afford to take a trip to Italy now – too bad! Actually I now realize following this discovery how much I had really been looking forward to it. I suppose I am indeed a true glutton for pleasure, who always wants to seize hold of everything.

I have not read much recently; unfortunately we did not take enough with us up there. An article by O. A. H. Schmitz, *Das Land ohne Musik* [The Country without Music], was very interesting as well as a few English novels, which, however, had little substance to them. Now, however, I will again have my time to read books, and I want to get several of those you listed for me from the castle library today. Mädy is still there and will probably stay until Easter, because it is really too lonely for her in Degenersh. in the winter.

I seem to recall that the Hellmanns happened to buy the first two nos. of the *Marsayas* edition from the Bodenhausens, which he had had from long ago; Luli still has the following nos. (3, 4, 5, 6) and would like very much to sell them. Would the Hellmanns want to take these as well? (Please give an answer to this.)

Thank Gerty *very* much for also sending a second package to my old Aunt Metzger; she is overjoyed and, at age 76, can use it.

Take care, dear Hugo. May our friendship remain intact in the years to come as it has up to now; this is my selfish wish.

Faithfully yours, O.

[Postcard] [Rodaun] 12 February 1924

I always feel concern when my thoughts wander there. As a result of the unspeakable amount of writing which is a consequence of having a birthday, I cannot write to you as I would like. I constantly wonder if it might not be possible, as you had to give up Italy, for you to come here during the second half of March – while Reinhardt's project is taking place here – for two weeks without the torturous back and forth between the city and Rodaun. Maybe I will find a way! Please do write me if the main part of the plan works out (renting your place).

Borchardt has created much ill-feeling in me as a result of a commemorative publication, and this has not diminished in twelve days (and half nights). To constantly be confronted everywhere by a lack of tact and a lack of sensitivity for what is proper does finally make one feel deathly exhausted.

Yours, Hugo

P.S. Please write me again soon, even if it is short.

❦ ❦ ❦

[Hinterhör] 21 February 1924

Your card made me very sad. What this unlucky man has staged again! Unfortunately I have not seen the thing; I only experienced once how enthused Borchardt and Wiegand were and imagined that it will be wonderful once it is finished and perhaps pleasing to you. Is it really *so* tactless that you are unable to forgive even partially? How is it possible for Wiegand not to feel this – I cannot imagine.

And now as far as I am concerned, Hugo, please do not worry; my situation is of course always so strange that even with almost no money, I can still lead a very comfortable life thanks to the castle. The place has not yet been rented, as the man who is interested did not want to come here to have a look at it until the weather was warmer. If he does not take it, then Herbst wants to rent part of it to a well-known doctor, who would like to create a small sanatorium there; not too nice either, but something must be done. The doctor is already here; however, it will take approximately two months before anything has been decided.

About my coming to Vienna, if I did not have the feeling that I would somehow be a burden on you, I would of course love to come. Couldn't Gerty find a room for me in a decent guesthouse or hotel, where I could live for 10 Marks a day; then it would be entirely possible for me to come, or is there nothing available of this kind? Mädy was summoned to Berlin per telegram yesterday, as Luli has come down with the flu. I hope it's nothing serious, for after all this child is now the only hold on life left for Mädy.

I read a lot in Goethe and am enjoying my little yellow room; now and then I have guests and am perfectly happy. And one can also go tobogganing and skiing.

Take care, Hugo. I hope your mood improves again.

Your faithful, Ottonie.

❦ ❦ ❦

[Rodaun] 17 March 1924

Dearest, I have been quite worried about you this year. I would really like you to come here, the sooner the better. Poor Marie;[252] and now Jeannette[253] is also ill! Is this dangerous? Will it lead to an operation?

No, please come here, if possible around the 25th or 26th for 10 days. On the 28th Reinhardt will be opening his theater, and on the 27th I believe the dress rehearsal will take place, and shortly thereafter, *Kabale und Liebe* and *Der Schwierige* will follow. We will manage to find a room in the city. As I know now that you take pleasure in the city, the stores, the collections of paintings – if you have your freedom and a little bit of contentment, then every burden is removed from my shoulders, and nothing but happiness remains. Material concerns will not cause any difficulties. The Rodaun community[254] gives a small stipend to nice (female) friends; it is quite within in its means to do so. It is also doing better now and is in the process of being reorganized; in the near future it will even be able to present seven German writers with 1,000 Swiss Francs apiece.

Write or send me a telegram the day of your arrival. A good train is running, which I believe departs from there around 9:20 in the morning.

Yours, Hugo

❦ ❦ ❦

[Rodaun] 1 April 1924

Dearest, our letters have crossed; still I am a little worried that you have not written again since then. It is tremendously difficult for me trying to organize everything; the theater, on which I am so dependent at times, is a hellish thing for my nerves. Now again I am having every imaginable "problem" with *Der Schwierige* – the actors, the schedule; everything is uncertain and difficult and an endless test of nerves, and for Reinhardt as well. The premiere is this evening; the theater perhaps the most beautiful in Europe; I look forward to showing it to you – perhaps in June. I believe R. will be presenting it until July.

One request now, the fulfillment of which would mean the world to me. If you cannot fulfill it, then you simply cannot; in which case the word "impossible" will suffice. Then I will have to try something else. The request is this: could you possibly keep Raimund there from around the 16th to the 27th of April? Maybe in the castle? Or in a peasant house – or

---

252. O. D. S.'s longtime cook in Hinterhör, who was ill with pneumonia.
253. O. D. S.'s personal maid.
254. H. v. H. means, jokingly, his own pocketbook.

wherever. For you, if it is at all possible, it certainly should not involve any inconvenience; for he is a charming and very entertaining person to live with, and he will adore your atmosphere there. As young as he is, he has experienced a lot, and he rates decency above all else. For I received a gift from foreign friends and can use this to go to Sicily. I would leave with Christiane and Gerty on the 18th – it would be the greatest favor to me if R. could be taken care of there for part of this time (the Easter vacations). For the rest of the time I will place him with someone in Vienna.

Please answer immediately.

Yours, Hugo.

P.S. If it is not possible, then please send a *telegram*.

[Hinterhör] 4 April 1924

You will have received my telegram. I am so sorry that I cannot take Raimund now, but we have Baby's confirmation on the 21st, and perhaps you know what something like this means for a family from Boll. All of Christoph's friends are coming from Württemberg, who will be staying in the castle, and Fräulein von Groth[255] will be staying in Hinterhör, as well as another teacher and friends of Baby, so that there would be no room for Raimund there. And right after this I have to go to Munich with the child to have her adenoids removed so she can then go to the Alm in Tyrol during the first days of May. I would have loved so much to have had Raimund here with us, and I also believe that we would get along very well with each other, however the time is not right.

How nice that you can go to Italy. Only it will unfortunately be too crowded there I suppose, from what I hear, and the trains crossing the Brenner Pass are so terribly crowded. Unfortunately nothing is going to come of our plans to establish a sanatorium; after discussing it with Müller, it turns out that it is not the right time now; all the patients are traveling south. So we will have to look again for another renter; I am enclosing an announcement, perhaps Gerty would be so kind as to give it to the *Neue Freie Presse* or some other acceptable newspaper and to let me know what it costs. I would be very grateful. I will still be in the castle until Thursday and will then be moving out with the children.

I can imagine what demands the theater places on you, however, I hope you are able to enjoy some good performances.

Kind regards,

Yours, Ottonie

---

255. Headmistress of M.-T.'s boarding school.

❦ ❦ ❦

[Rodaun] 26 May 1924

Dearest, I really hate it when I have no idea where you are or what you are doing. Of course it is entirely my fault this time – however, it was part of my travel plans not to receive or to write any letters. Until around the 27th of April I knew pretty much what you would be doing; I believe I should have sent a telegram that day, but a confirmation is something we absolutely cannot picture, and that is why I forgot. At any rate, I hope Baby knows that I will always be very fond of her when she is a grown-up person. A week ago we returned and spent the night in Villach – that is very close to Lienz (in a straight line), and I wished I had been able to picture you there above Windisch-Mattrei and that one could have come to see you by veering just slightly off course. For after all you are among the very few people whom I *wish* to see again, and this does not become less throughout the years, but rather becomes more so. However, it was simply impossible to know *whether* you were still there. Yesterday in the *Wiener Journal*, which contains all the social prattle, I suddenly came across the date of Franzl Pfetten's wedding somewhere out in the country in Upper Bavaria. So for a moment I believe to know where you are and am happy.

Ottonie, could you not come here in June for a few days? I can very easily have you as a guest in a hotel; everything has rather fallen into place (except for my assets which of course remain lost).[256] You could see a few of Reinhardt's performances, perhaps also *Der Schwierige* – and I wish to tell you so much and to see you. Ottonie, the true South is so beautiful; I want to show it to you so much. However, not until fifteen hours have passed in the express train south of Naples does the true beauty begin! I often think of the good Jeannette and *sincerely* hope that she is not seriously ill.

Yours, Hugo

❦ ❦ ❦

Red Cross Hospital [Hinterhör] 5 June 1924

Your letter was forwarded to me here, where I am staying not because of me rather because of Mädy. We spent ten rather tense days, as a sort of growth was suddenly discovered in Mädy's body; of course I had to think right away of Christoph. The operation had to be continually postponed because all sorts of things got in the way. Finally we came here, and after excruciating examinations, especially of her kidneys, etc., it turned out

---

256. Due to the rampant inflation in Austria as in Germany.

that she did not need an operation, but rather that her kidney had slipped to the pelvic girdle. Mädy was *marvelous*, as always in those kind of situations, but afterwards she suffered a true nervous breakdown. She will be coming to Hinterhör on Monday to rest a bit, and then she has to go to a sanatorium for kidney patients, where she has to have all kinds of baths and rub-downs, and also a Swedish massage. As she is supposed to stay at as high an altitude as possible, we are looking for something suitable, and I want to ask you if there might be something along the Semmering that would work out for her, or if you know of something above Bozen or somewhere? I think Irene Hellmann surely must know, so would Christiane perhaps be so kind as to give me an answer to these questions *right away*?

In the meantime I have arrived in Hinterhör; Mädy is coming on Monday, too. The children are here for four days of the Whitsun holiday and are of course overjoyed.

Yes, we really haven't heard from one another for a long, long time; how happy I am that Italy did you good and especially down there in the south. Hans Wilke also returned from Sicily recently feeling very excited. It was truly stimulating, everything he experienced; there was so much that he couldn't stop talking about it.

Yes, first, Baby's confirmation here was especially nice for me because I once again experienced a wave of devotion, which reached us from Württemberg and Christoph's world. Then I went to Degenersh. with Hans Wilke, where he showed me everything he had accomplished in the woods during the two years, and he really did accomplish a lot. We only stayed for two days, and he drove me by car through the incredible spring blossoms to Beichlingen to the charming Wertherns. A wonderful, old castle and beautifully situated. From there, we went to Sondersh. Then Hans Wilke continued on through the Eichsfeld to relatives'; unfortunately I could not join him. I stayed at my mother's for two weeks, who really is doing much better than one ever could have expected; she even plans to come see me again next winter. There I received the news about Mädy, and I of course gave up my plans to continue on to Mecklenburg and Hamburg. In Munich I was together with Rudi one evening, who rushed off to Fischhorn, because, as always, he was running late.

It seems rather questionable, though, whether I will be able to come to see you now, because for one thing, I was just gone for four weeks, and if having some vegetables in July means anything to us, I really must stay here; and secondly, I also don't know yet if we can let Mädy travel alone; and last but not least, these unnecessary 500 Marks, of course, stand obtrusively between here and Vienna.

There is supposed to be a very good book from Stegemann now, *Der Kampf um den Rhein* [Battle for the Rhine]. Are you familiar with it? Can you recommend it?

Take care, Hugo. I am afraid we will have to postpone seeing each other until the fall; maybe you can come here again in November.

Many, many kind regards from,

Yours, Ottonie

P.S. Are you working and on what, and how are your plans for Aussee coming?

❦ ❦ ❦

Bad Aussee, 27 August [1924]

Dearest,

Just a quick word regarding the idea of a spur of the moment visit in Basel. In the absence of Carl B., I do not think it looks good. Naturally I know that you would undertake this in a very straightforward and gracious manner; neither have I ever lost sight of the goal you have in mind here. However, I would very strongly not recommend it. It comes down to this: the helpful mother is a clumsy woman and not very useful. The children do not support her. That is why Carl has not been there the entire summer; he will not be returning there in the fall either but rather will be coming to our place. Dori von der Mühll is a charming person and very bright. Still I have the feeling it would be better if you did not do this under the circumstances. It is also extremely uncomfortable to travel there from Basel up to Schönenberg by train – and I somehow have the feeling that it would be unpleasant for Carl, in particular because he has tremendous admiration for you and wants nothing more than to see more of you. And herein of course lies the problem!

We had made such lovely plans, each of us with a project, to come to your place on the 10th of November for three or four weeks as "paying guests." How sad! It could have been such a wonderful and rich form of existence. Of course there is nothing to criticize here – what you did is certainly understandable. I hope it is not for more than a year. To see you a few weeks a year does not seem to be enough to me but much too little – in any case it is the very minimum.

So now I have one request: come here on the 15th or the 20th of October for two weeks. We will then manage very well the four of us together, Gerty, you, B. and I; the little house is easy to heat. We have a good cook! Please do not say no! For your train and so on, I will of course invite you (my material situation is much better now than during the absurd years of the past). Please say yes soon!

Yours, Hugo

❦ ❦ ❦

[Bad Aussee] Saturday evening, 27 [September 1924]

Yes, please see that you arrive here the evening of the 20th; that is a wonderful date. We will inquire at the station as to how the trains will be running then. I ask for your forgiveness if I repeat this (only in the thought of perhaps having thought but not yet expressed it) that you of course are my *guest* "on this trip."

I am, however, very happy that you saw the Hahnloser collection.[257] It was precisely this about which I had recently heard a great deal and very much regretted not knowing the people personally, and hence being able to pave the way for you to the Villa Flora; it seems that the pushy little bug from St. (incidentally, I have not seen him, it seems, since he ran me down in Rodaun as a sixteen or seventeen year old boy – that was a long time ago) had the right idea. You surely also instinctively treated him with the necessary prudence! Oh yes, we, too, have had the foehn here for the past ten days, which causes one's ideas to freeze within one's head instead of jostling around nicely, and I truly suffer very much during this time of year which is so crucial for my work – but the same thing happens every year, where one is brought rather close to the brink of despair, and in the end, one continues to live after all. By the way, I was in Vienna for four days in the meantime for the performance of *Ruinen von Athen* [Ruins of Athens]. Beethoven's music is wonderful, based on an old and rather flat festival play by Kotzebue, which Strauss and I tinkered around with so that it could once again be performed on the stage, where it should remain – most of all on account of the talented ballet director, Kroeller, who added one more thing to the program that same evening: a ballet, *Don Juan*, by Gluck; and this in particular turned out absolutely wonderfully – the colors, the lighting and the rhythm; and I suppose this will be the real joy of the evening. I have not seen anything as beautiful since the Russians, and as it will probably remain a part of the Viennese repertoire, I hope you will be able to see it in January. Mell's *Apostelspiel* will be performed at the beginning of October in the Josefstädter Theater; he will direct it himself. I hope it is well received and will perhaps be presented here later. We are also expecting Burckhardt at the beginning of October. We sent a telegram to Rudi, but he did not deem it worth answering.

Adieu, dearest. Please do write once in the meantime; there is no reason not to know anything of one another because we will be meeting soon.

Yours, Hugo.

---

257. One of the best Swiss private collections, specializing in French paintings of the nineteenth and twentieth centuries.

❦ ❦ ❦

[Rodaun] 24 January 1925

Dearest, such a good letter from you, in which you so completely reveal yourself. I would rather, if even in a few lines, respond immediately! On the other hand, I had heard absolutely nothing from you for so long! Not a word from Basel, not a word from the unknown place where you were staying afterwards. Completely unknown, and anonymous – so that I was unable even to think of writing to you. The anonymity was also underscored by the following: a card arrived from Marie-Therese for Raimund; it included neither the date, nor the place, nor the hotel – nothing. Can the dreadful child do nothing but mimic her mother *in this respect?*

I was in Leipzig in December. The main reason aside from a contract and quite a few business matters was that I asked Rudi to come and invited him to spend two days with me in Dresden. The two turned into four – and they were immensely beneficial days. I left feeling happy that the stiffness around him and in him was truly beginning to dissolve – that we will have him back again. That he can cast away the burden of this wretched craftsman's life. [Here, two ink blots appear on the letter.] (Gerty refilled my inkwell; now I am beginning to understand.) This provides him a second and exceedingly charming youth. The dear, exceptional, incomparable man!

Along with the same mail as yours there arrived a rather strange and beautiful letter from Burckhardt from Paris. He captures the city in his own way, which always has something human and grand about it, something very non-bourgeois and not up-to-date. I hope – if I arrive there around the middle of February for a few days – to find him there. I will then board a ship in Bordeaux and sail by way of Lisbon to Casablanca, the French harbor in West Africa, from where one can reach Morocco. Then across Morocco and Algiers to Tunis and back to Marseille. I have been invited by the *Compagnie transatlantique.* (How I would love to take you with me.) I will probably be accompanied by Dr. Zifferer from the Austrian Embassy in Paris. This is no goodbye, but rather something I just had to tell you.

Yours, Hugo

❦ ❦ ❦

Rabat, Morocco, Seaport on the Atlantic Ocean, 17 March 1925

I constantly think of this gift you have been given, perhaps the best of all – not for others but for yourself – this gift of being able to behold a thing and to experience profound and intense enjoyment through the sense of sight, which is granted to so few among our intellectual and sensuously poor people. Often I could not help thinking of you when, the hour before sundown – anticipating it – I sat on the tower of my battlement, twenty meters above the large market square of Marrakesh, with the turreted red walls of this enormous city below me – the Paris of the Sahara, the ancient Berber city, only superficially influenced by Arab culture. The flood of caravans of black and semi-black Negroes, who come to barter, to trade, to buy and to look around. And right beneath me the crowded square – "Square of the Dead" it is called, strangely enough, named after some mass killing many hundreds of years ago – and so full of life, five or ten thousand people shoving around the place, and so many mules, so many camels; and it is actually quiet, not a sound except of drums and archaic musical instruments, a monotonous, numbing and exciting rhythm – from here, and from there. Here the made-up little dancers dressed like girls and swaying their hips like girls; there the snake charmer with his assistants, who play the flute and beat tambourines. He is a giant from a valley high up in the Atlas Mountains, with a stiff, black upstanding mane – who has a certain grace in spite of his wildness, and a sense of humor; frightening yet magnificent, he waves someone forward from the seated circle, and then, breathing heavily on him, tells him his future. Then he acts like a wild clown when – while at first the wicked, sand-gray viper remains half-asleep on the tambourine, only occasionally darting forward – he pulls his assistant, the bald-headed one, back and forth as if he wanted to push him into the snake; and still the wonderful, perfectly formed circle of people sitting and standing around him, old men and youths, Arabs and Sudanese, high-ranking men with white beards and beggars in rags – all watching with the same tense attentiveness. And another such perfectly formed circle surrounds the old narrator of heroic deeds and merry tales; a smaller one surrounds the one partly reciting, partly singing a love story to the accompaniment of a flute – there are perhaps eight such circles which fill out the longest part of the market square. Here and there someone rides by and brings his mount to a stop and looks or listens over the shoulders of those standing around; others leave the circle and tend to their business again. Over on the other side where the market becomes wider, close to a hundred mules stand, laden with bundles of green barley, in a sun-drenched, dusty place; there the buyers constantly come and go.

If I divert my gaze somewhat away from the market, I look into a Fonduk, such an enormous, open yard, perhaps two hundred yards square; there they unload the merchandise; here and there a kneeling camel, and the gray, patient asses wait in the half shadow for the next load or even for a bit of rest. Surrounding this big yard – already darkening, with a light here and there – is the jumble of the narrow, reed-covered merchant alleys: the Suk. The stands there are now closing. During the daytime, there is a life there unlike any other in the narrowest of spaces. One alleyway full of tailors, another filled with dyers – or jewelers or smiths or slipper merchants or spice merchants. No store is bigger than a closet. They sit there on top of the spices, on top of the dates. And in such a spot, the silver smith works, a child blows the fire for him, and behind him an old man sleeps while the sparks fly around his beard.

If, however, I turn to look behind me, away from the market, the city is completely silent; a thousand flat roofs made of loam, here and there a palace with high walls, dark turrets, and in the back a garden. Encircling the town are two walls covered with dark turrets, and extending all the way around them is a cordon of palms. On the outside there are still nomadic villages for the itinerant tribes who camp in front of the gates. And further on stand the sultan's large oil palm groves reflected in the stone-edged pools. All around this lies the farthest horizon my eyes have ever beholden. Directly south of here is the glorious snow chain of the Atlas Mountains, close to twenty peaks eternally covered by snow – none much smaller than Mont Blanc. To the west – not visible, yet perceptible – lies the sea, into which the sun now abruptly plunges, so that the city is seized by a purple glow, and one part of the circle of palm trees dissolves into liquid gold. In the north, somewhat to the northeast, is a smaller mountain range, amethyst colored, with a light green sky. But who could ever describe this! Below, the market now becomes louder and louder, the hand drums and whistles more and more intense.

I did not write this letter in one sitting. Yesterday while I was writing, I was collected by some young officers of the government to go to tea, and in the meantime I have changed places and am writing this in Meknesch, an old sultan city 200 km inland in the mid-range mountains. Adieu. I hope you and the little one are well. I saw Burckhardt in Paris.

Yours, Hugo

❦ ❦ ❦

[Rodaun, 7 August 1925]

Of course, dearest, you absolutely must bring the child[258] with you! For whom else other than young people do we arrange such a feast anyway! And who should enjoy it now – and remember it later – except them!

So auf Wiedersehen! We are taking the automobile to Salzburg tomorrow, Gerty, Christiane, Raimund and I. Franzi will be coming later.

---

258. O. D. S. was asked to bring M.-T. along to the Salzburg Festival.

Countless times during these days I have thought of the days in July of 1920 and '21, those lovely weeks at your place, the days of hard work, the emergence, largely, of *Der Turm* and so many of my most important plans and sketches. I hope all there is well!

Yours, Hugo

❦ ❦ ❦

Bad Aussee, 5 December 1925. Rodaun, beginning the 7th

But no, dear beloved! No!

Several days before your letter arrived I said to Gerty: "Now the good Lord should give me three weeks – instead of being the last day of November it should be the 4th or 5th, when I could still go to Ottonie's and write the second act of the comedy. (The comedy[259] with Greek costumes, i.e. in the present but partially veiled – when the cocotte and the public speaker oppose one another, she for aristocracy, he for democracy.)

It is so wonderful to be with you in complete peace in late autumn or at the beginning of winter. (However, I do not even know if you are alone) – and it is now the beginning of December, and I have to go to Vienna. (And anyway the winter came terribly fast and early; we are stuck in deep snow, and at night it is 10 to 14 degrees below zero.)

However, this is how things were in the autumn: it was very uncertain whether or not Burckhardt would be coming, and not just for a short time, for he was finally supposed to write his post-doctoral thesis, and this required going to a Swiss library and it was supposed to be finished by Christmas. And Schröder promised to come sometime this autumn – it was truly an absolute nightmare! And Christiane wanted to stay with us here for a "long time" – so I was probably going to be there with two women, and perhaps three, the thought of this was too frightening. Then Burckhardt came around the 20th of September and stayed for about three weeks. However, it was not a good visit. His gloomy hypochondria took control of him – this terribly dark, subterranean streak – and ruined this time for him and for us. And then Rudi came, on the 15th of October, and was charming as only he can be (and his cheerfulness, despite the dismal background, was so touching); and he added on one day after another and stayed until All Saints' Day [1 November]. If one had known beforehand, indeed, if one might have known this at the start of his visit, how lovely it would have been to call you!

Then on All Souls' Day, Rudi left, Christiane left; Raimund had left earlier, and I stayed alone with Gerty during this gloomy, foggy month (it was so completely different from the previous one of ours). For me, how-

---

259. *Timon,* never completed.

ever, and for my work, this month was the best. I worked my way through the remaining acts of the comedy so that now they really only need to be covered by one more light coat in order to be complete. And then I spent many, many hours turning to an old project again – a novel-like story.[260] I had written a large part of it in 1912, the first book and the blueprint for its completion; I have now gained much greater sovereignty over such a plan. I hope I can come up with an exact plan for all four (or five?) books during the next half year, as well as for the individual chapters. Considering my life as a whole, I matured both early and late in my life.

Dearest, write a word to me in Rodaun; I wonder, have you received *Der Turm* (in book form) from Wiegand? Otherwise I will send it to you right away.

I received very nice letters recently from rather young people I did not know, scattered around here and there in the great and obscure Germany. I would like to write Hans Wilke a letter again sometime. But first, do tell me in a few words, so that I understand the situation: whatever does it mean that he is accepting a position in America, as he does after all have the estates, and thus also a profession?

Yours, Hugo

Vienna, 15 January 1926

Dearest, my talk with Franckenstein[261] did not yield anything for Luli. He does not have any vacancies (not a single "pigeonhole" is unoccupied at present); he advises against work as a volunteer with the possibility of occasionally playing some small role. Instead, he offers the following assistance: (Noting that this is on a "friendly" basis), Luli should write him a letter after the 22nd of this month which explains where and what kind of apprenticeship she has had, the roles she has already played, the roles she has studied. He will then strongly recommend her to several agents. (With a picture enclosed.) He says this is the only possible way.

If it works out that I am able to invite you for a stay in Sorrento or Amalfi from the 3rd to the 13th of March, could you come by yourself around the 3rd of March to Naples? In any case, please write me about this. I say the 3rd of March, but the 1st suits me just as well; only the end date (13th) is somewhat restricted.

Mädy and Christa are here and have found a flat. They wish that things did not cost so much, which is really not possible now. Does H. W.

---

260. *Andreas,* a fragment.
261. Clemens von Franckenstein, director of the Munich Opera.

really keep Mädy on such a tight shoestring that she is unable to spend more than 500 or 600 Marks a month?

Yours, Hugo

❦ ❦ ❦

Rodaun, 18 March [1926] evening

My dearest one, even though it is suddenly snowing like mad again, and I only have a third of my five senses at my disposal, I do not wish to allow myself to be prevented from writing you. I am enclosing what I wrote for the Zurich *Reading Circle* about Schröder as a poet, which seems to have pleased him a lot. They delivered the magazine to him the moment he arrived. It was of course rather hastily written; they scarcely left me any time with their order for the scantiest of thought and attention. So it just turned out the way it did; however, without such pressure, nothing would have come of it.

You wrote me several dear lines at the end of January from somewhere near the Pyrenees. I could not determine how you had gotten there, and with whom? To whom? However, this did not diminish the pleasure I derived from knowing that you were enjoying yourself in a sunny place. (But your letters are too *hard* to read. No other handwriting causes me such problems. You write one letter like the other; one word can be "liebt" or "Hund" or "Dampf" or "klebt" – one must simply guess. If you only wouldn't write quite so hastily, and would sometimes write one or the other letter with a bit more care!)

Well, it is hard to speak of myself and of a winter such as this. Really it has been an unproductive time, and sometimes it seems a completely miserable time to me – it was also an extremely terrible, humid, dark, endless winter – on the other hand, my inner tension is so great that a much younger man could not begin to bear it – as a result of the richness of the possibilities hovering inside of me. Compared to this, my self of twenty years ago seems rather poor and empty.

The theater is a terribly capricious device. All these things are so uncertain, so threatened in themselves; all of this has taken on a form which just twenty years ago would have seemed like the monstrous product of some kind of a crazy dream. Back then everything seemed so obvious, and everything seemed directed towards a dull, secure eternity – today everything is questionable, and one lives in grandiose uncertainty, as aboard a sinking ship. And now I must utter the peculiar truth, the strange experience of these last six years, since around 1920: that it is this that caused my powers to grow – and that it sometimes seems to me that I have only truly been alive since the world assumed this character. How much I would like to talk to Eberhard about all this. What a pity that one cannot speak to the dead about such things.

I now want to carry out this old plan I had for *Herbstmondnacht* [Moon Night in Autumn] sometime soon, in which a fifty-year-old man may have a quarter of an hour to talk to his much younger, yet deceased, wife.

I wanted to go down south, i.e. to Sicily, but circumstances got in the way. However, now an idea suddenly flashed through my mind: there may be a performance of *Cristina* here around the 20th of April – which, if it comes about, will be lovely. How would it be if you were invited for five or six days around that time? Would this be possible, in principle? Or do you have plans to go to Mecklenburg, Ireland, Swabia or Norway during this time?

Do you have *Der Turm* yet? Good night!

Yours, Hugo

P.S. I am having a little, exceedingly strange brochure sent to you, one written by a doctor named Kohnstamm, who died in 1917. Did I not hear Eberhard mention this name? In connection to what?

R., 9 April 1926

Dear Ottonie, that was a tremendously well-written letter; every word was legible, and for that reason, it also contained so much news and much beauty (and unfortunately also some sad things). That about the 20th being the day of the premiere of *Cristina* was not meant to be taken too literally; it might also be the 23rd or 26th, so one cannot plan for this, but perhaps for the one in May. Two ladies from Hamburg[262] is of course a lot; I imagine the whole thing as a municipal coat of arms, two walking towers and in the middle the little Ottonie. But could you not start the whole thing *a few days earlier*? For on the morning of the 17th, I will be driving with Gerty and Christiane in the automobile to central Germany – to Weimar by way of Regensburg and Bamberg, then down the Lahn to Koblenz by way of Kassel, and finally to Heidelberg. The date of departure cannot be changed as we must be at Roffredo Gaetani's opera in Weimar on the 21st.

So please think it over, and write me about it.

Yours, Hugo

---

262. O. D. S. had an informal finishing school for young ladies, and these were two tall girls who were arriving from Hamburg.

Rodaun, 30 July 1926

Dear Ottonie, that is a date, the 30th of July, that brings to mind many a memory. I was with you sometimes then. Once it was extremely hot. These were good days, though. I would like very much to be there in the peace and quiet with you again sometime – I am so fond of your calm, earnest, sincere nature; when it is noisy, which makes you loud, too, I can no longer recognize you; everything seems to change then, including your gestures; I cannot imagine that you are the same person with whom I have spent so very many hours.

This summer is terrible, simply without precedent. It is the worst summer I have ever experienced; I lead the life of an invalid, there is not a single hour when I am in possession of my intellectual powers. This is an inconspicuous yet severe test that has been imposed on me. I am going to rewrite *Der Turm* in the autumn. In particular the last two acts are going to undergo considerable change. I enjoy doing this. If only the atmosphere does not rob me of all my strength again.

I will take care of the matter with Madame de Planta,[263] however, I do not think that R. [Reinhardt] will be presenting anything before the 15th. The premiere of *Turandot* is of course not until the 13th, and up to then there will surely be rehearsals every evening and into the night.

We once had the idea of getting into Raimund's little car the day before you were to come to Salzburg – namely on the 16th or 17th to meet you in Neubeuern. Would it be possible to spend the night there? But what good does it do to make plans; the weather will be miserable. Also I am afraid Mädy is probably there, too! Carl Burckhardt now writes about Christa on occasion saying that she is such a smart child. He said nobody ever looked after her – what is going on here again?

Yours, Hugo

Bad Aussee, 8 September 1926

Ottonie, what shall we do now with Rudi again! Indeed, I have no greater desire than to ask you to come to Aussee today or tomorrow – although I really wanted to have both of you here together, and now again he is not answering me. He is probably sitting in a corner, fat and mad, hating the world and drinking cocktails; admiring his Dahlias, while hoping from one hour to the next that a telegram will arrive saying we have all died of the plague and he need not come, because it is too late to make the funeral anyway.

---

263. A friend of the Burckardt's in Geneva to whom M.-T. was introduced during her study year there.

What to do? Maybe you could help! Couldn't you call him on the phone? However, that may be too complicated. Perhaps you can tell or write Wiegand that *he* should call him and ask! I am very happy that I spent the twenty-four hours in Hinterhör. I was very moved by everything – and indeed you remain the same, and the little one is a dear, serious, and good child. I definitely want to come and stay with you this winter.

One other thing, Ottonie. You said you might be able to help out with a trip to America[264] for one or even both of the boys. I have suddenly been hit with a lot of expenses. The little one is also supposed to go there, and even further to the west. The first half of October or a bit later is the time I have in mind. Can you possibly arrange something then?

Yours, Hugo.

P.S. Carl unfortunately foolishly interrupted work on the novel, which was progressing so wonderfully, because of certain personal considerations. He does not know yet what dangers one is exposing oneself to.

Bad Aussee, 9 September 1926

Dearest, Rudi announces his arrival on the 22nd of Oct. (i.e. around this date, as I told him that I will be in Vienna from the 18th to the 21st of Oct.) I suppose that is rather late, but it is usually so lovely and peaceful during late autumn. Would that suit you? Maybe it will be possible for you to come with him from Munich, and perhaps I can fetch you both in Salzburg.

One more thing: please send me your copy of Kohnstamm's examination here quickly as registered printed matter.

Yours, Hugo

Aussee, 9 October 1926

Dearest, maybe I should just say it once, and not only to myself, that I am happy beyond words that I will have you and Rudi here at the same time at the end of this month – and that the thought of this has already lit up all the weeks that lie behind me, which were rather severe.

If only Rudi does not do anything to disappoint me this time! I wrote him over and over again; now that Wiegand is in Bremen, I again asked him to talk it over with Rudi, so that he will be sure to make plans to come here from Munich on the morning of the 22nd via Salzburg, and I hope *with you*! Do still write him in your own words in the same vein; it is

---

264. O. D. S. had good connections to the Hamburg-America Line.

much easier in life to do too little rather than too much to bring about a good thing.

The September weeks were severe because my domestic duties fought with those much more stringent ones of the artist; indeed they fought among themselves. For while I once again felt the need to dedicate all my strength and attention to *Der Turm* one final time, new material forced itself on me with such savagery that I nearly became ill; during all this, the rather difficult preparations for the departure of the two boys were underway. Both are facing a rather problematic future at the same time, although not together; Franz left on the 29th of Sept. from Hamburg, the younger one on the 1st of Oct. from Cherbourg.

The person who is suffering so miserably from migraines almost without interruption is Isepp's wife. Will you see Dr. Glaser and then write something?

These days call forth particularly vivid memories of certain long-past October months at the castle. What old friends we have become!

Yours, Hugo.

P.S. Because of an international congress over which I, taking turns with Seipel,[265] am to preside, I will be in Vienna (Stallburggasse 2) on the 18th, 19th, and 20th; on the 21st I will be back in Aussee.

Bad Aussee, 20 November [1926] In Rodaun beginning 26 November

Dearest, please read the enclosed essay first, then the letter written by someone I do not know, which I found very moving. Here one is searching for teachers, and the country's best and brightest young people are eking out an existence between starvation and serving as private tutors!

It makes me immensely happy to remember our conversations and to feel how you have given your life a wonderful new meaning through the school.[266]

Yours, Hugo

---

265. Ignaz Seipel (1876–1931) Chancelor of Austria.

266. In 1925 Julie started a boarding school for boys in part of the castle. O. D. S. was taking the ten- and eleven-year-olds to Hinterhör, and they lived in the same rooms H. v. H. always had inhabited. For O. D. S., this meant a very satisfying occupation; she shared the responsibility with the teacher in residence and became some sort of a mother for the boys who were for the first time away from home. In 1942, the Nazis suddenly closed the school. Later, many of the boys kept returning to Hinterhör and kept in close contact with O. D. S. until her death. After World War II ended, M.-T. returned to Neubeuern with her husband Ralph Miller, who advised her to go to the Military Government in Munich and have the sale of the school declared a "duress sale." With that, M.-T. was able to create a non-profit foundation, and deed the whole place to the school in 1948, when it reopened, now for boys and girls.

P.S. A book that will be sent to you by the Fischer Publishers is for you, but by no means for the schoolboys.

May I ask you to thank the poet,[267] who lived at Neubeuern, on my behalf for a few kind lines he wrote?

🌿 🌿 🌿

Girgenti, 19 February 1927

Dear, good Ottonie, I am rather unhappy and also somewhat ashamed to have to retract the invitation now after all. I see that it is very different regarding the time than one imagines in advance; four or five days in such a place doing nothing but recuperating really is a long time; planning in advance is hard, too, because everything is so overfull, and one often receives no response at all to telegraphic inquiries, and now I am quite certain that we will be in Milan around the 4th of March and very much on our way home! Please do not be angry with me – instead I am placing all my hope in your coming to visit us at the end of April or in May. I hope then to have an automobile and a decent chauffeur, so that Rodaun and the city are no longer separated, but rather that one can stay in both places at the same time.

Poor Mädy in Vienna was a terribly sad sight – the thought that this is Eberhard's wife, who flutters around in a city so senseless and without dignity – much like a bat, which also is such a poor little animal – and who, fluttering around, can indeed cause an entire room full of people to feel restless, bumping into everything, constantly becoming entangled, neither welcome nor comfortable anywhere. The poor, poor thing.

Good, dear Ottonie, it was so pleasant in Munich; I hope the child is once again completely well – and I hope to see you soon.

I can't give a better address now than Rodaun; everything is most likely to reach us from there.

In friendship,

Yours, Hugo

🌿 🌿 🌿

Neubeuern-Inn, Oberbayern, 8 March 1927

So finally we have peace again here, and the constant balls have come to an end.[268] Baby of course had a wonderful time, and, thank God, also managed to avoid the engagement everyone was expecting. I have to say

---

267. Albrecht Schaeffer.
268. O. D. S. had to spend three months with M.-T. in Munich for M.-T.'s coming-out in society.

that I am really tired, for it seems to me that something like that is much more of a strain on a mother.

It was really a pity that my coming to Italy did not work out; however, it couldn't be helped, as you had to return so early. I hope it was as nice as you had hoped and you were able to truly recuperate; it is just a pity that you had to return so soon and still have all of April ahead of you.

Mädy has finally resolved now to move to Munich and also found a very handsome flat in Widenmaierstrasse, close to the Wolffs. May she be somewhat happier there! I am going to Sondershausen to my mother with Christa in a few days and from there to Meineweh, in order to supervise the move,[269] which will not be very easy sorting through things in this house crammed so full. We also plan to go to see Hans Wilke in Degenershausen for two days, with whom all the negotiations have also finally come to an end now.

Luli has been offered[270] a three-year contract by the *Schauspielhaus* in Munich. Her agent came here today to help her with this; it seems she is considered in Munich to be a talent who only lacks a routine. She has turned into a rather intelligent creature with lots of ideas and a great deal of charm; we really had a lot of fun with her.

So, addio for now, Hugo. Many thanks to Gerty for her dear letter. Baby has been completely well for two weeks now; it was a stupid flu and throat infection.

Always yours, Ottonie

🌿 🌿 🌿

[Hinterhör] 5 May 1927

Dear Hugo, today Carl and Elisabeth[271] resumed their travels after we had spent several extremely delightful days with them. I find his little wife exceedingly charming; in my view, she is a very good addition to Carl's life in her quiet, balanced way. In many respects she is like a delightful little girl and then again surprisingly mature; she knows exactly what she wants. At first one does not find her very pretty at all, and then she starts to please you more and more. Carl told me that you want to go visit them in the automobile, sometime around the end of May. Couldn't you go by way of Hinterhör? I am all alone; Baby will be traveling to England via Hamburg on the 17th and I do not have any paying guests right now, so you would not have to have anything to do with strangers. Mädy will be busy in Munich for a while furnishing her flat, and by happy chance she

---

269. Of Mädy's furniture, which was stored there.
270. Luli Bodenhausen had become an actress.
271. Elisabeth Burckhardt, Carl's wife, née de Reynold.

found a gentleman lodger; this way she has somebody to take care of and cannot sit around here with us. I would be happy if you wrote me a line as soon as possible about whether you could come and when. Carl spent one evening conversing with the students[272]. I had once read aloud to them his *Reise* [Trip], which they had found very interesting. It was of course a major event for them to speak to the author. The school is growing, now there are already eighty-two boys here, and it will hardly be possible to accept any more, as every corner of the house is being used now.

I was in Zurich recently and saw Dori, who came from Basel to meet me; she was delighted by her stay in Vienna and recounted so delightfully all the things she had heard and seen. Christa spent several additional days in Basel at Dori's and left from there for England with friends.

Take care, Hugo. It would be so good if you came here for a little while.

Many regards, also to Gerty,

Yours, Ottonie

❦ ❦ ❦

Rodaun, 25 May 1927

My dearest one, maybe I already wrote everything that follows ten or twelve days ago – not only in my head, but also on paper – and sent it to you, that may very well be; I am very confused now due to a multitude of occupations and concerns (mostly about both the boys – how often am I reminded of Eberhard's fatherly concerns, which connects me to him all over again). If so, please excuse my confusion; but just in case, I will finally write it down today. If it is at all possible for me to visit Carl, then only for a short time (because I have to be back before Reinhardt leaves here; nothing has really been determined yet regarding *Der Turm*, despite R's more than good intentions, indeed his love for this work). And of course I will also be traveling by train; I never thought of driving there in an automobile, that was merely Carl daydreaming.

However, I am very glad that he came to visit you; the last thing he had said was that this would be impossible, that is the kind of panic his fear of Mädy engenders (which I understand, and which Eberhard would understand; and which perhaps a woman, you and Gerty or Julie, could never fully understand. For us it is the deepest of horrors that a woman can be like that.) But indeed he went there (maybe he noticed that I felt sad when he said this to me, although I did reply), and apparently he was

---

272. O. D. S. invited the senior class of the boys in the school to listen to Carl read from his "Reise," a trip to Turkey on which he had been sent by the International Red Cross to report on the Armenians there, who suffered terribly from Turkish atrocities.

very happy, as you were with him and Elisabeth (whom one is all the more fond of the better one gets to know her), and the school impressed him very much. I am glad about this and can now discuss it with him further.

My life is hard at the moment, and my unpredictable girlfriend and comforter — the imagination — gave way to her ugly half-sister: worry.

I will write again soon.

Yours, Hugo

❧ ❧ ❧

Rodaun, 8 January 1928

Dearest, I think I will arrive in Munich on the 23rd, will be staying in the Marienbad and hope very much to see you. I will try to see the various important people who live there and to bring some of them together now and again. I would stay until the 5th, assuming that the 4th remains the date of the premiere. Maybe afterwards I can come to Hinterhör with you for two or three days and see a bit of the boys. But above all I hope that you will come to Munich during this time!

Did you circulate the book by T. E. Lawrence[273] among the boys? It will show them an extraordinary man, who emerges from this book with exceptional force. At the beginning of November you promised that you would *soon* return the magazine *Kreatur* to me. Please do so now *immediately*.

Much love, Hugo

P.S. I will be going from Munich to Berlin via Frankfurt and would like to spend a few days in Degenershausen on the way to visit Eberhard's grave. Do you think that Hans Wilke will welcome my visit around 8 to 10 of February?

❧ ❧ ❧

Schönenberg, 19 February 1929

Dear Ottonie, we are three here together; however, we often speak so very animatedly of you that you are truly, at least every other day, a fourth among us. Elisabeth, who indeed of all of us has known you by far the shortest time, is extremely attached to you; in general this little person has such a keen sense for quality and calm and so consistently makes accurate judgments about people and relationships. She still has at least ten

---

273. *Seven Pillars of Wisdom.*

years ahead of her during which she can constantly continue to become wiser and nicer, and one cannot imagine how far she will go.

Our life is enormously peaceful; by contrast, Aussee was a Montmartre. Indeed we are rather the prisoners of the severe winter; the body needs every bit of strength it has to constantly and quietly defend itself, and little remains for the imagination. So it may be that one had already written a letter like this one in one's mind six or eight days ago, and then it freezes once again, with the ground, in the forests, where the old beech tree trunks crack from the cold and the deer lie dead in the bushes, and the frozen songbirds fall down on top of them.

During the past days, I have been especially sad about the death of poor old Zifferer.[274] Here this poor, sensible and loyal old man had to leave after five of the most excruciating months of suffering from a rare illness, whose name the doctors concealed from him; and he was scarcely ready or prepared to die, the poor fellow.

I think about Eberhard all the time; his grave is cold; however, he is somewhere else – there where he had already been at certain times during his life.

Mädy has now opened her main headquarters in Vienna, and Luli is performing in the theater, in the *Burgtheater* of all places – without any talent, and probably without believing to have any talent either. The whole thing is a symphony of false notes, everything about it is silly, every nuance wrong and undignified, and this appears under the name of Eberhard, who epitomized dignity and despised everything silly and unnecessary more than death. I did not see her.

Auf Wiedersehen, Ottonie; I think I will stop by there during the second half of March – will you be there?

Yours, Hugo

༃ ༃ ༃

Schönenberg, Thursday, 28 February 1929

Yes, dearest Ottonie, what a pity that Mädy is there, because I had hoped to visit you sometime around the 20th of March with Gerty on the way home from Heidelberg. But now maybe you can come to Munich as our guest for two days (where I must be for various meetings) – even spending a few hours together can be of immense importance for old friends joined together by so many ties; I realized this again yesterday when Rudi passed through and I, down in Basel, was able to spend five hours together with him. As is typically the case, we ended up discussing an effort on which we find ourselves in complete agreement to not only

---

274. Paul Zifferer (1874–1929), writer and Austrian cultural attaché in Paris.

keep the memory of Eberhard alive in our hearts, but also in the world; there we both achieved the same insight that Rudi did through assiduous reading of the correspondence, and through which something had become apparent to me long ago: Eberhard was not given the ability to express his true self in words – written words. If the books he wrote on the history of art do not reveal the rich and deep nature of the author, then the same may be said of his letters; they were and are precious for the recipient, who behind these dry and often ordinary lines could feel one of the kindest of friends speaking to him, or as if he had just received instructions from an incomparable superior; for someone with no connection to him they are ordinary letters. So the task remains to portray the figure of this unforgettable man through some medium. Rudi undertook this task[275] and has already found the solution: it is the most worthy of honors which he has bestowed upon Eberhard – he does a marvelous job of maintaining the limits between that which one could express to an intimate friend and the way in which one must present this strange, indeed, profoundly symbolic figure, to strangers. I hoped to set myself the goal of giving more. I took a lot of notes, from the intuition provided by loving reflection. Whether or not I am capable of bringing these notes together to form a true picture – today I ask myself. Missing is everything which gives color, everything which gives shape (herein, too, lies something symbolic). There is no anecdote, no special characteristic, no peculiarity; no visible success, no climax, no verdicts. Everything is rounded, shapeless, everything avoiding success or fulfillment – and in that respect it is so moving, and exemplary. But how to depict this? However, I shall not despair. I hope to discuss this unresolved, elusive "material" with Rudi. Auf Wiedersehen.

Yours, Hugo

❦ ❦ ❦

[Postcard]   [Rodaun] 15 July [1929]

My dear, good friend,
    Please write Rudi about what happened to us, and if you can, to Borchardt as well.
    His address is Candiglia *Pistoia*.

Yours, H.

❦ ❦ ❦

---

275. R. A. Schröder created a beautiful memorial of bronze and stone for E.'s grave.

It is the day of the annual sports festival at the Neubeuern school. Julie, Ottonie, and Marie-Therese are all there watching the boys perform at the high jump and broad jump. Suddenly, a messenger arrives with a telegram in hand, searching for Countess Degenfeld. Reading the text, she turns white as a sheet. M.-T. rushes to her and reads: "Franz has committed suicide, Hugo." M.-T. leads her mother back to the castle, helps her pack, drives her to the station, and puts her on the train to Vienna.

In Rodaun, so many of H. v. H.'s friends gather at the cemetery for Franz's funeral. It does not begin, since his parents have not arrived. People start getting nervous; something must be wrong. Then word comes: Hofmannsthal is dead. The shock of his son's suicide had been too much for his delicate nervous system. While dressing for the funeral, he had collapsed and died.

Upon returning to Neubeuern, Ottonie said: "If only Hugo could have been among us, there for once were nearly all his friends together; how often did he try to arrange such a gathering."

Index

Works by Hugo von Hofmannsthal

Abenteuer, 369
Die ägyptische Helena (The Egyptian Helena), xii, xxii, 399, 400, 401, 403, 404
Amor and Psyche, 121, 124
Andreas, 418
Arabella, xii, xxii, xxiii, 42
Arabian Nights, Introduction, 282
Ariadne auf Naxos, xii, xvi, xx, xxi, xxii, xlii, 66, 112, 114, 116, 132, 133, 135, 137, 150, 153, 164, 169, 175, 183, 200, 202, 208, 211, 214, 244, 285, 286, 401
"Beethoven," Speech, 366
Begegnungen, 296
Book of Friends, 375
Der Bürger als Edelmann, Translation, 302, 308, 346, 379
Cristinas Heimreise (Cristina's Homecoming), 4, 6, 9, 369, 420
Die deutschen Erzähler, Introduction, 198, 200
Elektra, xii, xvi, xxi
Florindoscenen, 369
Die Frau ohne Schatten, Libretto, xii, xxii, 112, 145, 158, 167, 198, 199, 245, 246, 336, 373, 374
Die Frau ohne Schatten, Fairy Tale, 238, 250, 251, 287, 298, 311, 313, 315, 336, 346, 354
Die Furcht (Fear), 296
Gespräche in Rodaun (Conversations in Rodaun), 366
"Harlekin," xlii, 66, 311
Herbstmondnacht (Moon Night in Autumn), 420
"Homer," Essay, 164, 176, 181
Jedermann, 112, 120, 121, 123, 128, 131, 133, 140, 148, 149, 150, 154, 162, 167, 176, 179, 180, 199, 204, 205, 240, 243, 360, 361, 381, 387
Josephslegende, 186, 255
Die Lästigen (Annoying People), 283, 307
"Maria Theresia," 299
La mort du jeune homme voluptueux, 187
Oedipus Rex, Translation, 8, 10, 14, 50, 63, 107
Orest, 187
Prosaschriften (Writings in Prose), 296, 368
"Reitergeschichte," xv
Der Rosenkavalier, Opera, xii, xxx, 4, 34, 39, 46, 51, 55, 59, 65, 99, 278, 301
Der Rosenkavalier, Film, 396
Ruins of Athens, Stage Performance, 413
Der Schwierige (The Problematic One), 287, 294, 295, 297, 344, 373, 374, 379, 383, 408, 410
Sophocles' Antigone, Prelude, xvi
Timon, 417
Der Tor und der Tod (Death and the Fool), 24
Der Turm (The Tower), 297, 375, 398, 400, 417, 418, 420, 421, 422, 426
Der Unbestechliche (The Incorruptible), 385, 386
"Der Wanderer," 204
Das Welttheater (The Theater of the World), 381, 382, 383, 386, 387, 391

General Index

(Includes persons and institutions, concepts and movements, and works by persons other than Hofmannsthal.)

Abeken, Rudolf; "On Goethe's *Elective Affinities*," 130
Adler, Augusta, 368
Adolf, Paul, 58, 68
Agnes, 213
Ahlers, Aida von, 100, 102, 103, 106
Ahlers, Carola von, 384
Albrecht, Duke of Württemberg, xvii
Almanach de Gotha, 60
Andrian, Leopold von, 87, 294, 295, 323, 345, 405; *Der Garten der Erkenntnis* (The Garden of Knowledge), 294
Angelus Silesius, 27
Angold, Mary, 20, 29, 69, 70, 72, 90, 100, 101, 105, 122, 123, 125, 146, 148, 150, 161, 176, 178, 186, 196, 198, 221, 227, 235, 247, 248, 395
Anna Amalia, Duchess of Sachsen-Weimar, 228
D'Annunzio, Gabriele, xxii, 164; *Vielleicht–vielleicht auch nicht* (Maybe–Maybe Not), 83, 91
Arabian Nights, 282
Art Nouveau Movement, xxiv, 56
Astruc, Gabriel, 216
Austin, Gerhard, xii

Balzac, Honoré de, 5, 6, 7, 11, 23, 75, 83, 102, 159, 161, 239, 240; *Albert Savarus* 23; *Le colonel Chabert*, 242; *La cousine Bette*, 5, 242; *Le cousin Pons*, 23; *Le curé de village*, 23, 105, 243; *Les employés*, 242; *Eugénie Grandet*, 240; *La femme de trente ans*, 9; *Histoire de la grandeur et la décadence de César Birotteau*, 144, 242; *Histoire de treize*, 243; *Illusions perdues*, 5, 144, 157, 159, 168; *L'illustre Gaudissart*, 168; *Louis Lambert*, 23; *Le lys dans la vallée*, 21, 23, 28; *La maison Nucingen*, 242; *Le médecin de campagne*, 5, 16, 21, 23, 24; *Le père Goriot* 5, 6, 242; *La recherche de l'absolu*, 23; *Séraphita*, 23; *La vieille fille*, 5, 242
Mrs. Banck, 150
Barbusse, Henri, 340; *Le feu*, 340
Mr. Barry, 241
Bassermann, Albert, 60
Mrs. Bauk, 100
Beaulieau, 257
Beethoven, Ludwig van, 137, 143, 342; *Eroica*, 278; *Hammerclavier Sonata* op. 106, 212; Piano sonatas op. 31, 212; *Ruinen von Athen*, 413
Behn, Fritz, 128, 142, 154, 155
Beinheimer Antique Shop, 142
Belke, 106
Berger, Lily 138
Bernauer, Georg, 21
Miss Bernhardt, 368
Bernsdorff, Count Albrecht von, 293, 319
Bernsdorff, Count Johann Heinrich von, 293, 319
Beroldingen, Count Egon von, 119, 284
Bethmann-Hollweg, Theobald von, 71
Bibliothek der Romane, 23
Biel, 72
Biermann, Leopold, 55
Binswanger, 208, 359, 360
Bismarck, Prince Otto von, 63
Björnson, Björnstjerne, 23
Blei, Franz, 70, 92
Blei, Sibylle, 324, 328

Blumhardt Christoph, 9
Boccaccio, Giovanni, 225
Bodenhausen, Baroness Christa von, 69, 261, 284, 287, 296, 332, 344, 371, 418, 421, 425, 426
Bodenhausen-Degener, Baroness Dora von (Mädy), 5, 6, 8, 13, 16, 17, 19, 24, 30, 34, 40, 59, 60, 68, 69, 70, 72, 77, 84, 90, 95, 98, 100, 107, 123, 125, 126, 127, 130, 131, 134, 135, 142, 145, 146, 149, 158, 160, 175, 176, 178, 179, 180, 181, 182, 185, 187, 192, 196, 207, 208, 209, 213, 216, 232, 233, 247, 248, 250, 251, 252, 253, 255, 257, 261, 266, 268, 270, 271, 280, 282, 293, 294, 303, 304, 305, 306, 309, 310, 311, 313, 315, 316, 321, 322, 323, 324, 326, 327, 329, 332, 335, 340, 349, 351, 357, 359, 360, 361, 363, 364, 367, 368, 372, 374, 377, 385, 394, 395, 396, 406, 407, 410, 411, 418, 419, 421, 424, 425, 426, 428
Bodenhausen-Degener, Baron Eberhard von (Bockelchen), xii, xviii, 3, 4, 5, 6, 10, 11, 12, 13, 14, 15, 19, 21, 24, 29, 30, 64, 68, 70, 72, 75, 77, 84, 95, 100, 107, 110, 111, 112, 113, 123, 125, 126, 129, 131, 133, 134, 135, 137, 145, 149, 150, 151, 153, 157, 164, 167, 169, 170, 174, 175, 176, 179, 180, 182, 184, 185, 192, 195, 197, 198, 199, 200, 204, 206, 213, 216, 221, 224, 225, 227, 230, 231, 232, 244, 245, 246, 248, 250, 252, 253, 255, 258, 261, 263, 267, 269, 270, 271, 272, 273, 274, 275, 277, 279, 280, 281, 285, 287, 288, 289, 291, 294, 295, 296, 297, 300, 301, 303, 304, 305, 306, 307, 308, 309, 310, 311, 312, 313, 315, 316, 317, 318, 319, 320, 322, 323, 325, 329, 330, 334, 342, 350, 354, 355, 357, 359, 360, 367, 372, 385, 388, 389, 390, 395, 397, 401, 420, 424, 426, 427, 428, 429
Bodenhausen, Baron Hans Wilke von, 80, 209, 211, 216, 251, 252, 255, 261, 287, 328, 360, 367, 368, 372, 373, 379, 384, 385, 390, 394, 404, 411, 418, 425, 427
Bodenhausen, Baroness Julie von (Luli), 94, 119, 261, 329, 352, 372, 384, 406, 407, 418, 425, 428
Bodenhausen, Baroness Karin von, 17, 98, 134, 196, 213, 252, 287, 294, 296, 299, 345, 359, 360
Bohlen, 71
Bonnard, Pierre, 217
Dr. von Boot, 259
Borchardt, Kaspar, 381
Borchardt, Marie Luise (Marel), 335, 340, 352, 365, 366, 377, 380, 381, 395
Borchardt, Rudolf, 187, 202, 212, 244, 274, 275, 291, 294, 297, 305, 306, 307, 310, 311, 315, 316, 317, 318, 319, 320, 321, 322, 323, 324, 327, 328, 329, 330, 331, 332, 333, 334, 335, 336, 338, 340, 342, 345, 350, 351, 352, 353, 354, 355, 357, 365, 366, 369, 370, 377, 380, 393, 394, 395, 397, 401, 404, 407, 429; *Der arme Heinrich,* 316, 317, 321; "Der Dichter und das Dichterische," 394; "Dichter und die Geschichte," 316, 321; "Der Durant," 320, 324, 333, 365, 377; *Die geliebte Kleinigkeit* (The Beloved Trifle), 401; "Die halbgerettete Seele" (Half-Saved Soul), 378, 380; "Der Krieg und die deutsche Selbsteinkehr" (War and Germany's Self-Examination), 274; "Rede am Grabe Eberhard Bodenhausens" (Eulogy

for Eberhard Bodenhausen), 310, 317, 321; *Verkündigung,* 365
Bosetti, Hermine, 60, 208, 211
Bräker, Uli, *Der arme Mann im Tockenburg,* 29, 194
Brandenstein-Zeppelin, Count Karl Alexander von, 284
Bremer Presse, 328
Brentano, Bettina, 129
Browning, Robert, xv, 22, 188, 189, 191, 198; *Dramatic Romances,* 22; *Men and Women,* 22; *The Ring and the Book,* 187, 199
Bruckmann, Elsa, 147
Bruckmann, Hugo, 24, 36, 147
Bruckmanns, 237
Buddha, Siddhartha Gautama, 253
Burckhardt, Carl Jacob, 348, 353, 371, 377, 383, 386, 388, 389, 391, 392, 397, 399, 400, 401, 403, 404, 412, 413, 414, 417, 421, 422, 425, 426; *Reise* (Trip), 426
Burckhardt, Elisabeth, 425, 427
Burckhardt, Helene, 393
Burnett, Frances H., *Little Lord Fauntleroy,* 228

Carl August, Duke of Sachsen-Weimar, 228
Carlyle, Thomas, *Geschichte der französischen Revolution* (The Revolution), 327
Carolin (maid), 145
Carossa, Hans, 27
Caruso, Enrico, 53
Casanova, Giacomo, 235, 237, 238, 278
Caspary (Art Dealer), 236, 289, 290, 291, 293
Chamberlain, Houston Stewart, *Goethe,* 208, 210
Collier, Price, 174, 240
Colloredo-Mansfeld, Count Ferdinand, 295
Commedia dell'arte, xx

Conard, Louis, 23
Conrad von Hötzendorf, Baron Franz, 402
Coster, Charles de, 237
Courbet, Gustave, 291
Courten, Count Carlo von, 275
Craig, Gordon, 63

Dabette, 100, 109
Dame Kobold, 365
Dandolo, 339
Daumier, Honoré, 390
Debussy, Claude, *L'après-midi d'un faune,* 219
Degas, Edgar, 122
Degenfeld–Schonburg, Count Alfred von, xvii
Degenfeld–Schonburg, Count Alfred von (Fredy), 258, 394
Degenfeld–Schonburg, Countess Anna von, 11, 16, 40, 69, 84, 105, 106, 117, 118, 178, 197, 198, 199, 200, 219, 223, 225, 227, 232, 233, 247, 251, 257, 258, 261, 262, 263, 264, 267, 268, 270, 272, 306
Degenfeld–Schonburg, Count Christoph Martin von, xvii, 16, 45, 78, 89, 95, 97, 163, 223, 252, 284, 301, 302, 305, 384, 409, 410, 411
Degenfeld, Konrad, 235
Degenfeld–Schonburg, Countess Marie Therese (Baby), xvii, xviii, 11, 13, 17, 20, 27, 29, 31, 40, 46, 58, 69, 77, 84, 88, 91, 92, 100, 101, 105, 110, 118, 119, 120, 123, 130, 133, 146, 148, 151, 159, 160, 161, 176, 187, 191, 201, 215, 235, 247, 248, 251, 257, 261, 263, 275, 278, 291, 293, 324, 326, 332, 338, 339, 340, 344, 345, 347, 351, 357, 358, 372, 387, 388, 390, 391, 392, 394, 395, 403, 405, 406, 409, 410, 411, 414, 416, 421, 423, 424, 425, 430

Delacroix, Eugène, 289, 290, 398
Delatour, 53
Delbrück, 365
Demogeot, Jacques, 23
Destinn, Emmy, 169
Deventer, Sam, 364
Diaghilev, Serge, 186; ballet (The Russians), 162, 175, 176, 177, 186, 205, 206, 207, 217, 219, 221, 413
Dickens, Charles, 338, 362; *Great Expectations,* 362; *Oliver Twist,* 338, 340
Dietrich-Schardt, Mary, 140
Dilthey, Wilhelm, 23; *Das Erlebnis und die Dichtung,* 23
Döring, Gertrud von, 34
Dörnberg, Baron von, 235
Dörner, 312
Dostoevsky, Feodor, 203, 223, 228, 402; *The Brothers Karamazov,* 201; *Crime and Punishment,* 206, 207; *The Demons,* 402; *The Idiot,* 247; *Memoirs from the House of the Dead,* 226
Douglas, Anga, 64, 351

Eckermann, Johann Peter, 21, 55, 279; *Eckermanns Gespräche mit Goethe,* (Eckermann's Conversations with Goethe), 55; Goethe-Eckermann letters, 21
Eckstein, 365
Eichendorff, Baron Joseph von, *The Life of a Good-for-Nothing,* 22
Elgin, Earl of, 53
Emin Pascha, 229
Esmond, 249, 250, 252
Eulenburg, Tora, 392
Euripides, *The Bacchae,* 140
Everyman, 112
Eysoldt, Gertrud, 121, 139, 140

Faistauer, Anton, 238
Faßbinder, Zdenka, 241
Fay, Maud, 211

Festspielgemeinde (Festival Organization), 386
Fink, 237
S. Fischer Publishing House, xi, 326, 424
Förster-Nietzsche, Elisabeth, 59, 62, 64, 92
Fontane, Theodor, 23
Forster, Herr von, 262
Fortuny, Mariano, 15, 186
Franckenstein, Baron Clemens von, 211, 226, 241, 418
Franckenstein, Baron Georg von, 147, 211, 226
Franz Ferdinand, Archduke of Austria, xix, 257
Franz Joseph I, xv
Freytag, Gustav, *Bilder aus der deutschen Vergangenheit* (Pictures from the German Past), 23, 268

Gaetani, Roffredo, 420
Gagliardi, 366
Gaisberg, Aribert von, 119
Gaisberg, Baron Armin von, 16, 406
Gandegg, 302
Gauguin, Paul, 217, 219
Gavarni, Paul, 390
Geiger, Benno, 294, 356
Gelder, Aert de, 298
Gemmingen, Baroness Dorothea von, 78, 213
Gemmingen, Baron Friedrich von, 78, 200, 213, 247
George, Stefan, 370
Géricault, Théodore, 289, 291
Gersdorf, Baron Karl von, 19, 24, 146, 147, 148, 149, 212, 216
Gicky 405
Gide, André, 92
Giorgione, 58
Glaser, Heinrich, 160, 178, 260, 261, 423
Gluck, Christoph Willibald, 413; *Don Juan,* 413; *Orpheus and Eurydice,* 127, 129, 136

Goethe, Johann Wolfgang von, xviii, 5, 17, 21, 22, 26, 27, 28, 29, 59, 61, 62, 69, 71, 73, 100, 129, 146, 161, 197, 203, 206, 224, 225, 273, 278, 290, 303, 325, 347, 407; *Alexis und Dora*, 22; *Briefe*, 228; *Dichtung und Wahrheit* (Poetry and Truth), 26, 28, 70; *Faust*, 220, 221, 222, 223, 224, 225, 226, 329; *Die Geheimnisse* (The Secrets), 76; *Gesellige Lieder*, 266; *Hermann und Dorothea*, 22; *Italienische Reise*, 188; *Die Leiden des jungen Werthers* (The Sorrows of Young Werther), 79, 80; "Lob der Mutter" (Mother's Praise), 26; *Römische Elegien*, 235; *Sprüche in Prosa* (Maxims and Reflections), 206, 240, 279; *Torquato Tasso*, 246; *Die Wahlverwandtschaften* (Elective Affinities), 125, 126, 129, 130, 136, 288; *West-östlicher Diwan* (West–Eastern Divan), 22, 237, 238, 240, 312; *Wilhelm Meister*, 100, 105
Gogh, Vincent van, 119, 217, 219, 283, 284, 288, 290, 293, 295, 298
Goldsmith, Oliver, *The Vicar of Wakefield*, 213
Gomperz, Max von, 239
Gotthelf, Jeremias, *Uli der Knecht*, 22, 23
Gourgaud, Caspar, 22
Gräf, Hans Gerhard, *Goethe über seine Werke* (Goethe on His Works), 125, 128, 130, 144
Greco, El, 122, 124, 125
Grillparzer, Franz, 301, 335
Grimm, Hermann, *Goethe*, 23
Grimm, Jacob and Wilhelm, *Fairy Tales*, 31, 188, 266
Grimmelshausen, Hans Jacob Christoph von, *Simplicius Simplicissimus*, 362
Grot, Martha von, 409
Groth-Oettingen, 403
Grünägl, 293
Grünewald, Matthias, *Isenheim Altar*, 339
Guizot, Guillaume, 28

Haas, Otto, 384, 391, 405
Hahnloser, 413
Hals, Frans, 199
Hamsun, Knut, *Mysterien*, 23, 253; *Pan*, 23, 253
Harrach, Count Hans Albrecht von, 63, 71
Harrach, Countess Helene von, 63, 71
Hauptmann, Gerhart, 138, 140, 203; *Gabriele Schillings Flucht*, 187; *Der Narr in Christo Emanuel Quint*, 66; *Die Ratten* (Rats), 60
Haydn, Joseph 53
Hearn, Lafcadio 253
Hebbel, Friedrich, xviii, 246, 247, 250, 290, 332, 333; *Aus meinem Leben* (Diaries), 144, 199, 331, 333; *Gedichte* (Poems), 338, 340; *Meine Kindheit*, 23
Hebra, Wilhelm von. 329
Heims, Else, 245
Heinemann, 292
Heinrich, 196
Heiseler, Emmy von, 100, 105, 241, 249, 344, 348, 400, 403, 404
Heiseler, Henry von, 32, 34, 105, 193, 249, 392, 400, 403, 404
Heiss, 90
Hellmann, Irene, 405, 406
Hellmann, Paul, 405, 406, 411
Hempel, Frieda, 169
Herbst, Hans, 310, 312, 314, 315, 319, 324, 326, 359, 363, 364, 366, 368, 372, 373, 374, 382, 407
Herder, Johann Gottfried von, 228
Herwarth von Bittenfeld, Hans Wolfgang, 285, 296, 302, 314, 348, 350, 380
Herzlieb, Minna, 347
Heye, Clara, 55, 266, 300, 302, 345

Heymel, Alfred Walter von, 58, 60, 70, 85, 91, 92, 120, 216, 266
Hildenbrandt, Wilhelm A., 16
Hindenburg, Paul von, 264
Hodler, Ferdinand, 202, 219, 290, 348, 350
Hohenberg, Baron Gottfried von, 384
Hölderlin, Friedrich, 119, 203, 240, 276, 401; *Hyperion,* 268, 269
Hofmann, Ludwig von, 236, 249, 252
Hofmann, Elly von, 252
Hofmannsthal, Christiane von, 156, 277, 297, 303, 323, 325, 330, 332, 335, 336, 338, 341, 343, 345, 347, 350, 353, 358, 360, 364, 370, 371, 374, 377, 378, 379, 383, 384, 387, 391, 392, 397, 403, 405, 409, 411, 416, 417, 420
Hofmannsthal, Franz von, xxii, 223, 386, 416, 423, 430
Hofmannsthal, Gertrud von (Gerty), xvi, 16, 17, 19, 20, 23, 25, 33, 36, 48, 50, 54, 59, 60, 61, 63, 64, 87, 94, 109, 114, 117, 121, 123, 126, 128, 131, 134, 135, 138, 139, 142, 147, 149, 153, 156, 163, 165, 166, 172, 176, 178, 180, 181, 182, 184, 186, 196, 198, 201, 212, 221, 225, 227, 228, 229, 230, 237, 238, 242, 244, 248, 250, 253, 254, 256, 258, 259, 260, 261, 272, 277, 282, 283, 287, 293, 297, 299, 310, 311, 312, 314, 323, 326, 330, 331, 343, 344, 346, 348, 350, 351, 353, 354, 355, 356, 357, 358, 359, 360, 363, 365, 366, 378, 381, 382, 385, 389, 392, 393, 394, 395, 397, 400, 403, 404, 406, 407, 409, 412, 414, 416, 417, 420, 425, 426, 428
Hofmannsthal Hugo August Peter von, 48, 59, 109, 128, 131, 135, 139, 161, 164, 166, 179, 180, 184, 198, 247, 248, 249, 258, 260, 261, 272, 273, 274, 275
Hofmannsthal, Raimund von, xviii, 163, 166, 238, 247, 248, 303, 395, 408, 409, 414, 416, 417, 421, 423
Hohnstein, Countess, 329
Homer, 143, 164; *Odyssey,* 11, 196
Hügel, Countess Huberta von, 178
Hügel, Fery von, 227, 270, 275

Ilse, 195
Impressionism, xii
Insel–Almanach, 148
Das Inselschiff, 351
Insel Publishing House, 23, 224, 292, 375, 386
Isenheimer Altar, 343
Mrs. Isepp, 423
Isepp, Sebastian, 382, 383, 384

Jacobi, Max, 228
Jeanne d'Arc, 249
Jeritza, Maria, 211
Jonson, Ben, 122
Josten, 242

Kahnweiler, 217
Kant, Immanuel, 144
Kanzler, R., 361
Karl I, Emperor of Austria, 257
Kassner, Rudolf, 154, 156, 211, 243, 340, 342, 345, 376, 377; *Der Tod und die Maske* (Death and the Mask), 342
Keats, John, 23, 334; *Isabella or the Pot of Basil,* 195; *Sonnets,* 334
Keller, Gottfried, *Zürcher Novellen,* 269
Kessler, Count Harry von, 5, 6, 19, 24, 25, 28, 55, 59, 62, 63, 64, 65, 67, 68, 71, 92, 112, 152, 153, 174, 184, 201, 205, 215, 216, 217, 218, 219, 254, 272, 321, 323
Mr. Keszycki, 28, 150, 155, 235
Mrs. Keszycki, 269

Keyserling, Count Hermann von, 347, 349, 374; *Die Indienreise*, 342
Kippenberg, Anton, 159, 161, 366, 367
Kleist, Heinrich von, 17, 336, 349, 386; *Letters*, 21, 139, 336; *Penthesilea*, 139, 140, 160
Dr. Kohnstamm, 420, 422
Kolb, Annette, 34, 146, 148, 207, 208, 212, 222, 224, 225, 230, 234, 248; *Das Exemplar*, 222, 224
Mrs. König, 374
König (painter), 138
Kotzebue, August von, 413
Kramer–Klett, Baron, 377
Kreatur, 427
Kreisler, Fritz, 103
Krisis, 345
Kroeller, Heinrich, 413
Kröller–Müller, Helene, 364
Kröller–Müller, Otto, 364
Kühlmann, Myra von, 314, 361
Kühlmann, Richard von, 295
Kunst und Künstler (Art and Artists), 292

Lagerlöf, Selma, *Nils Holgerson and the Trip of Wild Geese*, 228
Lampe, Walter, 193, 249
Lampe–von Guaita, Else, 266
Lang, Erwin, 116, 121, 123, 131, 134, 138, 140, 141, 143, 147, 154, 156, 163, 165, 167, 176, 179, 181, 183, 186, 187, 195, 196, 200, 202, 206, 212, 220, 229, 243, 254, 259, 260, 262, 264, 274
Lang, Karl Heinrich von, 27
Lawrence, D. H., xviii
Lawrence, Thomas E., *The Seven Pillars of Wisdom*, 427
Leden, Christian, 403, 404
Leibl, Wilhelm, 236, 238, 289
Lenau, Nikolaus, 144
Lénern, Maria, *Les affranchis* (The Emancipated), 62

Lenotre, Théodore, *Vieilles maisons, vieux papiers*, 21, 22, 26
Levin, Willy, 158, 164, 175, 205, 307
Liberty, 176
Lichnowsky, Duke Karl Max, 18, 63
Lichnowsky, Duchess Mechthild, 50, 55, 60, 63, 146, 152
Liebermann, Max, 205, 289
Liebknecht, Karl 326
Mrs. Lindemann, 127, 232
Lobkowitz, Prince Ferdinand, 211
Lorenz, Jeannette, 408, 410
Ludendorff, Erich von, 326
Ludwig, Emil, *Bismarck*, 213
Lully, xx

Mackensen, Fritz, 213
Madame Butterfly, 109
Mahler, Gustav, 113
Manet, Edouard, 289
Mann, Thomas, xix
Maria Theresia, Empress, 403
Marie, 408
Martens, Albertine von, 69, 106
Martin, Mabel, 112, 225
Marsyas, 287, 406
Massary, Fritzi, 405
Maupassant, Guy de, *Yvette*, 392; "Retour," 392
Mr. Mauracher, 302
Meid, Hans, 290
Meier–Graefe, Julius, 321, 367, 368, 391, 398; *Courbet and Corot*, 292; *History of the Development of Modern Art*, 289
Mr. Mell, 147
Mell, Max, 114, 175, 179, 181, 182, 183, 185, 186, 211, 225, 229, 288, 291 332, 348, 350, 370, 383, 397, 401, 413; *Das Apostelspiel*, 413
Melusine, 99
Mensdorf–Pouilly, Count Albert, 295, 402
Ms. Metzger, 406

Michelet, Jules, *Histoire de France*, 336
Mickelsch, 344
Milhaud, Darius, 177
Miller, Ralph, 423
Milton, John, 124, 126
Dr. Moeller, 89
Moissi, Alexander, 129, 139, 140, 179, 205, 246, 254, 369, 405
Molière, Jean–Baptiste Poquelin, 112, 302; *Le bourgeois gentilhomme*, 286, 302; *Le malade imaginaire*, 280
Montgelas, Albrecht von, 63
Montholon, Comte Charles Tristan de, 22
Mr. Morton, 182
Moussorgsky, Modest, *Boris Godunov*, 217
Mozart, Wolfgang Amadeus, 186, 281; *Letters*, 159; *Figaros Hochzeit* (The Marriage of Figaro), 120
Mühll, Dori von der, 412, 426
Müller, Karl von, 129
Müller, Margarethe (Eta), see von Schwartz
Müller, Marie, 129
Müller–Hofmann, Willy, 229, 243, 244, 247, 249, 252, 259, 264, 267, 324, 327, 328, 329, 340, 353, 357
Prof. Dr. Müller, 296, 372, 409
Münchhausen, Baron von, 82
Musset, Alfred de, 22, 150, 155, 161
Müssigbrot, 129
Mutzenbecher, Frau Heinrich, 261

Nadler, Joseph, 329, 331, 333, 362
Napoleon I, 21, 22, 26, 184; *Memoirs de Ste. Hélène*, 22
Neue freie Presse, 409
Der Neue Merkur, 348
Neumann, K. E., *Buddha Übertragungen* (Translations of Buddha's Sayings), 362; G.

Buddhas letzte Tage (Buddha's Last Days), 362
Nijinsky, Vaclav, 176, 205, 219
Nostitz, Alfred von, 157, 159, 160, 188, 204, 205, 281, 295, 298
Nostitz, Helene von, 55, 157, 159, 160, 202, 204, 205, 281, 295
Novalis, Friedrich Baron von Hardenberg, 29, 91, 240; *Fragmente*, 206; *Hymnen*, 194

Mrs. Odhner, 330
Oppenheimer Countess Gabriele von (Yella), 147, 163, 237, 243, 320, 336, 344, 346, 349, 397

Paléologue, Maurice, 402
Pallenberg, Max, 121, 388, 405
Pannwitz, Rudolf, 294, 295, 296, 297, 298, 299, 300, 301, 302, 303, 304, 305, 307, 309, 312, 313, 315, 317, 318, 319, 320, 321, 328, 342, 346, 347, 348, 349, 351, 353, 356, 358, 372, 373; *Die deutsche Lehre*, 347; *Die Befreiung des Oedipus*, 301; *Der Tod des Empedokles*, 301
Pepino, Anton Joseph, 16, 61, 66, 68, 235
Petra, 322, 327
Pfetten–Ansbach, Baron Franz von, 374, 379, 406, 410
Philippe, Charles–Louis, 125, 128, 137
Picasso, Pablo, 202, 217, 218, 219, 289, 374
R. Piper Publishing House, 363
Pipo, 150
Planta, Esther de, 421
Plato 144
Poussin, Nicolas, 292
Proust, Marcel, *A l'ombre des jeunes filles en fleurs*, (In the Shade of the Young Girls), 394; *Du côté de chez Swann* (Next to Swann), 394
Putlitz, Baron Joachim von, 200

Queen of Naples, 212
Queen of Württemberg, 97

Racine, Jean, *Andromaque,* 114
Rathenau, Walther, 188
Reading Circle of Zürich, 419
Reck, Carola von, 69
Redlich, Josef, 295, 300, 315, 320
Reiher, 145
Reinhardt, Edmund, 212
Reinhardt, Max, xii, xvi, xx, 5, 8, 14, 19, 24, 40, 43, 44, 50, 52, 53, 63, 66, 71, 98, 107, 109, 112, 119, 120, 121, 128, 129, 131, 139, 140, 142, 148, 152, 153, 160, 162, 164, 166, 169, 173, 174, 175, 179, 183, 186, 187, 205, 212, 240, 244, 245, 246, 247, 248, 249, 250, 254, 280, 281, 285, 294, 297, 302, 307, 308, 329, 343, 353, 356, 360, 361, 367, 368, 369, 370, 373, 374, 383, 388, 391, 406, 408, 410, 421, 426
Rembrandt, 58, 199, 203, 298, 339
Rémusat, Paul, 185, 187, 194, 198, 199; *Mémoires de Madame de Rémusat,* 185, 250
Renoir, Pierre Auguste, 289, 290
Reserl, 402, 404
Revue française, 137
Reymont, Vladislav, *Die polnischen Bauern* (The Polish Peasants), 327, 329, 333
Richter, Cornelia, 63
Richter, Raoul, 204
Rilke, Rainer Maria, xv, 222, 224, 232, 342; *Auguste Rodin,* 342
Robinson, Edward; 123, 125, 127, 130
Roller, Alfred, 53
Rousseau, Jean Jacques, *Les confessions,* 114
Rubens, Peter Paul, 339
Rubinstein, Ida, 176

The Russians, see Diaghilev
Rysselberghe, Elisabeth van, 216
Rysselberghe, Théo van, 16, 178, 215, 216, 217, 219

St. Denis, Ruth, 123, 124, 127, 130, 143
Salzburg Festival, xx, xxii
Sand, George, 347
Schaeffer, Albrecht, 338, 342, 345, 347, 424; *Gudula,* 342
Schaljapin, Fedor, 217
Schenk, Baron von 235
Schenker, 186
Schereschewsky, Arnold, 345
Schiller, Friedrich, 159; *Don Carlos,* 296; *Kabale und Liebe,* 285, 408; "Die Teilung der Erde," 311
Schillings, Max, 55, 59, 200
Schinckel, Joachim von, 341
Schlesinger, Franziska, 191, 192, 197
Schmitz, Aida, 105, 106
Schmitz, Carola, 24, 29
Schmitz, Oskar, *Das Land ohne Musik* (The Country Without Music), 406
Schmitz, Tanya, 384
Schmitz, Wolja, 384
Schnitzler, Arthur, xxii, 23, 403
Schröder, Dora, 356
Schröder, Clärchen, 55, 345
Schröder, Lina, 55, 345
Schröder, Rudolf Alexander (Rudi), xv, 11, 30, 38, 55, 63, 65, 85, 91, 94, 116, 131, 139, 147, 165, 177, 179, 180, 181, 182, 185, 201, 212, 213, 215, 216, 231, 243, 252, 253, 254, 255, 258, 263, 268, 274, 299, 300, 302, 303, 309, 310, 311, 313, 314, 315, 316, 318, 320, 321, 323, 324, 328, 329, 332, 334, 335, 336, 337, 339, 342, 345, 346, 348, 349, 350, 351, 352, 353, 354, 355, 356, 357, 358, 359, 363, 365, 367, 369, 370, 376, 388,

389, 390, 391, 392, 393, 394, 395, 397, 398, 400, 401, 411, 413, 414, 417, 419, 421, 422, 428, 429; *Ausseer Ode,* 358; *Deutsche Oden* (German Odes), 206
Schwartz, Adolf von, 259, 261
Schwartz, Albrecht von, 259, 261, 263, 267, 273, 340, 355, 361, 374, 388
Schwartz, Annemarie von, 396
Schwartz, Johann Friedrich von, 13, 39, 43, 45, 55, 59, 77, 95, 174, 175, 198, 199, 213, 262, 270, 271, 273, 287, 288, 310, 313
Schwartz, Margarete von, 44, 122, 220, 262, 372, 401
Schwartz, Margarete von (Eta), 222, 237
Schwartz, Oda von, 123, 125, 133, 406
Schwerin, Count Botho von, 175
Scott, Sir Walter, *Ivanhoe,* 213
Seebach, Count Nikolaus von, 53, 158, 161
Seipel, Ignaz, 423
Shakespeare, William, 5, 23, 60, 122, 124, 144, 194, 197, 402; *As You Like It,* 143; *A Winter's Tale,* 143; *Hamlet,* 246, 303; *King Lear,* 246; *Macbeth,* 280, 281; *Measure for Measure,* 197; *The Merry Wives of Windsor,* 62; *Much Ado About Nothing,* 174; *Othello,* 60, 197, 236; *Sonnets,* 194
Sisi, 193, 201
"Sleepers" (poem), 213
Slevogt, Max, 289, 292
Miss Smith, 100
Smith Elder & Co., 22, 199
Söhnlein and Cie., 326
Sophocles, *Oedipus Rex,* 8
Sossenks, 84
Spartakists, 335
Spenser, Edmund, 124

Spiegl von Thurnsee, Edgar, 244, 245, 246, 247, 248
Spitzemberg, Baroness Hildegard von, 63
Sprecher, Barbara von (Bärby), 344, 348, 355, 357
Stanley, Henry M., 229
Stauffenberg, Wilhelm Baron Schenk von, 213, 214, 233, 234, 245, 253
Stegemann, *Der Kampf um. den Rhein* (Battle for the Rhine), 412
Stein, Charlotte von, 228, 346, 347
Stein, Fritz von, 228
Steinitzer, Wilhelm, 196, 212, 215, 216, 235, 249, 378
Stelzer, 268, 270
Stendhal, 83, 91, 176, 327; *De l'amour,* 83; *Le rouge et le noir,* 98; *Vie de Napoléon* (Life of Napoleon), 327
Stern, Ernst, 169
Sternheim, Carl, 212
Stetten, Otto von, 249
Stifter, Adalbert, 44, 56, 75, 141, 146; *Abdias,* 79; *Der Hochwald* (The Timber Forest), 141; *Die Mappe meines Urgroßvaters* (Great-Grandfather's Folder), 79, 141; *Die Narrenburg* (Castle of Fools), 79; *Studien,* 384
Strauß, Richard, xv, xvi, xx, xxii, 25, 40, 43, 46, 52, 53, 54, 56, 59, 60, 98, 99, 112, 113, 115, 120, 121, 154, 158, 161, 164, 169, 173, 174, 175, 177, 179, 183, 200, 205, 212, 214, 244, 277, 278, 286, 329, 364, 399, 401, 403, 404, 413; *Salome,* 233, 234
Strauß, Richard–Hugo von Hofmannsthal, *Die ägyptische Helena,* xii, xxii, 399, 400, 401, 403, 404; *Arabella,* xii, xxii, xxiii, 42; *Ariadne auf Naxos,* xii, xvi, xx, xxi, xxii, xlii, 66, 112, 114, 116, 132, 133, 135, 137, 150, 153,

164, 169, 175, 183, 200, 202, 208, 211, 214, 244, 285, 286, 401; *Elektra*, xii, xxi; *Die Frau ohne Schatten*, xii, xxii, 112, 145, 158, 167, 198, 199, 245, 246, 336, 373, 374; *Josephslegende*, 186, 255; *Der Rosenkavalier*, xii, xxx, 4, 34, 39, 46, 51, 55, 59, 65, 99, 278, 301
Stravinsky, Igor, *Le sacre du printemps*, 219
Strindberg, August, 23
Studnitz, Ernst von, 58, 188
Süddeutsche Monatshefte, 11

Taine, Hippolyte Adolphe, 24 28; *Histoire de la littérature anglaise*, 21, 23, 122, 124, 126, 128, 130
Talenten, 290
Taube, Baron Otto von, *Der verborgene Herbst* (Lost Autumn), 241
Tessenow, Heinrich, 345
Thackeray, William Makepeace, *Pendennis*, 362
Thannhauser, 289
Thiers, Adolphe, *Histoire de la révolution française*, 21, 22
Thun–Hohenstein, Countess Christiane von, 238
Thurn und Taxis, Prince Alexander von, 163, 201, 211
Thurn und Taxis, Princess Marie von, 163, 201, 211
Thylla, 266
Tiersch, Frieda, 404
Till Eulenspiegel, 115, 242
Tintoretto, 58
Tirpitz, Alfred von, 402
Tolstoy, Leo, *Der Tod des Iwan Iljitsch* (Death of Ivan Ilitch), 227
Treitschke, Heinrich von, *Geschichte des 19. Jahrhunderts* (History of the Nineteenth Century), 327, 331, 333
Treskow, 360

Tschuang Tse, *Reden und Gleichnisse* (Talks and Parables), 372
Turandot, 421
Tyralla (banker), 364, 365, 366, 368, 382

Une caprice, 150
Upanishads, 253

Vandal, Albert, *L'avènement de Bonaparte* (Napoleon), 250
Varese, Edgar, 8, 105, 111, 113, 120
Varese, Suzanne, 105, 111, 114, 120
Varnbühler, Baron Axel von, 58
Velde, Helen van de (Puppy), 100, 118, 122, 192, 332, 341, 350
Velde, Henry van de, 6, 56, 57, 58, 60, 61, 62, 64, 65, 66, 68, 107, 109, 154, 175, 177, 182, 184, 187, 190, 193, 213, 215, 217, 222, 224, 241, 266, 340, 341, 350, 363, 387
Velde, Maria van de, 51, 53, 54, 56, 57, 58, 60, 61, 62, 63, 65, 67, 68, 107, 118, 175, 187, 189, 193, 213, 215, 249, 251, 266, 267, 340, 363, 366
Velde, Nele van de, 100, 118, 122, 241
Verdi, Guiseppe, *Falstaff*, 235
Vermeer, Jan, 58
Veronese, 58, 186
Verry, Amélie, 406
Victory of Samothrake, 177
Voigt, Marie–Luise (Marel), 335, 340, 352, 365, 366, 377, 380, 381, 395
Vollard, Ambroise, 217, 219
Vollmöller, Hans, 140; *Orestie*, 127, 128, 129, 132
Vossler, Karl, 382

Wagner (shopkeeper), 140
Wagner, Richard, *Der fliegende Holländer*, 145; *Tristan und Isolde*, 241

Waldhausen, Frau von, 384
Walter, Bruno, 231
Wassermann, Jakob, 119, 130, 136, 226, 243, 329, 332, 333; *Christian Wahnschaffe*, 340; *Die Schwestern* (The Sisters), 130
Weber, Eugène, xi
Wendelstadt, Baron Jan von, 3, 92, 192
Wendelstadt, Baroness Julie von, xviii, 4, 6, 8, 10, 16, 28, 31, 32, 34, 40, 55, 59, 60, 69, 75, 77, 78, 81, 83, 84, 88, 89, 92, 93, 94, 96, 97, 98, 99, 102, 103, 104, 105, 106, 108, 109, 110, 111, 113, 118, 119, 125, 130, 132, 133, 140, 145, 149, 150, 151, 152, 153, 154, 160, 166, 170, 175, 176, 177, 178, 179, 181, 182, 189, 192, 203, 208, 215, 223, 225, 227, 231, 232, 241, 249, 251, 256, 260, 261, 262, 269, 275, 279, 281, 282, 285, 290, 292, 296, 304, 308, 333, 345, 372, 374, 377, 380, 381, 383, 392, 394, 426, 430
Wengersky, Count Eberhard von, 68, 248
Wengersky, Countess Irmgard von, 65, 68, 69, 78, 80, 248
Whitman, Walt, xviii, xx, 22, 161, 162, 203, 206, 210, 222, 229, 274, 279, 332; "Drum Taps," 210;."Seashore Memories," 210; "Song at Sunset," 210; "Poem of Joys," 210
Wiecke, Paul, 61
Wiegand, Willy, 366, 370, 375, 376, 379, 389, 390, 392, 394, 404, 407, 418, 422
Wieland, 321
Wiener Journal, 410
Wiesenthal, Grete, 116, 121, 124, 130, 131, 134, 138, 140, 141, 143, 154, 156, 158, 160, 162, 163, 165, 167, 174, 175, 176, 179, 186, 187, 194, 195, 196, 200, 201, 202, 203, 204, 206, 211, 212, 220, 229, 236, 238, 243, 249, 252, 254, 255, 260, 262, 267, 270, 271, 273, 274, 276, 303
Wilde, Oscar, 233
Winkler, Josef, 21, 99, 104, 161
Wolde, Ludwig, 328, 365, 376, 377, 381
Wolff, Alfred, 200, 213, 235, 241, 425
Wolff, Hanna, 200, 213, 234, 235, 241, 425
Wolff, Otto, 384, 425

Zeppelin, Count Ferdinand von, 284
Zichy, Countess Margit von, 201
Zifferer, Paul, 414, 428
Zimmer, Andrew, xii
Zimmermann (banker), 382
Zumbusch, 287

OHIO UNIVERSITY LIBRARY